# Microsoft™ Outlook Programming

# Microsoft™ Outlook Programming

## Jumpstart for Administrators, Power Users, and Developers

Sue Mosher

**Digital Press**

An imprint of Elsevier Science

Amsterdam Boston Heidelberg London New York Oxford Paris San Diego San Francisco Singapore Sydney Tokyo

Digital Press is an imprint of Elsevier Science.

Recognizing the importance of preserving what has been written, Elsevier Science prints its books on acid-free paper whenever possible.

**Library of Congress Cataloging-in-Publication Data**

A catalog record for this book is available from the Library of Congress.

ISBN: 1-55558-286-9

**British Library Cataloguing-in-Publication Data**

A catalogue record for this book is available from the British Library.

The publisher offers special discounts on bulk orders of this book.

For information, please contact:

Manager of Special Sales
Elsevier Science
200 Wheeler Road
Burlington, MA 01803
Tel: 781-313-4700
Fax: 781-313-4882

For information on all Digital Press publications available, contact our World Wide Web home page at: http://www.digitalpress.com or http://www.bh.com/digitalpress

10 9 8 7 6 5 4

Printed in the United States of America

# *Contents*

# *Foreword*

How many times have you sat in front of your screen, thinking about that one feature you would add to Outlook—if you only had the chance?

One of the benefits of my job is that, in addition to helping to design each new version of Outlook, I meet a lot of people with ideas about how to make Outlook better. Some of these people I run across in the usual places—the seat in front of me on an airplane (inevitably with seatback reclined as far as possible), at the symphony ticket office, or in a local library. Other times, I meet people in places I'd never expect, doing things with Outlook we never imagined.

During a trade show that I used to attend every summer in New York City, I finished up early one afternoon and decided to return to my hotel. As I entered the lobby, I heard unmistakable techno music coming from the back of the hotel. Curious what kind of rave could be going on at 3 P.M., I walked down the hall to see what was going on. As I approached the grand ballroom, the music got louder, and I could see shadows from spinning disco lights under the door. I cracked the door open and peered into the room to find a bustling hive of pre-adolescent activity—a model search for girls 10–14 years old.

The far half of the ballroom was occupied by some sort of contest involving lip syncing and dancing, complete with flashing strobe lights, Britney Spears hits, and anxious mothers petitioning the judges. In another corner, a tropical island set had been constructed; girls in front of *faux* palm trees, intense lights, and painted ocean waves were being photographed by two or three professionals barking "energy, energy!" and "great, great, you're fantastic!"

In the corner nearest to me were several men, outfitted in California chic, sitting behind folding tables interviewing yet another group of would-be models for their agencies. What caught my eye was that in front of the agent nearest me was a laptop running Outlook. As each girl approached, he created a new contact in Outlook and entered information about her as she talked. When he finished asking his stock questions, he saved the contact, thanked the girl and her mother, and waved on the next person in line.

Intrigued, I came back later after the day's recruiting activities ended. I introduced myself and told the agent that I work on the Outlook team at Microsoft. The agent described to me how he was using Outlook to manage his talent search. He collected information about the girls—height, weight, age, hair color, etc., and typed it into the notes section at the bottom of the contact form. He also entered his own numerical values for more subjective criteria—how pretty the girl's face was, or how outgoing her personality seemed. At the end of the day, the agent went back to his hotel room and manually applied a secret formula to each model's statistical information. He then called the girls with the highest appeal quotient and attempted to sign them to his modeling agency.

"What would be really useful," he told me, "would be if I could have actual fields to enter the information for each girl, and then have Outlook calculate the desirability of the models automatically." He went on to confide: "I bet you could sell a lot more copies of Outlook if you built that right into the product."

Whatever the dubious merits of the agent's suggestion, how many times have you wished that Outlook could do something that there seems to be no way to do? Maybe you've thought about clicking a button to have Outlook automatically file old mail into separate folders for each month in which you received mail. Or maybe, you wish Outlook could validate ZIP codes for your contacts, or assign you a task when you have expense reports to approve, or manage vacation requests from your employees.

The good news is that you can do all of these things and more, and it doesn't take any existing programming expertise. Outlook has an easy-to-use but exceptionally powerful programming model that you can use to customize Outlook for your personal use or for the needs of the organization you administer.

Sue Mosher has been the high priestess of Outlook since before Outlook was even a product. From the first version of Outlook onward, Sue has been at the public forefront of all things Outlook and Exchange—first as an influential voice on the web and on newsgroups, more recently as a valued Microsoft Outlook MVP. Her Web site is so full of reliable information that I'll often try to find the answer I'm looking for there before using Microsoft's internal tools to research an issue.

Reading *Microsoft Outlook Programming: Jumpstart for Administrators, Power Users, and Developers* is a great way to get started with Outlook programming, especially for the beginner. The book is written in plain language, without complicated jargon or convoluted, abstract concepts to learn. Even if you've never written a line of code in your life, you will be able to follow the real-world examples in each chapter to rapidly gain knowledge and confidence. Before you know it, you will be crafting your own programs.

If you are experienced with VBA but have never programmed with Outlook, this book also makes a great starting point. You will apply your expertise to concepts unique to Outlook programming: custom forms, stores, the event model, integrating Outlook data with XML Web services, and more. Even if you are already a seasoned veteran, you will appreciate the technical depth of the information presented and the relevance of the examples therein. No matter what your skill level, you will learn how to program Outlook to work the way your business works—saving you time and helping you to manage your information more effectively.

Alas, I didn't make my usual trip to New York this summer, so I don't know for sure if the gaggle of starry-eyed girls took over the hotel again as in past years. I do know this much, however—when I eventually run into you at the airport or in your office and find out you've customized Outlook to, say, manage turtle breeding or keep track of what flavors of ice cream you own—sigh—at least I'll know who to blame.

Jensen Harris
Lead Program Manager
Microsoft Outlook
July 2002

# *Acknowledgments*

More people than I could ever name played a role in this book, but at the top of the list is Digital Press publisher Theron Shreve, who saw how much a new basic Outlook programming book was needed. Pam Chester at DP and my long-time friend and agent, Valda Hilley, also smoothed the way with incredible behind-the-scenes effort.

After answering thousands of Outlook programming questions in the Microsoft newsgroups, I must offer my thanks to all the Outlook administrators, users, and developers who have alternately stimulated and annoyed me. You constantly push me to find new techniques to work around Outlook's limitations and better ways to explain the basics.

A special debt of gratitude goes to all the Outlook MVPs (Most Valuable Professionals recognized by Microsoft for great practical knowledge and grace under fire when helping other users). Ken Slovak played a key role by reading every chapter and testing all the code, but if you find any code that won't run, it's my fault. I also need to single out Randy Byrne, Dmitry Streblechenko (developer of Outlook Spy and Redemption), and Siegfried Weber (an Exchange MVP), who sometimes talk way over my head but always remain a source of inspiration, and Steve Moede and Diane Poremsky, whose great code samples taught me a lot.

At Microsoft, many people contributed to my ability to shed light on Outlook programming, particularly Bill Jacob, Abdias Ruiz, John Eddy, and Paul Cornell. I'd also like to thank Outlook lead program manager Jensen Harris for his support and inspiration, and for writing the foreword to this book. People at other companies who inspired and instructed include Phil Seeman and Sandy Billingsley.

The physical production of this book began with much appreciated formatting assistance from Ann Gosnell. Final production was in the capable hands of Alan Rose, Harlan James, Lauralee Reinke, and Jordan Marx.

The following articles that originally appeared in *Windows & .NET Magazine* (http://www.winnetmag.com) or the *Exchange & Outlook Administrator* newsletter (http://www.exchangeadmin.com <http://www.exchangeadmin.com/>) provided portions of the content for this book. Copyright 2001–2002, Penton Media, Inc. Reused with permission:

"A Primer About Dates" (InstantDoc ID 16455)

"More Fun with Dates" (InstantDoc ID 20078)

"Taking Outlook to Task" (InstantDoc ID 19694)

"Making Contact" (InstantDoc ID 22254)

"Linking Outlook Contacts" (InstantDoc ID 20353)

"More About Links" (InstantDoc ID 20475)

"Improve your Custom Outlook Forms" (InstantDoc ID 23483)

My virtual assistant, Kathleen Redding, was indispensable in keeping the rest of my business organized while I filled my head with Outlook code. You are a treasure, and I am so blessed to have you as a friend!

My family, Robert and Annie, tolerated my long hours at the keyboard and helped me rejoice at the minor triumphs along the way. Those little celebrations really helped. I promise we'll have time to eat something other than pizza. Even Dymka the cat seems more relaxed now that she can stretch out on a desk that's not covered with page proofs and CDs.

Finally, I thank God for the opportunity to share this knowledge and help people connect with each other.

# Introduction

It's been more than three years since I first tried to explain how to program Microsoft Outlook in "Teach Yourself Microsoft Outlook 2000 Programming in 24 Hours" (Sams) in a way that would appeal to a wide range of Outlook users. I wanted potential power users to learn how to turn Outlook into a more productive desktop tool. I hoped to help administrators build forms that would enhance collaboration in their organizations and small personal tools to automate repetitive administrative tasks. To experienced developers, I aimed to explain the many quirks that can make programming Outlook difficult.

Since that time, of course, Outlook 2002 has been released, adding new programming features, but also new challenges. In the wake of LoveLetter and dozens of other viruses that targeted Outlook, Microsoft dramatically changed the functionality that makes it possible to work with email addresses and send messages programmatically. One of the goals of this book is to explain the new security features thoroughly and lay out your options, including a third-party library, Redemption. I also wanted to explain more of the architecture, especially the elements that tend to be stumbling blocks for new Outlook developers.

I've seen increasing interest in using Outlook forms in non-Exchange environments and expect this trend to continue, especially with recent third-party enhancements for Outlook that allow data sharing without Exchange. At the same time, Microsoft's .NET initiative has made XML Web services an incredibly easy-to-use development strategy for Outlook 2002, bringing new functionality to Outlook with just a couple of lines of code. Therefore, in this new book, I wanted to highlight a broader range of collaboration environments than just Exchange and database connections.

Another goal was to organize the material better so that you can find the building blocks you need to handle everyday Outlook tasks. For example, in

Chapter 14, "Working with Items," you'll find all the techniques for accessing a particular Outlook item. Be sure to check out Appendix C for a list of key procedures you'll want to reuse in your own projects.

I think it's important to say what this book is not: It is not a complete reference to the Outlook object model, nor is it a guide to building complex applications for installation in an enterprise or distribution to the general public. Excellent resources are available on both those topics, and you'll find them listed in Appendix A.

But what you won't find anywhere other than in this book is a balance between deep discussions of the practical aspects of Outlook development and the programming basics that make it possible for someone with no prior code-writing experience to get a great start. Instead of explaining everything there is about Outlook folders, for example, I'll show you the most important techniques—the building blocks that you'll use over and over again—and explain the best practices gleaned from years of listening to other Outlook developers. I have tried throughout the book to provide examples of these techniques that you can use immediately and then combine with other processes into new applications that you build yourself.

## Conventions used in this book

This book uses different typefaces to differentiate between code and regular text, and also to help you identify important concepts.

Code appears in `monospace` font:

```
Item.BodyFormat = olFormatRichText
```

Placeholders for various expressions appear in *`monospace italic`* font. You should replace the placeholder with the specific value that it represents.

Text that you type is presented within quotation marks. New terms appear in *italics*.

The Notes, Tips, and Cautions scattered through the book try to call attention to information that will help you become a better Outlook programmer. A Note presents interesting information related to the surrounding discussion. A Tip offers advice or teaches an easier way to do something. A Caution advises you of potential problems and helps you steer clear of disaster.

1

# *What You Can Do with Outlook*

Welcome to Microsoft Outlook's world of programming possibilities! Both Outlook 2000 and Outlook 2002 make it easier than ever to customize the program. This chapter gets you started by introducing the tools for Outlook programming and suggesting ways to start thinking about projects you want to try.

The highlights of this chapter include discussions of the following:

- What kinds of projects are possible in Outlook 2000 and 2002
- What tools you will use the most
- How to decide which tool to use
- How to determine which version of Outlook you have installed
- How to sketch out your plans for Outlook programming projects

## 1.1 Why program with Outlook?

Whether you have been using Microsoft Outlook for just a few days or more than a year, you've certainly figured out that it does more than e-mail—much, much more. It's not unusual to find people who have organized their entire lives with Outlook.

But if you asked each Outlook user how he or she puts the program to work, you would receive a different answer every time because people have their own ideas on how to organize the critical information in their lives. Wouldn't it be great if Microsoft could make Outlook so customizable that everyone could use it his or her own way? It might not be 100 percent possible, but the programming environment included with Outlook 2000 and 2002 is rich enough to let you make major strides toward bending Outlook to your will—or that of the organization you work for.

This book shows you how to use the programming tools in Outlook to make it your own. It's OK if you have never programmed before—this book shows you how! It's much easier than you might think. If you are an experienced programmer, you will see how to put Outlook's special features to work and how to work around its many quirks.

To help you get excited about the chapters ahead, take a look at this list of things you can do when you learn how to program with Outlook:

- Distribute a list of company holidays to people in the office so that they can instantly add them to their Outlook calendars
- Create your own custom rules to handle incoming e-mail
- Search and replace data, such as telephone area codes
- Create custom reports by integrating Outlook data with Word layouts
- Schedule a follow-up call for a meeting easily
- Create Outlook forms that duplicate the paper phone message, vacation request, and other business forms you use

Are you excited yet?

## 1.2 Outlook programming tools

Before digging into the details of Outlook programming, here is a preview of the primary tools you will be using:

- Visual Basic for Applications
- Outlook forms
- Visual Basic Scripting Edition (VBScript)
- Object models, not just for Outlook, but also for Collaboration Data Objects, Redemption, Scripting Runtime, Word, and Excel

### 1.2.1 Visual Basic for Applications

Outlook includes one of the richest available development environments—*Visual Basic for Applications* (or VBA for short). Outlook shares it with not only the other Office programs, but also programs such as AutoCAD that have licensed VBA as their programming environment.

The VBA programming environment is shown in Figure 1.1. (The screen shots in this book were taken using Windows XP. If you use a different operating system, your screen may look slightly different, but will

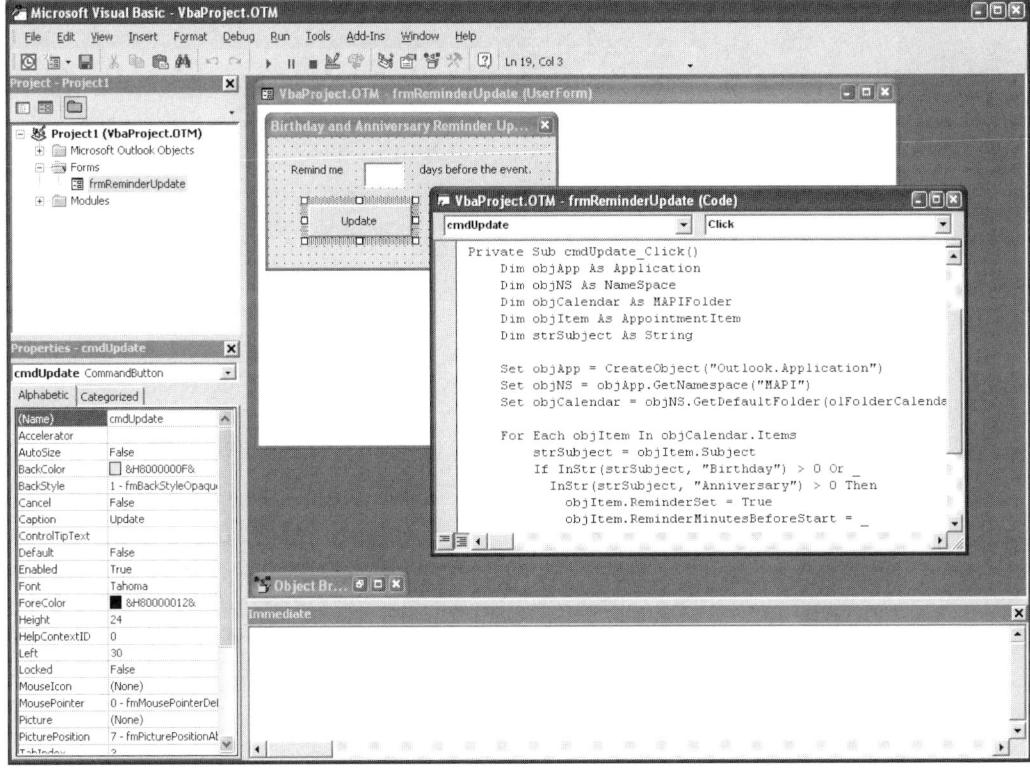


**Figure 1.1** *VBA includes a rich form and code environment (compare with Figure 1.4).*

function the same.) Figure 1.1 includes all the tools a professional developer might want:

- Visual forms designer (for Windows dialogs, not for Outlook forms)
- Intelligent editor with color coding and dropdown lists to avoid code errors
- Detailed help on the things you can do with Outlook
- Debugging windows and other tools

VBA allows you to write code that handles the many events that take place when you work with your Outlook information—such as creating new items or switching from one folder to another.

VBA also gives you the ability to design dialog boxes that pop up to get information from the user and windows that stay on the screen to provide information to the user. For example, you might build a VBA form to display how many vacation days you have used so far this year or the time that you last received messages in your Inbox.

Furthermore, you can use VBA to create macros that you can add to the Outlook toolbar to launch a telephone message form, search for and replace text in all the items in a folder, and expand Outlook's capabilities in many other ways. In Outlook 2002, the Rules Wizard can run a macro in response to a condition that you set in a rule.

You might have created macros in Word or Excel by turning on a macro recorder that watches your actions and then builds the appropriate code. Outlook does not include a comparable macro recorder, but the examples in this book show you how to use VBA to perform all the basic actions of creating messages and other items, addressing them, and sending them.

Note that the VBA techniques discussed in this book also apply if you want to move up from Outlook's integrated development environment to building more sophisticated Outlook tools with Microsoft's Visual Basic development program. (Visual Basic .NET requires different techniques that are beyond the scope of this book. We'll stick to VBA and, by extension, Visual Basic.)

### 1.2.2 Customized forms

The second stop on the road to Outlook programming proficiency is learning how to customize the basic Outlook forms.

Every item that you open in Outlook—whether it's an e-mail message, a contact, or an appointment—uses a particular form to display its data. (If you have programmed in Microsoft Access or Visual Basic, you may already be familiar with using forms as templates to display different data items.) You can customize these forms to show or hide fields, respond to user input and actions, and control other Outlook tasks. Customized forms can be shared with other users, both within your organization and across the Internet.

In many programming environments, you must start from scratch every time you want to create a new window for the user to interact with. Outlook is different in that it presents you with a group of built-in forms. To build a custom form, you start with one of the built-in forms and then add your own special touches.

For example, Figure 1.2 shows the default Contact form as it normally looks when you add a new item to the Contacts folder. Notice that the E-mail field shows only one address and provides no clue that as many as three addresses can be associated with this contact. In Figure 1.3, you see

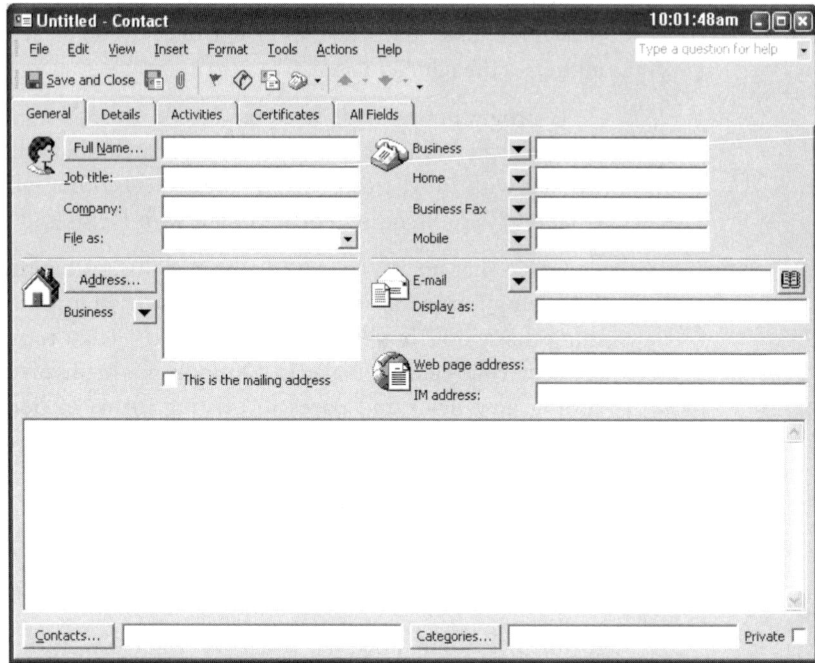

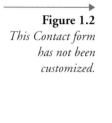

**Figure 1.2** *This Contact form has not been customized.*

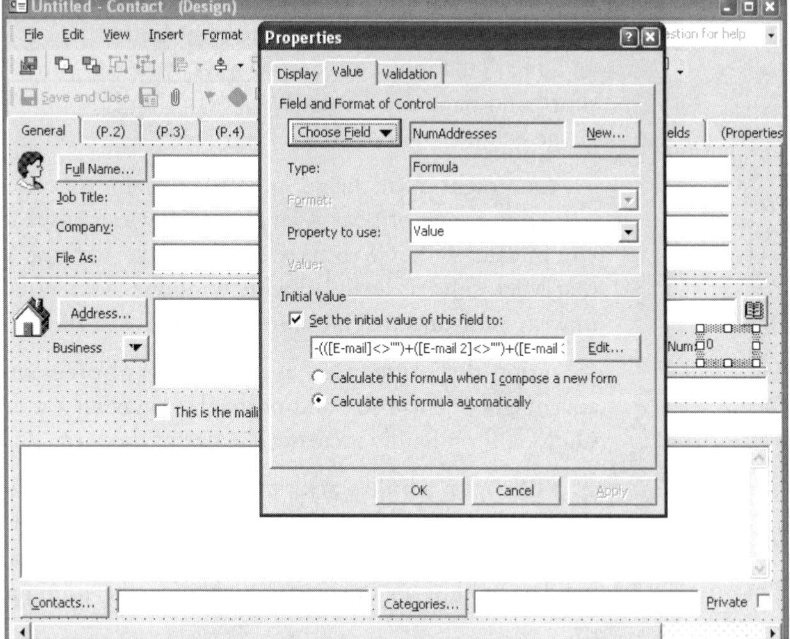


**Figure 1.3** *This Contact form has been customized to show the number of e-mail addresses for any contact item displayed using this form.*

the same form, this time as it's being redesigned and customized with a `NumAddresses` property and text box to indicate how many e-mail addresses the contact has.

Is programming code necessary to do this? Not really. All it takes is a fairly simple formula, no more complicated than those you might have worked with in Microsoft Excel spreadsheets. You will see how it works in Chapter 17, "Extending Form Design with Fields and Controls."

Given that no real code is involved, is this really programming? Sure it is! Designing forms for user interaction is such an important part of programming that whole books have been devoted to that topic alone. Many of the changes you want to make to Outlook might involve nothing more than adding new fields and pages to existing forms to hold the data. Without writing any code at all, you can perform simple validation to make sure that the data meets your criteria for correctness and develop simple formulas such as the one for counting e-mail addresses.

### 1.2.3 Visual Basic Scripting Edition

A time will come, however, when you want your forms to do more. Maybe you will want to generate a task for a follow-up telephone call from an appointment and have Outlook automatically fill in the contact name for you, or perhaps you would like to be reminded to add a category to each outgoing message you send. When you are ready to go beyond entering data and manipulating it in simple ways, you can move up to *VBScript*, the shorthand name for Visual Basic Scripting Edition, the programming language behind Outlook forms.

You might have heard of VBScript in the context of Web pages. VBScript is one of several languages that can control what you see when you interact with a Web page. It also works with the Windows Script Host that Microsoft has included with Windows since Windows 98 to allow you to write programs that are stored as simple text files.

Scripts don't run as fast as other kinds of programs, but they enjoy the advantages of small size and portability. Having a script associated with an Outlook form hardly increases the size of the form at all.

VBScript is a little scary, though. It's like working without a net, because the built-in editor for building VBScript programs is, well, a text editor. Figure 1.4 shows a sample script for a form to distribute a list of company holidays within an organization. Notice the minimal toolbar. The form

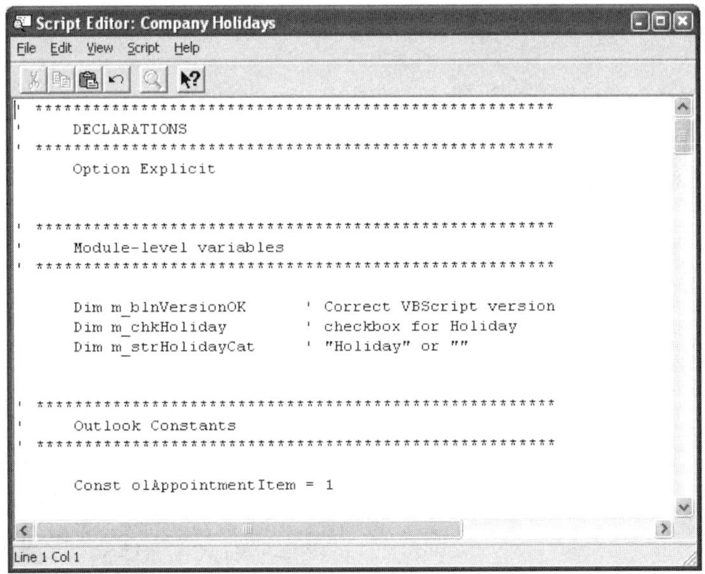


**Figure 1.4** *The Outlook form script editor is just a text editor (compare with Figure 1.1).*

script editor also has none of the color-coding or automatic syntax checking found in VBA.

One sneaky technique you will learn in this book is to write and test your Outlook form code in the superior VBA code environment, make a few minor adjustments to adapt it to VBScript, and then copy and paste it into the script window of an Outlook form. This method cuts down on programming time immensely.

### 1.2.4 Office integration, object models, and beyond

Outlook can create Word or Excel documents, and Microsoft Office programs such as Excel and Word can create messages, appointments, and other Outlook items. You can even integrate Outlook with a Microsoft Access database. This integration occurs thanks to something called the *Outlook object model.* All the Office programs and many other Windows components have object models that reveal what these programs can do, the types of items they can work with, and the characteristics of those items.

Besides the Outlook object model, you also work with the Collaboration Data Objects (CDO) model. CDO can reach some corners of e-mail that Outlook by itself can't, such as the fields in the Global Address List on Microsoft Exchange Server. You will see several examples of how CDO delivers details that Outlook can't access.

**Table 1.1** *Object Models Commonly Used When Programming with Outlook*

| Object Model | Description |
|---|---|
| ActiveX Data Objects (ADO) | Exchange information with Access and other databases |
| Active Directory Services Interface (ADSI) | Interact with the Exchange and Windows 2000 directory |
| Collaboration Data Objects (CDO) | Access MAPI properties of Outlook items, as well as many Exchange Server properties |
| Outlook object model | Create and manipulate Outlook items, as well as react to application-level events |
| Other Office application object models | Work with Excel, Word, PowerPoint, and Access objects from within Outlook |
| Redemption | Access features that secure versions of Outlook may block and use some MAPI features for which the Outlook object model has no equivalent |
| Scripting Runtime | Working with Windows files and folders |

CDO is sometimes thought of as a "light" version of MAPI, which is short for Messaging Application Programming Interface and is the foundation on which Outlook is built. You cannot use VBA to use Extended MAPI directly, but Redemption is an object model that wraps around MAPI, provides access to features that secure versions of Outlook may block, and exposes features for which the Outlook object model has no equivalent.

As you read what other people have done with Outlook programming—in this book and others, on the Web, or in newsgroups—you might hear about other object models relevant to designing with Outlook, such as those listed in Table 1.1.

For example, you will be using the Excel and Word object models to write reports from Outlook objects because Outlook has fairly limited print layout functions. You also will see how to write code that populates a list box from an Access database.

## 1.3 New programming features in Outlook 2002

The biggest change in Outlook 2002 is the addition of strict security features aimed at preventing a virus from using Outlook to propagate itself. We will cover this topic in depth in Chapter 13, "Understanding Outlook

**Table 1.2** *Major Additions to the Outlook Object Model in Outlook 2002*

| Component | Description |
|---|---|
| `ItemProperties` collection, `ItemProperty` object | Provides a single collection that contains all properties on an Outlook item, unlike `UserProperties`, which covers only custom properties |
| `Search` object, `Results` collection | Allows you to perform complex searches—across multiple folders in a Personal Folders file or Exchange mailbox—using SQL-like syntax |
| `Views` collection, `View` object | Allows you to create, delete, and modify Outlook folder views |
| `Reminders` collection, `Reminder` object | Provides objects, events, and methods for building custom handlers for Outlook reminders |

Security." In addition, Table 1.2 lists the four main additions to the Outlook object model.

In addition to the objects and collections in Table 1.2, Outlook 2002 also adds a cancelable `BeforeDelete` event for Outlook items; a number of properties and methods to assist in deploying applications based on items in Outlook folders; events triggered by Cut, Copy, and Paste commands on a folder; a property to set the format of a message to plain text, HTML, or rich text; and many more small, but welcome additions. As we encounter them in later chapters, we'll make sure to note that they work only for Outlook 2002.

## 1.4 How to start

At this point, you might feel the hardest task in Outlook programming is knowing where to start. Do you start with VBScript or VBA? Do you work with the form first and then write the program code, or vice versa?

Start by choosing one or more compelling projects—ideas that will save you time in the long run, make repetitive tasks less burdensome, or perhaps just display information that is hard to get to in the basic Outlook interface. Try to be as specific as possible. Don't decide to build a project to make Outlook work just like GoldMine (a popular sales contact management program). Instead, pick a particular GoldMine feature you want Outlook to duplicate.

When you choose a project, don't start writing code or moving fields around on a form right away! Instead, take some time to outline what you want the project to accomplish, using what programmers call *pseudo code*.

But wait! You say you don't know how to write programming code. (That's why you bought this book, you protest.) No, we're not asking you to write a program (not yet), only to lay the groundwork. When you write pseudocode, you're walking through the logic of what you want to happen, without worrying about the exact language required to make it work.

For example, say you want to enhance Outlook's appointment form with a button that would create a new task for a follow-up telephone call to the person you met with. The pseudocode might look something like this:

```
User clicks button
    Show task form
    Copy details of meeting to task body
    Copy contact from meeting to the task's Contact field
    Set task due date for one week from the meeting date
    If task due date falls on a weekend, holiday, or vacation
    day, then adjust the due date to the next business day
    ...and so forth
```

Nothing in this list looks like programming, but it describes in detail what you want Outlook to do when the user clicks the follow-up call buttons. It won't take much to move from this pseudocode to the program code to implement these steps.

Which tool is appropriate for a particular project? Table 1.3 provides some recommendations of the tools you are most likely to use in particular

**Table 1.3** *Choosing Outlook Tools*

| If You Want To . . . | You Will Probably Use This Approach |
|---|---|
| Show additional information on an Outlook form | Modify an Outlook form |
| Make something happen in response to something the user does with an Outlook item | Modify an Outlook form with VBScript code |
| Write a macro that can be run from the Outlook toolbar | Write a routine in VBA |
| Make something happen when the user starts Outlook, switches to a different folder, or performs other actions that don't involve a particular Outlook item | Write a routine in VBA |
| Display status information as the user performs various Outlook tasks | Create a form in VBA with a routine to show the status information |

situations. Don't take these recommendations as hard and fast rules. In many cases, you can approach a project in several ways. As you work through the examples in the chapters that follow, you will develop a better feel for which Outlook tool works best where.

## 1.5 A word on Outlook versions and setup

This book aims to cover the basics of programming for Outlook 2000, which was the first version to include an integrated VBA environment, and Outlook 2002. Much of the content is also relevant to Outlook 97 and Outlook 98, especially the chapters on designing Outlook forms. You can also run code to automate Outlook from VBA in Word or Excel, from Visual Basic, or even from Windows Script Host scripts, so you shouldn't feel left out if you don't have Outlook 2000 or 2002 yet. You just won't be able to program for those versions' application-level events or use objects, methods, or properties introduced in the newer versions.

Among Microsoft Office programs, Outlook 2000 and Outlook 98 have the peculiar distinction of being two applications in one. Depending on how you install Outlook, you may be working in Internet Mail Only mode or in Corporate or Workgroup mode. Each mode includes features not available to the other. For example, Outlook 2000 includes a Send Plain Text Only check box on the Contact form, but that feature works only in Internet Mail Only mode. To check your version, choose Help, About. In Outlook 2000 or 98, the second line will tell you whether you are in Internet Mail Only or Corporate Workgroup.

Another factor that makes a difference in how Outlook operates is whether you connect to a Microsoft Exchange Server, Microsoft's enterprise

**Table 1.4** *Key Outlook Development Components*

| Component | Features |
|---|---|
| Microsoft Outlook | VBScript support<br>CDO |
| Office Shared Features | Digital Signature for VBA Projects<br>Office XP Web Components (optional)<br>Office 2000 Web Components (optional)<br>VBA/Visual Basic Help |
| Office Tools | HTML Source Editing/Web Scripting/Web Debugging |

e-mail and collaboration server. In Chapter 23, "Exchange Server, Databases, and XML Web Services," you will look at some particular issues related to creating applications for Exchange Server users.

The default Office or Outlook installation does not include all the development tools that you might want to be able to use. You can use Control Panel, Add/Remove Programs to modify your installation of Outlook or Office to make sure that the components in Table 1.4 are available. Select Office or Outlook, then Change. When the Installer opens, choose the Add or Remove Features option to add these components.

## 1.6 Summary

At first, Microsoft Outlook programming can seem complex because there is more than one tool and no clear picture of where to start. However, by modifying Outlook forms and creating custom programs in VBA, you can build powerful applications that use electronic messaging as a vehicle for all kinds of other interactions.

This book is divided into sections that introduce Outlook skills one at a time with examples that you can easily try on your own computer. After an introduction in Part 1 to VBA design, in Part II you learn programming code techniques frequently used in Outlook. Experienced programmers who want to incorporate Outlook automation into their projects may want to skip ahead to Part III, which presents the key techniques related to working with Outlook folders and items. You'll also learn about the security features in Outlook that make some properties and methods difficult to use and about how to use events in VBA to run your Outlook code automatically. Part IV covers Outlook form design with many examples. Finally, in Part V, you'll find out how to integrate Outlook with Word, Excel, Access, and Exchange to print reports, connect to databases, and build collaboration tools. We also discuss how to share your Outlook forms and VBA applications with other users and how to manipulate menus, toolbars, and the Outlook Bar

Code samples specifically related to this book can be found at http://www.outlookcode.com. See Appendix A for other Outlook development resources on the Web and elsewhere.

# *Outlook VBA Design*

# 2

# *The VBA Design Environment*

Visual Basic for Applications (or VBA as I'll call it from now on) is the programming environment where you will write and test macros and procedures that respond to various events that occur when you use Outlook. VBA was added to Outlook 2000, although other Office applications have had it for some time. If you have an older version of Outlook, you can still use VBA in other Office applications to perform some of the automation tasks you'll learn about in this book.

The highlights of this chapter include discussions of the following:

- How to start and end a VBA session
- What the basic windows in VBA are used for
- Where to enter program code
- How to add a new form
- How to avoid a security message when you start VBA
- How to determine where Outlook saves your VBA projects

## 2.1 VBA security

The default VBA security setting in Outlook 2002 or in Outlook 2000 with the Service Pack 2 or the Outlook Email Security Update does not allow you to run VBA code. Therefore, before starting VBA, you should check the security settings by choosing Tools, Macro, Security. If the setting on the Security dialog (see Figure 2.1) is High, set it to Medium, then restart Outlook.

With security set to Medium, once you write some VBA code, Outlook will prompt you (see Figure 2.2) each time it starts to confirm that you

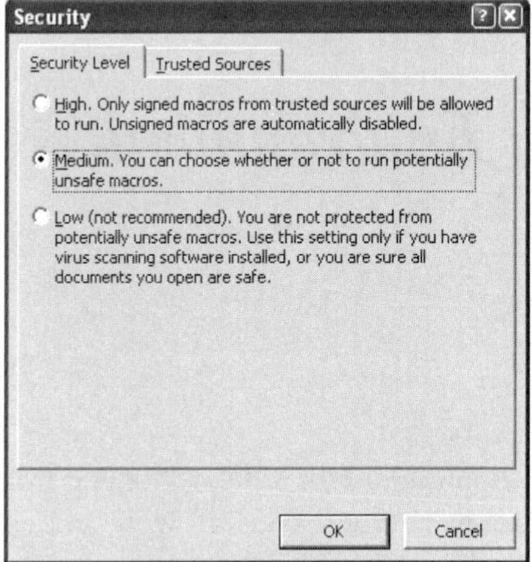


**Figure 2.1** *Adjust macro security to Medium before you first run Outlook VBA.*

want to allow that code to run. At the end of this chapter, you'll learn how to sign your VBA project digitally to avoid that prompt.

CAUTION: If you choose Disable Macros in the dialog shown in Figure 2.2, you can still work on your VBA project, but you will not be able to run any program code until you exit and restart Outlook, then choose Enable Macros.

## 2.2 Starting VBA

Once you have adjusted Outlook VBA security, you can start a VBA session by pressing Alt+F11. Alternatively, choose Tools, Macro, Visual Basic Editor. A new window opens, as shown in Figure 2.3. It may look terribly complex if you haven't previously worked with Visual Basic or with VBA in other programs. Don't worry. In this chapter, you will learn about those two

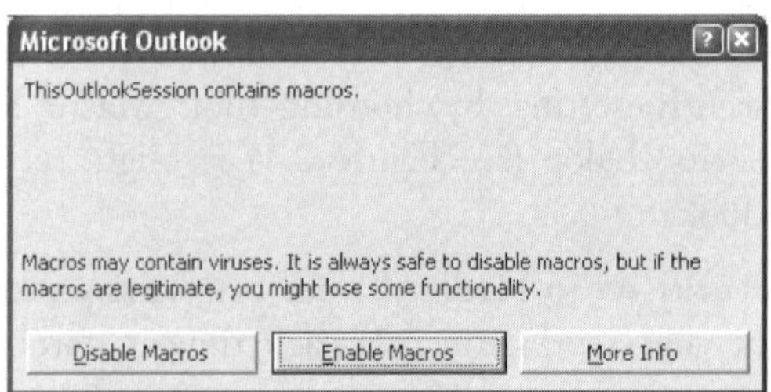


**Figure 2.2** *This message appears when you start VBA after creating any code modules or forms if your macro security setting is Medium.*

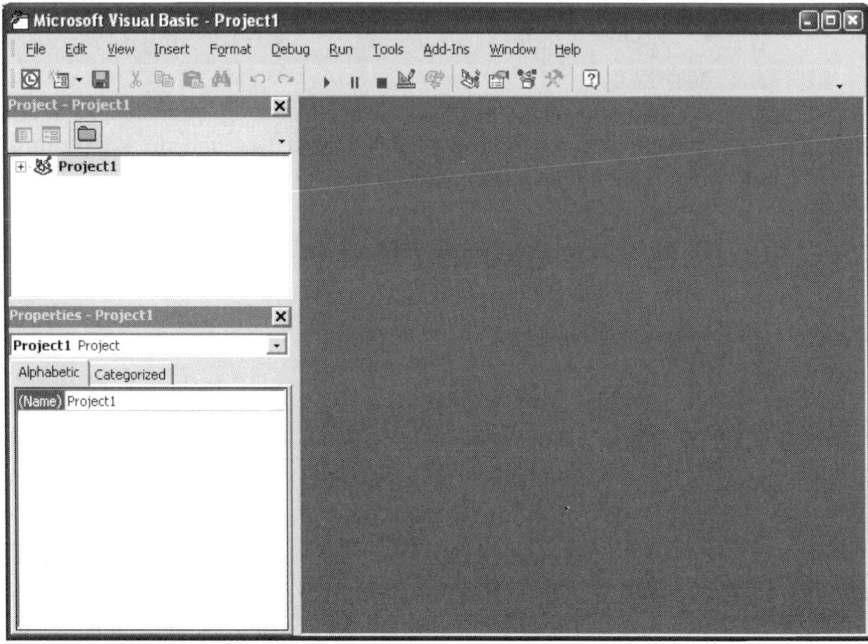


**Figure 2.3** *The VBA environment contains no program code and forms when you first start it.*

windows on the left and fill out the blank space on the right with a form and a module, your first VBA programming components.

---

**Tip:** Working in VBA does not mean you can't get your e-mail messages. Outlook remains open. Just click the View Microsoft Outlook button on the VBA toolbar or click the Outlook icon in the Windows Taskbar.

---

## 2.3 Saving your work and ending a VBA session

You should save your work periodically, perhaps after you finish positioning controls on a form or after you finish coding a module. You do this by clicking the Save button, pressing Ctrl+S, or choosing File, Save.

To end a VBA session, click the close (x) button in the upper-right corner of the VBA window, or choose File, Close and Return to Microsoft Outlook. If any modules or forms are unsaved when you leave VBA, Outlook prompts you to save the VBA project VbaProject.OTM when you exit Outlook. This saves all modules and forms in a single project file.

---

**Note:** Outlook always stores its VBA project in a file named VbaProject.OTM on your system; the exact location depends on your Windows configuration. Unlike Office programs (such as Word and Excel) that allow you to have a VBA project for each document and template, Outlook allows only this one project. You cannot change the file name or the location.

---

## 2.4 VBA windows

When you use VBA, the first two windows that appear are the Project Explorer and Properties windows. You can close either of them with the close (x) button in the upper-right corner of the window. Probably, you will want to keep them open, unless you have limited space on your screen.

---

**Tip:** If the Properties or Project Explorer window is not visible, you can restore either window with the appropriate command on the View menu or the corresponding toolbar button.

---

Besides these two, you will also look at module and form windows (the windows you use to create Outlook applications) and the Object Browser, which helps you discover what you can do with Outlook.

### 2.4.1 Project Explorer

The Project Explorer window lists the currently loaded VBA elements that make up your programming application. For example, compare Figure 2.4 with Figure 2.3. Figure 2.4 shows the Project Explorer after I added a form and a module (more on those shortly). You will always see `ThisOutlookSession`, because this module is built into Outlook. You will use the `ThisOutlookSession` module to build code routines that handle Outlook events.

The three buttons at the top of the Project Explorer are (left to right) View Code, View Object, and Toggle Folders. When working with a form, use the View buttons to switch between its code and layout. The Toggle Folders button flattens the list of elements in the project, hiding the folders and listing everything in alphabetical order.

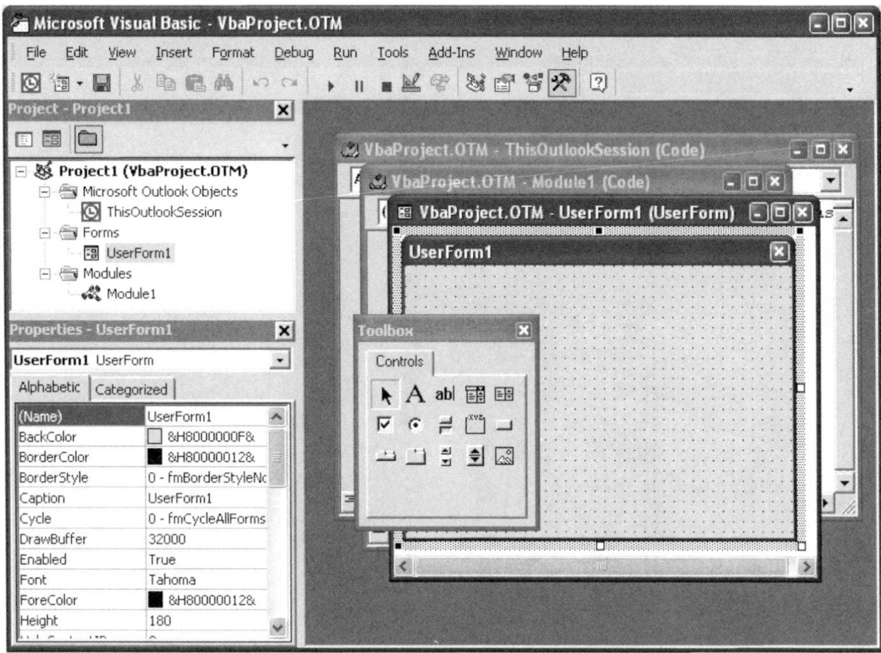


**Figure 2.4** *Use the Project Explorer as a map or index to the components you are currently working on.*

## 2.4.2 Properties window

The Properties window, which appears below the Project Explorer window lists all the attributes of any project elements.

In Figure 2.5, you see the properties for a code module (more on those shortly) created by choosing Insert, Module. The only property is its name, `Module1` by default. To change the `Name` property, click next to (Name) and replace `Module1` with a different name.

When you start designing VBA forms, you will see that VBA form controls have many, many properties. Some properties you change by typing in a new value. Others you pick from a list. Most can also be changed with program code. An example would be turning the text in a control red when the value of the control meets certain criteria.

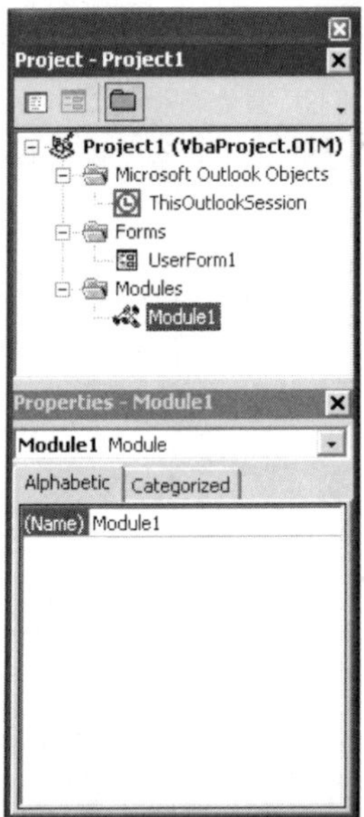


**Figure 2.5** *Every programming component in VBA has properties.*

---

**Tip:** If you drag the Properties window by its title, you can float it over another part of the VBA environment. Both the Properties window and the Project Explorer (and most other VBA windows) are dockable; you can either park them against one side of the main window or float them anywhere inside the VBA window.

---

### 2.4.3 Forms

Now, add your first form to the VBA environment by choosing Insert, UserForm. You should see something like the form in Figure 2.6

VBA forms use controls to display information to the user and gather data. No data resides in the form itself, except during the short time that the form is visible. Most of the VBA forms you will build in Outlook are called *dialog boxes* because they force the user to carry on a conversation with the program. The user can't return to the Outlook application until the conversation ends with the user clicking OK, Cancel, or some other button that closes the dialog box.

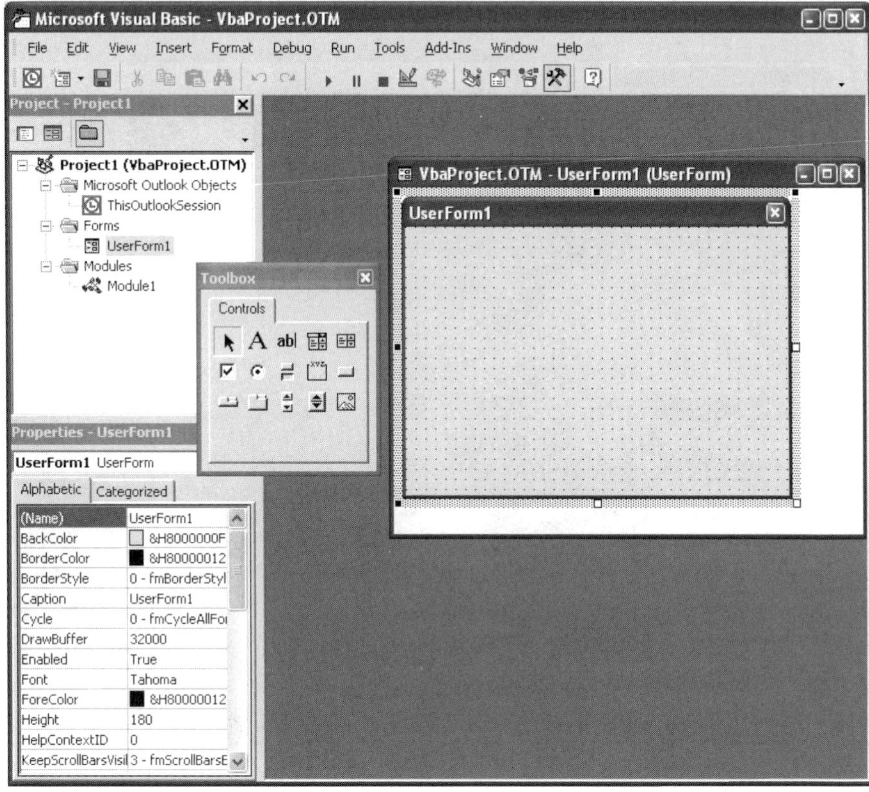


**Figure 2.6** *The design tools for VBA forms include a toolbox.*

## 2.4.4 Modules

Now, add a module. A *module* is a collection of programming procedures. Choose Insert, Module, and you should see something like Figure 2.7, only your module will be totally blank.

The module window is a rather smart text editor. It checks your code against the VBA programming language, reminds you of the parameters of every function, and colors your text to distinguish different code elements. For example, the text shown at the top of Figure 2.7 appears in VBA in green because it is a *comment*, text in a program module that is not executed as code. To create a comment, start a line of text with an apostrophe (').

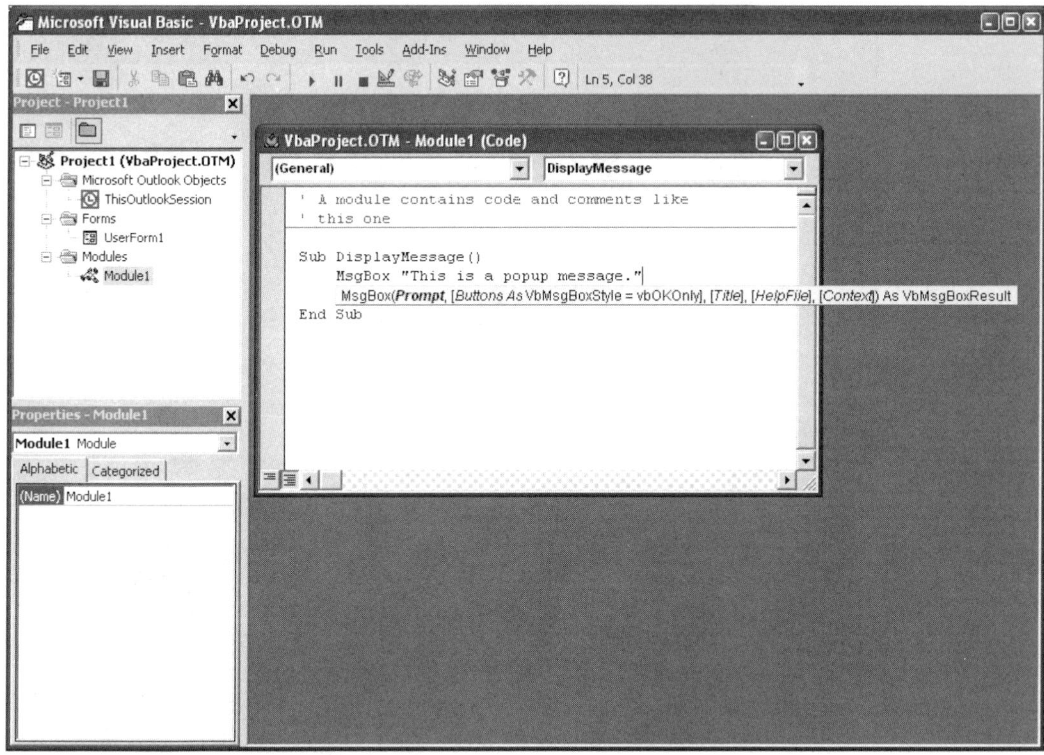


**Figure 2.7** *Modules contain programming procedures.*

---

**Note:** You can also insert another kind of module called a *class module*. You will learn more about class modules in Chapter 11, "Responding to Outlook Events in VBA."

---

In Figure 2.7, notice the pop-up about the `MsgBox` function that tells you what parameters it can use and in what order to use them to pop up a message box on the user's screen. This information appears as you type the name of a function that VBA recognizes, and then disappears automatically after you finish typing the current function. If you find this distracting, you can turn it off by choosing Tools, Options and clearing the box for Auto Quick Info.

---

**Tip:** Choose Tools, Options if you want to experiment with the settings for the code editor.

---

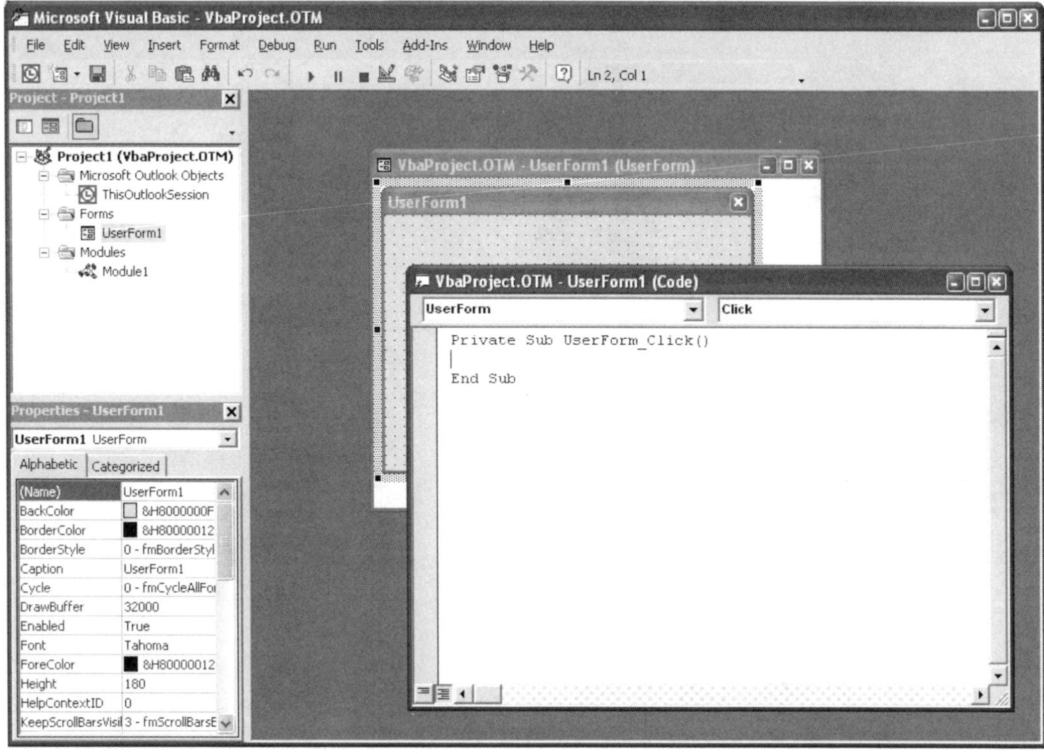


**Figure 2.8** *Forms also include programming code, shown in a separate window.*

Did you know that you already have another place to write programming code for your project? Select `UserForm1` in the Project Explorer, and then double-click anywhere on the blank form. A code window like the one in Figure 2.8 appears, ready for you to type in the first procedure that applies directly to the form. (Don't be concerned just yet about what to type; that's coming in the next few chapters.)

---

**Tip:** You can toggle between the forms and modules either with the Project Explorer or by using the Window menu.

---

### 2.4.5 Object Browser

You need to take a look at one more window, the Object Browser. Choose View, Object Browser, or click the Object Browser toolbar button. You will probably want to maximize it so that it fills whatever space is not occupied

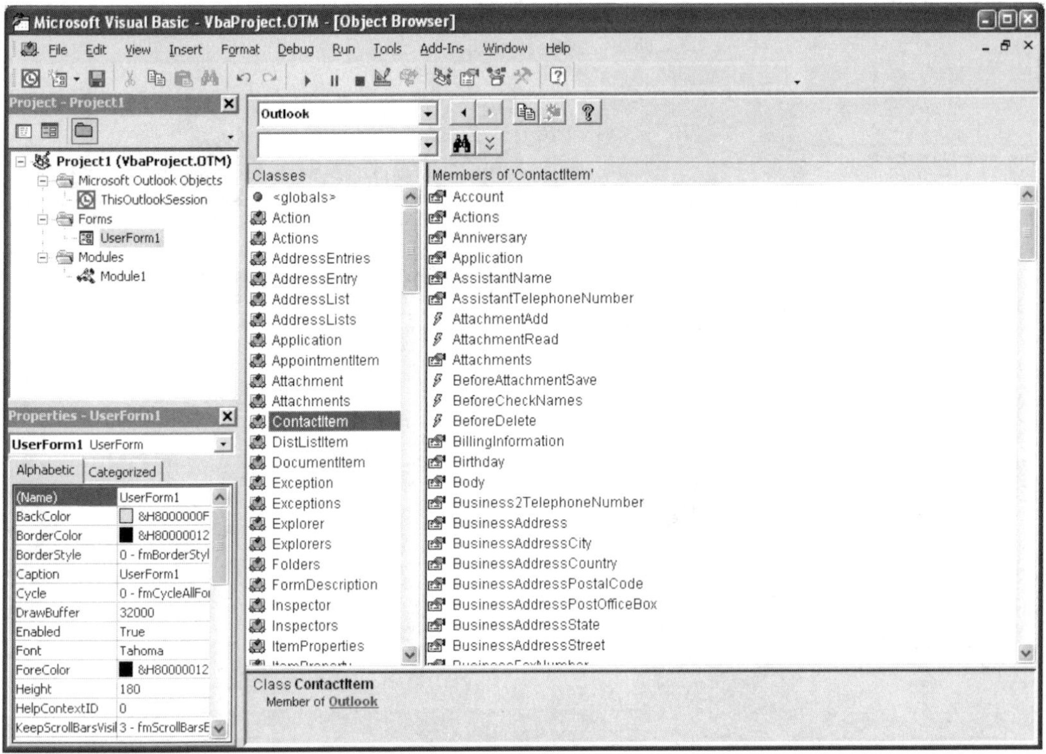


**Figure 2.9** *The Object Browser describes the various objects you can program with and their properties, methods, and events.*

by the Project Explorer and Properties windows, as shown in Figure 2.9. In the dropdown list at the top of the Object Browser, switch from <All Libraries> to Outlook.

---

**Note:** From now on, most figures illustrating work in VBA will show only the particular form or code window, not the entire VBA environment.

---

The Object Browser is your cookbook, your road map, and your index to the world of Outlook items, folders, and other components. Under Classes, you see each Outlook object. Click on `ContactItem`, for example, and under Members of 'ContactItem' on the right, you see the characteristics of Contact items: what they can do, what you can do to them, and their properties. After you select a class or member, click the question-mark button to read the help topic about the item. For many topics, you will find a link to examples that contain sample code you can copy and paste into your application.

Similarly, you can use the Object Browser to explore the characteristics of VBA forms or of other Office applications. We will look at the Object Browser in more detail in Chapter 10, "Working with the Object Models." However, you should go ahead and start browsing it to learn more about what you can do in Outlook.

---

**Tip:** The fields you see in the (All Fields) page on an Outlook form generally match the object properties for different items, although not always exactly. For example, the Company field on a Contact form is actually the `CompanyName` property of a `ContactItem` object. In a formula on a form, you would use `Company`, but in VBA or VBScript code, you would have to use `CompanyName`.

---

## 2.5 Working with VBA projects

Take a look at the project in more detail. Both the Project Explorer and the title bar for the Microsoft Visual Basic window include the name VbaProject.OTM. This is the actual name of the file that contains your Outlook VBA project.

You can't change the default name of this file or store it in a different location. You can, however, exit Outlook, rename the VbaProject.OTM file, restart Outlook, and start VBA. This will create a new, empty project. To return to the original project, exit Outlook, rename the current VbaProject.OTM, and then rename the original project back to VbaProject.OTM.

---

**Note:** Unlike other Office applications (such as Excel or Word) that include a VBA project for each document, Outlook allows you to work only on one project at a time.

---

### 2.5.1 Backing up your work

Because the VbaProject.OTM file contains all your Outlook VBA work, including it in your regular system backup is a good idea. You can also make copies of individual modules and forms, either as backups or for reuse on a different computer. In the Project Explorer, select any form or module, and then choose File, Export File. Outlook exports modules as .bas files, forms as .frm files, and the `ThisOutlookSession` module as a .cls file.

The File menu has an Import command for bringing in a module or form that was previously saved, as well as a Remove command. When you remove a module or form from the project, Outlook asks whether you want to export it first. It's a good idea to go ahead and export, just in case you want to recover the routines in that module or form later.

Another way to back up your work is to run the Save My Settings Wizard included with Office XP and downloadable for Office 2000 from http://office.microsoft.com. This tool backs up your Outlook VBA project, as well as other key files and registry settings.

### 2.5.2 Signing your project

The Office 2000 and 2002 CDs include a tool called Selfcert.exe that you can use to sign your Outlook VBA project digitally, so that you will not see the Disable Macros/Enable Macros prompt (Figure 2.2) when you start Outlook. The Selfcert tool creates a digital certificate, similar to that which you can get from providers like Verisign, only it's free and doesn't reflect a trusted hierarchy of other certificates. After you run the tool, restart Outlook and switch into the VBA environment. Then choose Tools, Digital Signature, and click Choose to sign your project with the new certificate.

After you sign the project, you can switch back to the main Outlook window, choose Tools, Macros, Security and set security to High if you want maximum protection. Also, your new certificate will appear on the Security dialog's Trusted Sources tab. To put your new security settings into effect, restart Outlook one more time.

## 2.6 Getting help in VBA

Like all Microsoft Office programs, Outlook includes a detailed system of help topics designed to assist you in various tasks. One way to access Help is to press F1, and if the Office Assistant appears, type your search words in the assistant's box, then press Enter or click Search. If you see the Microsoft Visual Basic Help window instead of the Office Assistant, switch to the Answer Wizard tab, type your search words there, then click Search.

To obtain help with a VBA function, select text in your code and press F1 to get details about it. For example, in the routine in Figure 2.7, select `MsgBox` and then press F1 to see the MsgBox Function help topic shown in Figure 2.10. Topics on functions always give their basic syntax, and most also include hints on how to use them, notes on situations where they might be appropriate, and one or more code examples.

If you want information on a function that isn't already in your code, click the Help button on the toolbar. Then, type the text you want to search for and click OK (or Search if you're using the Office Assistant) to see a list of related topics.

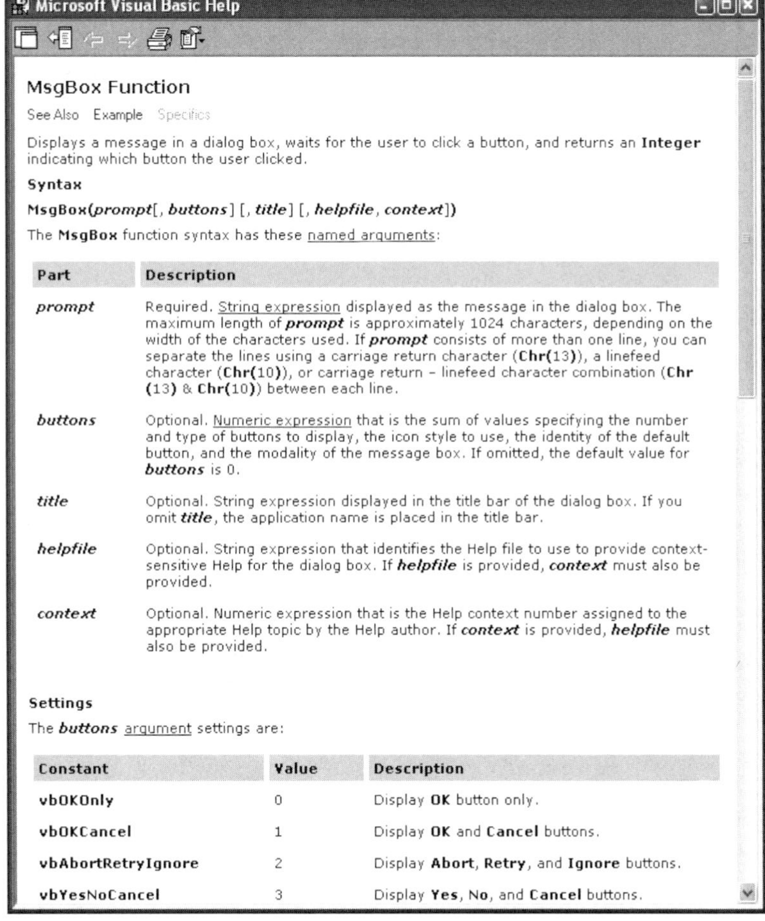


**Figure 2.10** *Detailed help topics on VBA functions help you learn programming fast.*

**CAUTION:** Unfortunately, Outlook VBA Help is known not to be 100 percent accurate. Some flaws are documented in the Microsoft Knowledgebase, but others have persisted through several versions. Test any code sample that you want to copy from Help into your own project. If it doesn't work, consult the resources listed in Appendix A for possible workarounds.

## 2.7 Summary

The VBA environment allows you to create dialog boxes and other user input and display forms, as well as to program code modules that you can run as macros from the toolbar or, in Outlook 2002, even as part of Rules Wizard rules. In Chapter 3, you will learn how to create forms with VBA. Some of these new techniques can be eventually transferred to the Outlook forms design environment, which is covered later in the book.

# 3

# *A VBA Birthday/Anniversary Reminder Form*

Now that you know your way around the VBA design environment, you are going to build a form to add a new feature to Outlook—setting reminders for birthday and anniversary events that Outlook creates automatically from corresponding dates in contact items. In the process, you will learn the basics of designing VBA forms.

The highlights of this chapter include discussions of the following:

- How to add controls to a form using the VBA Toolbox
- Which controls can be useful for data entry tasks
- How to start adding code to a form
- What makes a good dialog box or other VBA form
- When to use option button and check box controls
- How to work with list box and combo box controls
- How to manage the way users move around in a form

## 3.1 Understanding Outlook birthdays and anniversaries

Whenever you add a birthday or anniversary on the Details page of the built-in Contact form, Outlook automatically creates a corresponding recurring event in your Calendar folder and adds a shortcut to that event in the contact item. However, the events that Outlook adds to the Calendar folder don't have reminders. Therefore, unless you check the Calendar well in advance, those birthdays could sneak up on you.

---

**Note:** Entering a date does not automatically create a matching Calendar entry for user-defined date/time fields added to the Contact form. If you want this kind of functionality, you must add it in VBScript code. In Chapter 14, "Working with Items and Recipients," you will learn how to create new items with code, using information from an existing item.

---

You can use VBA to build a tool to globally update all the birthdays and anniversaries to make sure that they have reminders. You can use it periodically to ensure that any newly added anniversaries or birthdays also have reminders.

## 3.2 Step 1: What controls do you need?

The birthday/anniversary reminder tool consists of an Outlook VBA form and accompanying program code. Key first steps in designing any form are to decide what the form will do and what information it needs to complete its task.

The purpose of your form has already been decided—to add a reminder to all birthdays and anniversaries. To accomplish this, the form requires information from the user on when to set the reminder a specific number of days, weeks, or months in advance of the event.

---

**Note:** Another key decision you will make in designing forms is what kind of feedback to provide the user as the form goes about its work. This is discussed in Chapter 9, "Handling User Input and Feedback."

---

How many ways are there to enter the reminder interval? You might consider the following:

- A text box control in which the user enters the number of days
- A text box control in which the user types "3 days," "2 wks," or "1m," and so on, as in Outlook's built-in date/time- and duration-type fields
- A spin button control that the user clicks until the desired number of days is shown
- A spin button control to show the number, as well as option button controls to select days, weeks, or months

- Option button controls to select from the most frequently used reminder intervals (as you want to define them)

Which approach would be best? The first and third approaches are somewhat limited because they count only days, not weeks or months. The second approach takes some work because you would have to write code to convert what the user types into the corresponding number of days. (Controls bound to duration-type data fields on Outlook items perform this conversion automatically, but VBA controls do not include that feature.) The fourth approach might be a little too complicated. The last approach is too limited if you later decide to share the form with other people, who might have other preferences for reminders.

**Tip:** If you are designing a form for your personal use, don't feel that you have to cover every possible option or exception. You would, of course, in a program for wider distribution, but for a personal application, it might be easier to create a form that doesn't offer unlimited options for setting reminders.

In other words, it's hard to know which option would be best without creating the form and using it for a while (or being a mind reader). Few programming projects have one single best solution. Brainstorm a number of approaches, then evaluate their pros and cons.

Since this is our first VBA form, we'll keep it simple and use the first approach—a text box in which users enter the number of days before the event that they want to be reminded of. The form, therefore, will use these controls:

- A text box in which the user enters the number of days
- At least one label to cue the user how to use the form
- A command button the user can click to perform the reminder updates
- A second command button the user can use to close the form

## 3.3 Step 2: Create the form

After you have a general plan, the next step is to create the form and set its particular properties. You will have to start VBA, which you learned how to do in Chapter 2.

**Table 3.1** *VBA Form Properties to Set Immediately*

| Property | Description | Suggested Value |
|---|---|---|
| `(Name)` | The form name as shown in the Project Explorer and as used in program code | `ReminderUpdate` |
| `Caption` | The name shown in the title bar of the form | `Birthday and Anniversary Reminder Update` |

To add a form, choose Insert, UserForm. A blank form appears, along with the Toolbox. The Properties window shows the properties for the form. Table 3.1 lists key properties you should set right away.

**Tip:** If you plan to work with the same form for a while, you don't have to keep the Project Explorer on the screen. Choose View, Project Explorer to hide it, or click the Project Explorer's close (x) button. The Properties window will grow taller, making it easier to use. To see the values for the properties more easily, make the Properties window wider by dragging its right border toward the right.

**CAUTION:** Make sure that you set the `(Name)` property before you start writing program code. If you change the `(Name)` after you write code for the form, you must use search and replace in your code to update the form name wherever it appears.

The value for the `(Name)` property must follow the naming convention for objects, which allows internal capitalization, but no spaces. You can (and should) include spaces in the `Caption` property.

## 3.3.1 Exploring form properties

Click on the Categorized tab of the Properties window to see the properties organized into different groups: Appearance, Behavior, Font, Misc, Picture, Position, and Scrolling. Because the properties in a group are often related, viewing the categories helps to remind you to change those allied properties. For example, if you change the `BackColor` property, you might also want to change the `BorderColor`.

---

**Tip:** If you are not familiar with a particular property, select it, and then click F1 to bring up a Help topic that explains it.

---

As you explore the form properties, notice that different properties use different methods to enter new values. For some properties, such as `BackColor` or `Enabled`, you click on a dropdown list and select a value. For others, you type in the value; `Caption` is a good example. In other cases, such as `Font` and `Picture`, you click a button with an ellipsis (...) to get a dialog from which you can select the new value.

What about those cryptic values for some of the Appearance properties? What does `&H8000000F&`, the value for `BackColor` mean? The value for each color property is a *long integer*, a number whose value can range from –2,147,483,648 to 2,147,483,647, but the Properties window shows those values in *hexadecimal* format, in which numbers are expressed in base 16 notation (i.e., 20 in the decimal notation we normally use is equivalent to 14 in hex, whereas 30 in decimal would be 1E in hex).

Don't worry, you don't have to know the values for all the colors, nor do you need the ability to convert a decimal number to hexadecimal. VBA makes it easy to select colors with a couple of mouse clicks. For example, click on the `BackColor` property to select it, and then click the arrow button at the right side of the property's value box. A list of colors appears, as is shown in Figure 3.1.

Now, look at the `SpecialEffect` property shown in Figure 3.2. First, notice that it supports only a few values: `0`, `1`, `2`, `3`, and `6`. Also, see how each numeric value has a word associated with it. For example, the value `1` also has the word `fmSpecialEffectRaised`. This is an example of an *intrinsic constant*, a value built into VBA that doesn't change and has a special keyword associated with it.

You use intrinsic constants in VBA code to work with the property values for forms, controls, and other objects. Hundreds of intrinsic constants are associated with VBA itself and with various Outlook components. As you might imagine, they make it much easier to read and write program code. For example, for a form named `ReminderUpdate`, this line of code changes the form from flat to raised:

```
ReminderUpdate.SpecialEffect = 1
```

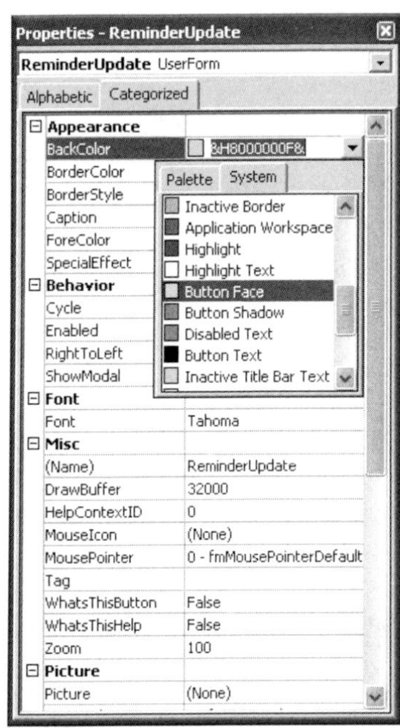


**Figure 3.1**
*Select colors for the form and its controls from among the System colors for the current Windows color scheme or by using the Palette.*

**Figure 3.2**
*Many properties allow only certain values, which have equivalent intrinsic constants.*

This line does the same thing, but is much easier to understand because it contains an intrinsic constant instead of a number:

```
ReminderUpdate.SpecialEffect = fmSpecialEffectRaised
```

You can change many form and control properties with program code while the form is running. The help topic on each property tells you whether or not that's possible.

---

**Note:** You can use only a limited set of intrinsic constants in VBScript code on Outlook forms—only those that VBScript supports.

---

### 3.3.2 Should you use a modal or modeless form?

Another important form property is `ShowModal`, which can have the value `True` or `False`. While a modal form is on the screen, you cannot return to the main application window. This is the typical behavior of a dialog box: The dialog box opens, the user makes a change, and then the user closes the dialog to return to the application. From a programming standpoint, modal forms are important to controlling program flow. No other code executes until the modal form is either hidden or unloaded.

If a form is modeless, the user can work both with the main application windows and with the form. An example would be a form that provides information to the user, either on demand or according to a schedule. (How about a form that counts down the number of minutes until your own birthday?)

Because the `ReminderUpdate` form is designed to perform a quick, occasional update, no need exists to make it a modeless form. Because the default for `ShowModal` is `True`, you don't have to make a property change for this form.

## 3.4 Step 3: Add user input controls

Ready for the next step? Now that you have a blank form and understand some of its properties, you can add controls to it. You will use the simplest of the approaches described previously—a text box in which the user types the number of days. There are two ways to add a text box to the form:

- To get a standard size text box, drag from the TextBox tool on the Toolbox to the form.

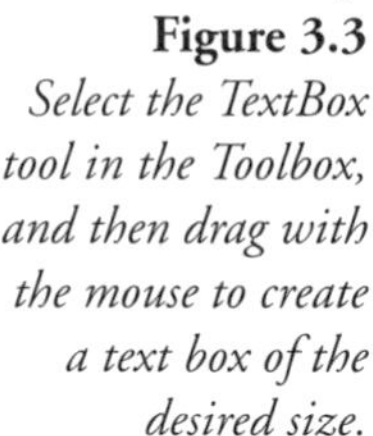

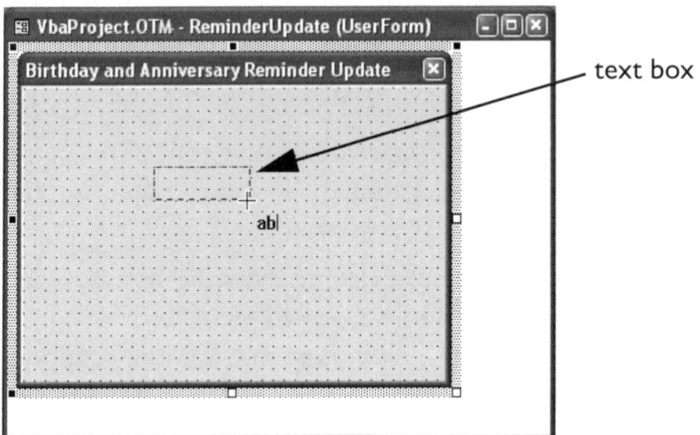


**Figure 3.3** *Select the TextBox tool in the Toolbox, and then drag with the mouse to create a text box of the desired size.*

- To set a custom size, select the TextBox tool in the Toolbox. Position the mouse pointer over the form where you want one corner of the text box to go. Hold down the left mouse button, and drag the mouse to trace a rectangle the size of the text box you want, just as shown in Figure 3.3.

Don't forget to leave room for label controls that indicate how to use the text box. You can always reposition any of the controls later if you need to.

It is important to give a name to each control that holds data, using the Properties dialog. For the text box that will display the number of days, use the name `txtDays`. You might also want to add a value for the `ControlTipText` property to pop up information when the user pauses the mouse over the control.

Now, use the Label (to the left of the TextBox tool in the Toolbox) tool to add two label controls, one to the left and one to the right of the text box. The form should look like that shown in Figure 3.4.

To add your own text to the `Label1` control, click the Select Objects tool in the Toolbox to switch the mouse pointer back to an arrow. Click the `Label1` control once to select it; then click a second time. When you see the blinking vertical insertion point inside the control, you can delete the `Label1` text and replace it with your own, as shown in Figure 3.5.

**Tip:** That's click once to select the `Label1` control, pause briefly, and then click again to edit its caption. The timing is important. If the clicks are too close together, VBA interprets them as a double-click and opens a program code window for the form.

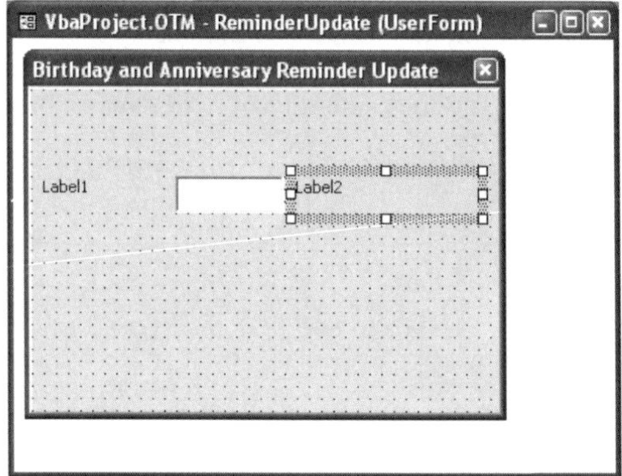


**Figure 3.4** *Change the text for a label control by typing it into the control or updating the Caption property.*

You can also enter text for a label control by typing in the text as the value for the `Caption` property.

To make the form look better, you might want to resize or move the labels. You could also change the `TextAlign` property of the label on the left from `1 - fmTextAlignLeft` to `3 - fmTextAlignRight` to right-align the caption so that it appears closer to the text box. Look in the Format menu for essential layout commands to help you size and position VBA form controls.

## 3.5 Step 4: Add command buttons

The form in Figure 3.5 now has a text box and two label controls to give the user an idea of what kind of information to enter. What's missing? There's no way to actually start the process of updating the Calendar events to add a

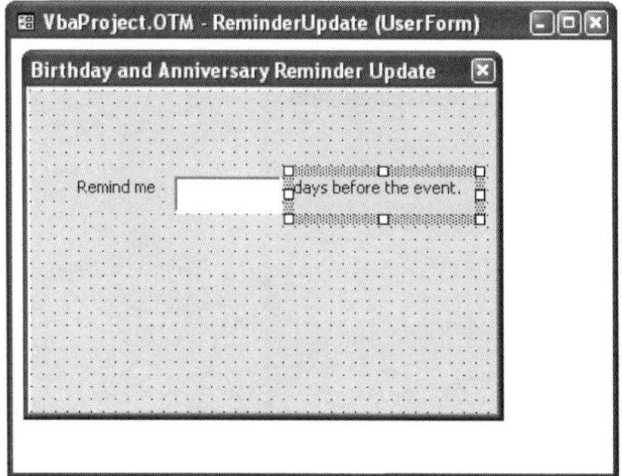


**Figure 3.5** *Combine a data-entry control with one or more explanatory label controls.*

**Table 3.2** *Properties for ReminderUpdate Command Buttons*

| Property | CommandButton1 | CommandButton2 |
|---|---|---|
| `(Name)` | `cmdUpdate` | `cmdClose` |
| `Accelerator` | `U` | |
| `Cancel` | `False` | `True` |
| `Caption` | `Update` | `Close` |
| `Default` | `True` | `False` |

reminder. You need at least one command button control to run the code you will be adding to the form. Command buttons are those ubiquitous form controls that make things happen. The code associated with a button runs when you click it.

You can add two command button controls, one to run the update and the other to close the form. Use the Command Button tool from the Toolbox to drag two buttons to your form. Set the properties shown in Table 3.2.

**Tip:** The form has a close (x) button in the upper-right corner, but putting a command button on the form as well makes it just a little more obvious to the user that the form should be closed when the update has completed.

The most important of these properties are (`Name`) and `Caption`. To see the effect of the other properties in Table 3.2, you must see what the `ReminderUpdate` form will look like to a user. Click the Run button on the toolbar, or choose Run, Run Sub/UserForm. Your form should look like the one in Figure 3.6.

**Figure 3.6** *The ReminderUpdate form is starting to look like a real user form, buttons and all.*

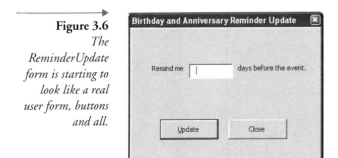

---

**Tip:** You can select the form or any control on it by picking it from the dropdown list at the top of the Properties window.

---

Until now, you have been working in design mode. Figure 3.6 shows the form in run mode. In other words, the form is active. If the buttons had program code associated with them, that code would run when you click them. However, if you click the buttons, nothing happens because you have not added code to the form yet.

### 3.5.1 Basic command button properties

Take a closer look at the Update and Close buttons in Figure 3.6. The property settings from Table 3.2 are responsible for giving them a look similar to that common to dialog box command buttons in most Windows programs.

First, setting the `Accelerator` property for the `cmdUpdate` button to `U` causes the letter U to be underlined. This means the user can press Alt+U as an alternative to clicking the button. Keyboard accelerators such as this make forms more usable and friendlier to those who prefer the keyboard to the mouse.

See how the `cmdUpdate` button has a dark border, whereas the `cmdClose` button doesn't. This is a visual clue that you set the `cmdUpdate` button as the default button by setting its `Default` property to `True`. Pressing the Enter key is the same thing as clicking on the default button. This means that to use your form, the user just has to enter the number of days, then press Enter.

Similarly, pressing the Esc key is equivalent to clicking on the `cmdClose` button, because you set the `Cancel` property of that command button to `True`. This made `cmdClose` the cancel button.

A form can have only one default button and one cancel button. Neither is required. Setting a command button's `Default` or `Cancel` property for a button to `True` makes it the new default or cancel button.

---

**CAUTION:** In this example, you made `cmdUpdate` the default button so that you could see what a default button looks like. In reality, though, the default button should never be a button that runs code that can make irreversible changes to many items.

---

Because the cmdClose button does not do anything yet when you click it, click the close (x) button in the upper-right corner of the ReminderUpdate form to close the running version and return to the design environment. Alternatively, switch back to the design environment, and click the Design Mode button.

### 3.5.2 Adding code

Making the command buttons do something is a matter of adding code. You can start with an easy routine to close the form when the user clicks the cmdClose button.

To add code to any command button, double-click the button on the form. A code window, such as that in Figure 3.7, appears. VBA automatically creates the first and last lines of the subroutine that runs when you click the cmdClose button. The name of the routine is cmdClose_Click. The keyword Private means that this routine runs only in the context of the current form; no other components in your VBA project can use it.

Notice the two dropdown lists at the top of the code window. The one on the left includes the name of every control on the form, as well as UserForm to represent the form itself and a (General) section in which you declare variables and constants (more on that in Chapter 5, "Code Grammar 101."

The list on the right includes Click, as well as all the other events that can take place on the form or relative to a control. You learn more about events in Chapter 4, "Code Basics." For now, you will work just with the Click event for your two command buttons.

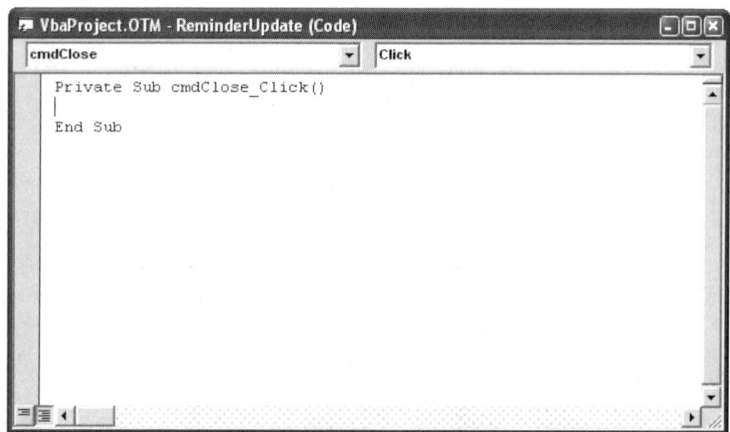
VbaProject.OTM - ReminderUpdate (Code)
cmdClose
Click
Private Sub cmdClose_Click()
End Sub

**Figure 3.7** *A form's code window gives you quick access to all the controls and the events they support.*

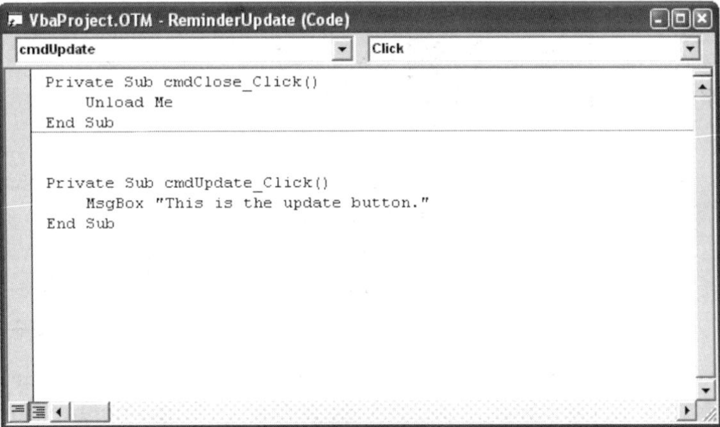
```
Private Sub cmdClose_Click()
    Unload Me
End Sub

Private Sub cmdUpdate_Click()
    MsgBox "This is the update button."
End Sub
```

**Figure 3.8** *The two command buttons now have code that will run when the user clicks each button.*

In the space between `Private Sub cmdClose_Click()` and `End Sub`, type

```
Unload Me
```

`Unload` is the command to remove a form from memory and from the computer display. You can use `Me` instead of the full name of the form, `ReminderUpdate`, because this code is running behind one of the controls on the form that you want to unload.

To add code for the other command button, you do not have to switch back to the form. Instead, choose `cmdUpdate` from the dropdown list of controls at the top of the code window. This will add the shell for the `cmdUpdate_Click()` procedure. Inside that procedure, type

```
MsgBox "This is the update button."
```

This is the code to pop up a simple message to the user. The code window should now look like that shown in Figure 3.8.

---

**Tip:** The indenting in Figure 3.8 helps make the code more readable, but doesn't affect how it runs.

---

Congratulations! You have written your first program code! Click the Run button on the toolbar, or choose Run, Run Sub/UserForm to see the form in action. First, click the Update button. You should see a message box such as the one shown in Figure 3.9.

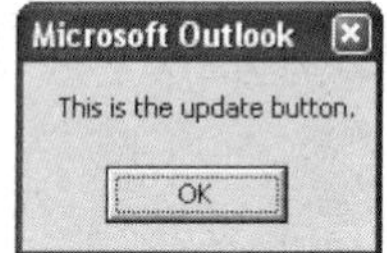


**Figure 3.9**
*It's easy to pop up a simple message box.*

---

**Note:** Message boxes are useful not only for displaying information to the user, but also for forcing the user to make a choice. You will look at message boxes in more detail in Chapter 9, "Handling User Input and Feedback."

---

After you click OK to dismiss the message box, click the Close button or press Esc. The `cmdClose_Click()` procedure runs, unloading the form.

### 3.5.3 Anatomy of a procedure

No doubt, you're eager to design applications that do more than just open message boxes. To give you some additional practice adding code to a command button, replace the `cmdUpdate_Click()` procedure with the procedure shown in Listing 3.1.

The `cmdUpdate_Click()` procedure is divided into three sections. The first section, in which each line begins with `Dim`, defines the variables used. The next section, in which each line begins with `Set`, is a series of assignment statements setting up the Outlook object variables. You will learn how to set up variables and work with objects in Chapter 5, "Code Grammar 101."

The real work is done by the `intMinutes =` ... line and the `For Each ... Next` loop. The line

```
intMinutes = 24 * 60 * txtDays.Value
```

calculates the number of minutes (24 hours in a day times 60 minutes in an hour times the number of days specified on the form) and places the result in a variable named `intMinutes`. This is the value the code uses to set the reminder and is the only place where the procedure has to use a value from the form.

The `For Each ... Next` loop examines each item in the Calendar folder and tests whether the word "Birthday" or "Anniversary" is part of the item's Subject, using the very useful `Instr()` function, which you'll learn more about in Chapter 6, "Working with Expressions and Functions." For

**Listing 3.1** *Code for the cmdUpdate_Click() Procedure*

```
Private Sub cmdUpdate_Click()
    Dim objApp As Application
    Dim objNS As NameSpace
    Dim objCalendar As MAPIFolder
    Dim objItem As AppointmentItem
    Dim strSubject As String
    Dim intMinutes as Integer

    Set objApp = CreateObject("Outlook.Application")
    Set objNS = objApp.GetNamespace("MAPI")
    Set objCalendar = objNS.GetDefaultFolder(olFolderCalendar)

    intMinutes = 24 * 60 * txtDays.Value
    For Each objItem In objCalendar.Items
        strSubject = objItem.Subject
        If InStr(strSubject, "Birthday") > 0 Or _
          InStr(strSubject, "Anniversary") > 0 Then
            objItem.ReminderSet = True
            objItem.ReminderMinutesBeforeStart = intMinutes
            objItem.Save
        End If
    Next
    Beep
End Sub
```

those appointments identified as birthdays or anniversaries, it adds a reminder based on the value in the `intMinutes` variable.

---

**Note:** `For Each ... Next` loops, which are covered in Chapter 7, "Controlling Program Flow," get a real workout in Outlook. You use them extensively to cycle through every subfolder in a parent folder, every item in a folder, every recipient in a message, and so on.

---

**Tip:** Did you recognize `olFolderCalendar` as another intrinsic constant?

---

The `Beep` statement gives you an audible indicator that the code has finished running.

Try running the form again, as you did earlier, but with the new code for the `cmdUpdate` button. (Be sure to back up your Calendar folder, as noted in the next Caution.) Does it operate as you expected, creating reminders in birthday and appointment events?

CAUTION: Although Outlook has an Undo command for single actions, you cannot undo bulk changes made by procedures such as the preceding one. Before you run any procedure that alters all the items in a folder, you should back up the contents of that folder. You can use Outlook's File, Import and Export command to export the folder to a Personal Folders file, or you can copy the items to another folder.

## 3.6 Step 5: Plan the next development stage

In one sense, no development project is ever finished because you can always think of ways to improve it. Here are some possible ways to enhance the `ReminderUpdate` form:

- Allow the user to update just birthdays, just anniversaries, or both. (Hint: This requires two check boxes and a little more code.)
- Before running the update routine, validate the entry in the `txtDays` control to make sure that a number greater than zero is present.
- Don't update any Calendar item that already has a reminder.
- Speed execution of the update routine by examining only all-day events, instead of every item in the Calendar folder.
- Add feedback to tell the user how many items were updated.
- Ask the user to confirm each change to a birthday or anniversary.

As you consider possible enhancements, consider not just the functionality, but also the look of the form. Does it make sense to the user? A dialog box should be logical, unambiguous, and consistent. The user should have no doubt about what kind of data to enter in each control. Validation code behind the form should protect the user from "wrong" entries. Controls should be grouped in a clear sequence. They might follow a cycle that mimics the boxes on a paper form, or they might just be grouped in an orderly fashion, either from left to right or top to bottom. Lining up controls and using similar size controls makes it visually easy for the user to follow the sequence visually. If your application uses several dialog boxes, they should have the same color scheme, unless you vary the colors for a particular reason.

# 3.7 More on VBA form controls

The `ReminderUpdate` form is certainly functional, but it would be hard to find a more unsightly form. We're going to implement some of the enhancements suggested in Step 5 above by adding more controls to the form.

## 3.7.1 Check box controls

Our first enhancement is to allow the user to choose whether to update just birthdays, anniversaries, or both. This takes just a couple of check box controls.

When you add a check box control to a form, you don't have to drag a box on the form to trace out the size of the control. Just select the CheckBox tool in the Toolbox and then click on the form where you want the check box to appear. Check boxes do not need separate label controls to identify them because they include their own `Caption` property.

Figure 3.10 shows the `ReminderUpdate` form with two check boxes added, one for birthdays and one for anniversaries.

The properties of the first check box should be as follows:

```
(Name)              chkBirthdays
Accelerator         B
Caption             Birthdays
Value               True
```

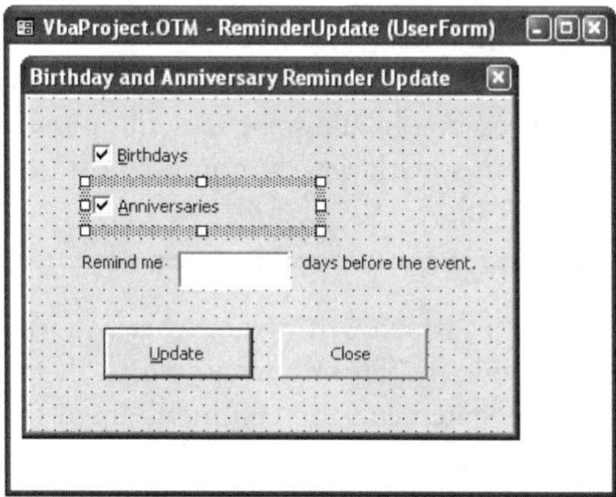


**Figure 3.10** *Check box controls give users more choices.*

For the second check box, use the following properties:

| | |
|---|---|
| `(Name)` | `chkAnniversaries` |
| `Accelerator` | `A` |
| `Caption` | `Anniversaries` |
| `Value` | `True` |

---

**Note:** The `Accelerator` property is case sensitive. If you enter `a`, instead of `A`, for the accelerator letter for the `chkAnniversaries` box, the second *a* in the word will be underlined, instead of the initial capital *A*.

---

Why set the `Value` for the check boxes to `True`? This is where you must know your users—or your own needs, if you are designing in VBA for yourself. Most people probably want to update both birthdays and anniversaries. Setting the `Value` for the check boxes to `True` means that most people won't have to interact at all with the check boxes. They can go straight to the text box and type in the reminder period.

An initial value such as this is called the *default* for the control. Setting the right defaults so that users have to enter as little new information as possible is a key technique for making highly usable forms.

You're probably wondering how to change the code from the original reminder update form to use the information in these check boxes. Most check boxes can contain only one of two values, either `True` or `False`. If the `chkBirthdays` box is checked and the user's Calendar folder includes a birthday event, you want to add a reminder. The same goes for anniversaries.

---

**Note:** The check box control includes a property, named `TripleState`, that changes a check box to allow the user to set the value to `Null`. In this situation, `Null` means neither `True` nor `False`. In other words, the check box has no value at all.

---

This is one case in which writing out what you want to happen provides a clue to how to code it. Notice how we wrote "If the `ChkBirthdays` box . . ." `If ... Then` statements are commonly used to program exactly this type of situation—when you know the values in question are either `True` or `False`. You have already seen an `If ... Then` statement in the code for the

**Listing 3.2** *Use If… Then Statements To Test Conditions*

```
Sub cmdUpdate_Click()
    Dim objApp As Application
    Dim objNS As NameSpace
    Dim objCalendar As MAPIFolder
    Dim objItem As AppointmentItem
    Dim strSubject As String
    Dim intMinutes as Integer

    Set objApp = CreateObject("Outlook.Application")
    Set objNS = objApp.GetNamespace("MAPI")
    Set objCalendar = objNS.GetDefaultFolder(olFolderCalendar)
    intMinutes = 24 * 60 * txtDays.Value

    For Each objItem In objCalendar.Items
        strSubject = objItem.Subject
        If InStr(strSubject, "Birthday") > 0 And _
          chkBirthdays.Value = True Then
            objItem.ReminderSet = True
            objItem.ReminderMinutesBeforeStart = intMinutes
            objItem.Save
        End If
        If InStr(strSubject, "Anniversary") > 0 And _
          chkAnniversaries.Value = True Then
            objItem.ReminderSet = True
            objItem.ReminderMinutesBeforeStart = intMinutes
            objItem.Save
        End If
    Next
End Sub
```

ReminderUpdate form, where you tested whether an item is a birthday or anniversary. You must update the For Each ... Next loop to integrate the new check boxes into the procedure. Replace the original code for the Click event for the cmdUpdate button with the new code in Listing 3.2.

As you saw in earlier in the chapter, you use the Value property of a control to get the data the user has entered. For a check box control, the Value indicates whether the user has checked the box (chkBox.Value = True) or not (chkBox.Value = False).

**Note:** You probably noticed that the steps inside the two If ... End If code sequences are exactly the same. Normally, you wouldn't have such repetition in a routine. In Chapter 7, "Controlling Program Flow," you will look at ways to streamline such code.

### 3.7.2 Option buttons

Check box controls are ideal for obtaining information from the user when the desired answer is Yes or No, True or False, or On or Off. If more than two answers are possible, option button controls might work better.

Option button controls are sometimes called *radio buttons* in reference to older car radios, which had buttons you pushed to change stations. The last button pressed remained pushed in, until you pressed another button for another station. Only one button at a time could be pushed in.

Option buttons on forms work the same way: No more than one option button can be selected. In other words, whether it's a choice of five radio stations or four flavors of ice cream at a picnic, you can choose only one.

You may see option buttons when you need to choose among three or more different selections. Option buttons are also sometimes used when only two choices exist, but they don't reduce so easily to a True/False selection.

To see how option buttons work, you can use them instead of check boxes on the ReminderUpdate form. Here are three choices:

- Update birthdays only
- Update anniversaries only
- Update both birthdays and anniversaries

---

**Tip:** Option buttons are a good way to force the user to make a choice. If one button is already selected when the form opens, the user has to either select another button or be content with the default.

---

To replace the check boxes with option buttons, select and delete the check boxes. Next, before you put the buttons on the form, you're going to add a frame control to hold them. Select the Frame tool in the Toolbox, and then drag a rectangular shape in the blank area at the top of the form. Set these properties for the frame:

```
(Name)          fraOptions

Caption         Add reminders to:
```

If you look at the properties for the frame, you will see that it has no `Value` property. The frame itself doesn't hold data. Instead, it lassos the controls you put inside it and either organizes them visually or, in the case of option buttons, coordinates their operation.

---

**Tip:** If you have only one set of option buttons on a form, putting a frame around them is optional. If you have two sets of buttons, however, at least one set requires a frame to indicate which buttons work together. Using frames for both sets makes your form more consistent.

---

Add option buttons to the frame by selecting the Option Button tool in the Toolbox and then clicking inside the frame. You might have to rearrange controls to make more room or enlarge the frame by dragging the white size handle boxes on each side and at each corner of the frame. Give your option buttons these properties:

- Option button 1:

| | |
|---|---|
| `(Name)` | `optBirthdays` |
| `Caption` | `Birthdays` |
| `Value` | `False` |

- Option button 2:

| | |
|---|---|
| `(Name)` | `optAnniversaries` |
| `Caption` | `Anniversaries` |
| `Value` | `False` |

- Option button 3:

| | |
|---|---|
| `(Name)` | `optBoth` |
| `Caption` | `Both` |
| `Value` | `True` |

---

**Note:** From now on, the suggested property settings shown for new controls won't include the `Accelerator` property. You already know how to set it and know that it makes forms easier for keyboard users to navigate.

---

Setting the `Value` property for the `optBoth` button to `True` makes it the default choice for the form. Run your form. It should look like that shown

**Figure 3.11** *Option buttons make it easy to select among three or more choices*

in Figure 3.11. Try clicking on each of the three option buttons. Can you select more than one at a time?

To make the `chkUpdate` button use the information from the option buttons, you would need to use the code in Listing 3.3.

**Listing 3.3** *Use Option Button Values to Get the User's Choice*

```
Sub cmdUpdate_Click()
    Dim objApp As Application
    Dim objNS As NameSpace
    Dim objCalendar As MAPIFolder
    Dim objItem As AppointmentItem
    Dim strSubject As String
    Dim intMinutes As Integer

    Set objApp = CreateObject("Outlook.Application")
    Set objNS = objApp.GetNamespace("MAPI")
    Set objCalendar = bjNS.GetDefaultFolder(olFolderCalendar)
    intMinutes = 24 * 60 * txtDays.Value

    For Each objItem In objCalendar.Items
        strSubject = objItem.Subject
        If InStr(strSubject, "Birthday") > 0 And _
            (optBirthdays.Value Or optBoth.Value) Then
            objItem.ReminderSet = True
            objItem.ReminderMinutesBeforeStart = lngMinutes
            objItem.Save
        End If
        If InStr(strSubject, "Anniversary") > 0 And _
            (optAnniversaries.Value Or optBoth.Value) Then
            objItem.ReminderSet = True
            objItem.ReminderMinutesBeforeStart = lngMinutes
            objItem.Save
         End If
    Next
End Sub
```

Compare the first `If` statement in Listing 3.3 with the same lines in Listing 3.2. Both check the subject of a Calendar folder item for the text "Birthday" and the value of one or more controls on the `ReminderUpdate` form. Listing 3.2 checks for the value of the `chkBirthday` control with this expression:

```
chkBirthdays.Value = True
```

whereas Listing 3.3 uses this expression:

```
(optBirthdays.Value Or optBoth.Value)
```

Like check boxes, option buttons on VBA forms can have a value of `True` or `False`. Therefore, the syntax `optBirthdays.Value` is shorthand for `optBirthdays.Value = True`. The `Or` in the above statement means that the expression returns `True` if the value of either `optBirthdays` or `optBoth` is `True`.

### 3.7.3 List box and combo box controls

Check boxes and option buttons make it easy for users to choose among several preferences. However, these can take up a lot of space on a form. Sometimes, you have so many choices that no room would be left for other controls if you used an option button to show each choice.

This is where list box and combo box controls come in. These controls, which are very similar, let users select from a potentially large number of choices. List boxes restrict users to the range of choices you provide. Combo boxes can allow users to either pick from a list or type in a new value. The familiar dropdown list boxes that you see in many Windows programs (e.g., the Priority list on any Outlook item) are a special type of combo box. Figure 3.12 shows various styles of list and combo boxes on an Outlook Post form. The style and behavior of list and combo boxes are controlled by the properties listed in Table 3.3.

---

**Note:** If you set the `MultiSelect` property to anything other than `0 - Single`, you cannot use the `Value` property of the control to find out what the user has chosen. Instead, you must check the `Selected` property to find out whether each row is marked. `lstbox.Select(`*`index`*`)` returns `True` if the *`index`* number row is selected. Chapter 7, "Controlling Program Flow," includes an example of how to check the `Selected` property with a `For ... Next` loop.

---

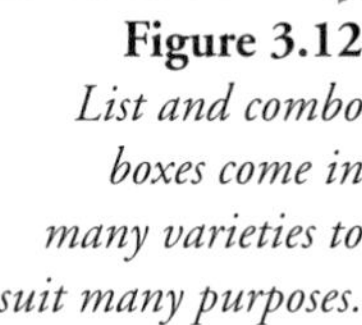

**Figure 3.12** *List and combo boxes come in many varieties to suit many purposes.*

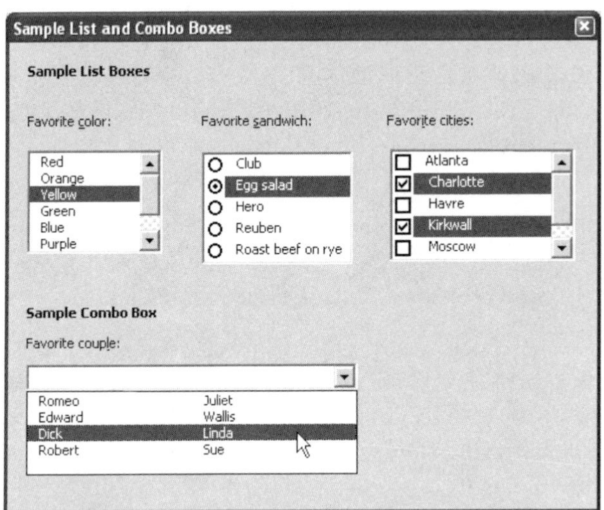


---

**Tip:** For properties that support only specific values, like many of those in Table 3.3, try double-clicking in the VBA Properties window or Outlook form Advanced Properties dialog to cycle through all the possible values.

---

You can use the `AddItem` method to fill a list box, one row at a time. Here is the code to fill the `lstColors` list box for Favorite Colors, shown in Figure 3.12:

```
lstColors.AddItem "Red"
lstColors.AddItem "Orange"
lstColors.AddItem "Yellow"
lstColors.AddItem "Green"
lstColors.AddItem "Blue"
lstColors.AddItem "Purple"
lstColors.AddItem "Black"
lstColors.AddItem "Brown"
```

The code to initialize a list box like this usually runs in the `UserForm_Initialize` event handler of a VBA form.

---

**Tip:** For multiple column list and combo boxes, such as the Favorite Couple list in Figure 3.12, you would use a different method to fill the list box: the `List` method, which fills it from a two-dimensional array. See Chapter 6, "Working with Expressions and Functions," for an example.

---

**Table 3.3** *Key List and Combo Box Properties*

| Property | List | Combo Box | Description |
|---|---|---|---|
| `BoundColumn` | X | X | In a multicolumn list or combo box, which column is bound to a data field (default = `1`). |
| `ColumnCount` | X | X | Number of columns (default = `1`). |
| `DropButtonStyle` | | X | Sets the symbol on a combo box's button (default = `1 - Arrow`). |
| `ListRows` | | X | Number of rows to display in a combo box's dropdown list. |
| `ListStyle` | X | X | Shows the list with or without a check box or option button for each item. Use `0 - Plain` for no check boxes and `1 - Option` for option buttons on single-selection lists and combo boxes, and check boxes on multiselect list boxes. |
| `MatchEntry` | X | X | Controls how the list or combo box tries to match what the user types. Use `0 - FirstLetter` to display the next entry on the list matching the last character the user typed, `1 - Complete` to search for an entry matching all user-typed characters, and `2 - None` not to try to match what the user types. |
| `MatchRequired` | | X | Determines whether the user's text must match an item on the list (default = `False`) |
| `MultiSelect` | X | | Determines whether the user can select more than one item from a list box. Use `0 - Single` to restrict the user to one selection, `1 - Multi` to allow multiple selections with additional mouse clicks, and `2 - Extended` to allow the user to click and then Shift+click to select a range from within the list. |
| `ShowDropButtonWhen` | | X | Determines when the user sees a combo box's button. Use `0 - Never` to always hide the button, `1 - Focus` to show it only when the user is in the control, and `2 - Always` to always show it. |
| `Style` | X | | Determines whether a user both types in a value and picks from the list. Use `0 - DropDownCombo` to allow both and `2 - DropDownList` to allow the user only to pick from the list. |
| `TextColumn` | X | X | In a multicolumn list or combo box, determines which column to use for the `Value` property of the control. |

### 3.7.4 Acceleraters and tab order

Earlier in this chapter, you saw that the `Accelerator` property of VBA forms is one means of helping keyboard-preferring users to get around your form easily. Another key technique for controlling navigation is to set the tab order in a logical fashion. You've probably noticed that as you press Tab in a dialog box or other form, you can enter information in each control in turn. The current control is said to be the one with the *focus*. The tab order determines which control gets the focus as the user presses Tab to move through the controls.

---

**Note:** You can direct the user's attention to a particular control programmatically using the `SetFocus` method.

---

First, return to the `ReminderUpdate` VBA form. Right-click on any empty area of the form, and then choose Tab Order to display the Tab Order dialog (see Figure 3.13). (You can also choose View, Tab Order.) Now you see why it's so important to give distinctive names to your controls! If we had left the command buttons as `CommandButton1` and `CommandButton2` instead of renaming them to `cmdUpdate` and `cmdClose`, it would have been much harder to figure out how to adjust the tab order.

---

**Tip:** Did you notice that the Tab Order dialog consists of a list box control and four command button controls?

---

Use the Move Up and Move Down buttons to rearrange the Tab Order list to match the order in which controls appear on the form itself. The final order should be

```
fraOptions
txtDays
cmdUpdate
cmdClose
```

---

**Tip:** To exclude a control from the tab order, set its `TabStop` property to `False`. The control will still appear in the Tab Order window but will be bypassed when the user presses Tab or Enter to move through the form's controls.

---

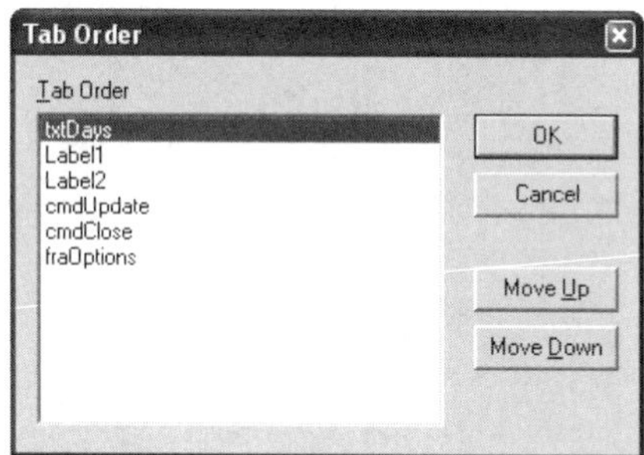


**Figure 3.13** *Compare the order of controls listed here with the form shown in Figure 3.11.*

What happened to the option buttons? They are actually inside the `fraOptions` frame, which has its own tab order. To set the tab order inside a frame, right-click the frame, then choose Tab Order and make the necessary adjustments.

After you change the tab order, run the form and press Tab to move through the controls. Does the order seem logical to you?

---

**Note:** Most forms use a left-to-right tab order, moving through the controls at the top of the form and then going to the next row of controls. However, some forms use a clockwise order. Others go from top to bottom for the set of controls on the left and then start at the top again for the next column of controls. The important thing is to be consistent, both within a form and within a group of forms in an application.

---

## 3.8 Summary

You should be proud of your accomplishment—building your first working Outlook application in VBA, one that performs a very useful function that is not built into Outlook. In the process, you learned how to add many types of controls to a VBA form; how to work with VBA form and control properties; and how to add code to a command button control. The code demonstrated one of the key Outlook techniques that you will use time and time again—looping through a folder in order to examine each item in the folder. Don't worry if you don't know how to write such code from scratch. Subsequent chapters will cover all the details. Chapter 4 explores the different ways you can run VBA code in Outlook and gets you started writing functions and subroutines.

# *Adding VBA Code*

# 4

# Code Basics

Get ready to dig into coding. In this chapter and the others that follow in this section, you will learn the basics of writing VBA programming code in Microsoft Outlook. Most of the techniques will also be applicable to VBScript code behind Outlook forms.

The highlights of this chapter include discussions of the following:

- What triggers program routines to execute
- When to use a function versus a subroutine
- How to run an Outlook subroutine from a toolbar button
- In Outlook 2002, how to run an Outlook subroutine from a Rules Wizard rule

## 4.1 Understanding when code runs

Think about the Windows applications you use every day. If you have a money-management program, take that as an example. When you start the program, it probably pops up reminders that you have bills to pay or investments to check on. You click a button or maybe a menu command to enter a new transaction. Perhaps you can type "May 15," and the program converts it to `May 15, 2003` (or whatever the current year might be). Although virtually all of the program runs out of sight, it depends on you, the user, for the key interactions that tell it what to do.

Each time you interact with the program—choosing a menu item, clicking a button, saving an item, and even pressing Tab to move from one control to another—you cause one or more events to fire. Each event can have a programming routine associated with it.

Each type of object (VBA forms, command buttons, text boxes, Outlook folders and items, and so on) has its own set of possible events. Not every event will have code related to it. As you build Outlook programs, you must decide which events are important to your program and which you can ignore.

Outlook as an application has events, too. You use these events, for example, to perform certain tasks every time you start Outlook or every time you end the program.

In addition to routines that run when events are triggered, you can have other procedures that launch directly from the macros list or a toolbar button. Finally, you will write many nonevent procedures that support macros and event procedures by performing calculations and automating routine tasks.

### 4.1.1 VBA form events

Let's take a closer look at events that take place on VBA forms. An easy way to see what events a form supports is to use View, Code to display the code window for the form (see Figure 4.1). From the left dropdown list at the top of the form, choose UserForm. (This will place the `Sub ... End Sub` shell for a subroutine named `UserForm_Click` in the code window; you can delete or ignore it.) Use the right dropdown list to see all the events for the `UserForm` object, in other words, for the current form.

It's important to distinguish between form-level events and control events. For example, the `Click` event for a form fires only when you click outside the area of any of the controls. If you click on a control, the `Click` event for that control fires, not the `Click` event for the form. Initially, you

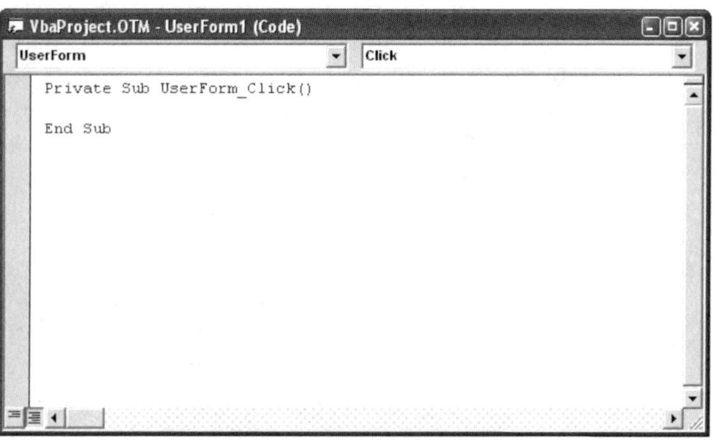
VbaProject.OTM - UserForm1 (Code)
UserForm
Click
Private Sub UserForm_Click()
End Sub

**Figure 4.1** *The dropdown lists at the top of the code window help you understand what events are supported by your form and its controls.*

**Table 4.1** *Key VBA Form Events*

| Event | Occurs |
|---|---|
| `Initialize` | After the VBA form is loaded, but before it becomes visible |
| `Activate` | When a VBA form becomes the active, visible window in Outlook |
| `Terminate` | After the VBA form has been unloaded, but before it is removed completely from memory |

will probably find the form events listed in Table 4.1 the most useful. Note that the `Initialize` event fires before the `Activate` event.

---

**Tip:** With most of the forms you create in Outlook VBA, you will be more interested in control events than form events.

---

Controls on forms have their own events, too. In Chapter 3, "A Birthday/Anniversary Reminder Tool," you saw an example of code attached to the `Click` event for a command button. Table 4.2 lists `Click` along with other important events for VBA controls.

Here are some notes on control events:

- The `BeforeUpdate` event is often used to validate the data entered in a control because it can be cancelled to roll back the control to its previous value.
- Command buttons support only the `Click` event.
- Text boxes do not support the `Click` event.

**Table 4.2** *Key VBA Control Events*

| Event | Occurs |
|---|---|
| `Enter` | Just before the focus enters a control |
| `Click` | When a user clicks on a control |
| `BeforeUpdate` | Before the user's change to a control takes effect |
| `AfterUpdate` | After the user's change to a control takes effect |
| `Exit` | When the focus leaves a control |

- For check boxes, the `Click` event occurs not only when the user clicks in the box, but also when the user changes the value by pressing the spacebar or the accelerator key for the control.
- The `Exit` event can be cancelled if you want the user to remain in the control.
- Visual Basic programmers will recognize that the `Enter` and `Exit` events in VBA are analogous to the `GotFocus` and `LostFocus` events in Visual Basic.

A good way to become acquainted with the order in which form and form control events fire is to create a simple form with one check box, one text box, and one command button. Don't worry about changing the default names of the controls; this is just a test form. To enter code for each event for each control and for the form itself, in the code window, follow these steps:

1. Select the control or form from the left dropdown list.
2. Select the event from the right dropdown list.
3. Between the `Private Sub` and `End Sub` statements, enter one line for each event to pop up a message box with the name of the event. You can use the code in Listing 4.1 as a model.

After you enter the code, run the form, and use the mouse and keyboard to move through the various controls, enter data, delete data, and so forth. Each event will pop up a message box to tell you which event is occurring.

### 4.1.2 What is a Sub anyway?

After entering the code in the preceding section, you're probably wondering about the `Private Sub` and `End Sub` statements. These mark the beginning and end, respectively, of a code procedure called a *subroutine*. The `Private` keyword means that each of these routines runs only in the context of the particular VBA form. That's appropriate for forms because the event won't have any meaning without the control or form that it is related to. However, as you will see, in other code modules, you may choose to make a subroutine public so that it can be used elsewhere.

To start a new subroutine, just type "Sub" on a new line in the code editor, followed by the name you want to use for the procedure. Procedure names can't contain spaces. When you press Enter at the end of the `Sub` line, VBA adds an `End Sub` statement automatically.

**Listing 4.1** *A Series of Message Boxes Shows the Sequence in Which Control and Form Events Fire*

```
Private Sub CheckBox1_AfterUpdate()
    MsgBox "CheckBox After Update"
End Sub

Private Sub CheckBox1_BeforeUpdate(ByVal Cancel)
    MsgBox "CheckBox Before Update"
End Sub

Private Sub CheckBox1_Click()
    MsgBox "CheckBox Click"
End Sub

Private Sub CheckBox1_Enter()
    MsgBox "Checkbox Enter"
End Sub

Private Sub CheckBox1_Exit(ByVal Cancel)
    MsgBox "Checkbox Exit"
End Sub

Private Sub CommandButton1_Click()
    MsgBox "Command Button Click"
End Sub

Private Sub TextBox1_AfterUpdate()
    MsgBox "Text Box After Update"
End Sub

Private Sub TextBox1_BeforeUpdate(ByVal Cancel)
    MsgBox "Text Box Before Update"
End Sub

Private Sub TextBox1_Enter()
    MsgBox "Text Box Enter"
End Sub

Private Sub TextBox1_Exit(ByVal Cancel)
    MsgBox "Text Box Exit"
End Sub

Private Sub UserForm_Activate()
    MsgBox "Form Activate"
End Sub

Private Sub UserForm_Initialize()
    MsgBox "Form Initialize"
End Sub

Private Sub UserForm_Terminate()
    MsgBox "Form Terminate"
End Sub
```

Did you notice that each subroutine name is followed by a pair of parentheses? These contain the arguments for the subroutine—any inputs to the routine.

In most cases, form and control events have no arguments. `BeforeUpdate` and `Exit` are exceptions. They both have `Cancel` as an argument. If you set `Cancel` to `True`, you cancel the event. In the case of `BeforeUpdate`, the control returns to the value it had before the user updated it. With `Exit`, setting `Cancel` to `True` makes the focus stay on the control, rather than move on to the next control.

Here is some code you can use with the `txtDays` control on the `ReminderUpdate` form from Chapter 3, "A VBA Birthday/Anniversary Reminder Tool." It uses the `BeforeUpdate` event to make sure that the user enters a valid number:

```
Private Sub txtDays_BeforeUpdate(ByVal Cancel _
  As MSForms.ReturnBoolean)
    If IsNumeric(txtDays.Value) = False Then
        Cancel = True
        MsgBox "Please enter a number."
    End If
End Sub
```

**Note:** `IsNumeric()` is a built-in function that is `True` if its argument is a number and `False` if not.

Also, note that this validation procedure runs only when the user actually enters data in the `txtDays` control. You may also want to add similar validation, using `IsNumeric()`, in the `Click` event for the `cmdUpdate` button to handle the case of the user leaving `txtDays` blank and then clicking the Update button.

Performing validation with cancelable events can make a form friendlier to the user because you can use message boxes and other clues to tell the user precisely what to do.

### 4.1.3 Application-level events

Application-level events allow you to create procedures to initialize Outlook with particular settings; perform actions against outgoing messages; automatically process incoming messages; and respond to synchronization, switching views, switching folders, and many other interesting events. For example, you can use the `FolderSwitch` event to display a custom toolbar when the user switches to a particular folder.

Programming responses to application-level events is more complicated than programming VBA forms and simple macros. Therefore, a discussion of this topic is deferred until Chapter 11, "Responding to Outlook Events in VBA."

### 4.1.4 Code modules

You first encountered modules in Chapter 2, "The VBA Design Environment," while exploring the VBA programming environment. Any code that is not associated with a particular form is stored in a module. You can keep everything in just one module or, more likely, organize your procedures into several modules. You can use the built-in `ThisOutlookSession` module for application-level event code.

### 4.1.5 Macros to run programs on demand

People frequently ask whether they can create toolbar buttons to perform particular tasks (such as launching a custom form or switching to a particular view). With VBA, the answer is yes, you can run macro subroutines from toolbar buttons.

*Macros* are simply subroutines that are stored in VBA modules, not forms, and have no arguments. If a macro requires some input information, you cannot pass that information as an argument to the macro. Instead, the macro must either display a VBA form to get the information from the user or use one of the other methods discussed in Chapter 9, "Handling User Input and Feedback."

Any argumentless subroutine in a VBA module that does not use the `Private` keyword is automatically listed among the macros that you see when you choose Tools, Macro, Macros (see Figure 4.2). You don't have to do anything special to get your subroutines on the list.

---

**Tip:** Press Alt+F8 to open the Macros dialog quickly.

---

Don't look for a macro recorder, such as the ones in Microsoft Word and Excel. You must write all Outlook macros from scratch.

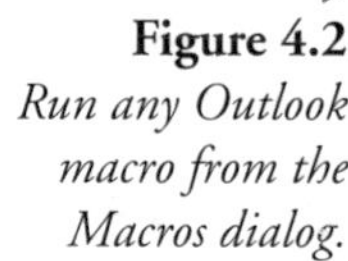

**Figure 4.2**
*Run any Outlook macro from the Macros dialog.*

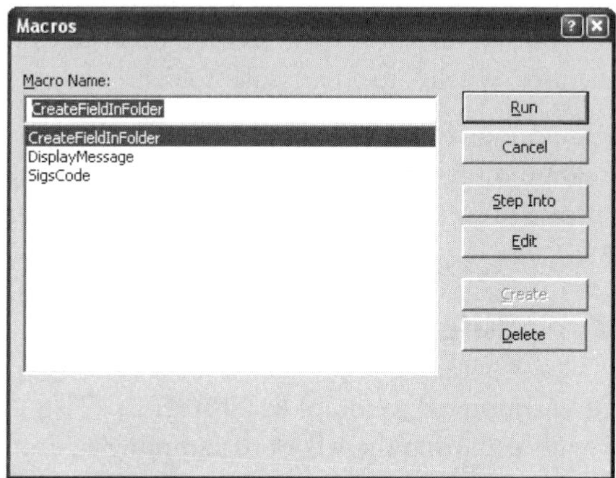


To add any macro to an Outlook toolbar, follow these steps:

1. Close the VBA window, if it's open.
2. In the main Outlook window, choose View, Toolbars, Customize. (If you want to run the macro from the toolbar of an Outlook item, open an item first, and then choose View, Toolbars, Customize.)
3. From the Commands tab in the Customize dialog box (see Figure 4.3), drag the macro from the Commands list to the toolbar where you want it to appear. This will create a button for that macro on the toolbar.

**Figure 4.3**
*Add any macro to your Outlook toolbars.*

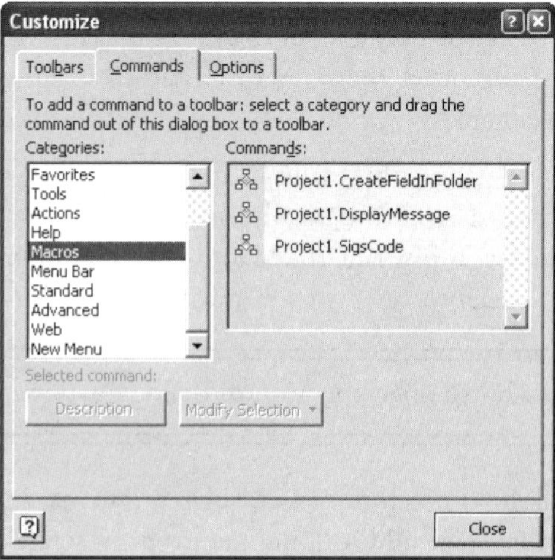

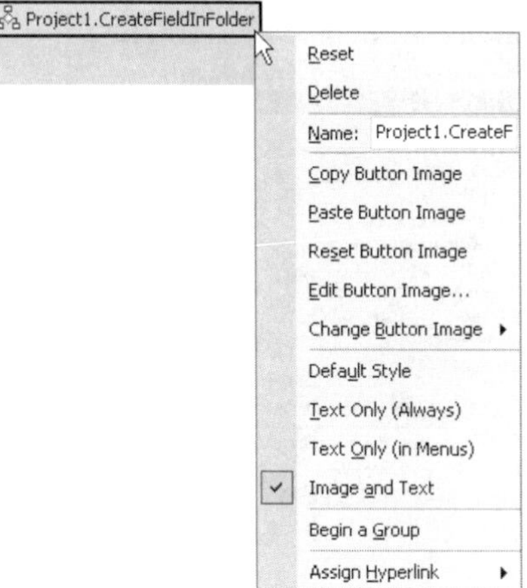


**Figure 4.4** *Customize the macro toolbar button by changing its name and icon.*

4. With the Customize dialog still open, right-click the new button to pop up a menu of commands for customizing it (see Figure 4.4). You will certainly want to change the name to remove the `Project1.` prefix. You might also want to choose Change Button Image to pick an icon.
5. When you finish customizing the button and toolbar, close the Customize dialog box.

---

**Tip:** When you're customizing toolbar buttons, the Default Style command (see Figure 4.4) really means *image only—show this button only as an icon.*

---

### 4.1.6 Subroutines that run from a rule

Outlook 2002 (but not Outlook 2000) allows you to write a VBA subroutine and call it from a Rules Wizard rule using a new "run a script" rule action. The procedure can be either in the built-in ThisOutlookSession module or any custom module, but it must include a `MailItem` or `MeetingItem` argument. This argument represents the incoming message or meeting request that triggers the rule.

After you create a subroutine with a `MailItem` or `MeetingItem` argument, you can use it in a "run a script" action in a Rules Wizard rule, as shown in Figure 4.5.

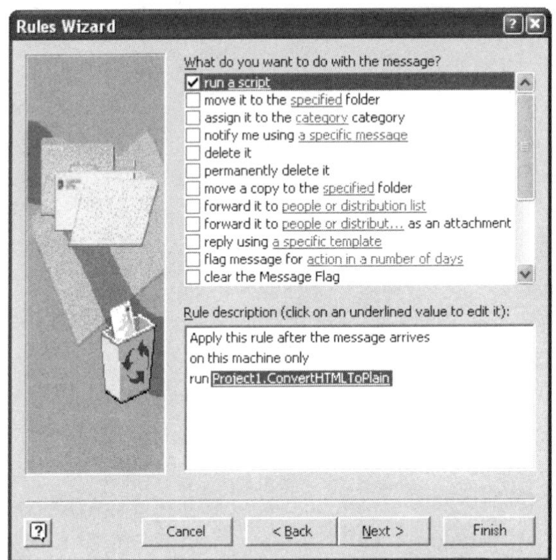


**Figure 4.5** *The "run a script" rule action doesn't actually run a script. Instead, it runs a specially constructed VBA subroutine.*

This short example shows a subroutine that can be used in a Rules Wizard rule to convert incoming HTML messages to plain text:

```
Sub ConvertHTMLToPlain(objMsg As MailItem)
    If objMsg.GetInspector.EditorType = olEditorHTML Then
        objMsg.BodyFormat = olFormatPlain
        objMsg.Save
    End If
End Sub
```

The other new Outlook 2002 feature that makes this work is the `BodyFormat` property, which allows you to set a message's format. Using this technique to convert a message to plain text removes any danger from malicious HTML code. However, it also makes any embedded image attachments inaccessible from the user interface. The images are still stored in the message, however, and can be accessed via code.

---

**CAUTION:** Microsoft suggests that this type of rule should not be run by Exchange Server users who normally work offline.

---

## 4.2 Writing VBA code

Now, to write some VBA code! If you don't already have an empty module in the Project Explorer, choose Insert, Module to add one.

You will write a macro to launch a Task form with certain fields already filled in, in this case, the due date already assigned to one week from today. You will be able to run this macro from a toolbar to create a task that you are due to finish in the next week.

To start, type "Sub CreateOneWeekTask" into the code window, and then press Enter. `Sub` indicates that this is a subroutine, not a function (you will get to functions shortly). `CreateOneWeekTask` is the name of the procedure. Procedure names can't contain spaces and must be unique within a module. When you press Enter, VBA automatically adds the `End Sub` statement marking the end of the procedure and adds parentheses after the procedure name. Because this is a macro that you're going to run from a toolbar button, you don't want to put any arguments inside the parentheses.

---

**Note:** `Public` procedures, those that don't start with `Private Sub`, but with just `Sub`, need names that are unique not only within the current module, but also within your project. Don't worry too much about this. VBA will warn you if you create a public procedure with a duplicate name.

---

The next step is to initialize an object variable that Outlook VBA uses every time you need to work with Outlook data. Add this line:

```
Set objApp = CreateObject("Outlook.Application")
```

Next, add the line below to create the task:

```
Set objTask = objApp.CreateItem(olTaskItem)
```

These two lines are *boilerplate*. You use them so many times in Outlook VBA applications that you might want to create a separate module containing sample procedures with these statements and other standard object variable assignment statements used to get the current Outlook folder, the current Outlook item, and so forth. If you have Office Developer Edition, you can use its Code Librarian to store boilerplate code snippets.

How do you know that this statement creates a task? The key is the `olTaskItem` keyword in the `Set objTask` statement. `olTaskItem` is an example of the intrinsic constants built into Outlook. They are great coding shortcuts because they usually have very descriptive names. For example, it's not difficult to remember that `olTaskItem` is a constant that represents an Outlook task when used with the `CreateItem` method.

---

**Note:** VBScript on Outlook forms does not support the intrinsic Outlook constants. You must explicitly declare these constants or use their literal values. As you will see in Chapter 10, "Working with the Object Models," you can use the Object Browser to see all the intrinsic constants and get their values.

---

### 4.2.1 Variables

Both `objApp` and `objTask` are *variables*. Variables have names and hold the data used in your procedures. Many statements in programming code manipulate variables and then return new values based on those operations. In the next chapter, you will look in more detail at variables.

Both the above statements require a `Set` keyword because they create object variables that represent complex programming constructs, rather than set the value of variables that hold simple numeric or text data. That's the way the VBA programming language works. It has a very specific syntax or grammar, just like English, Russian, or any spoken language. To make yourself understood, you must follow the VBA syntax. The VBA Editor makes it easy, as you will see, because it often suggests the right words and warns you when you make common mistakes.

Using `obj` as a prefix for all object variables helps you remember to initialize them with a `Set` statement and release them later with a statement that sets the object to `Nothing` (e.g., `Set objApp = Nothing`). You should always set an object variable to `Nothing` when your code has finished using it, as we've done with the procedure shown in Figure 4.6.

### 4.2.2 Outlook properties and methods

Next, add these two lines:

```
objTask.StartDate = Date
objTask.DueDate = Date + 7
```

Both of these statements are assignment statements. They assign values to the `StartDate` and `DueDate` properties of the task.

**Figure 4.6** *This procedure to create a new task creates two objects, sets two properties, and runs a method to display a task due one week from today.*

```
Sub CreateOneWeekTask()
    Set objApp = CreateObject("Outlook.Application")
    Set objTask = objApp.CreateItem(olTaskItem)
    objTask.StartDate = Date
    objTask.DueDate = Date + 7
    objTask.Display
    Set objApp = Nothing
    Set objTask = Nothing
End Sub
```

The standard syntax for referring to properties of an Outlook item or other object, such as a folder, is

```
object.propertyname
```

For custom properties that you create for Outlook items (see Chapter 17, "Extending Form Design with Fields and Controls"), the syntax is slightly different:

```
item.UserProperties.Find("propertyname")
item.UserProperties("propertyname")
```

The two variations above are equivalent.

Once you have created the new task, you will want Outlook to show it. To make the new item appear takes just one line:

```
objTask.Display
```

The `Display` keyword is called a *method*. By applying a method to an object, you make something happen—display a form, save an item, and so forth. Earlier you used the `CreateObject()` and `CreateItem()` methods to get an Outlook `Application` object and create a new task. Notice that a method uses a syntax similar to a property: *`object.method`*.

You've not only written a very useful macro, shown in its entirety in Figure 4.6, you've also seen how assignment statements, methods, and intrinsic constants comprise key code building blocks. Reward yourself by running the procedure and watching your new task appear! If you find this procedure useful, add it to the toolbar so you can click a button any time to get a new task due one week from today.

### 4.2.3 Subroutines versus functions

Not every procedure you write is a subroutine. You also write *functions*. These are procedures that return data to the program, usually by performing some operation on data you provide to the function.

---

**Tip:** Think of a function as a magic box with an opening at the top, an opening at the bottom, and a crank on the side. Pour something into the top, turn the crank, and something completely different comes out the bottom. Your job as a programmer is to supply the magic that makes the box perform its trick.

---

Here's an example:

```
Public Function Quote(varInput)
    Quote = Chr(34) & varInput & Chr(34)
End Function
```

This `Quote()` function can take anything as its argument (`varInput`) and returns that data surrounded by quotation marks. `Chr()` is a built-in function that returns a string consisting of the single ASCII character corresponding to a given number. (In this case, an ASCII 34 is a quotation mark.) The ampersand (`&`) is an operator used to concatenate (or join) two bits of text. You'll learn more about operators in the next section.

A function always includes one or more statements that assign the value of the function to some expression. Here, that `Quote =` statement is the only statement in the whole function. Table 4.3 shows the results the `Quote()` function delivers for various sample arguments.

---

**Tip:** A function can have more than one assignment statement, and assignment statements can occur anywhere in a function. However, for beginners, it's easiest to always make the assignment statement the last line in a function's code. That way, you will be able to spot a function with a missing assignment statement easily.

---

If you add the `Quote()` function to the module you're building in VBA, you can reuse it in other procedures. You will definitely use it later in message boxes and in searching and filtering for particular Outlook items.

**Table 4.3** *Sample Results for the Quote() Function*

| Argument | Result |
|---|---|
| `Quote("Microsoft Outlook")` | `"Microsoft Outlook"` |
| `Quote(2)` | `"2"` |
| `Quote(Null)` | `""` |

### 4.2.4 Operators

Operators are symbols that perform various mathematical and data operations, such as addition, division, joining strings, or comparing two numbers to find out whether one is greater than the other. Table 4.4 lists those you are most likely to use in Outlook. Many of them should be familiar from your earliest arithmetic books.

**Table 4.4** *Commonly Used Operators*

| Operator | Description |
|---|---|
| + | Addition |
| - | Subtraction |
| * | Multiplication |
| / | Division |
| & | String concatenation |
| = | Equal to |
| > | Greater than |
| >= | Greater than or equal to |
| < | Less than |
| <= | Less than or equal to |
| <> | Not equal to |
| `And` | True if both expressions are true; otherwise, false |
| `Or` | True if either expression is true; otherwise, false |
| `Not` | True if the expression is false; false if the expression is true |

**Tip:** For the complete list of operators or to learn more about any particular operator, open the Outlook VBA window and, in Help, ask about "Operator Summary."

### 4.2.5 Referring to VBA forms and controls

You have one more VBA issue to address: how to refer to VBA forms and controls in your code. It's really simple. You use the name you give the form or control.

You saw an example of this in Section 3.5.3 in the `cmdUpdate_Click` procedure on the `ReminderUpdate` form. In the following statement

```
objItem.ReminderMinutesBeforeStart = _
  24 * 60 * txtDays.Value
```

`txtDays.Value` represents the `Value` property of the `txtDays` text box on the form. You don't have to use the name of the form anywhere because the code is running inside the form, attached to the `Click` event for one of the form's command buttons.

If the code is in a separate module or behind a different form, refer to the form and the control on that form with the syntax *`formname.controlname`*. For example, the `RunReminderUpdate` subroutine loads the `ReminderUpdate` form, displays it to the user with the `Show` method, and then disables the `cmdUpdate` button by setting its `Enabled` property to `False`. You would put `RunReminderUpdate` not in the `ReminderUpdate` form's code, but in a separate normal code module:

```
Sub RunReminderUpdate()
    Load ReminderUpdate
    ReminderUpdate.cmdUpdate.Enabled = False
    ReminderUpdate.Show
End Sub
```

Did you notice that `RunReminderUpdate` is a macro that you can run from a toolbar button or by pressing Alt+F8? That will make it easier to update your birthdays and appointments.

Why would you disable the `cmdUpdate` button? Now that you know how to work with VBA form events, you can write code that watches what the user enters into the `txtDays` box and enables the `cmdUpdate` button only if a valid number is present. You already created a validation procedure in this chapter. You can just enhance that subroutine, replacing your earlier `txtDays_BeforeUpdate` procedure with the code below:

```
Private Sub txtDays_BeforeUpdate(ByVal Cancel _
  As MSForms.ReturnBoolean)
    If IsNumeric(txtDays.Value) = False Then
        Cancel = True
        MsgBox "Please enter a number."
    Else
        cmdUpdate.Enabled = True
    End If
End Sub
```

Notice that because the `txtDays.BeforeUpdate` procedure is an event handler on the `ReminderUpdate` form, you do not need to specify the name of the form in the `cmdUpdate.Enabled` statement.

---

**Note:** You will learn about `If ... Then ... Else ... End If` statement blocks in Chapter 7, "Controlling Program Flow."

---

## 4.3 Summary

This has been a busy chapter in which you have learned how program code consists of subroutines and functions. You have written code to react to events and used object methods to make something happen. In particular, you used the Outlook `Application` object and its `CreateItem` method to create a new task. Other new concepts are constants to store data that doesn't change and operators to combine multiple bits of information.

In Chapter 5, you will continue learning code basics by learning about variables and refining your understanding of modules and constants.

# 5

# Code Grammar 101

So far, your excursion into Outlook programming code has been a lot like beginning language lessons. Most of the initial work in learning a language is oral: You work with a teacher or tape, memorizing phrases and repeating them. Sooner or later, though, you have to learn more about the structure of a language; you have to study grammar. Welcome to Code Grammar 101, the chapter in which you study the basic syntax of VBA, much of which you will be able to apply later to VBScript.

Highlights of this chapter include discussions of the following:

- How to make a procedure available to any VBA routine
- Where and when to add global constants
- What data types VBA supports
- How to name your variables
- Which features of the VBA editor make it easier to write accurate code quickly

## 5.1 Option Explicit

I'm going to let you in on a little secret: To create the macro in Chapter 4, "Code Basics," you did more typing than you had to. Outlook can do more of the work for you and at the same time avoid common errors. The key is to set up VBA so that it forces you to declare all your variables.

First, it helps to see what happens when you have a mistake in your code. Go back to the `CreateOneWeekTask` macro in Chapter 4, and change `the objTask.Display` line to `objMyTask.Display`, then run the routine. You should receive an Object Required error message, shown in Figure 5.1. Click the Debug button, and VBA takes you directly to the statement with a problem—the one you changed. It's wrong because

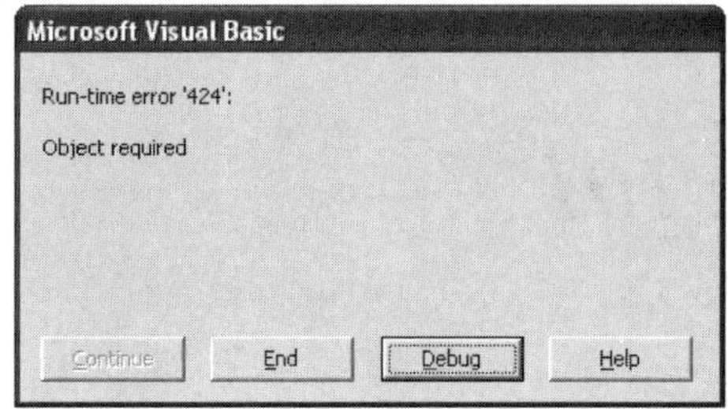


**Figure 5.1** *A wrong variable name causes an error.*

`objMyTask` isn't the right name for the object variable for the new item; it should be `objTask` instead.

I want you to notice this error because it's a common one—you might change a variable name midprocedure or just make a typo. You're going to make a couple of changes to the macro code to help prevent such errors.

Reset your procedure to get out of debug mode and back to design mode: Click the Reset button, or choose Run, Reset.

Press Ctrl+Home to move to the top of the module containing the `CreateOneWeekTask` procedure. The dropdown lists at the top of the code window should show `(General)` and `(Declarations)`. You are now in the declarations section of the module, before the first procedure. This is where you place statements that affect the entire module and declare variables and constants that you want to use in more than one procedure.

Make this statement the first line in the declarations section: `Option Explicit`. The `Option Explicit` statement tells VBA that, within this particular module, all variables must be declared before you use them. This

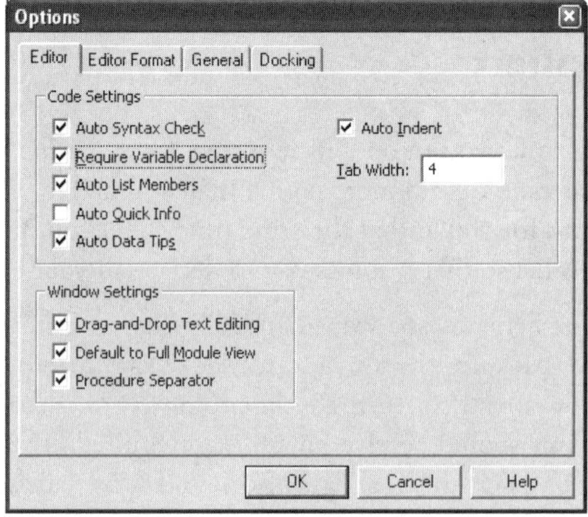


**Figure 5.2** *Options for the VBA code editor include requiring all variables to be explicitly declared.*

means that you can't just throw in a new variable any time you need it. You must declare it first, either in the declarations section if it's a global-level or module-level variable or at the beginning of a procedure. Using `Option Explicit` forces VBA to check all your variable names to make sure they're declared when it compiles your code before it runs any procedure. Detecting an error early, at the compile stage, is better than finding the error only when you run the procedure.

To add `Option Explicit` automatically to the declarations for any new module, choose Tools, Options. In the Options dialog box, shown in Figure 5.2, check Require Variable Declaration. This change affects only new forms and modules. If you want to use `Option Explicit` in an existing module, you must add it to the declarations section of the code module.

## 5.2 Declaring variables

After adding `Option Explicit` to the module, if you now try to run the `CreateOneWeekTask` macro you will receive a compile error because you didn't declare any variables. Use the `Dim` statement to declare any variable at the beginning of the procedure, right after the `Sub` or `Function` statement that marks the beginning of the procedure. To declare all the variables used in the `CreateOneWeekTask` macro, add these statements to your code:

```
Dim objApp As Outlook.Application
Dim objTask As Outlook.TaskItem
```

**Tip:** If you write code only inside the Outlook VBA environment, you can omit the Outlook prefix on data type declarations and use just `Dim objApp as Application` or `Dim objTask as TaskItem`. However, it's a good idea to get into the habit of using a fully qualified declaration in case you later expand your programming efforts to Visual Basic or to VBA in other Office programs.

Did you notice that, when you type the space after `As`, VBA pops up a list of possible ways to complete the `Dim` statement? This feature, Auto List Members, will save you hours of typing and avoid many errors. It helps you complete a statement or expression by offering a set of appropriate choices. Select an item from the list, and then press Enter to add that text to the current statement. If you press Enter, VBA completes the statement and puts the cursor on the next line. Try Tab or the spacebar instead of Enter. If you press Tab, VBA completes the statement, but leaves you on the same statement line, immediately after the added text. If you press the spacebar, VBA completes the statement, leaves the cursor on the same line, and adds a space at the end.

For example, if you type "Dim objApp As Outlook.ap," you see Application selected in the list of data and object types. Press Enter to select Application, completing the `Dim` statement, and to get a new blank line where you can enter your next `Dim` statement.

### 5.2.1 Variable data types

When you declare a variable in VBA, you normally specify a data type. If you don't, the variable uses the Variant data type. Because variant-type variables can support all kinds of operations, VBA cannot optimize the code when it compiles it, as it can if you use explicit data types. Therefore, using explicit data types can make your VBA code run more efficiently. Table 5.1 lists the data types that VBA supports.

---

**Note:** In Table 5.1, *E+38* means that you multiply by a factor of *10 to the power of 38*, and *E–45* means *10 to the power of –45*. This scientific notation, as it's called, is used to simplify the writing of very large and very small numbers.

---

You should use the variant data type in VBA for variables that hold data from a form control (where users can type numbers and letters or leave the control blank) and other situations where the exact data type is not known at design time.

---

**CAUTION:** Date/time fields in Outlook items do not support the full range of dates that a VBA date variable can hold. Dates on Outlook forms must fall between April 1, 1601, and August 31, 4500, inclusive. Dates that appear in Outlook form fields and folder views as None are usually January 1, 4501, although there also are some cases where no date is present in the field.

---

Even though VBA includes an object data type, most of the time you should declare an object variable as a specific type of object, as you saw in the `Dim` statements earlier in this section. Use the object data type when you don't know what type of object you might be dealing with. For example, when accessing items in an Outlook Contacts folder, you don't know in advance

**Table 5.1** *VBA Data Types*

| Data Type | Prefix | Can Contain |
|---|---|---|
| Boolean | `bln` | `True` (–1) or `False` (0) |
| Byte | `byt` | Any nondecimal number between 0 and 255 |
| Integer | `int` | Any nondecimal number between –32,768 and 32,767 |
| Long | `lng` | Any nondecimal number between –2,147,483,648 and 2,147,483,647 |
| Single | `sng` | Numbers from –3.402823E+38 to –1.401298E-45 for negative values and from 1.401298E-45 to 3.402823E+38 for positive values (single-precision floating point) |
| Double | `dbl` | Numbers from –1.79769313486231E+308 to – 4.94065645841247E-324 for negative values and from 4.94065645841247E-324 to 1.79769313486232E+308 for positive values (double-precision floating point) |
| Currency | `cur` | Numbers between –922,337,203,685,477.5808 to 922,337,203,685,477.5807 (limit of four decimal places) |
| Decimal | `dec` | Any integer up to +/–79,228,162,514,264,337,593,543,950,335; any decimal number up to +/–7.9228162514264337593543950335 with 28 places to the right of the decimal; smallest nonzero number is +/–0.0000000000000000000000000001 |
| Date | `dte` | Date and time values from January 1, 1000 to December 31, 9999; time values are resolved to the second |
| Object | `obj` | Reference to any object |
| String | `str` | For variable-length strings, from 0 to approximately 2 billion alphanumeric characters; for fixed-length strings, from 1 to 65,400 characters. |
| Variant | `var` | Any kind of data, including numbers, strings, and objects |

whether any given item is a `ContactItem` or a `DistListItem` (distribution list) object. In that case, you'd declare a variable `As Object`: `Dim objItem As Object`. The same is true of the Outlook Inbox, which can contain task requests, meeting requests, nondelivery reports, and other types of items besides messages. If you're looping through all the items in the Inbox, use an object variable declared `As Object` for each individual item.

### 5.2.2 Variable naming conventions

Variable names must follow certain rules. They must begin with a letter, not a number, and cannot contain a period. Most programmers use a naming convention—a specific pattern for variable names—for a variety of reasons:

- To distinguish variables from constants and intrinsic objects

- To provide a reminder of the type of data a variable contains
- To make the code easier to read, especially if someone else might be maintaining it in the future

Don't invent your own naming convention. Use one of the accepted methods. The simplest is to begin a descriptive name of a variable with a prefix (e.g., those in Table 5.1) that gives the data type.

**Tip:** Being consistent with a naming convention is like sticking to your weekly exercise routine. If you keep it simple and manageable, you're more likely to succeed.

For example, the `strMessageClass` variable is used to hold the `MessageClass` property of a form, and it's a string variable. Therefore, its name is `str & MessageClass` or `strMessageClass`.

## 5.3 Understanding scope

The examples you have seen so far deal with variables only as they occur inside a particular procedure. Sometimes, though, you want variables to be in wider use. For example, you might want to *instantiate* (or create a new instance of) an object variable to represent the current Outlook folder in one procedure, then perform some operations on that folder (or the items in it) in several other procedures, some of which may be in different modules. Therefore, you would declare it as a global variable, using code like this:

```
Public g_objMyFolder as Outlook.MAPIFolder

Sub SetMyFolder()
    Dim objApp As Outlook.Application
    Dim objExplorer As Outlook.Explorer
    Set objApp = CreateObject("Outlook.Application")
    Set objExplorer = Application.ActiveExplorer
    Set g_objMyFolder = objExplorer.CurrentFolder
    Set objExplorer = Nothing
    Set objApp = Nothing
End Sub
```

The `ActiveExplorer` represents the folder window that the user is currently viewing, while its `CurrentFolder` property corresponds to the folder displayed. Therefore, the code above sets a global `MAPIFolder` object to the folder currently being displayed in Outlook.

**Table 5.2** *Variable Scope Definitions*

| Scope | Description |
|---|---|
| Procedure | Available only within the current procedure. Declare with a `Dim` statement at the beginning of the procedure. |
| Module | Available only to procedures within the current module. Declare with a `Dim` or `Private` statement in the declarations section of the module. |
| Global | Available to procedures in any module in the VBA Project Explorer. Declare with a `Public` statement in the declarations section of any module. |

In VBA, variables can be procedural or global or have module-level scope. Table 5.2 summarizes the scopes a variable can have.

In the `SetMyFolder` subroutine, the `objExplorer` and `objApp` procedural variables are set to `Nothing` at the end of the procedure. The global `g_objMyFolder` variable is not set to `Nothing` because it will be used in other procedures. Some other procedure will need to include `Set g_objMyFolder = Nothing` when that variable is no longer needed.

**Tip:** You can use either `Dim` or `Private` to declare private scope variables in modules, but `Private` makes your intent perfectly clear.

**Note:** Some VBA documentation uses the term *public module scope* instead of *global scope,* or *private scope* instead of *module scope.* I think it's easier to think in terms of *global* versus *module,* than *public* versus *private,* especially if you are in the habit of using `g_` and `m_` as prefixes to denote the different scopes.

Scope also affects variable names. You should not have a module-level variable named `strMsg` and also use a procedure variable with the same name. (VBA will use the local procedure variable, not the module-level variable, but the overlapping names have the potential to cause confusion.) Repeated variable names are OK, however, if the variables are all local to the procedures in which they are used. For example, it's common to use variable names such as `intAns` and `strAns` across many procedures to hold the results from `MsgBox()` and `InputBox()` functions (`Ans` being short for

"Answer"). This isn't a problem if you declare the variable as a local variable inside the procedure each time.

These two lines of code, placed in the declarations section of a module, declare a module-level date variable, using a prefix of `m`, and a global-level string variable with a `g` prefix:

```
Private m_dteLastVacationDay
Public g_strUserName
```

Why care about scope at all? For two main reasons: to make code run more efficiently and to keep two procedures from inadvertently changing the same variable.

The efficiency issue involves memory. The broader the scope, the longer the variable remains in memory. A variable is removed from memory when it goes out of scope—in other words, when all the code in the procedure or module has run and the variable is no longer needed.

**Note:** The same scope concepts apply to procedures. In VBA, you can have `Private` procedures, available only in the current module (such as event handlers in form code modules) and `Public` procedures available to any other module. Use `Private` if you have an argumentless procedure that you do not want to appear in the macros list.

In general, you should use the tightest scope possible. Because you can use arguments to pass variables from one procedure to another (as you will see shortly), global and module variables should be the exception, not the rule.

## 5.4 Declaring constants

Constants can have scope, too. You can have constants that are available only to a procedure's code, others that work in the current module, and still others that are global. You declare a constant with a `Const`, `Private`, or `Public` statement that also assigns its value.

Names for constants follow the same pattern as variable names, using `M` as a prefix for module constants and `G` for global constants. Common practice is to use all caps for constants.

For procedure constants, place the `Const` statement at the beginning of a procedure, along with any `Dim` statements. For module constants in VBA, place the `Const` statement in the declarations section of the module, and use the optional `Private` or `Public` keyword to define the scope. For global constants in VBA, use a constant assignment statement with the Public keyword in the declarations section of the module. These are all examples of constant declaration statements:

```
Const ATTEMPTS = 5

Private Const M_COMPANYNAME = "Turtleflock, LLC" as String

Public Const G_VACATIONDAYS = 10 As Integer
```

Notice that constants can hold any kind of data; they're not limited to just numbers.

Both VBA and VBScript support some intrinsic constants whose names begin with `vb`. The names of these built-in constants are easier to remember than their corresponding values. Table 5.3 lists many you're likely to use. You will see others in Chapter 9, where you learn more about message boxes.

---

**Note:** Color constant values listed in Table 5.3 with &h prefixes are long integers written in hexadecimal format. The `Chr()` function returns a character with a particular ASCII value. For example, 9 is the ASCII value for the character placed in a document when you press the Tab key.

---

**Table 5.3** *Key Intrinsic Constants*

| Constant | Value | Description |
|---|---|---|
| *Color Constants* | | |
| `vbBlack` | &h00 | Black |
| `vbRed` | &hFF | Red |
| `vbGreen` | &hFF00 | Green |
| `vbYellow` | &hFFFF | Yellow |
| `vbBlue` | &hFF0000 | Blue |
| `vbMagenta` | &hFF00FF | Magenta |
| `vbCyan` | &hFFFF00 | Cyan |
| `vbWhite` | &hFFFFFF | White |

**Table 5.3** *Key Intrinsic Constants (continued)*

| Constant | Value | Description |
|---|---|---|
| *Date Constants* | | |
| vbSunday | 1 | Sunday |
| vbMonday | 2 | Monday |
| vbTuesday | 3 | Tuesday |
| vbWednesday | 4 | Wednesday |
| vbThursday | 5 | Thursday |
| vbFriday | 6 | Friday |
| vbSaturday | 7 | Saturday |
| *Date Format Constants* | | |
| vbGeneralDate | 0 | Displays a date and/or time formatted according to your system settings |
| vbLongDate | 1 | Displays a date using your computer's long date format |
| vbShortDate | 2 | Displays a date using your computer's short date format |
| vbLongTime | 3 | Displays a time using your computer's long time format |
| vbShortTime | 4 | Displays a time using your computer's short time format |
| *String Constants* | | |
| vbCr | Chr(13) | Carriage return |
| vbCrLf | Chr(13) & Chr(10) | Carriage return+linefeed |
| vbLf | Chr(10) | Line feed |
| vbTab | Chr(9) | Horizontal tab |

In Outlook VBA code, you will often see constants that begin with `ol`. However, VBScript does not support these. In VBScript, you must either use the actual value of the constant or include constant declarations in your code. To make it easier to write and test code ported to VBScript from VBA, many Outlook programmers include key Outlook constants at the beginning of every script. You will look at this in more detail in Chapter 18, "Writing Code to Respond to Outlook Form Events."

## 5.5 Coding style

Most programmers follow two style conventions that tend to make code easier to read:

- Keeping statements together in blocks indented the same amount of space. (Press Tab at the beginning of a line to indent the default four characters.)
- Using an underscore (_) as a continuation character at the end of a line when the statement code would otherwise run off the screen.

---

**Tip:** In the VBA code editor, to change the indent of a group of statements at one time, select the statements. Then, press Tab to increase the indent, or press Shift+Tab to decrease the indent.

---

The order in which procedures occur in a module doesn't really matter to VBA, but it does matter to someone (you!) who's trying to understand the code. The dropdown list on the upper-right corner of the code window keeps track of procedures in alphabetical order. Within a module, you might want to keep them in order of importance: main procedure first and then subsidiary subroutines and functions.

At the beginning of this chapter, I promised that you could cut down on the amount of typing you do in the VBA code window if you declare all your variables. As you use any declared object variable, VBA displays a list of *members* of that object class. Members include the events, methods, and properties—in other words, everything you might be able to do with or find out about an object.

You saw a small demonstration of this when you added `Dim` statements earlier; VBA helped you pick the right data or object type. It gets even better when you start using those object variables. To see how this feature works, create a new VBA procedure, and add the following code:

```
Dim objApp As Outlook.Application
Dim objAppt As Outlook.AppointmentItem
Set objApp = CreateObject("Outlook.Application")
```

**Figure 5.3** *The Auto List Members feature helps automatically complete your VBA code statements.*

On a new line, type "Set objAppt = objApp." (with a period at the end) and then pause for a moment. After you type the period, you will see a list of all the methods, properties, and events for an `Application` object variable (see Figure 5.3).

Type "cr," and the members list jumps to `CreateItem`, which is the method you want for this example. Press Tab to paste `CreateItem` into the text of the statement. Then, type an open parenthesis. As soon as you type the parenthesis, VBA again pops up a list—this time one of appropriate intrinsic constants—as well as information on the `CreateItem` method and its parameters (see Figure 5.4).

To finish the statement, press the down arrow key to select `olAppointmentItem`, press Tab to add it to the code window, and type a closing parenthesis. The code statement you entered looks like this:

```
Set objAppt = objApp.CreateItem(olAppointmentItem)
```

but all you typed was

```
Set objAppt = objApp.cr[Tab]([Down Arrow])
```

That's 27 keystrokes using the Auto List Members feature (as it's called), versus 50 keystrokes to type the entire statement by hand. See, it really will save you lots of typing and prevent many mistakes!

Before leaving general style issues, I want to introduce one more concept that makes your code infinitely more readable when you work with object

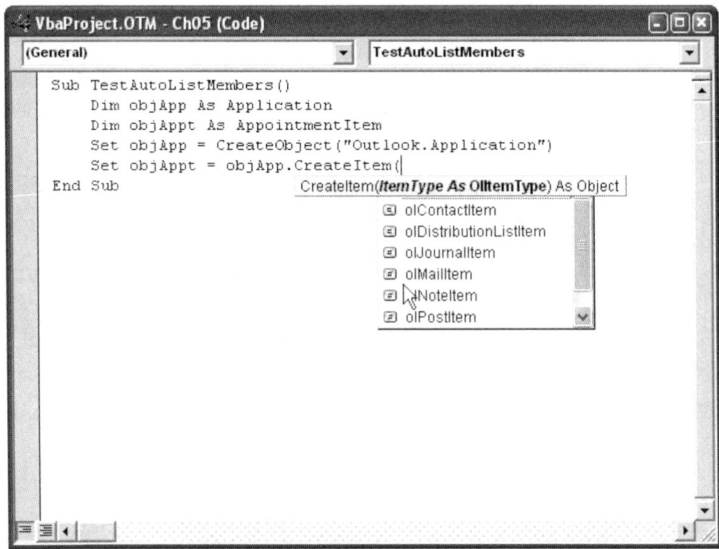


**Figure 5.4** *The Auto Quick Info feature provides the syntax for functions, methods, and their parameters as you type in the code window.*

variables. You can use a `With ... End With` code block to set properties and invoke methods on a single object. For example, if you have a `ContactItem` object variable named `objContact` (in other words, an Outlook Contact item), you can set the name and other properties and then save the item using a block of statements like this:

```
With objContact
    .FullName = "Sue Mosher"
    .Company = "Turtleflock, LLC"
    .BusinessAddressCity = "Arlington"
    .Save
End With
```

You can even nest `With ... End With` blocks. If you use a property of the outer `With` object in the code for the inner `With` block, you'll need to provide the fully qualified *`object.property`* expression, as long as the inner block refers to an object that is a child of the object referred to with the outer block.

## 5.5.1 Calling procedures

You've probably heard of programs that number thousands or millions of lines of code. All that code is not contained in just one procedure. Programs typically break down into many small chunks, each of which performs a certain role in the larger application.

To transfer control from one procedure to another, one procedure in the program *calls* another procedure. A procedure that invokes another subroutine or function is the *calling procedure*, and the other procedure is the *called procedure*. Most functions and many subroutines have one or more arguments that pass a value from one procedure to another.

User-defined functions are called the same as built-in functions, by giving the function name and then any arguments in parentheses.

Subroutines can be called with the subroutine name, followed by arguments separated by commas, or with the `Call` keyword and the arguments in parentheses. Both these statements call the same subroutine:

```
MyProc arg1, arg2, arg3

Call MyProc(arg1, arg2, arg3)
```

Using the `Call` type of statement to call a subroutine is less ambiguous and makes it easier to spot the points in your code where you branch to a different procedure.

When you call a subroutine, the code in the called procedure executes, and then control returns to the next line of the calling procedure. For example, in these two procedures,

```
Sub ProcOne()
    Dim intA as Integer
    intA = 10
    Call ProcTwo()
    intA = 10 * 10
End Sub

Sub ProcTwo()
    Dim intB as Integer
    intB = 20
    intB = 20 * 20
End Sub
```

the value of `intA` is set to `10`. Then, `ProcTwo` executes and sets the value of `intB`. Finally, execution returns to `ProcOne` to change the value of `intA` once more.

### 5.5.2 Passing arguments

For procedures with arguments, the default in VBA is to pass the variable by reference, which means that the value of the original variable can be changed through the statements inside the called procedure. The alternative

**Listing 5.1** `ByVal` *Makes a Difference in How VBA Code Runs*

```
Sub ByValDemo()
    Dim R As Integer, V As Integer
    R = 10
    V = 10
    Call ByRefSub(R, V)
    Debug.Print R, V
End Sub

Sub ByRefSub(X, ByVal Y)
    X = X + 20
    Y = Y + 20
End Sub
```

is to pass variables by value, which means that the original variable remains unaltered, no matter what happens in the procedure to which it is passed. VBA makes a copy of the original variable, so only the copy gets passed to the called procedure. This is a concept that's easier to see in action than to read about. Listing 5.1 contains a demonstration you can add to a VBA module and run to see for yourself what happens.

The code sets the value of two variables, `R` and `V`, each to `10`, and then calls the `ByRefSub` procedure, passing `R` by reference to the `X` argument and `V` by value to the `Y` argument. Because `V` is passed by value to the `Y` variable in the second procedure, the statement `Y = Y + 20` has no effect on the value of `V`. However, the statement `X = X + 20` not only changes `X` in the `ByRefSub` procedure, but also changes the value of `R` in the calling procedure to `30` because `R` was passed to the `X` variable by reference.

You could have used a `ByRef` keyword in the `Sub ByRefSub()` statement to make it perfectly clear that you're passing `R` by reference. However, because passing variables by reference is the default in VBA, you didn't have to.

**Tip:** `Debug.Print` is a convenient method for seeing the result of VBA code. It shows the data in columns in the Immediate window, which you can view by pressing Ctrl+G or choosing View, Immediate Window. Make sure, though, that you take `Debug.Print` statements out of your final code because they can slow down the program.

### 5.5.3 Adding data types to arguments and functions

In VBA, you can improve the efficiency and consistency of your code by declaring the data type not just for variables in procedures, but also for the functions you create and for the arguments for both subroutines and functions. Use the same `As` data type syntax as you learned for `Dim` statements. For example, it's obvious from the data type declarations in this `MailAddr()` function that you have to supply an Outlook Contact and an integer as arguments.

```
Function MailAddr(obj As Outlook.ContactItem, _
                  int1 As Integer) As String
    Dim strAddress as String
    Select Case int1
        Case 1
            strAddress = obj.Email1Address
        Case 2
            strAddress = obj.Email2Address
        Case 3
            strAddress = obj.Email3Address
        Case Else
            strAddress = ""
    End Select
    MailAddr = strAddress
End Function
```

The function always returns a string value, corresponding to the first, second, or third e-mail address in the item (if there is one), or an empty string if you use a number other than 1, 2, or 3 for the `int1` argument.

## 5.6 Summary

Knowledge of key code syntax elements, such as variable and constant declarations, scope, and data types, will enable you to write efficient and effective code. The VBA code window has several features that help automatically complete statements with a minimum of typing and a maximum of accuracy. You also saw a brief introduction to the `ActiveExplorer` object and its `CurrentFolder` object property, which together allow you to get the folder that the user is currently viewing in Outlook.

In Chapter 6, you turn to functions and expressions, including those useful for working with the many dates you'll find in Outlook items.

# 6

# *Working with Expressions and Functions*

Much of the work of programming involves performing calculations and updating variables with new values. The key tools for this work are expressions, built-in functions, and functions you create yourself. Outlook, like most programming environments, includes a variety of functions for manipulating dates and text, as well as doing math.

Highlights of this chapter include discussions of the following:

- How to tell variables and functions from literals
- Which functions can help you work with text
- How to add and subtract dates
- How to create a follow-up task for a certain number of days after a meeting
- How to replace one category with another
- How to use an array to fill a list box

We can't cover all of Outlook's functions in just one chapter—only those you're most likely to use. You can find out about others by reading the Help topics.

## 6.1 Elements of an expression

You have seen that many programming statements include a variable on the left side of an equals sign and terms on the right side that comprise an *expression*. The expression may be a string value or a number or a date, but the key concept is that it can be reduced to some finite value. A statement like

```
strPhoneNumber = "+1 (" & strAreaCode & ") " & strNumber
```

means "set the value of the `strPhoneNumber` variable equal to the expression on the right side of the equals sign." The expression itself consists of four terms joined by ampersand (`&`) string concatenation operators:

| | |
|---|---|
| `"+1 ("` | string literal |
| `strAreaCode` | string variable |
| `") "` | string literal |
| `strNumber` | string variable |

---

**Tip:** A phone number is a string, not a numeric value, because it contains characters as well as numbers.

---

**Note:** Not all programming statements set a variable equal to an expression, of course. Some statements control program flow or set object variables.

---

A *literal* value is a specific value that doesn't change, but is expressed in programming statements as the value itself, not as a programming constant. You must enclose string literals in quotation marks and date literals (including time values) with number (`#`) signs. Here are more examples of literals:

```
"tomorrow"

#March 2, 2003#

#3/2/2003#

#10:00 a.m.#

3298
```

The last item is a literal, too—a number literal. You do not need to enclose numbers with special characters when you use their literal values.

---

**Tip:** The `#3/2/2003#` literal always means March 2, 2003 even if your system is set to use a day/month/year short date format. We look at this issue later in Section 6.4.4, "Time zones and international dates."

---

If you use the naming conventions introduced in the previous chapter, you should have no problem distinguishing literals from variables and functions. Variable names and constants should follow the naming rules with prefixes that indicate their scope and content. String and date literals have their surrounding quotation marks and number signs, and number literals are, well, just numbers. You can combine functions, literals, variables, and constants in expressions.

## 6.2 Using mathematical expressions

You encountered the principal mathematical operators earlier in Chapter 4, "Code Basics." You actually do less math in Outlook programming than in some other applications because most of the time you are manipulating Outlook items and working with text and dates.

When working with mathematical expressions, remember that mathematical expressions are evaluated from left to right. Also, if an expression contains more than one operator, the terms involving operators are evaluated in a particular sequence, according to the operator precedence order, which you can look up in Help. However, it's much better to control the order by adding parentheses to group related terms.

Text boxes on VBA forms and many Outlook item properties can hold several different kinds of data. If you set a variable to a text box or property value, you can't always be sure of what type of data you're working with. Even if you give the variable a name that indicates it should contain numeric data, there could be something wrong with your code, or the variable could contain a value of `Null`—in other words, it could contain no data. To avoid an error, you can perform a test first, using the built-in `IsNumeric()` function, which returns `True` or `False`, to find out whether the variable can be evaluated to a number, as you did in this code snippet from the VBA birthday/anniversary reminder form that you enhanced in Chapter 4, "Code Basics":

```
If Not IsNumeric(txtDays.Value) Then
    Cancel = True
    MsgBox "Please enter a number."
End If
```

**Note:** The expression `Not IsNumeric(txtDays.Value)` is equivalent to `IsNumeric(txtDays.Value) = False`.

---

**Tip:** The presence of `Null` in any mathematical expression causes the entire expression to resolve to `Null`. For example, `Null + 2` is not the same as `0 + 2`. `Null + 2` resolves to `Null`, not 2.

---

You might be puzzled by statements such as `D = D * 1.20`. Why does the variable `D` appear on both sides of the equals sign? This statement updates the value of `D` by multiplying `D` by 1.20. If `D` equals 100, then the new value of `D` after the statement runs is 120.

## 6.3 Working with strings

A great deal of Outlook programming code is devoted to manipulating text—or more precisely, manipulating string variables—by breaking them into parts and putting them back together. For example, if you have a variable named `strPhoneNumber` that contains a number using the standard pattern *`+xx (yyy) zzz-zzzz`* or *`(yyy) zzz-zzzz`*, this code extracts the area or city code from within the parentheses and assigns it to a new variable, `strAreaCode`:

```
intLeftPar = InStr(strPhoneNumber, "(")
intRightPar = InStr(intLeftPar, strPhoneNumber, ")")
strAreaCode = Mid(strPhoneNumber, intLeftPar + 1, _
  intRightPar - intLeftPar - 1)
```

Did you notice the string literals for the parenthesis characters?

### 6.3.1 Extracting string parts

The preceding code uses two important string functions, `Instr()` and `Mid()`. `Instr()` finds the occurrence of a single character or string within another string, while `Mid()` returns text from inside a string, starting at a particular position and continuing for a specific number of characters. Table 6.1 lists these and other essential string functions. The examples assume that `strPhoneNumber = "+1 (203) 555-7890"`.

### 6.3.2 Comparing strings

Often you want to know whether one string is the same as another or is contained inside another. Table 6.2 lists three essential functions for comparing strings. The arguments listed in brackets (`[ ]`) are optional; you do not include the brackets when you use these functions.

**Table 6.1** *Functions to Extract String Parts*

| Function | Example | Evaluates To |
|---|---|---|
| `Left(string, length)` | `Left(strPhoneNumber,3)` | `"+1"` |
| `Right(string, length)` | `Right(strPhoneNumber,8)` | `"456-7890"` |
| `Mid(string, start, length)` | `Mid(strPhoneNumber, 5, 3)` | `"203"` |

Comparisons are case-sensitive by default. To make string comparisons ignore upper and lower case, set the optional *`compare`* argument to 1, as shown in the example for the `StrComp()` function in Table 6.2.

**Tip:** You can use the intrinsic constants `vbTextCompare (=1)` and `vbBinaryCompare (=0)` in functions that take a *`compare`* argument.

`InStrRev()` works like `InStr()`, only it starts from the end of *`string1`*, not the beginning. Its arguments are in a different order, too.

The `StrComp()` function returns these values:

| | |
|---|---|
| If *`string1`* is less than *`string2`* | `-1` |
| If *`string1`* is equal to *`string2`* | `0` |
| If *`string1`* is greater than *`string2`* | `1` |
| If *`string1`* or *`string2`* is `Null` | `Null` |

In VBA, you can set an entire module to use case-insensitive string comparison by adding an `Option Compare Text` statement to the declarations section of the module. To use case-sensitive comparisons, add `Option Compare Binary`, which is the default if no `Option Compare` statement is present.

**Table 6.2** *Functions for Comparing Strings*

| Function | Example | Evaluates to |
|---|---|---|
| `InStr([start,] string1, string2[,compare])` | `InStr(3, "repeated","e")` | 4 |
| `InStrRev(string1, string2 [, start[,compare]])` | `InStrRev("repeated","e")` | 7 |
| `StrComp(string1, string2[, compare])` | `StrComp("ABCDE","AbCdE",0)` | 0 |

---

**Note:** Using text comparison, rather binary comparison, may flatten the difference between letters in the standard English alphabet and letters from other languages that use diacritical marks. However, the result will depend on your Windows language settings, so you may need to experiment.

---

### 6.3.3 Replacing parts of a string

There are three basic ways to replace one part of a string with another:

- Break the string into substrings, change or substitute one or more substrings, and then join the substrings back together using the ampersand (`&`) concatenation operator.
- Use the `Replace()` function to create a new string that replaces part of the original string with another.
- In VBA (but not VBScript code on Outlook forms), use the `Mid` statement to replace part of one string with another.

Let's go back to telephone numbers for some examples. Consider a situation in which your local area code, 717, is being split into 717 and 570. The fact that telephone numbers use a standard format with area/city and country code—for example, +1 (717) 555-1234—makes it easy to parse the different parts of the number. For a variable named `strPhoneNumber`, the three lines below return the updated number to a variable named `strNewPhoneNumber` by breaking out three characters on the left (the country code) and the eight characters on the right (the local number), then concatenating them with the new area code in the middle.

```
strCountryCode = Left(strPhoneNumber, 3)
strNumber = Right(strPhoneNumber, 8)
strNewPhoneNumber = strCountryCode & "(507) " & strNumber
```

The same operation performed with the `Replace()` function takes just one line of code:

```
strNewPhoneNumber = Replace(strPhoneNumber,"(717)","(507)")
```

---

**Tip:** `Replace()` also supports optional *`start`*, *`count`*, and *`compare`* arguments to return only the portion of the string beginning at *`start`*, make a specific *`count`* of replacements, and set the comparison type as with the `InStr()` function.

---

The final method is the `Mid` statement in VBA:

```
Mid(strPhoneNumber, 5) = "507"
```

---

**CAUTION:** Don't confuse the `Mid` statement in VBA with the `Mid()` function, which works in both VBA and VBScript.

---

While `Mid` works much like `Replace()`, there are some significant differences:

- You can't use the `Mid` statement in VBScript.
- `Replace()` allows you to replace a string that is *`count`* characters long with a string of a different length.
- `Mid` makes only one replacement, while `Replace()` can make multiple replacements within a string.
- `Mid` alters the original string variable, while `Replace()` leaves the original intact and returns a new value.

### 6.3.4 Other useful string functions

Not all string functions extract, compare, or combine text. Table 6.3 illustrates functions to fill a string with a particular character, return the length of a string, remove leading or trailing spaces, and change a string to upper or lower case.

**Table 6.3** *Other Useful String Functions*

| Function | Example | Evaluates to |
|---|---|---|
| `String(number, character)` | `String(4,"+")` | `"++++"` |
| `Space(number)` | `Space(10)` | `"          "` |
| `Len(string)` | `Len("Microsoft Outlook")` | `17` |
| `Trim(string)` | `Trim("  sloppy text ")` | `"sloppy text"` |
| `LTrim(string)` | `LTrim("  sloppy text ")` | `"sloppy text "` |
| `RTrim(string)` | `RTrim("  sloppy text ")` | `"  sloppy text"` |
| `UCase(string)` | `UCase("Microsoft Outlook")` | `"MICROSOFT OUTLOOK"` |
| `LCase(string)` | `LCase("Microsoft Outlook")` | `"microsoft outlook"` |

## 6.4 Working with dates

Date manipulation skills are critical to Outlook programming because virtually every Outlook item has one or more important dates associated with it—the date an e-mail message was received, the due date for a task, a friend's birthday, the time of your appointment tomorrow, and so on. In this section, you learn how to extract components from dates and perform date arithmetic. We also briefly visit issues related to time zones and international dates. But first, let's start with three basic date-related functions: `IsDate()`, `CDate()`, and `FormatDateTime()`.

**Note:** This section covers time issues, too, because the VBA date type and the Outlook date/time field type can contain both date and time data.

### 6.4.1 Basic date-related functions

What is a date? In the context of Outlook, a date is any built-in or custom property designed to handle dates or times. In addition to working with such properties, Outlook programs often need to get dates from users through controls on a form. How can you tell whether the user has entered a valid date?

You can use the built-in `IsDate()` function to test for a valid date. `IsDate()` takes any date or string expression as its argument and returns `True` if the expression represents a valid date between January 1, 1000 and December 31, 9999. `IsDate()` is smart about handling dates in a variety of formats. Any of the following expressions returns `True`:

```
IsDate("3/31/01")
IsDate("31 Mar 2001")
IsDate("10:00")
IsDate(#3/31/01#)
```

You might wonder why `IsDate("10:00")` returns `True`. Remember a time always has a date component (and a date always has a time component), even if Outlook displays only the date.

`CDate()` is one of several available functions to convert values from one data type to another, in this case to a date value. Normally, you would use it with `IsDate()` because you will get an error if you try to convert a non-

**Table 6.4** *NamedFormat Arguments for FormatDateTime()*

| Constant | Value | Example |
|---|---|---|
| `vbGeneralDate` | 0 | `12/31/2002 6:30:00 PM` |
| `vbLongDate` | 1 | `Tuesday, December 31,2002` |
| `vbShortDate` | 2 | `12/31/2002` |
| `vbLongTime` | 3 | `6:30:00 PM` |
| `vbShortTime` | 4 | `18:30` |

date value to a date. The `MakeDate()` function returns today's date if the *`somedate`* argument is not a valid date:

```
Function MakeDate(somedate) As Date
    If IsDate(somedate) Then
        MakeDate = CDate(somedate)
    Else
        MakeDate = Date
    End If
End Function
```

Finally, the `FormatDateTime()` function is useful for returning any date or time as text, using the user's Windows preferences for formatting dates. Its basic syntax is:

```
FormatDateTime(Date [, NamedFormat])
```

You can use it in both VBA and VBScript. (The `Format()` function offers even more flexibility in arranging date elements in a string, but VBScript does not support it.) Table 6.4 shows the available options for the *`NamedFormat`* argument and gives examples using the default Windows settings for U.S. users. The constants are valid in both VBScript and VBA.

### 6.4.2 Date extraction functions

Being able to extract components from dates means that you can find out whether Valentine's Day falls on a weekend or what journal entries you made on Monday. Table 6.5 lists functions you can use to get just the date or just the time portion of a date or extract any particular date component. Optional arguments are in brackets.

**Table 6.5** *Functions to Extract Date Parts*

| Function | Returns |
|---|---|
| `Date` | Current system date |
| `DatePart(`*`interval,date[,firstday[,firstweek]`*`)` | Part specified by the interval string:<br>`"yyyy"` Year<br>`"q"` Quarter<br>`"m"` Month<br>`"y"` Day of the year<br>`"d"` Day<br>`"w"` Day of the week<br>`"ww"` Week of the year<br>`"h"` Hour<br>`"n"` Minute<br>`"s"` Second |
| `DateValue(`*`date`*`)` | Date component without any time value |
| `Day(`*`date`*`)` | Day of the year |
| `FormatDateTime(`*`date/time`*` [,`*`NamedFormat`*`)` | The date/time formatted as text with optional *`NamedFormat`* |
| `Hour(`*`time`*`)` | Hour of the day, from 0 to 23 |
| `Minute(`*`time`*`)` | Minute of the hour, from 0 to59 |
| `Month(`*`date`*`)` | Month of the year, from 1 to 12 |
| `MonthName(`*`month[,abbreviate]`*`)` | Name of the month, given the number of the month |
| `Now` | Current system date and time |
| `Second(`*`time`*`)` | Second of the minute, from 0 to 59 |
| `Time` | Current system time |
| `Timer` | Number of seconds since midnight |
| `TimeValue(`*`time`*`)` | Time component without any date value |
| `Weekday(`*`date[,firstdayofweek]`*`)` | Number from 1 to 7 representing the day of the week counting from *`firstdayofweek`* |
| `WeekdayName(`*`weekday[,abbreviate[,firstday]]`*`)` | Name of the day, given its number |

---

**Note:** Unlike most other functions, the `Date`, `Now`, `Time`, and `Timer` functions do not use parentheses after the function name.

---

Here is an example of a function to check for weekend days. It evaluates to `True` if the `dteDate` argument falls on a Saturday or Sunday.

```
Function IsWeekend(dteDate As Date) As Boolean
    Dim intWeekday as Integer
    intWeekday = Weekday(dteDate, vbMonday)
    IsWeekend = (intWeekday >= 6)
End Function
```

The `IsWeekend` function uses the optional *`firstday`* parameter of the `Weekday()` function to set Monday as the first day of the week, using an intrinsic constant, `vbMonday`, so that Saturday is the sixth day of the week and Sunday the seventh. That makes it easy to test for Saturday or Sunday with the `(intWeekday >= 6)` expression, which evaluates to `True` or `False`.

### 6.4.3 Performing date arithmetic

Date arithmetic involves calculating the time elapsed between two dates (or times) or adding time to or subtracting time from a particular date to get a new date. Possible uses include

- Figuring the number of weeks since your last vacation day
- Calculating how long since you had any interaction with a contact
- Projecting the next date you should call a contact

Outlook stores dates in the same format as double-type numbers—the integer portion representing the date and the decimal portion representing the time. This means that for the simplest sort of date arithmetic, you can just add the number of days. For example, `Now() + 3` is three days from the current date/time.

For more complicated calculations—such as the number of weeks between two dates or a date 13 months in the future—you use the `DateAdd()` and `DateDiff()` functions:

```
DateAdd(interval, number, date)
DateDiff(interval, date1, date2[, firstday, [,firstweek]])
```

The *interval* argument takes the same values as in the `DatePart()` function in Table 6.5. In the `DateAdd()` function, the *number* argument is the number of *interval* periods you want to add. To get a date in the future, add a positive number. To get a date in the past, add a negative number.

The following function calculates the next business day that occurs *intAhead* days from *dteDate*, by combining the `Weekday()` and `DateAdd()` functions and adding one or two days if the date falls on a weekend:

```
Function NextBusinessDay(dteDate As Date, _
                         intAhead As Integer) As Date
    Dim dteNextDate as Date
    dteNextDate = DateAdd("d", intAhead, dteDate)
    Select Case Weekday(dteNextDate)
        Case 1
            dteNextDate = dteNextDate + 1
        Case 7
            dteNextDate = dteNextDate + 2
    End Select
    NextBusinessDay = dteNextDate
End Function
```

`DateDiff()` returns a negative number if *date1* is later than *date2*. For example, `DateDiff("d", Now(), #1/1/2001#)` returns a negative number telling you the number of days since the millennium began.

A common application of `DateDiff()` in Outlook is to calculate the age of someone whose birthday is coming up. `DateDiff()` can't do this by itself because it rounds up to the nearest year if you compare two dates where the day and month of the earlier date fall after the day and month of the later date in the comparison. To avoid that rounding and get an accurate count, you can use the `YearsSinceDate()` function in Listing 6.1. (Since this is a common need on Outlook forms, the function is written without data typing, so you can use it in VBScript.)

The `YearsSinceDate()` function uses many of the date functions discussed in this section: `DateDiff()` for comparisons; `Month()`, `Day()`, and `Year()` to extract date parts; and `CDate()` to create a valid date from a concatenation of those parts.

### 6.4.4 Time zones and international dates

If you have to deal with users in multiple time zones or in different countries, Outlook presents some challenges. For one thing, Outlook has no

**Listing 6.1** *Calculating the Number of Years Between Two Dates*

```
Function YearsSinceDate(dteDate1, dteDate2)
    Dim dteEarlyDateInLateYear
    Dim dteEarly
    Dim dteLate
    If DateDiff("d", dteDate1, dteDate2) >= 0 Then
        dteEarly = dteDate1
        dteLate = dteDate2
    Else
        dteEarly = dteDate2
        dteLate = dteDate1
    End If
    dteEarlyDateInLateYear = _
        CDate(Month(dteEarly) & "/" & _
              Day(dteEarly) & "/" & _
              Year(dteLate))
    If DateDiff("d", dteEarlyDateInLateYear, _
                dteLate) >= 0 Then
        YearsSinceDate = _
          DateDiff("yyyy", dteEarly, dteLate)
    Else
        YearsSinceDate = _
          DateDiff("yyyy", dteEarly, dteLate) - 1
    End If
End Function
```

concept of an all-day event that is time-zone independent. For example, if you make New Year's Day a holiday in the eastern time zone of the United States and put that on a company calendar in an Exchange Server public folder, your office in London will see it not as an all-day event, but as an event running from 5 A.M. January 1 to 5 A.M. January 2. There are no easy solutions to this issue within the scope of this book.

While U.S. users are accustomed to entering dates in month/day/year format, many people in other countries use day/month/year instead. In general, Outlook and VBA will correctly interpret whatever the user enters in a date/time field as the correct date that the user intended, according to the user's Windows regional settings. However, you may want to provide a nonambiguous display for date information. For example, you might want to display the fourth day of March as "04 Mar 2003," instead of "3/4/2003," which could mean March 3 or April 3, depending on the country. The `FormatDateTime()` function listed in Table 6.5 is available in both VBA and VBScript for use on Outlook forms to turn any date or time into text formatted with the user's own Windows regional preferences.

## 6.5 Using user-created functions

The `NextBusinessDay()` function is a good example of the kind of function you can create in Outlook and use over and over again. User-defined functions help keep your code readable by breaking tasks down into manageable chunks. To help you see how this works, look at the code in Listing 6.2. The `CreateFollowUpTask` macro is designed to run when you have an Outlook appointment item open. The macro will create a follow-up task, based on an appointment's start date and other information.

When you run the `CreateFollowUpTask` macro, either from the Macros window or from a toolbar button, the code creates a new task item five

**Listing 6.2** *Incorporating a Function Makes It Easier To Follow the Code Logic*

```
Sub CreateFollowUpTask()
     Dim objApp As Outlook.Application
     Dim objItem As Object
     Dim objTask As Outlook.TaskItem
     On Error Resume Next
     Set objApp = CreateObject("Outlook.Application")
     Set objItem = objApp.ActiveInspector.CurrentItem
     If objItem.Class = olAppointment Then
          Set objTask = objApp.CreateItem(olTaskItem)
          With objTask
               .StartDate = NextBusinessDay(objItem.Start, 5)
               .Subject = "Follow up"
               .Body = "Follow up to appointment on " & _
                        FormatDateTime(objItem.Start, vbLongDate) & _
                        vbCrLf & vbCrLf & "APPOINTMENT NOTES:" & _
                        vbCrLf & objItem.Body
               .Display
          End With
     End If
End Sub

Function NextBusinessDay _
   (dteDate As Date, intAhead As Integer) As Date
    Dim dteNextDate As Date
    dteNextDate = DateAdd("d", intAhead, dteDate)
    Select Case Weekday(dteNextDate)
        Case 1
            dteNextDate = dteNextDate + 1
        Case 7
            dteNextDate = dteNextDate + 2
    End Select
    NextBusinessDay = dteNextDate
End Function
```

business days from the date of the appointment, copies information from the appointment to the task, and then displays the task for further modification.

Someone reading the code sees the `With ... End With` block in the `CreatFollowUpTask` macro as a single set of logical steps, without any diversion into the details on how the `NextBusinessDay()` function works.

---

**Note:** The code uses the expression `objApp.ActiveInspector.CurrentItem` to get the item that Outlook currently has open, if any, and then checks to make sure that it is an appointment before proceeding further. The `objItem` object variable is declared `As Object` because you don't know what kind of item it is until you test its `Class` property. You'll learn more about this technique in Chapter 14, "Working with Items and Recipients."

---

To create other kinds of follow-up items, you could add more macros that create different kinds of items, but you could call the same `NextBusinessDay()` function from each one, passing it different arguments as needed. You need to know, however, that Outlook items don't always use the same field name for the same kind of information. While the `AppointmentItem` object has a `Start` field, the `TaskItem` object has a `StartDate` field. However, the `Body` field always represents the large text box on the main page of any Outlook item. Chapter 10 will show you how to use the Object Browser in VBA to look up property names.

With more complex functions, you can use a feature called *named arguments* to make the calling code a little bit clearer. With named arguments, you can specify the arguments for a function in any order. For example, you may have noticed that the `InStr()` and `InStrRev()` functions for searching inside one string for the presence of another use the same arguments, but in a different order. If you are used to the order in `InStr()`, it's easy to make a mistake when using `InStrRev()`. You can avoid that kind of error if you specify the arguments by name. Get the names from the Auto Quick Info text that VBA pops up for each function, then use a colon followed by an equals sign (`:=`) to assign a value to each named argument—`StringCheck`, `StringMatch`, and `Start` in this example for `InStrRev()`:

```
Sub NamedArgsDemo()
    Dim strLookIn As String
    Dim strLookFor As String
    Dim lngFromRight As Long
    strLookIn = "Able I was ere I saw Elba."
    strLookFor = "I"
```

```
        lngFromRight = InStrRev(StringCheck:=strLookIn, _
                           StringMatch:=strLookFor, Start:=20)
        Debug.Print lngFromRight
    End Sub
```

## 6.6 Using Split() and Join() functions, and arrays

I'd like to finish this chapter with two more string functions, `Split()` and `Join()`, to help introduce the topic of *arrays*. You use these functions to tinker with the `Categories` field on every Outlook item and also with the `Companies` field that appears on all but note items. `Categories` is a keyword field; it consists of multiple string values. When you view this property in the Categories dialog or in a text box on an Outlook form, you'll see the individual categories separated by a character called a *delimiter.* On most systems in the United States, a comma is used as the delimiter, but the delimiter in other countries (set in the Windows regional settings) may be a semicolon or some other character.

The `Split()` and `Join()` functions are designed to make it easy to handle such a delimited list and its component substrings. The full syntax for the `Split()` function is `Split(`*`expression`*`[, `*`delimiter`*`[, `*`limit`*`[, `*`compare`*`]]])`, where

| | |
|---|---|
| *`expression`* | is a delimited string expression |
| *`delimiter`* | is a single character; the default is the space character (" ") |
| *`limit`* | number of substrings to be returned; the default is `-1`, which means return all. |
| *`compare`* | comparison option, same as for `InStr()` |

A statement such as `arr() = Split(objItem.Categories, ",")` returns an array. An array holds one or more values as separate elements. Refer to the elements of an array by subscript, starting with `0` for the first element. The first element in the array in Listing 6.3 would be `arr(0)`, the second `arr(1)`, and so forth.

---

**Tip:** VBA allows you to create arrays that use `1` as the lowest subscript, but since VBScript doesn't support this type of array, we'll stay away from it.

---

`Join()`, the opposite of `Split()`, uses this syntax: `Join(array, delimiter)`. It returns a string consisting of the items in *array*, separated by the *delimiter* character.

### 6.6.1 A macro to replace one category with another

Outlook does not include a feature to replace one category with another, but it's easy to build a macro to perform the replacement using the `Split()` and `Join()` functions. Take a look at the example in Listing 6.3.

The `For Each ... Next` loop is the heart of the procedure. It gets each item in the current folder, uses the `Split()` function to convert the `Categories` field to an array, and then checks each element of the array to see whether it needs to be updated. After the entire array has been checked, the `Join()` function reassembles the `Categories` for the item and then closes and saves the item.

**Listing 6.3** *Use the Split() and Join() Functions To Work with Categories*

```
Sub ReplaceCat()
     Dim objApp As Outlook.Application
     Dim objFolder As Outlook.MAPIFolder
     Dim objItem As Object
     Dim arr() As String
     Dim strOldCat As String
     Dim strNewCat As String
     Dim I As Integer
     strOldCat = "Customer"
     strNewCat = "Client"
     Set objApp = CreateObject("Outlook.Application")
     Set objFolder = objApp.ActiveExplorer.CurrentFolder
     For Each objItem In objFolder.Items
         arr() = Split(objItem.Categories, ",")
         For I = 0 To UBound(arr)
             If arr(I) = strOldCat Then
                 arr(I) = strNewCat
                 Exit For
             End If
         Next
         objItem.Categories = Join(arr, ",")
         objItem.Save
     Next
     Set objApp = Nothing
     Set objFolder = Nothing
     Set objItem = Nothing
End Sub
```

**Note:** The `Exit For` statement inside the `If ... End If` loop allows the program to go directly to refreshing the `Categories` field once it finds and updates the category value in the array. Because each category appears only once in the `Categories` field, once we find the category to be updated, it is not necessary to look at the other values in the array.

In this case, we don't even need to know how many categories each item has. The `For I = 0 To UBound(arr) ... Next` loop cycles through all the elements of the array. `UBound()` is a function that returns the largest subscript for a particular array.

**Tip:** We look at `For ... Next` loops, `If ... End If` blocks, and other ways to control program flow in the next chapter.

The statement `If arr(I) = strOldCat Then` checks to see whether a given array element matches the old category (`strOldCat`). If there is a match, the routine changes that category to the new category with the statement `arr(I) = strNewCat`. Finally, the `objItem.Categories = Join(arr, ",")` statement puts the now updated elements of the array back into the `Categories` field. The default delimiter for `Join()` is the space character (`" "`); don't forget to specify the comma delimiter when working with the `Categories` field.

### 6.6.2 More on arrays

An array requires a slightly different `Dim` statement from the one you used for other variables. For a dynamic array such as the one in Listing 6.3—one that could be any size depending on the number of categories—use a `Dim` statement, following the variable name with empty parentheses, like this: `Dim arr() As String`. The `As` *`datatype`* keywords indicate the type of elements the array will contain. Later use `ReDim arr(`*`x`*`)` to set or change the exact size of the array; *x* is not the number of elements but the upper bound of the array, the largest subscript. If you have 10 elements in the array, the upper bound is 9. If you add the `Preserve` keyword, as in `ReDim Preserve ...`, any existing data in the array is kept; otherwise, a `ReDim` statement reinitializes the array, and any existing data is lost.

For fixed-dimension arrays, use `Dim arr(`*`y`*`)`. You can also create multidimensional arrays. One convenient use of this type of array is to initialize list box controls that contain data in more than one column. Here is the code used to initialize the `cboCouples` list box ("Favorite couples") that you saw in Figure 3.12.

```
Dim arrCouples(4, 2)
arrCouples(0, 0) = "Romeo"
arrCouples(0, 1) = "Juliet"
arrCouples(1, 0) = "Edward"
arrCouples(1, 1) = "Wallis"
arrCouples(2, 0) = "Dick"
arrCouples(2, 1) = "Linda"
arrCouples(3, 0) = "Robert"
arrCouples(3, 1) = "Sue"
cboCouples.List = arrCouples
```

Compare the code above with the code in Chapter 3 that fills the `lstColors` list box for Favorite Colors using the `AddItem` method.

## 6.7 Summary

With an arsenal of string and date functions, plus functions to handle arrays, you are well equipped to start building routines to work with Outlook items. User-created functions enhance programs with reusable procedures that cut down the time needed to build new applications.

Just as in the previous chapter you saw what programming code is required to retrieve the Outlook folder that the user is viewing, in this chapter, you encountered the `ActiveInspector` object and its `CurrentItem` property, which together allow you to get the item that a user currently has open in Outlook. You also created a new task item with the `CreateItem` method, which you first saw in Chapter 4, and set some key properties for the task.

In Chapter 7, you learn more about controlling the flow of a program with different types of loops and other techniques.

# 7

# *Controlling Program Flow*

It's hard to write code without running into issues of program flow. How do you get the program to perform a certain action in one situation and a different action under other conditions? How do you work through all the items in an Outlook folder, examining each in turn? You've already looked at passing arguments from subroutine to subroutine as one way of controlling the flow of a program. You will learn several more methods in this chapter.

Highlights of this chapter include discussions of the following:

- How to use `If ... Then ... Else` statements to create branches in your program
- When to use `For Each ... Next` versus `For ... Next` loops
- How `GoTo` statements open the door to proper error handling

## 7.1 If ... Then statements

You have already seen several examples of `If ... Then` statements in earlier chapters. The basic syntax is simple:

```
If expression Then
    code to perform actions
End If
```

The expression in the first part of the `If ... Then` statement must evaluate to `True` or `False`. These are good examples of such expressions:

```
IsNumeric(txtDays.Value)

InStr(strSubject, "Birthday") > 0

strAddress <> ""

intDoIt = vbYes
```

---

**Tip:** The intrinsic constant `vbYes` is used with message boxes, as you will see in Chapter 9, "Handling User Input and Feedback."

---

Typically, the `If ... Then` expression will be either a function that returns either `True` or `False` or an expression using one of the comparison operators you encountered in Chapter 4, "Code Basics."

You can also have a more complex expression involving more than one condition linked with the comparison operators `And`, `Or`, or `Not`, such as this one from the `ReminderUpdate` form in Chapter 3, "A VBA Birthday/Anniversary Reminder Tool":

```
If InStr(strSubject, "Birthday") > 0 And _
  chkBirthdays.Value Then
```

Why didn't the above expression use `chkBirthdays.Value = True`? Because that would be redundant. Assuming that `chkBirthdays` represents a normal check box control, its `Value` property always evaluates to either `True` or `False`. You don't need to write `chkBirthdays.Value = True`; just `chkBirthdays.Value` is sufficient. Similarly, an equivalent for `chkBirthdays.Value = False` would be `Not chkBirthdays`, because the `Not` keyword turns `True` into `False` and vice versa.

After the `If ... Then` statement, you must supply the statements that you want the program to run if the expression is `True`. If you have only one statement to run, you can include it with the `If ... Then` statement on a single line:

```
If D > 10 Then D = D * 1.20
```

Notice that you leave out the `End If` when you create an `If ... Then` statement on a single line.

The single-line format works only for the simplest of `If ... Then` statements. Most of the time, you have more than one code statement to execute and, therefore, must place each statement on a separate line after the `If ... Then` statement and end the block with an `End If` statement. This example of an `If ... End If` block tests whether a given Outlook item is a contact and, if it is, assigns values to two string variables for the parent folder's `StoreID` and the item's `EntryID`, which together uniquely identify the item.

```
If objItem.Class = olContact Then
    Set objFolder = objItem.Parent
```

```
    strStoreID = objFolder.StoreID
    strItemID = objItem.EntryID
End If
```

You saw a similar usage in Listing 6.2, where we tested whether an item was an appointment before proceeding to work with its properties.

---

**Tip:** If you wanted to use the above code in VBScript, you'd want to declare `olContact` as a constant first or substitute its literal value, 40, in the code.

---

---

**Note:** The `StoreID` of an Outlook folder and `EntryID` of an Outlook item can be used with the `GetFolderFromID` and `GetItemFromID` methods of the `NameSpace` object to retrieve a folder or item. You'll see these techniques in Chapter 12, "Working with Stores and Folders," and Chapter 14, "Working with Items and Recipients."

---

You can nest `If ... Then` statement blocks inside each other, as in this example, to manage the foreground and background colors for a text box control named `txtOldCategory`:

```
If txtOldCategory.ForeColor = vbRed Then
    If txtOldCategory.BackColor = vbRed Then
        txtOldCategory.BackColor = vbBlack
    End If
End If
```

---

**Tip:** VBA and VBScript provide constants, such as `vbRed` and `vbBlack`, for eight commonly used colors.

---

Too many levels of nesting make `If ... End If` blocks very difficult to read and debug, especially when you start nesting them with other kinds of program control statements. All it takes is one extra or one missing `End If` to make your procedure stop dead in its tracks. When you find it necessary to use nested `If ... End If` blocks, take extra care to indent all the statements within each block to make them look consistent. This will also make it easier to see that each block has the correct starting and ending statement and that they match.

A common variation on `If ... Then` expressions adds an `Else` block so that you perform one set of actions if the expression is `True` and a second set if the expression is `False`. Expanding on the earlier code to manage the foreground and background colors in a `txtOldCategory` control, you might have

```
If txtOldCategory.ForeColor = vbRed Then
    If txtOldCategory.BackColor = vbRed Then
        txtOldCategory.BackColor = vbBlack
    End If
Else
    txtOldCategory.BackColor = vbYellow
End If
```

A less common variation uses `ElseIf` to test for another condition. In fact, you can add several `ElseIf` statements, as shown in Listing 7.1.

The logic in `If ... Then ... ElseIf` statements is often difficult to follow. A more readable way to accomplish the same result is to use a `Select Case` statement, which is covered in the following section.

`If ... End If` blocks sometimes offer clues as to where your code can be simplified. Take, for example, this code from Listing 3.2:

```
If InStr(strSubject, "Birthday") > 0 And _
  chkBirthdays.Value Then
    objItem.ReminderSet = True
    objItem.ReminderMinutesBeforeStart = intMinutes
    objItem.Save
End If
If InStr(strSubject, "Anniversary") > 0 And _
  chkAnniversaries.Value Then
    objItem.ReminderSet = True
    objItem.ReminderMinutesBeforeStart = intMinutes
    objItem.Save
End If
```

Each `If ... End If` block contains the same three `objItem` statements. You can simplify the code by using the original `If ... End If`

**Listing 7.1** `ElseIf` *Statements Provide More Complex Branching*

```
If txtOldCategory.ForeColor = vbRed Then
    If txtOldCategory.BackColor = vbRed Then
        txtOldCategory.BackColor = vbBlack
    End If
ElseIf txtOldCategory.Forecolor = vbWhite Then
    txtOldCategory.BackColor = vbBlack
ElseIf txtOldCategory.Forecolor = vbBlue Then
    txtOldCategory.BackColor = vbWhite
End If
```

blocks to set a Boolean variable, `blnUpdate`, that indicates whether to proceed with the update. Then, you add a third `If ... End If` block to perform the actual update, only if `blnUpdate` is `True`:

```
If InStr(strSubject, "Birthday") > 0 And _
  chkBirthdays.Value = True Then
    blnUpdate = True
End If
If InStr(strSubject, "Anniversary") > 0 And _
  chkAnniversaries.Value = True Then
    blnUpdate = True
End If
If blnUpdate Then
    With objItem
        .ReminderSet = True
        .ReminderMinutesBeforeStart = intMinutes
        .Save
    End With
End If
```

This version is about the same length as the preceding code, but much easier to maintain. If you later decide to change the statements updating the item's reminder settings, you have to make the changes in only one location, in the `If blnUpdate Then ... End If` block, not in two separate `If ... End If` blocks.

**Tip:** Did you notice that we also streamlined the new version by adding a `With ... End With` block?

## 7.2 Select Case statements

The next program flow control tool is the `Select Case` statement. Use this when you want to test a particular variable or property that could have several values, not just `True` or `False`. The syntax of `Select Case` looks as follows:

```
Select Case expression
    Case value1
        code to perform actions
    Case value2
        code to perform actions
    Case value3, value4
        code to perform actions
    ...
```

```
        Case Else
            code to perform actions
    End Select
```

---

**Note:** On Outlook forms, the `Select Case` statement is essential to event handlers for the `PropertyChange` and `CustomPropertyChange` events. You will see these in Chapter 18, "Writing Code to Respond to Outlook Form Events."

---

The expression in a `Select Case` statement can be a variable, an object property, or a more complex expression. Each `Case` statement handles one or more values that the expression can take on. You can even include more than one value on the same line, as shown in the `Case` *`value3, value4,`* statement above. Because you can't always anticipate every possible value, the optional `Case Else` statement provides a way to handle exceptions to the known values. If you don't include `Case Else` and the expression does not match any of the given `Case` values, the program control moves directly to the statement following `End Select`.

The code in Listing 7.1 uses too many `ElseIf` statements to be readable. However, if you transform it to a `Select Case` block, it is very easy to follow. Compare the version in Listing 7.2 with the original.

Notice that you can nest `If ... End If` blocks inside `Case` blocks. The reverse is also true; you can nest a `Select Case` block inside an `If ... End If` block. Be careful, though, to get the ending statements in the correct order. The following would trigger a compile error because the `End Select` statement appears before the `End If` of the nested `If ... End If` block.

```
    Select Case expression1
        Case value1
            your code here
        Case value2
            If expression2 Then
                your code here
    End Select
    End If
```

---

**Note:** VBA supports a couple of refinements to `Case` statements, such as `Case` *`expression1`* `To` *`expression2`* to specify a range of values and the `Case Is` *`comparisonoperator`* expression to allow the use of comparison operators in a `Case` statement. These are not available in VBScript.

---

**Listing 7.2** *Test Possible Values With a Select Block*

```
Select Case txtOldCategory.ForeColor
    Case vbRed
        If txtOldCategory.BackColor = vbRed Then
            txtOldCategory.BackColor = vbBlack
        End If
    Case vbWhite
        txtOldCategory.BackColor = vbBlack
    Case vbBlue
        txtOldCategory.BackColor = vbWhite
End Select
```

## 7.3 Do loops

The next program flow tool is the venerable `Do` loop. The basic principle of a `Do` loop is that it continues to run a series of statements until a certain condition is met. Here are several variations:

```
Do Until expression1
    code block 1
Loop

Do While expression2
    code block 2
Loop

Do
    code block 3
Loop While expression3

Do
    code block 4
Loop Until expression4
```

The first example repeats the statements in *`code block 1`* until *`expression1`* returns `True`. The second example repeats the statements in *`code block 2`* as long as *`expression2`* remains `True`. The third example always runs at least once, but repeats only if *`expression3`* is still `True`. Similarly, the fourth example always runs at least once and keeps looping until *`expression4`* returns `True`.

Use a `Do` loop when you don't know how many times a block of statements should run. If you want the loop to run at least once, consider using the syntax in the preceding third and fourth examples. If you can't be sure whether the loop will have to run at least once, the first or second version might be more appropriate. Somewhere inside the loop, you'll need one or more statements to change the value of the test expression. Otherwise, there may be no way for the code to exit the loop. In the example below, code inside the loop changes the value of both `X` and `Y`:

```
X = 2
Y = 1
Do Until Y > X
    X = X - 2
    Y = Y + 1
    lngReps = lngReps + 1
Loop
```

Execution of the loop stops after seven repetitions when `X` reaches a value of 6 and `Y` is 8. The `lngReps = lngReps + 1` statement counts the number of repetitions.

---

**CAUTION:** Think through the logic of your `Do` loops carefully, and make sure that it includes a way for the procedure to exit the loop. Otherwise, the routine might find itself in an infinite loop. If you run VBA code that you suspect is trapped in an infinite loop, press Esc or Ctrl+Break to break out of the routine.

---

In addition to the `Until` expression or `While` expression keywords that control when looping stops, you might want to provide an additional test that causes the routine to exit the loop. For example, if you want to limit the operation to a particular amount of time, you can use the `Timer` function, which returns a value (using the single data type, a numeric type that can include decimals) representing the number of seconds elapsed since midnight. This code stops the loop after 60 seconds pass:

```
sngStart = Timer
Do While X > Y
     your code that might take
       a long time to execute
       runs here
    If Timer - sngStart > 60 Then
        Exit Do
    End If
Loop
```

The `Exit Do` statement causes program control to pass to the first statement after the `Loop` statement.

The `Timer` function is available only in VBA, not in VBScript on Outlook forms.

CAUTION: Because the `Timer` function resets to `0` each day at midnight, if a procedure using `Timer` runs just before midnight, and then again right after midnight, the results may not be what you expect.

## 7.4 For ... Next loops

Another type of loop is the `For ... Next` loop. These loops cycle through either a known quantity of items or all the items within a set.

One type of `For ... Next` loop continues until a particular number of iterations has occurred. Its syntax looks like this:

```
For I = intStart To intEnd
    your code runs here
Next
```

This type of `For` statement requires three elements:

- A numeric variable to hold the current value of the iteration (`I` is a customary choice)
- A numeric expression, `intStart`, that evaluates to an integer and represents the starting value for `I`
- A numeric expression, `intEnd`, that evaluates to an integer and represents the ending value for `I`

Both `intStart` and `intEnd` can be literal integers, or you could substitute any expression that evaluates to an integer. For example, if you want to fill a message box (which you'll learn more about in Chapter 9) with the contents of an array, you can use code that looks like this:

```
strOldList = "red, blue, green"
arr() = Split(strOldList, ",")
For I = 0 To UBound(arr)
    strNewList = strNewList & vbCrLf & Trim(arr(I))
Next
MsgBox Mid(strNewList, 3)
```

Instead of counting up—for example, from `0` to `UBound(arr)` as in the previous example—you can count down by specifying a `Step` parameter. For example, Listing 7.3 illustrates how to use this technique using a `Step` parameter with a value of –1 to delete all the attachments in any Outlook item.

**Listing 7.3** *Delete All Attachments in an Outlook Item using a For ... Next Loop*

```
Sub DeleteAttachments(objItem As Object)
    Dim objAtt As Outlook.Attachment
    Dim intCount As Integer
    Dim I As Integer
    intCount = objItem.Attachments.Count
    If lngCount > 0 Then
        For I = intCount To 1 Step -1
            Set objAtt = objItem.Attachments.Item(I)
            objAtt.Delete
        Next
        objItem.Save
    End If
    Set objAtt = Nothing
End Sub
```

**Note:** If the code in Listing 7.3 counted up instead of down, it would remove only half the attachments from the item because each time an attachment was deleted, Outlook would recalculate the `Index` property used to get the next attachment with `objItem.Attachments.Item(`*`index`*`)`. If you delete the attachment with an `Index` of 1, the attachment whose `Index` was 2 now has an `Index` of 1, and the attachment whose `Index` was 3 now has an `Index` of 2. When the `Next` statement increments the value of `I` from 1 to 2, the original second attachment is skipped and the code deletes the third attachment, the one whose `Index` is now 2. In short, never mess with the loop counter inside the loop.

## 7.4.1 Handling multiselect list boxes

The code inside a `For ... Next` loop typically does something with the `I` counter value. In Listing 7.3, `objItem.Attachments.Item(I)` represents the *I*th attachment in the Outlook item.

Another practical example occurs if you have a multiselect list box. On list boxes where only one selection is allowed, you can use the `Value` property of the control to find out what the user has selected. With a multiselect list box, you must check the `Selected` property of each item in the list to learn whether the user has chosen it. This code displays each selected item in a list box in its own message box:

```
For I = 0 To (lstBox.ListCount - 1)
    If lstBox.Selected(I) = True Then
```

```
        MsgBox lstBox.List(I)
    End If
Next
```

A loop for a list box named `lstBox` should begin with the statement:

```
For I = 0 to (lstBox.ListCount - 1)
```

because the index number for items in the list box begins with `0`. The syntax for getting a particular item from the list box is `lstBox.List(`*`index`*`)`.

### 7.4.2 For Each ... Next loops for collections

The other type of `For ... Next` loop works with collection objects. A *collection* is an object that itself contains a set of other objects of a particular type. For example, each Outlook folder (listed in the object browser as a `MAPIFolder` object) has an `Items` property that comprises the collection of all items in the folder. The `MAPIFolder` also has a `Folders` property—a collection of all subfolders. Listing 7.3 illustrates another collection—the `Attachments` collection on most individual Outlook items.

Collection objects typically have a `Count` property, just as list boxes do, but you can work with them more efficiently by using this type of `For ... Next` loop:

```
For Each object In collection
    your code runs here
Next
```

If, for example, you want to change one or more properties for all items in a folder, you use a `For Each ... Next` loop to get each item in turn, alter the property, and then save the item. Listing 7.4 is a generic routine for working with the properties of items in the currently displayed Outlook folder.

The `WorkWithCurrentFolderItems` procedure performs this sequence of operations:

1. Get the currently displayed folder (`ActiveExplorer.CurrentFolder`).
2. Get the first item in the folder.
3. Change some properties on the item.
4. Save the item.
5. Repeat with the next item in the folder until all items have been used.

---

**Tip:** If you have not already started building a library of generic VBA code modules, now is a good time to begin. Create a module named `Generic`, and then add the procedure in Listing 7.4. The next time you have to work with the properties of items in a folder, just make a copy of the `WorkWithCurrentFolderItems` procedure, change the name of the procedure, and update lines in the `With objItem ... End With` block to set the item properties for your specific application.

---

At the end of a `For Each ... Next` loop, you might want to report back to the user on the operations performed on the items in the collection. One way is to increment a variable each time an operation occurs.

For example, the code in Listing 7.5 is based on the `For Each ... Next` loop in the `ReplaceCat` subroutine in Listing 6.3. It omits the `Dim` statements to save space but has been updated to add a `intCount` variable to keep track of how many items were changed and to open a message box with the result at the end. (Note that this code also illustrates both types of `For ... Next` loops!)

The statement

```
intCount = intCount + 1
```

is a typical statement for keeping a running count. It takes the current value of `intCount`, adds one, and returns the incremented value to the `intCount`

**Listing 7.4** *Use This Generic Code To Work with Item Properties in the Current Outlook Folder*

```
Sub WorkWithCurrentFolderItems()
    Dim objApp As Outlook.Application
    Dim objItem As Object
    Set objApp = CreateObject("Outlook.Application")
    Set objFolder = objApp.ActiveExplorer.CurrentFolder
    For Each objItem In objFolder.Items
        With objItem
            .property1 = newvalue1
            .property2 = newvalue2
            more property changes
            .Save
        End With
    Next
    Set objApp = Nothing
    Set objFolder = Nothing
    Set objItem = Nothing
End Sub
```

**Listing 7.5** *Track the Number of Items Where a Category Was Replaced*

```
Sub ReplaceCatCh07()
    strOldCat = "Customer"
    strNewCat = "Client"
    Set objApp = CreateObject("Outlook.Application")
    Set objFolder = objApp.ActiveExplorer.CurrentFolder
    intCount = 0
    For Each objItem In objFolder.Items
        arr() = Split(objItem.Categories, ",")
        For I = 0 To UBound(arr)
            If arr(I) = strOldCat Then
                arr(I) = strNewCat
                intCount = intCount + 1
                Exit For
            End If
        Next
        objItem.Categories = Join(arr, ",")
        objItem.Save
    Next
    MsgBox intCount & " items were changed"
    Set objApp = Nothing
    Set objFolder = Nothing
End Sub
```

variable. Because it resides within the `If ... End If` loop, the statement updates `intCount` only when a match is found for the category you want to replace.

The `Exit For` statement that follows works like the `Exit Do` statement you saw earlier for `Do` loops. It terminates the `For I = 0 To UBound(arr) ... Next` loop after a matching value has been found in the array. Note that it terminates only the one `For I ... Next` loop. The `For Each ... Next` loop in which it is nested continues to operate until all items in the folder have been processed.

## 7.5 GoTo statements

The last program flow technique discussed in this chapter is the `GoTo` statement, which applies only to VBA, not VBAScript, and is used primarily for error handling. A `GoTo` statement works in conjunction with labels that set off subsections in your subroutines. Here's an example:

```
Sub GoToDemo()
    Dim intAns As Integer
    On Error GoTo Err_Handler
    intAns = MsgBox("Do you want to simulate an error?", _
                    vbYesNo)
```

```
    If intAns = vbYes Then Err.Raise 1
    MsgBox "No error occurred."
    Exit Sub
Err_Handler:
    MsgBox "Error Number " & Err & " occurred."
End Sub
```

The statement `On Error GoTo Err_Handler` tells the routine to branch to the section labeled `Err_Handler:` whenever it encounters an error. Program flow continues with the statements in the `Err_Handler` section until the end of the subroutine. An `Exit Sub` statement is placed before the `Err_Handler:` label so that if no error has occurred, the program exits from the subroutine before running the statements in the `Err_Handler:` section.

---

**Note:** `Err.Raise` is a method for simulating an error so that you can find out what your program will do when an error occurs. You will look in detail at error handling and debugging in the next chapter.

---

You could also use `GoTo` statements by themselves to branch from one portion of a procedure to another section. However, the other program flow methods you've studied in this chapter produce much clearer code. The `GoTo` statement, therefore, is pretty much relegated to use just in error handling in VBA.

## 7.6 Summary

In this chapter, you picked up a variety of ways to control the way your program flows within a particular subroutine or function. Along the way, you also learned how to deal with selected items in multiselect list boxes and how to work with collections, such as all Outlook items in a folder. Chapter 8 continues the discussion of general VBA coding techniques with methods for debugging programs and handling errors, both expected and unexpected.

# 8

# *Handling Errors and Debugging VBA Applications*

This chapter gives you a break from writing procedures. It explores what might go wrong with your Outlook VBA code and how to fix it. Outlook includes many tools to assist you in tracking down such problems in VBA. We'll look at analogous techniques for VBScript on Outlook forms in Chapter 18, "Writing Code to Respond to Outlook Form Events."

Highlights of this chapter include discussions of the following:

- What types of errors you are likely to encounter
- What debugging techniques Outlook VBA supports
- How to handle errors you can't avoid
- Why it's worth taking the time to add comments to your application

In addition, you will get a few tips on how to make things go right.

## 8.1 Understanding errors

If you're going to learn how to debug Outlook applications, you need to understand that many types of errors can occur in the course of designing and running a VBA procedure. One classification scheme might divide them into five varieties:

- Simple syntax errors
- Compile errors
- Runtime errors
- Logic errors
- Outlook application bugs

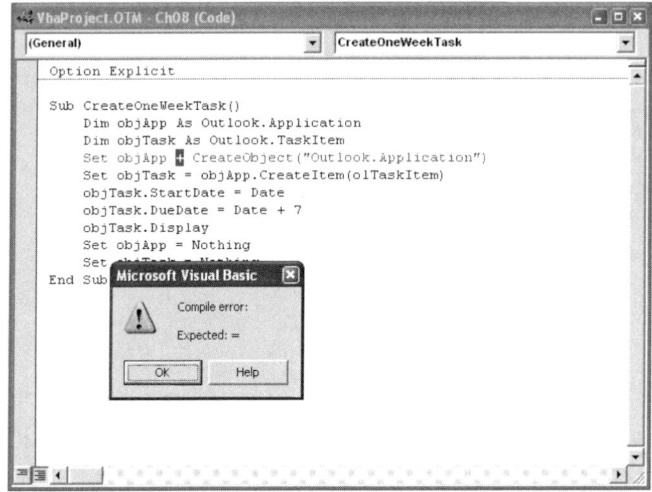


**Figure 8.1** *VBA tries to help you correct simple syntax errors as you type.*

Simple syntax errors occur as you type code statements in VBA. For example, you might enter this statement:

```
Set objApp + CreateObject("Outlook.Application")
```

when what you mean is:

```
Set objApp = CreateObject("Outlook.Application")
```

When you press the Enter key at the end of the statement, VBA pops up a message such as that in Figure 8.1, colors the problem statement in red, and highlights the portion of the statement that appears to be in error.

This kind of error checking is analogous to the spelling and grammar checker in Microsoft Word. Like Word's spell check, you can turn off VBA's syntax checker if you find it intrusive. Choose Tools, Options, and then clear the box for Auto Syntax Check.

The Auto Syntax Check feature detects errors only in single statements. It doesn't alert you to missing `End If` statements or undeclared variables in modules where `Option Explicit` is set. To find those kinds of errors, you can *compile* your VBA procedure. A procedure must be compiled before it can run. VBA automatically compiles procedures when you run them, but you can also manually compile the entire Outlook VBA project, including all modules, by choosing Debug, Compile.

Errors detected when you compile may not be as easy to fix as simple syntax errors. For example, take a look at Figure 8.2. The error message indicates that something is wrong with the `If ... End If` block. However, you can see clearly that you have both an `If` statement and an `End If`

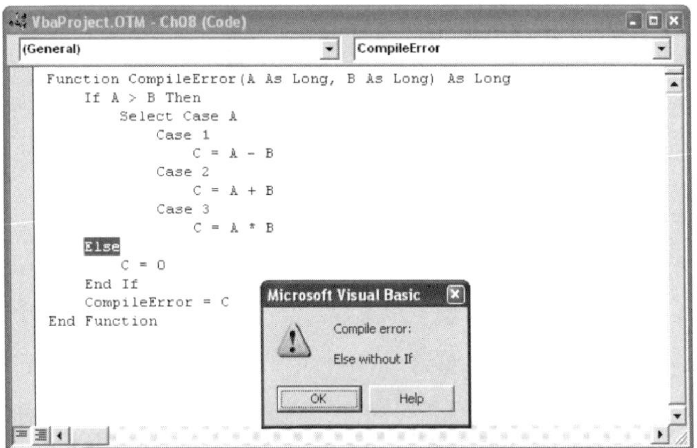


**Figure 8.2** *Some errors, such as a missing End Select statement, are detected only when you compile.*

statement. So what's the problem? In a case like this, examine the statements above the highlighted statement to find the error. In the code in Figure 8.2, the problem is a missing `End Select` statement.

If you are using `Option Explicit` in your modules to force variable declaration, compiling will also find any undeclared variables, as well as any typos in variable names. When you compile, only one error is highlighted at a time. After correcting the first error, compile again to see whether additional errors are present. Keep compiling until you receive no error messages.

The third type of error, a runtime error, comes to light only when a procedure runs and a statement with an error executes—making this type of error potentially difficult to find. The following procedure contains one of the most common runtime errors you are likely to encounter in Outlook programming. Can you find it?

```
Sub NoObjectError()
    Dim objApp As Outlook.Application
    Dim objNS As Outlook.NameSpace
    Dim objFolder As Outlook.MAPIFolder
    Dim objMsg As Outlook.MailItem
    Set objApp = CreateObject("Outlook.Application")
    Set objNS = objApp.GetNamespace("MAPI")
    Set objFolder = _
       objNS.GetDefaultFolder(olFolderDrafts)
    objMsg = objFolder.Items.Add("IPM.Note.Sales")
    objMsg.Display
    Set objApp = Nothing
    Set objNS = Nothing
    Set objFolder = Nothing
    Set objMsg = Nothing
End Sub
```

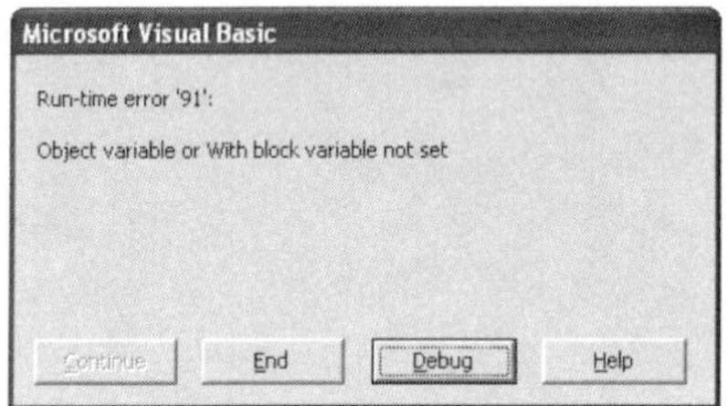


**Figure 8.3**
*Runtime errors usually halt the execution of your procedure.*

The error is in the statement

```
objMsg = objFolder.Items.Add("IPM.Note.Sales")
```

Because `objMsg` is an object variable, you cannot assign it a value with a simple = statement. It requires a `Set` keyword. If you run the `NoObjectError` subroutine, when the program gets to that statement, it cannot continue and pops up the error message shown in Figure 8.3.

The runtime error dialog gives you several choices. The Continue button is usually unavailable because most runtime errors are so bad that the program cannot continue to run until you correct the problem.

If you choose End, program execution halts. After you correct the problem, you can run the procedure again from the beginning.

If you choose Debug, VBA pauses program execution, switching to what's called *break mode.* (Notice the word "[break]" in the title bar in Figure 8.4.) The next statement to be executed is highlighted in yellow and marked with an arrow to the left. This is the statement you must fix before the program can continue. After you correct it, click the Continue button on the toolbar, or choose Run, Continue to pick up execution with the highlighted statement.

If you are unsure about the meaning of a runtime error, click the Help button on the dialog (refer to Figure 8.3). In most cases, a Help topic (see Figure 8.5) appears, explaining why the error may have occurred and how you might correct it.

**Note:** Some runtime errors are unavoidable. You learn how to build error handling into your Outlook applications later in this chapter.

The next type of error is the logic error or, as many programmers call them, dumb mistakes. You can't blame the program for these. They represent flaws in the logic of your procedures.

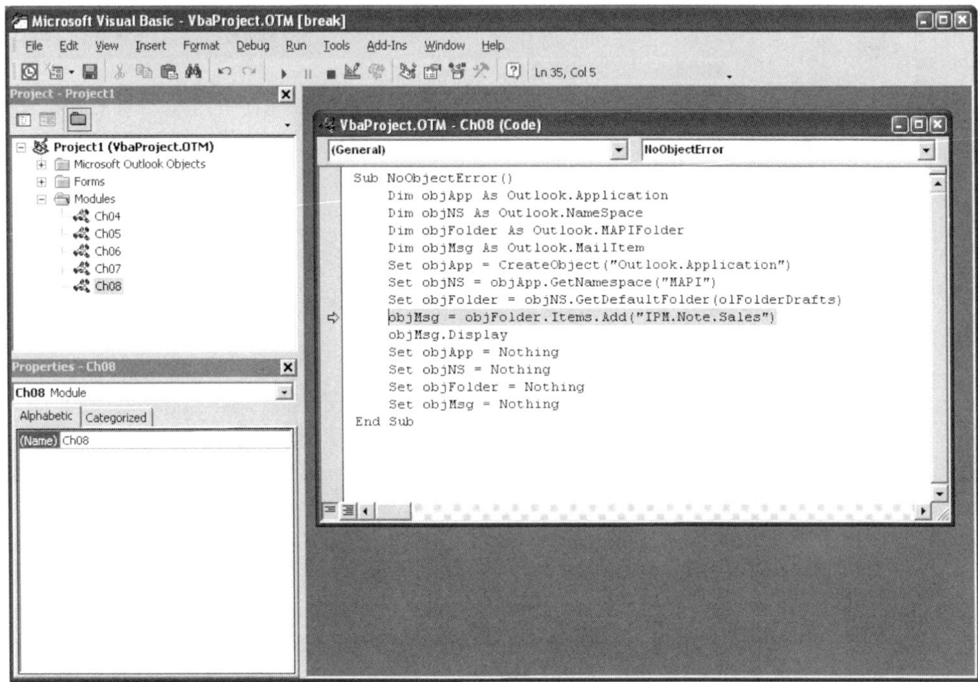


**Figure 8.4** *In break mode, VBA highlights the next statement to be executed.*

For example, an application includes a VBA form containing two text box controls, `txtStart` and `txtEnd`, where the user enters start and end dates. Before processing Outlook items in that date range, your code uses a `DatesOK()` function to make sure that both entries are dates and that the end date is later than the start date. At least, that's what you think your code does. However, when you run the form and enter what seem to be valid dates, `DatesOK()` often returns a value of `False`. Take a look at the code for `DatesOK()`, and see whether you can pick out the logic error:

```
Function DatesOK() As Boolean
    If IsDate(txtStart.Value) And IsDate(txtEnd.Value) Then
        If txtEnd.Value >= txtStart.Value Then
            DatesOK = True
        Else
            DatesOK = False
        End If
    End If
End Function
```

Did you find it? The problem is with the expression `txtEnd.Value >= txtStart.Value`. The `Value` for each text box control is not date/time

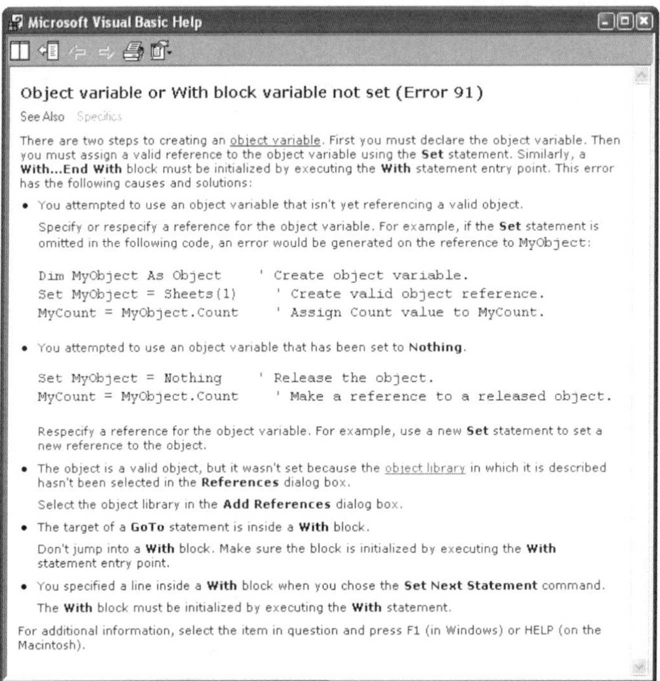

Microsoft Visual Basic Help
Object variable or With block variable not set (Error 91)
See Also Specifics
There are two steps to creating an object variable. First you must declare the object variable. Then you must assign a valid reference to the object variable using the Set statement. Similarly, a With...End With block must be initialized by executing the With statement entry point. This error has the following causes and solutions:
You attempted to use an object variable that isn't yet referencing a valid object.
Specify or respecify a reference for the object variable. For example, if the Set statement is omitted in the following code, an error would be generated on the reference to MyObject:
Dim MyObject As Object ' Create object variable.
Set MyObject = Sheets(1) ' Create valid object reference.
MyCount = MyObject.Count ' Assign Count value to MyCount.
You attempted to use an object variable that has been set to Nothing.
Set MyObject = Nothing ' Release the object.
MyCount = MyObject.Count ' Make a reference to a released object.
Respecify a reference for the object variable. For example, use a new Set statement to set a new reference to the object.
The object is a valid object, but it wasn't set because the object library in which it is described hasn't been selected in the References dialog box.
Select the object library in the Add References dialog box.
The target of a GoTo statement is inside a With block.
Don't jump into a With block. Make sure the block is initialized by executing the With statement entry point.
You specified a line inside a With block when you chose the Set Next Statement command.
The With block must be initialized by executing the With statement.
For additional information, select the item in question and press F1 (in Windows) or HELP (on the Macintosh).


**Figure 8.5** *Click Help on a runtime error message dialog to see more information on the problem.*

data; it's a variant, like the values returned by all form controls. This means that when you apply a comparison operator such as >=, the two terms are compared as if they were string values, a fatal flaw when you're trying to compare dates. For example, 4/10/03 may be a later date than 4/4/03, but the expression `"4/10/03" >= "4/4/03"` is `False`.

To fix this logic error, you must make sure that you are actually comparing dates. The `CDate()` date conversion function does the trick. Change the errant expression to:

```
CDate(txtEnd.Value) >= CDate(txtStart.Value)
```

As you can see, logic errors can be tough to track down. These defensive strategies can help prevent them:

- Plan your procedures well before coding
- Use properly declared and typed variables
- Test with lots of different data

The final type of error can be the most frustrating—the bug built into Outlook. No matter how much testing takes place before the product is released, some problems known to Microsoft always remain. Others may come to light only after thousands of developers begin putting all the new features to use. When you encounter a suspected program bug, you don't have to suffer in silence and solitude. The resources listed in Appendix A, "Resources for Outlook Programming," can help you confirm whether you've run up against a program limitation and whether a patch or workaround is available.

## 8.2 Debugging in VBA

*Debugging* is the process of tracking down errors—mainly logic and run-time errors—by following the sequence in which code statements execute and monitoring the resulting changes in the values of your variables. VBA includes several tools that allow you to set the location where you want to start debugging and follow the variable values. These include

- Breakpoints
- The Immediate window
- The Watch window and Quick Watch feature
- The Locals window
- The Call Stack

These tools are found on the Debug and View menus in VBA.

### 8.2.1 Using breakpoints

The idea of a breakpoint is to pause program execution so that you can take a look at the code and variable values and make any necessary changes before continuing with the next statements. You can set manual breakpoints or have VBA switch to break mode automatically under conditions that you set.

---

**Note:** As you saw in the previous section, you can switch to break mode by clicking Debug if a runtime error message appears. You can also get into break mode by pressing Ctrl+Break while the program is executing. However, this method provides no control over which procedure will be interrupted.

---

To set a breakpoint, click in the gray left margin of the module window next to the line of code where you want to place the breakpoint. You can also click in the code line and then press F9, or choose Debug, Toggle

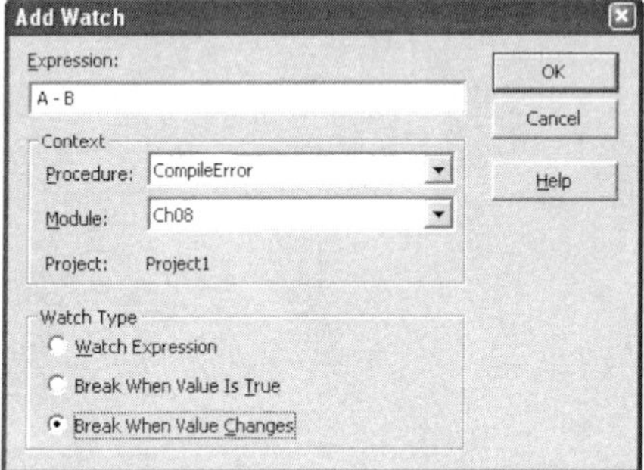


**Figure 8.6** *Watch expressions can switch VBA to break mode automatically while your code is executing.*

Breakpoint. Follow the same procedure to remove a breakpoint. To remove all breakpoints in your project, choose Debug, Clear All Breakpoints.

To have VBA switch to break mode automatically under a certain condition, you must set a *watch* for a particular variable. The easiest way is to select, then right-click on the variable or expression that you want to watch and choose Add Watch. The Add Watch dialog (see Figure 8.6) appears. Check to make sure that you picked the right variable and context and then set the Watch Type at the bottom. You can have VBA go into break mode either when the value in the Expression box is `True` or when it changes.

Watches are shown in the Watches window (see Figure 8.7). You can toggle this window on and off with the View, Watch Window command. To change or remove a watch, right-click it in the Watches window; then choose Edit Watch or Delete Watch. When VBA is in break mode, you can use the Watches window to examine the values of the watch expressions. For object variables, you will see a + sign to the left of the expression. Click it to expand the information about the object to show all its properties and their values.

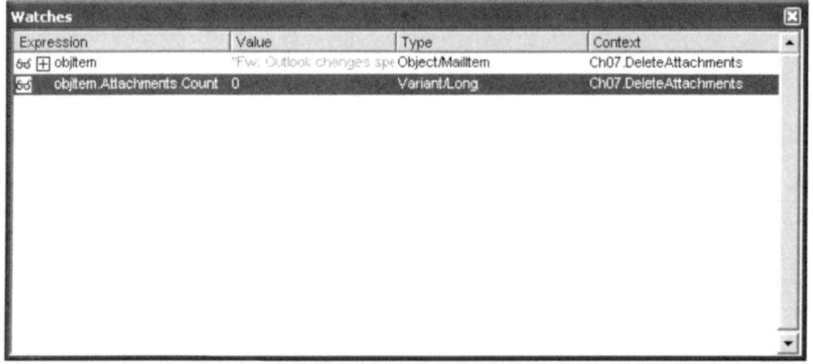


**Figure 8.7** *The Watches window shows each expression for which you have set a watch, along with its current value if VBA is in break mode.*

---

**Tip:** If you just want to add a watch without setting it to break, select a variable or expression and then choose Debug, Quick Watch.

---

### 8.2.2 Working in break mode

What can you do when you're in break mode in VBA? Here are some of the techniques that programmers use in break mode to work out the problems in their code:

- Check the sequence of procedures that have already run
- Edit code to correct problems
- Examine and change the values of variables
- Restart the procedure from the breakpoint or another statement
- Step through the code, statement by statement or procedure by procedure

To check what procedures ran before the break occurred, choose View, Call Stack. The Call Stack window shows the sequence of procedures, with the most recent at the top of the list.

While in break mode, you can edit your program code. Some changes may cause a message to appear that the project will be reset. This means that program execution will halt and VBA will return to design mode.

As you saw in Figure 8.7, the Watches window shows the current values of any variables or expressions for which you set a watch. Another way to see the value of any variable or object variable property is to pause the mouse pointer over the variable. After a second or two, a screen tip will appear, giving the current value (see Figure 8.8).

To see more values, choose View, Locals. The Locals window (see Figure 8.9) works much like the Watches window, only it shows all variables, not just those for which watches were set.

### 8.2.3 Using the Immediate window

Another VBA tool for examining variables is the Immediate window, which you can display by choosing View, Immediate Window. In the Immediate window, you can not only check the value of any variable, but also change values and even evaluate functions or run code statements.

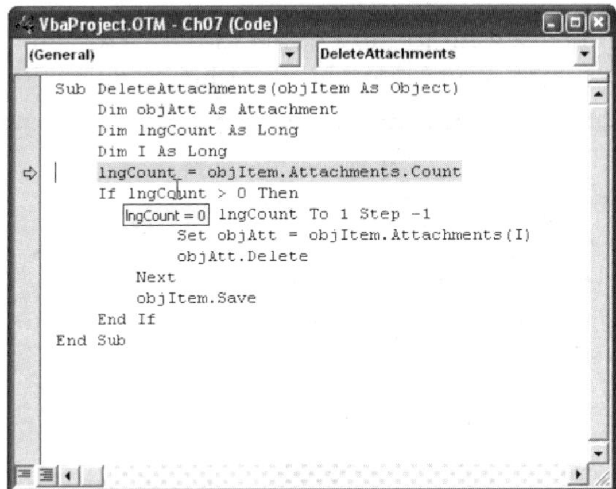


**Figure 8.8** *Screen tips pop up with the current variable values.*

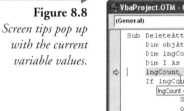

To check the value of any variable or expression, in the Immediate window type `?` or `Print`, followed by the variable or expression, and then press Enter. The value appears on the next line in the Immediate window.

---

**Note:** One advantage of the Immediate window over the Watches or Locals window is that it's easier to see the value of string variables containing long blocks of text—even multiple lines of text.

---

You can also add a `Debug.Print` statement to your program code and have it print information to the Immediate window as the code executes. In Figure 8.10, we've taken the `ReplaceCatCh07` subroutine from Listing 7.5 and replaced the `MsgBox` statement at the end of the procedure with a `Debug.Print` statement. When the procedure finishes, it puts a report of its actions in the Immediate window.

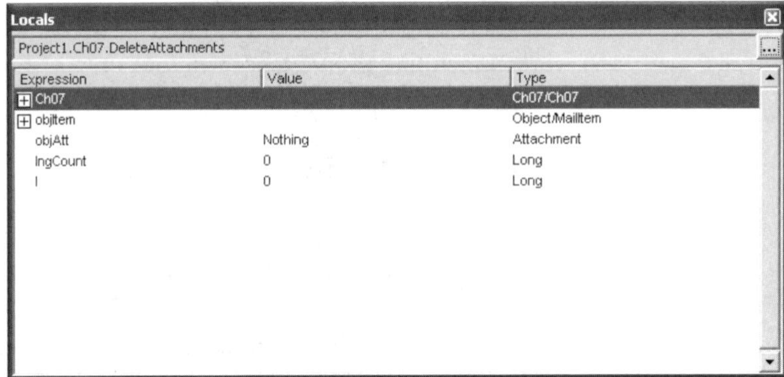


**Figure 8.9** *The Locals window tracks all variable values.*

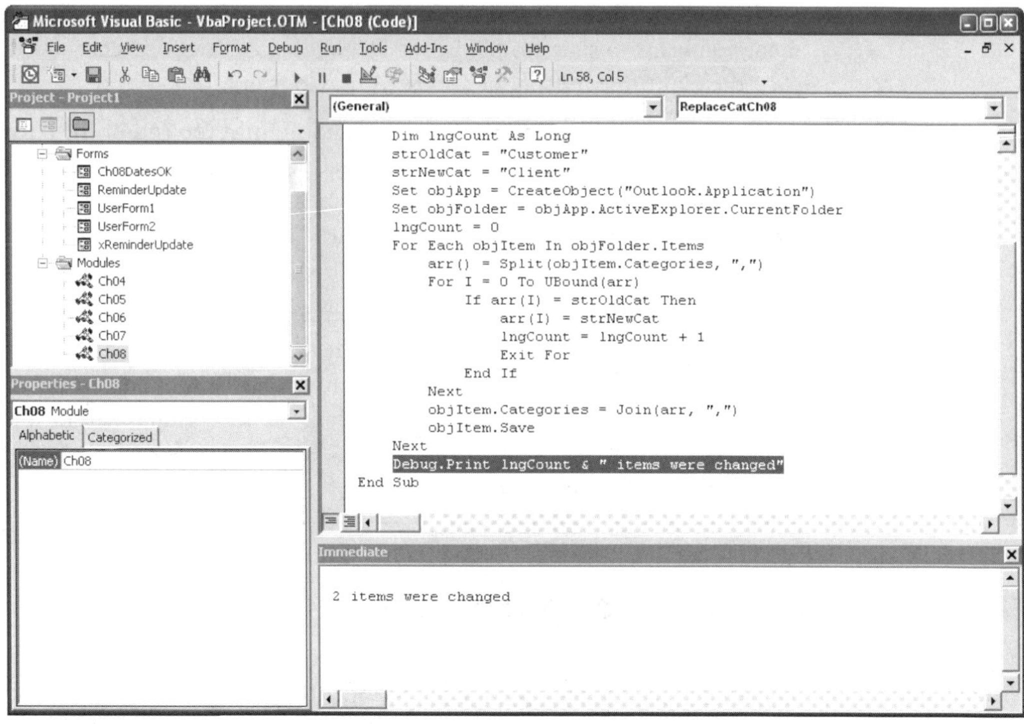


**Figure 8.10** *Use the Immediate window to evaluate functions, check the values of variables, and execute single code statements.*

While in break mode, you can change the value of any variable by typing the appropriate `Set objVariable = newvalue` or `variable = newvalue` statement in the Immediate window and then pressing Enter. When you continue with code execution, the code runs with the new value of the variable.

### 8.2.4 Continuing program execution

After making changes to your code in break mode, checking variable values, and executing statements in the Immediate window, you may want to continue running the procedure. To continue from the breakpoint, click the Continue button or choose Run, Continue.

To restart from the beginning, click the Reset button or choose Run, Reset. You can then restart the current procedure or any other procedure with the Run button.

To continue from a statement other than the breakpoint, select the statement you want to start from; choose Debug, Set Next Statement; and then click the Continue button, or choose Run, Continue.

These methods continue program execution until the end of the current procedure (or its calling procedure) or the next breakpoint. You can also step through the code, statement by statement, to get a feeling for exactly what happens when each statement executes. To continue program execution in this fashion, press F8 or choose Debug, Step Into.

**Tip:** If you want to step through a procedure without setting a breakpoint or a watch first, choose Debug, Step Into instead of Run to begin execution of the procedure in step mode. The Debug menu includes several other commands to help you step through your code in various ways: Step Over, Step Out, and Run to Cursor.

## 8.3 Creating clean applications

This chapter on debugging concludes with some tips on avoiding problems with your Outlook applications by writing error handlers, documenting the application, and writing reusable code.

Testing is another important issue. Remember that Outlook 2000 has two modes. Unless you know for certain that your application will be used only in Outlook 2002 or only in one of Outlook 2000's two modes, you should test it in both modes. You may also want to test against both types of information stores—Exchange Server mailboxes and Personal Folders files.

**Tip:** Microsoft Office XP Developer—a special edition of Office XP for developers—includes several add-ins to help you create cleaner applications: Code Librarian, VBA Code Commenter, and VBA Error Handler.

### 8.3.1 Adding error handlers

The runtime error message that you saw in Figure 8.3 doesn't tell an end user what went wrong or how to fix it. To provide a friendlier message, you can add general error handling to any VBA procedure. The following procedure includes an error handler to display a message box whenever an error occurs:

```
Sub ErrorHandlerDemo()
    On Error GoTo MyError
    program code goes here
    Exit Sub
MyError:
    MsgBox "Error number " & Err.Number & _
           vbCrLf & vbCrLf & Err.Description, , _
           "Error in ErrorHandlerDemo"
End Sub
```

The `On Error GoTo` *`linelabel`* specifies that, if an error occurs, program execution continues with the section named *`linelabel`*. In general, named sections appear at the end of a procedure with an `Exit Sub` statement before the named section, so that the statements in the named section do not execute except as the result of a `GoTo` statement. The linelabel itself must be followed by a colon.

The `MsgBox` statement, which you will learn more about in Chapter 9, uses two properties of the intrinsic `Err` object representing the error that occurs: `Number` and `Description`. Compare Figure 8.11 with Figure 8.3.

---

**Note:** `Err.Number` and `Err` by itself can be used interchangeably because `Number` is the default property of the `Err` object. If you have an error, the possible values for `Err.Number` are greater than zero. If `Err = 0`, you know that no error has occurred.

---

You are not limited just to displaying message boxes in response to errors, of course. If you want to trap particular known errors, you can expand the error-handling block with a `Select ... End Select` block such as this one, in which *`err1`* and *`err2`* represent specific errors that you want to address:

```
Select Case Err.Number
    Case err1
        error-handling code goes here
    Case err2
        error--handling code goes here
        additional Case statements
    Case Else
        error-handling code goes here
End Select
```

In such an error-handling block, a useful statement is `Resume Next`. This causes program execution to continue with the statement immediately following the one in which the error occurred.

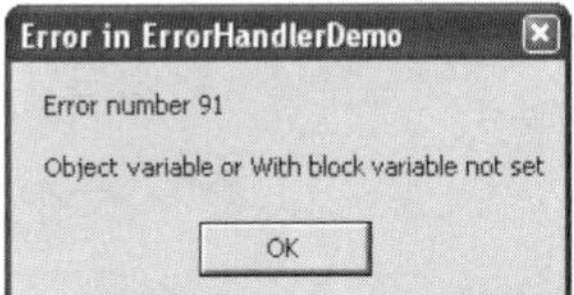
Error in ErrorHandlerDemo
Error number 91
Object variable or With block variable not set
OK

**Figure 8.11** *Your application can display its own message boxes in response to errors.*

**Note:** You will see examples of error-handling to deal with known errors in Chapter 10, "Working with the Object Models," when we cover Collaboration Data Objects (CDO), and in Chapter 13, "Understanding Outlook Security."

**Tip:** To test how your code responds to a particular error, add an `Err.Raise` *`errnum`* statement to your code, in which *`errnum`* is the specific number for the error. The statement `Err.Clear` clears the current error number.

## 8.3.2 Documenting your application

To document your application, add comments to your program code. A *comment* is any text preceded by an apostrophe ('). VBA shows comment text in green.

Comments can introduce sections of your code and explain what each section does and also provide remarks on variables as you declare them. In complex modules, you may want to provide the author, purpose, history, arguments, and other information about each procedure. The following code provides an example of each of these types of comments:

```
' ***********************************************************
' Name:      CommentTextExample
' Author:    Sue Mosher
' History:   Version 1.0, 8 Apr 2002
' Purpose:   Demonstrate placement of different types of
'            comments
' Args:      None
' Returns:   Nothing
' ***********************************************************
Sub CommentTextExample()
    Dim strStart As String          ' start date from form
    Dim strEnd As String            ' end date from form
```

```
    ' get dates from form
    frmReminderUpdate.Show
    strStart = frmReminderUpdate.txtStartDate
    strEnd = frmReminderUpdate.txtEndDate
    Unload frmReminderUpdate
End Sub
```

You don't have to comment everything in every procedure, but try to provide enough comments so that you (or another developer) will be able to follow the code logic at any time in the future.

### 8.3.3 Making code reusable

Typos are one of the biggest sources of code errors. Therefore, one way to avoid many errors is to avoid typing. For example, going back to the first example in the chapter, you really should never have to type the following:

```
Set objApp = CreateObject("Outlook.Application")
```

because this commonly used statement should be in a boilerplate module of frequently used Outlook code that you can copy and paste whenever you need it. If you don't have such a module, start one, or at least start copying statements like this from another procedure, rather than retyping them every time.

Using variables instead of literals also makes it more likely that you will be able to reuse code between forms and modules. For example, Outlook provides a `Selection` object that represents the items that the user has selected in an Outlook folder. (You will learn more about it in Chapter 14, "Working with Items and Recipients.") Listing 8.1 is a boilerplate subroutine for working with a maximum number of selected items. You would enter your code for processing the items immediately after the `' program code continues here` comment statement.

---

**Note:** Notice the use of an `ExitSub:` block and `GoTo ExitSub` statements to ensure that the program runs the code to dereference all objects, regardless of whether the full selection processing code runs.

---

In the second `Case` statement, you could include the literal value for the maximum number of selected items you want to process, rather than use the `intMaxItems` variable. However, whenever you copy that code to another module, you would have to dig down to the `Case` statement to change the maximum number of items. Including the `intMaxItems =`

**Listing 8.1** *The intMaxItems Variable Makes It Easy To Adapt This Code Any Time You Need to Work with Selected Items*

```
Sub ReusableSelectionExample()
    Dim objApp As Outlook.Application
    Dim objItem As Object
    Dim objSelection As Outlook.Selection
    Dim intMaxItems As Integer
    ' *** Use next line to set maximum number ***
    ' *** of items this routine is allowed to ***
    ' *** process.                            ***
    intMaxItems = 5
    Set objApp = CreateObject("Outlook.Application")
    Set objSelection = objApp.ActiveExplorer.Selection
    Select Case objSelection.Count
        Case 0
            MsgBox "No items were selected"
            GoTo ExitSub
        Case Is > intMaxItems
            MsgBox "Too many items were selected"
            GoTo ExitSub
    End Select
    ' program code continues here

ExitSub:
    Set objApp = Nothing
    Set objItem = Nothing
    Set objSelection = Nothing
End Sub
```

`value` statement near the beginning of the procedure makes it much easier to reuse this code in a variety of modules that process `Selection`. The comment lines call attention to the statement setting the variable's value.

You could also pass `intMaxItems` as an argument, instead of setting it in the body of the procedure. Streamlined to ignore the `Dim` and `Set` *`obj`* `= Nothing` statements, the revised procedure would look like this:

```
Sub ReusableSelectionExample(intMaxItems as Integer)
    Set objApp = CreateObject("Outlook.Application")
    Set objSelection = objApp.ActiveExplorer.Selection
    Select Case objSelection.Count
        Case 0
            MsgBox "No items were selected"
            Exit Sub
        Case Is > intMaxItems
            MsgBox "Too many items were selected"
            Exit Sub
    End Select
    ' program code continues here
End Sub
```

Finally, if you have a routine that you want to run from the toolbar on either the main Outlook window or an open item window, don't write two complete versions—one for `ActiveExplorer.Selection` and another for `ActiveInspector.CurrentItem`. You'll have nightmares trying to keep the code consistent in the two procedures.

This is a case where three procedures are more efficient than two. One contains the code that you want to run against a particular item. The other two—one to run from a folder window, the other from an item window—call that procedure, passing the item as an argument.

For example, in Listing 8.2, the `SetFlag` procedure sets a message flag to remind you to make a decision on an item one week from today. The

**Listing 8.2** *Running a Procedure from an Open Item or Folder Selection*

```
Sub FlagOpenItem()
    Dim objApp As Outlook.Application
    Dim objOpenItem As Object
    Set objApp = CreateObject("Outlook.Application")
    Set objOpenItem = objApp.ActiveInspector.CurrentItem
    Call SetFlag(objOpenItem)
    Set objApp = Nothing
    Set objOpenItem = Nothing
End Sub

Sub FlagSelectedItems()
    Dim objApp As Outlook.Application
    Dim objSelItem As Object
    Dim objSelection As Selection
    Set objApp = CreateObject("Outlook.Application")
    Set objSelection = objApp.ActiveExplorer.Selection
    For Each objSelItem In objSelection
        Call SetFlag(objSelItem)
    Next
    Set objApp = Nothing
    Set objSelItem = Nothing
    Set objSelection = Nothing
End Sub

Sub SetFlag(objItem As Object)
    With objItem
        If .Class = olMail Then
            .FlagStatus = olFlagMarked
            .FlagRequest = "Make Decision"
            .FlagDueBy = Now + 7 ' one week from today
            .Save
        End If
    End With
End Sub
```

FlagOpenItem procedure calls SetFlag for the item in the ActiveInspector window, while the FlagSelectedItems procedure calls SetFlag for each item selected in the ActiveExplorer window.

---

**Note:** ActiveExplorer and ActiveInspector are objects that represent the current folder window and current item window, respectively.

---

You can put FlagOpenItem and FlagSelectedItems on separate toolbar buttons for the item window and main Outlook window, respectively. If you ever want to change the text of the message flag, you need to change it in only one place—in the SetFlag procedure.

Remember that any kind of item can be open or selected. If you use this technique, object variables representing items should be declared as Object, not as MailItem or another specific type. If your procedure uses methods or properties that apply only to certain kinds of items—such as the message flag properties in this example—you should check the Class of the item first. Otherwise, you run the risk of getting a runtime error when the code encounters an item that doesn't support the FlagStatus, FlagRequest, and FlagDueBy properties.

## 8.4 Summary

Producing reliable applications means testing your code and fixing problems as you go along. Outlook provides many debugging tools in the VBA environment. Error handlers and comments also help fill out your code and make it more professional. In addition, you've worked with code for handling the Selection object, which is frequently used in Outlook VBA macros that make changes to all selected items in a folder.

In Chapter 9, you will wrap up this survey of general coding techniques with a look at various ways to gather user input and provide feedback.

# 9

# Handling User Input and Feedback

This chapter deals with the practical matters of giving the user choices and receiving other input from the user. Your code will often need to ask the user what to do with a particular Outlook item: whether to proceed if a certain condition is met, how many days ahead to set a reminder, or what the due date and flag should be for a message flag.

Highlights of this chapter include discussions of the following:

- How message boxes and input boxes differ
- When you should use message boxes, input boxes, and VBA dialogs to get information from the user
- How to gather input from a VBA form and pass it to a VBA procedure
- How to use a VBA form to provide feedback to the user

## 9.1 Getting user input

In previous chapters, you have seen code samples that used a `MsgBox` statement to pop up a message to the user. You can use a message box also to get a response from the user that you can then use to decide what your program should do next. Other methods for getting user input include input boxes and integrating a VBA dialog form into a calling procedure.

### 9.1.1 Using message boxes

In several procedures in previous chapters, you have seen `MsgBox` statements displaying pop-up messages to the user. The syntax for this type of statement is

```
MsgBox prompt, , title
```

where *prompt* is the text you want the user to see and *title* is an optional title for the message box. If you omit the *title* argument, the title of the message box defaults to "Microsoft Outlook." (In VBScript code on Outlook forms, it defaults to "VBScript.")

Used in an expression, the MsgBox() function also provides a way to get a Yes or No answer from the user. A typical series of statements using a MsgBox() function in this fashion looks like this:

```
intAns = MsgBox(prompt, buttons, title)
If intAns = vbYes Then
    your code runs here
Else
    alternative code runs here
End If
```

The arguments for the MsgBox( ) function include

- *Prompt*—String expression for the text that you want the user to see in the message box
- *Buttons*—Optional numeric expression that determines the number of command buttons, their labels, and the default button
- *Title*—Optional string expression for the title of the message box

If you omit the *buttons* argument, but want to include a title, you must leave the comma delimiter in place inside the parentheses. These are all valid MsgBox() expressions:

```
MsgBox("Will you be gone all day?")
MsgBox("Will you be gone all day?", , "Take a Day Off")
MsgBox("Will you be gone all day?", 36, "Take a Day Off")
MsgBox("Will you be gone all day?", _
       vbQuestion + vbYesNo, _
       "Take a Day Off")
```

However, `MsgBox("Will you be gone all day?", "Take a Day Off")` would not be a valid expression because it omits the comma that occurs after the optional *buttons* argument.

---

**Note:** The MsgBox() function also supports two optional arguments to supply the name of a Windows Help file and the context number for the help topics you want to display. The creation of Help files is not covered in this book, however, so we'll ignore those arguments.

---

**Table 9.1** *Message Box Constants*

| Constant | Value | Description |
|---|---|---|
| *Button Type Constants* | | |
| `vbOKOnly` | 0 | Display OK button only (default). |
| `vbOKCancel` | 1 | Display OK and Cancel buttons. |
| `VbAbortRetryIgnore` | 2 | Display Abort, Retry, and Ignore buttons. |
| `vbYesNoCancel` | 3 | Display Yes, No, and Cancel buttons. |
| `vbYesNo` | 4 | Display Yes and No buttons. |
| `vbRetryCancel` | 5 | Display Retry and Cancel buttons. |
| *Icon Constants* | | |
| `vbCritical` | 16 | Display Critical Message icon (refer to Figure 9.1). |
| `vbQuestion` | 32 | Display Warning Query icon. |
| `vbExclamation` | 48 | Display Warning Message icon. |
| `vbInformation` | 64 | Display Information Message icon. |
| *Default Button Constants* | | |
| `vbDefaultButton1` | 0 | First button is default. |
| `vbDefaultButton2` | 256 | Second button is default. |
| `vbDefaultButton3` | 512 | Third button is default. |

The easiest way to get the value for the `buttons` argument is to use the sum of three numbers:

```
buttontypes + icon + defaultbutton
```

where each of these values is a Visual Basic constant from one of the three groups listed in Table 9.1.

**Figure 9.1** *From left to right, the Critical Message, Warning Query, Warning Message, and Information Message icons.*

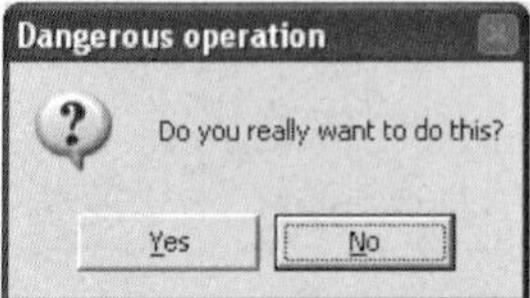


**Figure 9.2** *For risky operations, make No the default message box button.*

---

**Tip:** The possible values for the `MsgBox()` arguments make it possible to show 65 different kinds of message box. You don't have to learn 65 different parameters or even the numeric values in Table 9.1 because you can use the intrinsic constants in both VBA and VBScript.

---

Use only one constant from each group to build the *buttons* argument value. This message box asks users whether they really want to proceed:

```
intAns = MsgBox("Do you really want to do this?", _
         vbYesNo + vbQuestion + vbDefaultButton2, _
         "Dangerous operation")
```

and sets the default button to the second button, No, so that the user must actively decide to proceed by clicking the Yes button. Figure 9.2 shows what the user sees.

If the prompt for the message box is lengthy or is itself an expression, don't use a string literal. Instead, use a separate string variable to build it. In Listing 8.1 in the previous chapter, you encountered the `Selection` object that represents the items a user has highlighted in an Outlook folder view. Instead of just telling users that they've selected too many items for processing, you might give them more specific information and ask whether they want to proceed. This code snippet assumes that you have already set an `objSelection` variable and builds a `strMsg` string from two bits of text and the number of items selected (`objSelection.Count`):

```
strMsg = "This selection includes " & _
         objSelection.Count & " items. " & _
         "Do you want to continue?"
intAns = MsgBox(strMsg, _
         vbYesNo + vbQuestion + vbDefaultButton2, _
         "Process Selection")
```

Figure 9.3 shows what the user sees—the specific number of items selected and an option to proceed.

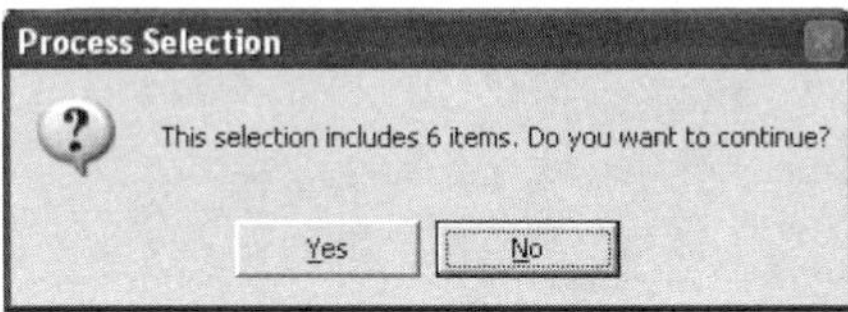


**Figure 9.3** *When you ask users to make a choice, provide enough information for them to make a decision; in this case, provide the number of selected items.*

The `intAns` variable in all the message box examples is the key to getting the user's response. The `MsgBox()` function returns one of the integers in Table 9.2, all of which have Visual Basic intrinsic constant equivalents.

Always ask for confirmation for risky operations, especially those with the potential for data loss. Removing attachments from items is an example. Listing 9.1 provides an updated version of the `DeleteAttachments` subroutine in Listing 7.3. It asks for user input in three places:

- If the item contains only one attachment, the first `MsgBox()` function asks whether the user really wants to delete it.
- For items with multiple attachments, the second `MsgBox()` function asks whether the user wants to be prompted to remove each attachment. The prompt includes the number of attachments.
- If the user does choose to be prompted, the code uses the name of the file to build the prompt message for the third `MsgBox()` function.

**Table 9.2** *Return Values for the MsgBox() Function*

| When the User Presses | MsgBox( ) Constant | Returns |
|---|---|---|
| OK | 1 | `vbOK` |
| Cancel | 2 | `vbCancel` |
| Abort | 3 | `vbAbort` |
| Retry | 4 | `vbRetry` |
| Ignore | 5 | `vbIgnore` |
| Yes | 6 | `vbYes` |
| No | 7 | `vbNo` |

**Listing 9.1** *Adding User Input to the DeleteAttachments( ) Subroutine*

```
Sub DeleteAttachmentsCh09(objItem As Object)
    Dim objAtt As Outlook.Attachment
    Dim intCount As Integer
    Dim i As Integer
    Dim strMsg As String
    Dim intResAsk As Integer
    Dim intResDel As Integer
    intCount = objItem.Attachments.Count
    If intCount > 0 Then
        If intCount = 1 Then
            strMsg = "Do you really want to remove " & _
                     "the attachment from this message?"
            intResAsk = MsgBox(strMsg, _
              vbQuestion + vbYesNo + vbDefaultButton2, _
              "Remove Attachments")
            If intResAsk = vbYes Then
                objItem.Attachments(1).Delete
            End If
        Else
            strMsg = "This message has " & intCount & _
                     " attachments. Do you want to be " & _
                     "prompted to remove each one?"
            intResAsk = MsgBox(strMsg, _
                          vbQuestion + vbYesNo, _
                          "Remove Attachments")
            For i = intCount To 1 Step -1
                Set objAtt = objItem.Attachments(i)
                If intResAsk = vbYes Then
                    strMsg = "Do you want to delete " & _
                      "the " & objAtt.filename & " file?"
                    intResDel = MsgBox(strMsg, vbQuestion _
                      + vbYesNo + vbDefaultButton2, _
                      "Remove Attachments")
                Else
                    intResDel = vbYes
                End If
                If intResDel = vbYes Then
                    objAtt.Delete
                End If
            Next
        End If
        If objItem.Attachments.Count < intCount Then
            objItem.Save
        End If
    End If
    Set objAtt = Nothing
End Sub
```

### 9.1.2 Using input boxes

The `MsgBox()` function provides a limited number of possible responses—basically Yes, No, Cancel, and variations on those themes. If you want some other kind of input from the user, you need another method. The `InputBox()` function provides an easy way to get a single number, string, or date from the user.

---

**Note:** Try not to beleaguer the user with a series of input and message boxes. If you need more input data or confirmations than a single `InputBox()` or `MsgBox()` function can provide, use a VBA form.

---

The basic `InputBox()` syntax looks like this:

```
InputBox(prompt, title, default, xpos, ypos)
```

All arguments except *`prompt`* are optional. The *`prompt`* and *`title`* arguments work as in the `MsgBox()` function. The *`default`* argument is an optional string expression for the text you want to display in the input box as the default response in case the user types nothing in.

The *`xpos`* and *`ypos`* arguments are optional numeric expressions that govern the screen location of the input box. They use the distance from the left and top of the screen, respectively, measured in twips; there are 1,440 twips to an inch. If you omit these arguments, Outlook centers the input box horizontally, about one-third of the way down the screen.

---

**Note:** Like the `MsgBox()` function, the `InputBox()` function also supports additional optional arguments that let you call a Windows Help file.

---

An input box returns a string consisting of whatever the user types into the box. Here is the code that created the input box in Figure 9.4.

```
Dim strAns As String
strAns = InputBox("Flag message(s) for:", _
           "Flag Selected Message(s)", _
           "Follow up")
```

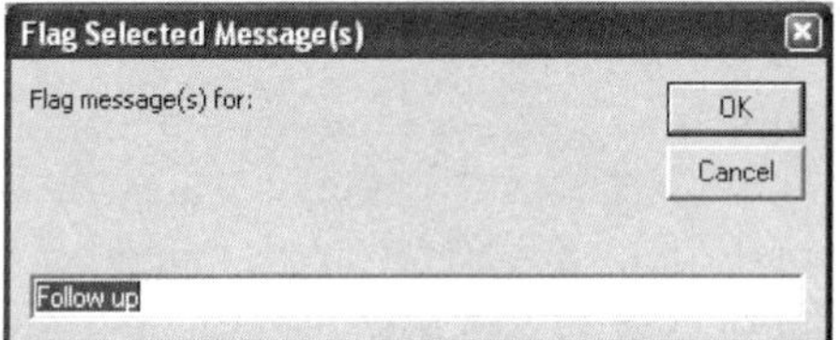


**Figure 9.4** *An input box asks the user for one piece of information.*

---

**Tip:** A statement using `InputBox()` is often followed by one or more statements that test the value returned by the function to make sure that it's more than an empty string, that it's a number, and so on.

---

You could add the above code to the `FlagSelectedItems` subroutine from Listing 8.2 to get the user's flag preference as a `strAns` variable. Then,

**Listing 9.2** *Using an InputBox() to Prompt the User*

```
Sub FlagSelectedItemsCh09()
    Dim objApp As Outlook.Application
    Dim objSelItem As Object
    Dim objSelection As Outlook.Selection
    Dim strAns As String
    Set objApp = CreateObject("Outlook.Application")
    Set objSelection = objApp.ActiveExplorer.Selection
    strAns = InputBox("Flag message(s) for:", _
               "Flag Selected Message(s)", _
               "Follow up")
    If strAns = "" Then
        strAns = "Follow up"
    End If
    For Each objSelItem In objSelection
        Call SetFlagCh09(objSelItem, strAns)
    Next
    Set objApp = Nothing
    Set objSelItem = Nothing
    Set objSelection = Nothing
End Sub

Sub SetFlagCh09(objItem As Object, strFlag As String)
    With objItem
        If .Class = olMail Then
            .FlagStatus = olFlagMarked
            .FlagRequest = strFlag
            .FlagDueBy = Now + 7 ' one week from today
            .Save
        End If
    End With
End Sub
```

you could use `strAns` in the statement that sets the flag. Listing 9.2 presents an updated version.

Here are a few notes on the code in Listing 9.2:

- The `If ... End If` block in the `FlagSelectedItemsCh09` procedure handles the case in which the user deletes the default text from the input box and leaves it blank; it reverts to the default "Follow up."
- The `Call` statement passes both the item to be updated and the flag text.
- The `SetFlagCh09` subroutine has been updated to handle the flag text as an argument.

### 9.1.3 Using VBA forms

What if you want the user to provide both a message flag and a due date to the `FlagSelectedItemsCh09` subroutine? Can you do that with an `InputBox()` function? No, each input box returns only one piece of information, and popping up one input box after another is not considered good design. The solution is to display a VBA form to gather the extra information.

A VBA form for user input should be modal with controls where the user enters data or makes selections, as well as an OK button. The code behind the form should set a global variable that the calling subroutine can use to determine whether the user clicked OK or canceled the form dialog. To make use of the form's data, the calling subroutine should follow these steps:

1. Use the `Show` method to display the form.
2. After the user interacts with the form, check the global variable to see whether the user clicked OK.
3. If the user did click OK, get data from the (now hidden) form's controls.
4. After obtaining all the necessary data from the form, unload the form.

### 9.1.4 A macro to set a flag on selected messages

In many cases, you can largely duplicate the look of Outlook's own dialog boxes with VBA forms of your own. In this example, you will create a macro to set a message flag on selected items, after prompting the user for the flag text and due date. Here's what you have to do:

1. Create a new VBA form named `Ch09FlagOptions` with the caption "Flag for Follow Up".

2. Add a text box named `txtFlagTo` and a matching label with the caption "Flag to".

3. Add a text box named `txtDueBy` and a matching label with the caption "Due by".

4. Add a command button named `cmdOK` with the caption "OK", and set its `Default` property to `True`.

5. Add a command button named `cmdCancel` with the caption "Cancel", and set its `Cancel` property to `True`.

6. In the form's code windows, add the code in Listing 9.3. When clicked, the command buttons set the value of a global variable (`g_blnCancel`) and then hide or unload the form. The `UserForm_Terminate` subroutine is necessary to make sure that the global variable is set even if the user clicks the form's Close (x) button.

7. Add the code in Listing 9.4 to a VBA module.

Here's how it works: The `Ch09FlagOptions.Show` statement in the `FlagSelectedItemsCh09Ver2` module in Listing 9.4 displays the Flag for

**Listing 9.3** *Basic Code for a VBA Form for User Input*

```
Dim blnUserChose As Boolean

Private Sub cmdCancel_Click()
    g_blnCancel = True
    blnUserChose = True
    Unload Me
End Sub

Private Sub cmdOK_Click()
    g_blnCancel = False
    blnUserChose = True
    Me.Hide
End Sub

Private Sub UserForm_Terminate()
    If blnUserChose = False Then
        g_blnCancel = True
    End If
End Sub
```

Follow Up form shown in Figure 9.5. Because the form's `ShowModal` property is set to `True` (the default), execution of the `FlagSelectedItemsCh09Ver2` procedure halts until the user interacts with the form by pressing one of the buttons or closing the form.

**Listing 9.4** *A Procedure Calls a Modal VBA Form and Gets Its Data Before Unloading It*

```
Public g_blnCancel As Boolean

Sub FlagSelectedItemsCh09Ver2()
    Dim objApp As Outlook.Application
    Dim objSelItem As Object
    Dim objSelection As Outlook.Selection
    Dim strFlag As String
    Dim strDue As String
    Dim dteDue As Date
    Set objApp = CreateObject("Outlook.Application")
    Set objSelection = objApp.ActiveExplorer.Selection
    Ch09FlagOptions.Show
    If g_blnCancel = False Then
        strFlag = Ch09FlagOptions.txtFlagTo.Value
        If strFlag = "" Then
            strFlag = "Follow up"
        End If
        strDue = Ch09FlagOptions.txtDueBy.Value
        If IsDate(strDue) Then
            dteDue = CDate(Ch09FlagOptions.txtDueBy.Value)
        Else
            dteDue = #1/1/4501#
        End If
        For Each objSelItem In objSelection
            Call SetFlagCh09Ver2(objSelItem, strFlag, dteDue)
        Next
    End If
    Unload Ch09FlagOptions
    Set objApp = Nothing
    Set objSelItem = Nothing
    Set objSelection = Nothing
End Sub

Sub SetFlagCh09Ver2 _
  (objItem As Object, strFlag As String, dteDate As Date)
    With objItem
        If .Class = olMail Then
            .FlagStatus = olFlagMarked
            .FlagRequest = strFlag
            .FlagDueBy = dteDate
            .Save
        End If
    End With
End Sub
```

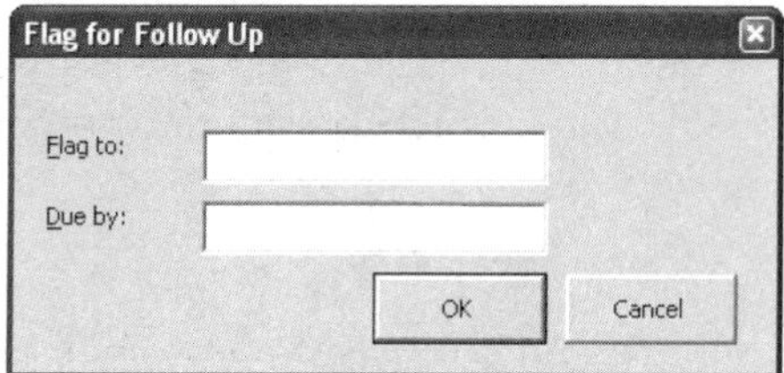


**Figure 9.5** *A VBA dialog can look very much like one of Outlook's built-in dialog boxes.*

If the user clicks the OK button, the `g_blnCancel` variable is set to `False`. If the user clicks the Cancel button or clicks the Close (x) button (which triggers the `UserForm_Terminate` procedure), `g_blnCancel` is set to `True`. After the user finishes with the form, control returns to the `FlagSelectedItemsCh09Ver2` procedure. If `g_blnCancel = False` (in other words, if the user clicked the OK button), the procedure gets the values from the list boxes on the form (which was just hidden, not unloaded) and uses those values to set a message flag on each selected item.

---

**Note:** The `dteDue = #1/1/4501#` statement may look peculiar. It runs if the user enters something in the `txtDueBy` text box that is not a date. This date `#1/1/4501#` actually means "no date" to Outlook, not January 1, 4501. You can use this special date when you need a date/time field in an Outlook item to show "None" on the screen.

---

The other new line is `Unload Ch09FlagOptions`, which terminates the form and releases its memory. In Listing 9.3, you see a variation, `Unload Me`, in which a form unloads itself.

## 9.2 Providing feedback

VBA provides two main methods for providing feedback to the user: message boxes triggered by `MsgBox` statements and VBA forms. A third—and very simple—method is to use a `Beep` statement to get the user's attention with an audible alert when a long series of operations finishes or an error occurs.

### 9.2.1 Feedback with message boxes

For the full syntax for `MsgBox` statements, refer back to Section 9.1.1 on "Using message boxes" earlier in this chapter. While most feedback message boxes show only an OK button, you can use the *buttons* parameter to call attention to a message with a warning icon.

Message boxes have several disadvantages as a feedback mechanism:

- Execution of your code halts while the message box is on the screen. It restarts only when the user clicks OK.
- You cannot control the look of the message box, only the text. There is no way, for example, to turn the text red if something is going wrong.
- A message box can show only one piece of information at a time. If you want to provide feedback on two different operations, you would have to combine that information into one text for the message box.

### 9.2.2 Feedback with VBA forms

Providing feedback with a VBA form avoids the limitations of message boxes. You can use multiple controls to provide information on different operations. Controls can change color or font size to call attention to critical feedback. You can even use graphics on the form to provide a different kind of visual feedback. In the next section, we'll explore how to provide feedback with a text box by modifying the birthday/anniversary reminder form you saw in Chapter 3.

The basic technique is to change the text in the text box as a procedure runs. From working with VBA form controls in Chapter 3, you already know that the syntax for the data in almost any control is `control.Value`, where *control* is the name of the control. If you want to change the text in a text box named `txtProgress` to show when an update procedure started running, you could put this statement in the procedure, assuming that the procedure is running from code behind the form:

```
txtProgress.Value = "Update started at " & _
  FormatDateTime(Now, vbShortTime)
```

If the procedure is running from another module, as could be the case with a nonmodal form, you would need to specify the name of the form. If the form were named `MyForm`, you would use `MyForm.txtProgress.Value` instead of `txtProgress.Value`.

One variation is to use a text box where the `Multiline` property is set to `True` and add a line to that control every time something happens in your procedure that you want to notify the user about. Use the `vbCrLf` constant to put each new addition on its own line at the top of the text box, so the user sees the most recent progress report at the top:

```
txtProgress.Value = "Update started at " & _
  FormatDateTime(Now, vbShortTime)
txtProgress.Value = "Finished at " & _
  FormatDateTime(Now, vbShortTime) & _
  vbCrLf & txtProgress.Value
```

After you update the control value, you need to give Windows an opportunity to update the screen display with these statements:

```
DoEvents
formname.Repaint
```

where *formname* is the name of the form. The `Repaint` method redisplays the form on the screen. `DoEvents` is a method that yields processing time to the operating system. If you don't include these statements, users will never see the feedback until the main procedure finishes.

Obviously, updating the form control adds extra processing time, but in many cases it's worth it. If you don't provide feedback, especially for lengthy processes, you run the risk of the user deciding that Outlook is hung and shutting down the program or even the entire computer.

### 9.2.3 Adding feedback to the birthday/anniversary reminder form

Let's see how you might apply that kind of feedback to a form that you're already familiar with—the birthday/anniversary reminder form created and customized in Chapter 3.

Figure 9.6 shows the form modified to add a new text box at the bottom and rearrange the command buttons. The new text box should have these properties:

| | |
|---|---|
| `(Name)` | `txtProgress` |
| `BackColor` | `Button Face (&H8000000F&)` |
| `Locked` | `True` |
| `Multiline` | `True` |

The `Locked` and `BackColor` properties ensure that the text box is both read-only and has a gray background so that users don't automatically assume that it's a text box that they should type in.

You need to make a few changes in the code for the `cmdUpdate_Click` event handler, as shown in Listing 9.5, and to add a new procedure, `UpdateProgress`.

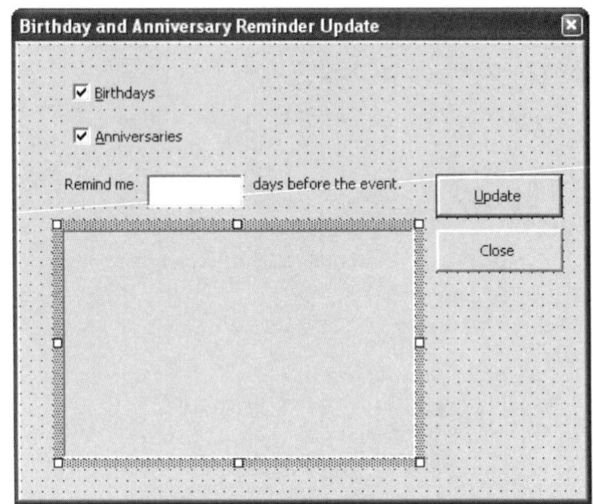


**Figure 9.6** *The large text box is gray because its Backcolor property was set to match that of other controls where the user is not allowed to type.*

The `UpdateProgress` subroutine adds a timestamp to the text for the update, posts it to the text box, then updates the screen. Using a separate procedure to perform the details of the feedback update makes it easy to put a minimal amount of code in the main procedure—just a single call for each update to the `UpdateProgress` procedure.

**Listing 9.5** *The Birthday/Reminder Form Code, Updated To Include Feedback on the Form*

```
Private Sub cmdUpdate_Click()
    Dim objApp As Outlook.Application
    Dim objNS As Outlook.NameSpace
    Dim objCalendar As Outlook.MAPIFolder
    Dim objItem As Outlook.AppointmentItem
    Dim strSubject As String
    Dim intMinutes As Integer
    Dim intCount As Integer
    Dim intCountBA As Integer
    Set objApp = CreateObject("Outlook.Application")
    Set objNS = objApp.GetNamespace("MAPI")
    Set objCalendar = objNS.GetDefaultFolder _
                      (olFolderCalendar)
    Call UpdateProgress("Update started")
    Call UpdateProgress("Processing " & _
                        objCalendar.Items.Count & " items")
    intMinutes = 24 * 60 * txtDays.Value
    intCountBA = 0
    intCount = 0
```

**Listing 9.5** *The Birthday/Reminder Form Code, Updated To Include Feedback on the Form (continued)*

```
    For Each objItem In objCalendar.Items
        strSubject = objItem.Subject
        If InStr(strSubject, "Birthday") > 0 Or _
          InStr(strSubject, "Anniversary") > 0 Then
            objItem.ReminderSet = True
            objItem.ReminderMinutesBeforeStart = intMinutes
            objItem.Save
            intCountBA = intCountBA + 1
        End If
        intCount = intCount + 1
        If intCount Mod 100 = 0 Then
            Call UpdateProgress _
              (intCount & " items processed")
        End If
    Next
    Beep
    Call UpdateProgress _
      ("Finished: " & intCountBA & " items updated")
    Set objApp = Nothing
    Set objNS = Nothing
    Set objCalendar = Nothing
    Set objItem = Nothing
End Sub

Private Sub UpdateProgress(strUpdate As String)
    txtProgress.Value = _
      FormatDateTime(Now, vbShortTime) & vbTab & _
      strUpdate & vbCrLf & txtProgress.Value
    Me.Repaint
    DoEvents
End Sub
```

You can see the results in Figure 9.7—a line corresponding to each time the `UpdateProgress` procedure was called. Notice that the lines for number of items processed increment in hundreds. This code snippet shows why:

```
If intCount Mod 100 = 0 Then
    Call UpdateProgress(intCount & " items processed")
End If
```

`Mod` is a special operator that returns just the remainder from a division operation, so it will equal 0 only when `intCount` is an even multiple of 100. You can use this technique to provide periodic updates when processing large numbers of items.

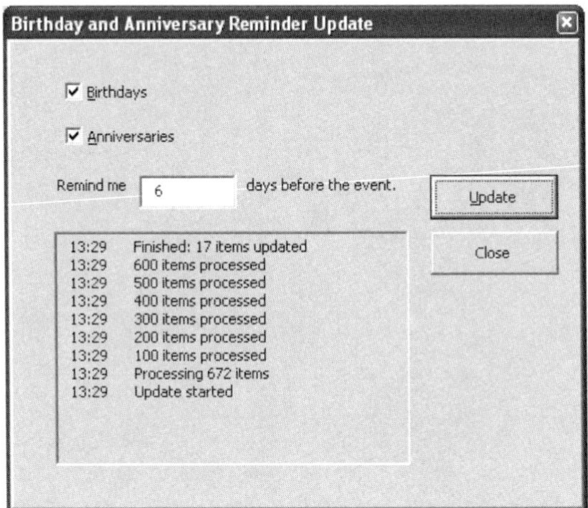


**Figure 9.7** *Even though this update finished in less than a minute, the feedback about its progress is reassuring to the user.*

## 9.3 Summary

This chapter concludes the section on code essentials with techniques for handling user input through `MsgBox()` and `InputBox()` functions and VBA forms. You can also use `MsgBox()` and `InputBox()` with VBScript on Outlook forms. Instead of gathering information from a VBA dialog, VBScript code behind an Outlook form will normally use information that the user has entered in fields on the form.

You also now know how to update a text box on a VBA form to provide feedback to users while a process is under way. In Chapter 10, you will look in more detail at different object models at work in Outlook programming.

# *Special Outlook Techniques*

# 10

# *Working with the Object Models*

You've seen the term *object* many times in the course of the book so far. In this chapter, you dive deeper into the subject of object models, not only for Outlook but also for other programming interfaces you might want to use to build Outlook applications.

Highlights of this chapter include discussions of the following:

- How to include additional object models in your Outlook project
- How to use the Object Browser to discover what you can accomplish with Outlook
- What you can do with the Collaboration Data Objects (CDO) and FileSystemObject models that you can't do with the Outlook object model
- How to create a message with voting buttons through code
- How to use the Windows Script Host to read the Windows registry or launch a program, file, or Web page

Objects are special because they contain not only data, but also specific methods, events, and properties that determine how that data behaves and what you can do with it. Those shared characteristics define the object class. The methods, events, and properties are called *members* of the class.

Often, objects of different classes act much the same. For example, the different Outlook item objects support sets of properties that largely overlap, and all include many of the same events and methods.

Objects often exist in a parent-child relationship. An Outlook `JournalItem` object, for example, has a parent `MAPIFolder` object.

Trying to understand the concept of objects might seem like a lot of trouble when what you really want to do is write Outlook applications, but the effort pays off in the end. Grasping the core of the object model helps you know what you can do in Outlook—and how to accomplish it.

# 10.1 Using the VBA Object Browser

The main tool for exploring the object models is VBA's Object Browser. To display the Object Browser, choose View, Object Browser. You can also press F2 or click the Object Browser button on the toolbar. When the Object Browser appears, you might want to maximize it to be able to see more information on the screen.

When you start the Object Browser, it presents information on all the programming libraries available to you (more on that in the next section). To look at just the Outlook objects, in the dropdown list at the top of the Object Browser (the one that defaults to <All Libraries>), select Outlook.

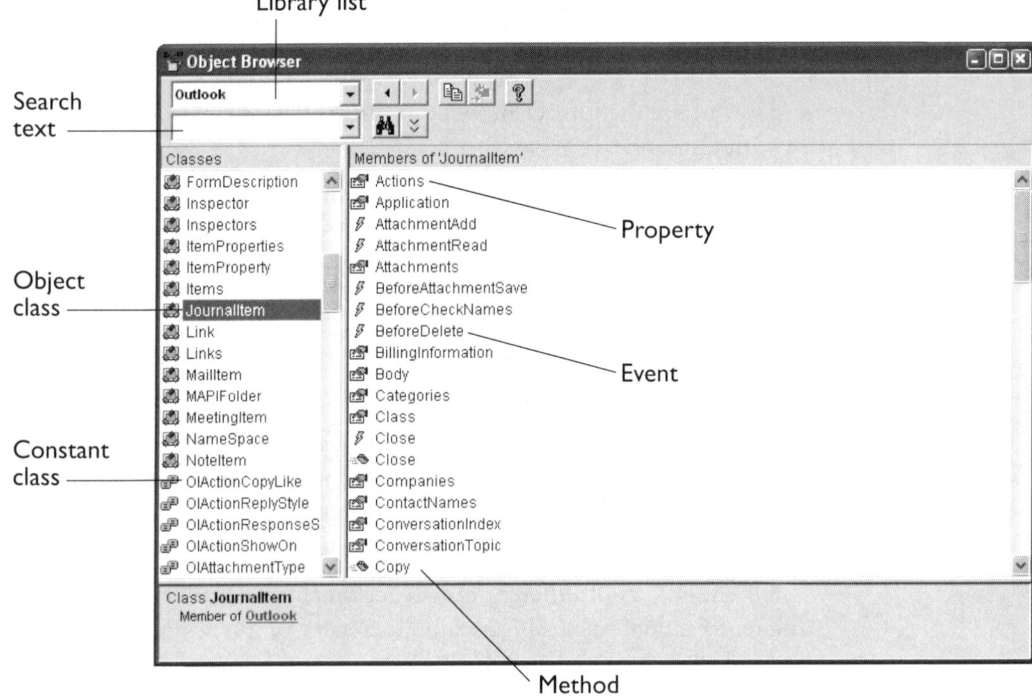


**Figure 10.1** *Use the Object Browser to explore Outlook's objects and their methods, properties, and events.*

Your screen should now look something like Figure 10.1, which shows the `JournalItem` class.

Pay close attention to the different icons that help distinguish the types of object classes and their members. For example, the `JournalItem` object class includes both a `Close` event and a `Close` action, but it's easy to tell them apart by the icon. If you prefer to see all the properties together, followed by methods, then events, right-click the list of members and choose Group Members.

### 10.1.1 Understanding and adding libraries

The Object Browser displays information about not only Outlook objects, but also other objects you use in VBA, including any modules or forms you have created. Information about each basic set of objects is contained in a library that loads when you start VBA. You can also add more libraries when you want to work with other object models—for example, with Word or Excel to generate reports from Outlook data.

To see the libraries currently installed and add more, choose Tools, References. In the References dialog box, shown in Figure 10.2, the items at the top marked with check marks are already installed and part of your VBA environment.

To add another reference, scroll down the alphabetical list of unchecked items until you find the library you want to use. Then, click the desired

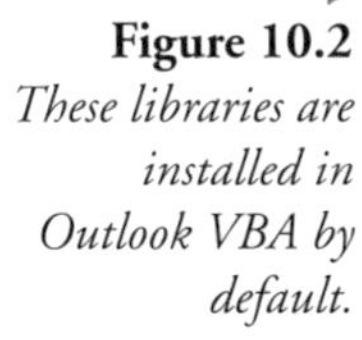

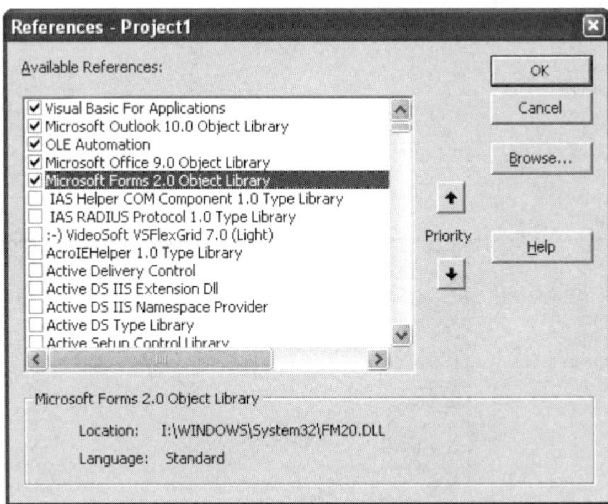


**Figure 10.2** *These libraries are installed in Outlook VBA by default.*

library's check box. You can also install new references by clicking the Browse button and finding the appropriate reference file on your system. Reference files can include the following:

- Outlook VBA files: .otm files
- Object Type libraries: .olb, .tlb, .dll files
- Executable files: .exe, .dll files
- ActiveX controls: .ocx files

To remove a reference if you're no longer using its objects in your project, clear its check box.

Two libraries can contain objects with the same name. To avoid conflicts, use a fully qualified declaration for each object. For example, use `Outlook.Recipient` instead of `Recipient`, especially when working with the CDO library, which we'll cover later in the chapter. It, too, has a `Recipient` object. Another good example is `Selection`, which without being fully qualified could be a Word, Excel, or Outlook object. If you don't use a fully qualified declaration, VBA will use the library closest to the top of the reference list that has a matching member.

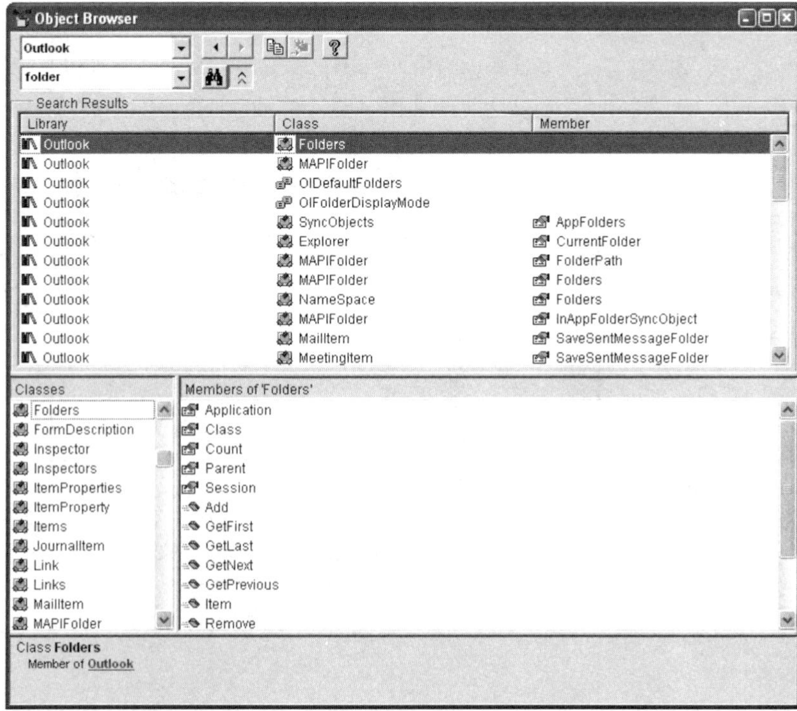


**Figure 10.3** *Search the Object Browser to find classes and members containing particular text.*

## 10.1.2 Searching for objects and getting help

You can search the Object Browser for classes and members related to particular topics. Type a word in the second dropdown list box, the one marked Search Text in Figure 10.1, and then press Enter or click the Search Text button. Figure 10.3 shows the results of a search of the Outlook library for the word "folder." It turns up a long list of objects, methods, events, properties, and constants whose names contain `Folder`.

To hide the search results, click the Hide Search Results button next to the Search Text button. You can see the search results again by clicking the same button (now the Show Search Results button).

If you've been browsing an object model for a while and want to retrace your steps, use the right and left arrow buttons at the top of the Object Browser window, above the Search button.

One great use of the Object Browser is as an index to the Help topics on the object models. Select any class or member, and then click the Help button or press F1 to get help on that item, including related properties, methods, and events.

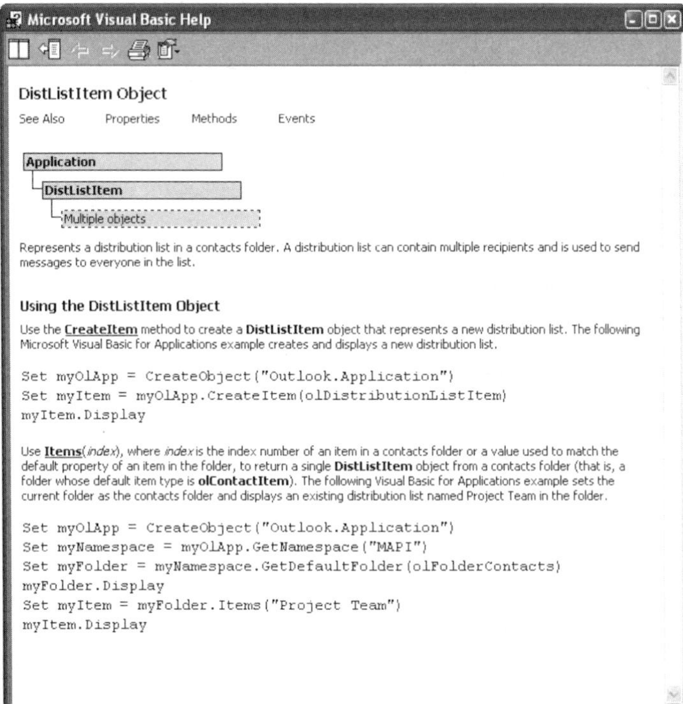


**Figure 10.4** *Help topics tell you how to create and use Outlook objects.*

**Note:** Not all libraries shown in the Object Browser have help files associated with them. Sometimes, you will have to refer to a separate help file or other documentation.

Figure 10.4 shows a typical help topic for the `DistListItem` (distribution list) object. Notice the links for Properties, Methods, and Events at the top. The diagram showing the `DistListItem` object in context with its parent and child objects is also clickable, enabling you to explore the object hierarchy in the Help system. You can also start at the top by searching in Help for "Microsoft Outlook Objects." That topic shows the overall map of the Outlook object model, seen in Figure 10.5.

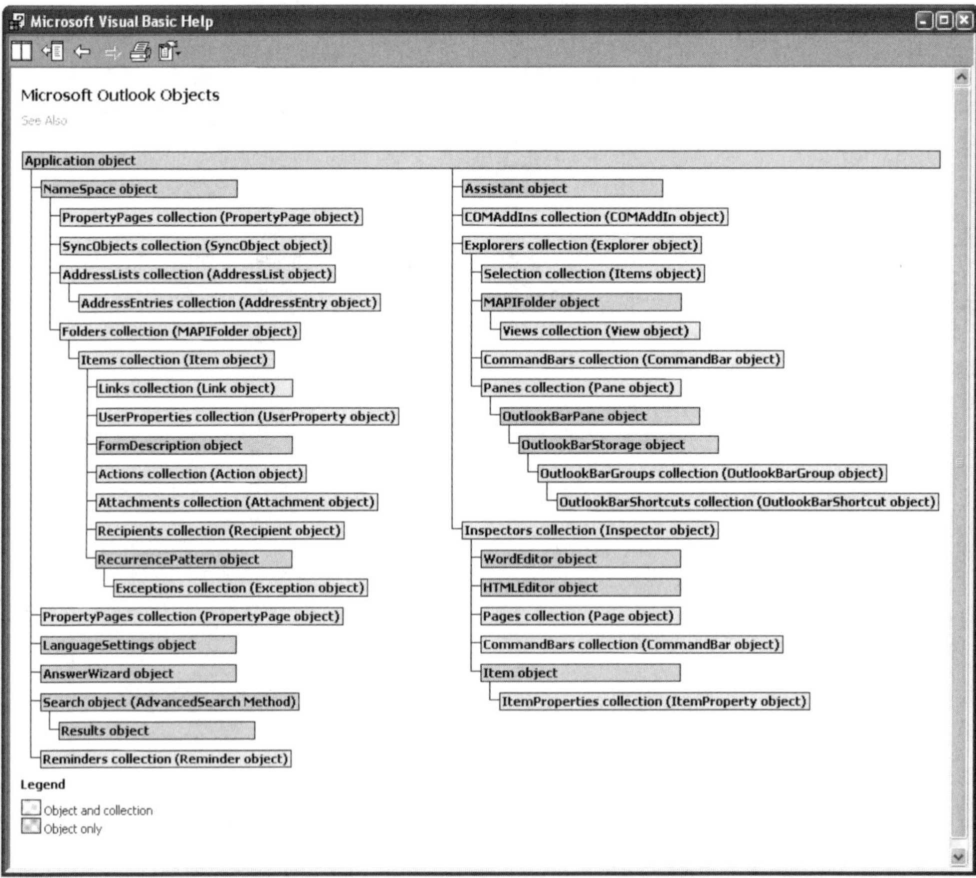


**Figure 10.5** *Click on any branch in the Help topic about the Outlook object model to learn how to use the various objects.*

Always closely examine and test any code that you take from Help topics, since the code samples are not always 100 percent correct.

## 10.2 Object and collection code techniques

Programming with objects requires some special code techniques. You've already learned three:

- Using a `Set` statement to initialize an object variable
- Using a `Set obj = Nothing` statement to dereference and release an object variable
- Using a `With ... End With` block to work with the properties and methods of a particular object

When you worked with items in a folder, you saw an example of an object *collection*, a set of objects of the same class that can be accessed through the properties and methods of the collection, not just via the individual item members. In the object model map in Figure 10.5, all the objects that include a name in parentheses are collections. For example, the `PropertyPages` collection is a set of `PropertyPage` objects.

Using `For Each ... Next` blocks to loop through all the objects in a collection is one important collection technique. You're going to look at others as you explore the properties, events, and methods you can expect to find in any collection.

A typical Outlook collection object includes the `Application`, `Class`, `Count`, `Parent`, and `Session` properties, listed in Table 10.1.

The `Count` property is probably the most often used.

**Table 10.1** *Standard Collection Properties*

| Property | Returns |
|---|---|
| `Application` | Parent `Application` object (Microsoft Outlook) |
| `Class` | Constant representing the collection's class |
| `Count` | Number of objects in the collection |
| `Parent` | Parent object of the collection |
| `Session` | NameSpace object for the current Outlook session |

One thing that bewilders some new Outlook developers is that every collection is listed in Help as read-only. What this means is that you cannot directly set any of the above properties. For example, you cannot change the value of the `Count` property to add a new item to the collection. Instead, you use specific collection methods to change the contents of the collection or retrieve any particular item in the collection.

Most Outlook collections include these three methods:

- `Add` to add a new object to the collection
- `Item` to refer to a specific object in the collection
- `Remove` to delete an object from the collection

However, some collections, such as `AddressLists`, do not support the `Add` or `Remove` methods, only the `Item` method.

## 10.2.1 Item method

To use the `Item` method to return a specific object, you must know either the index for the object or the value of its default property. The index is the position of the object in the collection, starting with 1. For example, the following code uses the syntax `objFolder.Items.Item(1)` to open and display the first item in the Inbox:

```
Set objApp = CreateObject("Outlook.Application")
Set objNS = objApp.GetNamespace("MAPI")
Set objFolder = objNS.GetDefaultFolder(olFolderInbox)
Set objMessage = objFolder.Items.Item(1)
objMessage.Display
```

**Note:** The collection of all items in a folder is `*folder*.Items`, not `*folder*`, so the `Item` method syntax is `*folder*.Items.Item(*index*)`, even though that might seem redundant.

The problem with using an index is not knowing exactly which object you might get. In the preceding example, the oldest message in the Inbox is displayed because it has index position 1.

The other method is to use the default property for an item to look it up. This property varies from object to object. For Outlook messages, contacts, and other data items, it's the `Subject` property. This variation on the

`Item` method prompts the user for the subject of a message and then displays that message:

```
strSubject = InputBox("Subject of message to open:", _
             "OpenFirstInboxItem")
If strSubject <> "" Then
    Set objApp = CreateObject("Outlook.Application")
    Set objNS = objApp.GetNamespace("MAPI")
    Set objFolder = objNS.GetDefaultFolder(olFolderInbox)
    Set objMessage = objFolder.Items.Item(strSubject)
    If Not objMessage Is Nothing Then
        objMessage.Display
    End If
End If
```

This version of the `Item` method has its limitations, too. It requires an exact match for the text used as the argument for `Item`, and if there is more than one matching object, only the first object is returned. You will learn some alternatives for finding particular items in Outlook folders in Chapter 14, "Working with Items and Recipients."

`Item` is the default property for a collection, which means that, strictly speaking, you don't have to use the word `Item` in your code. These two expressions, for example, are equivalent:

```
objFolder.Items.Item(strSubject)
objFolder.Items(strSubject)
```

### 10.2.2 Add method

The `Add` method creates a new object in the collection and returns that new object to an object variable. The syntax looks like this:

```
Set obj = collection.Add(arguments)
```

Some objects support arguments in their `Add` method to set properties for the new object. In other cases, you create the object with the `Add` method first and then set properties separately.

One key Outlook collection is the `Explorers` collection of available Outlook folder windows. Listing 10.1 illustrates the `Add` method by adding a new `Explorer` object to open a new Outlook window with the Calendar folder displayed. The `Explorers.Add` method requires one argument—the `MAPIFolder` object representing the folder to be displayed. You can also include an optional *`displaymode`* argument that specifies whether the view should include such navigation tools as the Outlook Bar.

**Listing 10.1** *Displaying a Folder in a New Window*

```
Sub ShowCalendar()
    Dim objApp As Outlook.Application
    Dim objNS As Outlook.NameSpace
    Dim objExplorers As Outlook.Explorers
    Dim objFolder As Outlook.MAPIFolder
    Dim objExplorer As Outlook.Explorer

    Set objApp = CreateObject("Outlook.Application")
    Set objNS = objApp.GetNamespace("MAPI")
    Set objExplorers = objApp.Explorers
    Set objFolder = _
      objNS.GetDefaultFolder(olFolderCalendar)
    Set objExplorer = objExplorers.Add(objFolder, _
                        olFolderDisplayFolderOnly)
    objExplorer.Activate
    Set objApp = Nothing
    Set objNS = Nothing
    Set objExplorers = Nothing
    Set objFolder = Nothing
    Set objExplorer = Nothing
End Sub
```

**Tip:** You can also use the `Display` method, as well as `Activate`, to show an `Explorer` or `Inspector` object.

Flip ahead to Section 10.2.4 for another example of the `Add` method.

### 10.2.3 Remove method

The `Remove` method is the opposite of `Add`. It deletes an object from the collection, using this syntax:

```
collection.Remove index
```

Normally, however, you don't know the position of any particular item in the collection, so you don't know the *`index`* that `Remove` requires. If you want to get rid of a particular object, it's usually easier to get the object with the `Item` method and then use the `Delete` method on the object to delete it from the collection.

`Remove` comes in handy for bulk deletion operations, such as removing all controls from a form. In Listing 7.5, you learned how to use a `For Each ... Next` loop and the `Delete` method to remove all attachments from an Outlook item. Listing 10.2 shows a different removal tech-

**Listing 10.2** *Removing All Custom Properties from the Currently Open Outlook Item*

```
Sub RemoveUserProps()
    Dim objApp As Outlook.Application
    Dim objInsp As Outlook.Inspector
    Dim objItem As Object

    Set objApp = CreateObject("Outlook.Application")
    Set objInsp = objApp.ActiveInspector
    If Not objInsp Is Nothing Then
        Set objItem = objInsp.CurrentItem
        Do While objItem.UserProperties.Count > 0
            objItem.UserProperties.Remove 1
        Loop
    End If

    Set objApp = Nothing
    Set objInsp = Nothing
    Set objItem = Nothing
End Sub
```

nique, using the Remove method and a `Do` loop to remove all user-defined properties that make up the `UserProperties` collection.

**CAUTION:** Avoid using the `Remove` method to try to remove attachments from Outlook items. It works OK in Outlook 2002, but not in Outlook 2000. Use the code in Listing 7.3 instead.

**Tip:** You may find it useful to prefix your collection variables with `col`, to make them stand out from object variables and normal variables.

### 10.2.4 Creating a voting button message

Outlook includes a useful feature for creating *voting button messages* that allow users to ask recipients to vote on a finite list of choices. Unfortunately, Outlook 2000 in Internet Mail Only (IMO) mode does not include a Voting Buttons option in its Options dialog. (Microsoft must have mistakenly thought that Internet mail users would not find this feature useful.) IMO users can, however, create a voting button message with a little bit of VBA code that uses the `Add` method to create several new `Action` items in the `Actions` collection.

**Listing 10.3** *Add Action Objects to Create a Voting Button Message*

```
Sub CreateVoteMessage()
    Dim objApp As Outlook.Application
    Dim strMsg As String
    Dim strActions As String
    Dim arrActions() As String
    Dim I As Integer
    Dim objMessage As Outlook.MailItem
    Dim objAction As Outlook.Action
    strMsg = "Enter voting button titles, " _
              & "separated by commas."
    strActions = InputBox(strMsg, "CreateVoteMessage")
    If strActions <> "" Then
        arrActions = Split(strActions, ",")
        Set objApp = CreateObject("Outlook.Application")
        Set objMessage = objApp.CreateItem(olMailItem)
        For I = 0 To UBound(arrActions)
            Set objAction = objMessage.Actions.Add
            With objAction
                .CopyLike = olRespond
                .Enabled = True
                .Name = arrActions(I)
                .Prefix = ""
                .ReplyStyle = olOmitOriginalText
                .ResponseStyle = olPrompt
                .ShowOn = olMenuAndToolbar
            End With
        Next I
        objMessage.Display
    End If
 Set objApp = Nothing
 Set objMessage = Nothing
 Set objAction = Nothing
End Sub
```

In most cases, the `Add` method requires one or more arguments, as you saw in the code for adding and displaying an `Explorer` object. In a few cases, though, you use the `Add` method with no argument and then work with the returned object's properties. Listing 10.3 illustrates the use of the `Actions` collection to create a message and add voting buttons after the user types in a comma-delimited list of voting button titles.

---

**Tip:** In Chapter 20, "Common Outlook Form and Item Techniques," you learn more about working with voting buttons and the `Actions` collection.

---

Notice the syntax for the `Add` method:

```
Set objAction = objMessage.Actions.Add
```

This is equivalent to these two statements:

```
Set colActions = objMessage.Actions
Set objAction = colActions.Add
```

In other words, you do not have to declare an object variable to represent the collection. Instead, you can use its parent object with the syntax `parent.collection.Add`.

The `With ... End With` block sets all the necessary properties with the default values that Outlook normally uses for voting buttons.

### 10.2.5 Releasing objects

If you pay attention to scope when writing your procedures and declare variables with the narrowest scope possible, you shouldn't have any problem with procedure-level object and collection variables staying in memory and using system resources after you need them. However, it doesn't hurt to release them anyway, as part of the end of each procedure, using a `Set object = Nothing` statement. `Nothing` is a special keyword that disassociates the variable from the object to which it refers.

---

**Tip:** Use the statement `If Not object Is Nothing Then` to test whether a previous `Set object . . .` statement was successful before you try to use any of the properties or methods of *`object`*.

---

Always use a `Set object = Nothing` statement to release any module or global object variables when your code no longer needs them. In certain cases, you may want to preset the value of an object or collection to `Nothing` after initializing the variable, so there is no ambiguity as to the value of the object or collection. You will see an example of this when you are walking the folder hierarchy in Chapter 12, "Working with Stores and Folders."

## 10.3 Programming with Collaboration Data Objects

So far in this book, you've been working mainly with the Outlook object model, with a brief side trip to the MSForms model when you were working with VBA forms and the events available for forms and controls. One other major object model deals with messages and contains some very useful methods that are not in the Outlook Model. Support for this model—called Collaboration Data Objects (CDO)—is not included in Outlook's default setup. If you don't find the Microsoft CDO 1.21 Library in the list of available references (refer to Figure 10.2), rerun the Outlook setup and select the Collaborative Data Objects component. Then, return to VBA and use Tools, References to include the Microsoft CDO 1.21 Library (cdo.dll) in your projects when you need it.

---

**Note:** If Windows 2000 or Windows XP is your operating system, you will also see a Microsoft CDO for Windows 2000 Library. This library is used mainly for creating outgoing messages for delivery by the SMTP service included with those operating systems and does not have any direct connection with Outlook.

---

Among the useful things you can do with CDO are delete an Outlook item permanently, rather than send it to the Deleted Items folder, and open a Select Names dialog, asking the user to choose recipients. You will look at the first task in this chapter and then work with the Select Names dialog in Chapter 14, "Working with Items and Recipients," after you become familiar with recipient concepts. CDO can also expose many more properties of individual items and folders than Outlook can, making it possible to perform tasks that otherwise might seem impossible. However, such properties are officially undocumented, so any work that you do in that area is somewhat at your own risk. Tools like Mdbvu32.exe and Outlook Spy, discussed in Appendix A, are invaluable to exploring the hidden behavior of Outlook items and folders.

To browse the CDO object hierarchy, choose MAPI in the Library drop-down list. (CDO is largely a wrapper around the Extended Messaging Application Programming Interface (MAPI) at the heart of Outlook.) The CDO library does not include a Help file integrated with the Object Browser. See Appendix A for sources for help on CDO.

Before you can use CDO in a VBA or VBScript procedure, you must start a CDO session using this code:

```
Dim objSession As MAPI.Session
Set objSession = CreateObject("MAPI.Session")
objSession.Logon "", "", False, False
```

The `Logon` method initializes the CDO session using the currently active Outlook session, which means that you work in CDO with exactly the same items and folders as you would access with Outlook's objects. For VBScript, use just `Dim objSession` instead of `Dim objSession As MAPI.Session`.

**Listing 10.4** *Initialize an MAPI.Session Object Variable Before Using CDO Methods*

```
Public g_CDOSession As MAPI.Session

Sub DoCDOLogon()
    Set g_objSession = CreateObject("MAPI.Session")
    g_objSession.Logon , , False, False
End Sub

Sub DoCDOLogoff()
    g_objSession.Logoff
    Set g_objSession = Nothing
End Sub
```

**Note:** CDO supports other logon parameters as well, but they are used mainly in more advanced applications beyond the scope of this book.

If you use CDO methods frequently, you may find it convenient to declare a public `MAPI.Session` object variable and initialize it before running any other routines that need CDO. Then, use another subroutine to log off from CDO when you have finished using it. As you will see in Chapter 11, "Responding to Outlook Events in VBA," the Outlook Application object has a `Startup` event appropriate for initializing public object variables. The code in Listing 10.4 shows the declaration and subroutines to initialize a CDO session and end it.

### 10.3.1 Passing an item between Outlook and CDO

CDO's main job is as a server component. It's a key element of Microsoft Exchange Server. Because CDO is intended as a server component, it has no direct link to the user interface, as the Outlook object model does through its `Inspector` and `Explorer` objects. Therefore, you must provide code to pass a particular Outlook item or folder to CDO. Fortunately, Outlook and CDO items share a key property in common—an `EntryID` that uniquely identifies an item within a particular folder hierarchy (or *information store*). Since Outlook may be using multiple information stores—Personal Folders files or Exchange Server mailboxes—you also need to use the `StoreID`, which is a property of the parent folder of the item.

**Note:** Only items that have been saved will have `EntryID` and `StoreID` properties that you can use to pass the item to CDO and back again.

**Listing 10.5** *A Procedure to Return a CDO Message Object from an Outlook Item*

```
Function GetCDOItemFromOL(objOLItem As Object) _
  as MAPI.Message
    Dim objApp As Outlook.Application
    Dim strEntryID As String
    Dim strStoreID As String
    Set objApp = CreateObject("Outlook.Application")
    strEntryID = objOLItem.EntryID
    strStoreID = objOLItem.Parent.StoreID
    If g_CDOSession Is Nothing Then
        Call DoCDOLogon
    End If
    Set GetCDOItemFromOL = _
      g_CDOSession.GetMessage(strEntryID, strStoreID)
    Set objApp = Nothing
End Function
```

You can use the `GetCDOItemFromOL()` function in Listing 10.5 any time that you have an Outlook object and you want to work with that item as a CDO `Message` object. The `GetOLItemFromCDO()` function in Listing 10.6 does just the opposite; given a CDO `Message` object, it returns the corresponding Outlook object by passing the `Message` object's `ID` and `StoreID` property values to Outlook's `Namespace.GetItemFromID` method.

**Listing 10.6** *A Procedure to Return an Outlook Item from CDO Message Object*

```
Function GetOLItemFromCDO(objCDOItem As MAPI.Message) _
  As Object
    Dim objApp As Outlook.Application
    Dim objNS As Outlook.NameSpace
    Dim strEntryID As String
    Dim strStoreID As String
    Set objApp = CreateObject("Outlook.Application")
    Set objNS = objApp.GetNamespace("MAPI")
    strEntryID = objCDOItem.ID
    strStoreID = objCDOItem.StoreID
    If g_CDOSession Is Nothing Then
        Call DoCDOLogon
    End If
    Set GetOLItemFromCDO = _
      objNS.GetItemFromID(strEntryID, strStoreID)
    Set objApp = Nothing
    Set objNS = Nothing
End Function
```

---

**Note:** In addition to the `Session.GetMessage` method to return a `Message` object, CDO also includes a similar `Session.GetFolder` method that returns a `CDO.Folder` object, given the `EntryID` and `StoreID` from an `Outlook.MAPIFolder` object.

---

The next section demonstrates how to use `GetCDOItemFromOL()`; you'll see an example of `GetOLItemFromCDO()` in Chapter 14, "Working with Items and Recipients."

### 10.3.2 Permanently deleting an item

When working with Outlook items, you occasionally want to delete an item. Using Outlook's `Delete` method sends the item to the Deleted Items folder. To remove the item completely, you would have to remove the item from that folder, too. However, CDO's `Delete` method works differently. Instead of moving the item to Deleted Items, it deletes the item completely. Listing 10.7 deletes the first item selected in the current folder.

**Listing 10.7** *Delete an Item Completely with CDO*

```
Sub DeleteOneItem()
    Dim objApp As Outlook.Application
    Dim objItem As Object
    Dim objCDO As MAPI.Message
    Set objApp = CreateObject("Outlook.Application")
    Set objItem = objApp.ActiveExplorer.Selection.Item(1)
    If Not objItem Is Nothing Then
        If g_CDOSession Is Nothing Then
            Call DoCDOLogon
        End If
        Set objCDO = GetCDOItemFromOL(objItem)
        If Not objCDO Is Nothing Then
            objCDO.Delete
        End If
    End If
    Set objItem = Nothing
    Set objCDO = Nothing
    Set objApp = Nothing
End Sub
```

# 10.4 Using the Scripting Runtime Library

Another object library that you will find useful for certain Outlook chores is the Scripting Runtime Library, which is part of Windows Script Host, a component for running scripts included with every version of Windows since Windows 98. A key object in the Scripting Runtime Library is the `FileSystemObject`. This object allows you to work with drives, files, and folders. Since it can be used from both VBA and VBScript, it is more useful to learn to program it than to use the `FileSystem` object that VBA provides. Some of the things you can do with the `FileSystemObject` include

- Checking whether a particular file exists
- Getting the user's Temp or other special folder
- Reading data
- Transfering attachments from one Outlook item to another

To use the `FileSystemObject` in your VBA code, use the Tools, References command to the Microsoft Scripting Runtime library (scrrun.dll). The Library list will then show Scripting as an available library. To instantiate a `FileSystemObject` variable, use this code:

```
Dim fso as Scripting.FileSystemObject
Set fso = CreateObject("Scripting.FileSystemObject")
```

Appendix A lists additional resources for learning about the `FileSystemObject`.

## 10.4.1 Working with folders and files

The `FileSystemObject` offers a variety of methods for working with drives, files, and folders, including those that return a particular `Folder` or `File` object from a path. A special object is the `TextStream`, a text file that has been opened for reading, writing new data, or appending to existing data. Tables 10.2 through 10.4 list the `FileSystemObject` methods you are most likely to use in Outlook programming.

## 10.4.2 Writing data to a log file

When performing a complex Outlook operation, you may want to create a log file on the user's computer that your routines can write to as needed. Once you have a `TextStream` object, you can use the methods listed in Table 10.5 to read and write data and close the stream.

**Table 10.2** *Key FileSystemObject Methods*

| Method | Returns | Outlook Usage and Notes |
|---|---|---|
| `BuildPath(`*`path, filename`*`)` | String with full filename path | Build a path from a special folder and a file name. |
| `CreateFolder(`*`path`*`)` | `Scripting.Folder` | Create a new folder for storing attachments, logs, etc. |
| `CreateTextFile(`*`filename, [overwrite, [unicode]`*`)` | `Scripting.TextStream` | Create a new file for storing logs, etc., and open it for reading and writing. (*`unicode`* option available only on supported operating systems.) |
| `DeleteFile(`*`filespec, [force]`*`)` | n/a | Delete a file—for example, an attachment being copied between items. (*`force`* option determines whether read-only files are deleted. Default is `false`.) |
| `FileExists(`*`filespec`*`)` | `True` or `False` | Check whether a file with the same name already exists before saving an attachment as a file. |
| `GetFile(`*`filepath`*`)` | `Scripting.File` | Get a file you can examine for version number, created or modified date, etc. |
| `GetSpecialFolder(`*`specialfolder`*`)` | `Scripting.Folder` | Get the user's temporary folder for saving files for short-term use. See Table 10.3 for possible values for *`specialfolder`*. |
| `GetTempName()` | String | Get a name for a temporary file. |
| `OpenTextFile(`*`filename, [IOMode], [create], [format]`*`)` | `Scripting.TextStream` | Open a text file for reading or writing. |

**Table 10.3** *Values for the specialfolder Argument in GetSpecialFolder()*

| Folder | Constant | Literal Value |
|---|---|---|
| Temporary folder | `TemporaryFolder` | 2 |
| System folder (e.g., C:\Windows\System) | `SystemFolder` | 1 |
| Windows folder | `WindowsFolder` | 0 |

**Table 10.4** *Values for Arguments in OpenTextFile ()*

| Argument | Description | Constant | Literal Values |
|---|---|---|---|
| `IOMode` | Add text at the end of the file | `ForAppending` | 8 |
| | Read the file | `ForReading` | 1 |
| | Write data to the file | `ForWriting` | 2 |
| `Create` | Create a new file if it doesn't already exist | `True` | |
| | Don't create a new file | `False` | |
| `Format` | Open the file as Unicode | `TristateTrue` | –1 |
| | Open the file as ASCII | `TristateFalse` | 0 |
| | Open the file using the system default | `TristateUseDefault` | –2 |

Listing 10.8 illustrates a structure for a complex procedure that includes logging errors to a text file. The `ComplexProcedure` subroutine instantiates the `m_objLogStream` object using the `GetLogFileStream()` function, then calls the `WriteErr` subroutine to write to the log file whenever an error occurs.

Notice that the `GetLogFileStream()` function can either use a full path (though it does not check for the validity of the path) or, if only the log file name is supplied, can create the log in the user's temporary folder.

**Table 10.5** *Key Methods for the TextStream Object*

| Method | Description |
|---|---|
| `Close` | Close the `TextStream`, saving any new data written to it. |
| `Read(chars)` | Read a specified number of characters from the text file. |
| `ReadAll` | Read all data from the text file. |
| `ReadLine` | Read one line from the stream. Repeat `ReadLine` to read each line in succession. |
| `Write` | Write a string of text to the stream. |
| `WriteBlankLines(lines)` | Write a number of blank lines to the stream. |
| `WriteLine` | Write a string of text, plus an end of line character to the stream. |

**Listing 10.8** *Log Errors to a Text File*

```
Dim m_objLogStream As Scripting.TextStream

Sub ComplexProcedure()
    On Error GoTo Err_ComplexProcedure
    Set m_objLogStream = GetLogFileStream("mylog.txt")
    If Not m_objLogStream Is Nothing Then
        m_objLogStream.WriteBlankLines 1
        m_objLogStream.WriteLine "Procedure started"
        additional code for the complex procedure
        m_objLogStream.WriteLine "Procedure finished"
        m_objLogStream.Close
    End If

Exit_ComplexProcedure:
    Set m_objLogStream = Nothing
    Exit Sub

Err_ComplexProcedure:
    Call WriteErr("ComplexProcedure")
    Err.Clear
    Resume Next
End Sub

Function GetLogFileStream(strFilePath As String) _
  As Scripting.TextStream
    Dim fso As Scripting.FileSystemObject
    Dim fld As Scripting.Folder
    Set fso = CreateObject("Scripting.FileSystemObject")
    If InStr(strFilePath, "\") = 0 Then
        Set fld = fso.GetSpecialFolder(TemporaryFolder)
        strFilePath = fso.BuildPath(fld.Path, strFilePath)
    End If
    Set GetLogFileStream = _
      fso.OpenTextFile(strFilePath, ForAppending, True)
    Set fso = Nothing
    Set fld = Nothing
End Function

Sub WriteErr(strProc As String)
    Dim strErr As String
    strErr = FormatDateTime(Now, vbShortDate) & " " & _
             FormatDateTime(Now, vbShortTime) & "  " & _
             "ERR " & Err.Number & ": " & Err.Description & _
             " (" & strProc & ")"
    m_objLogStream.WriteLine strErr
End Sub
```

### 10.4.3 Copying attachments between Outlook items

Outlook does not provide any way to copy an attached file directly between Outlook items. Instead, you need to save the attachment from the first item to a system folder, then attach it to the second item. Being able to find the user's temporary folder and delete files makes it possible to perform this operation without leaving a mess of files on the user's system.

Listing 10.9 includes two subroutines. The `CopyAttachments` subroutine is a reusable procedure you can use any time you need to copy attachments from one Outlook item to another. Before it saves the file attachment, it checks whether a file with the same name exists in the target folder. If there is such a file, the procedure changes the file name of the temporarily saved attachment to make sure there are no conflicts. To see how it

**Listing 10.9** *Copy Attachments from One Outlook Item to Another*

```
Sub CopyAttachmentsDemo()
    Dim objApp As Outlook.Application
    Dim objItem As Object
    Dim objTask As Outlook.TaskItem

    Set objApp = CreateObject("Outlook.Application")
    Set objItem = objApp.ActiveExplorer.Selection.Item(1)
    Set objTask = objApp.CreateItem(olTaskItem)
    objTask.Save
    Call CopyAttachments(objItem, objTask)
    objTask.Display

    Set objApp = Nothing
    Set objItem = Nothing
    Set objTask = Nothing
End Sub

Sub CopyAttachments(objSourceItem As Object, _
  objTargetItem As Object)
    Dim fso As Scripting.FileSystemObject
    Dim fldTemp As Scripting.Folder
    Dim objAtt As Outlook.Attachment
    Dim strFilePath As String
    Dim strFileExt As String
    Dim strFileName As String
    Dim intLoc As Integer
    Dim i As Integer
    Set fso = CreateObject("Scripting.FileSystemObject")
    Set fldTemp = fso.GetSpecialFolder(TemporaryFolder)
```

**Listing 10.9** *Copy Attachments from One Outlook Item to Another (continued)*

```
    For Each objAtt In objSourceItem.Attachments
        If objAtt.Type = olByValue Then
            strFilePath = fso.BuildPath(fldTemp.Path, _
                                        objAtt.FileName)
            If fso.FileExists(strFilePath) Then
                intLoc = InStrRev("objAtt.FileName", ".")
                strFileName = Left(objAtt.FileName, _
                                   intLoc - 1)
                strFileExt = Mid(objAtt.FileName, _
                                 intLoc + 1)
                i = 1 Do
                    strFilePath = _
                      fso.BuildPath(fldTemp.Path, _
                      strFileName & CStr(i) & _
                      "." & strFileExt)
                    i = i + 1
                Loop While fso.FileExists(strFilePath)
            End If
            objAtt.SaveAsFile strFilePath
            objTargetItem.Attachments.Add strFilePath, _
              olByValue, , objAtt.DisplayName
            fso.DeleteFile strFilePath
        End If
    Next
    Set objAtt = Nothing
    Set fldTemp = Nothing
    Set fso = Nothing
End Sub
```

works, from any Outlook folder select an item that has one or more attachments, then run the `CopyAttachmentsDemo` subroutine. This procedure creates a new task item and copies the attachments from the selected item to the task.

## 10.5 More useful object model techniques

This chapter concludes with a brief look at some other practical Windows Script Host (WSH) and Internet Explorer object model techniques for launching programs, files, and Web pages; getting the user's logon name; and reading the Windows registry. Since these models are used extensively for applications other than Outlook, you will find a wealth of material on the Internet to help you explore them further.

### 10.5.1 Launching a program or file

WSH includes a feature that makes it easy to launch a program or open a file in its native application. If you have WSH installed, you can launch any other program with code like this:

```
Dim objWSHShell As IWshRuntimeLibrary.IwshShell
Set objWSHShell = CreateObject("WScript.Shell")
objWSHShell.Run "notepad.exe"
```

The `Run` method can take as its argument any program file, document file, or URL that you can successfully launch with Windows' Start, Run command. For most documents, you will need to specify a full file path, not just the file name. To be able to declare an `IWshShell` object, add a reference to the WSH Object Model (wshom.ocx) to your Outlook VBA project.

### 10.5.2 Launching a Web page

The `IWshShell.Run` method allows you to launch Internet Web pages, as well as files, but it's not the only method available. If you add a reference to Microsoft Internet Controls (shdocvw.dll), you gain access to the entire Internet Explorer object model. This code snippet opens a page in a new Internet Explorer window:

```
Dim objIE As SHDocVw.WebBrowser
Set objIE = CreateObject("InternetExplorer.Application")
objIE.Navigate "http://www.outlookcode.com"
objIE.Visible = True
```

By contrast, using the `IWshShell.Run` method described in the previous section launches a Web page in an existing browser window.

### 10.5.3 Getting the user's logon name

Both Outlook and CDO provide techniques to obtain the current user's name (`Namespace.CurrentUser.Name` in Outlook and `Session.CurrentUser.Name` in CDO), but they trigger the Outlook security prompts that you will learn about in Chapter 13, "Understanding Outlook Security." WSH provides an alternative, shown in Listing 10.10, that returns the ID that the user entered to log onto Windows.

---

**Note:** You will see another method for getting the user's name in Chapter 12, "Working with Stores and Folders," that involves walking up the folder hierarchy to the root folder of the user's Exchange mailbox.

---

**Listing 10.10** *Use WSH to Get the User's Windows Logon Name*

```
Function WSHUserName() As String
    Dim objWSHShell As IWshRuntimeLibrary.IwshShell
    Set objWSHShell = CreateObject("WScript.Shell")
    WSHUserName = _
      objWSHShell.ExpandEnvironmentStrings("%username%")
    Set objWSHShell = Nothing
End Function
```

`ExpandEnvironmentStrings` method can also work with other environment variables besides `%username%` to return information about the user's computer, folder locations, etc.

### 10.5.4 Reading the Windows registry

The Windows registry contains a huge amount of information about user and computer settings that can come in handy. You can read the registry with the WSH `RegRead` method.

`WSHListSep()` function in Listing 10.11 is a practical example—reading the character that Windows uses to separate items in a list. The default separator setting for many countries, including the United States and English-speaking Canada, is to use a comma as the separator, but the default for French-speaking Canada is a semicolon. If you are writing code that could be used in different countries, you'll need to know the separator character if you want to work with the `Categories` property available on every Outlook item or with other keywords-type properties.

**Note:** The `IWshShell` object also includes `RegWrite` and `RegDelete` methods for modifying the Windows registry. Those techniques, however, are beyond the scope of this book. Changing the registry should always be approached with caution.

**Listing 10.11** *Use WSH to Get the User's List Separator*

```
Function WSHListSep() As String
    Dim objWSHShell As IWshRuntimeLibrary.IwshShell
    Dim strReg As String
    strReg = "HKCU\Control Panel\International\sList"
    Set objWSHShell = CreateObject("WScript.Shell")
    WSHListSep = objWSHShell.RegRead(strReg)
    Set objWSHShell = Nothing
End Function
```

**Listing 10.12** *Use WSH to Get the User's Time Zone Offset*

```
Function WSHTimeZoneOffset() As Integer
    Dim objWSHShell As IWshRuntimeLibrary.IwshShell
    Dim strReg As String
    strReg = "HKLM\System\CurrentControlSet\Control\" & _
             "TimeZoneInformation\ActiveTimeBias"
    Set objWSHShell = CreateObject("WScript.Shell")
    WSHTimeZoneOffset = objWSHShell.RegRead(strReg)
    Set objWSHShell = Nothing
End Function
```

Another example is to find out about the user's time zone. The `WSHTimeZoneOffset()` function in Listing 10.12 returns the number in minutes by which the user's time zone differs from Greenwich Mean Time.

You will use this function in Chapter 13 to work with follow-up flag due dates on contact items.

## 10.6 Summary

This chapter has used the Object Browser in VBA to explore new facets of the Outlook object model and introduce Collaboration Data Objects and other models. You also learned the standard methods and properties for the collection objects found throughout Outlook. This chapter contains a great deal of practical code that you can incorporate into your projects to display a folder in a new window; pass an Outlook item to CDO and vice versa; delete Outlook items; copy attachments between items; create voting button messages; log errors to a text file; launch documents, programs, and Web pages; and read the Windows registry.

You will see other object models in subsequent chapters, starting with SafeOutlook (or Redemption) in Chapter 13, "Understanding Outlook Security." In Chapter 12, we continue discussing key Outlook coding concepts, in particular the information stores that hold Outlook data and the folders into which stores are organized.

# 11

# *Responding to Outlook Events in VBA*

Before Outlook 2000, the only way to respond to events in Outlook was through VBScript code on a form. Programmers were limited to just the few item events. Outlook 2000 opened the door to programming event handlers at the application level with the more powerful VBA language. Although not every possible event is included in the Outlook object model, the range of available events is enough to keep any programmer busy for a long, long time. Here are just a few of the events for which you can write code:

- Starting Outlook
- Sending an item
- Receiving new mail
- Creating or modifying items or folders
- Switching to a different folder or to a different view

Highlights of this chapter include discussions of the following:

- What event code to place in the `ThisOutlookSession` module
- How to set up folders for monitoring new and changed items
- How to automatically add reminders to birthdays and anniversaries

If you skipped ahead to this chapter, you might want to make sure you understand the material in Part II, "Adding VBA Code," because this chapter requires a good understanding of basic coding techniques.

## 11.1 Application object events

The `Application` object stands at the top of the object model hierarchy and offers events that are useful to any Outlook 2000 or 2002 programmer,

**Table 11.1** *Key Application Object Events*

| Event | Description |
|---|---|
| `ItemSend` | Occurs when you send an item. Includes the item as an argument. Can be canceled. |
| `MAPILogonComplete` | Occurs after the `Startup` event fires, when Outlook has logged on to all services and accounts (Outlook 2002 only). |
| `NewMail` | Occurs when new mail arrives, even if a Rules Wizard rule moves the message out of the Inbox. Does not fire for each new message. |
| `Quit` | Occurs when Outlook shuts down, after all `Explorer` and `Inspector` windows have closed. |
| `Reminder` | Occurs when a reminder is triggered by an appointment or task item or for a flagged message or contact item. If the option to display reminders is turned on, the event occurs just before the reminder is displayed. Includes the item that triggered the reminder as an argument. |
| `Startup` | Occurs when Microsoft Outlook starts, after all add-in programs have loaded. |

plus one (`OptionsPagesAdd`) of interest mainly to developers building COM add-ins (which is beyond the scope of this book). Table 11.1 lists the key events. Only `ItemSend` can be canceled. The arguments for both `ItemSend` and `Reminder` include the associated item so that you can work with it in your code.

**Note:** Two other `Application` object events, `AdvancedSearchComplete` and `AdvancedSearchStopped`, work with the `Search` object added in Outlook 2002 to make it possible to perform more precise data searches, in some case across multiple folders. You will see how to build these searches in Chapter 14, "Working with Items and Recipients."

**Tip:** In the Object Browser, you can see the events for various Outlook objects more easily if you right-click in the Members pane on the right and choose Group Members.

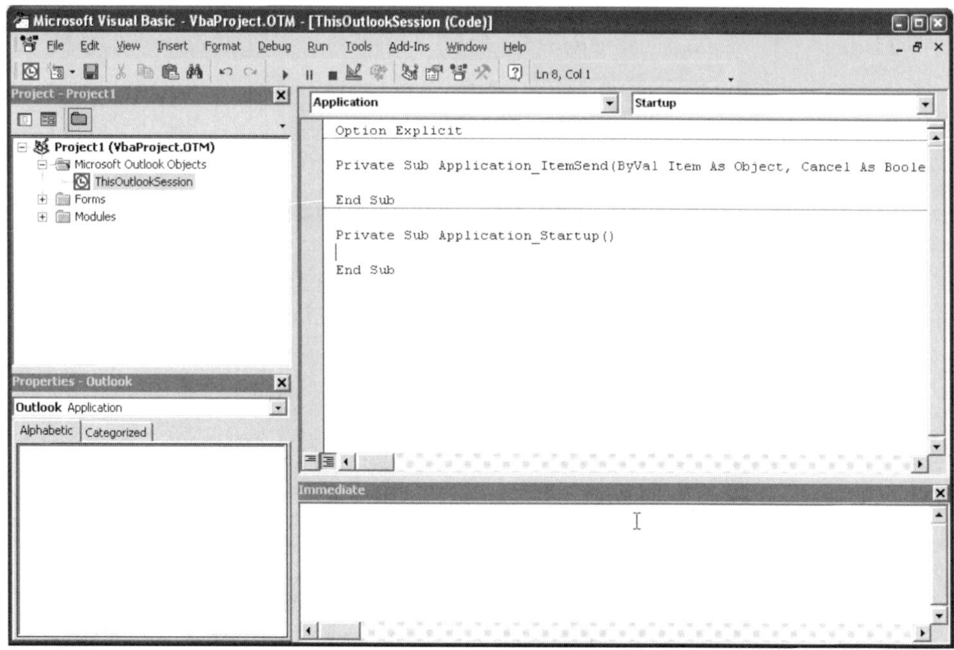


**Figure 11.1** *Place application-level event code in the ThisOutlookSession class module.*

Build code for any of these events in the `ThisOutlookSession` module found in the Project Explorer under Project1 and then Microsoft Outlook Objects, as shown in Figure 11.1. Double-click `ThisOutlookSession` to open it in a module window. This is a special kind of module, called a *class module*, that can respond to events. We'll come back to class modules when we consider handlers for events for objects other than `Application` object.

Since the `ThisOutlookSession` module was created automatically, it will not include an `Option Explicit` statement to force you to declare variables. You should go ahead and add that to the module's declarations section.

To add an `Application` event handler, select `Application` from the list at the top left of the module window. Then, from the list on the right, select the event for which you want to write code. VBA places a wrapper for the procedure in the module window with the correct syntax. Figure 11.1 depicts wrappers for the `ItemSend` and `Startup` events.

**Listing 11.1** *Initialize Key Object Variables*

```
Private Sub Application_Startup()
    g_strUser = WSHUserName()
End Sub
```

### 11.1.1 Startup, MAPILogonComplete, and Quit events

One use for the `Startup` event and, in Outlook 2002, `MAPILogonComplete`, is to initialize global variables. For example, in any module (a regular module, not `ThisOutlookSession` or another class module), add this declaration:

```
Public g_strUser as String
```

Then use the code in Listing 11.1 to initialize this variable when Outlooks starts. That way, you can use it in any VBA procedure. (See Listing 10.10 for the code for the `WSHUserName()` function.)

As you will see later in the chapter, another important use of the `Startup` event is to instantiate other Outlook objects that you plan to write event handlers for. In Outlook 2002, you can also use the `MAPILogonComplete` event instead of `Startup`, especially if you are using a profile that connects to Microsoft Exchange Server.

The `Quit` event is not very useful because all Outlook windows have already closed by the time the `Quit` event fires as you exit Outlook. Therefore, you no longer have access to Outlook items and folders. Also, by the time `Quit` fires, Outlook has already released any global variables.

### 11.1.2 Using NewMail to trigger a new mail pop-up

Outlook offers several built-in options for notifying the user that new mail has arrived, but maybe you want something more customized. Try creating a VBA form such as that in Figure 11.2, which pops up when new mail arrives and displays the time of the latest mail delivery. If you're often out of

**Figure 11.2** *This VBA form is displayed whenever the NewMail event fires.*

your office during the day, this form will make it easy to see at a glance whether any new messages arrived while you were gone—and at what time.

The form in Figure 11.2 has just two label controls. The one to hold the date and time information is named `lblReceived`. Name the form `Ch11NewMail` and set its `ShowModal` property to `False`. Add a command button named `cmdHide`, and add this code to the form:

```
Private Sub cmdHide_Click()
    Me.Hide
End Sub
```

To make the form display the most recent mail delivery time, add the following code to the `Application_NewMail` event in the `ThisOutlookSession` module:

```
Private Sub Application_NewMail()
    Ch11NewMail.Show
    With Ch11NewMail
        .lblReceived.Caption = Now
        .Repaint
    End With
End Sub
```

**Note:** The new mail notification options that you can set through the Outlook user interface do not fire on every incoming message. This applies to both the Rules Wizard and code that you supply to the `NewMail` event handler. We will look at another way of processing new mail by monitoring the Inbox, later in this chapter.

If you set the `ShowModal` property to `False`, you can leave the form on the screen while you do other work. Click the Hide button to make the form disappear until the next new mail comes in.

### 11.1.3 Using Reminder to put reminders in the Inbox

Not everyone likes to be reminded of tasks and appointments with a pop-up message. Some people prefer to see reminders as items in their Inbox. Because the `Reminder` event gives you access to the item that triggered the reminder, you can place a message in your own Inbox. The code in Listing 11.2 creates a new message from the reminder item and then places the new message in the Inbox. Place the code in the `ThisOutlookSession` module.

**Listing 11.2** *Placing Reminders in the Inbox*

```
Private Sub Application_Reminder(ByVal Item As Object)
    Dim objNS As Outlook.NameSpace
    Dim objItem As Outlook.MailItem
    Dim objFolder As Outlook.MAPIFolder
    Dim strDue As String
    Dim objCDOItem As MAPI.Message
    Set objNS = Application.GetNamespace("MAPI")
    Set objItem = Application.CreateItem(olMailItem)
    Select Case Item.Class
        Case olMail
            strDue = " Due " & Item.FlagDueBy
        Case olAppointment
            If Item.Location <> "" Then
                strDue = " (" & Item.Location & ")"
            End If
            strDue = strDue & " At " & Item.Start
        Case olContact
            Set objCDOItem = GetCDOItemFromOL(Item)
            If Not objCDOItem Is Nothing Then
                strDue = " Due " & _
                  objCDOItem.Fields(CdoPR_REPLY_TIME)
            End If
        Case olTask
            strDue = " Due " & Item.DueDate
    End Select
    If Item.Importance = olImportanceHigh Then
        strDue = strDue & " (High)"
    End If
    With objItem
        .Subject = Replace(TypeName(Item), "Item", "") & _
                     ": " & Item.Subject & strDue
        .Body = Item.Body
        .Save
        Set objFolder = _
          objNS.GetDefaultFolder(olFolderInbox)
        .Move objFolder
    End With
    Set objNS = Nothing
    Set objItem = Nothing
    Set objFolder = Nothing
    Set objCDOItem = Nothing
End Sub
```

Because the `Application_Reminder` subroutine is in the `ThisOutlookSession` module, `Application` is an intrinsic object; you do not have to declare an object variable for it.

If you look in the Object Browser, you'll see that the `ContactItem` has no `FlagDueBy` property like the `MailItem` has. The due date is, however, stored in the item in a field that CDO can access, so the code passes the item to CDO, using the GetCDOItemFromOL() function from Listing 10.5, and obtains the value for the flag's due date with the expression objCDOItem.Fields(CdoPR_REPLY_TIME). The CdoPR_REPLY_TIME constant represents the due date for the flag set on the contact. Appendix A has information on resources for learning more about CDO fields and how they are related to Outlook items.

TypeName() is a function that returns a string with the type of object (e.g., "ContactItem" for an Outlook contact).

---

**Note:** Outlook automatically saves unsent messages in the Drafts folder. That's why the code uses the Move method to get the reminder notice into the Inbox. Moving an item to the Inbox does not trigger the NewMail event.

---

There are lots of variations on this technique for processing reminders. For example, you could substitute this code for the With ... End With block to put a shortcut to the original item into the Inbox message:

```
objItem.Subject = "Reminder - " & Item.Subject & strDue
objItem.Body = Item.Body
Set objAttachment = _
  objItem.Attachments.Add(Item, olEmbeddeditem)
objItem.Save
objItem.Move objFolder
```

Only items in your default Outlook Inbox, Calendar, Contacts, and Tasks folders will trigger the Application.Reminder event.

Another possible application for the Reminder event is to forward reminders to another e-mail account or perhaps even to an e-mail address for a mobile phone. However, as you will see in Chapter 13, "Understanding Outlook Security," many Outlook installations cannot send items automatically without user intervention or use of the Redemption programming library.

### 11.1.4 Using the ItemSend event

When the ItemSend event fires, Outlook has not yet sent the item. This means that you can use the ItemSend event to change the item before it leaves your Outbox.

Some mail applications, such as Lotus Notes, can prompt the sender to specify what folder a message should be saved in. In Outlook, you can set

**Listing 11.3** *Setting the Folder for Saving an Outgoing Message*

```
Private Sub Application_ItemSend(ByVal Item As Object, _
                                 Cancel As Boolean)
    Dim objNS As Outlook.NameSpace
    Dim objFolder As Outlook.MAPIFolder
    Set objNS = Application.GetNamespace("MAPI")
    Set objFolder = objNS.PickFolder
    If Not objFolder Is Nothing Then
        If IsInDefaultStore(objFolder) Then
            Set Item.SaveSentMessageFolder = objFolder
        End If
    End If
    Set objFolder = Nothing
    Set objNS = Nothing
End Sub
```

the storage folder for an individual message on the message's Options dialog. If you want to approximate the way Notes works, you can use the code in Listing 11.3 to pop up a dialog box when the user sends the message and then set the `SaveSentMessageFolder` property to whatever folder the user chooses. Place the code in the `ThisOutlookSession` module.

**Note:** Listing 11.3 uses a `IsInDefaultStore()` function, which you will see in Chapter 12, to comply with Outlook's requirement that the `SaveSentMessageFolder` be in the same information store as the Sent Items folder.

Since you are working in the `ThisOutlookSession` module, you can use the same `Application` object that fires the `ItemSend` event. The `PickFolder` method of the `Namespace` object is one of several techniques for getting a particular `MAPIFolder` object, which we'll cover in Chapter 12, "Working with Stores and Folders." Did you notice that setting the `SaveSentMessageFolder` property required the `Set` keyword because it's an object property?

Another common use for the `ItemSend` event is to check for conditions under which you might want to cancel sending the item—such as a message that says it contains an attachment, but doesn't. To cancel the sending on an item in the `ItemSend` event handler, add this statement to your code:

```
Cancel = True
```

For example, Outlook 2002 introduces a new `ShowCategoriesDialog` method that pops up the Categories dialog, where the user can choose to

**Listing 11.4** *Require a Category on All Outgoing Items*

```
Private Sub Application_ItemSend(ByVal Item As Object, _
                                 Cancel As Boolean)
    If Item.Categories = "" Then
        Item.ShowCategoriesDialog
        If Item.Categories = "" Then
            Cancel = True
            MsgBox "This item can't be sent " & _
                   "until you choose a category."
        End If
    End If
End Sub
```

apply one or more categories to an item. If you want to make sure that all outgoing items have a category, you could use the code in Listing 11.4.

---

**CAUTION:** Be careful with the technique in Listing 11.4, because the categories you choose will be visible to recipients who also have Outlook. Don't use category names that you might find embarrassing.

---

## 11.2 Writing handlers for other object events

VBA handling of Outlook events is not limited to events associated with the `Application` object. You can write event handlers for other Outlook objects, too. Setting this up is a little more involved because you must first declare object variables using a `Dim WithEvents` statement. `WithEvents` can be used only in *class modules*—special code modules that establish and work with object classes and their methods, events, and properties. The `ThisOutlookSession` module itself is a class module.

---

**Tip:** VBA forms also have associated class modules. The code placed behind forms like the birthday/anniversary reminder form that you worked on in earlier chapters is actually code in a class module. You can also declare `WithEvents` statements in VBA form code.

---

Follow this basic procedure to set up an event handler for any Outlook event other than `Application` events:

1. Declare an object variable `WithEvents` in the `ThisOutlookSession` module or in a class module that you add with the Insert, Class Module command in the VBA environment.

2. Initialize the declared object with a statement in either the `Application_Startup` procedure, if you always want it to run, or some other procedure, if you want to run it only on demand or in certain situations.

3. Write code in the `ThisOutlookSession` module or the added class module to respond to the declared object's events.

**Note:** The individual Outlook items—`MailItem`, `ContactItem`, etc.—all have their own set of events. However, handling events for Outlook items in VBA is beyond the scope of this book because it involves a fairly complex class module and detection of each item that the user selects in a folder or opens in its own window. We will deal with events for Outlook items solely in the context of Outlook forms in Chapter 18, "Writing Code to Respond to Outlook Form Events."

## 11.3 Explorer events

You should remember by now that each window with an open Outlook folder is represented by an `Explorer` object in the `Explorers` collection. Events related to the `Explorer` object fire when the user changes views, selects items, or switches to a new folder. Table 11.2 summarizes the `Explorer` events.

**Table 11.2** *Explorer Events*

| Event | Description |
|---|---|
| `Activate` | Occurs when the user switches to the `Explorer` |
| `BeforeFolderSwitch` | Occurs just before the `Explorer` displays a new folder; includes the new folder as an argument; cancelable |
| `BeforeViewSwitch` | Occurs just before the `Explorer` displays a new view; includes the new view as an argument; cancelable |
| `Close` | Occurs when the `Explorer` closes |
| `Deactivate` | Occurs just before the focus switches from the `Explorer` to another window |
| `FolderSwitch` | Occurs just after the `Explorer` displays a new folder |

Table 11.2 *Explorer Events (continued)*

| Event | Description |
|---|---|
| SelectionChange | Occurs when the user selects different items. Does not apply to Outlook Today or file system folders |
| ViewSwitch | Occurs after the Explorer displays a new view |
| *Added in Outlook 2002* | |
| BeforeItemCopy | Occurs when the user copies an item; cancelable |
| BeforeItemCut | Occurs when the user cuts an item; cancelable |
| BeforeItemPaste | Occurs when the user pastes an item; cancelable |
| BeforeMaximize | Occurs when the user maximizes the window; cancelable |
| BeforeMinimize | Occurs when the user minimizes the window; cancelable |
| BeforeMove | Occurs when the user moves the window; cancelable |
| BeforeSize | Occurs when the user resizes the window; cancelable |

The BeforeFolderSwitch, BeforeViewSwitch, FolderSwitch, and ViewSwitch events can be triggered either by the user changing the folder or view or by code that assigns a new value to the Explorer's CurrentFolder or CurrentView property.

To make use of these events, you must declare appropriate object variables in the ThisOutlookSession module or another class module and should initialize those variables with code in the Application_Startup event handler in ThisOutlookSession. If you want to detect when a user has opened a new window and then change the appearance of that window, SelectionChange is the best event to use because it ensures that the full user interface is available.

## 11.3.1 Automatically showing the Outlook Bar on new folder windows

You might have discovered that you can open multiple Outlook windows by right-clicking on the name of any folder, then choosing Open in New Window. However, these windows do not show the Outlook Bar. To show how you can use the SelectionChange event to work with the appearance of an Explorer window, we will create the Explorer event handlers in a separate class module. This will also give you a little practice working with class modules and make it easier to back up your event handler module by exporting the class module from VBA.

---

**Note:** You can export the `ThisOutlookSession` module, but when you try to import it, it doesn't replace or update the existing `ThisOutlookSession` module. Instead, it imports as `ThisOutlookSession1`. You then have to copy and paste the code from `ThisOutlookSession1` into `ThisOutlook-Session`.

---

Follow these step-by-step instructions to create your class module and update `ThisOutlookSession` with the necessary code:

1. Choose Insert, Class Module to create a new class module in VBA.
2. In the Properties window, change the value of the `(Name)` property to `ExplEvents`.

**Listing 11.5** *Class Module Code to Handle Explorer and Explorers Events*

```
Private WithEvents m_colExplorers As Outlook.Explorers
Private WithEvents m_objExplorer As Outlook.Explorer

Private Sub Class_Terminate()
    Call DeRefExplorers
End Sub

Public Sub InitExplorers(objApp As Outlook.Application)
    Set m_colExplorers = objApp.Explorers
    If m_colExplorers.Count > 0 Then
        Set m_objExplorer = objApp.ActiveExplorer
    End If
End Sub

Public Sub DeRefExplorers()
    Set m_colExplorers = Nothing
    Set m_objExplorer = Nothing
End Sub

Private Sub m_colExplorers_NewExplorer _
  (ByVal Explorer As Explorer)
    Set m_objExplorer = Explorer
End Sub

Private Sub m_objExplorer_SelectionChange()
    If Not m_objExplorer.IsPaneVisible(olOutlookBar) Then
        m_objExplorer.ShowPane olOutlookBar, True
    End If
End Sub
```

3. Add the code in Listing 11.5 to the ExplEvents module.
4. Edit the ThisOutlookSession module to include the code in Listing 11.6. If you already have an Application_Startup procedure, do not create a new one. Simply add the code from the procedure in Listing 11.6 to your existing routine.

Either exit and restart Outlook, or run the Application_Startup procedure to initialize the new event handlers.

It is possible to start Outlook without first displaying a folder—for example, by using a shortcut to display a new message window. Therefore, the InitExplorers procedure only instantiates the m_objExplorer if it can confirm that at least one Explorer object (i.e., Outlook folder window) is available.

Listing 11.6 introduces a new declaration technique—the New keyword. When you use the New keyword in a declaration, you are creating a new instance of a class, in this case the class module that you named ExplEvents. We need to create an instance of the class before we can call any of the procedures in that class module—for example, the m_events.InitExplorers procedure called in Application_Startup.

---

**Note:** Explorer events allow you to gain sure access only to the last Explorer window opened. Handling all events for all open Explorer windows requires a "wrapper" class module and is beyond the scope of this book. Appendix A has further resources.

---

Other practical applications for Explorer events include the following:

- Turning off the preview pane when you switch to a view with "AutoPreview" in its name so that you don't have two different kinds of preview in a single view
- Turning on a custom toolbar when you switch to a particular folder and turning it off again when you switch to a different folder

**Listing 11.6** *ThisOutlookSession Code to Handle an Explorers Collection*

```
Dim m_explevents As New ExplEvents

Private Sub Application_Startup()
    m_explevents.InitExplorers Application
End Sub
```

- Automatically showing a certain view when you switch to a folder, rather than showing the last view used on that folder

### 11.3.2 Setting a default folder view

If you're like me and have several thousand items in your Sent Items folder, viewing just the last few days' worth makes the folder seem to run faster. Outlook includes a Last Seven Days view that filters out all but the last week's worth of items.

**Tip:** You may want to create your own custom Sent in Last Seven Days view, replacing the Received and From fields with the Sent and To fields.

To make Outlook automatically turn on the Last Seven Days view, you must create an event handler for the `FolderSwitch` event. Add the code in Listing 11.7 to your `ExplEvents` class module.

This code depends on having an m_`objExplorer` object declared `WithEvents` and initialized, as described in the previous section.

## 11.4 Inspector events

Just as Outlook has an `Explorers` collection with each individual `Explorer` object representing a folder window, it also has an `Inspectors` collection, where each individual `Inspector` object represents an individual Outlook item window. The `Inspectors` collection has one event,

**Listing 11.7** *Enforcing a Default Folder View*

```
Private Sub m_objExplorer_FolderSwitch()
    Dim objApp As Outlook.Application
    Dim objNS As Outlook.NameSpace
    Dim objSentItems As Outlook.MAPIFolder
    Set objApp = CreateObject("Outlook.Application")
    Set objNS = objApp.GetNamespace("MAPI")
    Set objSentItems = _
      objNS.GetDefaultFolder(olFolderSentMail)
    If m_objExplorer.CurrentFolder = objSentItems Then
       m_objExplorer.CurrentView = "Last Seven Days"
    End If
    Set objApp = Nothing
    Set objNS = Nothing
    Set objSentItems = Nothing
End Sub
```

NewInspector, which fires whenever a new Inspector opens. Unfortunately, the NewInspector event does not fire in all cases when the user opens a new Outlook message. In Outlook 2000, it does not fire when Word is used as the editor (a configuration known as WordMail). In both Outlook 2000 and 2002, you will get no NewInspector event when you invoke a Send or Send To command from other Office programs, Windows Explorer, or Internet Explorer. Furthermore, using the Next or Previous buttons in an open item window reuses the corresponding Inspector, so you don't get a NewInspector event there either, even though the item being viewed changes.

Further complicating the picture is the fact that, like NewExplorer, the NewInspector event provides only the most recently opened Inspector. To handle events for all open Outlook Inspector windows would require a "wrapper" class module, which is beyond the scope of this book.

**Table 11.3** *Inspectors and Inspector Events*

| Event | Description |
|---|---|
| *Inspectors Event* | |
| NewInspector | Occurs when an item opens in its own window (but not for Send or Send To commands from Office programs, Windows Explorer, or Internet Explorer or in WordMail in Outlook 2000) |
| *Inspector Events* | |
| Activate | Occurs when the user switches to the Inspector window or when the Next or Previous button is used to view another item in an open window |
| Close | Occurs when the Inspector closes |
| Deactivate | Occurs just before the focus switches from the Inspector to another window or when the Next or Previous button is used to view another item in an open window |
| *Added in Outlook 2002* | |
| BeforeMaximize | Occurs when the user maximizes the window; cancelable |
| BeforeMinimize | Occurs when the user minimizes the window; cancelable |
| BeforeMove | Occurs when the user moves the window; cancelable |
| BeforeSize | Occurs when the user resizes the window; cancelable |

Perhaps the most practical use of the `NewInspector` event is to make sure that a particular custom toolbar or toolbar button is visible.

An individual `Inspector` object has the events shown in Table 11.3, including several that apply only to Outlook 2002.

## 11.5 Folders and Items events

Another major category of events is those that affect the `Folders` and `Items` collections—in other words, Outlook folders and the items they contain. This is where Outlook reacts to the creation of a new folder or item, a change to an existing folder or item, or the deletion of a folder or item. Table 11.4 summarizes these events.

The `FolderRemove` and `ItemRemove` events have a severe limitation in that they fire only after the folder or item has been deleted—in other words, when it's too late to do anything about it! One workaround is to set up event handlers on the Deleted Items folder itself to watch for the addition of new folders and items. You will do a folder deletion monitor in the next section.

---

**Note:** Putting an event handler on the Deleted Items folder's `Items` collection to watch for deleted items does not help you recover data if the user presses Shift+Delete to delete the item without going through Deleted Items. Outlook 2002 introduces a `BeforeDelete` event for each type of Outlook item. You may want to incorporate it into your code for custom forms, as discussed in Chapter 18, "Writing Code to Respond to Outlook Form Events."

---

### 11.5.1 Preventing folder deletion

If you work in Outlook with the Folder List turned on, sooner or later you're bound to delete a folder accidentally. Outlook is good about asking whether you really want to delete a folder, but it doesn't hurt to have extra protection. One application of `Folders` events is to monitor the Deleted Items folder for any new folders added to it and ask users whether they really want to delete that folder.

As with other events, you must declare a `Folders` or `Items` object variable `WithEvents`, initialize it, and write code for the event handler. As with

**Table 11.4** *Folders and Items Events*

| Event | Description |
|---|---|
| *Folders Events* | |
| `FolderAdd` | Occurs when a new folder is created; includes the new `MAPIFolder` as an argument |
| `FolderChange` | Occurs when a folder is modified; includes the modified `MAPIFolder` as an argument |
| `FolderRemove` | Occurs after a folder has been deleted |
| *Items Events* | |
| `ItemAdd` | Occurs when a new item is created; includes the new item as an argument |
| `ItemChange` | Occurs when an item is modified; includes the modified item as an argument |
| `ItemRemove` | Occurs after an item has been deleted |

the `Explorer` and `Explorers` events, we will create a new class module for folder events. Follow these steps:

1. Choose Insert, Class Module to create a new class module in VBA.
2. In the Properties window, change the value of the `(Name)` property to `FolderEvents`.
3. Add the code in Listing 11.8 to the `FolderEvents` module.
4. Edit the `ThisOutlookSession` module to include the code in Listing 11.9. If you already have an `Application_Startup` procedure, do not create a new one. Simply add the code from the procedure in Listing 11.9 to your existing routine.

Either exit and restart Outlook, or run the `Application_Startup` procedure to initialize the new event handlers.

It's too bad that Outlook can't remember the original location of the folder before it was deleted. That's why Listing 11.8 must include a `PickFolder` method (which you first saw in Listing 11.3), so the user can indicate where the folder should be relocated.

**Listing 11.8** *Watching for Deleted Folders*

```
Private WithEvents m_colDeletedItemsFolders _
  As Outlook.Folders

Private Sub Class_Terminate()
    Call DeRefFolders
End Sub

Public Sub InitFolders(objApp As Outlook.Application)
    Dim objNS As Outlook.NameSpace
    Set objNS = objApp.GetNamespace("MAPI")
    Set m_colDeletedItemsFolders = _
      objNS.GetDefaultFolder(olFolderDeletedItems).Folders
    Set objNS = Nothing
End Sub

Public Sub DeRefFolders()
    Set m_colDeletedItemsFolders = Nothing
End Sub

Private Sub m_colDeletedItemsFolders_FolderAdd _
  (ByVal Folder As Outlook.MAPIFolder)
    Dim objNS As Outlook.NameSpace
    Dim objDestFolder As Outlook.MAPIFolder
    Dim strMsg As String
    Dim intRes As Integer
    If Folder.Items.Count <> 0 Then
        strMsg = "Did you really mean to delete the " & _
                 Folder.Name & " Folder?" & vbCrLf & _
                 vbCrLf & "If you click No, you " & _
                 "will need to choose the parent " & _
                 "folder where it belongs."
        intRes = MsgBox(strMsg, _
                 vbYesNo + vbDefaultButton2 + vbQuestion, _
                 "Delete Folder?")
        If intRes = vbNo Then
            Set objNS = _
              Folder.Application.GetNamespace("MAPI")
            Set objDestFolder = objNS.PickFolder
            If Not objDestFolder Is Nothing Then
                Folder.MoveTo objDestFolder
            End If
        End If
    End If
    Set objNS = Nothing
    Set objDestFolder = Nothing
End Sub
```

**Listing 11.9** *ThisOutlookSession Code To Handle Folders Events*

```
Dim m_folderevents As New FolderEvents

Private Sub Application_Startup()
    m_folderevents.InitFolders Application
End Sub
```

### 11.5.2 Automatically adding reminders to birthdays and anniversaries

In Chapters 3 and 9, we worked on a birthday/anniversary reminder tool, a VBA form that updated all existing birthdays and anniversaries in your Calendar folder. But wouldn't it be nice if Outlook would automatically add a reminder without the need to run the VBA form periodically? This is a perfect job for event handlers that monitor the Calendar folder for new and modified items.

Add the code in Listing 11.10 to the `FolderEvents` class module created in the previous section. If you created the `InitFolders` and `DeRefFolders` procedures in Listing 11.8, you don't need to add new ones. Just update the existing procedures to include the code from the corresponding subroutines in Listing 11.10. You can put all the initialization code for the various objects declared `WithEvents` in this module into the `InitFolders` and `DeRefFolders` procedures.

Also put the code in Listing 11.9 in the `ThisOutlookSession` module, if you haven't done so already. Restart Outlook or run the `Application_Startup` procedure, then add a new birthday to a contact, and check the corresponding entry in the Calendar folder.

Here are a few things worth noticing in the code in Listing 11.10:

- Even though it's rare for a nonappointment item to get added to the Calendar folder, it's still a good idea to always check the `Class` property of an item of unknown type, as we do with the `If Item.Class = olAppointment Then` statement, before using any properties specific to a certain type of item.
- The `*** USER OPTIONS ***` section calls attention to the key setting for your reminder updates—the number of days ahead of the event.

- The statement `ElseIf Item.ReminderMinutesBeforeStart < 24 * 60 Then` checks whether a reminder has been set for less than a day before the event.

**Listing 11.10** *Adding Reminders to Birthday and Appointments Events*

```
Private WithEvents m_colCalendarItems As Outlook.Items

Private Sub Class_Terminate()
    Call DeRefFolders
End Sub

Public Sub InitFolders(objApp As Outlook.Application)
    Dim objNS As Outlook.NameSpace
    Set objNS = objApp.GetNamespace("MAPI")
    Set m_colCalendarItems = _
      objNS.GetDefaultFolder(olFolderCalendar).Items
    Set objNS = Nothing
End Sub

Public Sub DeRefFolders()
    Set m_colCalendarItems = Nothing
End Sub

Private Sub m_colCalendarItems_ItemAdd _
  (ByVal Item As Object)
    Call UpdateReminder(Item)
End Sub

Private Sub m_colCalendarItems_ItemChange(ByVal Item As Object)
    Call UpdateReminder(Item)
End Sub

Sub UpdateReminder(Item As Object)
    Dim intDays As Integer
    Dim strSubject As String
    Dim blnDoUpdate As Boolean
    ' *** USER OPTIONS ***
    ' set number of days before event that the
    '   reminder should fire
    intDays = 5
    If Item.Class = olAppointment Then
        strSubject = Item.Subject
        If (InStr(strSubject, "Birthday") > 0 Or _
          InStr(strSubject, "Anniversary") > 0) Then
            blnDoUpdate = False
            If Item.ReminderSet = False Then
                blnDoUpdate = True
            ElseIf Item.ReminderMinutesBeforeStart _
              < 24 * 60 Then
                blnDoUpdate = True
            End If
```

**Listing 11.10** *Adding Reminders to Birthday and Appointments Events (continued)*

```
                If blnDoUpdate Then
                    With Item
                        .ReminderSet = True
                        .ReminderMinutesBeforeStart = _
                          intDays * 24 * 60
                        .Save
                    End With
                End If
            End If
        End If
End Sub
```

### 11.5.3 Processing new items in the Inbox

Just as you might use the `ItemAdd` event to monitor the Calendar folder for new birthdays or anniversaries, you can also monitor the Inbox for new incoming mail messages and, thus, build your own alternative to the Outlook Rules Wizard. There are a few caveats: If too many messages are received at once, Outlook will not fire the `ItemAdd` event for each one. Also, it is not a good idea to mix Rules Wizard rules and VBA processing of the Inbox because it's not possible to predict which will process a message first. You might even see the extreme case: A rule fires and performs part of its actions, then `ItemAdd` fires, and then the rule finishes.

For a demonstration of the `ItemAdd` technique, create a new subfolder under your Inbox named "Quarantine." (If you don't create the folder, the code in Listing 11.11 will create it for you.) Then add the code in Listing 11.11 to the `FolderEvents` module, adding to the `InitFolders` and `DeRefFolders` subroutines if you already created those following the steps in the previous two sections, rather than adding new ones. The `DoQuarIFrame` subroutine moves any HTML mail message that contains an <iframe> tag into the Quarantine folder; such messages often carry viruses.

This time, instead of calling a subroutine as the event handlers in Listing 11.10 called the `UpdateReminder` procedure, the `m_colInboxItems_ItemAdd` event handler gets the value of a function `QuarIFrame()`, which returns `True` whenever it moves a suspicious message containing an `<iframe>` tag to the Quarantine folder. This modular approach sets up a framework for putting several VBA-based rules in the `m_colInboxItems_ItemAdd` event handler. If an item has already been handled and moved from the Inbox, you probably don't want to handle it again, so

**Listing 11.11** *Moving Suspicious Mail Messages to a Quarantine Folder*

```
Private WithEvents m_colInboxItems As Outlook.Items

Private Sub Class_Terminate()
    Call DeRefFolders
End Sub

Public Sub InitFolders(objApp As Outlook.Application)
    Dim objNS As Outlook.NameSpace
    Set objNS = objApp.GetNamespace("MAPI")
    Set m_colInboxItems = _
      objNS.GetDefaultFolder(olFolderInbox).Items
    Set objNS = Nothing
End Sub

Public Sub DeRefFolders()
    Set m_colInboxItems = Nothing
End Sub

Private Sub m_colInboxItems_ItemAdd(ByVal Item As Object)
    Dim blnItemMoved As Boolean
    blnItemMoved = QuarIFrame(Item)
End Sub

Function QuarIFrame(objItem As Outlook.MailItem) As Boolean
    Dim objNS As Outlook.NameSpace
    Dim objInbox As Outlook.MAPIFolder
    Dim objQuarFolder As Outlook.MAPIFolder
    On Error Resume Next
    Set objNS = objItem.Application.GetNamespace("MAPI")
    Set objInbox = objNS.GetDefaultFolder(olFolderInbox)
    Set objQuarFolder = objInbox.Folders.Item("Quarantine")
    If objQuarFolder Is Nothing Then
        Set objQuarFolder = _
          objInbox.Folders.Add("Quarantine")
    End If
    If Not objQuarFolder Is Nothing Then
        If objItem.Class = olMail Then
            If InStr(1, objItem.HTMLBody, _
                     "<IFRAME", vbTextCompare) > 0 Then
               objItem.Move objQuarFolder
               QuarIFrame = True
            End If
        End If
    End If
    Set objNS = Nothing
    Set objInbox = Nothing
    Set objQuarFolder = Nothing
End Function
```

you can check the value of `blnItemMoved` before proceding to a second function:

```
blnItemMoved = QuarIFrame(Item)
If blnItemMoved Then Exit Sub
blnItemMoved = SecondRule(Item)
```

If `blnItemMoved` is `True`, code execution exits the subroutine and does no further processing on the message. If `blnItemMoved` is `False`, the `SecondRule()` function is processed.

---

**Note:** Building an `ItemAdd` event handler for the Items collection of the Inbox folder is not your only option for automatically processing incoming items. You could also use the `Application.NewMail` event. However, since the `NewMail` event does not provide any details about the arriving item(s), you would have to keep track of what items were previously processed and, if you are also running Rules Wizard rules, examine multiple folders for new items.

In Outlook 2002, you have the option of running a VBA subroutine from a rule, as described in Chapter 4, "Code Basics."

A fourth approach is to use the `NewMail` event provided by the Redemption library. Redemption is a third-party programming library normally used to lessen the impact of Outlook's security prompts, but which also provides some useful techniques that go beyond Outlook's object model. Unlike the analogous event in Outlook, Redemption's `NewMail` event passes the incoming item as an argument. We cover Redemption in Chapter 13, "Understanding Outlook Security."

---

## 11.6 Reminders events

Outlook 2002 adds a new `Reminders` collection of `Reminder` objects with associated events that fire when reminders are created, modified, or removed; when reminders fire; and when the user snoozes or dismisses a reminder. Table 11.5 lists the `Reminders` events.

For those events with a *`ReminderObject`* argument, this argument represents a `Reminder` object. Keep in mind that only items in the default Inbox, Calendar, Contacts, and Tasks folders can have reminders associated with them.

**Table 11.5** *Reminders Events*

| Event | Description |
|---|---|
| BeforeReminderShow | Occurs before Outlook displays a reminder (before ReminderFire); cancelable |
| ReminderAdd | Occurs after a new reminder has been created; includes the item that fired the reminder as an argument |
| ReminderChange | Occurs after a reminder has been changed; includes the item that fired the reminder as an argument |
| ReminderFire | Occurs right before a reminder fires; includes the item that fired the reminder as an argument |
| ReminderRemove | Occurs when a user dismisses a reminder, deletes an item that contains a reminder, or turns off the reminder for an item; also occurs when a reminder is dismissed programmatically with the Reminder.Dismiss method or removed from the Reminders collection |
| Snooze | Occurs when the user clicks the Snooze button on the Reminders dialog or when a reminder is snoozed programmatically with the Reminder.Snooze method; includes the item that fired the reminder as an argument |

To work with Reminders events, you must declare a Reminders object WithEvents and instantiate it, just as you did with the Explorers, Folders, and Items collections. Follow these steps to create a RemindersEvents class module and update ThisOutlookSession with the necessary code:

1. Choose Insert, Class Module to create a new class module in VBA.
2. In the Properties window, change the value of the (Name) property to RemindersEvents.
3. Add the code in Listing 11.12 to the RemindersEvents module.
4. Edit the ThisOutlookSession module to include the code in Listing 11.13. If you already have an Application_Startup procedure, do not create a new one. Just add the code from the procedure in Listing 11.13 to your existing routine.
5. Either exit and restart Outlook, or run the Application_Startup procedure to initialize the new event handlers.

**Listing 11.12** *Reminders Event Handlers and Initialization Code*

```
Dim WithEvents m_colReminders  As Outlook.Reminders
Dim m_intBusyStatus As Integer

Private Sub Class_Terminate()
    Call DeRefReminders
End Sub

Public Sub InitReminders(objApp As Outlook.Application)
    Set m_colReminders = objApp.Reminders
    m_intBusyStatus = 0
End Sub

Public Sub DeRefReminders()
    Set m_colReminders = Nothing
End Sub

Private Sub m_colReminders_ReminderFire _
  (ByVal ReminderObject As Outlook.Reminder)
    Dim strMsg As String
    Const ME_BUSY = vbYes
    Const ME_NOT_BUSY = vbNo
    Const ME_UNKNOWN_BUSY = 0
    If m_intBusyStatus = ME_UNKNOWN_BUSY Then
        strMsg = "Are you really busy today?"
        m_intBusyStatus = MsgBox(strMsg, _
          vbYesNo + vbDefaultButton2 + vbQuestion, _
          "Busy Day?")
    End If
    If m_intBusyStatus = ME_BUSY Then
        If ReminderObject.IsVisible Then
            ReminderObject.Snooze (24 * 60)
        End If
    End If
End Sub

Private Sub m_colReminders_Snooze _
  (ByVal ReminderObject As Outlook.Reminder)
    Dim objItem As Object
    Dim dteNextReminder As Date
    Dim strItemType As String
    Dim strMsg As String
    Dim intRes As Integer
    Set objItem = ReminderObject.Item
    dteNextReminder = ReminderObject.NextReminderDate
    If objItem.Importance = olImportanceHigh Then
        If DateDiff("h", Date, dteNextReminder) >= 24 Then
            strMsg = Replace(TypeName(objItem), "Item", "")
             strMsg = "You just snoozed the reminder " & _
```

**Listing 11.12** *Reminders Event Handlers and Initialization Code (continued)*

```
                        " for " & vbCrLf & vbCrLf & vbTab & _
                        strMsg & ": " & objItem.Subject & _
                        vbCrLf & vbCrLf & " until " & _
                        FormatDateTime(dteNextReminder) & _
                        "." & vbCrLf & vbCrLf & _
                        "Did you really want to do that? " & _
                        "Click No to edit the item and " & _
                        "change the reminder."
                intRes = MsgBox(strMsg, _
                  vbYesNo + vbDefaultButton2 + vbQuestion, _
                  "You Snoozed an Important Reminder !")
                If intRes = vbNo Then
                    objItem.Display
                End If
            End If
        End If
        Set objItem = Nothing
End Sub
```

Notice that using `Reminder.Snooze` in a `ReminderFire` event handler means that the reminder will not be displayed to the user.

## 11.7 Other events

A few more sets of events deserve attention. Outlook supports several events associated with synchronization of Outlook with an Exchange Server mailbox using a `SyncObject` object. The `SyncObject` object is a named set of synchronization settings or, in Outlook 2002, send/receive group settings. Table 11.6 lists its events.

An event handler for a `SyncObject` event might be initialized in a procedure that uses the `Start` method to perform synchronization using a particular `SyncObject` object. You could also choose to initialize it in the `Application_StartUp` procedure by referencing a particular item in the `Application.Session.SyncObjects` collection.

**Listing 11.13** *ThisOutlookSession Code To Handle Reminders Events*

```
Dim m_remindevents As New RemindersEvents

Private Sub Application_Startup()
    m_remindevents.InitReminders Application
End Sub
```

**Table 11.6** *SyncObject Events*

| Event | Description |
|---|---|
| `OnError` | Occurs when an error occurs during synchronization; includes the error's *`Code`* and *`Description`* as arguments |
| `Progress` | Occurs periodically during a synchronization session; includes several arguments providing information on the process, including the number of items to be synchronized |
| `SyncEnd` | Occurs after synchronization has completed |
| `SyncStart` | Occurs when synchronization begins |

Outlook 2002 adds a `Views` collection of all folder views plus `ViewAdd` and `ViewRemove` objects that fire, respectively, when a new view is added or an existing view is removed.

Finally, in Chapter 21, "Menus, Toolbars, and the Outlook Bar," you will examine events related to the Outlook Bar.

## 11.8 Summary

VBA event handling takes Outlook programming to a new level of utility not available in versions before Outlook 2000. Through events related to the application itself—and Outlook's folders, windows, reminders, and other components—you gain much greater control over what happens in Outlook.

Beyond the events, you also learned two useful methods for popping up dialogs in which users can select a folder or choose categories—`PickFolder` and `ShowCategoriesDialog` (which is available only in Outlook 2002). Furthermore, you saw an example of working with the CDO `Fields` collection to access a property that the Outlook object model does not expose.

In Chapter 12, you will learn more techniques for working with folders and the `Explorer` windows that display folders.

# 12

# *Working with Stores and Folders*

This chapter is devoted to techniques for working with Outlook information stores and folders—creating them, exploring their properties, and accessing folders beyond the default set. Not every user sees the same set of folders. Some may work only with Exchange Server mailboxes and public folders, while others use a mixture of Personal Folders files, IMAP folders, and HotMail or other HTTP mail service folders. The methods you learn in this chapter apply to all kinds of folders.

Highlights of this chapter include discussions of the following:

- Which types of information stores users are likely to see
- How to access the default information store
- When you might want to use a new `Explorer` object to display a different folder
- How to access a folder that resides anywhere in the folder tree
- How to create, copy, move, and delete folders

## 12.1 Information store concepts

Messages and other Outlook items are stored in folders. Folders are kept in what is known as an *information store.* Every Outlook user has at least one information store. For a standalone user, the basic store is a Personal Folders .pst file. (*PST* stands for *personal store.*) For a user connected to Microsoft Exchange Server, the basic store is the Exchange Server mailbox, but an Exchange Server user may also have a .pst file. Users with Hotmail and IMAP accounts are actually using .pst files to work with the data in the folders for those accounts. Outlook synchronizes the data from the server mailbox down to a local .pst file.

If the user has multiple information stores, one will be designated the default. Within the default store, you can always find the default Outlook folders, such as Inbox and Calendar. These are the folders you can access with the `GetDefaultFolder` method on the `NameSpace` object, which you have seen in several earlier chapters. The .pst file for a Hotmail or IMAP account cannot be the default store because these accounts do not support the appointment, contact, and other special Outlook items.

Users connected to Microsoft Exchange Server also have access to *public folders*, a hierarchy of folders for shared access. Exchange Server users may have access to additional user mailboxes, each with its own Inbox and other default folders. For example, an executive assistant may have access to the boss's folders.

---

**Note:** When working with Exchange Server folders outside the basic mailbox store, you must allow for the possibility that the user might not have full access to a folder. A user might be able to see the folder in the hierarchy, but not be able to work with the items within the folder because of permission restrictions on the folder.

---

Regardless of whether the default store is an Exchange Server mailbox or a Personal Folders .pst file, any user may have several .pst files open in Outlook. For instance, I have a .pst file holding materials related to this book and several .pst files filled with archived items.

## 12.2 Information store techniques

You can access any Personal Folders .pst file and create a new one through the Outlook object model. The code in Listing 12.1 prompts the user to enter the path for a file and then uses the `AddStore` method on the `NamesSpace` object to access an existing Personal Folders file or create a new one at the designated location if one does not already exist.

Users will see this .pst file in the folder hierarchy if they choose View, Folder List.

In the Outlook object model, all further work with stores—including removing a .pst file from the current Outlook session—takes place through `Folders` collections and `MAPIFolder` objects that represent individual Outlook folders. The root of any information store is represented by a `MAPIFolder` object, which has a `Folders` collection representing the first level of folders in the store (for example, the Calendar, Inbox, etc., in the

**Listing 12.1** *Add a New Personal Folders .pst File*

```
Public Sub AddPST()
    Dim objApp As Outlook.Application
    Dim objNS As Outlook.NameSpace
    Dim strPath As String
    Set objApp = CreateObject("Outlook.Application")
    Set objNS = objApp.GetNamespace("MAPI")
    strPath = InputBox("Enter the full name and path " & _
                       "for a new or existing .pst file", _
                       "Add Personal Folders")
    If Right(strPath, 4) <> ".pst" Then
        strPath = strPath & ".pst"
    End If
    objNS.AddStore strPath
    Set objApp = Nothing
    Set objNS = Nothing
End Sub
```

default store). To remove a store from the current Outlook session, use the `Namespace.RemoveStore` method, which takes a `MAPIFolder` argument—the root of the store:

```
objNS.RemoveStore objFolder
```

To find out what kind of stores are currently available, you have to use CDO.

The code in Listing 12.2 uses CDO to get the display name of each available store from its `Name` property. The `ProviderName` property of the store indicates what kind of store it is, returning "Microsoft Exchange Server" and "Personal Folders" for the two most common sources of stores. Exchange mailboxes and the public folder store both return "Microsoft Exchange Server" as the `ProviderName`.

As you can see, in CDO, you use the `Session.InfoStores` to access the collection of stores.

---

**Note:** Remember that CDO is not part of the default Outlook installation and that you must add a reference to the Microsoft CDO 1.21 Library before you can use CDO objects in VBA code.

---

In the Outlook object model, the Stores collection is represented by the `Namespace.Folders` object. You can get the names of the stores with the code in Listing 12.3, but you don't get the additional information on the type of store that CDO can provide.

**Listing 12.2** *Enumerate Information Stores with CDO*

```
Sub EnumStoresCDO()
    Dim objSession As MAPI.Session
    Dim objStore As MAPI.InfoStore
    Dim strMsg As String
    Set objSession = CreateObject("MAPI.Session")
    objSession.Logon "", "", False, False
    strMsg = ""
    For Each objStore In objSession.InfoStores
        strMsg = strMsg & objStore.Name & " (" & _
                 objStore.ProviderName & ")" & vbCrLf
    Next
    strMsg = "These stores are available:" & vbCrLf & _
             vbCrLf & strMsg
    MsgBox strMsg, , "Available Stores"
    Set objStore = Nothing
    objSession.Logoff
    Set objSession = Nothing
End Sub
```

If you have multiple Personal Folders files or an Exchange Server mailbox plus at least one Personal Folders file, it is often essential to know which is the default store or whether a particular folder or item is located in the default store because there is nothing to prevent you from having folders or items with the same name in different stores. Listing 12.4 shows

**Listing 12.3** *Enumerate Information Stores with the Outlook Object Model*

```
Sub EnumStoresOOM()
    Dim objApp As Outlook.Application
    Dim objNS As Outlook.NameSpace
    Dim colFolders As Outlook.Folders
    Dim objFolder As Outlook.MAPIFolder
    Dim strMsg As String
    Set objApp = CreateObject("Outlook.Application")
    Set objNS = objApp.GetNamespace("MAPI")
    Set colFolders = objNS.Folders
    strMsg = ""
    For Each objFolder In colFolders
        strMsg = strMsg & objFolder.Name & vbCrLf
    Next
    strMsg = "These stores are available:" & vbCrLf & _
             vbCrLf & strMsg
    MsgBox strMsg, , "Available Stores"
    Set objApp = Nothing
    Set objNS = Nothing
    Set colFolders = Nothing
    Set objFolder = Nothing
End Sub
```

**Listing 12.4** *Test Whether an Item or Folder Is in the Default Information Store*

```
Public Function IsInDefaultStore(objOL As Object) _
  As Boolean
    Dim objApp As Outlook.Application
    Dim objNS As Outlook.NameSpace
    Dim objInbox As Outlook.MAPIFolder
    On Error Resume Next
    Set objApp = CreateObject("Outlook.Application")
    Set objNS = objApp.GetNamespace("MAPI")
    Set objInbox = objNS.GetDefaultFolder(olFolderInbox)
    Select Case objOL.Class
        Case olFolder
            If objOL.StoreID = objInbox.StoreID Then
                IsInDefaultStore = True
            Else
                IsInDefaultStore = False
            End If
        Case olAppointment, olContact, olDistributionList, _
             olJournal, olMail, olNote, olPost, olTask
            If objOL.Parent.StoreID = objInbox.StoreID Then
                IsInDefaultStore = True
            Else
                IsInDefaultStore = False
            End If
        Case Else
            IsInDefaultStore = False
            MsgBox "This function isn't designed to work " & _
                   "with " & TypeName(objOL) & _
                   " items and will return False.", _
                   , "IsInDefaultStore"
    End Select
    Set objApp = Nothing
    Set objNS = Nothing
    Set objInbox = Nothing
End Function
```

an `IsInDefaultStore()` function that returns a Boolean value by matching the `StoreID` of any item with the `StoreID` for the default Inbox folder.

Every Outlook folder in a particular information store shares the same `StoreID` property. Therefore, by checking the `StoreID` for a folder or for the parent folder of an Outlook item and comparing it with the Inbox folder's `StoreID`, you can determine whether an item is in the default store.

## 12.3 Working with Explorers

The `Explorers` collection is part of the `Application` object and represents all the windows currently displaying folders in Outlook. For example, it's not unusual to have both the Inbox and Calendar open in separate windows so that you can switch back and forth between your mail and appointments. Each `Explorer` has a `CurrentFolder` property that returns a `MAPIFolder` object representing the displayed folder.

The `ShowCalendar` subroutine in Listing 10.1 demonstrated how to display a folder in a new Explorer window. However, for efficiency's sake, if your program needs to display the Calendar folder, it should first check whether an `Explorer` displaying the calendar is already available.

The `ShowCalendarCh12` subroutine in Listing 12.5 checks the `CurrentFolder` property of each `Explorer` object and compares it with the `objCalendar` object representing the default Calendar folder to make sure

**Listing 12.5** *Check Whether the Folder Is Already Displayed Before Opening a New Explorer*

```
Public Sub ShowCalendarCh12()
    Dim objApp As Outlook.Application
    Dim objNS As Outlook.NameSpace
    Dim colExplorers As Outlook.Explorers
    Dim objExpl As Outlook.Explorer
    Dim objCalendar As Outlook.MAPIFolder
    Dim strStoreID As String
    Dim strEntryID As String
    Dim blnIsCalOpen As Boolean
    Set objApp = CreateObject("Outlook.Application")
    Set objNS = objApp.GetNamespace("MAPI")
    Set objCalendar = _
      objNS.GetDefaultFolder(olFolderCalendar)
    strStoreID = objCalendar.StoreID
    strEntryID = objCalendar.EntryID
    blnIsCalOpen = False
    Set colExplorers = objApp.Explorers
        For Each objExpl In colExplorers
        If objExpl.CurrentFolder.StoreID = strStoreID And _
          objExpl.CurrentFolder.EntryID = strEntryID Then
            blnIsCalOpen = True
            objExpl.Activate
            Exit For
        End If
    Next
    If blnIsCalOpen = False Then
        objCalendar.Display
    End If
    Set objApp = Nothing
    Set objNS = Nothing
    Set colExplorers = Nothing
    Set objExpl = Nothing
    Set objCalendar = Nothing
End Sub
```

that any visible Calendar folder is the real default Calendar folder, not a folder named Calendar from somewhere else in the hierarchy. If the default Calendar is available, the `objExpl.Activate` statement shows it. If not, the `objCalendar.Display` statement shows the Calendar folder in a new window.

To use the currently active `Explorer` to display a different folder, include a statement that sets the `CurrentFolder` on the `ActiveExplorer` object to a different `MAPIFolder` object:

```
Set objApp.ActiveExplorer.CurrentFolder = objFolder
```

You can use the `Close` method to close any Explorer. However, if you close all `Explorer` objects, including the `ActiveExplorer` (i.e., the currently active folder window), the user may no longer have any Outlook windows open.

## 12.4 Accessing folders

In preceding chapters, you have seen several different techniques for accessing folders:

- The `Namespace.GetDefaultFolder` method to get one of the default Outlook folders
- The `Namespace.PickFolder` method to allow the user to choose a folder
- The `Application.ActiveExplorer.CurrentFolder` object to get the folder currently displayed in the Outlook viewer

The previous section on `Explorer` objects also showed how to use the `Explorer.CurrentFolder` property to get a folder displayed in a window other than the active folder viewer. In this section, you take a closer look at the methods above and learn two more folder retrieval methods: getting a folder from another Exchange Server user's mailbox and getting a folder when you know the full path to the folder through the hierarchy.

Because you can have duplicate folder names and duplicate information store names, just knowing a folder's name isn't enough. In fact, if you look at Table 12.1, which summarizes methods that return a folder, you will see that there is no direct way to retrieve a folder with only its name. You need to know either the mailbox in which it resides—if you're getting another Exchange Server user's folder—or IDs for both the information store and the folder.

**Table 12.1** *Methods That Return an MAPIFolder Object*

| Method | Returns |
|---|---|
| `Application.ActiveExplorer.CurrentFolder` | Folder the user most recently accessed |
| `Namespace.GetDefaultFolder(`*`FolderType`*`)` | Any of the default Outlook folders |
| `Namespace.GetFolderFromID(`*`EntryIdFolder, EntryIDStore`*`)` | Any folder from any information store |
| `Namespace.GetSharedDefaultFolder (`*`Recipient, FolderType`*`)` | Any default Outlook folder from another Exchange Server user's mailbox |
| `Namespace.PickFolder` | The folder chosen by the user from the folder hierarchy |

**Note:** The `GetFolderFromID` method is less useful than the other methods, which are more direct. One situation in which `GetFolderFromID` can be useful is when you are working with a folder using CDO techniques and then want to pass it to the Outlook object model as an object variable, using code similar to the `GetOLItemFromCDO()` function in Listing 10.6.

### 12.4.1 Getting a default folder

The following ten default folders are always present in Outlook's default information store:

- Calendar
- Contacts
- Deleted Items
- Drafts
- Inbox
- Journal
- Notes
- Outbox
- Sent Items
- Tasks

**Table 12.2** *Intrinsic Constants for Default Folders*

| Folder | Constant | Value |
|---|---|---|
| Calendar | `olFolderCalendar` | 9 |
| Contacts | `olFolderContacts` | 10 |
| Deleted Items | `olFolderDeletedItems` | 3 |
| Drafts | `olFolderDrafts` | 16 |
| Inbox | `olFolderInbox` | 6 |
| Journal | `olFolderJournal` | 11 |
| Notes | `olFolderNotes` | 12 |
| Outbox | `olFolderOutbox` | 4 |
| Sent Items | `olFolderSentMail` | 5 |
| Tasks | `olFolderTasks` | 13 |

It's simple to get any of these default folders using the `GetDefaultFolder` method of the `NameSpace` object. Here's how to set an object variable named `objCalendar` to the Calendar folder:

```
Set objApp = CreateObject("Outlook.Application")
Set objNS = objApp.GetNamespace("MAPI")
Set objCalendar = objNS.GetDefaultFolder(olFolderCalendar)
```

Remember that folders are objects in Outlook. Declare folder object variables as the `Outlook.MAPIFolder` type. Then, set the folder object variable to a particular folder, using the `GetDefaultFolder` method.

**Tip:** The `NameSpace` object itself represents the message store—either a Personal Folders file or an Exchange Server mailbox. But you don't have to worry about what it means. Just learn to use its methods and properties.

The single argument for `GetDefaultFolder` is an intrinsic constant; possible values are shown in Table 12.2.

### 12.4.2 Getting the current folder

As discussed earlier in the chapter, Outlook includes `Explorer` objects that represent the Outlook windows the user has open. Because you can have more than one Outlook window open, more than one `Explorer` object may be available.

To access the folder window the user is currently using, use the `ActiveExplorer` method of the `Application` object. To get the folder displayed in the window, use the `CurrentFolder` property of the `Explorer`, as in this example:

```
Set objApp = CreateObject("Outlook.Application")
Set objCurrentFolder = _
  objApp.ActiveExplorer.CurrentFolder
```

You don't necessarily have to use a separate object variable for the `Explorer` object. The above code simply uses `objApp.ActiveExplorer.CurrentFolder` to get the folder that the `Explorer` displays.

---

CAUTION: Don't assume that the `ActiveExplorer` method always returns an actual window displaying a folder. If the user has not yet started Outlook but uses a mailto: link from a Web page to create a new message, a new message item is displayed, but no folder window is visible.

Also, remember that the user can switch folders unless a modal dialog box is active. This means that you should use the `ActiveExplorer` method carefully. For example, if you want to know the folder from which the user opened an item, use the `ActiveExplorer` method in the `Open` event that fires when the Outlook item opens. Don't wait and try to get it in a later procedure; the user might have switched folders by then.

---

### 12.4.3 Letting the user choose a folder

You've seen how to get any Outlook default folder or the currently displayed folder. You can also allow the user to choose from any folder in the Outlook hierarchy using the `PickFolder` method of the `NameSpace` object. A typical application looks like this:

```
Set objApp = CreateObject("Outlook.Application")
Set objNS = objApp.GetNamespace("MAPI")
Set objFolder = objNS.PickFolder
If Not objFolder Is Nothing Then
    code to do something with the folder
End If
```

**Figure 12.1** *Use the PickFolder method to pop up this dialog.*

When this code runs, it pops up the Select Folder dialog, shown in Figure 12.1, in which the user can create a new folder or select a folder. Select Folder is a modal dialog, which means that code execution stops until the user clicks OK or Cancel.

Because the user can click Cancel in the dialog, code using the `PickFolder` method must handle the possibility that the user may choose no folder at all. The expression `Not objFolder Is Nothing` returns `True` if a folder was selected or `False` if the user clicked Cancel. `Nothing` is a keyword with a special meaning—that the object variable is currently set to no particular object.

### 12.4.4 Getting a default folder from another Exchange mailbox

To get a default Outlook folder from another Exchange Server user's mailbox, you must have a resolved `Recipient` object before you can use the `GetSharedDefaultFolder` method. You will look in more detail at `Recipient` objects in Chapter 14, "Working with Items and Recipients." Listing 12.6 uses a dummy message to allow you to get a `Recipient` from a name entered in an input box. After creating the message, the code adds the name to the `Recipients` collection, and then uses the `Resolve` method. Resolving a recipient compares the display name to the names in the Address Book. If the `Resolved` property is `True`, you have a valid recipient and can continue with the `GetSharedDefaultFolder` method.

**Listing 12.6** *Using a Dummy Message to Resolve a Recipient Before Getting Another User's Calendar*

```
Function GetOtherUserCalendar() As MAPIFolder
    Dim objApp As Outlook.Application
    Dim objNS As Outlook.NameSpace
    Dim objFolder As Outlook.MAPIFolder
    Dim strMsg As String
    Dim strName As String
    Dim objDummy As Outlook.MailItem
    Dim objRecip As Outlook.Recipient
    Set objApp = CreateObject("Outlook.Application")
    Set objNS = objApp.GetNamespace("MAPI")
    Set objFolder = Nothing
    strMsg = "Whose folder do you want to open?"
    strName = InputBox(strMsg, "Get Other User Folder")
    If strName <> "" Then
        Set objDummy = objApp.CreateItem(olMailItem)
        Set objRecip = objDummy.Recipients.Add(strName)
        objRecip.Resolve
        If objRecip.Resolved = True Then
            On Error Resume Next
            Set objFolder = _
              objNS.GetSharedDefaultFolder(objRecip, _
                olFolderCalendar)
            On Error GoTo 0
        Else
            MsgBox "Could not find " & Quote(strName), , _
                   "User not found"
        End If
    End If
    Set GetOtherUserCalendar = objFolder
    Set objApp = Nothing
    Set objNS = Nothing
    Set objFolder = Nothing
    Set objDummy = Nothing
    Set objRecip = Nothing
End Function

Function Quote(MyText) As String
    Quote = Chr(34) & MyText & Chr(34)
End Function
```

---

**Note:** If you are using Outlook 2002 or any version of Outlook 2000 later than build 9.0.0.4201, when you use the `GetOtherUserCalendar()` function, you will probably see a dialog asking you to authorize access to your address book. Click Yes to allow the code to run. You will learn more about such security prompts and how to code around them in Chapter 13, "Understanding Outlook Security."

---

**Tip:** The `Quote()` function in Listing 12.6 is helpful whenever you want to put quotation marks around some text (e.g., for use in a message box or in a search string).

It's important to understand that there is every possibility that you won't get a valid recipient or, for some other reason, will not be able to get the folder. If that happens, the statement

```
Set GetOtherUserCalendar = objFolder
```

results in the `GetOtherUserCalendar()` function returning `Nothing`. The calling subroutine has to test for that possible result, as in the following example:

```
Set objFolder = GetOtherUserCalendar()
If objFolder Is Nothing Then
    your code to handle the "no folder" case here
Else
    your code to work with folder here
End If
```

**Tip:** The `On Error Resume Next` and `On Error GoTo 0` statements turn error handling on, then back off. This allows the code to keep running without displaying an error to the user, even if it can't open the other user's folder.

### 12.4.5 Walking the folder tree to get any folder

What if you know the full path and name of the folder? How can you open it? Your code has to start at the top of the folder tree, walk through each level to find a matching folder, and then move on to the subfolders at the next level. Each level has a `Folders` collection from which you can pull a single folder with the `Item` method. For example, if you wanted to look for a folder whose full path is Public Folders/All Public Folders/Mailing Lists/Msexchange list, you could use code like this:

```
Set objApp = CreateObject("Outlook.Application")
Set objNS = objApp.GetNamespace("MAPI")
Set objFolder = objNS.Folders.Item("Public Folders"). _
                Folders.Item("All Public Folders"). _
                Folders.Item("Mailing Lists"). _
                Folders.Item("Msexchange list")
```

Not only is the full `Set objFolder` statement hard to type, but it's also difficult to debug if there is something wrong with the path string—for example, one of the folder names in the middle of the path might be missing.

Instead of using specific code like that in the preceding example whenever you need to get a nondefault folder from the hierarchy, you can use the generic `GetFolder()` function in Listing 12.7.

Do you recognize the `Split(strFolderPath, "\")` expression from Chapter 6? It breaks the path into a string array. Each entry in the array represents a different level of the folder hierarchy. With each iteration of the `For ... Next` loop, the code works its way down the path, attempting to get the corresponding folder by name from the `colFolders` collection. If there is no matching folder, the function exits the `For ... Next` loop and returns `Nothing`.

**Listing 12.7** *Walk the Folder Tree by Parsing the Path*

```
Public Function GetFolder(strFolderPath As String) _
  As Outlook.MAPIFolder
    Dim objApp As Outlook.Application
    Dim objNS As Outlook.NameSpace
    Dim colFolders As Outlook.Folders
    Dim objFolder As Outlook.MAPIFolder
    Dim arrFolders() As String
    Dim i As Long
    On Error Resume Next
    strFolderPath = Replace(strFolderPath, "/", "\")
    arrFolders() = Split(strFolderPath, "\")
    Set objApp = CreateObject("Outlook.Application")
    Set objNS = objApp.GetNamespace("MAPI")
    Set objFolder = objNS.Folders.Item(arrFolders(0))
    If Not objFolder Is Nothing Then
        For i = 1 To UBound(arrFolders)
            Set colFolders = objFolder.Folders
            Set objFolder = Nothing
            Set objFolder = colFolders.Item(arrFolders(i))
            If objFolder Is Nothing Then
                Exit For
            End If
        Next
    End If
    Set GetFolder = objFolder
    Set colFolders = Nothing
    Set objNS = Nothing
    Set objApp = Nothing
    Set objFolder = Nothing
End Function
```

**Listing 12.8** *Walk up the Folder Tree to Get the Exchange Mailbox Name*

```
Function GetMailboxUserName()
    Dim objApp As Outlook.Application
    Dim objNS As Outlook.NameSpace
    Dim objInbox As Outlook.MAPIFolder
    Dim strName As String
    Dim intPos As Integer
    Set objApp = CreateObject("Outlook.Application")
    Set objNS = objApp.GetNamespace("MAPI")
    Set objInbox = objNS.GetDefaultFolder(olFolderInbox)
    strName = objInbox.Parent.Name
    intPos = InStr(1, strName, "Mailbox - ", vbTextCompare)
    If intPos > 0 Then
        GetMailboxUserName = Right(strName, intPos + 9)
    End If
    Set objInbox = Nothing
    Set objNS = Nothing
    Set objApp = Nothing
End Function
```

### 12.4.6 Getting the user's mailbox name

As you will learn in Chapter 13, "Understanding Outlook Security," certain properties and methods trigger a security prompt that requires the user's approval before the program code can proceed. Among these is the `Namespace.CurrentUser` property, which would otherwise be very useful—for example, for providing a name you can stamp on an Outlook item to show who last modified it.

In an Exchange environment, an alternative to the `CurrentUser` property is use the `GetMailboxUserName()` function in Listing 12.8 to walk up the folder hierarchy from the Inbox to get the user's name from the top level of the mailbox, which the user sees as Outlook Today.

This technique works only when the user's default store is an Exchange Server mailbox. For other Outlook configurations, you can use Windows Script Host to get the user's Windows logon name, as you saw in Listing 10.10.

## 12.5 Folder techniques

You already know many useful techniques for working with Outlook folders because you know about collections. An Outlook `MAPIFolder` object is a member of a `Folders` collection. Therefore, you can use the `Add` or `Remove`

**Table 12.3** *Folders and MAPIFolder Object Methods*

| Method | Description | Returns |
|---|---|---|
| `CopyTo` | Copies the entire folder | The `MAPIFolder` object representing the newly copied folder. |
| `Delete` | Deletes the folder | N/A |
| `Display` | Shows the folder | N/A |
| `GetExplorer` | Initializes an `Explorer` object for the folder | The `Explorer` object representing the folder; use the `Activate` method to show it. |
| `MoveTo` | Moves the entire folder | N/A |

method on the parent `Folders` collection to create or delete a folder. We will look at this in more detail in the next section.

You can use the `Item` method to retrieve a folder by name or index. The `Folders` collection also includes `GetFirst`, `GetLast`, `GetNext`, and `GetPrevious` methods for moving through the collection.

For an individual Outlook folder, which is represented by a `MAPIFolder` object, Table 12.3 lists available methods.

---

CAUTION: The Outlook object model and the CDO model use two different types of objects for folders. In the Outlook object model, a folder uses the `MAPIFolder` object. With CDO, a folder uses the `Folder` object. They have different properties and methods. When declaring object folder variables, be sure to use the correct type—`Outlook.MAPIFolder` or `MAPI.Folder`—in your `Dim` statement.

---

### 12.5.1 Creating and deleting folders

To create a folder, use the `Add` method on the parent folder where you want to create the new folder. The `Add` method takes two arguments: the name of the folder and an optional *`type`* constant that defines what kind of items the folder can hold. Table 12.4 lists the possible values for *`type`*.

For example, this statement creates a new folder within an `objFolders` collection to hold Contact items in a folder named Old Contacts:

```
Set objFolder = _
  objFolders.Add("Old Contacts", olFolderContacts)
```

**Table 12.4** *Add Folder Types*

| Folder Contains | Type Constant | Value |
|---|---|---|
| Appointment items | `olFolderCalendar` | 9 |
| Contact items | `olFolderContacts` | 10 |
| Journal items | `olFolderJournal` | 11 |
| Message items | `olFolderInbox` or<br>`olFolderDrafts` | 6<br>16 |
| Note items | `olFolderNotes` | 12 |
| Task items | `olFolderTasks` | 13 |

If you omit the second argument, the folder *type*, the new folder inherits its *type* setting from the parent folder. The following code creates a new folder named Subscriptions as a subfolder of the Inbox folder. Because the *type* argument is omitted, the new folder will be a folder to hold Message items.

```
Set objApp = CreateObject("Outlook.Application")
Set objNS = objApp.GetNamespace("MAPI")
Set objFolder = objNS.GetDefaultFolder(olFolderInbox)
Set objNewFolder = _
  objFolder.Folders.Add("Subscriptions")
```

**Note:** You will get a runtime error if you try to add a new folder with the same name as an existing folder in the same `Folders` collection.

Notice the use of `objFolder.Folders.Add` to add a new folder to the `Folders` collection of the `objFolder` object. You don't add the folder to the `objFolder` itself, but to its `Folders` collection.

To remove a folder, use the statement `objFolder.Delete`. You can also use the `Remove` method on its parent `Folders` collection.

## 12.5.2 Moving and copying folders

You can copy or move entire folders, with all their items, to a new location in the folder hierarchy. Folders contain more than just the visible items. They may also contain hidden items including custom Outlook forms published to the folder and custom views on the folder. Copying or moving the entire folder, rather than just the items in the folder, ensures that those hidden items are also copied or moved.

To copy or move a folder, you need two `MAPIFolder` object variables: one for the folder being moved or copied and a second for the destination parent folder. The syntax for these two methods is similar, but `CopyTo` operates as a function, returning the newly copied folder as a new `MAPIFolder` object:

```
Set objNewFolder = objFolder.CopyTo(objDestFolder)
objFolder.MoveTo objDestFolder
```

### 12.5.3 Folder deployment features in Outlook 2002

Several new properties and one new public method in Outlook 2002 greatly improve the ease with which you can configure an Exchange Server public folder to be available offline and, if it is a Contacts folder, exposed in the Outlook Address Book. The `MAPIFolder.AddToPFFavorites` method adds the folder to the user's Public Folders\Favorites hierarchy, making it possible to monitor the folder's unread items count and use the folder offline. New properties allow you to display the folder as a list in the Outlook Address Book and include it in a special Application Folders send/receive group that Outlook can create automatically. Table 12.5 lists the key new `MAPIFolder` properties for deployment.

**Note:** `AddToPFFavorites` is available in Outlook 2000 as a hidden method of the `MAPIFolder` object. (You can see hidden methods in the Object Browser by right-clicking in the right-hand pane and choosing Show Hidden Members. However, the other deployment-related properties are new to Outlook 2002 and have no equivalents in Outlook 2000.

Outlook 2002 uses *send/receive groups* to combine both account data transfer settings and Exchange synchronization settings that were managed in synchronization groups in previous versions. Normally, an application cannot create a new send/receive group, but there is one exception. Outlook can automatically create an Application Folders send/receive group if you set a `SyncObject` object to `Namespace.SyncObjects.AppFolders`. The `HasAppFolders()` function in Listing 12.9 determines whether the user already has an Application Folders group and, if not, automatically creates it with this statement:

```
Set objSync = objNS.SyncObjects.AppFolders
```

**Table 12.5** *Deployment-related MAPIFolder Properties, New in Outlook 2002*

| Property | Description |
|---|---|
| `AddressBookName` | String; display name used if `ShowAsOutlookAB = True` |
| `CustomViewsOnly` | Boolean; if `True`, shows only views created specifically for the folder |
| `InAppFolderSyncObject` | Boolean; if `True`, includes the folder when performing a send/receive with the Application Folders send/receive groups |
| `ShowAsOutlookAB` | Boolean, for contacts folders only; if `True`, displays the folder in the Outlook Address Book with the display name set in `AddressBookName` |

Once you have an Application Folders send/receive group, you can populate it with folders from the Public Folders\Favorites hierarchy, either manuall or by setting a folder's `InAppFolderSyncObject` to `True`.

Before you can set up a folder for synchronization, the Exchange Server service in the Outlook mail profile must be configured with an offline folders .ost file and Send/Receive must be run at least once to initialize the .ost

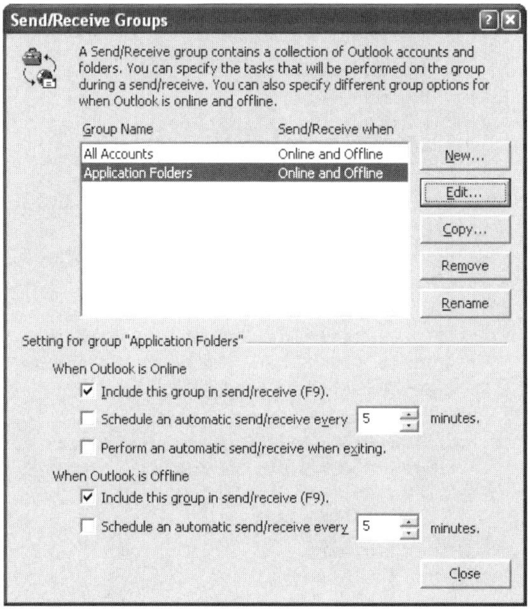

**Figure 12.2** *Use the Application Folders send/receive group to automatically synchronize public folder applications for offline use.*

**Listing 12.9** *Checking the Availability of the Application Folders Send/Receive Group*

```
Function HasAppFolders() as Boolean
    Dim objApp As Outlook.Application
    Dim objNS As Outlook.NameSpace
    Dim objSync As Outlook.SyncObject
    Set objApp = CreateObject("Outlook.Application")
    Set objNS = Outlook.GetNamespace("MAPI")
    Set objSync = objNS.SyncObjects("Application Folders")
    If objSync Is Nothing Then
        Set objSync = objNS.SyncObjects.AppFolders
        If Not objSync Is Nothing Then
            HasAppFolders = True
        End If
    Else
        HasAppFolders = True
    End If
    Set objNS = Nothing
    Set objSync = Nothing
    Set objApp = Nothing
End Function
```

file. Otherwise, setting the `InAppFolderSyncObject` property to True will not turn on synchronization for the folder in the Application Folders send/receive group. Even if `InAppFolderSyncObject = True`, the folder will not have a check mark next to it in the Application Folders send/receive

**Listing 12.10** *Configure a Public Contacts Folder for Offline and Address Book Use*

```
Sub ConfigurePublicContacts()
    On Error Resume Next
    Dim objFld As Outlook.MAPIFolder
    Dim objFavFld As Outlook.MAPIFolder
    Set objFld = GetFolder _
      ("Public Folders\All Public Folders\Public Contacts")
    If Not objFld Is Nothing Then
        With objFld
            .AddToPFFavorites
            If HasAppFolders() Then
                .InAppFolderSyncObject = True
            End If
            Set objFavFld = GetFolder _
              ("Public Folders\Favorites\Public Contacts")
            objFavFld.ShowAsOutlookAB = True
            objFavFld.AddressBookName = "Company Contacts"
        End With
    End If
    Set objFld = Nothing
    Set objFavFld = Nothing
End Sub
```

group. This means that once you set a folder for synchronization programmatically, you can't accidentally turn off synchronization.

The `ConfigurePublicContacts` subroutine in Listing 12.10 demonstrates just how much you can do in Outlook 2002 to make an Exchange public folder available to users. It adds a folder to the user's Favorites hierarchy, sets the folder for synchronization, and adds it to the Outlook Address Book.

Set the `AddressBookName` property if you want the folder to be viewed in the address book with a name different from the folder name.

## 12.6 Summary

We've covered many new concepts and methods in this chapter. You should have a good understanding of the various information stores you might encounter and the relationship between `Explorer` objects and the `MAPIFolder` objects they display. Your toolkit now includes a host of methods for creating, deleting, moving, and locating folders. If you are using Outlook 2002, you can also set up public folders for offline synchronization and make them visible in the address book.

# 13

# *Understanding Outlook Security*

The world changed for Outlook developers in May 2000, when the LoveLetter virus pushed Outlook into the headlines for weeks. Microsoft responded with a security update that not only blocked file attachments that might be viruses, but drastically changed the behavior of Outlook applications by putting up prompts for the user. The two main features of the Outlook E-mail Security Update are as follows:

- Blocking of attachments that Microsoft considers dangerous because they can be used to propagate viruses
- An object model guard that pops up user confirmation dialogs whenever a program accesses address-related properties or attempts to send a message

The Outlook E-mail Security Update also prevents script and ActiveX controls in HTML messages from working by forcing HTML messages to run in the Restricted Sites zone of Internet Explorer and by disabling scripting for the Restricted Sites zone. (The original default setting for Outlook 2000 was for HTML messages to run in the relatively insecure Internet zone.)

Some users and organizations ignored the security patch for Outlook 2000 when it was available only as a separate download. However, since it is part of Service Pack 2 for Office 2000, chances are that many, if not most, will have it installed eventually.

The security patch for Outlook 2000 is optional, but the security features are built into Outlook 2002. While end users can customize the list of blocked file attachments in Outlook 2002, the object model guard can be reversed only in an Exchange Server environment. In this chapter, you will learn the following:

- How Outlook security affects file attachments and object model programming

- How to use the administrative tools for managing Outlook security settings in an Exchange Server environment
- How to use the third-party Redemption library to write code that does not trigger the object model guard
- What other methods are available for coping with Outlook's object model security

When we refer to the Outlook E-mail Security Update or the security update in this chapter, we mean all versions of Outlook that include the enhanced features—Outlook 2002, Outlook 2000 with Office 2000 Service Pack 2 or a later service pack applied, and Outlook 2000 with the Outlook E-mail Security Update applied.

## 13.1 Attachment security

Systems running the Outlook E-mail Security Update can no longer open or save certain file attachments that Microsoft considers dangerous because they could potentially be used to transmit viruses. Appendix B contains a list of these file types. Outlook messages and other items will still contain the blocked attachments, and other programs may be able to access them, but the files will be invisible to Outlook itself, both to users and to code that uses either the Outlook object model or the Collaboration Data Objects (CDO) object model.

Users will also see a warning if they try to send an e-mail message that contains a blocked file attachment. However, the warning message is misleading because Outlook does not actually strip the attachment from the outgoing message. If the recipients are not running Outlook with the security update, they will see the attachment as they normally do.

On the other hand, if the user tries to forward a message containing a blocked file, Outlook strips the attachment from the forwarded copy.

In addition to these Level 1 attachments, as Microsoft calls them, the Outlook E-mail Security Update also supports a Level 2 list. To open a Level 2 file attachment, users must save it to disk first. End users in Outlook 2002 can use a registry value (HKEY_CURRENT_USER\Software\Microsoft\Office\10.0\Outlook\Security\Level1Remove) to demote file types from Level 1 to Level 2. For Outlook 2000 users with Office Service Pack 3 applied, the registry key is HKEY_CURRENT_USER\Software\Microsoft\Office\9.0\Outlook\Security\Level1Remove. (There is no comparable registry key for earlier versions of Outlook 2000.) Level1Remove is a string value; you will need to create it if it does not already exist. Enter the exten-

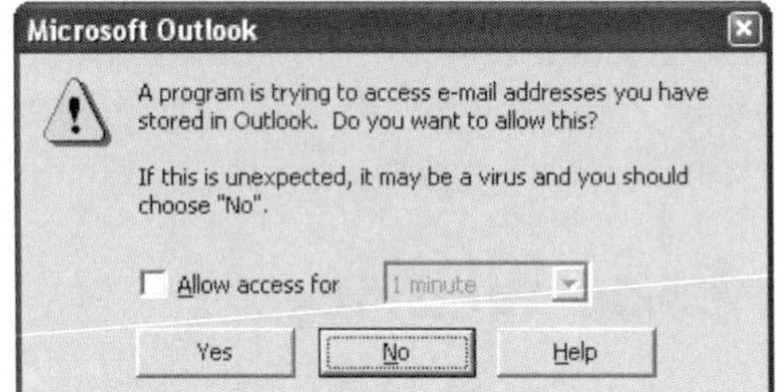


**Figure 13.1** *Users see this prompt when programs try to access address-related properties and methods.*

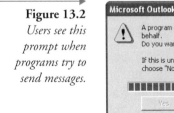

sions you want to unblock, separated by semicolons—for example, `"url;lnk"`—and then restart Outlook. Only administrators in an Exchange Server environment can modify the Level 2 list, as is described later in this chapter.

## 13.2 Automation security

The object model guard feature of the Outlook E-mail Security Update imposes two extreme restrictions on automating Outlook via either the Outlook object model or CDO:

- If a program (including VBA code or code on an Outlook form) tries to access address information in an Outlook item or the address book or to save an Outlook item as a file, the user gets a prompt (Figure 13.1) and can deny access, authorize a one-time access, or extend access for a period of up to 10 minutes.
- If a program tries to send an Outlook message, the user sees a prompt (Figure 13.2) and must explicitly authorize or deny each attempt to send. The user must wait five seconds before the Yes button becomes available to click.

Since neither prompt can be customized, there is no way for the user to know whether the request for access comes from a legitimate program, VBA macro, or Outlook form or from some rogue virus. The object model guard

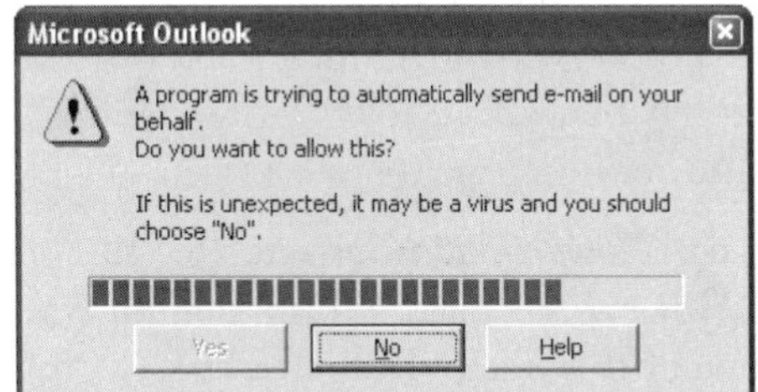


**Figure 13.2** *Users see this prompt when programs try to send messages.*

prompts appear even if your code is digitally signed, as described in Chapter 2, "The VBA Design Environment," or running from a published Outlook form. The only way to modify the object model guard is via the administrative security options for Exchange Server, which are discussed below.

## 13.3 Outlook form code security

Although we don't cover Outlook forms design until Part IV of this book the Outlook E-mail Security Update has a big effect on forms, too. Script on unpublished or one-off Outlook forms does not run at all. This means that you should never check the Send Form Definition with Item box on the Properties page of a message form that includes VBScript code because this will cause the form to one-off. Instead, you should make sure that the recipient has access to the published form.

## 13.4 Customizing Outlook security

Microsoft has provided two ways to customize the security settings:

1. In a Microsoft Exchange Server environment, administrators can customize the security settings by installing a special Outlook custom form in a public folder and using it to configure security options.
2. As noted earlier in the chapter, in Outlook 2002 and Outlook 2000 Service Pack 3, end users can use a registry value to allow access to particular file attachment types that Outlook normally blocks.

You can download the administrative security components from Microsoft (see Appendix A). They include instructions for creating the Outlook Security Settings public folder, setting permissions on that folder, publishing the security form, updating clients so they are aware of the security folder, and trusting Outlook 2002 COM add-ins.

The latest version of the security form consists of three pages. The first page (Figure 13.3) deals with attachments and other miscellaneous settings. Most of the settings that affect how Outlook and CDO code runs are on the Programmatic Settings page (Figure 13.4).

The third page allows an administrator to trust specific Outlook 2002 COM add-ins. However, detailed information on creating COM add-ins is beyond the scope of this book. The references in Appendix A on building

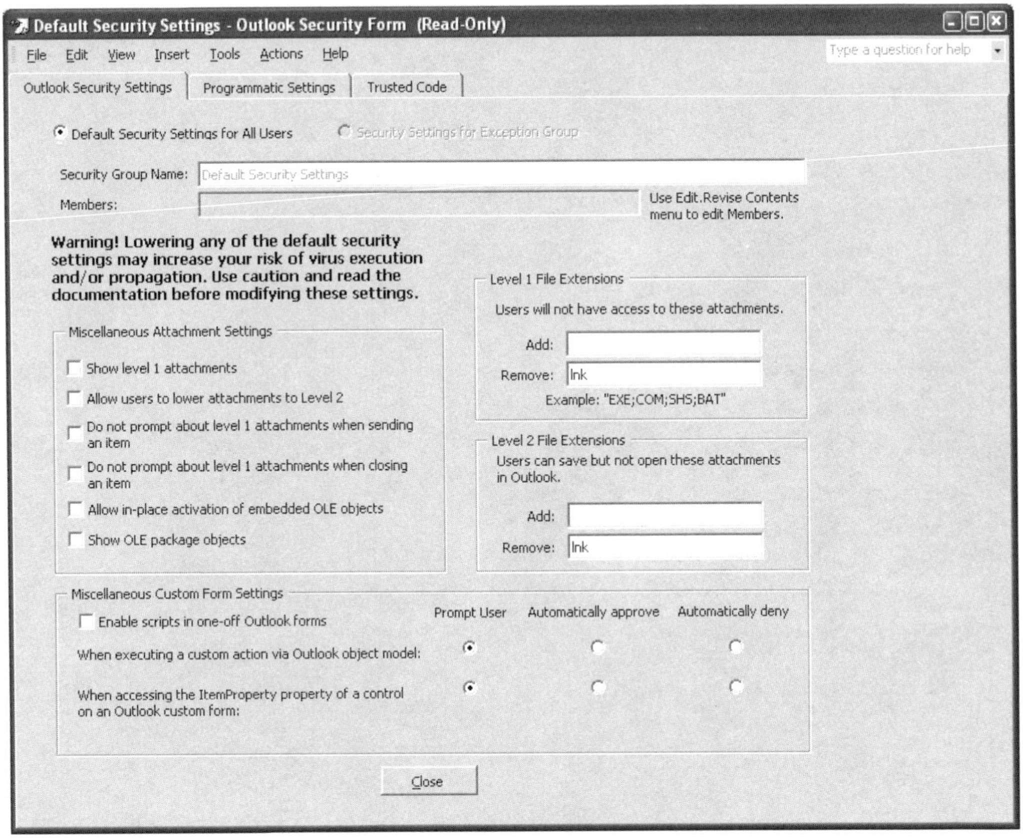

**Figure 13.3** *Attachment and miscellaneous settings on a default security form.*

Outlook 2002 COM add-ins will also show you how to use the Trusted Code page of the security form.

## 13.5 Coping with the security features

How you adapt to the security features in Outlook depends largely on how you're using Outlook's programming features. If you are a fairly casual user with a few helpful macros, you may be able to live with the security prompts. If you are an administrator processing large numbers of items automatically, you may need to avoid properties and methods that trigger the prompt so your code can run smoothly. If you design Outlook forms for use in a multiversion Outlook environment, you may want to test whether the user has a secure version of Outlook.

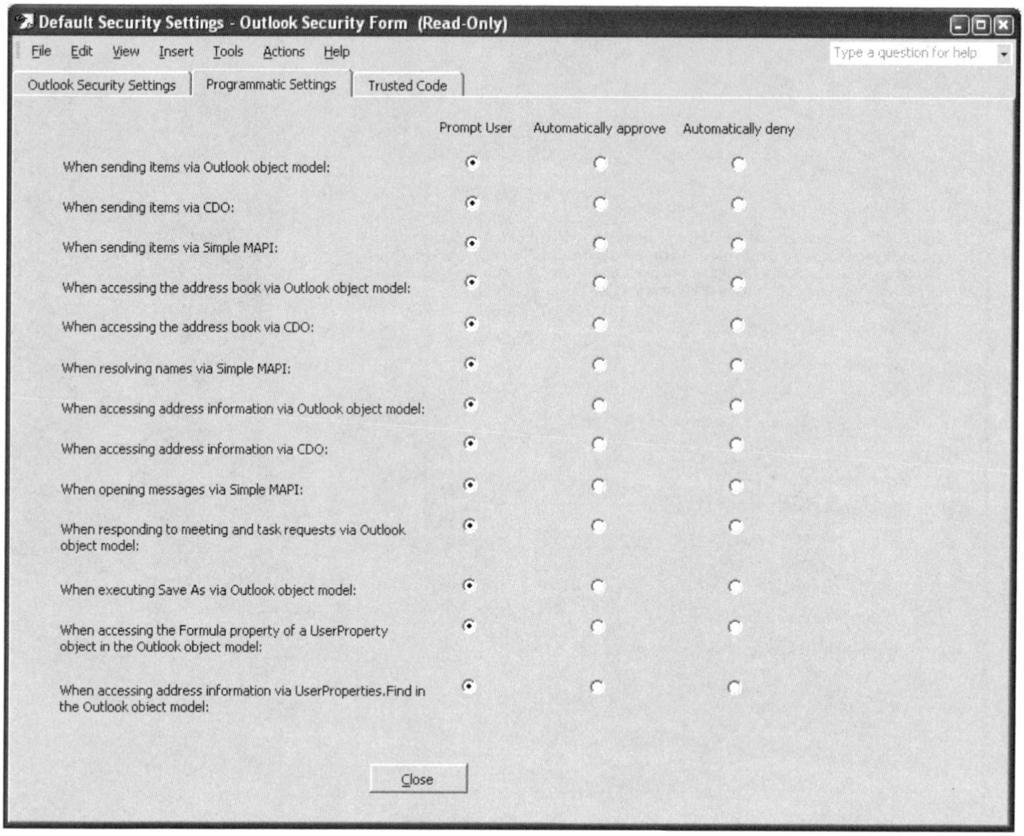

**Figure 13.4** *Settings for controlling the object model guard.*

Ideally, an application that you're planning to share with other Outlook users should never cause any of the security prompts to appear. If users constantly see security prompts and get accustomed to automatically clicking the Yes button, there's a higher risk that one day they'll click Yes and allow a virus to propagate. In practice that means either working closely with the mail administrator in a corporate environment to adjust the Outlook security settings or rewriting your program to avoid the properties and methods that trigger the prompts.

## 13.5.1 Detecting the Outlook version

If you're programming for other people—perhaps for an Outlook form—a minimum strategy might be to provide users with a one-time warning, using a `MsgBox`, that your program will cause certain security-related

**Table 13.1** *Outlook Versions with the E-mail Security Update*

| Product | Versions with E-mail Security Update |
|---|---|
| Outlook 97 | Not applicable because the security update is not available for Outlook 97 |
| Outlook 98 | Version 8.5.7806 and later |
| Outlook 2000 | Version 9.0.0.4201 and later |
| Outlook 2002 | All versions (10.0.x.x) |

prompts to appear. You would then make sure your code can handle the case in which the user answers No to a security prompt. Table 13.1 lists the different versions and which are secure.

You can use the `IsOLSecure()` function in Listing 13.1 to determine whether the user is running a secure version of Outlook in VBA. Listing 13.2 is the same function modified for use in VBScript code on an Outlook form.

**Listing 13.1** *VBA Function To Determine Whether the User Is Running a Version of Outlook with the E-mail Security Update*

```
Function IsOLSecure() As Boolean
    Dim objApp As Outlook.Application
    Dim strVersion As String
    Dim arrVer() As String
    On Error Resume Next
    Set objApp = CreateObject("Outlook.Application")
    strVersion = objApp.Version
    If Err Then Exit Function ' Outlook 97
    arrVer = Split(strVersion, ".")
    Select Case CInt(arrVer(0))
        Case 8 ' Outlook 98
            If CInt(arrVer(2)) >= 7806 Then
                IsOLSecure = True
            End If
        Case 9 ' Outlook 2000
            If CInt(arrVer(3)) >= 4201 Then
               IsOLSecure = True
            End If
        Case 10 ' Outlook 2002
            IsOLSecure = True
    End Select
    Set objApp = Nothing
End Function
```

**Listing 13.2** *VBScript Version of the IsOLSecure() Function for Use in Outlook Form Code*

```
Function IsOLSecure()
    Dim strVersion
    Dim arrVer
    On Error Resume Next
    strVersion = Application.Version
    If Err Then Exit Function ' Outlook 97
    arrVer = Split(strVersion, ".")
    Select Case CInt(arrVer(0))
        Case 8 ' Outlook 98
            If CInt(arrVer(2)) >= 7806 Then
                IsOLSecure = True
            End If
        Case 9 ' Outlook 2000
            If CInt(arrVer(3)) >= 4201 Then
                IsOLSecure = True
            End If
        Case 10 ' Outlook 2002
            IsOLSecure = True
    End Select
End Function
```

### 13.5.2 Anticipating security-related errors

If a user responds No to a security prompt, Outlook returns error 287. The code for the `MsgToContactWithErrorHandling` subroutine in Listing 13.3 creates a new message to the currently selected contact and shows how you might handle this error and encourage the user to click Yes.

If you run the code in Listing 13.3, you should see two security prompts: first the address book access prompt when the code tries to access the `Email1Address` property of the selected contact, and then the send prompt when the code tries to use the `Send` method of the newly created message. You will not see a security prompt when the code sets the `To` property of the message. You can set the `To`, `Cc`, and `Bcc` properties on a message without triggering security prompts.

## 13.6 Using the Redemption Library

Obviously, because not all programs that work with Outlook contact addresses and other properties affected by the object model guard produce security prompts (PDA synchronization utilities, for example), there must be some way to write code that avoids the prompts. Microsoft's official

**Listing 13.3** *Create a Message to the Selected Contact and Handle Possible Security Prompt Error*

```
Public Sub MsgToContactWithErrorHandling()
    Dim objApp As Outlook.Application
    Dim objItem As Object
    Dim objMsg As Outlook.MailItem
    Dim strAddr As String
    Dim strMsg As String
    Dim intRes As Integer
    Set objApp = CreateObject("Outlook.Application")
    Set objItem = objApp.ActiveExplorer.Selection.Item(1)
    If objItem.Class = olContact Then
        Set objMsg = objApp.CreateItem(olMailItem)
        With objMsg
            .Subject = "Test of Outlook Security"
            .Body = _
              "Prompts from objItem.Email1Address, Send"
            On Error GoTo Err_MsgToContactWithErrorHandling
            strAddr = objItem.Email1Address
            .To = strAddr
            .Send
            On Error Resume Next
        End With
    End If

Exit_MsgToContactWithErrorHandling:
    Set objMsg = Nothing
    Set objItem = Nothing
    Set objApp = Nothing
    Exit Sub

Err_MsgToContactWithErrorHandling:
    Select Case Err
        Case 287 ' object model guard - user said "No"
            strMsg = "If you want this to work, you " & _
                "must click Yes at the prompt. Do you " & _
                "want to try again?"
            intRes = MsgBox(strMsg, _
                            vbYesNo + vbDefaultButton2, _
                            "Outlook Security ")
            If intRes = vbYes Then
                Resume
            Else
                GoTo Exit_MsgToContactWithErrorHandling
            End If
    End Select
End Sub
```

solution is to use Extended MAPI (Messaging Application Programming Interface), which won't work with VBA because it requires C++ or Delphi. However, a third-party COM wrapper for Extended MAPI, Outlook Redemption (http://www.dimastr.com/redemption/) provides safe analogs of Outlook item and recipient objects, plus some additional features for Outlook developers that were previously available only with Extended MAPI or CDO.

Once you have downloaded and installed Redemption, you will need to use Tools, References to add the SafeOutlook Library to your VBA project references. Updating Outlook code to use Outlook Redemption requires just a few changes. If, for example, you wanted to work with the `Email1Address` property of an Outlook `ContactItem`, in the presecurity world, as in Listing 13.3 above, you would use

```
strAddr = objItem.Email1Address
```

To perform the same operation with Redemption, you first create a safe Redemption object corresponding to the Outlook object, and then set its `Item` property to the Outlook object:

```
Set objSafeContact = _
  CreateObject("Redemption.SafeContactItem")
objSafeContact.Item = objContact
```

You can then access virtually any property of the object, using code almost identical to the normal Outlook code, without incurring a security prompt:

```
strAddr = objSafeContact.Email1Address
```

The few unsupported properties are documented at the Redemption Web site.

Compare the `MsgToContactRedemption` procedure in Listing 13.4, which does not trigger any security prompts, with the `MsgToContactWith-ErrorHandling` subroutine in Listing 13.3.

One oddity that you will see with Redemption is that when you use its `Send` method, outgoing messages are placed in the Drafts folder, not the Outbox folder. They will, however, be transmitted just as if they were in the Outbox.

In the sections that follow, you'll see a few specific applications of Redemption to common Outlook programming tasks. Throughout the remainder of the book, where appropriate, we'll show alternative code using Redemption to avoid security prompts.

**Listing 13.4** *Use the Redemption Library to Avoid Outlook Security Prompts*

```
Sub MsgToContactRedemption()
    Dim objApp As Outlook.Application
    Dim objItem As Object
    Dim objSafeContact As Redemption.SafeContactItem
    Dim objMsg As Outlook.MailItem
    Dim objSafeMsg As Redemption.SafeMailItem
    Dim strAddr As String
    Set objApp = CreateObject("Outlook.Application")
    Set objItem = _
      objApp.ActiveExplorer.Selection.Item(1)
    If objItem.Class = olContact Then
        Set objSafeContact = CreateObject _
          ("Redemption.SafeContactItem")
        objSafeContact.Item = objItem
        strAddr = objSafeContact.Email1Address
        Set objMsg = objApp.CreateItem(olMailItem)
        With objMsg
            .Subject = "Test of Redemption"
            .Body = _
              "No prompts from objItem.Email1Address, Send"
            .To = strAddr
        End With
        Set objSafeMsg = _
          CreateObject("Redemption.SafeMailItem")
        objSafeMsg.Item = objMsg
        objSafeMsg.Send
    End If
    Set objMsg = Nothing
    Set objItem = Nothing
    Set objSafeContact = Nothing
    Set objApp = Nothing
End Sub
```

### 13.6.1 Virus risks with Redemption

Does using Redemption leave you open to a virus attack? I believe that the risk is minimal. Most recent viruses have already adapted to the Outlook E-mail Security Update. They can harvest addresses from sources other than Outlook address lists and carry their own SMTP engine so that they don't need to send through Outlook. Yes, a savvy, malicious programmer could write a virus that would exploit the presence of Redemption on a system, but such hackers are more likely to go for bigger targets.

Furthermore, the best tactic is to avoid contracting viruses, not to block their ability to run code on your system. Outlook's attachment blocking is actually a good first line of virus defense if your mail server doesn't block potentially dangerous attachments. Coupled with the latest Internet Explorer updates to plug vulnerabilities in HTML-format messages and a good virus scanner to monitor your mail, you should be well protected.

If you do want to add an extra layer of security, the Redemption Web site includes instructions on a couple of its security features that may help.

### 13.6.2 Getting the sender's address

The Outlook `MailItem` object has a `Sender` property but no property that you can use to obtain the From address for a message. Before the Outlook E-mail Security Update, the standard method for getting the sender's address was to use the CDO `GetFromAddressCDO()` function shown in Listing 13.5. (You can test it with the `TestGetFromAddressCDO` subroutine.)

Notice the error-handling to deal with the possible case where the user says No to the address book security prompt. The error number in CDO is different from that provided by Outlook objects.

An alternative `GetFromAddressR()` function using Redemption is shown in Listing 13.6, along with a subroutine you can use to test it. Redemption objects use `Fields` collections in much the same way as CDO objects to access MAPI properties that don't have friendly names. (You might want to turn back to Listing 11.2 to see a CDO example of `Fields`.)

The `GetFromAddressR()` function uses an object you have not seen before—`AddressEntry`. This object is present in Outlook, CDO, and Redemption and represents the details of a resolved recipient, which appears in the user interface as underlined. The `GetFromAddressR()` function also goes one step further than the CDO function and checks to see whether the item had an Internet (SMTP) or Exchange (EX) sender. If it's an EX sender, the code uses a specific field on the `AddressEntry` object to get the default SMTP address from the Exchange user's address record. If you use the `AddressEntry.Address` property on an EX recipient or sender, you get an address in X.400 format, not an easily understandable SMTP address.

---

**Note:** In Chapter 14, you will see Outlook and Redemption code for getting the Reply-to address from a message, which can sometimes be more useful than the From address.

---

**Listing 13.5** *Use CDO To Get the Sender's Address If You Don't Mind a Security Prompt*

```
Function GetFromAddressCDO(objMsg As Outlook.MailItem) _
  As String
    Dim objSession As MAPI.Session
    Dim objCDOMsg As MAPI.Message
    Dim strEntryID As String
    Dim strStoreID As String
    Set objSession = CreateObject("MAPI.Session")
    objSession.Logon "", "", False, False
    strEntryID = objMsg.EntryID
    strStoreID = objMsg.Parent.StoreID
    Set objCDOMsg = objSession.GetMessage(strEntryID, _
                                          strStoreID)
    On Error Resume Next
    GetFromAddressCDO = objCDOMsg.Sender.Address
    If Err = 80070005 Then
        MsgBox "The Outlook E-mail Security Update " & _
               "is apparently installed on this " & _
               "machine. You must response Yes to " & _
               "the prompt about accessing e-mail " & _
               "addresses if you want to get the " & _
               "From address.", vbExclamation, _
               "GetFromAddressCDO"
    End If
    Set objCDOMsg = Nothing
    objSession.Logoff
    Set objSession = Nothing
End Function

Sub TestGetFromAddressCDO()
    Dim objApp As Outlook.Application
    Dim objItem As Object
    Set objApp = CreateObject("Outlook.Application")
    Set objItem = objApp.ActiveExplorer.Selection.Item(1)
    If objItem.Class = olMail And objItem.Sent Then
        MsgBox GetFromAddressCDO(objItem)
    End If
    Set objItem = Nothing
    Set objApp = Nothing
End Sub
```

### 13.6.3 Sending reminders as mail messages

In Chapter 11, "Responding to Outlook Events in VBA," you saw how to use the `Application.Reminder` event to create reminder messages in the Inbox. Another useful application might be to send reminder messages to another mail address, perhaps a mobile phone compatible with Short Mes-

**Listing 13.6** *Use Redemption To Get the Sender's Address Without a Security Prompt*

```
Function GetFromAddressR(objMsg As MailItem) _
  As String
    Dim strType As String
    Dim objSenderAE As Redemption.AddressEntry
    Dim objSMail    As Redemption.SafeMailItem
    Const PR_SENDER_ADDRTYPE = &HC1E001E
    Const PR_EMAIL = &H39FE001E
    Set objSMail = CreateObject("Redemption.SafeMailItem")
    objSMail.Item = objMsg
    strType = objSMail.Fields(PR_SENDER_ADDRTYPE)
    Set objSenderAE = objSMail.Sender
    If Not objSenderAE Is Nothing Then
        If strType = "SMTP" Then
            GetFromAddressR = objSenderAE.Address
        ElseIf strType = "EX" Then
            GetFromAddressR = objSenderAE.Fields(PR_EMAIL)
        End If
     End If
     Set objSenderAE = Nothing
     Set objSMail = Nothing
End Function

Sub TestGetFromAddressR()
    Dim objApp As Outlook.Application
    Dim objItem As Object
    Set objApp = CreateObject("Outlook.Application")
    Set objItem = objApp.ActiveExplorer.Selection.Item(1)
    If objItem.Class = olMail And objItem.Sent Then
        MsgBox GetFromAddressR(objItem)
    End If
    Set objItem = Nothing
    Set objApp = Nothing
End Sub
```

sage Service (SMS) messages. Without Redemption, this type of application would be impractical because you wouldn't necessarily be at your desk to click the prompt (refer back to Figure 13.2) every time Outlook needed to send a message. Place the code in Listing 13.7 in the `ThisOutlookSession` module in VBA, replacing any other `Application_Reminder` event handler you might already have.

Redemption handles calls to blocked properties and methods, but for built-in properties that aren't blocked, such as `Body` or `Subject`, it forwards the request to the Outlook object assigned with the `Item` property.

**Listing 13.7** *Use Redemption To Forward Reminder Notices to Another E-mail Address*

```
Private Sub Application_Reminder(ByVal Item As Object)
    Dim objMail As Outlook.MailItem
    Dim objSafeMail As Redemption.SafeMailItem
    Dim objSafeCont As Redemption.SafeContactItem
    Dim strAddress As String
    Dim strDue As String
    Dim dteDue As Date
    Const PR_REPLY_TIME = &H300040
    ' *** USER OPTIONS ***
    strAddress = "sms@outlookforms.com"
    Select Case Item.Class
        Case olMail
            strDue = " Due " & Item.FlagDueBy
        Case olAppointment
            If Item.Location <> "" Then
                strDue = " (" & Item.Location & ")"
            End If
            strDue = strDue & " At " & Item.Start
        Case olContact
            Set objSafeCont = _
              CreateObject("Redemption.SafeContactItem")
            objSafeCont.Item = Item
            dteDue = objSafeCont.Fields(PR_REPLY_TIME)
            strDue = " Due " & DateTZAdjust(dteDue)
        Case olTask
            strDue = " Due " & Item.DueDate
    End Select
    If Item.Importance = olImportanceHigh Then
        strDue = strDue & " (High)"
    End If
    Set objMail = Application.CreateItem(olMailItem)
    With objMail
        .Subject = Replace(TypeName(Item), "Item", "") & _
                    ": " & Item.Subject & strDue
        .Body = Item.Body
        .To = strAddress
    End With
    Set objSafeMail = _
      CreateObject("Redemption.SafeMailItem")
    objSafeMail.Item = objMail
    objSafeMail.Send
    Set objMail = Nothing
    Set objSafeMail = Nothing
    Set objSafeCont = Nothing
End Sub

Function DateTZAdjust(dteDate) As Date
    Dim lngMinutes As Long
    lngMinutes = WSHTimeZoneOffset()
    DateTZAdjust = DateAdd("n", -lngMinutes, dteDate)
End Function
```

**Note:** If you set any properties of an Outlook item, save the item before assigning it to a Redemption object with the Redemption object's `Item` property. Otherwise, any changes that you made to the Outlook item will not be accessible in the Redemption item.

`WSHTimeZoneOffset()` is a function from Listing 10.12 that returns the number of minutes that the user's time zone differs from Greenwich Mean Time. It's needed here to adjust the due date for a flagged contact, because Outlook stores and the Redemption `Fields` collection returns the date in Greenwich Mean Time. Compare with the `Application_Reminder` event handler in Listing 11.2.

### 13.6.4 Handling new mail

In addition to its ability to work around the object model guard, Redemption's tight connection with Extended MAPI gives it the ability to do some things that Outlook can't. Some of these features are quite advanced; others are useful to even the novice Outlook developer.

For example, as you saw in Chapter 11, Outlook does not provide an easy, sure way to deal with all new incoming messages. Although Chapter 4 showed how to write VBA code to run from an Outlook rule, you might want a completely VBA solution. To that end, Redemption provides a `NewMail` event that returns the actual new message as the `Item` argument. Listing 13.8 shows the `ConvertHTMLToPlain` subroutine from Chapter 4

**Listing 13.8** *Use Redemption to Process Incoming Messages Individually*

```
Dim WithEvents m_red As Redemption.MAPIUtils

Private Sub Application_Startup()
    Set m_red = CreateObject("Redemption.MAPIUtils")
End Sub

Private Sub m_red_NewMail(ByVal Item As Object)
    If Item.GetInspector.EditorType = olEditorHTML Then
       Item.BodyFormat = olFormatPlain
       Item.Save
    End If
    Debug.Print Item.Subject & vbTab & _
      FormatDateTime(Now, vbShortTime)
End Sub
```

converted into an event handler for Redemption's `NewMail` event. All the code in Listing 13.8 should go in the `ThisOutlookSession` module; if you already have an `Application_Startup` event handler, edit it to include the code in Listing 13.8 rather than replacing it.

Processing messages with `NewMail` may not be appropriate if you tend to receive a large number of messages all in one batch because it may put too great a burden on your system.

## 13.7 Summary

The enhanced security in Outlook 2002 and the most recent versions of Outlook 2000 may require you to rethink your approach to programming Outlook. At the very least, your code will need to handle any errors that occur when the user chooses not to authorize access to blocked properties and methods. In an Exchange Server environment, you may have the option to use administrative tools to adjust the security settings both for attachments and for the object model guard. Another option is to rewrite portions of your code to the third-party Redemption programming library, which offers analogs to Outlook item objects that do not trigger security prompts on blocked properties and methods.

# 14

# *Working with Items and Recipients*

In Chapter 12, you explored the workings of Outlook folders and the Explorer windows that display them. In this chapter, you will work with individual Outlook items and their Inspector windows. You will learn about the many methods available for Outlook items and get some tips for dealing with recipients and item bodies.

Highlights of this chapter include discussions of the following:

- How to work with the Inspector objects that display Outlook items
- How to create, move, copy, delete, and perform other common item tasks
- How to display the Select Names dialog box from code
- Where to find the e-mail address for the sender or recipient of a message
- How to build a better `NextBusinessDay()` function

## 14.1 Working with Inspectors

The `Inspectors` collection is part of the `Application` object and represents all Outlook items displayed in their own windows. You have seen the `ActiveInspector` object in several previous chapters where it was used to create macros that operate on the currently displayed item. You can use this code to set an object variable to the current item:

```
Set objApp = CreateObject("Outlook.Application")
Set objInsp = objApp.ActiveInspector
If Not objInsp Is Nothing Then
    Set objItem = objInsp.CurrentItem
End If
```

**Table 14.1** *The savemode Argument Values for the Close Method*

| Option | *savemode* | Value |
|---|---|---|
| Close without saving changes | `olDiscard` | 1 |
| If the item was changed, prompt the user to save changes | `olPromptForSave` | 2 |
| Close and save changes | `olSave` | 0 |

If an `Inspector` showing the desired item is already available, you can use the `Activate` method to switch to that `Inspector`:

```
objInsp.Activate
```

Use the `Close` method to close any `Inspector`, using this syntax:

```
objIns.Close savemode
```

You must supply a value for the *`savemode`* argument. Table 14.1 lists possible values.

The code in Listing 14.1 closes all `Inspector` windows then redisplays the last item viewed. It uses the `GetInspector` method on the item most recently displayed (`ActiveInspector.CurrentItem`) to get a new `Inspector` and applies the `Activate` method to show it.

**Listing 14.1** *Close All but the Current Inspector Window*

```
Sub CloseAllButCurrentInspector()
    Dim objApp As Outlook.Application
    Dim objInspectors As Outlook.Inspectors
    Dim objInspector As Outlook.Inspector
    Dim objItemKeep As Object
    Set objApp = CreateObject("Outlook.Application")
    Set objInspectors = objApp.Inspectors
    Set objItemKeep = objApp.ActiveInspector.CurrentItem
    Do Until objInspectors.Count = 0
        objInspectors.Item(1).Close olPromptForSave
    Loop
    Set objInspector = objItemKeep.GetInspector
    objInspector.Activate
    Set objApp = Nothing
    Set objInspectors = Nothing
    Set objInspector = Nothing
    Set objItemKeep = Nothing
End Sub
```

You do not actually need to invoke an `Inspector` in order to show a particular item, because you can use the `Display` method to show any item. In the `CloseAllButCurrentInspector` subroutine, you could replace these two lines:

```
Set objInspector = objItemKeep.GetInspector
objInspector.Activate
```

with this single line:

```
objItemKeep.Display
```

In the following sections, we'll review the wide range of techniques for creating new items and accessing existing Outlook items. You will also see what methods Outlook items have in common and which are particular to specific item types.

## 14.2 Creating items

Outlook has three main methods for creating new items. Which one should you use? It depends on whether you are creating a standard item or using a custom template or form. (You will learn about creating custom forms in Part IV of this book.) Table 14.2 summarizes the available methods. Listing 14.2 provides an example of each creation method.

The `CreateItem` method creates an item in the default folder for that type of item (for example, the Tasks folder). If you need to create an item in a different folder or need to create an item that uses a custom form, you must use one of the other two methods.

**Table 14.2** *Item Creation Methods*

| Method | Use |
|---|---|
| `Application.CreateItem(`*`itemtype`*`)` | Create a new Outlook item, using one of the constants in Table 14.3 as the *`itemtype`* argument |
| `Application.CreateItemFromTemplate (`*`templatepath`*`, [`*`infolder`*`])` | Create a new item from an Outlook template .oft file or a saved .msg message file, using the *`templatepath`* to the file and optionally specifying the *`infolder`* (a `MAPIFolder` object) where the item should be created |
| `MAPIFolder.Items.Add([`*`type`*`])` | Create a new item in the folder, with the option of specifying a published custom form or a particular Outlook item type as an argument |

**Listing 14.2** *Create New Outlook Items by Three Methods*

```
Function NewStandardTask() As TaskItem
    Dim objApp As Outlook.Application
    Set objApp = CreateObject("Outlook.Application")
    Set NewStandardTask = objApp.CreateItem(olTaskItem)
    Set objApp = Nothing
End Function

Function NewCustomAppointment() As AppointmentItem
    Dim objApp As Outlook.Application
    Dim objNS As Outlook.NameSpace
    Dim strPath As String
    Set objApp = CreateObject("Outlook.Application")
    Set objNS = objApp.GetNamespace("MAPI")
    strPath = _
      "C:\Program Files\Microsoft Office\Templates\" & _
      "MyAppt.oft"
    Set NewCustomAppointment = _
      objApp.CreateItemFromTemplate(strPath)
    Set objApp = Nothing
    Set objNS = Nothing
End Function

Function NewCustomContact() As ContactItem
    Dim objApp As Outlook.Application
    Dim objNS As Outlook.NameSpace
    Dim objFolder As Outlook.MAPIFolder
    Dim objNewContact As Outlook.ContactItem
    Set objApp = CreateObject("Outlook.Application")
    Set objNS = objApp.GetNamespace("MAPI")
    Set objFolder = _
      objNS.GetDefaultFolder(olFolderContacts)
    Set objNewContact = _
      objFolder.Items.Add("IPM.Contact.MyContact")
    Set NewCustomContact = objNewContact
    Set objApp = Nothing
    Set objNS = Nothing
    Set objFolder = Nothing
    Set objNewContact = Nothing
End Function
```

The `CreateItemFromTemplate` method is rarely used because there are significant problems with using items created from .oft template files, as you will learn in Chapter 20, "Common Outlook Form and Item Techniques." You may, however, find it useful for opening copies of .msg files, Outlook items that have been saved as system files.

The `Items.Add` method can take any of the following values as its *`type`* argument:

- The message class of a custom form (which you set when you publish the form)
- Any of the constants in Table 14.3, except `olDistributionListItem`
- For Outlook 2002, `olExcelWorkSheetItem` (literal value 8), `olPowerPointShowItem` (10), or `olWordDocumentItem` (9) to create a new Office document in the folder

If you omit the *`type`* argument from `Items.Add`, Outlook creates a new item in the folder using the default item type for that folder—for example, a Contact item in a folder created to hold contacts.

**Note:** If you create an Outlook item using code on a VBA form, make sure that either the VBA form is modeless or that you unload it before you display the new Outlook item. Otherwise, you will get a Dialog Box is Open error.

If the newly created item is an Outlook item, it is not permanently stored in an Outlook folder until it is saved or sent, either by the user or via code. After creating a new item, you may also want to use code to set certain properties before you display the item to the user or save it. This code

**Table 14.3** *Constants for Use with the CreateItem Method*

| Item | *type* | Value |
|---|---|---|
| Message | `olMailItem` | 0 |
| Appointment | `olAppointmentItem` | 1 |
| Contact | `olContactItem` | 2 |
| Task | `olTaskItem` | 3 |
| Journal entry | `olJournalItem` | 4 |
| Note | `olNoteItem` | 5 |
| Post | `olPostItem` | 6 |
| Distribution list | `olDistributionListItem` | 7 |

snippet creates a new task using the `NewStandardTask()` function in Listing 14.2, sets the due date for one week from today, then displays the task:

```
Set objTask = NewStandardTask()
objTask.DueDate = Date + 7
objTask.Display
```

In Outlook 2002 only, if the newly created item is an Office document, it is saved automatically.

In addition to the three methods listed in Table 14.3, a number of other methods return new items, including `Copy`, `Reply`, `ReplyToAll`, `Forward`, `ForwardAsVcal`, and `ForwardAsVcard`. As you will see in Chapter 20, "Common Outlook Form and Item Techniques," voting buttons and other custom actions on Outlook forms also create new items.

## 14.3 Accessing items

In the code samples in previous chapters, you have seen several methods to access a particular existing item—especially an item selected in a folder and a currently displayed item. This section explains all the different ways to access items, including search methods.

### 14.3.1 Getting the current item

Where `Explorer` objects represent Outlook folder windows, `Inspector` objects correspond to Outlook item windows. Because you can have more than one Outlook window open, more than one `Inspector` object may be available.

To access the item window that the user is currently using, use the `ActiveInspector` method of the `Application` object. To get the actual item that the user sees in that window, use the `CurrentItem` property of the `Inspector`, as in the following example:

```
Dim objApp As Outlook.Application
Dim objItem As Object
Set objApp = CreateObject("Outlook.Application")
Set objItem = objApp.ActiveInspector.CurrentItem
```

The current item could turn out to be any kind of Outlook item—a message, a contact, even a note. Because you can't predict the type of item, you must use the generic `Dim objItem as Object` statement to declare the object variable. In most cases, your code will need to check what kind of

**Table 14.4** *TypeName() and Class Values for Outlook Item Object Variables*

| Object | TypeName(*object*) | *object*.Class | Class Value |
|---|---|---|---|
| Message | "MailItem" | olMail | 43 |
| Appointment | "AppointmentItem" | olAppointment | 26 |
| Meeting request | "AppointmentItem" | olMeetingRequest | 53 |
| Contact | "ContactItem" | olContact | 40 |
| Distribution list | "DistListItem" | olDistributionList | 69 |
| Journal | "JournalItem" | olJournal | 42 |
| Note | "NoteItem" | olNote | 44 |
| Post | "PostItem" | olPost | 45 |
| Task | "TaskItem" | olTask | 48 |
| Task Request | "TaskItem" | olTaskRequest | 49 |
| No object set | "Nothing" | error occurs | |

object it is before working with properties and methods. For this, you can use either the `TypeName()` function or the `Class` property of the item.

`TypeName()` returns a string value providing information about the variable. For object variables, it returns the type of object. Table 14.4 lists the intrinsic constants for the `Class` property values for different types of Outlook items and their literal values.

**Tip:** Table 14.4 lists just some of the `TypeName()` and `Class` values. To learn about other intrinsic constants for the `Class` property, look up `OlObjectClass` in the Object Browser.

If you try to access the `Class` property for an object variable that has not been set to an object, Outlook generates an error. Therefore, if there is any chance that the object might not have been set, it might be better to use the `TypeName()` function to find out what kind of item you have, instead of the `Class` property. Alternatively, you can use the expression *`object`* `Is Nothing` to test whether you have a valid object. Note also that the `Class` property can help you distinguish between an appointment and a meeting request or between a task and a task request.

## 14.3.2 Getting a particular item

In Listing 10.6, you saw an example of how to retrieve a particular item, given the two IDs that uniquely identify it—the `EntryID` and the `StoreID`—using the `Namespace.GetItemFromID` method:

```
Set objApp = CreateObject("Outlook.Application")
Set objNS = objApp.GetNamespace("MAPI")
Set objItem = objNSGetFolderFromID(entryID, storeID)
```

---

**Note:** An item does not have an `EntryID` until it has been saved. The `EntryID` for an item changes if you move the item to a different folder.

---

## 14.3.3 Working with all the items in a folder

In Chapter 12, "Working with Stores and Folders," you learned many techniques for getting any particular folder as a `MAPIFolder` object. Once you have a `MAPIFolder` object, you can work with its `Items` collection, which comprises all the Outlook items in the folder, often by looping through it with a `For Each ... Next` loop, as you saw in Chapter 7, "Controlling Program Flow." This code snippet puts a list of all items in the current folder in the VBA Immediate window:

```
Set objApp = CreateObject("Outlook.Application")
Set objFolder = objApp.ActiveExplorer.CurrentFolder
For Each objItem In objFolder.Items
    Debug.Print objItem.Subject
Next
```

Whenever you are looping through items in a folder, be sure to check the `Class` property or use the `TypeName()` function as described in the previous section. For example, when working in a contacts folder, Contact and Distribution List items have very different sets of properties. Only a Contact Item has a `FullName` property:

```
Set objApp = CreateObject("Outlook.Application")
Set objNS = objApp.GetNamespace("MAPI")
Set objFolder = objNS.GetDefaultFolder(olFolderContacts)
For Each objItem In objFolder.Items
    If objItem.Class = olContact Then
        Debug.Print objItem.FullName
    End If
Next
```

---

**CAUTION:** Depending on your computer configuration, Outlook may bog down or even produce errors when handling very large `Items` collections. CDO is an order of magnitude faster for processing large numbers of items.

---

The `Items` collection supports several very useful techniques to help you access Outlook items more efficiently—the `Sort` and `SetColumns` methods and the `IncludeRecurrences` property.

The `Sort` method comes into play when you not only want to retrieve certain items, but you also want to get them in a particular order. Use `Sort` like this:

```
objItems.Sort property, descending
```

The *`property`* argument is a string value—the name of the property you want to sort by. You can enclose a built-in property's name in brackets if you prefer. However, if you sort by a user-defined field, do not enclose the name in brackets. The *`descending`* argument is optional. The default is `False`. Set it to `True` if you want the returned `Items` collection to be sorted in descending order—for example, with the most recent dates first. Here are two examples from a contacts folder, the first using a built-in property, the second using a custom property:

```
objItems.Sort "[FullName]"
objItems.Sort "Spouse Birthday", True
```

You cannot use `Sort` on keywords fields, such as `Categories`, on custom formula or combination fields, or on certain other properties listed in the Help topic for `Sort`.

If your code needs to access only a subset of properties, you may be able to speed up your code by using the `SetColumns` method to cache certain built-in properties from the `Items` collection. You cannot use it with user-defined properties. Use `SetColumns` like this, specifying the properties you need in a single string, separated by commas:

```
objItems.SetColumns "FullName, CompanyName"
For Each objItem In objItems
    Debug.Print objItem.FullName, objItem.CompanyName
Next
```

As with `Sort`, there are some properties that don't work with `SetColumns`. After you apply `SetColumns`, Outlook will ignore any request for uncached properties. To discard the cache and return to accessing all properties, use `ResetColumns`:

```
objItems.ResetColumns
```

Calendar folders can contain recurring appointments—those that happen weekly, monthly, or at other intervals—but normally, the `Items` collection does not include each instance of a recurring appointment. If you need to see all recurrences, you can set the `IncludeRecurrences` property to `True`. First, however, you must sort the `Items` collection by the `Start` property:

```
objItems.Sort "Start"
objItems.IncludeRecurrences = True
```

---

CAUTION: Never use `Count` with an `Items` collection for which you've set `IncludeRecurrences` to `True`, except to test whether the collection has anything in it at all, using `Items.Count > 0`. The presence of appointments with no end date means that you'll get a meaningless number for the count. Likewise, a `For Each ... Next` loop may be never ending. Generally, you'll use `IncludeRecurrences` along with the `Find` or `Restrict` method discussed later in the chapter.

---

You will see two more `Items` methods later in this chapter—`Find` and `Restrict`.

### 14.3.4 Working with selected items

Listing 8.1 introduced the `Selection` object, which represents the items selected by the user in a folder window. A common application of `Selection` is within VBA macros to perform batch operations that you can't do with Outlook's built-in menu and toolbar button commands. This code sets an `objSelection` variable to the items selected in the current folder (the `ActiveExplorer` window's folder):

```
Set objApp = CreateObject("Outlook.Application")
Set objSelection = objApp.ActiveExplorer.Selection
```

If you want just one selected item, add this line:

```
Set objItem = objSelection.Item(1)
```

**Note:** The `Selection` object supports the `Item` and `Count` properties like many other collections, but not the `Add` and `Remove` methods. You cannot programmatically expand or contract the user's selection to include more or fewer items.

Because you have no way to know whether the user has selected one item or 100, you generally use a `For Each ... Next` loop to work with each item in turn. Depending on the operation you plan to perform on the selection, you might want to check the count first with the `Count` property of the `Selection` object. Listing 14.3 provides a framework you can use to determine the number of items selected and proceed accordingly.

**Listing 14.3** *Process Selected Items in a Folder*

```
Sub SelectionFramework()
    Dim objApp As Outlook.Application
    Dim objSel As Outlook.Selection
    Dim objItem As Object
    Dim intMaxItems As Integer
    '*** USER OPTION ***
    intMaxItems = 30
    Set objApp = CreateObject("Outlook.Application")
    Set objSel = objApp.ActiveExplorer.Selection
    Select Case objSel.Count
        Case 0
            MsgBox "No items were selected"
        Case 1 To intMaxItems
            For Each objItem In objSel
                Call ProcessSelection(objItem)
            Next
        Case Is > intMaxItems
            MsgBox objSel.Count & " items is too big " _
              & "a selection for this operation.", _
              vbExclamation, "SelectionFramework"
    End Select
    Set objApp = Nothing
    Set objSel = Nothing
    Set objItem = Nothing
End Sub

Sub ProcessSelection(objItem As Object)
    Debug.Print objItem.Subject
End Sub
```

The ProcessSelection subroutine included in the listing is just an example to show how each object in the Selection can be passed to a separate procedure that does the actual processing. This results in modular, reusable code. Set the value for intMaxItems to whatever number you feel is appropriate for your application.

---

**Tip:** Every Outlook item, regardless of what type of item it is, has a Subject property, so it's safe to use objItem.Subject without checking the type of item first.

---

## 14.3.5 Using Find and Restrict to filter items

Find, FindNext, and Restrict are three methods that work with a folder's Items collection to provide some control over what items are available. Find returns the first item that meets your conditions; FindNext returns the next matching item in the collection. Restrict is another type of filter that returns a subset of the Items collection.

---

**Note:** Find, Restrict, and Sort do not change the way a folder is displayed in an Explorer window.

---

Here is the basic syntax for Find and its associated method, FindNext:

```
Set objItem = objFolder.Items.Find(filter)
Set objItem = objFolder.Items.FindNext
```

The Restrict method uses a similar syntax, but returns an Items collection, instead of a single object representing an Outlook item:

```
Set objItems = objFolder.Items.Restrict(filter)
```

You work with the Items collection returned by the Restrict method just as you would work with the Items collection that comprises all items in a folder, often processing all the items with a For Each ... Next loop.

The filter argument is a string expression that evaluates to True or False. It includes at least one field, a comparison operator, and the value you want to find for that field. Field names are in brackets. The field can be either intrinsic or user-defined. String values must be surrounded by either one set of single quotation marks or two sets of double quotation marks. date/time values must be expressed as strings and surrounded with quotes;

they must not contain any seconds element, only day, month, year, hour, and minutes. Here are some examples of simple filters:

```
"[City] = 'Moscow'"
"[Unread] = True"
"[Start] >= ""March 3, 2003"""
```

**Note:** Only user-defined fields that are part of the folder definition can be used in `Find` and `Restrict` filters. This means that you must take special care to define custom fields on a folder, rather than just on items in the folder or on a form. We'll explore this issue in Chapter 17, "Extending Form Design with Fields and Controls," and Chapter 24, "Deploying Forms and Applications."

Filters can be difficult to build because of the need to surround the entire expression with quotation marks and enclose string and date/time literals in quotation marks. That's one reason you created the `Quote()` function in Chapter 12, "Working with Stores and Folders." Another trick to making filters easier to work with is to build the filter as a separate series of statements and then apply it with the `Find` or `Restrict` method. This code builds a filter to obtain all items during the months of June, July, and August 2002.

```
strFilter = "[Start] >= " & Quote("6/1/2002") & _
            " And [Start] < " & Quote("9/1/2002")
Set objItems = objFolder.Items.Restrict(strFilter)
```

The complete `strFilter` expression is

```
"[Start] >= ""6/1/2002"" And [Start] < ""9/1/2002"""
```

If you use a `Debug.Print` statement in your code to display the result of the `strFilter` expression, the Immediate window will show this text with all the doubled quotation marks resolved:

```
[Start] >= "6/1/2002" And [Start] < "9/1/2002"
```

**Note:** See the Help topics on the `Find` and `Restrict` methods for important information on what fields cannot be used in filters.

You can use variables, constants, or functions in the filter expression itself, but they must evaluate to a string. For example, in the filter `"[Start] >= Now"`, the expression `Now` is not equivalent to the `Now` function.

A filter that looks for items with a `Start` date later than right now is quite a bit more complicated:

```
strFilter = "[Start] >= " & _
          Quote(FormatDateTime(Now, vbShortDate) & _
          " " & FormatDateTime(Now, vbShortTime))
```

You cannot simply use `Quote(Now)`, because `Now` defaults to the general date format, which on most machines includes a seconds element. To work with only the date, hours and minutes, the filter uses the `FormatDateTime()` function twice, first to get the date, then to get the time in just hours and minutes.

---

**Tip:** You can use a filter such as `"[Categories] = 'mycat'"` to look for a single category, even if the items in question fall into more than one category.

---

Does it make any difference whether you use `Find` or `Restrict`? If you want to return only one particular item from a folder, `Find` is the logical choice. If your code needs to work with all the items in a folder that meet specific criteria, `Restrict` makes more sense. However, in an Exchange Server environment—especially in public folders—be wary of using `Restrict`. Exchange caches restrictions on its folders. Whenever an item is created or modified, it is matched against existing restrictions on the folder. While this can improve performance if a folder has a few cached restrictions that are used repeatedly, it can greatly increase the time required to save items if a folder has many restrictions.

You can use any of the techniques described in Section 14.3.3 with the `Items` collection returned by the `Restrict` method. You will see more examples of `Find` and `Restrict` in this and subsequent chapters.

### 14.3.6 A better NextBusinessDay() function

Back in Chapter 6, "Working with Expressions and Functions," you saw a very simple `NextBusinessDay()` function that skips weekend days. With the new techniques you've encountered in this chapter, you can now build a better the `NextBusinessDay()` function that is also aware of holidays and vacations. Listing 14.4 combines `Restrict`, `Sort`, and `IncludeRecurrences` to accomplish this and also introduces two new methods you can use on `Items` collections—`GetFirst` and `GetNext`.

This version of the `NextBusinessDay()` function makes several key assumptions:

- Both vacation and holiday days are marked with corresponding Vacation and Holiday categories
- Your business does not operate on holiday days
- Holidays and vacations are listed as all-day events

In your own business world, some or all of these assumptions might not hold. The code would be more complex in that case. For example, if you don't have vacation days marked with the Vacation category, you might have to rely on the `Subject` or some other property to indicate that a particular Appointment item is a vacation day. However, you could build on the basic techniques in Listing 14.4.

If the `dteDate` argument is `3/15/2003`, the filter constructed as `strFilter` looks like as follows:

```
"[AllDayEvent] = True And [End] > '3/15/2003' And
([Categories] = 'Holiday' Or [Categories] = 'Vacation')"
```

The `Restrict` method using this filter returns all holiday and vacation events that don't occur before the date in question.

The outer `Do` loop uses a variable, `intDayCount`, to keep track of the number of valid business days encountered. It is incremented only for days that are not weekends and do not overlap any appointments in the `objItems` collection.

---

**Tip:** When testing a filter in VBA code, add a `Debug.Print strFilter` statement so that you can see the results in the Immediate window.

---

The `objItems` collection was filtered to eliminate events that were too early and was sorted on the `Start` property. It also uses the `IncludeRecurrences` property to include individual instances of recurring events.

In the inner `Do` loop checks whether the date currently under consideration overlaps with any holiday or vacation events. The `GetFirst` method returns the first item in the `objItems` collection, and the `GetNext` method returns subsequent items. The expression `objAppt Is Nothing` tests whether the loop has exhausted the supply of events in `objItems`; if so, it exits the loop.

**Listing 14.4** *Account for Holidays and Vacations As Well As Weekends*

```
Function NextBusinessDay2 _
  (ByVal dteDate as Date, intAhead as Integer) as Date
    Dim objApp As Outlook.Application
    Dim objNS As Outlook.NameSpace
    Dim objFolder As Outlook.MAPIFolder
    Dim objItems As Outlook.Items
    Dim objAppt As Outlook.AppointmentItem
    Dim strFilter As String
    Dim intDayCount As Integer
    Dim blnSkip As Boolean
    strFilter = "[AllDayEvent] = True And " & _
      "[End] > " & Quote(Format(dteDate, "Short Date")) & _
      " And ([Categories] = " & Quote("Holiday") & _
      " Or [Categories] = " & Quote("Vacation") & ")"
    Set objApp = CreateObject("Outlook.Application")
    Set objNS = objApp.GetNamespace("MAPI")
    Set objFolder = objNS.GetDefaultFolder(olFolderCalendar)
    Set objItems = objFolder.Items.Restrict(strFilter)
    objItems.Sort "[Start]"
    objItems.IncludeRecurrences = True
    intDayCount = 1
    Do
        dteDate = dteDate + 1
        blnSkip = False
        If Weekday(dteDate, vbMonday) >= 6 Then
            blnSkip = True
        ElseIf objItems.Count > 0 Then
            Set objAppt = objItems.GetFirst
            Do While objAppt.Start <= dteDate
                If objAppt.End > dteDate Then
                    blnSkip = True
                End If
                Set objAppt = objItems.GetNext
                If objAppt Is Nothing Then
                    Exit Do
                End If
            Loop
        End If
        If blnSkip = False Then
            intDayCount = intDayCount + 1
        End If
    Loop Until intDayCount > intAhead
    NextBusinessDay2 = dteDate
    Set objApp = Nothing
    Set objNS = Nothing
    Set objFolder = Nothing
    Set objItems = Nothing
    Set objAppt = Nothing
End Function
```

**Tip:** You can also use the `GetLast` and `GetPrevious` methods on an `Items` collection. Always use `GetFirst` before `GetNext`, and `GetLast` before `GetPrevious`.

Filters can become complicated, but this example should help you see how the combination of the `Restrict` and `Sort` methods can bring order to what can seem at first like an impossibly complex task.

### 14.3.7 Using Search in Outlook 2002

Outlook 2002 introduces a new `Search` object that allows you to duplicate the behavior of the Advanced Find function in code. You can build more complex filters and even search across multiple folders within a single Exchange mailbox or Personal Folders .pst file. It will not, however, conduct searches across multiple Exchange Server public folders or folders in more than one mailbox or .pst file.

These searches use a totally different syntax, however, that ignores the usual Outlook property names. Instead, it uses the Distributed Authoring Search and Location (DASL) syntax employed by Exchange 2000. The best way to learn about this syntax is to experiment, using the dialog for building filters on folders. You can add a new key to the Windows registry to display an officially undocumented Query Builder tab to the Filter dialog (View, Current View, Customize Current View, Filter). Make a backup of your registry, then run Regedit and add a key named QueryBuilder to the HKCU\Software\Microsoft\Office\10.0\Outlook key; no value is required.

**CAUTION:** I recommend that you use the Query Builder just for investigating the query syntax, not for actually building queries for saved views. It is an undocumented feature, and there are reports that it sometimes might cause Outlook to crash.

In the next section, we'll return to the birthday and anniversary reminder tool that you built in Chapters 3 and 9 to enhance it with a search. So, let's use the Filter dialog to build the required search string. Follow these steps:

1. Switch to your Calendar folder.
2. Choose View, Current View, Customize Current View, Filter, and then switch to the Query Builder tab.

3. Under Field, choose Subject from the Frequently Used Fields list. For the Condition, choose "contains," and for the Value, type in "Birthday."
4. Click Add to List to add the Birthday condition to the filter.
5. Repeat steps 3 and 4, substituting "Anniversary" for "Birthday."
6. Under Logical Group, choose OR. The Query Builder should look like Figure 14.1.
7. Switch to the SQL tab and check the box for Edit These Criteria Directly. You should see the criteria shown in Figure 14.2.

You can ignore the (`"DAV:isfolder" = false AND "DAV:ishidden" = false`) portion of the criteria, because Outlook includes that expression by default on each filter. The important part is the expression

```
(("urn:schemas:httpmail:subject" LIKE '%Birthday%' OR
"urn:schemas:httpmail:subject" LIKE '%Anniversary%'))
```

The `urn:schemas:httpmail:subject` field is the DASL name for the `Subject` property. The `"urn:schemas:httpmail:subject" LIKE '%Birthday%'` expression means find all items with Birthday in the subject. You can see that there is a similar expression for Anniversary, and that the two expressions are joined with `OR`, which means that any item with either "Birthday" or "Anniversary" in the Subject will satisfy the condition.

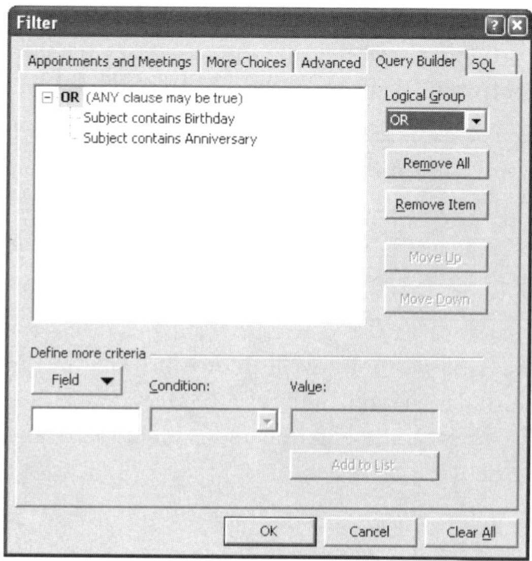


**Figure 14.1** *Add a Query Builder tab to help you work with Outlook 2002 Search filters.*

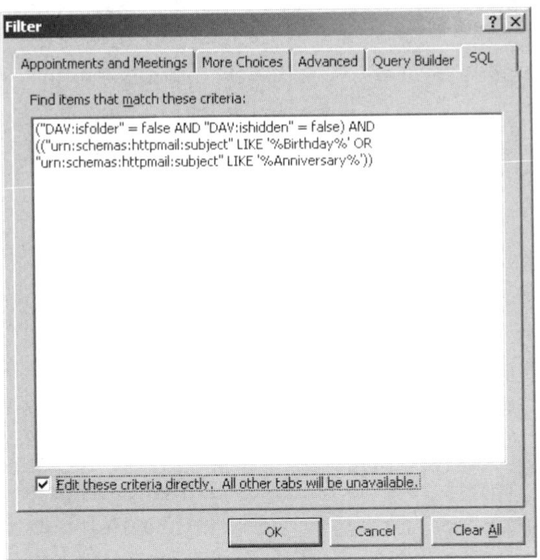


**Figure 14.2** *The SQL syntax uses field names related to the Exchange 2000 schema.*

Just as the `Subject` property is represented by the DASL schema name `urn:schemas:httpmail:subject`, every Outlook property has a corresponding DASL schema name. Appendix A includes resources for learning about DASL and getting a list of Outlook properties and their corresponding schema names.

The technique for using the `Search` object is more complex than `Find` or `Restrict`, because the search actually runs in the background. Therefore, your code needs to wait for the event that signals that the search has completed. In a nutshell, the steps are as follows:

1. Build the filter string and a string to define the scope of the search (i.e., what folders to search).
2. Start the search using the `Application.AdvancedSearch` method.
3. Wait for the `Application.AdvancedSearchComplete` or `Application.AdvancedSearchStopped` event.
4. Identify the search by a unique `Tag` that you set when you start the search (since you can run multiple searches simultaneously) and use the `Search.Results` collection just as you would an `Items` collection.

The next section walks through these steps with a specific example that you're already familiar with—the birthday/anniversary updater.

### 14.3.8 Updating all birthday and anniversary events

If you look back at the code for the birthday/anniversary reminder form in Chapters 3 and 9, you'll see that it had to loop through all the items in the Calendar folder, because you cannot use `Find` or `Restrict` to search for a substring. You can, however, use the Search object to perform a substring search.

To demonstrate this, you can make a copy of the ReminderUpdate form from Chapter 9: Export the original form, so that you have a saved copy. Then change the name of the form to `Ch14ReminderUpdate`. Place the code in Listing 14.5 in the `ThisOutlookSession` module. Replace the `cmdUpdate_Click` subroutine on the form with the corresponding procedure in Listing 14.6.

Here's how it works: When the user clicks `Update` in the birthday/anniversary reminder form, the code in Listing 14.6 builds a filter to match the SQL you saw in Figure 14.2. It then launches the search, setting the *`scope`* argument to the Calendar folder and the *`Tag`* to `"Reminders"`. How does the routine know when the search is complete? The event handlers for the `AdvancedSearchComplete` and `AdvancedSearchStopped` in Listing 14.5 change the value of the `Tag` property of the `txtProgress` control on the form when those events fire. A `Do` loop in the `cmdUpdate_Click` procedure keeps looping until it sees a change in `txtProgress.Tag`. If the `txtProgress.Tag` property indicates that the search completed successfully, it checks the number of items returned (`objSearch.Results.Count`) and proceeds to update those items, using the same code as in previous versions of this form.

**Listing 14.5** *Application Events to Work with a Search Object*

```
Private Sub Application_AdvancedSearchComplete _
  (ByVal SearchObject As Search)
    If SearchObject.Tag = "Reminders" Then
        Ch14ReminderUpdate.txtProgress.Tag = "complete"
    End If
End Sub

Private Sub Application_AdvancedSearchStopped _
  (ByVal SearchObject As Search)
    If SearchObject.Tag = "Reminders" Then
        Ch14ReminderUpdate.txtProgress.Tag = "stopped"
    End If
End Sub
```

**Listing 14.6** *Code for the ReminderUpdate Form*

```
Private Sub cmdUpdate_Click()
    Dim objApp As Outlook.Application
    Dim objSearch As Outlook.Search
    Dim objItem As Outlook.AppointmentItem
    Dim strFilter As String
    Dim strScope As String
    Dim strSubject As String
    Dim intMinutes As Integer
    Dim lngCountBA As Integer
    Call UpdateProgress("Update started")
    Set objApp = CreateObject("Outlook.Application")
    strFilter = _
      "(" & Quote("urn:schemas:httpmail:subject") & _
      " LIKE '%Birthday%' OR " & _
      Quote("urn:schemas:httpmail:subject") & _
      " LIKE '%Anniversary%')"
    Debug.Print strFilter
    strScope = "Calendar"
    Set objSearch = objApp.AdvancedSearch(strScope, _
                    strFilter, , "Reminders")
    Call UpdateProgress("Running search")
    txtProgress.Tag = ""
    Do While txtProgress.Tag = ""
        DoEvents
    Loop
    Call UpdateProgress("Search " & txtProgress.Tag)
    If txtProgress.Tag = "complete" Then
        intMinutes = 24 * 60 * txtDays.Value
        lngCountBA = objSearch.Results.Count
        If lngCountBA > 0 Then
            For Each objItem In objSearch.Results
                objItem.ReminderSet = True
                objItem.ReminderMinutesBeforeStart _
                  = intMinutes
                objItem.Save
            Next
            Call UpdateProgress ("Finished: " & _
             lngCountBA & " items updated")
        Else
            Call UpdateProgress _
             ("Finished: No items found to update")
        End If
    End If
    Beep
    Set objApp = Nothing
    Set objSearch = Nothing
    Set objItem = Nothing
End Sub
```

Whether or not the `Search` method is faster than `Find` or `Restrict` will depend on each particular application. You may find that the key advantage of `Search` is that it can perform more complex searches than `Find` or `Restrict`.

## 14.4 Using item methods

The different Outlook items have many methods in common. Table 14.5 provides a summary. Not all methods apply to every item. See the Help topic for an individual method for details.

**Table 14.5** *Common Item Methods*

| Method | Description |
|---|---|
| `Close` | Closes the item, saving changes if desired, using the same *`savemode`* argument values shown in Table 14.1 |
| `Copy` | Returns a copy of the item |
| `Delete` | Deletes the item |
| `Display` | Displays the item in an Inspector |
| `Forward` | Executes the `Forward` action, returning a new `Mail-Item` object |
| `Move` | Moves the item to a different folder, returning the moved item |
| `PrintOut` | Prints the item with default settings |
| `Reply` | Returns a `MailItem` addressed to the original sender |
| `ReplyAll` | Returns a `MailItem` addressed to the original sender and any Cc recipients |
| `Save` | Saves the item to the folder from which it was opened or to which it was added or, for a new item, to the default folder for the item type |
| `SaveAs` | Saves the item to a system file using the specified path and file format |
| `Send` | Sends the item (appointment, meeting item, message, or task request) |
| `ShowCategoriesDialog` | Displays the Categories dialog so the user can modify the categories for the item (Outlook 2002 only) |

To copy an item to another folder, first use the `Copy` method to get a copy of the item, and then use the `Move` method to place the copy in the destination folder, as in the following example:

```
Sub CopyToFolder(objItem as Object, _
                 objFolder as Outlook.MAPIFolder)
    Dim objApp As Outlook.Application
    Dim objNewItem As Object
    Set objApp = CreateObject("Outlook.Application")
    Set objNewItem = objItem.Copy
    objNewItem.Move objFolder
    Set objNewItem = Nothing
    Set objApp = Nothing
End Sub
```

Outlook can save items as files in system folders in the formats shown in Table 14.6. The format(s) available for any given item depend on the type of item and, in the case of mail and post items, whether the format is plain text, rich text, or HTML.

If you do not specify the format with the `SaveAs` method, the default Message (.msg) format is used.

**Note:** The vCard, vCal, and iCal formats are Internet standards for exchanging contact and schedule data and are used by many programs besides Outlook. Appendix A has more information on these standards.

**Table 14.6** *SaveAs Format Constants*

| Format | Constant | Value |
|---|---|---|
| Text only (.txt) | `olTXT` | 0 |
| Rich text format (.rtf) | `olRTF` | 1 |
| Outlook template (.otf) | `olTemplate` | 2 |
| Message format (.msg) | `olMSG` | 3 |
| HTML format (.htm) | `olHTML` | 5 |
| vCard file (.vcf) | `olVCard` | 6 |
| vCal format (.vcs) | `olVCal` | 7 |
| iCal format (.ics)—Outlook 2002 only | `olICal` | 8 |

The various Outlook items have their own specific methods, many of which apply to only one or two item types. Table 14.7 summarizes these methods. For more information and usage examples, see the Help topic for each method.

**Table 14.7** *Item-Specific Methods*

| Item Type | Method | Description |
|---|---|---|
| `AppointmentItem` | `ClearRecurrencePattern` | Changes an appointment to a single occurrence |
| | `ForwardAsVcal` | Returns a `MailItem` object with an attached vCal file for the appointment |
| | `GetRecurrencePattern` | Returns the `RecurrencePattern` object defining a recurring appointment |
| | `Respond` | Responds to an `AppointmentItem` contained in a meeting request |
| `ContactItem` | `ForwardAsVcard` | Returns a `MailItem` object with an attached vCard file for the contact |
| `DistListItem` | `AddMember` | Adds a single `Recipient` to a distribution list (Outlook 2002 only) |
| | `AddMembers` | Adds a specified `Recipients` collection of members to a distribution list |
| | `GetMember` | Returns a `Recipient` object representing a distribution list member |
| | `RemoveMember` | Removes a `Recipient` object from a distribution list (Outlook 2002 only) |
| | `RemoveMembers` | Removes a specified `Recipients` collection of members from a distribution list |
| `JournalItem` | `StartTimer` | Starts the timer on a Journal item |
| | `StopTimer` | Stops the timer on a Journal item |
| `MailItem` | `ClearConversationIndex` | Clears the `ConversationIndex` property |
| `MeetingItem` | `GetAssociatedAppointment` | Returns the `AppointmentItem` object associated with a meeting request |
| `PostItem` | `ClearConversationIndex` | Clears the `ConversationIndex` property |
| | `Post` | Saves the item to the target folder |

**Table 14.7** *Item-Specific Methods (continued)*

| Item Type | Method | Description |
|---|---|---|
| `TaskItem` | `Assign` | Assigns a task and returns a `TaskItem` object that can be sent to the assignee |
| | `CancelResponseState` | Resets the `ResponseState` property to its original value before responding to a task request |
| | `ClearRecurrencePattern` | Changes a task to a single occurrence |
| | `GetRecurrencePattern` | Returns the `RecurrencePattern` object defining a recurring task |
| | `MarkComplete` | Updates `PercentComplete` to 100%, `Complete` to `True`, and `DateCompleted` to the current date |
| | `Respond` | Responds to a `TaskItem` contained in a task request |
| | `SkipRecurrence` | Clears the current instance of a recurring Task and sets the recurrence to the next instance (Outlook 2002 only) |
| | `StatusReport` | Sends a status report to all recipients listed in the `StatusUpdateRecipients` property |
| `TaskRequestItem` | `GetAssociatedTask` | Returns the `TaskItem` object associated with a task request |

## 14.5 Working with the item Body property

For all Outlook items, when you want to modify the text in the large text box on the item, you always work with the `Body` property. `Body` is a string property, so you can use all the normal string parsing and manipulation functions on it. For example, the `StampDate` macro in Listing 14.7 adds the current date/time and user name to the bottom of the currently open item. It's designed to be run from a toolbar button.

If you wanted the stamp to appear at the top of the item instead of the bottom, you'd use this variation:

```
objItem.Body = Now & " - " & strUser & vbCrLf & objItem.Body
```

**Listing 14.7** *Stamp the Date and Current User on an Outlook Item*

```
Sub StampDate()
  Dim objApp As Outlook.Application
  Dim objItem As Object
  Dim strUser As String
  strUser = WSHUserName()
  Set objApp = CreateObject("Outlook.Application")
  Set objItem = objApp.ActiveInspector.CurrentItem
  objItem.Body = objItem.Body & vbCrLf & Now _
                 & " - " & strUser
  Set objItem = Nothing
  Set objApp = Nothing
End Sub
```

**Note:** If you are working in an Exchange Server environment, you can use the `GetMailboxUserName()` function from Listing 12.8 instead of the `WSHUserName()` function from Listing 10.10.

### 14.5.1 Body property limitations

All Outlook items other than the Message and Post items use rich text format (RTF) for the item body. If you set the `Body` property on any such item, any formatting that the user may have applied is lost.

Message and post items behave differently depending on whether you're running Outlook 2000 or Outlook 2002. Under Outlook 2000, setting the `Body` property automatically sets the format of the item to RTF. In Outlook 2002, setting `Body` causes the format to revert to the default format that the user set in the Tools, Options, Mail Format dialog. As you'll see in the next section, you can use the `BodyFormat` property in Outlook 2002 to set an item to a specific format.

Although you can manipulate the `Body` property itself, you cannot do much with the control that displays it on an Outlook form. You cannot position the insertion point in the control at a particular location, nor can you change the formatting of text using Outlook objects.

### 14.5.2 Working with the message Body property

Working with the `Body` property of a Message or Post is more complicated than working with that of a Contact or Appointment. Outlook supports

**Table 14.8** *Values for Inspector.EditorType*

| Editor | EditorType | Value |
|---|---|---|
| Plain text | `olEditorText` | 1 |
| HTML | `olEditorHTML` | 2 |
| Rich text | `olEditorRTF` | 3 |
| WordMail | `olEditorWord` | 4 |

three formats for messages and posts (plain text, rich text, and HTML) and two editors (the built-in editor and WordMail—Microsoft Word as the editor). In addition to the `Body` property, the `MailItem` and `PostItem` objects also have an `HTMLBody` property for storing text and formatting using HTML syntax.

The `EditorType` is a read-only property of the item's `Inspector` and may have the values shown in Table 14.8.

A user sets the default format and editor by choosing Tools, Options and changing the options on the Mail Format tab.

Although `EditorType` itself is read-only, certain code statements can have the effect of changing the editor or format for a particular item. If you set the `HTMLBody` property, the `EditorType` automatically changes to `olEditorHTML` and the `Body` property is updated automatically with plain text that matches the text you placed in the `HTMLBody` property. If you set the `Body` property, the `EditorType` reverts to `olEditorRTF` in Outlook 2000 or to the user's default format in Outlook 2002. Furthermore, if you set the `Body` property, the `HTMLBody` property is cleared, losing any HTML formatting. All formatting is lost in rich text messages, also.

**Note:** The Redemption object model, discussed in Chapter 13, "Understanding Outlook Security," provides an `RTFBody` property for each Outlook object, which you can use to work with the raw RTF content of the item.

In Outlook 2002, you can explicitly set the format of an item using the `BodyFormat` property values shown in Table 14.9.

**Table 14.9** *Values for BodyFormat*

| Editor | EditorType | Value |
|---|---|---|
| Plain text | `olFormatPlain` | 1 |
| HTML | `olFormatHTML` | 2 |
| Rich text | `olFormatRTF` | 3 |
| Unspecified | `olFormatUnspecified` | 0 |

## 14.6 Working with recipients

Two more key Outlook objects are `Recipients` collections and `Recipient` items. These represent the people and e-mail addresses with whom you communicate with in Outlook. The principle use of a `Recipients` collection is to represent the addressees on a sent or received item—not just messages, but also appointments and assigned tasks as well.

Each `Recipient` in a `Recipients` collection includes the basic properties in Table 14.10. However, attempting to work with a `Recipient` or the `Recipients` collection triggers the Outlook security address book access prompt that you learned about in Chapter 13, "Understanding Outlook Security." If all you need to do is set the recipients for an item, you can set values for the `To`, `Cc`, and `Bcc` properties. Setting the values for these properties does not trigger the security prompt, although you will get a prompt if you try to read the values of those properties from an item.

**Table 14.10** *Key Recipient Properties*

| Property | Description |
|---|---|
| `Address` | E-mail address |
| `Index` | Position in the `Recipients` collection |
| `Name` | Display name |
| `Resolved` | `True`, if the recipient has been successfully validated against the Address Book |
| `Type` | Type of entry, such as `To`, `Cc`, or `Bcc`, using the constants in Table 14.11 |

### 14.6.1 Adding recipients

As noted previously, you can add recipients to an item and avoid security prompts by setting the `To`, `Cc`, and `Bcc` properties. Separate multiple addresses with semicolons:

```
objItem.To = "mswish@microsoft.com;outwish@microsoft.com"
objItem.Bcc = "webmaster@slipstick.com"
```

---

**Tip:** You can use the mswish@microsoft.com and outwish@microsoft.com addresses to send Microsoft suggestions for future Outlook versions.

---

Another way to add a recipient to an item is to use the `Add` method to supply the name of someone in your Contacts folder (or other Outlook address list) or the Internet address in *`name@domain`* format. You can then set the `Type`, using one of the constants in Table 14.11. You will need to use this method if you want to add one or more recipients to an item that already has at least one recipient of the type that you want to add. The following example adds a recipient by name, and uses the `Resolve` method to check it against the user's address book. Outlook sets `objRecip.Resolved` to `True` if there is a match in the address book, and you can then set the

**Table 14.11** *Recipient Type Constants*

| Item Type | Recipient Type Constants | Value |
|---|---|---|
| `MailItem` | `olTo` (default) | 1 |
| | `olCC` | 2 |
| | `olBCC` | 3 |
| `MeetingItem` | `olRequired` (default) | 1 |
| | `olOptional` | 2 |
| | `olResource` | 3 |
| `TaskItem` | `olUpdate` | 2 |
| | `olFinalStatus` | 3 |

`Type` to `olBCC` to make the recipient a Bcc address that the people listed as To recipients won't see:

```
Set objRecip = _
  objItem.Recipients.Add("webmaster@slipstick.com")
objRecip.Resolve
If objRecip.Resolved Then
    objRecip.Type = olBCC
End If
```

Since the `Recipient` and `Recipients` collections trigger security prompts, you might want to consider using the Redemption object model to add recipients. Just as Redemption provides a `SafeMailItem` object analogous to Outlook's `MailItem`, it also has a `SafeRecipient` that functions like Outlook's `Recipient`. Compare this code snippet to the one above; it assumes that you already have an Outlook `MailItem` (the `objMail` variable):

```
objSafeMail.Item = objMail
Set objSafeRecip = _
  objSafeMail.Recipients.Add("webmaster@slipstick.com")
objSafeRecip.Resolve
If objSafeRecip.Resolved Then
    objSafeRecip.Type = olBcc
End If
```

### 14.6.2 Automatically adding a Bcc recipient to outgoing messages

A common application is to automatically add a Bcc recipient to outgoing messages. Listing 14.8 shows how you might do it with Outlook alone.

The problem with this code is that setting the `Bcc` property removes any Bcc recipients that the user previously set for the message. If you want to add a Bcc recipient and preserve any existing Bcc addresses, you must use `Recipients.Add`. Because that triggers the security prompts, Listing 14.9 provides a Redemption version.

**Listing 14.8** *Set a Bcc Recipient for Outgoing Messages*

```
Private Sub Application_ItemSend _
  (ByVal Item As Object, Cancel As Boolean)
    Item.Bcc = "webmaster@slipstick.com"
End Sub
```

**Listing 14.9** *Set a Bcc Recipient for Outgoing Messages with Redemption*

```
Private Sub Application_ItemSend _
  (ByVal Item As Object, Cancel As Boolean)
    Dim objSafeMail As Redemption.SafeMailItem
    Dim objSafeRecip As Redemption.SafeRecipient
    Item.Save
    Set objSafeMail = _
      CreateObject("Redemption.SafeMailItem")
    objSafeMail.Item = Item
    Set objSafeRecip = _
      objSafeMail.Recipients.Add("webmaster@slipstick.com")
    objSafeRecip.Resolve
    If objSafeRecip.Resolved Then
        objSafeRecip.Type = olBCC
    End If
    Set objSafeRecip = Nothing
    Set objSafeMail = Nothing
End Sub
```

Note that you must save the Outlook `Item` object before passing it to the Redemption `SafeMailItem`.

### 14.6.3 Showing the Select Names dialog

The CDO object model provides an `AddressBook` method that displays a Select Names dialog, such as that shown in Figure 14.3. This is a powerful method that allows you to completely customize the look of the Select Names dialog: its title, the number of boxes for recipients, and the labels for

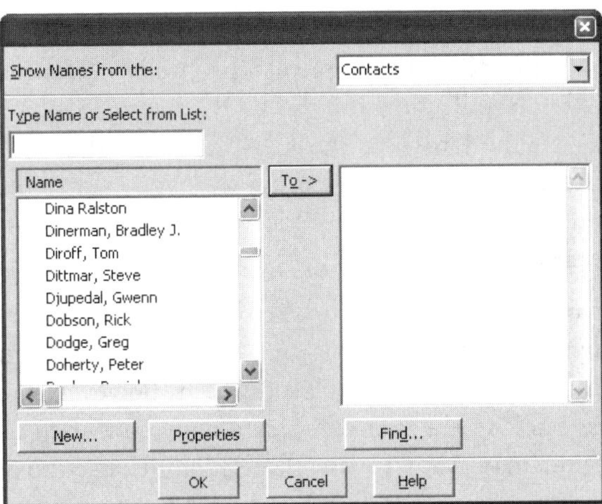


**Figure 14.3** *Use the AddressBook method to display the Select Names dialog.*

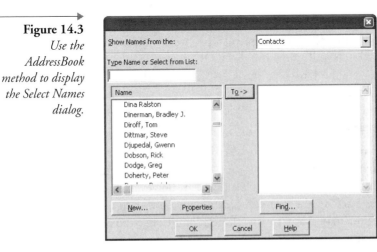

those boxes. The `AddressBook` method returns a CDO `Recipients` collection, which is not equivalent to the Outlook `Recipients` collection.

---

**Tip:** Don't forget that to use CDO methods you must use Tools, References to add the Microsoft CDO 1.21 Library to your Outlook VBA project references. Also, you must declare object variables with CDO data types, not data types for the Outlook object model equivalents.

In particular, note that both models use a `Recipient` object, but the two objects are not equivalent; you cannot set a CDO `Recipients` object equal to an Outlook `Recipients` object. The upcoming code example for the `AddressBook` method sets the `Recipients` collection on a CDO `Message` object, rather than trying to copy the recipients to an Outlook `MailItem` object.

The use of CDO is officially unsupported in Outlook 2000 in Internet Mail Only (IMO) mode, although most of the time, it works OK. However, using the *`OneAddress`* and *`ForceResolution`* parameters in the `Session.AddressBook` method in IMO mode will cause an error.

---

`AddressBook` is a relatively complex method with quite a few arguments listed in Table 14.12. In Listing 14.10, you use the named arguments method of specifying parameters to make it easier to follow the code.

The code in Listing 14.10 demonstrates how to use CDO to launch a customized Select Names dialog, add the chosen recipients to a CDO Message, then pass that message to Outlook for display.

Figure 14.4 shows the dialog that the user sees, with the title and the names of the different recipient type "wells" customized. After setting the `Recipients` collection for the CDO `Message` object, the code uses the `Update` method to save the CDO item so that you can get its `ID` and `StoreID` properties. You then use those properties in the `GetItemFromID` method on the `NameSpace` object to access an Outlook `MailItem` object (`objItem`) and display it.

If you use the `Session.AddressBook` method in this fashion—never actually working with the `Recipients` collection directly—you will not encounter Outlook security prompts. If, however, you want to display the address book so the user can pick a name and then use that name in your code, you may want to use the Redemption equivalent, which uses the same parameters as the CDO version, but returns a `SafeRecipients` col-

**Table 14.12** *AddressBook Arguments*

| Argument | Description |
|---|---|
| `Recipients` | Optional. `Recipients` collection holding initial values for the boxes in the Select Names dialog. |
| `Title` | Optional. Caption for the Select Names dialog box. |
| `OneAddress` | Optional. Boolean value for whether user can select only one address entry at a time. Default is `False`. |
| `ForceResolution` | Optional. Boolean value for whether the program should try to resolve all names before closing the Select Names dialog. Default is `True`. |
| `RecipLists` | Optional. How many recipient boxes to display. Default is 1. Possible values:<br>`-1`: Three boxes with default captions and `ForceResolu-tion:=False`<br>`0`: No boxes<br>`1`: One box for To recipients<br>`2`: To boxes for To and Cc recipients<br>`3`: Three boxes for To, Cc, and Bcc recipients |
| `ToLabel` | Optional. Label for To box. Default: `"To:"` |
| `CcLabel` | Optional. Label for Cc box. Default: `"Cc:"` |
| `BccLabel` | Optional. Label for Bcc box. Default: `"Bcc:"` |

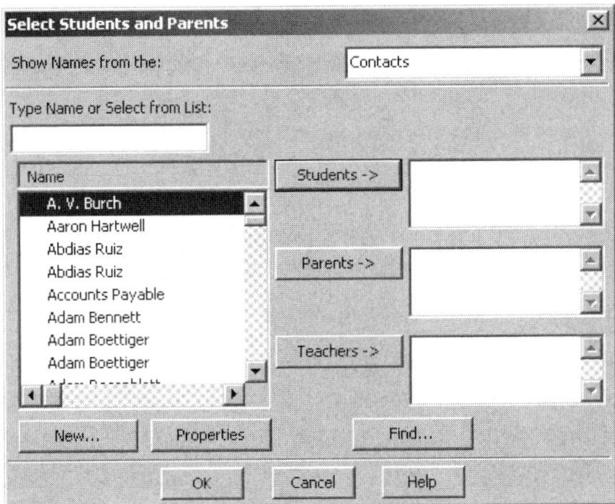


**Figure 14.4** *Display a customized recipient selection dialog with the CDO Session.AddressBook method.*

**Listing 14.10** *Using the AddressBook Method to Populate a Recipients Collection*

```
Sub AddressBookDemo()
    Dim objApp As Outlook.Application
    Dim objNS As Outlook.NameSpace
    Dim objItem As Outlook.MailItem
    Dim objMessage As MAPI.Message
    Dim objSession As MAPI.Session
    Dim objRecipients As MAPI.Recipients
    Dim strEntryID As String
    Dim strStoreID As String
    On Error Resume Next
    Set objSession = CreateObject("MAPI.Session")
    objSession.Logon "", "", False, False
    Set objRecipients = objSession.AddressBook( _
      Title:="Select Students and Parents", _
      OneAddress:=False, _
      ForceResolution:=True, _
      RecipLists:=3, _
      ToLabel:="&Students", _
      CcLabel:="&Parents", _
      BccLabel:="&Teachers")
    Set objMessage = objSession.Inbox.Messages.Add
    Set objMessage.Recipients = objRecipients
    objMessage.Update
    strEntryID = objMessage.ID
    strStoreID = objMessage.StoreID
    Set objApp = CreateObject("Outlook.Application")
    Set objNS = objApp.GetNamespace("MAPI")
    Set objItem = objNS.GetItemFromID(strEntryID, strStoreID)
    objItem.Display
    objSession.Logoff
    Set objApp = Nothing
    Set objNS = Nothing
    Set objItem = Nothing
    Set objMessage = Nothing
    Set objSession = Nothing
    Set objRecipients = Nothing
End Sub
```

lection that you can access without triggering security prompts. The function in Listing 14.11 provides a way to return one name from the address book dialog.

The actual format of the name that the `GetOneName()` function returns will vary the type of recipient (Exchange or Contact) and with the version of Outlook. For a Contact, Outlook 2002 returns the display name that you set for the particular e-mail address, while Outlook 2000 in Corporate/Workgroup mode returns the name followed with an "(Email)" suffix, assuming you choose an e-mail address rather than a fax address.

**Listing 14.11** *Use Redemption to Get the User to Choose One Name from the Address Book*

```
Function GetOneName() As String
    Dim objRUtils As Redemption.MAPIUtils
    Dim colSafeRecips As Redemption.SafeRecipients
    Dim strMsg As String
    Dim intRes As Integer
    On Error Resume Next
    Set objRUtils = CreateObject("Redemption.MAPIUtils")
    Set colSafeRecips = objRUtils.AddressBook(, _
                        "Pick a Name", , , 1, _
                        "My Choice")
    Do While colSafeRecips.Count <> 1
        strMsg = "You must choose exactly 1 name. " & _
                 "Do you want to try again?"
        intRes = MsgBox(strMsg, _
                        vbQuestion + vbYesNo + vbDefaultButton1, _
                        "GetOneName")
        If intRes = vbYes Then
            Set colSafeRecips = objRUtils.AddressBook(, _
                   "Pick a Name", , , 1, _
                   "My Choice")
        Else
            Exit Do
        End If
    Loop
    If colSafeRecips Is Nothing Then
        GetOneName = "Could not get a name"
    ElseIf colSafeRecips.Count <> 1 Then
        GetOneName = "Could not get a name"
    Else
        GetOneName = colSafeRecips.Item(1).AddressEntry.Name
    End If
    Set colSafeRecips = Nothing
    Set objRUtils = Nothing
End Function
```

### 14.6.4 Understanding address resolution

Before you send any Outlook item, all recipient addresses should be *resolved*, that is, validated against the user's Address Book. Internet addresses in `name@domain` format are resolved automatically. For other addresses, Outlook looks for a match in the various address lists in the Address Book.

Resolution occurs in any of these situations:

- The user clicks the Send button.
- The user clicks the Check Names button.

- Background name resolution is turned on, and Outlook finds a match as a background process.
- Program code uses the `Resolve` method on a `Recipient` item or the `ResolveAll` method on a `Recipients` collection.

In the first two situations, if Outlook does not find a match, it displays a dialog where the user can either try to find the recipient or create a new address. Using the Outlook object model's `Resolve` method does not provide an option for displaying that dialog, but the `Resolve` method in the CDO and Redemption object models and the `ResolveAll` method in CDO do. In a displayed Outlook item, resolved recipients are shown underlined. You can check the `Resolved` property for any recipient to find out whether address resolution was successful.

---

**Note:** In Listing 12.6 you saw an example using the `Resolve` method on a `Recipient` in a dummy `MailItem` before trying to use the `GetSharedDefaultFolder` method with that `Recipient`.

---

If you are creating a message programmatically, but not showing it to the user before sending it, you should use either CDO or Redemption to resolve the recipients to ensure that the message can actually be sent without triggering an error. The `ResolveAndSendViaCDO()` function in Listing 14.12 returns `True` if the recipients were all resolved and the message was sent, but it triggers security prompts both for the statements that refer to `Recipients` and the `objMsg.Send` statement.

The `ResolveAndSendViaRed()` function in Listing 14.13 does the same thing, only using Redemption, rather than CDO, thus avoiding the security prompts.

### 14.6.5 Adding senders to Contacts

On an open message, you can right-click the name in the From field and choose Add to Contacts to create a new item in the Contacts folder using the sender's information. However, if you read most of your messages in the preview pane, opening the message just to be able to save the sender might seem like a lot of trouble. Even though Outlook 2002 allows you to add a contact from the preview pane, it uses only the sender's From address. If the sender has a different reply-to address, the new contact won't capture that. Therefore, it might be useful to create a macro that works with a selected

**Listing 14.12** *Use CDO to Resolve Recipients Before Sending*

```
Sub ResolveAndSendViaCDODemo()
    Dim objApp As Outlook.Application
    Dim objMail As Outlook.MailItem
    Set objApp = CreateObject("Outlook.Application")
    Set objMail = objApp.CreateItem(olMailItem)
    objMail.To = "Someone somewhere"
    objMail.Save
    If Not ResolveAndSendViaCDO(objMail) Then
        objMail.Display
    End If
    Set objApp = Nothing
    Set objMail = Nothing
End Sub

Function ResolveAndSendViaCDO(objMail As Outlook.MailItem) _
  As Boolean
    Dim objSession As MAPI.Session
    Dim objMsg As MAPI.Message
    Dim strEntryID As String
    Dim strStoreID As String
    On Error Resume Next
    strEntryID = objMail.EntryID
    strStoreID = objMail.Parent.StoreID
    Set objSession = CreateObject("MAPI.Session")
    objSession.Logon "", "", False, False
    Set objMsg = objSession.GetMessage(strEntryID, strStoreID)
    objMsg.Recipients.Resolve True
    If objMsg.Recipients.Resolved Then
        objMsg.Send
    End If
    ResolveAndSendViaCDO = objMsg.Recipients.Resolved
    objSession.Logoff
    Set objSession = Nothing
    Set objMsg = Nothing
End Function
```

item in a folder and creates a new Contact item from the sender's information, using both the From and Reply-to addresses.

You already saw how to get the From address by using CDO or Redemption in Listings 13.5 and 13.6. To get the reply address, you create a reply message and get the address from the only `Recipient`. Listing 14.14 is the version using only Outlook objects, while Listing 14.15 is the Redemption version.

The principal difference between these two listings is in the use of the Redemption objects to get an object representing the recipient of the reply message. The `Recipients` collection of a Redemption `SafeMailItem` returns a `SafeRecipients` collection, access to which does not trigger security prompts.

Did you notice that the `CreateSenderContactOL` subroutine uses two different methods of creating new items—`Application.CreateItem` and `MailItem.Reply`?

**Listing 14.13** *Use Redemption To Avoid Security Prompts During Address Resolution*

```
Sub ResolveAndSendViaRedDemo()
    Dim objApp As Outlook.Application
    Dim objMail As Outlook.MailItem
    Set objApp = CreateObject("Outlook.Application")
    Set objMail = objApp.CreateItem(olMailItem)
    objMail.To = "Someone somewhere"
    objMail.Save
    If Not ResolveAndSendViaRed(objMail) Then
        objMail.Display
    End If
    Set objApp = Nothing
    Set objMail = Nothing
End Sub

Function ResolveAndSendViaRed(objMail As Outlook.MailItem) _
  As Boolean
    Dim objSafeMail As Redemption.SafeMailItem
    Dim objSafeRecip As Redemption.SafeRecipient
    Dim blnResolved As Boolean
    Dim blnSomeUnresolved As Boolean
    Set objSafeMail = CreateObject("Redemption.SafeMailItem")
    objSafeMail.Item = objMail
    blnSomeUnresolved = False
    For Each objSafeRecip In objSafeMail.Recipients
        blnResolved = objSafeRecip.Resolve(True)
        If Not blnResolved Then
            blnSomeUnresolved = True
        End If
    Next
    If Not blnSomeUnresolved Then
        objSafeMail.Send
    End If
    ResolveAndSendViaRed = (Not blnSomeUnresolved)
    Set objSafeMail = Nothing
    Set objSafeRecip = Nothing
End Function
```

**Listing 14.14** *Add a Contact with a Mail Message Sender's Information*

```
Sub CreateSenderContactOL()
    Dim objApp As Outlook.Application
    Dim objMail As Outlook.MailItem
    Dim objReply As Outlook.MailItem
    Dim objContact As Outlook.ContactItem
    Dim objRecip As Outlook.Recipient
    Dim strFrom As String
    On Error Resume Next
    Set objApp = CreateObject("Outlook.Application")
    Set objMail = objApp.ActiveExplorer.Selection(1)
    If Not objMail Is Nothing Then
        If objMail.Class = olMail Then
            Set objReply = objMail.Reply
            Set objRecip = objReply.Recipients(1)
            Set objContact = _
              objApp.CreateItem(olContactItem)
            objContact.FullName = objRecip.Name
            objContact.Email1Address = objRecip.Address
            strFrom = GetFromAddressCDO(objMail)
            If strFrom <> objRecip.Address Then
                objContact.Email2Address = strFrom
            End If
            objContact.Display
        End If
    End If
    Set objMail = Nothing
    Set objContact = Nothing
    Set objRecip = Nothing
    Set objReply = Nothing
    Set objApp = Nothing
End Sub
```

**Listing 14.15** *Add a Contact with a Mail Message Sender's Information Using Redemption to Avoid Security Prompts*

```
Sub CreateSenderContactRed()
    Dim objApp As Outlook.Application
    Dim objMail As Outlook.MailItem
    Dim objReply As Outlook.MailItem
    Dim objContact As Outlook.ContactItem
    Dim objSafeReply As Redemption.SafeMailItem
    Dim colSafeRecips As Redemption.SafeRecipients
    Dim objSafeRecip As Redemption.SafeRecipient
    Dim strFrom As String
    On Error Resume Next
    Set objApp = CreateObject("Outlook.Application")
    Set objMail = objApp.ActiveExplorer.Selection(1)
```

**Listing 14.15** *Add a Contact with a Mail Message Sender's Information Using Redemption to Avoid Security Prompts (continued)*

```
    If Not objMail Is Nothing Then
        If objMail.Class = olMail Then
            Set objReply = objMail.Reply
            objReply.Save
            Set objSafeReply = _
              CreateObject("Redemption.SafeMailItem")
            objSafeReply.Item = objReply
            Set colSafeRecips = objSafeReply.Recipients
            Set objSafeRecip = colSafeRecips.Item(1)
            Set objContact = _
              objApp.CreateItem(olContactItem)
            objContact.FullName = objSafeRecip.Name
            objContact.Email1Address = objSafeRecip.Address
            strFrom = GetFromAddressR(objMail)
            If strFrom <> objSafeRecip.Address Then
                objContact.Email2Address = strFrom
            End If
            objContact.Display
            objReply.Delete
        End If
    End If
    Set colSafeRecips = Nothing
    Set objSafeRecip = Nothing
    Set objSafeReply = Nothing
    Set objMail = Nothing
    Set objContact = Nothing
    Set objReply = Nothing
    Set objApp = Nothing

End Sub
```

## 14.7 Summary

You have furthered your understanding of Outlook items in this chapter by exploring the `Inspector` object, reviewing item methods, and working with `Recipient` objects using three different object models—Outlook, CDO, and Redemption. Keep in mind that not every item method works with each type of Outlook item.

You also combined your new skills in creating Outlook items and working with recipients to build a macro that can create a new Contact item that includes both the From and the Reply-to addresses from an incoming message.

This chapter concludes Part III. You now have all the basics necessary to work with many of the key Outlook objects. In Part IV, we'll tackle the task of creating Outlook forms and then writing code to automate them.

# *Outlook Form Design*

# 15

# Outlook's Six Basic Forms

This chapter gets you started with Outlook forms. You will take a guided tour of the six main built-in forms. This will give you an idea of which form would be the best fit for a particular project.

The highlights of this chapter include discussions of the following:

- How to start and end an Outlook forms design session
- Where to find forms you can use as models
- What information each form can store
- How to get help with forms design
- Where to save finished forms

## 15.1 Starting the forms designer

Every Outlook form starts from another Outlook form, rather than from a blank page. To start designing an Outlook form, choose Tools, Forms, Design a Form from the main Outlook menu. The Design Form dialog box shown in Figure 15.1 appears, listing the forms in the Standard Forms Library. This library holds the six basic forms that appear when you click the New button in any Outlook folder, as well as two hidden forms Outlook uses for meeting invitations and task assignments.

Select the form you want to use as the basis for your new form (for example, the Appointment form), and then click Open.

**Note:** The Look In list can show you other places where Outlook forms may be stored. The forms you find there have already been modified in some fashion. You can use them to create new forms, too. Later in this chapter you will learn more about where forms are stored.

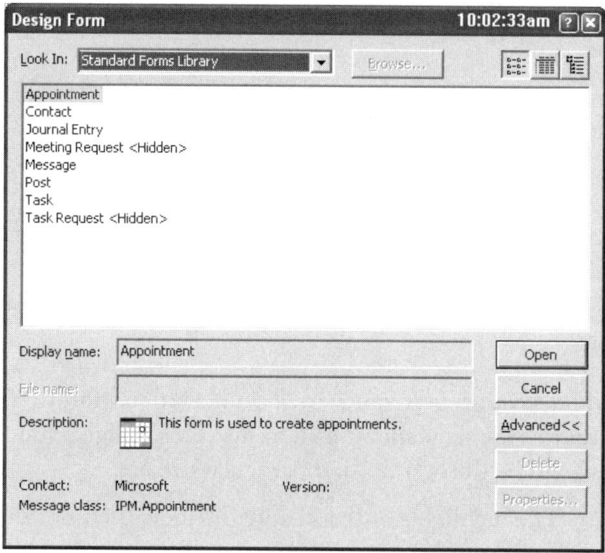


**Figure 15.1** *Select a form to modify for your project.*

You can also design a form based on an existing item—for example, a mail message to which you have added a Bcc recipient. Open the item, then choose Tools, Forms, Design This Form.

## 15.2 The basic Outlook forms

For many Outlook applications, you only have to make a few changes to an existing form. The next few sections introduce all six basic forms to help you understand which form would be best suited for a particular task.

### 15.2.1 The Appointment form

You will start with the Appointment form, opening it with the Tools, Forms, Design a Form command. Figure 15.2 shows the Appointment form open to the Appointment page. Each tab on the form, starting with Appointment and ending with (Actions), represents a page you can either show the user or hide. The pages whose names appear in parentheses are hidden by default. When users create new appointments in their Calendar folders, they normally see only the Appointment page and the Scheduling (called Attendee Availability in Outlook 2000) page, shown in Figure 15.3.

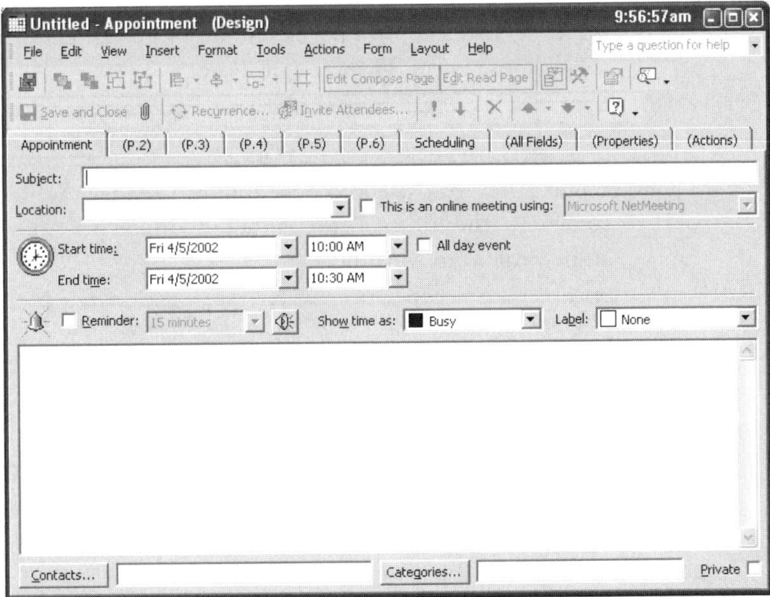


**Figure 15.2** *The Appointment form holds information about meetings and events.*

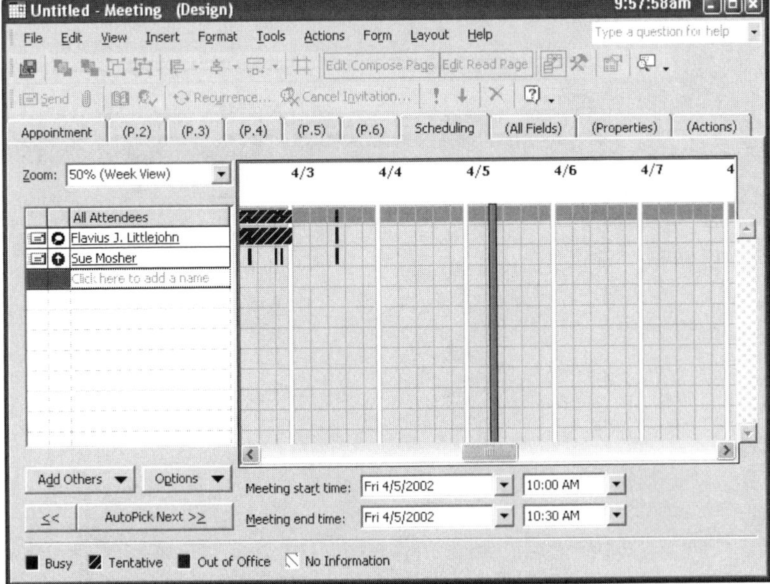


**Figure 15.3** *The Scheduling page of the Appointment form shows the times when people are free for meetings.*

**Note:** To toggle a form page's visibility to users, click on the page's tab, and then choose Form, Display This Page.

**Note:** After you use the Scheduling/Attendee Availability page to invite someone, the title of the window displaying the item changes from Appointment to Meeting.

You cannot customize the Appointment or Scheduling/Attendee Availability page of the Appointment form. Any customization takes place on the five pages labeled (P.2) to (P.6). Figure 15.4 shows the (P.2) page.

**Note:** In general, you cannot customize any page that contains a dropdown calendar control, apparently because Microsoft did not choose to make that control available to programmers. You can customize the first page of the Message, Post, and Contact forms. In addition, you can hide the built-in pages and use the same fields on your own custom pages. You can make the custom pages look very much like, if not exactly the same as, the built-in pages.

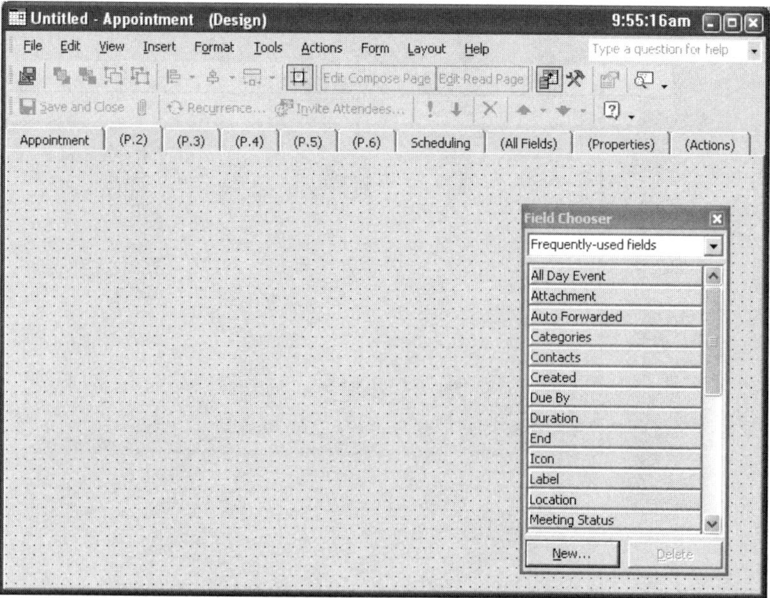


**Figure 15.4**
*Each form contains five blank pages you can customize.*

The (All Fields), (Properties), and (Actions) pages are common to all Outlook forms. You will look at them a little later in the chapter.

### 15.2.2 The Contact form

Next, take a look at the Contact form. Figures 15.5 to 15.8 show its built-in pages. Unlike the Appointment form, you can customize the first page of the Contact form, although you cannot make changes on the other built-in pages.

---

**CAUTION:** If you customize the first page of the Contact form, you cannot use the customized form with Outlook 97.

---

As you work with the various forms, you will discover that some features appear or disappear, depending on the version of Outlook you have. For example, Figure 15.5 shows an `IM Address` field that is present only in Outlook 2002. In Outlook 2000, the first page of the contact form shows a Send Plain Text Only checkbox that is not present in Outlook 2002 and does not appear to users with Outlook 2000 installed in Corporate or

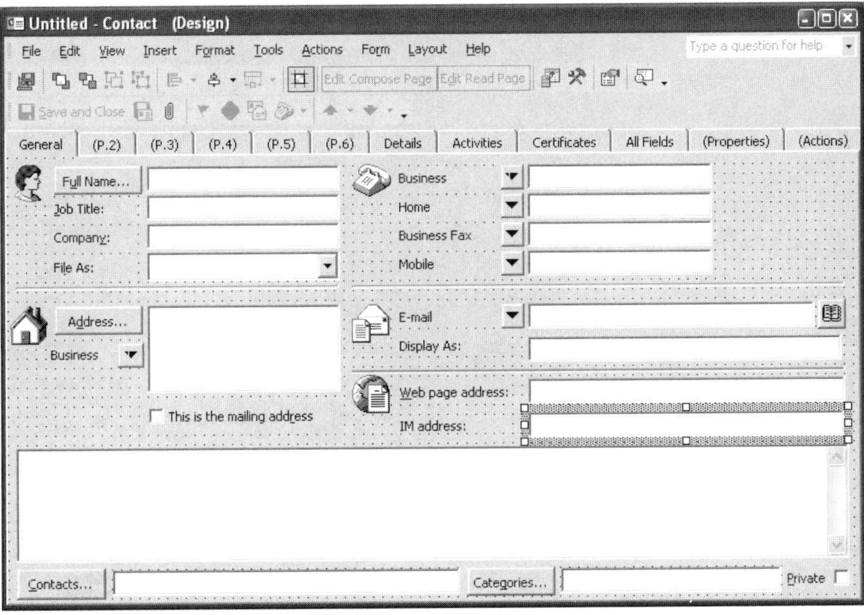


**Figure 15.5** *The grid of dots indicates that you can customize the General page of the Contact form.*

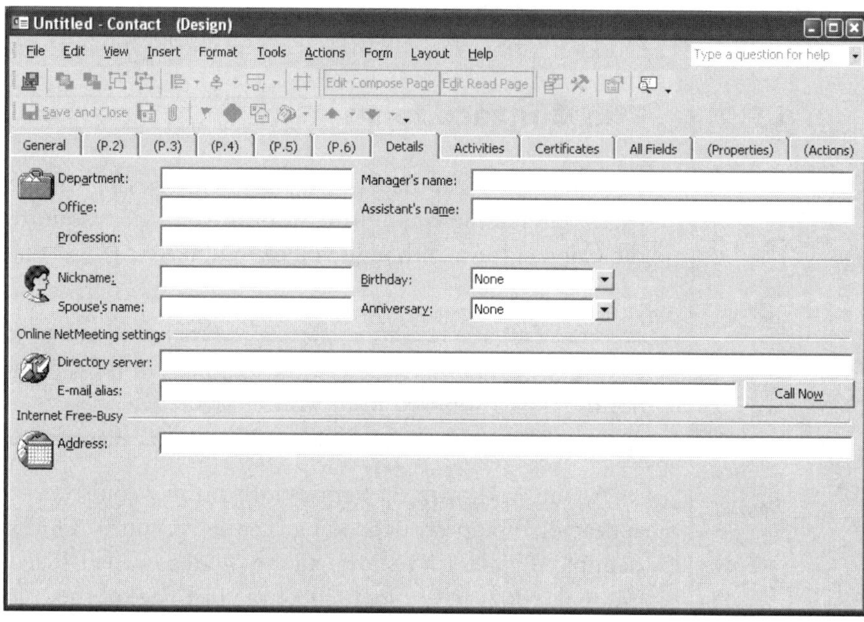


**Figure 15.6** *The Details page holds additional information about each contact.*

Workgroup mode. You should test your custom forms with the version of Outlook that users have.

The Activities page (see Figure 15.7) searches other Outlook folders to find items related to the current contact. The Show list normally defaults to All Items. If you change it—for example, to Upcoming Tasks/Appointments—Outlook does not save that change with the form. The default activities list is a property of the contacts folder, not the contacts form. On the contacts folder you can change the default list and create new activity groups that look at different combinations of folders.

---

**Note:** An activities group can show multiple folders only in a single Personal Folders file or Exchange Server mailbox. It cannot display multiple Exchange public folders or combine items from folders in different Personal Folders files or mailboxes.

---

The Contact form has a few limitations. If you customize the first page of the Contact form in Outlook 2000, the feature that automatically formats telephone numbers no longer works. This problem does not occur in Outlook 2002. In addition, you will also lose the button with a pencil icon

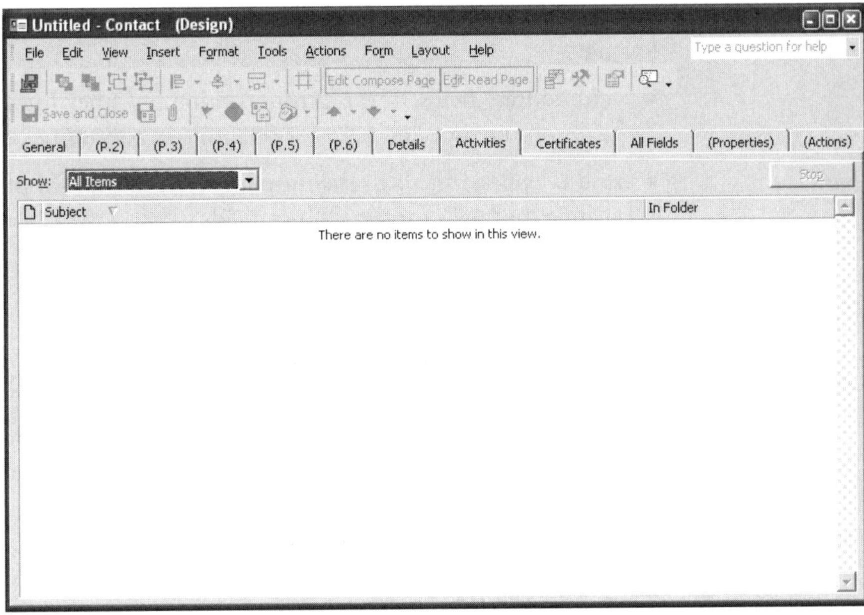


**Figure 15.7** *The Activities page of the Contact form tracks related items in other Outlook folders.*

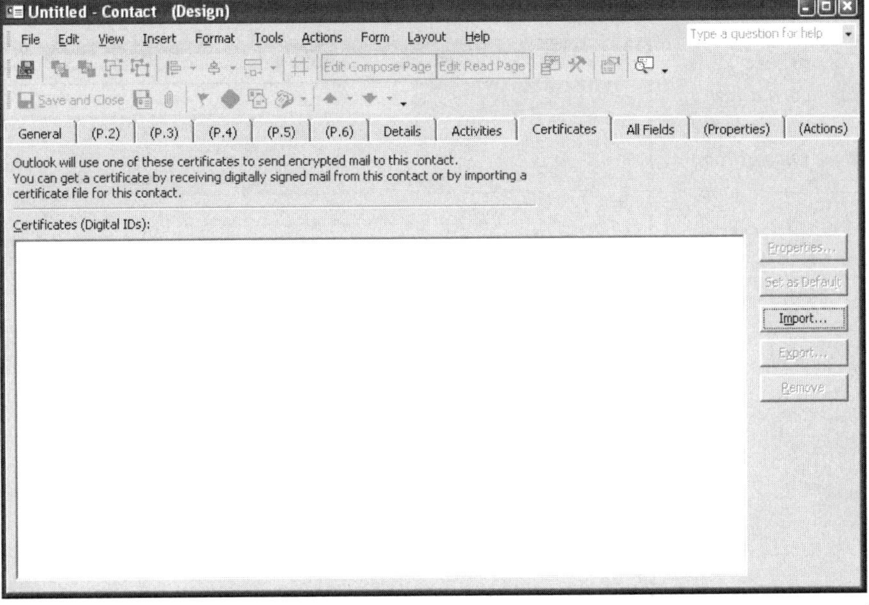


**Figure 15.8** *The Certificates page of the Contact form stores digital security certificate information.*

that displays the Check Phone Number dialog box. You cannot do the following:

- Add address fields to the Business, Home, Other list or change the labels on the dropdown list for the built-in address fields
- Add telephone fields to the dropdown list of built-in phone fields or change the labels for the built-in fields
- Add more e-mail address fields or change the labels for the three built-in e-mail address fields

## 15.2.3 The Journal Entry form

The Journal Entry form, shown in Figure 15.9, has just one built-in page, the General page, which you cannot customize. The unique feature of the Journal Entry form is that it includes buttons to start and stop a timer that keeps track of how much time you spend on a particular activity.

## 15.2.4 The Message form

The Message form, shown in Figure 15.10, is probably the most familiar of all the Outlook forms, because it appears every time you create a new e-mail

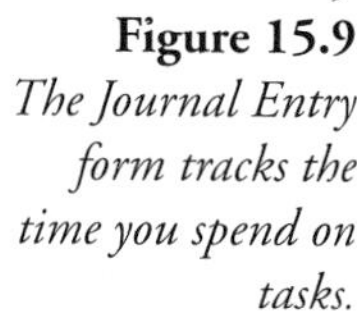

**Figure 15.9**
*The Journal Entry form tracks the time you spend on tasks.*

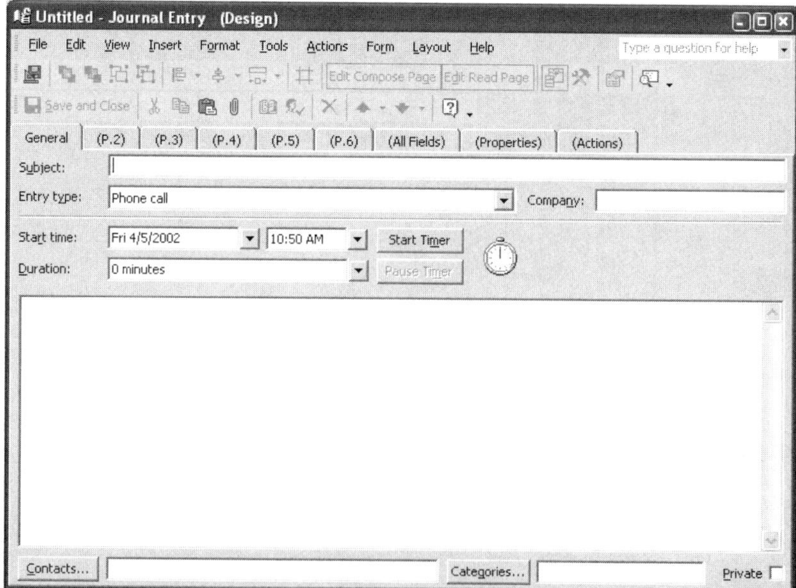

message. Because the built-in Message page of this form can be customized, it is used as the basis for many kinds of Outlook projects, especially those that involve routing information from one person to another.

Click the Edit Read Page button to see a different layout for the Message form, such as that in Figure 15.11. Click the Edit Compose Page button to return to the original layout. These two layouts help to explain why a message you compose looks different from a message you receive. If you add a field to the compose layout, Outlook does not automatically add it to the read layout for you.

All forms supporting individual compose and read pages, as you will see in Chapter 17, "Extending Form Design with Fields and Controls." However, only the Message and Post forms show separate compose and read pages by default.

---

**Tip:** Before opening a Message form for customization, turn off your Outlook automatic signature. Otherwise, the signature will become part of the message on your custom form. You also must turn off WordMail as the editor.

---

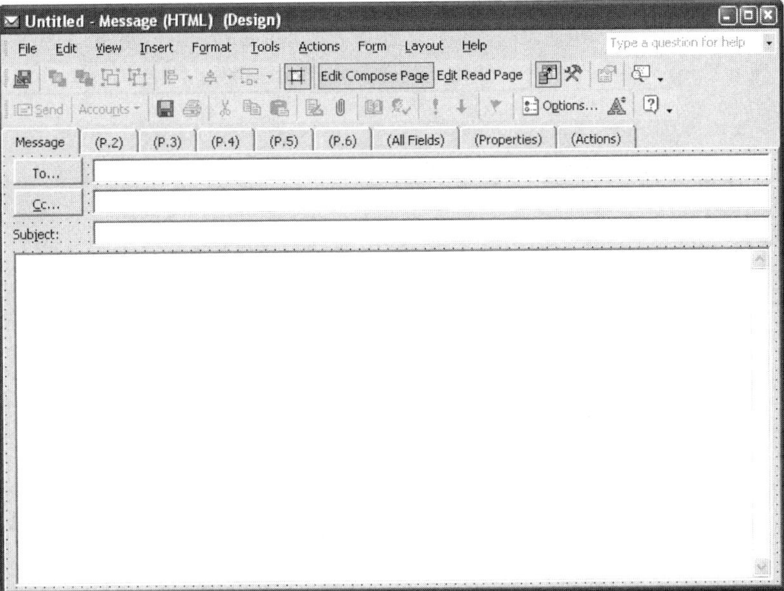


**Figure 15.10** *Use the Message form to create forms that exchange information with other Outlook users.*

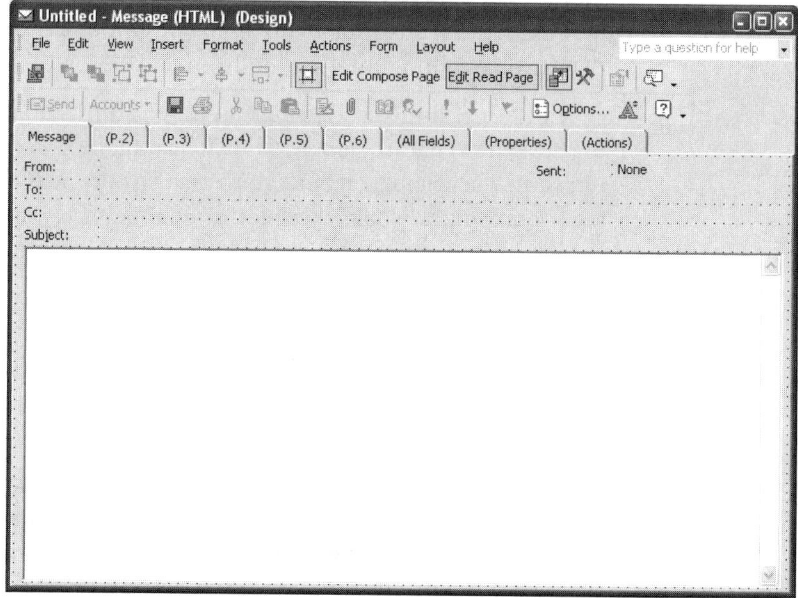


**Figure 15.11** *Message forms normally use distinct layouts for unsent and sent messages. This is the layout users see when they read messages.*

### 15.2.5 The Post form

The Post form, shown in Figure 15.12, is even simpler than the Message form. It is always used for posting information directly to a particular folder and, therefore, does not require the To or Cc buttons and boxes associated with the Message form.

### 15.2.6 The Task form

The last built-in form is the Task form. Its two pages, Task and Details, neither one customizable, are shown in Figures 15.13 and 15.14. Users typically create task items to build a to-do list for themselves or for the group of people they work with.

### 15.2.7 Hidden forms

In addition to the six basic forms, the Design Form dialog box (refer to Figure 15.1) also lists Meeting Request <Hidden> and Task Request <Hidden>. These are actually variations on the Appointment and Task forms and add a To button and box for addressing the form to meeting attendees or a task recipient. When you customize one of these forms, you are actually

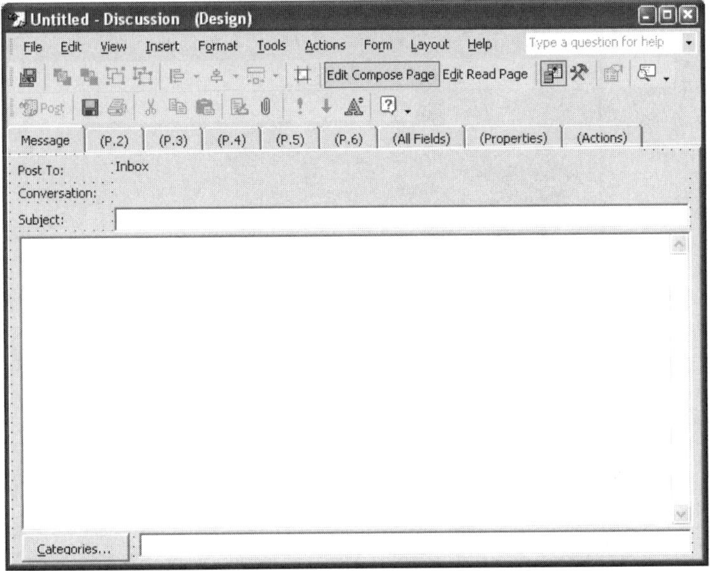


**Figure 15.12** *You can customize the Post form for use in Outlook discussion folders.*

customizing the Appointment or Task form. One important quirk to be aware of is that if you put VBScript code in an Meeting Request form, the code does not run when the user opens the meeting request item, but only when the user accepts the meeting.

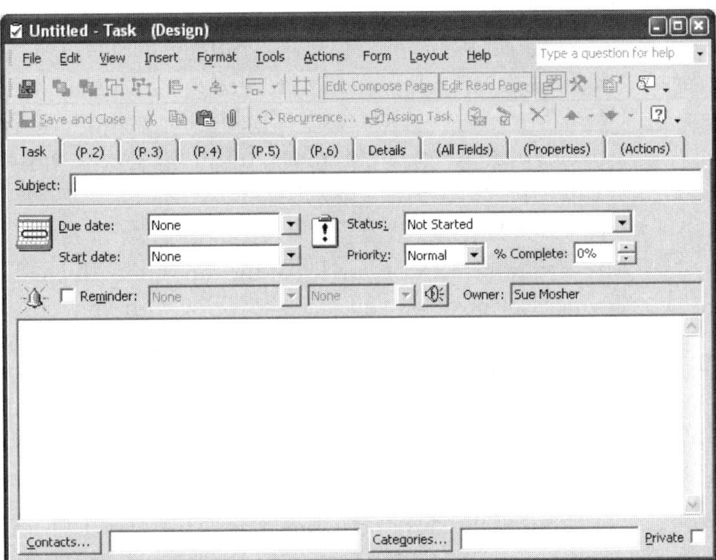


**Figure 15.13** *The first page of the Task form holds the most important information about each task.*

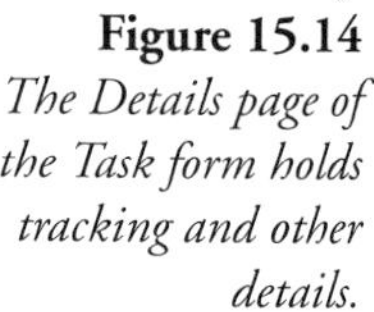

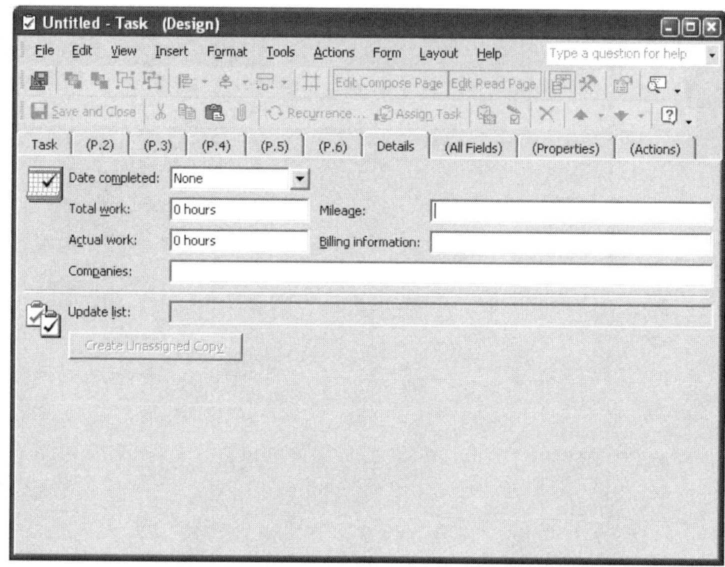


**Figure 15.14** *The Details page of the Task form holds tracking and other details.*

## 15.2.8 Common form pages

Here are the other pages every form includes: (All Fields), (Properties), and (Actions). The names appear in parentheses because these pages are normally hidden, except on the Contact form, which shows the All Fields page by default.

The All Fields page lists the fields available for use in the form. A *field* is a single piece of information related to an Outlook item. Each type of Outlook form uses a distinct set of fields. For example, a Contact form has three fields for holding fax numbers, but these do not appear on a Task form. A synonym for field is *property*. (Outlook uses field in its user interface, but property in developer documentation.)

From the Select From list at the top of the All Field page, you can choose which set of fields you want to work with and can see the names of the fields, along with their current values. For example, to see all the fields available in a Contact form, choose All Contact Fields. You then see the list shown in Figure 15.15. You can also choose Frequently Used Fields or Name Fields, and so on, to see a smaller subset of the many fields available in a Contact item.

You might also notice the choices for User-Defined Fields in This Item and User-Defined Fields in This Folder, as well as a New button at the bot-

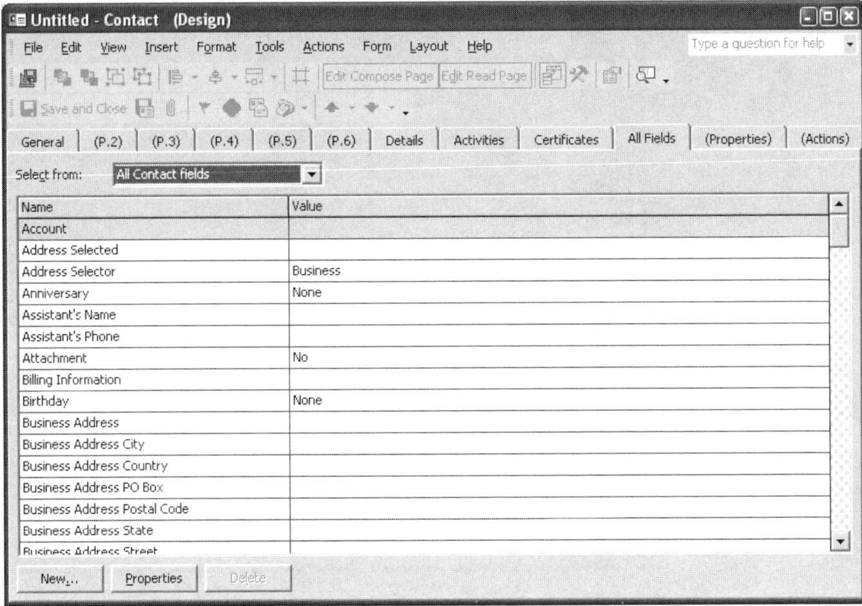


**Figure 15.15** *The All Fields page shows every field available in a form.*

tom of the page. You can create your own fields in Outlook (which you do in Chapter 17, "Extending Form Design with Fields and Controls").

On the (Properties) page, shown in Figure 15.16, you control various settings for the form, including the following:

- The icon it displays
- The version number
- An optional category and subcategory to help you track forms if you have many of them
- A contact for the form
- A description

Many of these properties, such as Contact and Description, are especially important if you are creating forms that other people will be using. You should always increment the version number when you change a form. You can start at 1 and add 1 each time that you change the form. Alternatively, you might use integers for major versions of the form and a decimal for minor changes. Incrementing the version number appears to help Outlook ensure that the user opens the latest version of a published form and

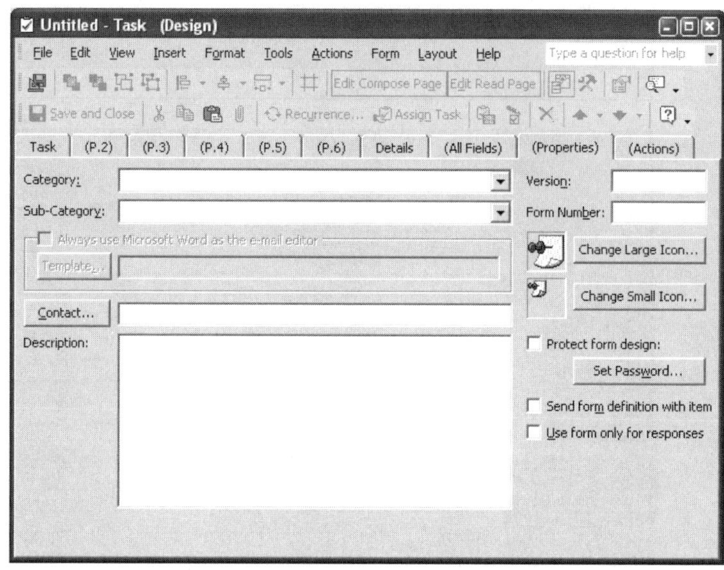


**Figure 15.16** *The (Properties) page allows you to control information that identifies the form.*

protect against corruption of the local forms cache; it is also useful for troubleshooting.

The last page is the (Actions) page, shown in Figure 15.17. It controls what happens when the user performs standard actions, such as Reply, Reply to All, Forward, and Reply to Folder. You can also add custom

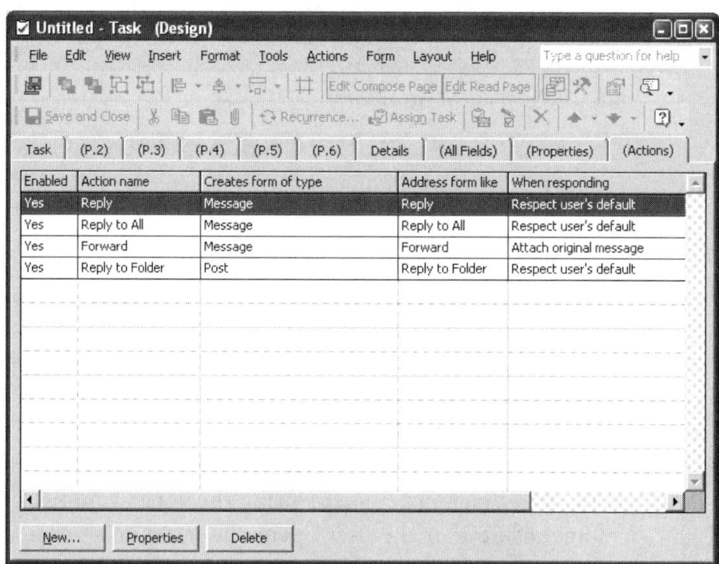


**Figure 15.17** *The (Actions) page controls commands that appear on the Actions menu.*

actions (as you learn in Chapter 20, "Common Outlook Form Techniques") that add new commands to the Actions menu and toolbar.

---

**Note:** Although every form lists the form actions shown in Figure 15.17, not every action is relevant to the current form. For example, the Reply action applies to a Message item, but not to a Task. On the other hand, the Forward action works on any form because you can forward any type of Outlook item to someone else.

---

## 15.3 When to use which form

How do you know which form to use? One approach is to make a pencil-and-paper sketch of the form you have in mind for your project and then find the closest match among the six Outlook forms. You can also look at the (All Fields) page for a sense of which forms include which fields. You should use the built-in fields as much as possible.

However, since you can always customize a form with additional fields, most of the time you should base your choice of form on its functionality. For example, if your project involves sending messages back and forth between people to gather and process information, you will probably use the Message form. If the information is gathered in one specific folder, rather than through an exchange of messages, the Post form is often appropriate.

However, don't feel that you have to use a particular form only for its original purpose. For example, if you want to keep track of how much time is spent on a project, you can use any of the three forms that include fields measuring time: the Appointment, Journal Entry, and Task forms. Since the Contact form is the only form with an Activities page, you could use it as the basis for a project form, with all the related components—people, meetings, tasks, etc.—containing a link back to an item using your project form. The parent project would then show on its Activities page all the linked items.

As you saw at the beginning of this chapter, the Design Form dialog box (refer to Figure 15.1) has a Look In list from which you can select various locations where forms are stored. Any form you previously modified can be located in one list or another. You can select that modified form and base a new form on it. For example, if you create a new Contact form that includes more fields and want to use those same fields in a new project, start with your modified form, rather than going back to the original Contact form.

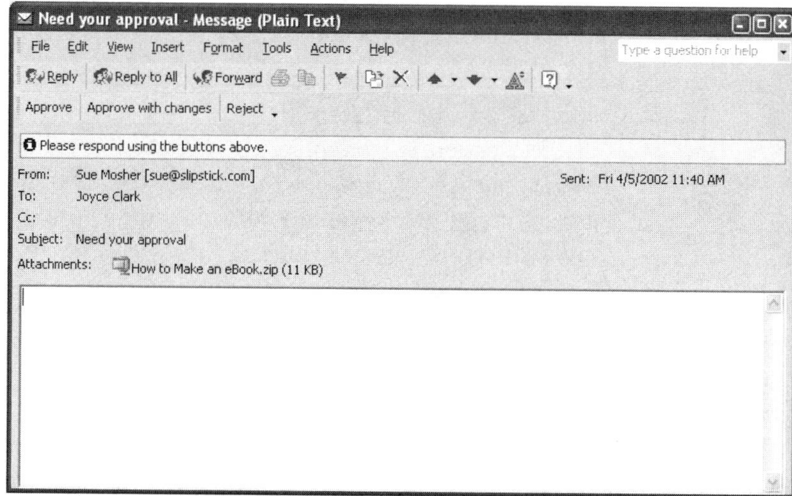


**Figure 15.18** *Voting buttons provide an easy method of creating a custom transmittal form.*

You can also open any Outlook item, make changes to it, and choose Tools, Form, Design This Form to use that particular item as the starting point for a custom form. This is a good approach when the form you want to customize is not in the Standard Forms list, such as the form for creating distribution lists in a Contacts folder. Another good example is a form with voting buttons. Although you can set the voting options in VBScript code, it's more often convenient to set the voting options in the normal message form by clicking the Options button. (You cannot create voting button messages with the Options button in Outlook 2000 in IMO mode.) You can then publish the form, as described later in this Section 15.6, to make it easy to reuse. Figure 15.18 shows a custom document transmittal form with three response buttons as the recipient would see it.

**Note:** If you customize the first page of a Message form, the infobar below the voting buttons will not appear.

## 15.4 Working in the forms designer

To complete this tour of the Outlook forms design environment, here are two of the tools you will be using: Field Chooser and Control Toolbox. Figure 15.19 shows the toolbar buttons for these and two other tools, Properties and View Code, which are covered in subsequent chapters.

**Figure 15.19** *The Field Chooser, Control Toolbox, Properties, and View Code buttons (left to right) display the form design tools.*

## 15.4.1 The Field Chooser

When you view any customizable page, the Field Chooser appears. As shown in Figure 15.20, it lists the fields you can add to the page. It defaults to Frequently Used Fields, but like the All Fields page, you can click the dropdown arrow at the top of the Field Chooser to see either all available fields or a particular subset.

To turn off the Field Chooser, click the Close button in its upper-right corner, or choose Form, Field Chooser from the menu. You can also click the Field Chooser button on the toolbar to turn it on and off.

## 15.4.2 The Control Toolbox

The buttons, check boxes, dropdown lists, and boxes for entering text on the form are all examples of *controls* that make up the form's user interface. To see the types of controls you can use, click the Control Toolbox button

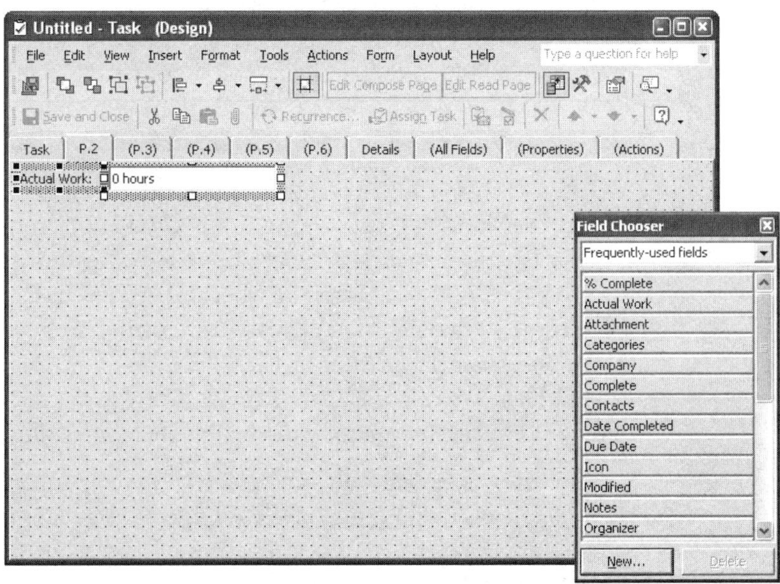


**Figure 15.20** *The Field Chooser provides a list of all fields available for the current form.*

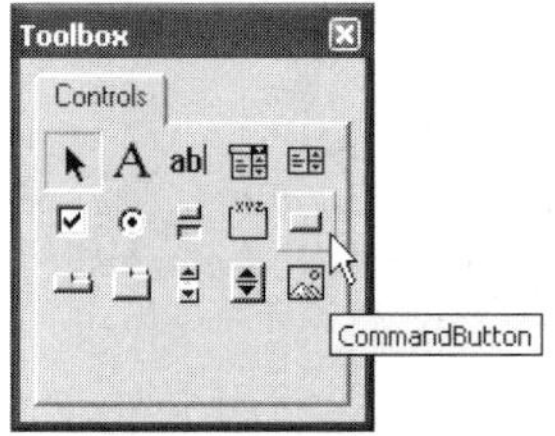


**Figure 15.21** *Pause the mouse pointer over any control in the Toolbox to see the name of the control.*

on the form's toolbar, or choose Form, Control Toolbox from the menu. This will display the Toolbox, shown in Figure 15.21. The easiest way to learn the names of the controls is to place your mouse pointer over a button without clicking. After a moment, the name of the control appears in a ToolTip.

**Tip:** In the next chapter, you will learn how to add ToolTip pop-up text to controls on your own customized form pages to make it easier for users to understand what each control does.

## 15.5 Getting help in Outlook forms design

Like all Microsoft Office programs, Outlook includes a detailed system of Help topics designed to assist you in various tasks, including designing forms. Getting to the Help on Outlook forms is a bit tricky, though. In Outlook 2002, the easiest method is to search your system for the file Olfm10.chm, which contains the Outlook forms help topics. Add a shortcut to that file either to your Programs menu or to your Windows desktop.

You can use a different method in Outlook 2000. Press Alt+F11 to start a VBA session. If you see a prompt for Disable Macros or Enable Macros, it doesn't matter which you choose because you will not be doing any macro editing in this lesson. After the Microsoft Visual Basic window opens, press F1; if the Office Assistant appears, type your search words in the assistant's box, and then press Enter or click Search. If you see the Microsoft Visual Basic Help window instead of the Office Assistant, switch to the Answer Wizard tab and type your search words there, then click Search.

In either version, you can also review the properties and methods of form controls by pointing the VBA Object Browser at the MSForms library. Note, however, that not all properties of form controls work the same on Outlook forms as they do on VBA forms.

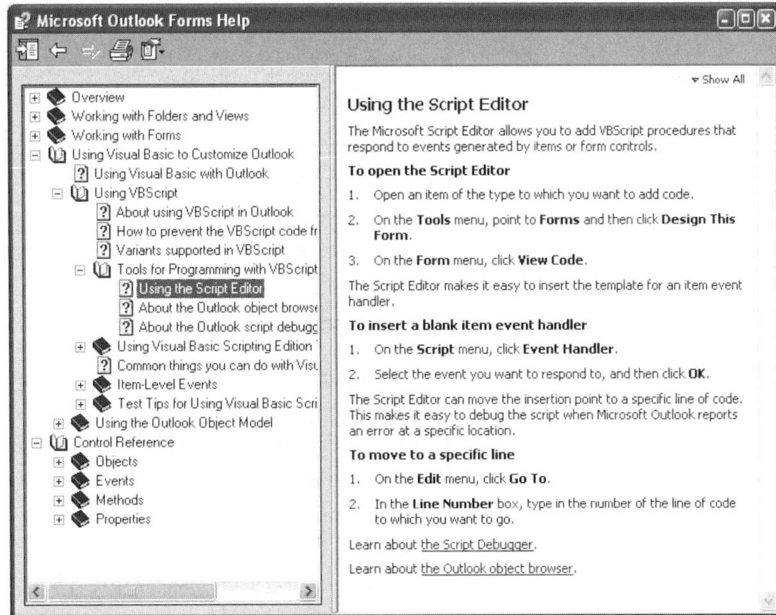


**Figure 15.22** *Don't overlook the notes and links to additional information at the bottom of many Help topics.*

Many help topics cover particular techniques. You usually see a series of numbered steps, such as that in Figure 15.22. Text shown in blue and underlined, as on a Web page, represents a linked topic. Click on the link to see the topic.

To close the Help window, click the Close (x) button in the upper-right corner. While you are working on forms design, you might want to leave Help open so that you can return to it if you have more questions.

## 15.6 Saving forms and ending a design session

When you have done enough work on a form for the day, you will want to save the form and end the forms design session. You can save the form in three ways:

- As an item in an Outlook folder
- As an Outlook template file anywhere on your computer
- As a published Outlook form, either in a forms library or in a particular folder

If you close the form with the Close (x) button in the upper-right corner, Outlook asks whether you want to save changes. If you respond Yes,

Outlook saves the item to the default folder for that type of item. For a Message form, this is the Drafts folder. For a Post form, it's the Inbox. Other forms go into the corresponding folder: an Appointment form to the Calendar folder, and so on.

---

**CAUTION:** I don't recommend storing custom forms as items in Outlook folders because it's too easy to delete them accidentally and not that easy to reuse them. You are better off saving them as template files or publishing them.

---

To save a form as a template file, choose File, Save As; under Save as Type, choose Outlook Template (*.oft). You also have to provide a filename. You can use the location that Outlook initially suggests (which will vary depending on your operating system and configuration—it's usually a folder named Templates under your Windows profile). This will correspond to the User Templates in File System location that appears in the Look In list on the Choose Form dialog (refer to Figure 15.1). If you are designing forms for use with a particular project, you might instead want to create a new folder on your system to hold that project's .oft files.

---

**Tip:** When you are designing a new form, you might want to save interim versions as .oft template files so that you can revert to a version without the most recent changes. Include the version number in the file name to make it easy to locate a particular version.

---

*Publishing a form* means saving it to a form library. Table 15.1 lists the three types of form libraries. If you don't use Microsoft Exchange Server, you won't see Organizational Forms.

When you publish a form to a library for an individual folder and have not checked the Use Form Only for Responses box on the (Properties) page, Outlook lists the form on the Actions menu for that folder as "New <name of form>."

---

**CAUTION:** Do not publish a form under the same name to two locations—for example, Personal Forms and a folder's form library. If you do, you run a high risk of corrupting the local forms cache. We'll discuss forms cache issues in more detail in Chapter 20, "Common Outlook Form and Item Techniques."

---

**Table 15.1** *Outlook Forms Libraries*

| Library | Description |
|---|---|
| Personal Forms | A library of forms stored in your Personal Folders or Exchange Server mailbox |
| Organizational Forms | A library of forms stored on the Exchange Server for group use; you need permission from the Exchange Server administrator to publish to this library |
| Libraries for individual Outlook folders | A library of forms associated with a particular folder, either in your mailbox or Personal Folders or in a public folder on the Exchange Server; you must have folder-owner permission to publish to a public folder |

**Note:** When you publish a message form, Outlook may display a message recommending that you check the Send Form Definition with Item box on the form's Properties tab. Generally, you should answer No. Checking that box means that any VBScript code on the form will not run under Outlook 2002 or versions of Outlook 2000 with the E-mail Security Update installed.

To publish a newly customized form based on one of the built-in forms, choose Tools, Forms, Publish Form. If you used a previously customized form as the basis for your new form, choose Tools, Forms, Publish Form As so that you can give it a new name. In the Publish Form As dialog box (see Figure 15.23), use the Look In dropdown list or the Browse button to select

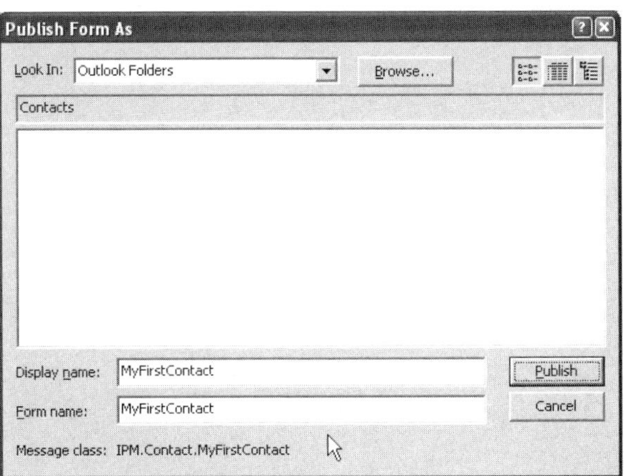


**Figure 15.23** *Publishing a custom Contact form to the Contacts folder.*

a location. Then, give the form a display name and form name, and click Publish.

---

**Tip:** In Chapter 24, "Deploying Forms and Applications," you learn how to remove old forms, make a form the default for new items in a folder, and convert old items to use the new form.

---

After you save a form as an .oft template file or publish it, you can end the design session by clicking the Close button and responding No to the Save Changes prompt. That prompt is for the Outlook item that you created in the process of building the form, not for the form design.

## 15.7 Summary

This chapter introduced you to the six basic Outlook forms you can customize and the techniques required to start and end a design session, save your design work, and display the Field Chooser and Control Toolbox. You also learned several methods and locations for saving forms. In Chapter 16, you will create your first customized form by modifying the Contact form in several ways.

# 16

# Creating Your First Custom Contact Form

In the previous chapter, you became acquainted with the Outlook forms design environment. Now, it's time to go to work and create your first custom Contact form. After a review of the overall process, you will get down to the business of adding and modifying form pages and controls.

The highlights of this chapter include discussions of the following:

- How to add controls to a form
- What constitutes a good control name
- Where to change control properties
- How to rename a page

## 16.1 The process in a nutshell

Creating a custom form involves a series of steps that occur in the same order every time:

1. Pick a form to start with, as discussed in Chapter 15, "Outlook's Six Basic Forms."
2. Add and modify controls on either built-in or customized pages.
3. Test the form.
4. Repeat steps 2 and 3 as necessary to complete the form.
5. Set the basic properties for the form.
6. Save or publish the form.

## 16.2 Add and modify controls and pages

Controls are the building blocks of your form's user interface. They determine how users will enter data, retrieve information, and otherwise interact with the form. A control can be linked, or *bound*, to an Outlook field; if the user changes the data shown in the control, the data in the Outlook field also changes. You can also have an *unbound* control, one whose data is not tied to an Outlook field. The contents of the unbound controls are temporary; when you close the item, the values from those controls are discarded.

Each form can display up to five custom pages, and on the Message, Post, and Contact forms, you can also modify the built-in first page. You will build a new page on a custom Contact form to learn about some of the frequently used fields that don't appear on either the General or the Details page.

---

CAUTION: If you modify the first page (the General page) of a Contact form, the form cannot be used with Outlook 97. If you must keep the form compatible with Outlook 97, leave the General page alone and do all your modifications on the available custom pages.

---

### 16.2.1 Add fields

To begin, open the Contact form in design mode and click on the (P.2) page. The Field Chooser should appear with the list of frequently used fields displayed. If it doesn't, click the Field Chooser button, or choose Form, Field Chooser.

To place a field on the form, drag it from the Field Chooser to the form page. Start with the Business Home Page field. Outlook automatically places the field at the top left of the blank page. Next, drag the Personal Home Page field to the form. See how Outlook places it directly beneath the first field. Check your form against Figure 16.1.

Also, notice that the name of the page, P.2, is no longer in parentheses. Outlook assumes that if you add fields to a custom page, you want users to see them, so it automatically sets the page to be visible to the user. Both these fields display their data in a control called a *text box* (because the user can normally type text into it). Text boxes are probably the most commonly used form control.

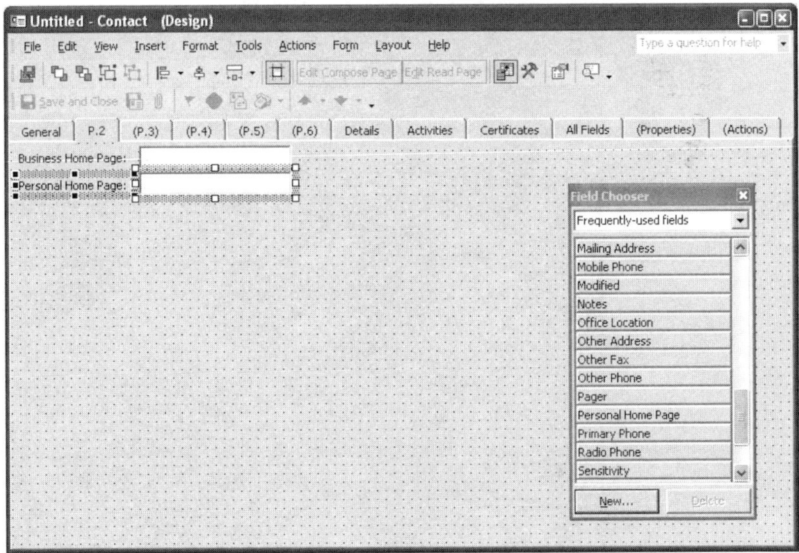


**Figure 16.1** *This custom page contains two fields dragged from the Field Chooser.*

The text that tells you the name of the field, such as Business Home Page for the first field, is called a *label*. Label controls are a key element in making forms easy to understand. Not only do they describe different controls, but you can also use them to provide detailed instructions on the form page.

---

**Tip:** Outlook saves you time by adding a label control for most fields that you drag from the Field Chooser. Some controls, such as check box controls, do not need label controls nearby because they include their own `Caption` property.

---

Now, drag two more fields from the Field Chooser: Flag Status and Follow Up Flag. Finally, in the Field Chooser, switch from the Frequently-Used Fields list to All Mail Fields (that's right, All Mail Fields), and drag the Due By field to your form. Your form should look like Figure 16.2

The Flag Status field uses a *combo box* control. This type of control combines elements of a text box control (users can type in it) with a *list box* control, where users pick an item from a list. Combo box controls usually work so that when users type the first letter or two of the item they want to select, the combo box control automatically selects that item without a mouse click.

Some Outlook fields do not appear in the fields list for the type of item you're working with. For example, the Due By field is used for both Mail

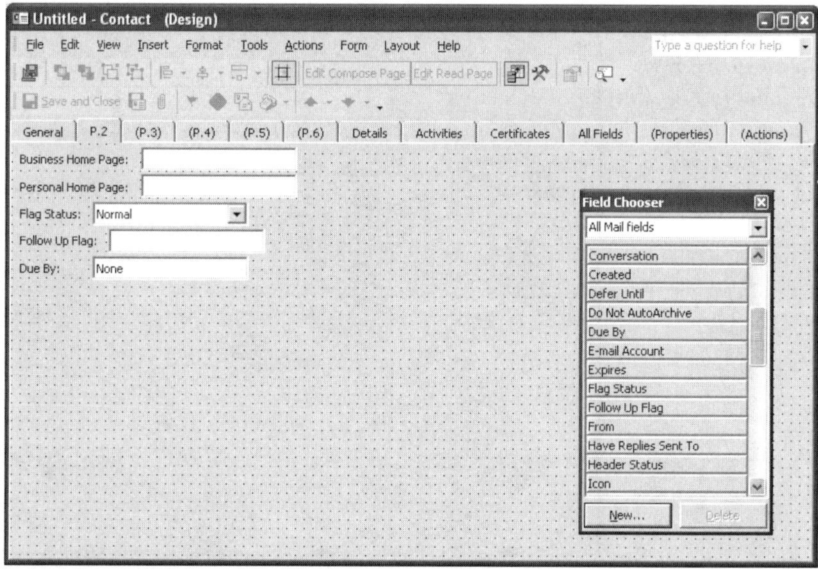


**Figure 16.2** *Now you have dragged five additional fields to the custom page.*

and Contact item message flags, but appears only on the list of Mail fields. It is worth experimenting to see what fields you can use from other types of items. Don't be surprised, though, if Outlook tells you that you cannot use a field from another type of item on your current form. Also, sometimes you get no warning; Outlook allows you to add the field to the form, but does not display the data you expect. There's no way to know which will work without trying. Chapter 10, "Working with the Object Models," provides information on how to explore the Outlook object model to learn what properties are available. Note, however, that the names you see in the Field Chooser are not always the same as the actual property names in the object model.

---

**Tip:** If you're eager to learn more about the different types of controls, you might want to peek ahead to Chapter 19, "More Controls for Outlook Forms."

---

## 16.2.2 Rearrange controls

When you drag fields from the Field Chooser, Outlook lines up any accompanying label controls on the left side of the form, then puts the text box and combo box controls adjacent to the label controls. Since the label controls have different widths, this leaves the right side looking sloppy. Your

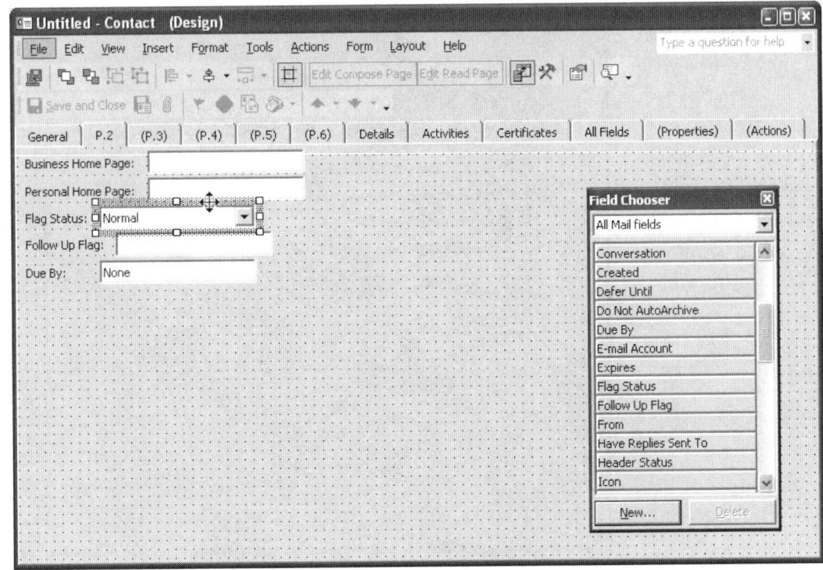


**Figure 16.3** *To move a single control, select it, move the mouse pointer until it turns into a four-headed arrow, and then drag the control to the new location.*

next task, therefore, is to make the Text and Combo Box fields align neatly along their right edges.

You could move each control individually. For example, click the box with the word Normal in it (in other words, the control for the Flag Status field) to select it. The box now appears with a gray line around it and eight white boxes called *drag handles* at the corners and sides; these are used for resizing the control. If you move the mouse pointer over one of the sides (but not over a drag handle), it turns into a four-sided arrow. When you see the four-sided arrow (see Figure 16.3), hold down the left mouse button and drag the field to a new location on the form.

There's an easier way to line up those controls, though. You can select a group of controls and then use a layout command to right-align them.

First, you have to know how to select multiple controls. Earlier, you clicked on one control to select it. To add another control to the selection, hold down the Ctrl key as you click it. Continue using Ctrl+click to include the four text boxes and the one combo box in your selection. If you select one of the labels by mistake, use Ctrl+click to deselect it. You can also click anywhere on the background of the form to clear all selections and start over completely.

Did you notice that the drag handles for the last control you clicked are white, whereas those for the others are black? The control with white drag handles acts as the model for alignment and resizing operations. In

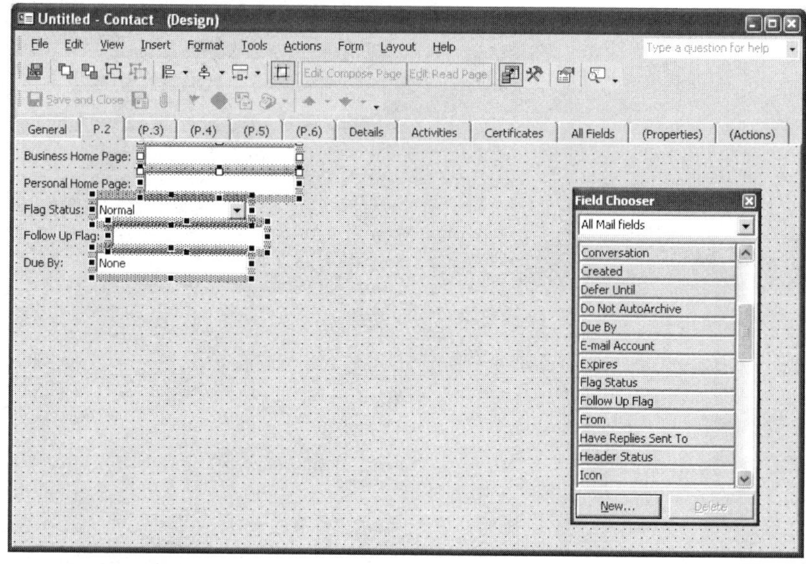


**Figure 16.4** *When multiple controls are selected, the one with the white drag handles controls any group sizing and alignment operations.*

this case, you want to line up everything along the right edge of the Business Home Page and Personal Home Page fields, so make sure that one of those fields has the white drag handles. If one of the other fields was the last selected, use Ctrl+click twice on the Business Home Page field to make it the last one selected. Figure 16.4 shows how the selected controls should look.

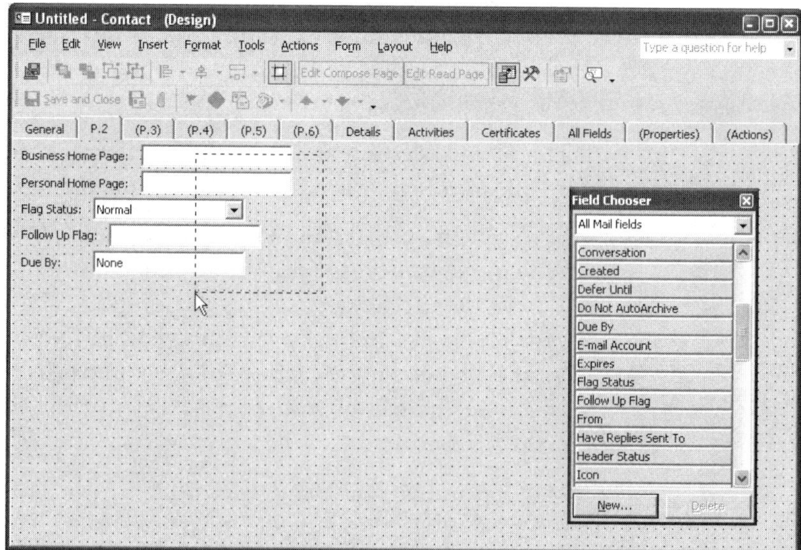


**Figure 16.5** *Quickly select adjacent controls by dragging across them.*

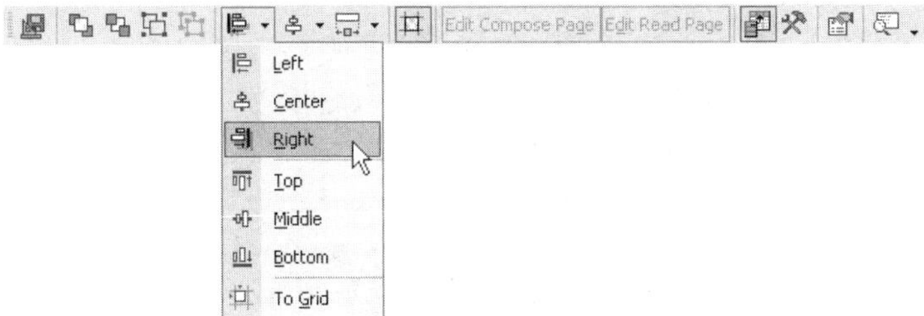


**Figure 16.6** *The Align commands on the Form Design toolbar.*

Here is a really quick method for selecting a group of adjacent controls: Drag a rectangular shape (with the mouse pointer) that covers a bit of each control you want to select and doesn't touch any other controls. For this form, position the mouse pointer slightly to the right of the Business Home Page field, the one you want to use as your alignment model. Then, hold down the left mouse button and drag the mouse diagonally toward the lower left until you see a rectangle touching all the text box and combo box controls, as shown in Figure 16.5. The control nearest the starting corner of the rectangle will be the one marked with the white drag handles. When you release the left mouse button, the controls will be selected, just as they were in Figure 16.4.

With the controls selected, click the small arrow next to the Align Left button on the toolbar (see Figure 16.6), and then click Right. You can also choose Layout, Align, Right from the menu. After aligning the controls, they should look like Figure 16.7.

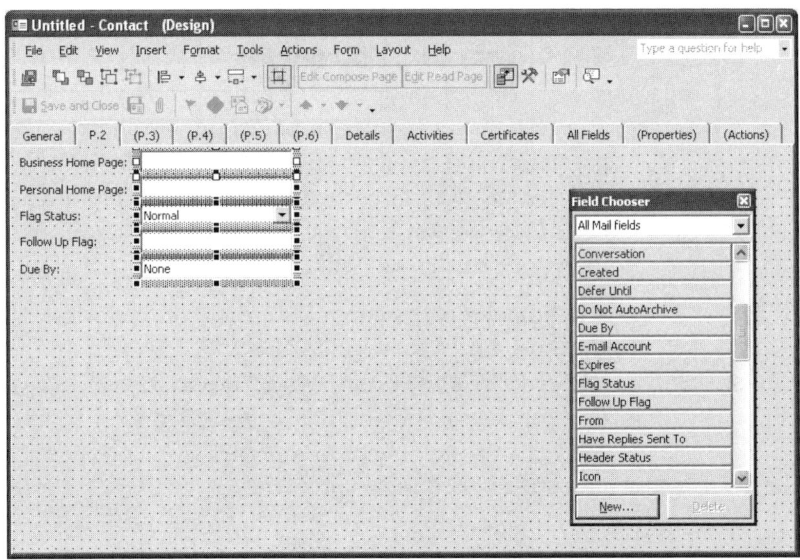


**Figure 16.7** *Controls that are the same size and aligned along their right edge are easier on the user's eye.*

**Tip:** Several buttons on the Form Design toolbar include small arrows that display a list of additional commands.

**Tip:** If you change the layout of your form and don't like the way it looks, press Ctrl+Z or choose Edit, Undo to reverse the last change you made.

The Layout menu and Form Design toolbar contain many other helpful commands for rearranging and resizing controls and setting the *tab order.* (The tab order controls what field gets the focus of the cursor when a user presses Tab or Shift+Tab to move out of a control.) To resize a control, select it and then drag it by one of the white drag handles.

### 16.2.3 Show, hide, and rename pages

Now that your five controls are looking neat, you can give that custom page a more descriptive name. To rename a page, choose Form, Rename Page, and type in the new name: "Home Pages & Flag" would be appropriate for this page.

To hide or show a page, choose Form, Display This Page. A check next to the Display This Page command indicates whether the user will see the current page. You can also look at the page name; the names of hidden pages are in parentheses.

### 16.2.4 Set control properties

To finish working with controls in this lesson, you have to learn about their properties. Just as an Outlook contact has built-in fields or properties that describe different facts about the contact record, properties on a control are the adjectives that describe the characteristics of the control. Forms have properties, too, as you will shortly see.

Outlook divides control properties into two groups: the basic ones you are most likely to want to use and advanced properties less commonly changed. To work with the basic properties, select a control and then click the Properties button on the Form Design toolbar. You can also right-click a control and then choose Properties from the pop-up menu. Figure 16.8 shows the basic Display properties.

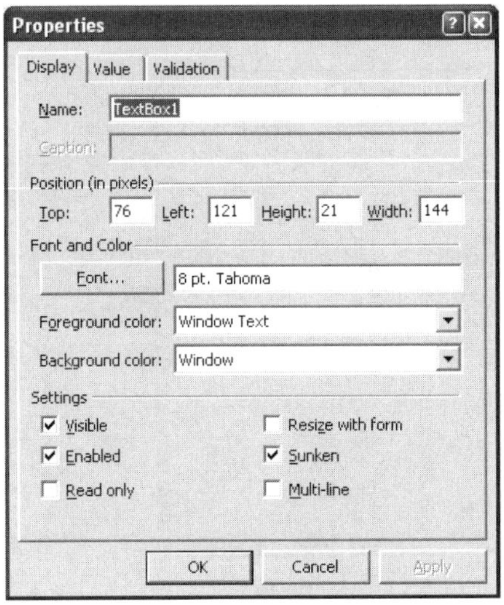

**Figure 16.8** *The basic control Display properties include name, position, font, and color.*

**Note:** You will learn about the properties on the Value and Validation tabs in the next chapter.

Every control needs a name to distinguish it from other controls in the tab order and in any programming code you write. Outlook assigns a name automatically. You should change the name, at least for text box controls and other controls where the user enters data. Changing the name of label controls is a less urgent task. Names should be descriptive, not cryptic, and should use the prefix from Table 16.1 appropriate for the control; no spaces are allowed in control names. A good descriptive name will help you remember the purpose for that control and make it easier to rearrange the tab order and to write code to work with the controls on the form.

**Table 16.1** *Outlook Form Control Name Prefixes*

| Control | Prefix |
|---|---|
| Label | `lbl` |
| Text Box | `txt` |
| Combo Box | `cbo` |
| List Box | `lst` |

**Table 16.1** *Outlook Form Control Name Prefixes (continued)*

| Control | Prefix |
|---|---|
| Check Box | `chk` |
| Option Button | `opt` |
| Toggle Button | `tgl` |
| Frame | `fra` |
| Command Button | `cmd` |
| Tab Strip | `tab` |
| Multipage | `mlt` |
| Scroll Bar | `hsb` (horizontal) or `vsb` (vertical) |
| Spin Button | `spn` |
| Image | `img` |

For example, on your form, Outlook gave the names `ComboBox1` to the combo box control for the Flag Status field and `TextBox1` to the text box control for the Follow Up Flag field. Good, clear names for these would be `cboFlagStatus` and `txtFollowUpFlag`. The prefix (`cbo` or `txt`) makes it easy, when you're writing code, to know whether you are working with a combo box or text box control. Since the two have different properties, it's important to keep track of what kind of control you're working with.

Figure 16.9 shows what the Tab Order dialog looks like after the names of the two controls described above are changed. It is easy to tell where the

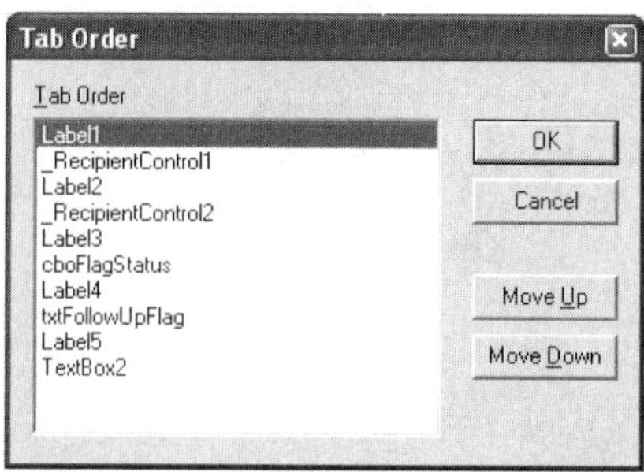


**Figure 16.9** *Use the Move Up and Move Down buttons on the Tab Order dialog to change the order in which the user moves through controls by pressing the Tab key.*

cboFlagStatus and txtFollowUpFlag controls appear in the tab order, but you have no way of knowing which fields are shown in the _RecipientControl1, _RecipientControl2, and TextBox2 controls, which still have the names that Outlook automatically assigned them.

Setting the tab order on Outlook forms is similar to the process for VBA forms. Flip back to Chapter 3, "A VBA Birthday/Anniversary Reminder Form," if you need a refresher.

Table 16.2 lists Name along with the other display properties you can set on the Display tab of the basic Properties dialog box for a form.

Outlook lists additional properties on a different Properties dialog box that appears when you right-click any control and then choose Advanced Properties from the pop-up menu. You can leave this Properties box open as you select controls, even multiple controls.

**Table 16.2** *Outlook Form Control Display Properties*

| Property | Description |
|---|---|
| Name | Unique descriptive name |
| Caption | Text on label, check box, option button, toggle button, frame, or command button |
| Position | Top, left, height, and width, measured in pixels |
| Font | Font size, style, and color |
| Foreground color | Text color, using the Windows color scheme |
| Background color | Background color, using the Windows color scheme |
| Visible | Can the user see the control? (Yes/No) |
| Enabled | Can the user click on or enter information in the control? (Yes/No) |
| Read only | Can the user change the control's data? (Yes/No) |
| Resize with form | Shrink and enlarge the control when the overall form changes size? (Yes/No) |
| Sunken | Add a 3-D look? (Yes/No) |
| Multi-line | Wrap text in a text box, and create a new line when the user presses Enter? (Yes/No) |

**Note:** The two Properties dialog boxes work differently with respect to multiple controls. If you select multiple controls and click Properties, the dialog box controls the properties only for the last control you selected. To set properties for a group of controls, select them. Then, right-click any selected control and choose Advanced Properties from the pop-up menu.

Text box controls have a total of 42 properties; combo and list box controls, even more; other controls have more or less, as needed. These properties include the Display properties from the basic Properties dialog, as well as many others. To change any property, select it in the Properties list and then look at the top of the Advanced Properties dialog box for either a drop-down list of choices or a text box where you can type in a value. Click the Apply button after you make your choice or type in a new property value.

For example, Figure 16.10 shows the Properties for the Follow Up Flag text box. Outlook provides this field so that you can specify how you want to follow up on a contact (or a mail message)—with a phone call, visit, reply, or some other activity. In case the user is not familiar with this feature, you can change the `ControlTipText` property to add text that pops up when the user pauses the mouse over the text box control. When you click the Apply button, Outlook adds the text in the box next to the Apply button to the properties for the text box as the new control tip. Figure 16.11 shows how a user will see the control tip on the finished form.

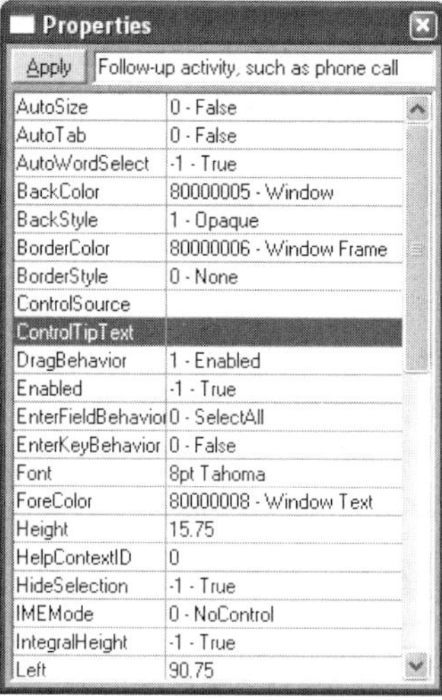


**Figure 16.10** *Set advanced properties for an Outlook Form control with this window.*

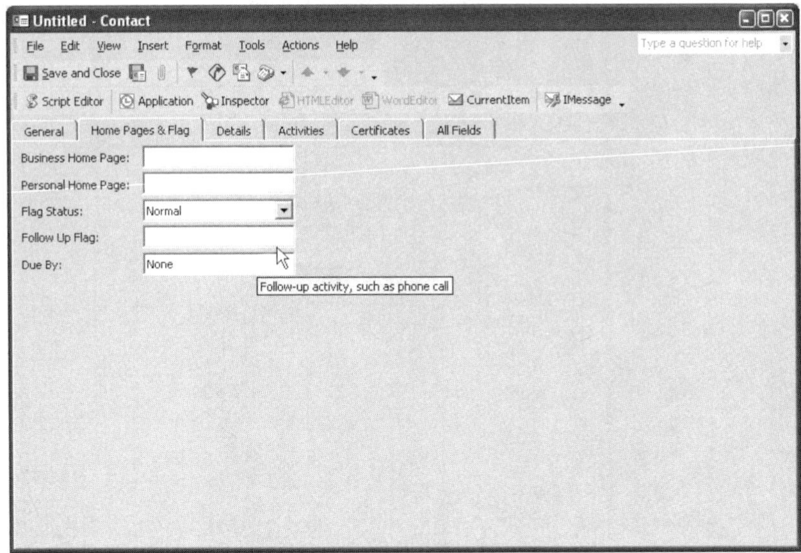

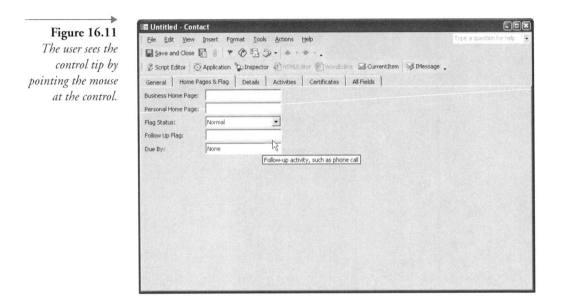

**Figure 16.11** *The user sees the control tip by pointing the mouse at the control.*

**Tip:** Control tips are a great way to document your custom form as you build it.

# 16.3 Complete the form

After you finish placing controls on the form and setting their properties, you need to test the form, set its properties, and then save or publish it.

## 16.3.1 Test the form

At any time, you can see how your form will look to a user by choosing Form, Run This Form. A new instance of the form appears, as in Figure 16.11, with all the changes you have made to the form so far. You can close it with the Close (x) button at the upper-right corner of the form and return to your working copy of the form, which remains open in design mode.

## 16.3.2 Set form properties

Forms have properties, too, just as controls do. Right-click on any blank area of the form background and then choose Advanced Properties to dis-

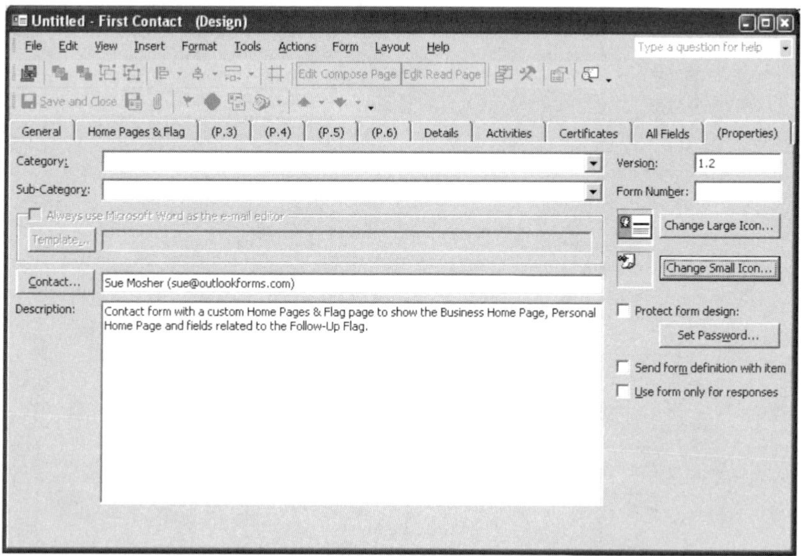


**Figure 16.12** *Set the form's operational properties on the (Properties) page.*

play the Properties window, where you can set the background color and other properties.

When you are satisfied with the form and have tested it, it's time to set the operational properties for the form before you save it. Click on the (Properties) tab to switch to that page, shown in Figure 16.12, which is normally hidden from users.

---

**Tip:** If the form is too wide for your display and you can't see the (Properties) tab or other tabs on the right side of the form, press Ctrl+Page Down to move through the different form pages one by one. You can use Ctrl+Page Up to cycle through the pages in the opposite order.

---

On the (Properties) page, you will almost always want to set the version, icons, contact, and description. Other settings may be optional, depending on the purpose of the form and the environment in which it will be used.

The version should be a number, increased every time you update the form with new enhancements. You can use a numbering sequence for the various versions, such as 1.0, 1.1, 1.2, and so on, or 1, 2, 3, 4, 5, and so on. Because of the way Outlook caches forms that the user recently opened, incrementing the number helps ensure that everyone who uses the form will have the latest version. It also helps with troubleshooting, since the user can choose Help, About This Form to get the version number of a published form.

By default, custom forms always use the icon for the Post form. To change either the large or small icon, click the appropriate button. Then, choose an icon from the *.ico files on your system in the C:\Program Files\Microsoft Office\Office10\Forms\1033\ folder. (Yours might be in a different location, depending on where you installed Outlook—for example, Office\Forms instead of Office10\Forms for Outlook 2000. In Outlook 2002, 1033 denotes the folder for U.S. English components. Figure 16.12 shows the Contactl.ico icon for the large icon. You will want to use the matching Contacts.ico for the small icon. The l and s at the end of the icon file name stand for the large and small versions of the same icon.

---

**Tip:** Use the Windows Start, Find, Files or Folders command to search for *.ico files located elsewhere on your system. You can use any icon with Outlook that is exactly 32 × 32 pixels in size. The small Outlook icon is 32 × 32, just like the large icon, but only the 16 × 16 pixels at upper left contain the icon image.

---

The Contact and Description fields should contain information about how the form should be used and whom to contact in case of questions or problems. This information appears when the user uses the Tools, Form, Choose Form command to run a published form. You also see it on the Help, About This Form dialog on a published form (see Figure 16.13).

Now, take a quick look at the less frequently used form properties. Set a Category and optional Subcategory if you use a hierarchy of categories to organize forms, either in your own folders or in the Organizational Forms

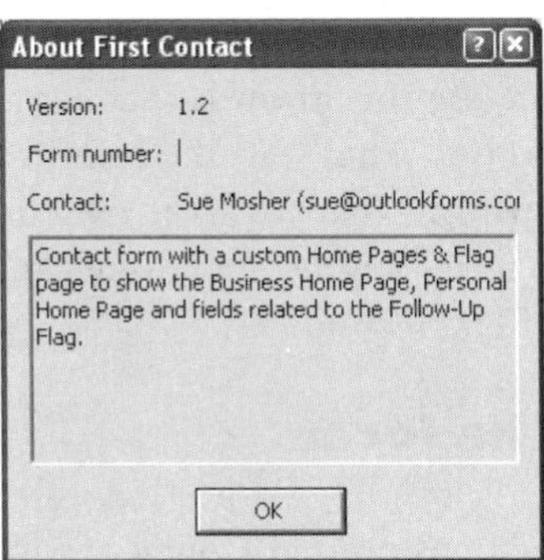


**Figure 16.13** *For published forms, when users choose Help, About This Form, they see the details you set on the (Properties) page.*

library. You can add a Form Number, in addition to the Version number, to identify your form as part of your organization's classification scheme.

Custom forms based on the Message or Post form can require the user to use Word as the e-mail editor, with a particular .dot Word template. These options are available only if the default message format is set to Microsoft Outlook Rich Text before you can open the form. (You can change the message format by choosing Tools, Options, and then switching to the Mail Format tab.) Set the Word as Editor options on your custom form with the Always Use Microsoft Word as the E-Mail Editor check box and the Template button.

If you want to discourage other people from changing your form design or seeing the code for your form, check Protect Form Design and click Set Password to give the form a password. Note, however, that it's very easy to retrieve the password with a bit of Outlook VBA code, so don't regard this password protection as foolproof.

Do not check the Send Form Definition with Item box; it is an obsolete setting held over from versions of Outlook without as much security as today's Outlook. If you check that box, code on the form will not run on Outlook 2002 or on Outlook 2000 or 98 with the Outlook Email Security Update installed. Items saved or sent with that form also will be much larger because they will include both the data and the form definition (a state known as a *one-off* form).

---

**Note:** Whenever you publish a message form, Outlook will suggest that you check the Send Form Definition with Item box to ensure that the recipient will have the form, especially if you're sending to someone via the Internet. We will cover the correct way to send messages using custom forms over the Internet in Chapter 20, "Common Outlook Form and Item Techniques."

---

If you want to prevent the user from launching a form directly, check Use Form Only for Responses. That way, the form works only in conjunction with another custom form that includes the current form among its custom actions. Custom form actions are covered in Chapter 20, "Common Outlook Form and Item Techniques."

### 16.3.3 Save or publish the form

You have finished your first customized Contact form! Now, save it by following the instructions in Chapter 15 for saving or publishing a form. Try both saving it as an Outlook template .oft file to a system folder and publishing it to your Personal Forms library. Remember that when you publish it, you must give it both a display name that will appear on the title bar of new instances of the form and a unique form name. Often, these are the same. In Figures 16.12 and 16.13 you can see that I used the name `First Contact` for the form created during this chapter.

## 16.4 Summary

Creating a custom form is simply a matter of adding controls, adjusting their properties and those of the form itself, and saving the form so that you can reuse it easily. How you lay out the form and the properties you set can make the form more pleasing to the eye and easier to use. In Chapter 17, "Extending Form Design with Fields and Controls," you'll learn how to create custom fields, add them to a form, set validation formulas, and build separate compose and read layouts.

# 17

# *Extending Form Design with Fields and Controls*

Now that you know how to create and save simple customized forms, you can add more controls and create some custom fields. You will also learn how to make Outlook forms display different information, depending on whether you are composing a new item or reading an existing item.

The highlights of this chapter include discussions of the following:

- How controls are linked to fields
- How to create custom fields and add them to forms
- Why it's a good idea to use Outlook's built-in fields whenever possible
- How to use formulas to combine information from various fields and prevent users from making data-entry mistakes
- What gives sent messages a different layout from newly composed messages

## 17.1 Understanding fields versus controls

In the previous chapter, you added several built-in fields to an Outlook form to make it easier for the user to store and retrieve the information in those fields. This is the key idea behind a field: It stores information permanently as part of an Outlook item.

Typically, each control on a form is bound to a particular field. In other words, the control shows the data in the field, and if you change the data in the control, it updates the information in the actual Outlook item when you save that item. Outlook also uses bound controls for fields that combine information from several fields or that calculate a value using a formula.

You will also find uses for unbound controls. These controls don't correspond to a particular field. Unbound controls store information, but only temporarily. The data they hold disappears when the user closes the current item unless the programmer adds code to the form to save it in an Outlook property first.

The fields you added to the form in Chapter 16 are all fields built into Outlook. Even the Due Date field is a built-in field, although the Field Chooser shows it as a Mail field rather than a Contact field.

You will probably want to use built-in fields as much as possible. For one thing, you cannot import from another data source into user-defined Outlook fields. The only way to import into user-defined fields is with programming code or a third-party tool. Therefore, using built-in fields can save you time if you plan to import or export data.

---

**Note:** You also cannot import directly into a custom form. However, as you will learn in Chapter 24, "Deploying Forms and Applications," changing the form for all items in a folder is a simple task.

---

**Tip:** The Billing Information and Mileage fields are text fields available on any Outlook form. The Contact form includes four extra generic fields listed in the Field Chooser as User Field 1, User Field 2, User Field 3, and User Field 4, for storing any kind of text information.

---

## 17.2 Creating user-defined fields

To explore user-defined fields, you can work with the Task form, creating a field and then adding a control to display it on a custom page. Use the Tools, Forms, Design a Form command to open the built-in Task form to get into design mode.

To add a new field, switch to one of the customizable pages and then click the New button on the Field Chooser. In the New Field dialog box, give the field a name, choose the type, and specify the format. Name the field "Project," and use the text type and text format, as shown in Figure 17.1.

This process creates a field in the parent folder for the form. Since you started from a new unmodified Task form, the `Project` field will appear in the User-defined Fields in Folder list for the Tasks folder. Drag the `Project` field to any customizable page. This adds the field to the form and, thus, to

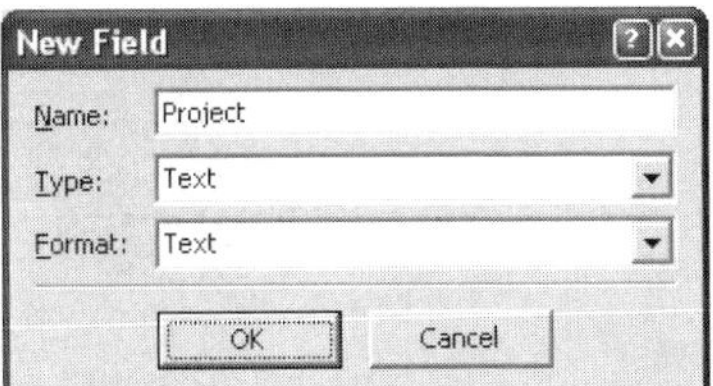


**Figure 17.1** *Specify the name, type, and format for a user-defined field.*

any items that you create with this form. The All Fields tab should show the `Project` field under both User-defined Fields in Folder and User-defined Fields in This Item.

---

**Note:** If a field exists only in a form and not in the folder, you cannot display the field in the folder view and use certain Outlook code methods. If you create a form and later want to use it in a different folder, chances are that the folder will not have the necessary field definitions. Chapter 24, "Deploying Forms and Applications," returns to this issue and provides code you can use to ensure that forms and folders have matching properties.

---

### 17.2.1 Field types

It's time to talk about the different types of fields that Outlook supports. Table 17.1 lists those available on the New Field dialog box. Experienced programmers might be perplexed because the user-defined field types available in Outlook are a little different from data types in VBA or other programming environments.

For example, Outlook lists a text type, instead of a string data type. To programmers, string data contains zero or more characters, and those characters can be numbers, letters, punctuation—any characters at all. Two Outlook field types can contain string data: the text type and the keywords type, which consists of several strings separated by commas.

---

**Note:** The separator used to distinguish the individual keywords in a keywords-type field depends on the regional settings for Windows. In U.S. English installations of Outlook, the separator is a comma, but in other countries, it might be a semicolon. Listing 10.11 shows how to obtain the user's list separator from the Windows registry.

---

**Table 17.1** *Types for Outlook User-Defined Fields*

| Field Type | Can Contain |
|---|---|
| Text | Any string |
| Number | Any number |
| Percent | Any number; displayed as a percentage |
| Currency | Any number involving money; displayed in the currency format for your country, as set in the Windows Control Panel under Regional Options. |
| Yes/No | Yes (–1)/No (0), True/False, or On/Off |
| Date/Time | Date and time data |
| Duration | The number of minutes |
| Keywords | Multiple strings, separated by commas (see Note below) |
| Combination | A combination of values from other fields, showing either all values or the first nonempty value |
| Formula | A calculation based on other fields and built-in functions |
| Integer | Any nondecimal number |

Notice the several types for holding numeric data: number, percent, currency, and integer. The yes/no type is actually a special number type that can hold either of just two values, -1 and 0, which stand for Yes, True, or On and No, False, or Off, respectively.

**CAUTION:** Outlook does not allow you to change the name or data type for a user-defined field after you create it. If you change your mind about the data type, you will have to delete the field from both the form and the parent folder and create it again. Make sure you have the type correct before you create any items with the form.

Fields using the date/time and duration types allow you to enter data using natural language, in other words, with ordinary words. For example, if you type "today" into a date/time field, Outlook converts that to the current date. You can type "next Tues", and it will calculate the date automatically. Try typing "2 wks from Fri", and you will get an idea of just how smart and useful this feature can be. (If you really want a thrill, type in "New Year's Eve".)

Duration fields store time measured in minutes, but allow you to enter it in days or hours as well. Use the letters "d" for day and "h" for hours. Try typing "2d" into any Duration field, and watch it turn into "2 days".

**Note:** To discover the type used by a built-in Outlook field, select the field on the All Fields page on the form and then click the Properties button. For example, the Categories field uses the keywords type. For some fields, you will see Internal Data Type listed as the type. The values and behavior of these fields are controlled by Outlook itself, not by the user directly, and they don't fit into any of the neat types in Table 17.1.

## 17.2.2 Combination fields

Combination fields let you combine the values in one or more fields with optional text. For example, you can use a combination field to show the first nonempty phone number or to put the text "This task is due:" in front of the due date.

You can add a combination field to show either the date a task was completed or the date it is due. As you did for the Project field, click the New button on the Field Chooser. Type "Completed or Due" for the Name, and choose Combination for the Type. Then, click the Edit button to display the Combination Formula Field dialog box in Figure 17.2. At the top, select Showing Only the First Non-Empty Field, Ignoring Subsequent Ones.

Before going further, take a moment to think through the logic of which field should come first. If the user has already finished the task, you don't

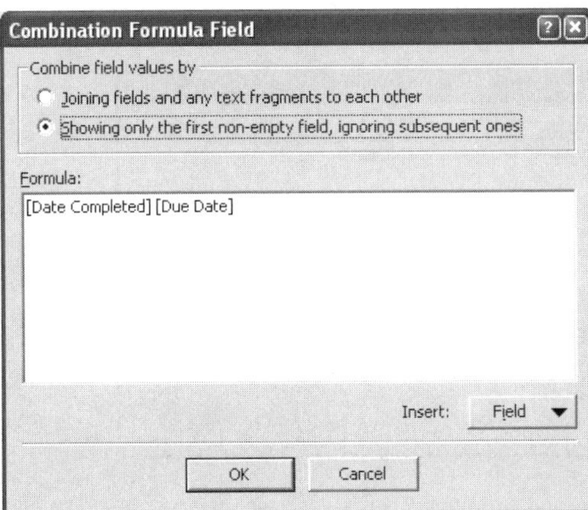


**Figure 17.2** *To create the formula for a Combination field, use several fields or combine fields and text.*

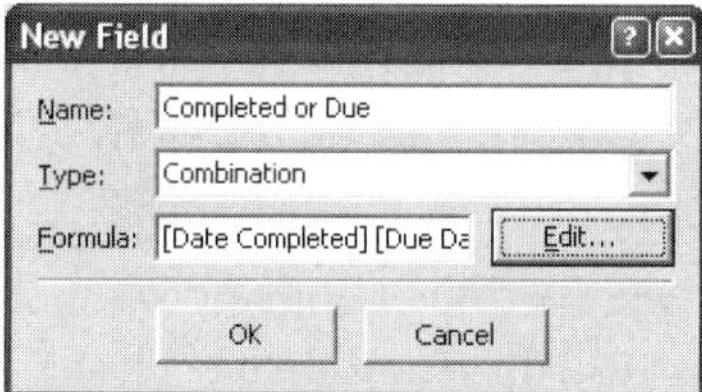


**Figure 17.3**
*Combination and formula fields have a Formula setting instead of a Format setting.*

have to see the due date, right? Therefore, the completed date should come first. After you decide on the field order, click the Field button, pick a field, and repeat until you see the fields you want in the Formula box. Click OK to save the combination formula. The New Field dialog box should look like Figure 17.3, using the formula `[Date Completed] [Due Date]`. Click OK to save the new field.

### 17.2.3 Formula fields

Next, you will create a Formula field that gives you the number of days until a task is due. Create the field by clicking the New button on the Field Chooser. Name the field `IsOverdue`, choose Formula for the Type, and then click Edit. In the Formula Field dialog box (see Figure 17.4), you will see not only the Field button that you saw when creating a combination field, but also a Function button. When creating formula fields on Outlook forms, you can use only intrinsic functions, those built into Outlook. The Outlook formula editor includes conversion, date/time, financial, general, math, and text functions.

To create a formula for a field, you combine fields, functions, and operators; such as + and /. You learned about operators in Chapter 4, "Code Basics."

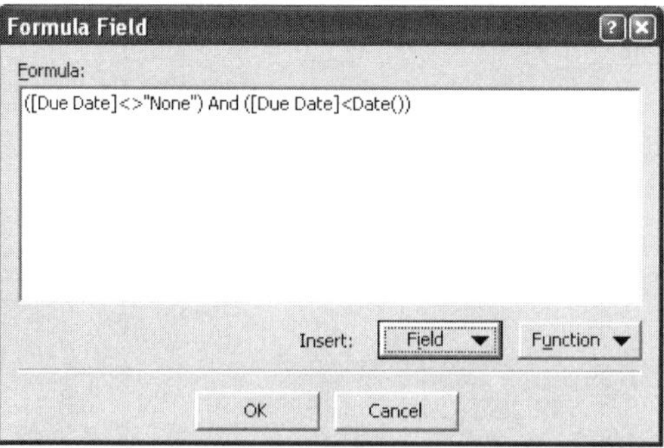


**Figure 17.4**
*Use text, fields, and functions to create a formula field.*

The `IsOverdue` field uses the task's built-in Due Date field to determine whether an item is overdue. To create the formula in the Formula Field dialog box, type in the formula shown in Figure 17.4. Click OK to save it as part of the definition of the `IsOverdue` field (see Figure 17.5). The formula uses one function, `Date()`, a simple function that returns today's date. For `IsOverdue` to return `True`, both `([Due Date]<>"None")` and `([Due Date]<Date())` must be true statements.

---

**Note:** The `IsOverdue` formula is an exception to the way you'll normally handle a "None" date in Outlook. Most of the time, when the user sees "None" on the screen, Outlook actually stores the date January 1, 4501, but here we need to test for the literal text "None."

---

The `IsOverdue` formula field is not limited to returning `True` and `False` values, of course. With the addition of a second function, `IIf()`, you could also use it to return specific text:

```
IIf(([Due Date]<>"none") And
([Due Date]<Date()),"OVERDUE!!!", "Not due yet")
```

The `IIf()` function is very useful for Outlook formula fields. When you add it to the Formula Field box by selecting it from the Function, General menu, you'll see that it consists of three parts—*`expr`*, *`truepart`*, and *`falsepart`*:

```
IIf( expr , truepart , falsepart)
```

For the first part, *`expr`*, the formula needs to provide an expression that evaluates to `True` or `False`–in our example, `([Due Date]<>"None") And ([Due Date]<Date())`. If there is a due date and the date is earlier than today's date, the *`truepart`* portion of our formula returns the text "OVERDUE!!!." If there is no due date or if the task is due today or in the future, the *`falsepart`* returns the text "Not due yet."

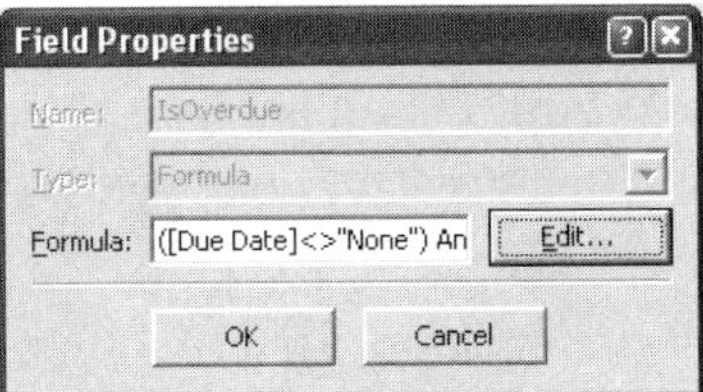


**Figure 17.5** *This Formula field returns either True or False.*

### 17.2.4 Working with formula and combination fields

If you make a mistake in a formula or combination field and want to change it later, after already adding it to a form, you can make your change through the control on the Outlook form that uses the field. Right-click the control, choose Properties, and then switch to the Value tab. Edit the formula under Set the Initial Value of This Field To. Your change will not be reflected in design mode. However, when you run the form, the new formula should be in effect.

If you have not yet added the field to the form, another way to edit the formula is to select it on the All Fields tab of the form, under User-defined Fields in Folder, then click the Properties button. If you use this method to change a formula for a field you have already added to a form, you should remove the field's control from the form, delete the field on the All Fields page, under User-defined Fields in This Item, and then add the revised formula field back to the form.

Formula fields present several limitations that you should be aware of. Outlook does not allow sorting and grouping on combination or formula fields in a view. One way around this limitation is to use a normal field of the appropriate type, and then put code behind the form or an initial value formula, covered later in this chapter, on the field's control to perform the calculation.

In addition, any formatting that you want on the item must be built into the formula since the New Field dialog replaces the normal Format list with the Formula box. For example, if you want a formula field named `OneWeekFromToday` to show the date one week from today, but in the format "Month day, year," you can use the `Format()` function to control the way the date looks to the user:

```
Format(Date() + 7 ,"mmm dd, yyyy")
```

This formula tells Outlook to take today's date—the `Date()` function again—add seven days, and then apply the `"mmm dd, yyyy"` format to the result. `Format()` is a very useful function available in Outlook formulas and VBA, but not in VBScript, that allows you to convert an expression into text in a specific format. For details on possible formats it can handle, look it up in Outlook VBA Help.

Finally, a formula or combination field is always read-only. Since the value of the field is determined by the formula, the user can alter the value only by changing the value of a field used in the formula. If you want to use a formula to suggest a value, but allow the user to override it, use a normal field and set its initial value, as described later in this chapter.

### 17.2.5 Counting e-mail addresses on a custom contact form

Let's look at one more example of a custom field. Do you remember the customized Contact form from Chapter 1, "What You Can Do with Outlook," that showed the number of e-mail addresses for a contact? It has another example of a formula field. Here is its formula:

```
-( ( [E-mail] <> "") + ( [E-mail 2] <> "" ) + ( [E-mail 3]
<> ""))
```

Each of the three expressions involving an e-mail field compares the value of the field to an empty string (`""`). For example, if there is no address in the `[E-mail]` field, the term `([E-mail] <> "")` returns `True`, which is actually the number `–1`. Each of the three expressions returns `–1` if there is an address and `0` if the field is blank. The minus sign (–) at the left of the formula changes the result from a negative to positive number. Therefore, the formula yields `0` if no e-mail address is present and a number between `1` and `3` if any of the fields is filled in.

---

**Tip:** If you know the functions and fields you want to use, you can type formulas directly rather than using the Field and Function buttons. For example, you could use the `Abs()` function to convert the sum of the three expressions above into a positive number. Also, feel free to put spaces around operators and fields to make the formula easier to read. Parentheses control the order in which expressions in a complex formula are evaluated, and they also enhance readability.

---

## 17.3 Adding fields to Outlook forms

After you create user-defined fields in the Field Chooser, you can add them to the task form's (P.2) page. If you haven't already done so, drag the `Project` and `IsOverdue` fields from the Field Chooser to the custom page so that it looks like Figure 17.6. Dragging a field to the form adds it to the User-defined Fields in This Item list on the All Fields tab. Any item created with this form will include that field.

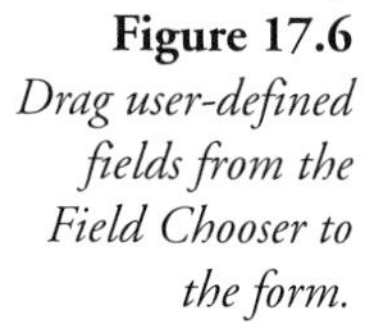

**Figure 17.6** *Drag user-defined fields from the Field Chooser to the form.*

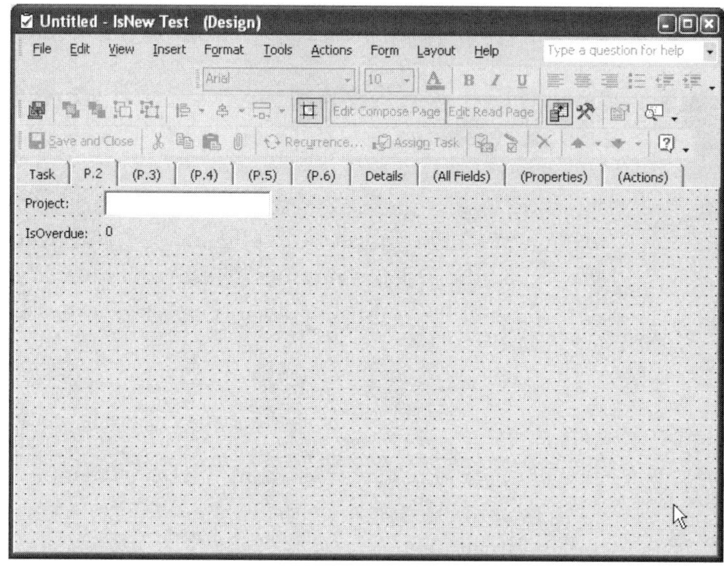


Where did the `IsOverdue` field's value of `0` come from? The formula for `IsOverdue` can return only `True` or `False`, that is, `–1` or `0`. Normally, you use a check box control to display the value in a Yes/No field because few users know that `True` equals `–1`. However, because `IsOverdue` is a formula field, not a yes/no field, Outlook does not automatically create a check box control when you drag `IsOverdue` to the form.

## 17.3.1 Binding a control to a field

If you want to use a check box control to display the `IsOverdue` field, you can't just drag the field from the Field Chooser. Instead, you place the check box control on the form, then bind it to the field. This is a technique you can use any time you want Outlook to display a field in a particular type of control.

First, select the `IsOverdue` text box and label controls that you added to the form, and delete them. Display the Toolbox, if you don't see it already, and then follow these steps:

1. Drag a check box control to the form, positioning it where the `IsOverdue` field originally appeared.
2. Right-click the check box and choose Properties to open the basic Properties dialog box for the control.

3. On the Value tab, click the Choose Field button, and select the `IsOverdue` field from the User-defined Fields in Folder list. Outlook fills in the details for the field automatically, as shown in Figure 17.7.

4. Switch to the Display tab, and enter "chkIsOverdue" for the Name of the control. You can leave the Caption as `IsOverdue`, which Outlook filled in for you, or change it to something more descriptive, such as "Task Is Overdue."

5. Click OK to save the changes to the control's properties.

---

**Tip:** When you drag a control from the Toolbox, you can place it precisely on the form.

---

The Value page in Figure 17.7 deserves a bit more explanation. All the controls on the Value page and the Validation page are disabled until you click the Choose Field button and bind a control to a field. You probably noticed the New button. Like the New button on the Field Chooser, this creates a new user-defined field. If you use the New button on the Value tab to create a new field, Outlook automatically creates it in the parent folder and in the form, all at the same time.

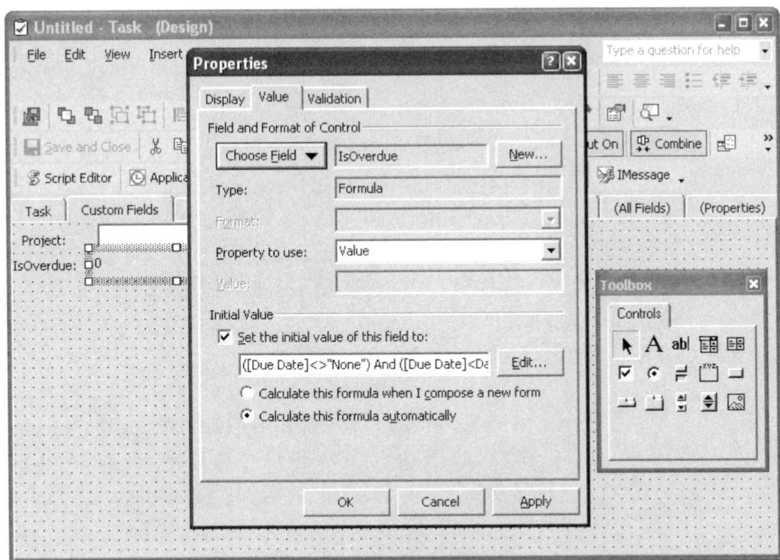


**Figure 17.7** *When you use the Toolbox to create a control on the form, you can bind an Outlook field to the control in the control's Properties dialog.*

For field types other than formula and combination, you can change the format setting for the field. Each data type has its own format choices. For example, there are 16 formats for date/time fields.

### 17.3.2 Initial value

Under Initial Value, you can set the initial value of any field (not just formula fields) to a formula. If you want the initial value to appear when you create a new item, but allow later changes, select Calculate This Formula When I Compose a New Form. If you always want to use a calculated value, select Calculate This Formula Automatically; users will not be able to change the value of the field.

For example, instead of creating the `OneWeekFromToday` field discussed earlier as a Formula field, you could create it as a Date/Time field, set an Initial Value formula to `Date( ) + 7`, select Calculate This Formula When I Compose a New Form, and choose the format that best suits your needs.

### 17.3.3 Simple validation

For fields other than combination and formula fields, you sometimes want to specify that a field must not be left blank or that it can accept only certain values. This technique, called *validation*, is an important method for preventing users (including yourself!) from making mistakes. Configure validation on the third page of the basic Properties dialog for each Outlook form control. Figure 17.8 shows a possible validation rule for the `Project` field created earlier.

If you just want to require a value, check the top box, labeled A Value Is Required for This Field. If the user leaves the field blank, a message pops up that a value is required for a field. Outlook doesn't tell you which field is missing a value, but when you click the OK button on the pop-up message, it does take you directly to the field that needs attention.

### 17.3.4 Validation formulas

It's nicer for the user, though, to know exactly how to correct a data entry problem, not to get some generic error message. Therefore, I recommend that instead of checking A Value Is Required for This Field, you check Validate This Field Before Closing the Form and provide a validation formula and a specific message to users. Also, you need to use this setting if you

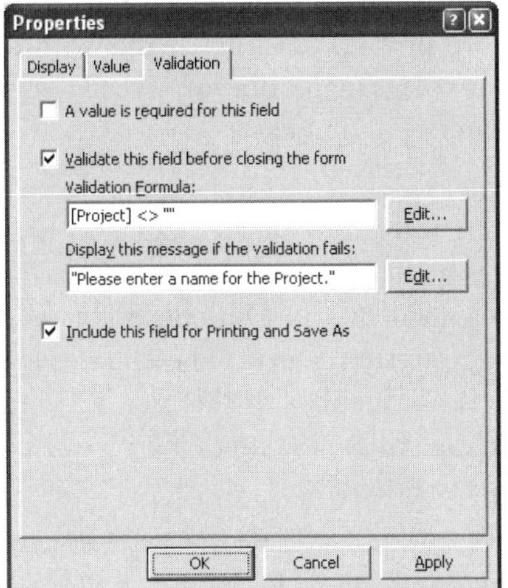


**Figure 17.8** *Validation rules help users enter data correctly.*

want to check the actual value of the field before the item is saved, not just that there is a value present.

Either type a validation formula in the Validation Formula box, or click the Edit button to see a Validation Formula dialog box similar to that for Formula fields. See Table 17.2 for examples of validation formulas. Notice that the `[Project] <> ""` validation formula is equivalent to checking the A Value Is Required for This Field box.

As you can see, validation formulas can use fields, functions, and operators. One thing these examples have in common is that the formula includes the field you want to validate. It wouldn't make any sense, would it, to have a validation formula that ignored the very value you wanted to test?

**Table 17.2** *Sample Validation Formulas and Failure Messages*

| Formula | Result | Suggested Validation Failure Message |
|---|---|---|
| `[Project] <> ""` | Requires that the Project field is not left blank | Please enter a name for the project. |
| `Len([Project Code]) = 10` | Requires that the Project Code field has exactly 10 characters | The project code must be exactly 10 characters long. |
| `([Due Date] = "None") OR ( [Start Date] <> "None")` | If the user has set a Due Date, the user must also set a Start Date. | Since you have set a due date for this task, you must also set a start date. |

The other thing they have in common is that every validation formula must evaluate to `True` or `False`. Contrast this with formula fields, where the result of the formula can be one of several kinds of data—`True` or `False`, a number, some text, or a date.

The third example in Table 17.2 illustrates a very common type of validation formula, where if the user enters a value for one field, you also want the user to provide a value for a second field. When a formula contains two or more expression joined by `OR`, Outlook evaluates each expression and returns `True` if any expression is true. Therefore, this formula evaluates to `True` if either there is no due date or the user has entered some start date. Otherwise, as in the case where the user enters a due date but no start date, the formula evaluates to `False`.

---

**Tip:** To enter a validation formula for a built-in field that appears on a form page that you can't edit, drag the field from the Field Chooser to any blank page on your custom form. You can then set up validation through the properties of the field's control on that page. You will want to choose Form, Display This Page to hide the page from users, since it duplicates fields they would see on other pages of the form.

Note that field names for built-in fields are language-specific. A validation formula that you create in Outlook set up for U.S. English users might fail for users working with Outlook in French.

---

If you use a validation formula, you should always add an expression in the box labeled Display This Message If the Validation Rule Fails. Otherwise, the user gets a cryptic, generic message that the field didn't pass the validation rule. In your validation failure message, don't just tell the user that something is wrong; explain how to fix it. Table 17.2 includes examples of validation failure messages that match the validation rule.

---

**CAUTION:** Before you delete a control from a form, check its Validation properties. If validation is active and you remove the field from the form, Outlook still tries to validate it. The user will almost always get an error message, but will not be able to correct the error, because the control is no longer present on the form. Therefore, you should clear the validation formula before you delete the control.

---

### 17.3.5 Control limitations

Outlook users can become spoiled by some elements of the application's user interface, particularly the dropdown calendar for picking dates, the automatic phone number formatting, and the automatic breaking of the Full Name and Address fields into their constituent parts.

The bad news is that you can't duplicate the dropdown calendar on your custom form pages (not without adding a component called an ActiveX control). Nor can you create new phone number fields and have Outlook include them in the dropdown list of phone numbers and format them into international style automatically.

The good news is that some fields, such as the Full Name field and the various address fields, do work the same on custom pages as on built-in pages. For example, if you type "Alex Smith" into a Full Name field on a custom page, Outlook stores `Alex` in the First Name field and `Smith` in the Last Name field. Also, as noted earlier, any user-defined date/time or duration fields support Outlook's shortcuts for entering dates and duration.

---

**Note:** When you work with the Message or Notes field in code, it has yet another name, the `Body` property. At least in that context, the property name is the same for every type of Outlook item.

---

If you want users to have the ability to add attachments to an item, you must have a page on your form that displays the Message or Notes field. The name in the Field Chooser varies, depending on the type of item. On Appointment, Message, and Post forms, it appears as the Message field. For Contacts, Journal Entry, and Task forms, Outlook calls it the Notes field. However, you can use this field only once on a form.

## 17.4 Laying out compose and read pages

Have you ever sent an e-mail message to yourself? Did you wonder why the message you receive looks different from the one you create? Outlook allows you to design two versions of every page, one used when you compose the item, the other when a user reads it. This applies not just to message forms, but to all Outlook forms.

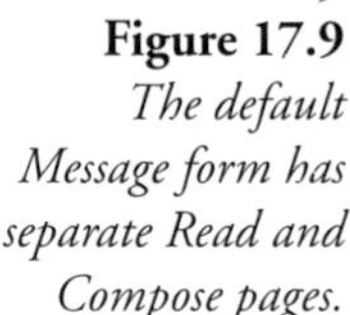

**Figure 17.9**
*The default Message form has separate Read and Compose pages.*

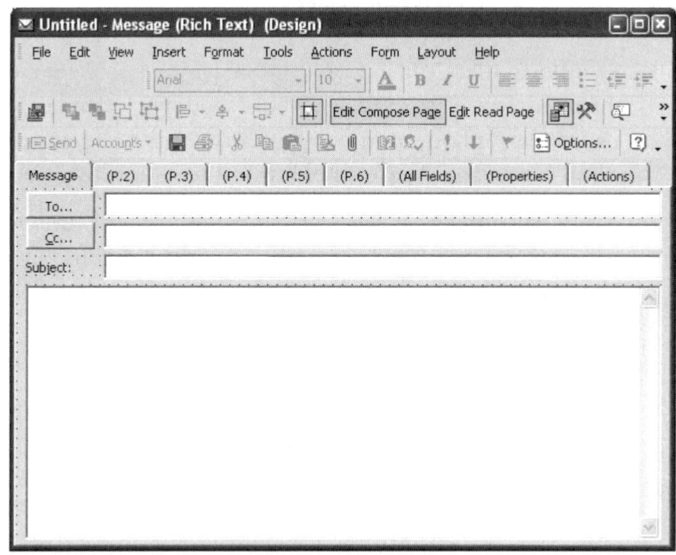


Open the standard Message form in design mode to see how this works. Figure 17.9 shows the Compose page for a new message, with the To, Cc, and Subject fields enabled for the user to fill in. Click the Edit Read Page to see the Read page (shown in Figure 17.10) for the same form. This time, you see the From and Sent fields, and all the fields in the header are displayed in gray, to indicate that they cannot be changed.

**Figure 17.10**
*Use the Edit Compose Page and Edit Read Page buttons to switch between layouts.*

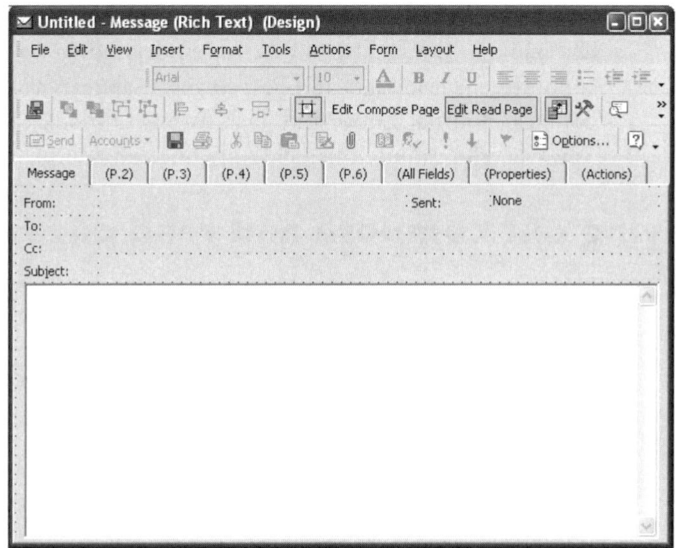

To set up a page with a single layout so that it has separate Compose and Read versions, choose Form, Separate Read Layout. Outlook copies all the fields from the original page (making it the Compose page) to the new Read page. Switch between the two layouts with the Edit Compose Page and Edit Read Page buttons. The page will have the same name in both layouts.

---

**Tip:** You can save yourself a lot of time if you refrain from separating the Compose and Read layouts until you have placed and configured all the controls that you want to appear on both versions. After you separate the layouts, if you want the same control on both layouts, you must add it to each layout separately.

---

**CAUTION:** Be extremely careful if you decide to use the Form, Separate Read Layout command to revert to a single page instead of two layouts. Outlook discards the page that is not currently visible.

---

No single property of an Outlook form can tell you whether it is open to the compose or read layout. In Chapter 18, you will see a function that provides this information.

## 17.5 Summary

In this chapter, you learned how to create your own custom fields and add them to Outlook forms. You also worked with validation rules and fields based on formulas. For additional flexibility, Outlook allows you to maintain separate Compose and Read layouts for each customized form page.

Ensuring that related forms, items, and folders have matching fields can be tricky. Chapter 24, "Deploying Forms and Applications," provides code you can use to add fields to folders, based on the custom properties present in a custom form. For more information on date and other functions commonly used in Outlook formulas, see Chapter 6, "Working with Expressions and Functions."

In Chapter 18, we will apply the VBA code-writing skills that you learned in Part II, "Adding VBA Code," to the task of writing code behind Outlook forms. Outlook forms use VBScript, not VBA, but you'll find that knowing VBA makes coding Outlook forms easy to do.

# 18

# *Writing Code to Respond to Outlook Form Events*

The chapters in Part II, Adding VBA Code, and Part III, Special Outlook Techniques, provided a solid grounding in both general and Outlook-specific programming methods, with a focus on the VBA environment. In this chapter, you will apply those methods to Outlook forms, which can also run code respond to events.

The highlights of this chapter include discussions of the following:

- What events you can use to program Outlook forms
- How to build user interaction and validation into a form
- How to write and test code in VBA so that you can transfer it to VBScript behind an Outlook form with as little effort as possible
- How to debug VBScript code

## 18.1 Outlook form code basics

To add code to an Outlook form, open the form in design mode; then, click the View Code button, or choose Form, View Code. All code on Outlook forms is event driven. A routine runs either from a form event (see Table 18.1) or from the `Click` event on a control. You can add other subroutines and functions, but they must be called from one of the event procedures.

To add code for a form event, in the code window, choose Script, Event Handler, and select from the list of events in the Insert Event Handler dialog box (see Figure 18.1). A `Function ... End Function` or `Sub ... End Sub` wrapper is added to the code window, depending on the event. Figure 18.2 shows the wrappers for the `Open` and `CustomPropertyChange` events.

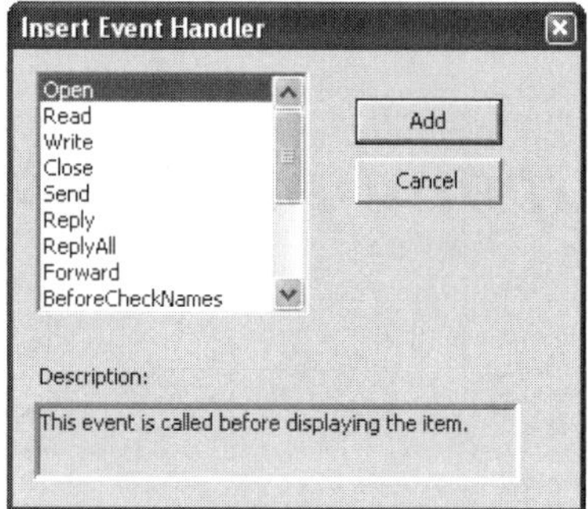


**Figure 18.1** *Add Outlook form-level event handlers through this dialog.*

---

CAUTION: The Insert Event Handler dialog does not check to see whether a particular event is already present in your script. It's possible to add duplicate event handlers. If you have more than one procedure with the same name, Outlook will not give you an error message when you try to run the form. Instead, it will simply skip any duplicates and run only the last procedure with a certain name.

---

Any declarations, such as `Option Explicit` or module-level variable declarations, should be placed before the first procedure. Each form has only one VBScript module.

### 18.1.1 Outlook form events

Outlook forms have their own set of events, but they're quite different from the VBA form events and from the Outlook application events you have

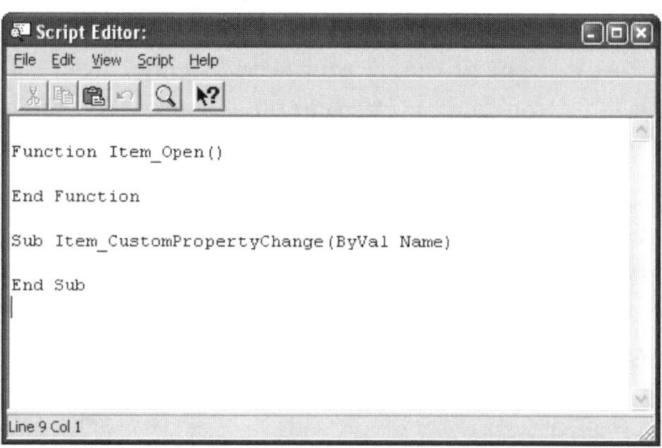


**Figure 18.2** *Outlook form event handlers in VBScript have their own specific syntax, just like VBA application event handlers.*

encountered so far. Table 18.1 lists the 16 Outlook form events and tells you which can be canceled.

---

**Note:** The syntax for canceling an event in VBScript code is different from that in VBA. You will see an example in the next section.

---

Outlook form controls have just one event, `Click`, which fires only on most (but not all) unbound controls, not on those linked to a particular

**Table 18.1** *Form Events (* = added in Outlook 2000, ** = added in Outlook 2002)*

| Event | Occurs |
|---|---|
| `AttachmentAdd*` | When an attachment is added to an item |
| `AttachmentRead*` | When the user opens an attachment. (In Outlook 2000, this event may not fire if the attachment is embedded in the body of a rich-text format message.) |
| `BeforeAttachmentSave*` | Just before an attachment is saved into the Outlook item (cancelable) |
| `BeforeCheckNames*` | Before Outlook starts to resolve names in the To, Cc, and Bcc fields against the Address Book after the user explicitly uses the Check Names command (cancelable) |
| `BeforeDelete**` | Before Outlook deletes the item (cancelable) |
| `Close` | When a displayed Outlook item is closed (cancelable) |
| `CustomAction` | When a custom action associated with an item occurs (cancelable). (See Chapter 20, "Common Outlook Form and Item Techniques," for details on custom actions.) |
| `CustomPropertyChange` | When the value of a user-defined property changes |
| `Forward` | When the user forwards the item (cancelable) |
| `Open` | Just before Outlook displays an item in its own window (cancelable) |
| `PropertyChange` | When the value of a built-in property changes |
| `Read` | When the user opens an item for editing, either in its own window or using in-cell editing in a folder view |
| `Reply` | When the user replies to the item (cancelable). |
| `ReplyAll` | When the user replies to the item using Reply to All (cancelable) |
| `Send` | When the user sends the item (cancelable) |
| `Write` | When an item is saved (cancelable) |

field. To detect changes in the data stored in controls (so that you can perform validation and other tasks), you must use the `CustomPropertyChange` and `PropertyChange` events. Outlook forms don't support the `BeforeUpdate` event that you find on VBA form controls.

### 18.1.2 Adding VBScript code to an Outlook form

Later in this chapter, you will learn how to use the VBA environment to create and test Outlook form VBScript code. However, to get started, we'll do a little programming in the VBScript environment.

One commonly used technique is to determine whether the user has just created a new item or is working with an existing item. This is important, for example, if you want to initialize certain property values and prefer to use code rather than the Value tab for a property's control on the form. The event that fires when the user creates a new item and displays it in a new Inspector window is the `Open` event. Therefore, your code to determine whether the item is new or existing should go in the `Open` event handler.

---

**Note:** The user may also be able to create a new item directly in a table view, if the view is displaying a new item row. In that case, the `Open` event does not fire on new items.

---

You can check either the `Size` property or the `EntryID` property to determine whether an item is new.

Listing 18.1 shows a typical structure for working with a new item. It checks whether the `Size` property is 0 and, if so, sets a module-level Boolean variable, which you can use in other routines in this script, to `True`. It also calls a separate subroutine, `InitForm`, that includes whatever code might be needed to initialize controls on the form; in this example, it just pops up a message box to let the user know that this is a new item.

Instead of `Item.Size = 0`, you could also use `Item.EntryID = ""` to test whether the item is newly created.

---

**Note:** Listing 18.1 includes an `Option Explicit` statement, which works the same in VBScript as in VBA—it raises an error if you try to run code that includes undeclared variables. You should add `Option Explicit` to each form script, but you will need to do that manually. Outlook cannot add it automatically as it can with VBA modules.

---

**Listing 18.1** *Determining Whether the User Is Creating a New Item*

```
Option Explicit
Dim m_blnIsNew

Function Item_Open()
    If Item.Size = 0 Then
        m_blnIsNew = True
    Else
        m_blnIsNew = False
    End If
    Call InitForm
End Function

Sub InitForm()
    If m_blnIsNew Then
        MsgBox "New item initialized"
    Else
        MsgBox "Existing item initialized"
    End If
End Sub
```

`Item` is an intrinsic object that you can use in any Outlook form code; it represents the actual item that the form is displaying. Outlook form code also supports an intrinsic `Application` object; this means that you do not have to declare and instantiate an Outlook `Application` object with a `CreateObject()` statement. For example, Listing 18.2 demonstrates how the `Item_Open` event handler can set a module-level object variable that represents the folder that the user is viewing. `Application.ActiveExplorer` represents the currently open folder window.

Referring back to Table 18.1, you'll see that `Open` is one of several events that can be canceled programmatically. To cancel an Outlook form event, set the return value of the event handler function to False. For example, if you want to require that all items using a particular form have some text in the `Subject` property, you could validate that property and prevent the user from saving an item with blank Subject by adding the code in Listing 18.3 to the `Item_Write` event handler.

**Listing 18.2** *Setting an Object Variable for the Currently Open Folder*

```
Dim m_objActiveFolder

Function Item_Open()
    Set m_objActiveFolder = _
      Application.ActiveExplorer.CurrentFolder
End Function
```

**Listing 18.3** *Canceling an Event in VBScript Form Code*

```
Function Item_Write()
    If Item.Subject = "" Then
        Item_Write = False
        MsgBox "Please fill in the Subject."
    End If
End Function
```

You will see more validation examples later in the chapter.

Another example of canceling an event applies only to Outlook 2002, which adds a `BeforeDelete` event. You could use the code in Listing 18.4 to ask the user to confirm the deletion.

You could include code to perform updates on related items or databases if the user confirms the deletion. Unfortunately, though, the `BeforeDelete` event fires only if the user has the item open in an `Inspector` window. It does not fire if the user deletes the item from a folder view.

### 18.1.3 Using the Outlook Object Browser (mini)

The VBScript environment also includes a smaller version of the Object Browser. From the code window for a form, choose Script, Object Browser to display the Object Browser, shown in Figure 18.3. Click Object Help to see the help topic for the selected item. Click Insert to paste the name of the selected class or member or a selected constant value into your script.

**Listing 18.4** *Asking the User to Confirm an Item's Deletion*

```
Function Item_BeforeDelete(ByVal Item)
    Dim strMsg, strTitle
    Dim intRes
    strMsg = "Do you really want to delete this item?"
    strTitle = "Delete " & Item.Subject & "?"
    intRes = MsgBox(strMsg, vbYesNo + vbQuestion, strTitle)
    If intRes = vbNo Then
        Item_BeforeDelete = False
    Else
        perform any related updates
    End If
End Function
```

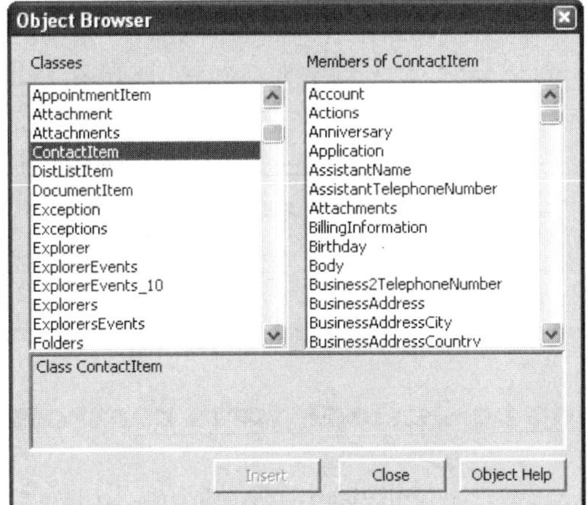


**Figure 18.3** *This minibrowser helps you keep track of Outlook objects when you're working on form code using VBScript.*

### 18.1.4 Referring to Outlook item properties

So far in this chapter, we have been working with built-in Outlook properties, such as `EntryID`, `Size`, and `Subject`. As you learned in Chapter 17, "Extending Form Design with Fields and Controls," you can create your own properties, too. These require a different syntax in your form code (and the difference extends to VBA code, too).

Where you can refer to a built-in property on the current item in VBScript simply with `Item.`*`property`*, for a custom property you need to use the `UserProperties` collection of all user-defined properties. For example, to work with the `IsOverdue` formula field that you created in Chapter 17, you would use any of these expressions, which are equivalent:

```
Item.UserProperties.Find("IsOverdue").Value
Item.UserProperties.Item("IsOverdue").Value
Item.UserProperties("IsOverdue").Value
Item.UserProperties("IsOverdue")
```

In Outlook 2002, you also have the option of using the `ItemProperties` collection to refer to both built-in and custom properties by name, for example:

```
Item.ItemProperties.Item("Subject").Value
Item.ItemProperties("Subject").Value
Item.ItemProperties("IsOverdue")
```

Including the `Item` method is optional, since it is the default method for the `ItemProperties` collection. Likewise, the `Value` property is the default property for the `ItemProperty` object, as well as for an individual `UserProperty` object.

---

**Tip:** Each `ItemProperty` object in the Outlook 2002 `ItemProperties` collection includes an `IsUserProperty` property to determine whether it is a built-in or custom property.

---

### 18.1.5 Referring to Outlook form controls

Sometimes your code will need to work directly with a control that is displaying an Outlook property or with a control that is unbound. Outlook uses a peculiar syntax to get a control object, one more complicated than a VB or VBA programmer might be accustomed to. You need to know not just the name of the control, but also the name of the page on the Outlook form where it appears. The following code snippet checks the value of a text box control named `txtDeficit` on a page named Budget and changes the color of the text in that control to red if the value of the control is less than zero:

```
Set objPage = _
  Item.GetInspector.ModifiedFormPages("Budget")
Set objControl = objPage.Controls("txtDeficit")
If objControl.Value < 0 Then
    objControl.ForeColor = vbRed
End If
```

Notice that in this example, you don't need to know what property the control is displaying, but you do need to know what page the control appears on.

In general, when your code needs to work only with the value of a property, you should use the `Item.`*`property`*, `Item.UserProperties("`*`property`*`")`, or, in Outlook 2002 only, `Item.ItemProperties("`*`property`*`")` syntax. If, however, your code needs to get the value from a control that is not bound to an Outlook property or to manipulate the appearance of a control, you should use the syntax shown above to set an object variable to the control itself.

In Chapter 17, "Extending Form Design with Fields and Controls," you learned how to design separate compose and read layouts on Outlook

**Listing 18.5** *Distinguishing Between the Compose and Read Layouts*

```
Private Function ShowsComposeLayout(objItem)
    Const olMail = 43
    If objItem.Class = olMail And _
       Not objItem.Sent Then
        ShowsComposeLayout = True
    ElseIf objItem.Size = 0 Then
        ShowsComposeLayout = True
    Else
        ShowsComposeLayout = False
    End If
End Function
```

forms. Outlook provides no special property or syntax to tell you that the user is viewing the compose or read page. In theory, you could name the controls differently on each page (e.g., `txtRDeficit` for the read page and `txtCDeficit` for the compose page), but this would soon become burdensome. An easier method is to use code to determine which layout the user might be working with, based on key Outlook properties. The `ShowsComposeLayout()` function in Listing 18.5 checks the `Sent` property of a message or the `Size` property of any other type of item to determine whether the item has already been sent or saved. If it hasn't been sent or saved, the item must be showing the compose layout. If it has, it must be displaying the read layout.

Note, however, that the `ShowsComposeLayout()` function cannot tell you whether a form supports separate compose and read layouts.

You would want to use `ShowsComposeLayout` in the `Item_Open` event handler, possibly to set a module-level Boolean variable.

## 18.2 Converting VBA code to VBScript

So far in this chapter, we have been working with very simple code written directly in the VBScript window on an Outlook form in design mode. Some Outlook forms, however, have complex code modules running into hundreds of lines. Writing that much code in the form code window, without the features you're accustomed to in VBA, makes it likely that you will make simple mistakes, if not grand ones. Therefore, I (and many other professional Outlook developers) recommend that you write as much of your form code as possible in VBA, test it in VBA, then make the few changes needed to convert it to VBScript before copying it into the code window.

Here are the key differences between VBScript and VBA code:

- VBScript does not support the Outlook intrinsic constants, only the VB constants. You must either include declarations for the Outlook constants in your module and procedures or use the actual literal values that correspond to the constants. Listing 18.5, for example, includes a declaration for the `olMail` constant.

  In VBScript on an Outlook form, you don't have to use a

  ```
  Set objApp = CreateObject("Outlook.Application")
  ```

  statement because the `Application` object is intrinsic to VBScript behind an Outlook form.

- The `Item` object representing the current item is also intrinsic to Outlook form code. In VBA, you must instantiate an object variable to represent any Outlook item.
- VBScript supports only the variant data type, which can represent any type of data. You do not use typed variable declarations, such as `Dim strMsg as String`, in VBScript.
- As you saw in the previous section, the syntax for referring to controls on Outlook forms is more complex than for VBA forms.
- A few VBA functions, such as `Format()`, have no VBScript equivalent.

As an example, the next section shows the VBScript version of a useful function that you first encountered in Chapter 12.

### 18.2.1 A GetFolder() function for VBScript

In Listing 12.7, you saw a `GetFolder()` function that can return a `MAPIFolder` object by parsing a path string and walking the Outlook folder hierarchy. The VBScript version of this function, shown in Listing 18.6 and designed for use in Outlook form code, is almost identical.

The VBScript version makes these changes:

- All the variable declarations are now untyped to reflect VBScript's limitation to the variant data type.
- To declare an array for use with the `Split()` function, instead of `Dim arrFolders() As String`, you use `Dim arrFolders`, omitting both the data type and the closing parentheses. Similarly, the `arrFolders = Split(strFolderPath, "\")` statement does not include parentheses on the array variable.

**Listing 18.6** *Walk the Folder Tree by Parsing the Path (VBScript Version)*

```
Public Function GetFolder(strFolderPath)
    Dim objNS
    Dim colFolders
    Dim objFolder
    Dim arrFolders
    Dim i
    On Error Resume Next
    strFolderPath = Replace(strFolderPath, "/", "\")
    arrFolders = Split(strFolderPath, "\")
    Set objNS = Application.GetNamespace("MAPI")
    Set objFolder = objNS.Folders.Item(arrFolders(0))
    If Not objFolder Is Nothing Then
        For i = 1 To UBound(arrFolders)
            Set colFolders = objFolder.Folders
            Set objFolder = Nothing
            Set objFolder = colFolders.Item(arrFolders(i))
            If objFolder Is Nothing Then
                Exit For
            End If
        Next
    End If
    Set GetFolder = objFolder
    Set colFolders = Nothing
    Set objNS = Nothing
    Set objFolder = Nothing
End Function
```

- Since this code is designed to run in an Outlook form, you can use the intrinsic `Application` object.

### 18.2.2 Writing form code in VBA

Let's examine some strategies for using the VBA environment to write and test VBScript code.

First, you can take advantage of VBA's Auto Syntax Check and Auto Complete Members features simply by writing your code in VBA with fully typed variables. For example, this subroutine, written in VBA, creates a new appointment from an existing task:

```
Sub CreateApptFromTask(Item As Outlook.TaskItem)
    Dim objAppt As Outlook.AppointmentItem
    Set objAppt = _
      Application.CreateItem(olAppointmentItem)
    With objAppt
        .Start = Item.DueDate - 2
        .End = Item.DueDate
        .Subject = Item.Subject
```

```
        .Body = Item.Body
        .Save
    End With
    Set objAppt = Nothing
End Sub
```

Because of the typed variable declarations (`Item As Outlook.TaskItem` and `Dim objAppt as Outlook.AppointmentItem`), VBA can help you write the code by suggesting property names and pointing out syntax errors.

To clean up this procedure so that you can use it in an Outlook Task form, all you have to do is take out the typed variable declarations and add one Outlook constant:

```
Sub CreateApptFromTask()
    Dim objAppt
    Const olAppointmentItem = 1
    Set objAppt = _
      Application.CreateItem(olAppointmentItem)
    With objAppt
        .Start = Item.DueDate - 2
        .End = Item.DueDate
        .Subject = Item.Subject
        .Body = Item.Body
        .Save
    End With
    Set objAppt = Nothing
End Sub
```

We also removed the `Item` argument for the subroutine because the procedure is designed to work upon the current task item (i.e., the one in which this code is running).

In the VBScript code, you'd also need an event to call the `CreateAppt-FromTask` subroutine, probably from a command button:

```
Sub cmdCreateAppt_Click ()
    Call CreateApptFromTask()
End Sub
```

As with all controls on an Outlook form, the only command button event you can use in VBScript code is `Click`.

### 18.2.3 Testing form code in VBA

You can push VBA even further by not just writing Outlook form code there, but also testing it. Take the `CreateApptFromTask` subroutine in the previous section, for example. You can test it in VBA by writing a little

**Listing 18.7** *Return the Currently Selected or Open Outlook Item*

```
Function GetCurrentItem() As Object
    Dim objApp As Outlook.Application
    Set objApp = CreateObject("Outlook.Application")
    On Error Resume Next
    Select Case TypeName(objApp.ActiveWindow)
        Case "Explorer"
            Set GetCurrentItem = _
              objApp.ActiveExplorer.Selection.Item(1)
        Case "Inspector"
            Set GetCurrentItem = _
              objApp.ActiveInspector.CurrentItem
    End Select
    Set objApp = Nothing
End Function
```

more code to get a `TaskItem` and then pass that object to the VBA version of `CreateApptFromTask` subroutine. The `GetCurrentItem()` function in Listing 18.7 returns the currently selected or open Outlook item. Because it's flexible about whether the user is working with an `Explorer` or `Inspector` window, you can reuse this function endlessly—whenever you need to return just one item. (It's also handy for macros you plan to run from a toolbar.) Listing 18.8 puts the `GetCurrentItem()` function together with the `CreateApptFromTask` subroutine in a testing subroutine that checks to make sure the current item is a `TaskItem` before calling the `CreateApptFromTask` subroutine.

To test code for form events, such as `Open` and `Write`, in VBA, you can use the same kind of class module that you used in Chapter 12, "Working with Stores and Folders." As an example, we'll create a class module for testing `MailItem` events.

Start by creating a new class module in VBA and giving it the name `MyMailItem`. Add the code shown in Listing 18.9. To a separate code module (not a class module), add the code in Listing 18.10. Run the `TestMail-`

**Listing 18.8** *Test Code Against the Current Outlook Item*

```
Sub TestCreateApptFromTask()
    Dim objItem As Object
    Set objItem = GetCurrentItem()
    If objItem.Class = olTask Then
        Call CreateApptFromTask(objItem)
    End If
    Set objItem = Nothing
End Sub
```

**Listing 18.9** *Use a Class Module To Test Outlook Form Events*

```
Dim WithEvents Item As Outlook.MailItem
Dim m_blnIsNew As Boolean

Private Sub Class_Initialize()
    Dim objItem As Object
    Set objItem = GetCurrentItem()
    If objItem.Class = olMail Then
        Set Item = objItem
        Debug.Print Item.Subject
    End If
End Sub

Private Sub Class_Terminate()
    Set Item = Nothing
End Sub

Private Sub Item_Open(Cancel As Boolean)
    If Item.Size = 0 Then
        m_blnIsNew = True
    Else
        m_blnIsNew = False
    End If
    Call InitForm
End Sub

Private Sub Item_Write(Cancel As Boolean)
    Cancel = Not IsValidated
End Sub

Private Function IsValidated() As Boolean
    If Item.Subject = "" Then
        MsgBox "Please fill in the Subject."
        IsValidated = False
    Else
        IsValidated = True
    End If
End Function

Private Sub InitForm()
    If m_blnIsNew Then
        MsgBox "New item initialized"
    Else
        MsgBox "Existing item initialized"
    End If
End Sub
```

**Listing 18.10** *Instantiate a Class Object*

```
Dim objMyMail As MyMailItem

Sub TestExistingMailEvents()
    Set objMyMail = New MyMailItem
End Sub

Sub EndTestMailEvents()
    Set objMyMail = Nothing
End Sub
```

`Events` subroutine when you want to test `MailItem` events. This procedure creates a new `MyMailItem` Class object, which in turn initializes the `Item` object declared `WithEvents` in the class module. Events for that `Item` object will continue firing until either the item no longer exists or you run the `EndTestMailEvents` procedure to dereference the Class object.

The code in Listing 18.9 does not perform any actual form initialization or validation. Instead, it just displays message boxes to demonstrate the different events firing.

Compare the `Item_Open` event handlers in Listings 18.1 and 18.9. When you add your own initialization, validation, or other event code, make it as modular as possible. Rather than writing many lines of code in the `Item_Open()` event handler (or any other event handler), use code that calls other procedures. That way, you will have a minimal amount of code that has to be reworked from VBA to VBScript format and a maximum amount of code that can be reused in other forms.

### 18.2.4 A recipe for VBA to VBScript code conversion

Here is a general list of steps to follow if you have a subroutine or function that works in VBA and you want to use it in an Outlook item's VBScript code:

1. Copy the VBA procedure code and paste it into an Outlook form's script window.
2. Comment the `As` data type portion of any `Dim` declarations, function statements, and procedure arguments. (Leaving the type information in the procedure as a comment makes your form code well documented.)

3. Remove any `Dim variable As Application` declarations.
4. Remove any statement that sets an `Application` object variable, such as

```
Set objApp = CreateObject("Outlook.Application")
```

   This statement is not necessary because `Application` is an intrinsic object in Outlook form code.
5. Change any reference to an `Application` object variable, such as `objApp`, to the `Application` intrinsic object.

---

**Tip:** An alternative to steps 4 and 5 is to replace any `Set objApp = CreateObject("Outlook.Application")` statement with `Set objApp = Application`.

---

6. If you used Outlook intrinsic constants, add `Const` statements at the beginning of the script to declare the constants you need. Placing them before any subroutines or functions makes them operate as module-level constants, available to any procedure on the form.

---

**Tip:** To get the value of any intrinsic constant, in the VBA code editor right-click the constant, and then choose Quick Info from the pop-up menu. You can also type "?" followed by the name of the constant in the Immediate window, and then press Enter.

---

7. Check all procedures with arguments to make sure that the arguments are being passed correctly. Remember that VBA passes arguments `ByRef` by default, while the default in VBScript is to pass arguments `ByVal`. If a VBA procedure passes a variable `ByRef`, then changes the value of that variable in the body of the procedure, you must add a `ByRef` keyword if you want it to work the same way in VBScript. You may want to get into the habit of specifying `ByRef` and `ByVal` on all VBA procedures that you plan to convert to VBScript. That way, they'll work the same in both languages.
8. If the procedure was created as a VBA macro, attach it to an event handler in VBScript, such as the `Click` event for a command button.

9. If the procedure was created as a VBA event handler in a Class module, use the Script, Event Handler command in the VBScript code window to insert the corresponding event handler. Copy only the body of the VBA procedure (not the `Sub`, `End Sub`, `Function`, or `End Function` statements) to the VBScript event handler. For cancelable events, replace any `Cancel = True` statements with an *`event_handler`* `= False` statement where *`event_handler`* is the name of the event-handling function.

## 18.3 Understanding event order

By investigating the order in which related events fire, you can gain better control over the behavior of Outlook forms. For example, you can prevent users from making changes to items in table views that have in-cell editing turned on, or you can force items created with a form to save in a particular folder, regardless of how the user launched the form. Try adding the code in Listing 18.11 to any form, then publish that form in the normal folder for that item.

After you publish the form, launch it from the Actions menu for the folder where you published it, and experiment with creating new items, opening existing items, and editing items in the table view with in-cell editing turned on. Make sure that you try different methods of saving and closing the item. See if you can duplicate the results shown in Table 18.2.

When opening an existing item, the `Read` event fires only once for the current item. The first time you open the item, `Read` and `Open` both fire. If

**Listing 18.11** *Investigate the Order in Which Key Events Fire*

```
Function Item_Open()
    MsgBox "Open fired"
End Function

Function Item_Read()
    MsgBox "Read fired"
End Function

Function Item_Write()
   MsgBox "Write fired"
End Function

Function Item_Close()
   MsgBox "Close fired"
End Function
```

**Table 18.2** *Event Firing Order for Opening and Closing Items*

| User action | Event Order |
|---|---|
| Display a new item with the `Actions` or `Choose Form` command | `Open` |
| Open an existing item | `Read`<br>`Open` |
| Create a new item in the new item row of a table view (only if custom form is default for folder) | `Write` |
| Make changes in an open item, then close it with the Close (x) button in the upper-right corner or the Esc button | `Close`<br>`Write` (if user answers Yes to the Do You Want to Save Changes? prompt) |
| Make changes in an open item, then close it with Save and Close button | `Write`<br>`Close` |
| Make changes in an open item, then save it with the File, Save command | `Write` |
| Make changes in existing item, using in-cell editing | `Read`<br>`Write` |

you close the item and then open it again, only `Open` fires. If you close the item, open a second item, and then open the first item again, `Read` and `Open` both fire once again. Something similar occurs if you open an item, close it, and then try to use in-cell editing to edit it—the `Read` event does not fire. This behavior occurs because Outlook caches the last opened item.

Even more confusing is the different order in which `Write` and `Close` can occur, depending on how the user closes the item. If the user clicks Save and Close, `Write` occurs first, then `Close`. However, if the user uses the Esc key or the Close button (x) in the upper-right corner of the item, `Close` fires; the `Write` event fires later, after the user answers Yes to the Do You Want To Save Changes? prompt.

When a user clicks Send on a message form, the `Send` event fires first, followed by `Write`, then `Close`.

---

**Note:** Sending a message places it in the Outbox. Only when the item has actually been delivered by the appropriate mail account does it move to the Sent Items folder and acquire a time stamp indicating when it was sent.

---

**Listing 18.12** *Force the User To Make Changes Only If the Item Is Displayed in a Form*

```
Dim m_blnOpenInsp

Function Item_Open()
    m_blnOpenInsp = True
End Function

Function Item_Write()
    If Not m_blnOpenInsp Then
        MsgBox "Please open the item to make changes."
        Item_Write = False
    End If
End Function

Function Item_Close()
    m_blnOpenInsp = False
End Function
```

### 18.3.1 Preventing the user from making changes with in-cell editing

As mentioned earlier in this chapter, the in-cell editing feature of table views allows users to edit items without opening them in a form. This might be undesirable if, for example, you provide a lot of feedback to the user in the form. The code in Listing 18.12 prevents the user from saving changes to an item that has not been opened.

Oddly enough, the module-level `m_blnOpenInsp` variable must be explicitly set to `False` in the `Close` event. Otherwise, Outlook caches the value, which would allow you to open an item, close it, and then edit the item in a view with in-cell editing turned on. This is the kind of Outlook oddity that you find only with thorough testing.

### 18.3.2 Saving an item in a specific folder

There are situations in Outlook where you may want items to save automatically in a particular folder. You might, for instance, want to allow users to launch a form regardless of what folder they are working in, but save the item created from that form to a specific Exchange Server public folder. A prime example would be a form that creates new journal items, but instead of saving them to the user's own Journal folder stores them in a public folder. (If you use forms substitution, as described in Chapter 24, "Deploying Forms and Applications," you can make such a custom form the default.)

What makes this relatively difficult to accomplish is that, as you saw in Table 18.2, the `Write` and `Close` events can fire in two different orders, depending on how a user chooses to save the item. The code in Listing 18.13 offers a solution by tracking whether the item is the original or a copy; note that it uses the `GetFolder()` function from Listing 18.6.

To see the code in action, put this code (and the code for the `GetFolder()` function) into a custom journal form or other custom form designed to be saved in a folder. (It will not work properly with a message

**Listing 18.13** *Force an Item To Save in a Particular Folder*

```
Dim mblnSaveInTarget
Const olDiscard = 1

Function Item_Open()
   If Item.BillingInformation <> "IsCopy" Then
       If Item.Size = 0 Then
           Item.Start = Now
       End If
       mblnSaveInTarget = True
   End If
End Function

Function Item_Write()
   Dim objCopy
   Dim objTargetFolder
   Dim objMoved
   Dim intRes
   If mblnSaveInTarget And Not Item.Saved Then
      Set objTargetFolder = GetFolder(Item.Mileage)
      If Not objTargetFolder Is Nothing Then
          Item.BillingInformation = "IsCopy"
          Set objCopy = Item.Copy
          Set objMoved = objCopy.Move(objTargetFolder)
          Item_Write = False
          Item.Close olDiscard
          intRes = _
            MsgBox("Do you need to keep this item open?", _
            vbYesNo + vbQuestion + vbDefaultButton2, _
            "Moving Item")
          If intRes = vbYes Then
              objMoved.Display
          End If
      End If
   End If
   Set objCopy = Nothing
   Set objMoved = Nothing
   Set objTargetFolder = Nothing
End Function
```

form.) Before publishing the form, go to the All Fields tab; for the `Mileage` property, enter the path to the folder you want the form to save to (e.g., Personal Folders\Journal\test).

Here's how it works: When the user creates a new item, the `Open` event fires. Since it's a new item, the `BillingInformation` property is empty, and, therefore, the `mblnSaveInTarget` module-level variable is set to `True`. Also, on new items, the `Start` date on the item is set to the current date/ time to compensate for an Outlook quirk—on new appointments and journal entries created with custom forms, the start date defaults to the date the form was published.

When the user saves the item, the `Write` event fires. If `mblnSaveInTarget` is `True` (as it will be only on new items) and the item has not yet been saved, the code uses the `GetFolder()` function to return the target folder for saving the item, based on the path in the `Mileage` property. It then creates a copy of the item. The copy also fires the `Open` event, but because the `BillingInformation` field now contains the value `IsCopy`, `mblnSaveInTarget` is set to `False` on the instance of the code running on the copy. This means that when the code saves the copy by moving it to the target folder, the `Item_Write` event handler code that ran on the original item does not run on the copy. Without some mechanism like this to keep track of the state of the item and its copy, you would wind up in an endless loop of copies.

At the time the item is copied and moved to the target folder (i.e., when the `Write` event fires) there is no way to know whether the user has clicked Save or Save and Close. Therefore, the code closes the original item, but displays the copy, now stored in the target folder, if the user responds Yes to the prompt.

## 18.4 Reacting to control and property changes

Another frequently used Outlook technique is to respond immediately to the user's interaction with a custom form without waiting for the user to save or send the item. As you might expect, this depends on the ability to fire events that detect when a user changes the value of a property or makes other changes to a form. Experienced VB and VBA developers may be disappointed here; the shortage of control events on Outlook forms means that there's no easy way to know what control currently has the user's focus or even what form page the user is viewing. However, you can respond precisely to changes made to built-in or custom properties and, to an extent, to unbound controls.

### 18.4.1 Using the PropertyChange and CustomPropertyChange events

To build code that responds to changes in Outlook properties, you use the `PropertyChange` and, for user-defined properties, `CustomProperty-Change` events. Each of these events passes the name of the changed property as an argument. You will have only one `PropertyChange` and one `CustomPropertyChange` event handler in the script for each form.

Since an Outlook item can have dozens of properties and you're probably interested in changes to only a few, you generally use a `Select Case ... End Select` block to pay attention to only those properties you want to respond to. To see how this works, open a new Outlook task item in design mode, display the code window, and insert an event handler for the `PropertyChange` event. Outlook pastes a

```
Sub Item_PropertyChange(ByVal Name)
```

statement into your code. `Name` is the expression you use in the `Select Case` statement. Add the following code, which reacts specifically to changes in the `DueDate` and `Complete` properties and also includes a generic property change handler under `Case Else`.

```
Sub Item_PropertyChange(ByVal Name)
    Select Case Name
        Case "DueDate"
            If DateDiff("w", Now, Item.DueDate) > 3 Then
                MsgBox "You shouldn't plan more than" _
                  & "3 weeks ahead."
            End If
        Case "Complete"
            If Item.Complete = True Then
              MsgBox "Congratulations! You finished " & _
                "this task!"
            End If
        Case Else
            MsgBox "You changed the " & Name & "property."
    End Select
End Sub
```

Run this form, and try changing values in different fields. You should find out several very interesting things about the `PropertyChange` event, as follows:

- The `PropertyChange` event fires not just for changes the user makes, but also when properties change because of actions that Outlook takes automatically.

- A change made to one property can cause a cascade of changes to several other properties. For example, changing the `Status` to `Complete` causes changes in the `ReminderSet`, `PercentComplete`, `DateCompleted`, and `Complete` properties, as well as the change to `Status`.
- Not all properties support the `PropertyChange` event. When you type in the large text box on the Task page, you are changing the `Body` property. However, you won't see a pop-up message saying, "You changed the Body property;" not even when you press Tab to move the focus off that control.

Another important observation is that the `Case` statements for the `PropertyChange` event routine require you to supply the property names as string literals. However, if you want to access the property values themselves, you use the familiar `Item.`*`property`* syntax.

---

**Note:** An event handler for the `PropertyChange` event provides one way to validate data entry on an Outlook form—immediately after the user makes a change to a property. Another validation method is to include code in the `Item_Write` event function to check values and use the statement `Item_Write = False` to cancel the write operation and allow the user to correct the error.

---

A `CustomPropertyChange` event handler looks almost exactly the same:

```
Sub Item_CustomPropertyChange(ByVal Name)
    Select Case Name
        Case "MyProp1"
            your code for a change in MyProp1 goes here
        Case "MyProp2"
            your code for a change in MyProp2 goes here
        ' continue with Case statements for other properties
        ' whose values you want to monitor
    End Select
End Sub
```

You can use the `PropertyChange` and `CustomPropertyChange` events to help you understand what happens when the user interacts with form controls showing both built-in and custom properties. Just add this code to your form to have a message box pop up every time a property changes:

```
Sub Item_PropertyChange(ByVal Name)
    MsgBox "The " & Name & " property changed."
End Sub
```

```
Sub Item_CustomPropertyChange(ByVal Name)
    MsgBox "The " & Name & " custom property changed."
End Sub
```

You may want to ignore any `PropertyChange` or `CustomPropertyChange` events that occur while your form is loading, since Outlook itself may set some properties at that time or you may be setting property values in the `Open` event handler. An easy solution is to set a Boolean `IsLoading` variable in the `Open` event handler and use that variable in the property event handler(s):

```
Dim blnIsLoading

Function Item_Open()
    blnIsLoading = True
    code to initialize form
    blnIsLoading = False
End Function

Sub Item_PropertyChange(ByVal Name)
    If Not blnIsLoading Then
        Select Case Name
            Case "prop1"
                code for a change in prop1
            Case "prop2"
                code for a change in prop2
        End Select
    End If
End Sub
```

After a form has loaded, the `PropertyChange` or `CustomPropertyChange` event fires only after the user presses Tab or Enter or otherwise moves the focus to another control. If the user changes the value of a property and then immediately saves the item, the `PropertyChange` or `CustomPropertyChange` event does not fire. Therefore, if you are using those events to perform validation, you may also want to run that same validation code from the `Item_Write` event handler.

There is one other major limitation of the `PropertyChange` event: it does not respond to changes in the `Body` property, which is shown in the large message box on all forms. A possible workaround is to create a custom formula field that uses the value of the `Body` property, and to monitor that property with the `CustomPropertyChange` event.

## 18.4.2 Firing events from changes to a control's value

As you learned earlier in this chapter, Outlook uses a peculiar syntax to get the value of a control, a more complicated syntax than a VB or VBA programmer might be accustomed to. You need to know not just the name of the control, but also the name of the page on the Outlook form where it appears. Another limitation is that the only event supported by controls on an Outlook form is the `Click` event. For example, you can use the `Click` event to track when a user selects a new value from a dropdown list (combo box):

```
Sub cboCompanies_Click()
    Set objPage = _
      Item.GetInspector.ModifiedFormPages("My Page")
    Set cboCompanies = objPage.Controls("cboCompanies")
    MsgBox "The value in the " & cboCompanies.Name & _
          "control has changed to " & cboCompanies.Value & "."
End Sub
```

However, not all controls support the `Click` event. The `Click` event fires on a dropdown list combo box, but not if the user types a value into a combo box with the style set to `DropDownCombo (0)`. It fires for label, list box, check box, option button, and command button controls, but not for text box or spin button controls. For list boxes, there must be at least one item in the list, and the user must click on a list item (not in a blank area in the list box), in order for the `Click` event to fire.

Another common application of the `Click` event is to use a combo box, list box, check box, or option buttons to change the appearance of another control. For example, you might want to change the items displayed in a list box or combo box or display a group of items that were previously hidden. In this example, `chkNeedCheck` is an unbound check box and `fraCheckData` is a frame on the General page containing bound controls where the user can enter additional information:

```
Sub chkNeedCheck_Click()
    Set objInspector = Item.GetInspector
    Set objPage = _
      myInspector.ModifiedFormPages("General")
    Set fraCheckData = objPage.Controls("fraCheckData")
    Set chkNeedCheck = objPage.Controls("chkNeedCheck")
    fraCheckData.Visible = chkNeedCheck.Value
End Sub
```

Clicking on the `chkNeedCheck` check box toggles the `frmCheckData` control's `Visible` property, alternately showing and hiding the frame and all the controls it contains.

---

**CAUTION:** Using a frame control to hide and show a group of controls is a good idea because it avoids the one-off problem that can plague forms in which individual controls are enabled and disabled. See Chapter 20, "Common Outlook Form and Item Techniques," for more on preventing one-off items.

---

Besides the `Click` event, you can use the `Write`, `Close`, or `Send` events to process information in unbound controls. Note, however, that if the user changes only the data in an unbound control—and not the data in any bound control—the `Write` event will not fire, even if the user clicks Save.

### 18.4.3 Creating a hyperlink on an Outlook form

A very practical use for the `Click` event on an unbound control is to create a control that launches a Web page in a browser. While the `ContactItem` has several properties with built-in hyperlink capability (`BusinessHomePage`, `FTPSite`, `PersonalHomePage`, `WebPage`), other forms don't have such suitable properties. A good workaround is to put the text for a hyperlink in the `Caption` property of a label control and use code such as the following to launch the link in the browser when the user clicks the label:

```
Sub lblWebPage_Click()
    Set objWeb = _
      CreateObject("InternetExplorer.Application")
    objWeb.Navigate Item.GetInspector.ModifiedFormPages _
      ("P.2").Controls("lblWebPage").Caption
    objWeb.Visible = True
End Sub
```

You may want to format the label control to show the link as blue and underlined so users will know to click on it.

### 18.4.4 Performing validation in Outlook form code

In Chapter 17, "Extending Form Design with Fields and Controls," you saw examples of validation using the Validation page of a control's Properties dialog. If you have more than one field to validate, you may want to let the Write event perform the validation, canceling the saving of the item at the first sign that all fields don't meet your conditions.

In some cases, you can use the SetFocus method of a control to point the user toward a property that needs a different value. This example assumes that you have customized the Message page on a message form:

```
Function Item_Write()
     Dim objPage
     Dim txtSubject
     If Item.Subject = "" Then
          Item_Write = False
          MsgBox "Please fill in the Subject."
          Set objPage = _
            Item.GetInspector.ModifiedFormPages("Message")
          Set txtSubject = objPage.Controls("Subject")
          txtSubject.SetFocus
     End If
     Set objPage = Nothing
     Set txtSubject = Nothing
End Function
```

However, to use SetFocus, you must have a valid control object, which implies that you have an object for the form page. Remember that not all form pages are customizable. The ModifiedFormPages collection contains only the pages that have been customized. Therefore, you will be able to use SetFocus only on customized pages.

### 18.4.5 A custom Contact form with required categories

Microsoft Outlook allows users to build a personal list of frequently used categories (the Master Category List), but does not provide for a master group list. One solution is to use a Contact form that requires the user to choose from a list of categories included as part of the form's code. Until the user picks one of the required categories, the contact item cannot be saved.

The only customized page of this form is the Categories page, shown in Figure 18.4. It contains three controls—an unbound label control (lbl-Categories) displaying the text on the left, a list box (lstCategories) bound to the Categories field, and a button dragged from the All Contact Fields list in the Field Chooser. If you drag the field shown as Categories …, Outlook creates a button that launches the Categories dialog. We've edited the caption of the button so that it reads More Categories … .

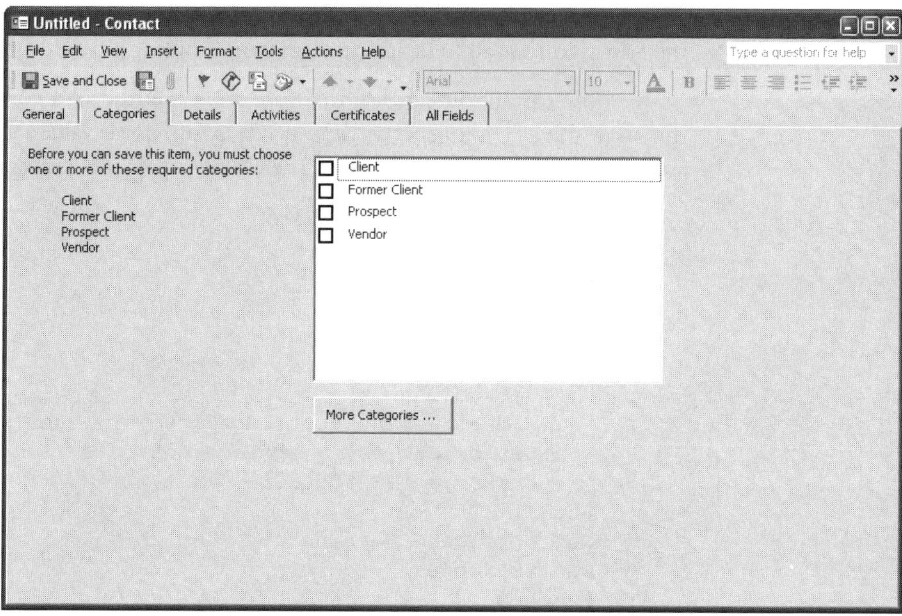

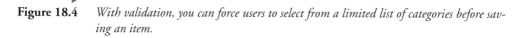

**Figure 18.4** *With validation, you can force users to select from a limited list of categories before saving an item.*

The code behind this form, shown in Listing 18.14, wraps up many of the concepts in this chapter: It uses the `Open` event handler to initialize the appearance of two controls and applies validation in the `Write` event.

The `HasRequiredCategory()` function provides a good example of comparing the contents of two arrays: the user's category choice(s) and the list of required categories from the `m_strRequiredCats` variable. The code also uses a VBScript version of the `WSHListSep()` that returns a user's list separator character. Compare with the version in Listing 10.11.

## 18.5 Debugging in VBScript

You have seen the form code samples get more and more complex throughout this chapter and are probably wondering what VBScript offers for debugging tools. For detailed debugging in VBScript, Outlook includes the Microsoft Script Debugger. The Script Debugger is available only when you are running an Outlook form and does not allow you to edit the actual form script code.

**Listing 18.14** *Force an Item To Save in a Particular Folder*

```
Option Explicit
Dim m_strRequiredCats

Function Item_Open()
    Dim objPage
    Dim lstCategories
    Dim lblCategories
    Dim arrRCats
    Dim strLabel
    Dim i
    ' *** USER OPTION ***
    ' list of categories in the order you want them to appear
    m_strRequiredCats = "Client;Former Client;Prospect"
    Set objPage = _
      Item.GetInspector.ModifiedFormPages("Categories")
    Set lstCategories = objPage.Controls("lstCategories")
    Set lblCategories = objPage.Controls("lblCategories")
    strLabel = "Before you can save this item, you " & _
               "must choose one or more of these " & _
               "required categories:" & vbCrLf
    arrRCats = Split(m_strRequiredCats, ";")
    lstCategories.List = arrRCats
    For i = 0 To UBound(arrRCats)
        strLabel = strLabel & _
                   vbCrLf & Space(10) & Trim(arrRCats(i))
    Next
    lblCategories.Caption = strLabel
    m_strRequiredCats = UCase(m_strRequiredCats)
    Set objPage = Nothing
    Set lstCategories = Nothing
    Set lblCategories = Nothing
End Function

Function Item_Write()
    Dim objPage
    Dim lstCategories
    If HasRequiredCategory() = False Then
        Item_Write = False
        Item.GetInspector.SetCurrentFormPage "Categories"
        Set objPage = _
          Item.GetInspector.ModifiedFormPages("Categories")
        Set lstCategories = _
          objPage.Controls("lstCategories")
        lstCategories.SetFocus
    End If
    Set objPage = Nothing
    Set lstCategories = Nothing
End Function
```

**Listing 18.14** *Force an Item To Save in a Particular Folder (continued)*

```
Function HasRequiredCategory()
    Dim objPage
    Dim lstCategories
    Dim arrCats
    Dim arrRequiredCats
    Dim strListSep
    Dim blnMatch
    Dim i, j
    blnMatch = False
    strListSep = WSHListSep()
    Set objPage = _
      Item.GetInspector.ModifiedFormPages("Categories")
    Set lstCategories = objPage.Controls("lstCategories")
    If m_strRequiredCats <> "" Then
        arrCats = Split(UCase(Item.Categories), strListSep)
        arrRequiredCats = Split(m_strRequiredCats, ";")
        For i = 0 To UBound(arrCats, 1)
            For j = 0 To UBound(arrRequiredCats, 1)
                If Trim(arrCats(i)) = _
                  Trim(arrRequiredCats(j)) Then
                    blnMatch = True
                    Exit For
                End If
            Next
            If blnMatch = True Then
                Exit For
            End If
        Next
    Else
        blnMatch = True
    End If
    HasRequiredCategory = blnMatch
    Set objPage = Nothing
    Set lstCategories = Nothing
End Function

Function WSHListSep()
    Dim objWSHShell
    Dim strReg
    strReg = "HKCU\Control Panel\International\sList"
    Set objWSHShell = CreateObject("WScript.Shell")
    WSHListSep = objWSHShell.RegRead(strReg)
    Set objWSHShell = Nothing
End Function
```

**Note:** The Script Debugger is part of Web Scripting, one of the Office Tools components included with Outlook 2000 and 2002. If Web Scripting is not already installed when you try to use the Script Debugger, you will be prompted to install it from your Outlook or Office CD-ROM or shared installation files on your network. If you have Microsoft Visual Studio installed, you will have the option of using the Visual Interdev debugger.

To start the Script Debugger, run any form that includes VBScript code and then choose Tools, Forms, Script Debugger. Another way to launch the Script Debugger is to place a `Stop` statement in your code. When the `Stop` statement executes, you receive a runtime error message and can choose to debug the application.

**Tip:** You can use a `Stop` statement in VBA code as well to force VBA to switch to break mode.

When form script code encounters an error, you may see a message (see Figure 18.5) asking whether you want to debug the script. This message will appear only if you have a script debugger on your system. If you don't have a script debugger or you choose No in response to the debug prompt,

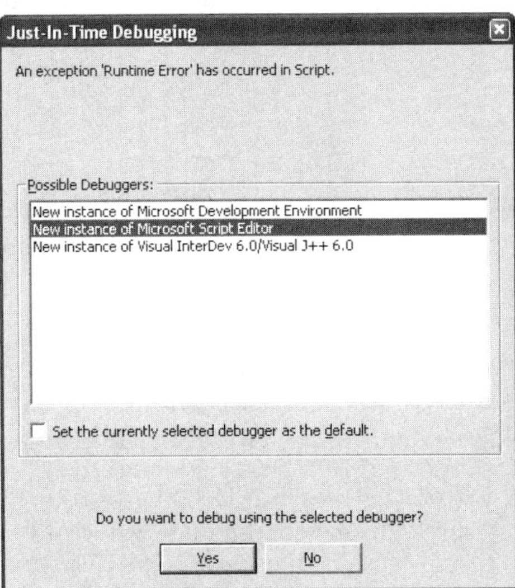


**Figure 18.5** *If you have a script debugger installed, form code errors will give you the opportunity to debug problem code.*

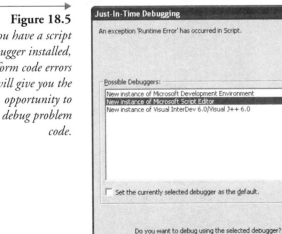

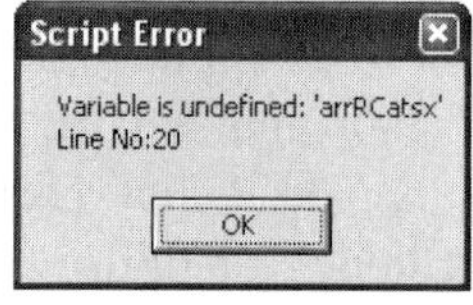
Script Error
Variable is undefined: 'arrRCatsx'
Line No:20
OK

**Figure 18.6** *Form code error messages will tell you what line is causing the problem.*

you'll see an error message (Figure 18.6) giving you the line number in which the error occurred. In the form code window, you can use the Edit, Go To command to go quickly to that line and fix the problem.

If you have more than one script debugger on your system, you can choose the one you prefer. Each script debugger should include many of the same debugging tools as VBA, including Watch and Locals. The Debug menu contains the same Step Into and Set Next Statement commands, as well as other functions. You also see toolbar buttons for the most frequently used debugging commands. However, the debugger may not have an Immediate window where you can write new code statements.

The one thing you cannot do in any script debugger is edit the Outlook form code directly. If you find a program statement with an error, you may need to skip it to see whether the rest of the code runs OK. If the debugger supports an Immediate window, try skipping the problem statement, running an alternative version from the Immediate window, then resuming code execution after the problem statement. If that works, copy the code from the Immediate window back into the form's code window.

## 18.6 Summary

In this chapter, you have encountered many techniques and code samples for dealing with Outlook form events and also for many common Outlook techniques, such as saving an item created with a custom form to a particular folder. The Outlook form code environment is nowhere near as rich as the VBA environment when it comes to coding and debugging tools. If you write your form code in the VBA environment and then port it to the form's script, you will encounter fewer mistakes that require debugging.

In Chapter 19, you will see how to enhance your forms with more controls that, for example, display pictures and views of Outlook folders.

# 19

# More Controls for Outlook Forms

Outlook forms provide a rich environment for creating forms to display data and interact with users because they can support many different types of controls. Chapter 3, "A VBA Birthday/Anniversary Reminder Tool," introduced many of the controls you will see in this chapter. Controls on Outlook forms, however, may behave differently than they do on VBA forms.

Highlights of this chapter include discussions of the following:

- How to use the `Click` event on controls to trigger changes in other controls or run other code
- What other controls are available in the Toolbox
- How to display the contents of an Outlook folder using the Outlook View Control on a form page
- How to add the ability to browse for files using the Common Dialog Control
- Why Outlook forms don't save changes that you make to the appearance of controls

## 19.1 Using the basic controls

You have already seen a lot of code samples using some of the basic controls, either in Outlook forms or in earlier chapters on VBA forms. The next few sections provide specific tips and techniques for using these controls in Outlook forms.

### 19.1.1 Command buttons

Command buttons are placed on Outlook forms so that users can perform certain tasks on demand (i.e. at the click of a button). As discussed in Chapter 18, "Writing Code to Respond to Outlook Form Events," the `Click` event on a command button control is the only event for that control available on an Outlook form. Here is the basic syntax for a `Click` event handler for a command button named `cmdRunCode`:

```
Sub cmdRunCode_Click()
    MsgBox "Running this code"
End Sub
```

Notice that the name of the command button is part of the name of the subroutine. If you change the name of the button, you must also change the name of the event handler.

### 19.1.2 Check boxes

Dragging any Yes/No Outlook property, such as the `Complete` property for a task, from the Field Chooser to a custom form page will result in a check box control being placed on the form. Check boxes are used whenever you want the user to have an easy way to toggle between the values of `True` and `False` for a property.

You will also find unbound check boxes useful for toggling the appearance of other controls on a form because, like command buttons, unbound check boxes support a `Click` event. For example, this code snippet for a check box named `chkShowMoreFields` shows or hides a frame control named `fraMoreFields` containing more controls. (Frames are covered in section 19.1.4.) Both controls are on a custom page named Key Data.

```
Sub chkShowMoreFields_Click()
    Dim objPage
    Dim chkShowMoreFields
    Dim fraMoreFields
    Set objPage = _
      Item.GetInspector.ModifiedFormPages("Key Data")
    Set chkShowMoreFields = _
      objPage.Controls("chkShowMoreFields")
    Set fraMoreFields = objPage.Controls("fraMoreFields")
    fraMoreFields.Visible = chkShowMoreFields.Value
    Set objPage = Nothing
    Set chkShowMoreFields = Nothing
    Set fraMoreFields = Nothing
End Sub
```

### 19.1.3 Option buttons

Also known as radio buttons, option buttons are a good choice if you need the user to pick from a small number of mutually exclusive choices. (For a Yes/No type of choice, a check box is usually preferable. For a long list of choices, you're better off with a list box or combo box.)

To use option buttons to set the value of an Outlook property, on the Value tab of each button's Properties dialog, bind each button in a set to the same Outlook property. The `Value` property can be any data type, but each button needs to have a different value. Figure 19.1 shows an option button being set up to handle a custom Estimated Work Time `Duration` property for a Task form.

Figure 19.2 shows three such buttons, along with a text box, all bound to the same Estimated Work Time property. The buttons have these properties:

- Option button 1:

  ```
  Name        OptEstWork1
  Caption     One day
  Value       1d
  ```

- Option button 2:

  ```
  Name        OptEstWork2
  Caption     Three days
  Value       3d
  ```

- Option button 3:

  ```
  Name        OptEstWork3
  Caption     One week
  Value       1w
  ```

Normally, you would not also display a text box bound to the same property. The text box in Figure 19.2 is present to illustrate how selecting one of the options sets the corresponding value for the bound property.

If you have more than one set of option buttons on a form, each set must be enclosed in a frame control. (Actually, you can leave one set without a frame; that set will use the form page as a whole as the equivalent of a frame.)

**Figure 19.1** *Assign a different value to each option button in a set for an Outlook property.*

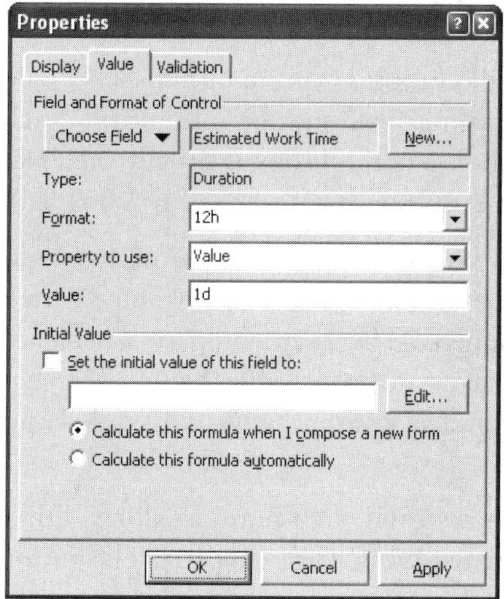


**Tip:** Place the frame control for a set of option buttons on the form, then create the buttons inside the frame. Don't try to move a set of already created option buttons into a new frame control.

**Figure 19.2** *Use option buttons to restrict users to a small number of choices.*

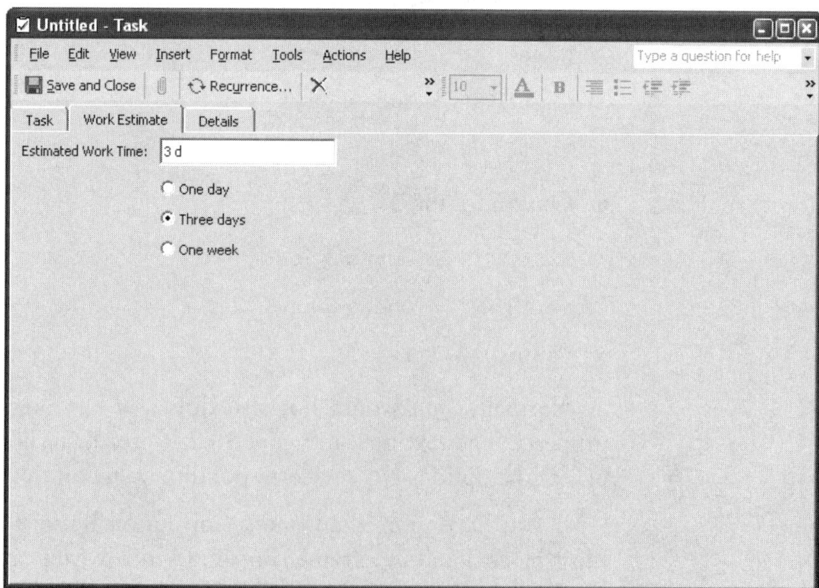

If you bind two option buttons to a Yes/No property, on the Value tab for each control, you should set the format to True/False. Set the `Value` property of one button to `True` and the other to `False`.

Bound option buttons will fire a `PropertyChange` or `CustomPropertyChange` event, depending on whether they are bound to a built-in property or a custom property.

If you are using a set of unbound option buttons, the value for each will be either `True` or `False`. You cannot set other values, as you can with buttons bound to Outlook properties. Your form code can either evaluate the values of each button in the set until it finds the one that's `True`, or it can use the `Click` event for each button. A good technique is to use the `Caption` or `Tag` property of the button to store a value that you can then use to set the value for another control or property on the form. To set the `Tag` property, you need to use the Advanced Properties dialog.

As an example, consider a form with a custom page named Color and three option buttons inside a frame named `fraColor` to allow the user to change the color of the caption for the frame. The `Caption` and `Tag` property of each button reflect that color; the `Tag` property holds the literal value of the `vbRed`, `vbBlack`, or `vbBlue` constant.

- Option button 1:

```
Name        OptColor1
Caption     Red
Tag         255
```

- Option button 2:

```
Name        OptColor2
Caption     Black
Tag         0
```

- Option button 3:

```
Name        OptColor3
Caption     Blue
Tag         16711680
```

In Listing 19.1, the `Open` and `Close` event handlers set and dereference a module-level variable, `m_objControls`, to make it easy to work with the

**Listing 19.1** *Using Option Buttons to Change the Appearance of Another Control*

```
Dim m_objControls

Function Item_Open()
    Dim objPage
    Set objPage = Item.GetInspector.ModifiedFormPages("Color")
    Set m_objControls = objPage.Controls
    Set objPage = Nothing
End Function

Function Item_Close()
    Set m_objControls = Nothing
End Function

Sub optColor1_Click()
   m_objControls("fraColor").ForeColor = _
     m_objControls("optColor1").Tag
End Sub

Sub optColor2_Click()
   m_objControls("fraColor").ForeColor = _
     m_objControls("optColor2").Tag
End Sub

Sub optColor3_Click()
   m_objControls("fraColor").ForeColor = _
     m_objControls("optColor3").Tag
End Sub
```

Color page's `Controls` collection in several different event handlers. Each of the `Click` event handlers for the option buttons changes the color of the frame to the value in the `Tag` property of the clicked option button.

### 19.1.4 Frames

Frame controls have two major uses on Outlook forms: (1) to provide grouping for option buttons and (2) to make it easy to show/hide or enable/disable a group of controls. In some versions of Outlook, enabling or disabling an individual control can cause the Outlook item to one-off, a problem we'll explore in more detail in Chapter 20, "Common Outlook Form and Item Techniques." Therefore, a good strategy when you want to toggle the display of some controls is to put them all in one frame and use code to set the `Visible` property of the frame, rather than the individual controls. You saw an example of this earlier in Section 19.1.2.

You can also use a frame control to add simple lines and boxes to a form, including boxes that logically group different sets of controls, such as one group related to e-mail and another related to calendars. Such groupings can help the user locate the right control more quickly.

### 19.1.5 List box and combo box controls

You learned about list box and combo box controls in the context of VBA forms in Chapters 3 and 6. The techniques for using these controls on Outlook forms are similar.

One difference on an Outlook form is that to populate a list or combo box, you can enter a Possible Values list on the Value page of the control, as shown in Figure 19.3. To build a list using code, use either the `AddItem` method or the `List` property, as covered in those earlier chapters. I think `List` is much easier—especially for multicolumn boxes or for single-column boxes, if you combine it with the `Split()` and `Join()` functions for working with arrays. Chapter 23, "Exchange Server, Databases, and XML Web Services," provides an example of filling a combo or list box from a database table using another property, `Column`.

In a combo box, if you want to require the user to use one of the listed choices, bring up the Advanced Properties dialog for the control and set `MatchEntry` property to `-1 - True`. If the user does not choose one of the listed choices, Outlook will pop up the message Invalid Property Value. Several properties that work in VBA forms are not supported in Outlook forms, including `ColumnHeads`, `ControlSource`, and `RowSource`.

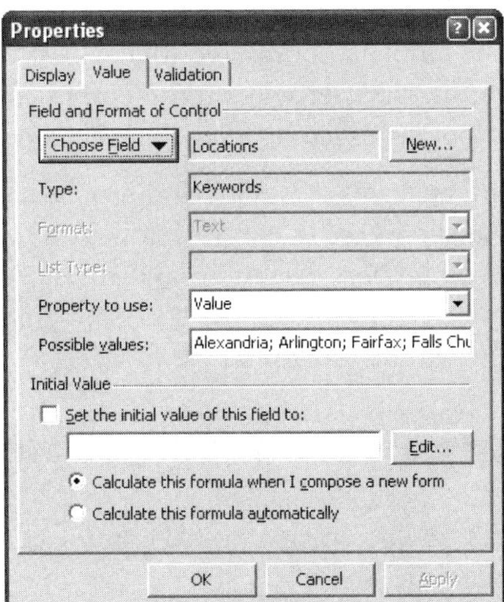


**Figure 19.3** *You can use the Possible Values property of the control to set up the list of values for a list box or combo box.*

To make a list box capable of capturing more than one user selection, on the Advanced Properties of the control, you must set the `MultiSelect` property to `1 - Multi`. Outlook will do this automatically when you bind a list box to a keywords property, such as `Categories`, `Company`, or a custom keywords property.

You should not bind a multiselect list box to anything but a keywords property. If you bind a multiselect list box to a normal text property, when the user moves the focus to another control, Outlook will no longer display the user's selections in the list box. It will store the selections in the property bound to the list box, separating the selections with a comma (or, more precisely, with the user's list separator character). However, when the user moves the focus back to the list box, the control will not redisplay the selections. The user probably will just get frustrated that the selections won't stick in the list box, even though Outlook actually is storing them as a delimited list.

If, for some reason, you decide that you need to use a multiselect list box with a nonkeywords property, use an unbound list box. You will need to provide code in the `Open` event handler to set the `Selected` property for each item you want to appear selected and in the `Write` event handler to build a delimited list of the user's selections.

### 19.1.6 Persisting control appearance

A key concept to keep in mind is that any changes you make to the appearance of a control by using code to change control properties while the user is working with the form are not persistent. The next time the user opens an item using that form, the user will see the published version of the form, with the controls looking exactly as they did when you published the form.

Usually, control appearance is related to some data values. For example, you might want to show certain controls only if the user has chosen a particular value in a combo box. The solution is to use the `Open` event handler to check the data values and make the corresponding changes in the controls' appearance when the user opens the item.

## 19.2 Using more controls from the Toolbox

The Outlook form Toolbox contains several more controls that you might find useful in certain situations:

- The tab strip control adds a strip of tabs to the form. The `Value` property of the control corresponds to the current tab, beginning with 0 for the first tab. However, the tab strip does not fire a `Click` event, making it impossible to use it to display and hide controls depending on which tab is chosen. (You can use the tab strip on a VBA form, however, and write code for the `Change` event, which will fire when a user switches between tabs.)
- The multipage control looks a bit like the tab strip, but you can add controls to each page. The `Value` property of the control corresponds to the current page, beginning with 0 for the first page. When you run the form, the `SelectedItem` property of the control indicates which page is currently selected and is used to access properties of that particular page.
- The scroll bar control can be set to appear as either a vertical or horizontal scroll bar. (On a VBA form, when the user scrolls, the `Change` event fires. No event fires on an Outlook form.)
- The spin button control is commonly used to set values in set increments, such as the number of copies to be printed.
- The image control can display many types of picture files. If you don't set its `Picture` property, you also can use it to enhance a form with simple lines and boxes in different colors.

### 19.2.1 Adding customized controls to the Toolbox

If you like consistent forms, you probably use exactly the same size command buttons on every form you create. You can make that task easier by adding your own customized versions of the standard controls to the Toolbox. Follow these steps:

1. In the design mode of a form that has the control looking the way you want, drag the control to the Toolbox.
2. Right-click the newly added Toolbox control, and choose Customize New. (For example, if you drag a command button to the Toolbox, you see Customize New CommandButton.)
3. In the Customize Control dialog box (see Figure 19.4), change the Tool Tip text to something appropriate for your control, and then click OK.

**Figure 19.4** *Drag customized controls to the Toolbox, then give them a distinctive Tool Tip.*

Optionally, if you have a .bmp, .dib, or .ico graphic that you want to use as a picture for the command button, you can click Load Picture in the Customize Control dialog to change the button's icon.

After you add a control to the Toolbox in this fashion, you can add it to any form just as you would a built-in control, but it will retain its customized properties.

To remove a customized control that you added to the Toolbox, right-click its Toolbox button, and then choose Delete New control.

---

**Tip:** If the Control Toolbox comes up blank, search your system for a file named Outlook.box. If it's present, delete or rename it. Then restart Outlook to recover the default Toolbox.

---

### 19.2.2 A Contact form with pictures

A common question about the Outlook Contact form is, Can I use it to display an employee or client's picture? That's exactly what the image control is designed to do. You can follow these steps to add an image control that loads a user's photo from a stored system file:

1. Open a Contact form in design mode, and switch to the (P.2) page.
2. Choose Form, Rename Page to change the name of the page to Photo.
3. From the Field Chooser, drag the User Field 1 to the page. Change the text of the label control to "Photo file:".
4. From the Toolbox, add a command button next to the text box for User Field 1. Give it the name `cmdRefresh` and the caption `Refresh`.

5. In the Toolbox, click on the image control, and drag a rectangle onto the form representing the size of the picture you want to display. (If you don't see the Toolbox, click the Toolbox button to display it.)
6. Change the name of the control to `imgPhoto`.
7. Add the code in Listing 19.2 to the form.
8. Publish the form as IPM.Contact.Photo.

**Listing 19.2** *Load a Picture from a System File into an Outlook Form*

```
Dim IsLoading
Dim imgPhoto

Function Item_Open()
    Dim objPage
    IsLoading = True
    Set objPage = Item.GetInspector.ModifiedFormPages("Photo")
    Set imgPhoto = objPage.Controls("imgPhoto")
    Call LoadPhoto()
    Set objPage = Nothing
    IsLoading = False
End Function

Function Item_Close()
    Set imgPhoto = Nothing
End Function

Sub Item_PropertyChange(ByVal Name)
    If Not IsLoading Then
        Select Case Name
            Case "User1"
                Call LoadPhoto()
        End Select
    End If
End Sub

Sub cmdRefresh_Click()
    Call LoadPhoto()
End Sub

Sub LoadPhoto()
    Dim strMsg
    On Error Resume Next
    If Item.User1 <> "" Then
        imgPhoto.Picture = LoadPicture(Item.User1)
        If Err = 481 Then
            strMsg = "Could not load " & Item.User1 & _
                     vbCrLf & vbCrLf & _
                     "Try a different format."
            MsgBox strMsg, , "Invalid Picture Error"
        End If
    End If
End Sub
```

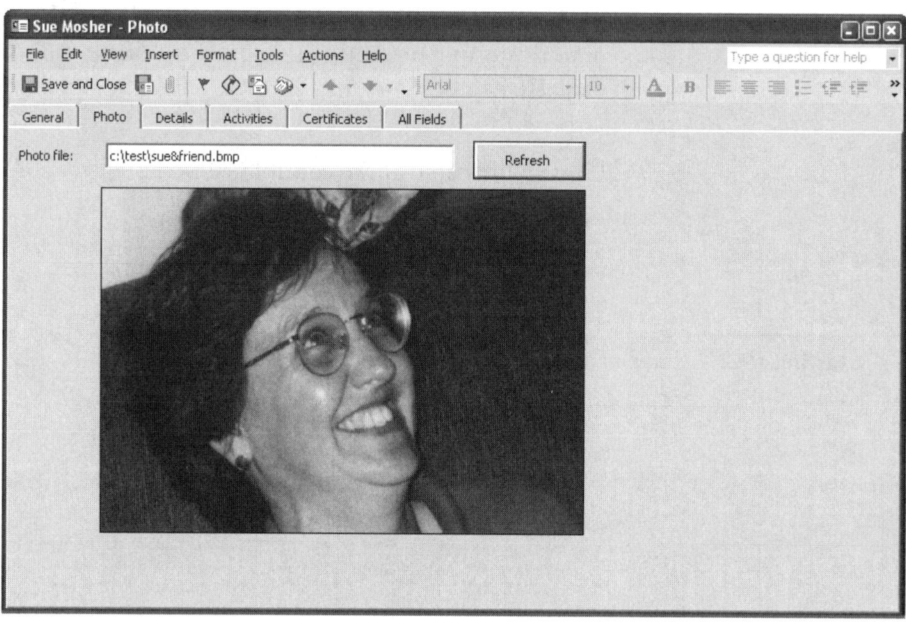


**Figure 19.5** *Use an image control to put a face with the name of a contact.*

Here's how to make it work: Use Tools, Forms, Choose Forms to create a new item using the IPM.Contact.Photo form. In the text box on the Photo page, type in the full path and file name of the picture you want to load for this contact. Click the Refresh button to load the picture. The `LoadPhoto` subroutine uses the data in `User Field 1` (the `ContactItem.User1` property in the object model) to set the control's `Picture` property and load the image from the file. Figure 19.5 shows the resulting Photo page.

A variation on this technique would be to keep images for all employees in a shared network drive with a file for each picture using each employee's full name (assuming you had no duplicate names). In that case, the `LoadPhoto` subroutine could construct the path to the picture from the contact's `FullName` property, as shown in Listing 19.3.

Notice the use of the `FileSystemObject`, covered in Chapter 10, "Working with the Object Models," to check whether a file exists corresponding to the contact's `FullName` property.

## 19.3 Adding more ActiveX controls

Beyond the standard Toolbox controls is a rich world of additional controls called ActiveX controls. Programmers use these not only to add new capa-

**Listing 19.3** *Load a Picture from a Shared Network Drive Using the Contact's FullName Property*

```
Sub LoadPhoto()
    Dim strFolder
    Dim strFile
    Dim fso
    Dim strMsg
    strFolder = "\\Server\Shared\Photos\"
    strFile = strFolder & Item.FullName & ".bmp"
    Set fso = CreateObject("Scripting.FileSystemObject")
    If fso.FileExists(strFile) Then
        On Error Resume Next
        imgPhoto.Picture = LoadPicture(strFile)
        If Err = 481 Then
            strMsg = "Could not load " & strFile & _
                     vbCrLf & vbCrLf & _
                     "Try a different format."
            MsgBox strMsg, , "Invalid Picture Error"
        End If
    End If
    Set fso = Nothing
End Sub
```

bilities to programs, but also to create Web pages. Many such controls are included with Windows, Microsoft Office, Outlook, or Internet Explorer, and third-party sources offer even more controls. Visual Basic and other development tools also let you create your own ActiveX controls; if you don't want users to see your VBScript form code, one possible solution is to build one or more ActiveX controls that encapsulate the functionality provided by your code.

**Note:** The drawback of using ActiveX controls besides those that come with Windows, Office, Outlook, or Internet Explorer is that you must install and register them on each computer that will run a form that uses them. If you do decide to use a control that isn't already installed on users' machines, check its documentation to make sure that you are licensed to redistribute the control.

To browse the ActiveX controls already available on your system, right-click anywhere on the Toolbox and then choose Additional Controls from the pop-up menu. You will see many controls (see Figure 19.6) that suggest interesting possibilities. For example, if the computer has the Windows Media Player installed on it, you can add a Windows Media Player control to play audio or video from an Outlook form. Not all ActiveX controls will work with Outlook, though.

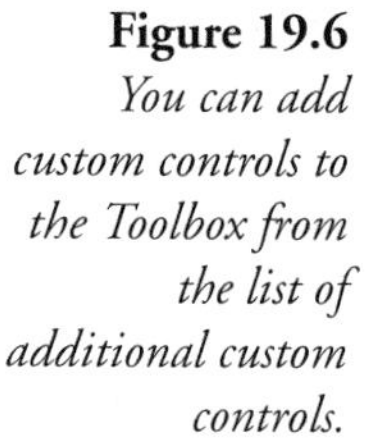

**Figure 19.6** *You can add custom controls to the Toolbox from the list of additional custom controls.*

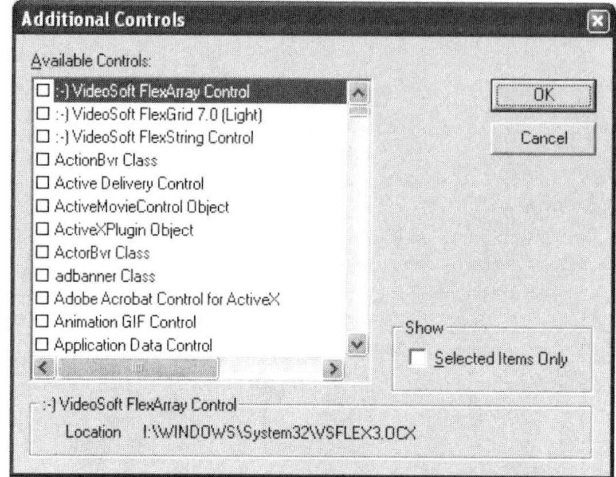


---

**Tip:** If you check the Selected Items Only box, you will see a list of Microsoft Forms 2.0 controls. These are the standard controls that the Toolbox normally contains.

---

Third-party controls that you download from the Internet or buy separately may include a setup program that registers the controls. If not, you must install and register the controls manually. Copy the controls to your \Windows\System or \Winnt\System32 folder, and then run this command:

```
regsvr32 mycontrol.dll
```

in which mycontrol.dll (or .ocx) is the file name of the control.

A common quandary for Outlook form designers is how to duplicate the dropdown calendar that appears on the Appointment, Journal, and Task forms. This calendar control is private to Outlook and cannot be added to your custom pages. (This also explains why pages using this control cannot be customized.) However, a similar date picker control is included with Office Developer Edition and Visual Studio 6.0, and variations are available from third-party developers.

## 19.3.1 Using the Outlook View Control

The Outlook View Control (OVC) is a free ActiveX control used to display Outlook 2000 or 2002 views in an Outlook form, a Web page, or a Visual Basic project. The OVC is included with Outlook 2002 and can be downloaded for use with Outlook 2000 (see Appendix A).

The OVC can display any Outlook folder view and can filter the folder to display only items meeting particular conditions. This makes it ideal for use on a form to show items in other folders that are related to the current item. Its main limitation is that it can show only one folder at a time. It cannot present a consolidated view of several folders, as the Activities page on a Contact form can. (Of course, the Activities page cannot be programmed like the OVC.)

For Outlook 2000, there is an additional limitation: The OVC does not expose a `Selection` object. This means that you cannot use it in an Outlook form to provide an easy way for the user to select one or more items that you will run additional code against. Users can, however, double-click or right-click items as they normally would in an Outlook folder. The Outlook 2002 version of the OVC does have a `Selection` object.

Since the OVC is very useful, you will probably want to add it to the Toolbox. Right-click the Toolbox, choose Custom Controls, check the box for the Microsoft Outlook View Control, and then click OK.

To add an instance of the OVC to an Outlook form, select the control in the Toolbox, then use the mouse to drag out a rectangle the size and shape

**Table 19.1** *User-Configurable Properties of the OVC*

| Property | Description |
|---|---|
| `DeferUpdate` | Makes Outlook wait to update the control only when the `ForceUpdate` method is called |
| `EnableRowPersistance` | If set to `True`, the OVC remembers the last item selected. (Outlook 2002 only) |
| `Filter` | Applies a DASL query to the view, using the syntax for `Search` discussed in Chapter 14, "Working with Items and Recipients" (Outlook 2002 only) |
| `FilterAppend` | Appends an additional DASL query to the view using a logical AND to join it to the existing filter (Outlook 2002 only) |
| `Folder` | Path for the folder displayed in the view as a string (e.g., \\Public Folders\All Public Folders\Sales\Prospects) |
| `Namespace` | Always equals `"MAPI"` |
| `Restriction` | Applies a filter to the view using the syntax for `Find` and `Restrict` discussed in Chapter 14, "Working with Items and Recipients" |
| `View` | Sets the name of the view for displaying the folder |
| `ViewXML` | Sets the XML for the view displaying the folder (Outlook 2002 only) |

**Listing 19.4** *Return a String Path for any MAPIFolder Object*

```
Function GetFolderPath(objFolder)
    Dim strPath
    Dim objParent
    On Error Resume Next
    strPath = "\" & objFolder.Name
    Do While Err = 0
       Set objParent = objFolder.Parent
       If Err = 0 Then
            strPath = "\" & objParent.Name & strPath
            Set objFolder = objParent
        Else
            Exit Do
        End If
    Loop
    GetFolderPath = "\" & strPath
    Set objParent = Nothing
End Function
```

**Listing 19.5** *Use the OVC To Display Vacation Days*

```
Const olFolderCalendar = 9

Function Item_Open()
    Dim objPage
    Dim ViewCtl1
    Set objPage = _
      Item.GetInspector.ModifiedFormPages("Vacations")
    Set ViewCtl1 = objPage.Controls("ViewCtl1")
    With ViewCtl1
        .Folder = GetCalFolderPath()
        .View = "Events"
        .Restriction = "[Subject] = ""Vacation"""
    End With
    Set objPage = Nothing
    Set ViewCtl1 = Nothing
End Function

Function GetCalFolderPath()
    Dim objFolder
    Dim objNS
    Set objNS = Application.GetNamespace("MAPI")
    Set objFolder = objNS.GetDefaultFolder(olFolderCalendar)
    GetCalFolderPath = GetFolderPath(objFolder)
    Set objFolder = Nothing
    Set objNS = Nothing
End Function
```

you want the control to display as. Usually, you'll make it fairly large, so that the user can see as much detail from the folder as possible. By default, the OVC displays the user's Inbox folder. If you want it to display a different folder, you will need to set the control's `Folder` property either through the Advanced Properties dialog or through form code.

Notice that the `Folder` property takes a string value, not a `MAPIFolder` object. Outlook 2002 provides a `MAPIFolder.FolderPath` property that returns the folder path for a specific folder. For Outlook 2000, you can use the `GetFolderPath()` function in Listing 19.4.

To demonstrate the OVC, consider a message form used to request approval of vacation time. You can add an OVC to a custom page and use code to display all the items in user's Calendar folder with the subject "Vacation," so that the user can see at a glance what vacation time has already been taken. The form code in Listing 19.5 assumes that you've added the OVC to a custom page named Vacations.

`ViewCtl1` is the default name that Outlook uses when you add the OVC to a form. The `GetCalFolderPath()` function uses the `GetFolderPath()` function in Listing 19.4 to return a path string for the user's default Calendar folder. Figure 19.7 shows the results after the user has run the form.

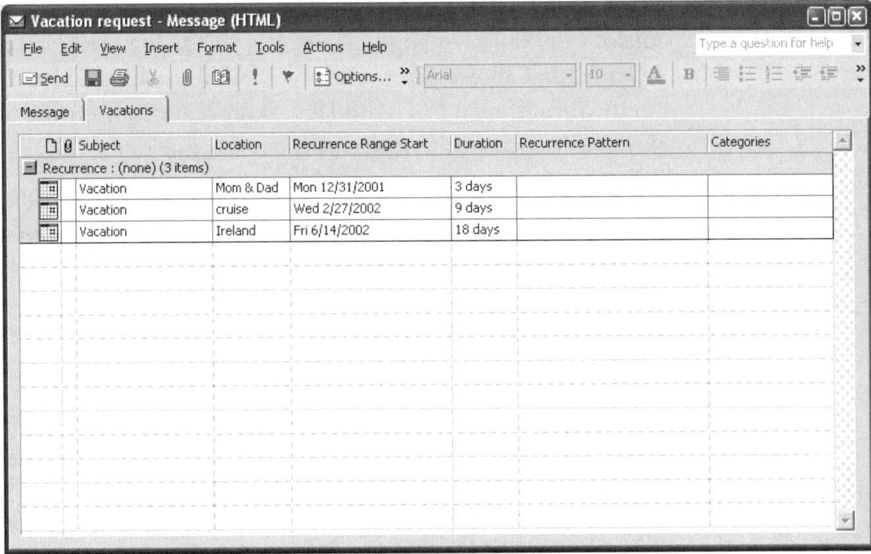


**Figure 19.7** *The OVC can provide a filtered view of any Outlook folder.*

Inside the OVC, users can double-click any item to display it, just as they would from a regular Outlook folder or right-click items for more options.

You can also use the OVC in VBA, VB, Web pages, and any other application that can use ActiveX controls. However, the functionality will differ, depending on the environment, in order to maintain Outlook security. The resources in Appendix A will give you more information on using the OVC. You will see the OVC again in Chapter 23, "Exchange Server, Databases, and XML Web Services," in the context of Outlook folder home pages.

---

**Tip:** If you are using the updated OVC in a Web page or other non-Outlook application, omit the View parameter (e.g., `<param name="View" value="By Category">`) in the initial settings for the control. If you set the `View` this way, even to `value=""`, more often than not it will cause the control to default to the user's Inbox rather than showing the folder you want.

---

### 19.3.2 Using the Common Dialog Control to pick a file

One control likely to be present on any system running Outlook is the Common Dialog Control. This control provides several commonly used dialogs to Windows applications, but the dialog most useful for Outlook is the one that allows you to pick files. We'll use it to add a Browse ... button to the form shown in Figure 19.5 to make it easier for the user to choose an image file to associate with a particular contact.

You must first add the Microsoft Common Dialog Control to your control Toolbox. Then add the control to the Photo page of the form. Don't worry about the position; this control will be invisible when you run the form. Change the `Name` property of the control to `ctlCommonDialog`. Also add a command button control named `cmdBrowse` and put the `cmdBrowse_Click` code from Listing 19.6 in your form.

This code sets the default filter for the Open dialog to show only image files that will work with the image control. The Open dialog is modal, which means the execution of the form's code pauses until the user selects a file or cancels the dialog. The code does not need to load the picture because setting the `Item.User1` property triggers the `PropertyChange` event, which will run the code in Listing 19.2.

**Listing 19.6** *Use the Common Dialog Control to Add an Open Dialog Box for Choosing Files*

```
Sub cmdBrowse_Click()
    Dim strPath
    Dim intPos
    Dim strFileName
    Dim objPage
    Dim strFileFilter
    Dim ctlCommonDialog
    Set objPage = Item.GetInspector.ModifiedFormPages("Photo")
    Set ctlCommonDialog = objPage.Controls("ctlCommonDialog")
    strFileFilter = "Pictures (*.bmp;*.gif;*.jpg;*.wmf)" _
                    & " | *.bmp;*.gif;*.jpg;*.wmf |" _
                    & "All Files (*.*) | *.*"
    ctlCommonDialog.Filter = strFileFilter
    ctlCommonDialog.ShowOpen
    If ctlCommonDialog.FileName <> "" Then
        Item.User1 = ctlCommonDialog.FileName
    End If
    Set objPage = Nothing
    Set ctlCommonDialog = Nothing
End Sub
```

# 19.4 Summary

Additional controls can enhance the functionality of Outlook forms. Sometimes they can even simplify what would be complex coding chores, such as duplicating an Open dialog for selecting files. If you use ActiveX controls beyond those available in the Outlook Toolbox, make sure that they are properly registered and installed on users' systems.

Chapter 20 concludes this section on Outlook forms with information on additional form techniques, such as showing and hiding pages, linking Outlook items, and using forms over the Internet.

# 20

# *Common Outlook Form and Item Techniques*

In the previous chapters in this section, you learned how to create simple Outlook forms and customize them with various controls and VBScript code. This chapter concludes the discussion of Outlook forms with more methods for making your forms more usable, a few architectural considerations, and some advanced techniques for creating more interactive forms, linking Outlook items, and exchanging Outlook forms over the Internet.

Highlights of this chapter include discussions of the following:

- What key architectural issues can cause problems for Outlook forms developers
- How to build a vacation approval form that sends back an Appointment item ready to save to the Calendar folder
- How to add a button to run VBScript code without using a command button on a custom page
- Why you need to use a linking mechanism when you want to create an item that automatically updates a public folder
- How to send either an HTML or plain-text message based on an Outlook form

In addition to the form code samples in this chapter, you will see a couple of VBA examples since some of the techniques can be applied either in a custom form or in VBA code that monitors a particular folder for new items.

## 20.1 Working with form layouts

As with VBA forms, you should pay attention to the ease of use of Outlook forms. Use fonts consistently. You can select multiple controls, then right-click and choose Advanced Properties to apply new font settings to all the selected controls. Also, line up the controls neatly. The Layout menu in design mode includes alignment, sizing, grouping, and other commands to help you build a consistent look.

On the Advanced Properties dialog for any control, you can set the `ControlTipText` property to display a tip to any user who pauses the mouse over the control. Other useful techniques include setting accelerators, managing the tab order, showing and hiding particular form pages, and setting the active page.

### 20.1.1 Setting control accelerators and tab order

You learned how to set the accelerators and tab order for controls on a VBA form in Chapter 3, "A VBA Birthday/Anniversary Reminder Form." The processes for creating an Outlook form are quite similar.

To set the tab order, choose Layout, Tab Order to access the Tab Order dialog, where you can use the Move Up and Move Down buttons to rearrange the order. Figure 20.1 shows the Tab Order dialog for the first page of the Contact form.

**Note:** When you use the Tab Order dialog, you are actually changing the `TabIndex` property of each control, which appears in the Advanced Properties dialog.

Notice how each text box control has a corresponding label. For example, you see `FileAsLabel`, followed by `FileAs`. Including the label properties in the tab order is critical to making accelerators (also known as

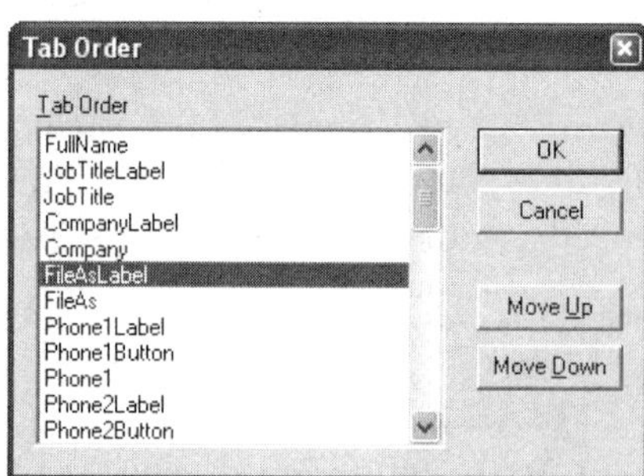


**Figure 20.1** *Compare the Tab Order dialog for a custom form with a VBA form's Tab Order dialog, shown in Figure 3.13.*

Full Name...

**Figure 20.2** *The accelerator key (or hotkey) appears as an underlined letter in the control's caption.*

hotkeys) work. If the user presses Alt+l—the accelerator key combination for the `FileAsLabel` control—the cursor moves to the `FileAs` control, the control that follows `FileAsLabel` in the tab order.

To set an accelerator, change the value for the `Accelerator` property on the Advanced Properties dialog for a control. Alternatively, you can use the Properties dialog and insert an ampersand (`&`) in the `Caption` property of the control before the letter that you want to function as an accelerator. For example, Figure 20.2 shows the command button that launches the Check Full Name dialog. On the Properties dialog, the `Caption` appears as `Full_ &Name ...`, but the Advanced Properties dialog shows it as Full Name, with the `Accelerator` property set to N.

### 20.1.2 Showing and hiding form pages

While you cannot change the order of pages on an Outlook form, you can show and hide pages using the methods of the `Inspector` object shown in Table 20.1.

A useful application of these techniques is to ensure that a properly published form is being used by showing the pages you want the user to interact with only if the form's code can run. Because in secure versions of Outlook, code behind unpublished forms does not run at all, the user won't see the necessary pages if the form is unpublished. Figure 20.3 shows a variation on the Vacation Request form that you first saw in Chapter 19. I've added a custom WARNING page and hidden the Message and Vacations pages.

**Table 20.1** *Inspector Methods for Form Pages*

| Method | Description |
|---|---|
| `HideFormPage(pagename)` | Hides the *pagename* page. |
| `SetCurrentFormPage(pagename)` | Switches to the *pagename* page. |
| `ShowFormPage(pagename)` | Shows the *pagename* page. |

The `Item_Open` procedure includes this code, which shows those two pages and hides the WARNING page:

```
Set objInsp = Item.GetInspector
With objInsp
    .ShowFormPage "Message"
    .ShowFormPage "Vacations"
    .SetCurrentFormPage "Message"
    .HideFormPage "WARNING"
End With
```

If someone tries to use an unpublished version of the form or if the form has one-offed for some reason (as described later in the chapter), the user sees only the WARNING page shown in Figure 20.3.

If you use code to hide and show form pages, make sure that your code uses the `ModifiedFormPages` collection to return only a visible page. If your code tries to return a page that is hidden, it will raise an error.

**CAUTION:** Using the `HideFormPage` and `ShowFormPage` methods causes forms to one-off in versions of Outlook that preceded Outlook 2000.

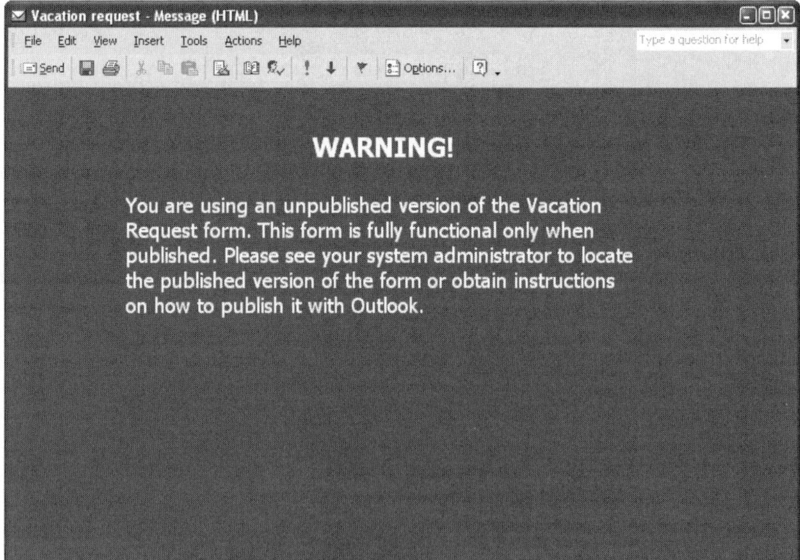


**Figure 20.3** *This warning page will be hidden once the form has been properly published and can run its VBScript code.*

## 20.2 Understanding Outlook forms architecture

You can build Outlook forms without understanding the underlying architecture, but if you are planning to use them to collaborate with other people, you'll need to know how forms interact with Outlook data items and what problems may arise. An Outlook form is a template that provides a managed view of the data in an individual Outlook item. The form designer decides what information should be displayed to the user, what it should look like, and what interactivity the form should offer.

Publishing the form creates a special hidden Outlook item in the folder in which the form was published, in the root of the user's default information store (for forms published to the Personal Forms library), or in a special system folder on an Exchange Server (for forms published to the Organizational Forms library). This helps explain why exporting items from an Outlook folder does not export any custom forms: Only the data items are exported, not the hidden form items.

The link between a data item and the form used to display it depends on the value of the `MessageClass` property of the data item. If you do not use a published form to create the item, the `MessageClass` is the default for that type of item (e.g., `IPM.Note` for a message). The `MessageClass` for an item created with a published message form would be `IPM.Note.`*`formname`*, where *`formname`* is the name you gave to the form when you published it. As you will see in Chapter 24, "Deploying Forms and Applications," forcing a folder full of items to use a particular custom form is a relatively simple matter of changing the value of each item's `MessageClass` property and saving the item.

Two specific architectural issues deserve special attention. Unexpected and unwanted effects occur in situations where the form becomes part of the data item, a situation known to Outlook developers as one-off forms. Also, for better performance, Outlook caches custom forms locally. Preventing and recovering from forms cache corruption are important techniques.

### 20.2.1 Preventing one-off forms

A one-off form is an item in which the form definition has become embedded in and saved with the data item. One telltale symptom is a vast increase in the size of the item, especially when compared with items of the same type that use the default form. The item may also revert to the default icon for that type of item and list the default `MessageClass` for that type of item. If the form has code behind it, in versions of Outlook that predate the Outlook Email Security Update (see Chapter 13, "Understanding Outlook Security"), users will see a prompt asking them to enable or disable macros—a confusing message since the user is not likely to know what that means. Secure versions of Outlook have a different symptom—code on a one-off form doesn't run at all, again causing potential confusion.

One of the most frequent causes of one-off forms is checking the Send Form Definition with Item box on the (Properties) page of the form. Unfortunately, Outlook strongly suggests checking this box whenever you publish a message form, especially if you want to use it over the Internet. Generally, you should ignore that suggestion. We will look at other ways to exchange Outlook data via Internet messages later in this chapter.

Another common cause is a mismatch between fields defined in the form and those defined in the folder where items created with the form are stored. Specifically, the folder may have a field that is not included in the form definition. If the user sets a value for this field, the item will one-off because it has to store the field definition in the item and can do that only if it also stores the custom form in the item. The solution, as you'll see in Chapter 24, "Deploying Forms and Applications," is to make sure that the fields in the folder are also defined in the form. One-offing also occurs if you programmatically add a new custom property to an item that uses a custom form.

Yet another cause of one-off forms is adding voting buttons to a custom message form. In general, you'll want to add any voting buttons as part of the overall form design, as described later in Section 20.4, "Working with custom actions."

Other causes of one-off form items relate to changing the form design in code, and these vary with the version of Outlook. The best prevention for this type of one-offing is to avoid known problem properties and test carefully before deploying the form.

For example, list box and combo box controls have a `PossibleValues` property that contains the list items. Setting this in VBScript code causes the form to one-off. Therefore, you should either set the possible values through the user interface or use the `List` property or `AddItem` method to populate the control.

Following are some other known coding techniques that may cause one-offing, depending on the version of Outlook. Outlook 2002 appears to have fewer problems with one-offing than Outlook 2000.

- Using the `UserProperties` collection to work with built-in properties
- Setting the `Enabled`, `Visible`, or `ReadOnly` properties of a control. Instead, you can use the `Locked` property to set a control for read-only use.
- Using methods related to an item's `FormDescription` object.
- Using methods related to the `Action` object (i.e., custom actions, discussed later in the chapter).
- Using the `PossibleValues`, `ItemProperty`, or `LayoutFlags` properties of a control

If you already have one-off items, resetting the `MessageClass` property to the custom form as shown in Listing 20.1 provides a partial cure. The form remains embedded in the item, so the size is still large, but the item will recover its connection to the published form so that the code will run again. See Appendix A for information on another recovery solution that requires CDO.

### 20.2.2 Managing the forms cache

When you open an item that requires a custom form, Outlook stores a copy of the form on your local hard disk. The next time you need to use the form, Outlook checks this forms cache. If the form is in the cache, Outlook goes to the form's original location to check the form's timestamp. If a user has modified the form since Outlook cached it, Outlook opens the form from its original location and updates the cache with the modified version. If no one has modified the form since Outlook cached it, Outlook loads the form from the cache, which is usually much faster than opening it from the original location.

**Listing 20.1** *Code in the Open and Write Event Handlers can use a Module-Level Variable to Maintain the Correct MessageClass Value*

```
Dim m_strMessageClass

Function Item_Open()
    m_strMessageClass = Item.FormDescription.MessageClass
End Function

Function Item_Write()
    Item.MessageClass = m_strMessageClass
End Function
```

If the required form isn't in the cache, Outlook looks in other locations in the following order:

- Current folder's forms library
- Personal Forms library
- Organizational Forms library

The version number on the (Properties) page of a custom form also seems to play a role in ensuring good cache behavior. Increment this number before you publish each new version of the form.

If the forms cache becomes corrupted, the user sees an error message that the form cannot be displayed and, instead of the custom form, the default form for that type of item loads. The one major known cause of forms cache corruption is publishing a form with the same `MessageClass` property in two different places—such as in two different public folders or in the Personal Forms library for testing and the Organizational Forms library for public use. Therefore, you should avoid publishing a form in two places unless you use a different `MessageClass` for each instance.

If the forms cache becomes corrupted, you will need to clear the forms cache. In Outlook 2002 and Outlook 2000 Service Release 1/1a in Corporate/Workgroup mode, you will find a Clear Forms Cache button on the Manage Forms dialog (Tools, Options, Other, Advanced Options, Custom Forms, then click Manage Forms).

Outlook 2000 in IMO mode does not have a Manage Forms dialog. Therefore, you will need to clear the cache manually. Exit Outlook, and delete the Frmcache.dat file. The Frmcache.dat file resides in the forms cache folder. Without Windows user profiles, the forms cache folder is C:\Windows\Local Settings\Application Data\Microsoft\Forms. With user profiles, look in C:\Windows\Profiles*username*\LocalSettings\Application Data\Microsoft\Forms, where *username* is the name you use to log onto Windows. (On Windows 2000 or Windows NT systems, the Windows directory could be C:\Winnt. You may find it easiest just to search your system for Frmcache.dat.)

When you restart Outlook, it will create a new Frmcache.dat file with information about the cached forms. If that technique doesn't resolve the problem, try deleting not just the Frmcache.dat file but also the subfolders in the Forms folder, one for each cached form.

Microsoft says that is has resolved the problem with forms cache corruption by adding a registry entry that will force Outlook to reload a form from the original source whenever it senses corruption. This solution requires Outlook 2002 with Service Pack 1 (or later) or the hotfix for Outlook 2000, described in Microsoft Knowledgebase article Q285219. In the HKEY_LOCAL_MACHINE\SOFTWARE\Microsoft\Office\10.0\Outlook key in the registry, you must add a DWORD value named ForceFormReload and set its value to 1. The same registry key works for both Outlook 2000 and 2002.

## 20.3 Linking Outlook items

Once you move beyond simple Outlook forms, you will probably encounter situations where you want to link different Outlook items together. For example, you might want to keep a master record for a company and be able to find the individual contacts at that company easily. Or, you might have a project going and want to collect all the items related to that project—messages, contacts, meetings, tasks, and so on.

While different types of Outlook items offer various methods for linking with other items, these have their limitations. Therefore, in this section, we'll look at both built-in methods and those you can create with programming.

### 20.3.1 Understanding the Activities page

As you learned in Chapter 15, "Outlook's Six Basic Forms," the Contact form has a special page called Activities that can display items related to the current contact. The different activities groups shown on the page are defined in the properties of the Contacts folder. An activities group cannot show multiple Exchange public folders, which limits the Activities page's usefulness in Exchange public-folder applications.

Outlook uses a variety of properties to build the Activities items lists—including the sender and recipients on mail messages, invitees on appointments, and people assigned to perform tasks. It also uses a special collection called `Links` that allows the user to make a connection manually between the current Outlook item and any contact.

### 20.3.2 Using the Links collection

What the user sees as a Contacts button and text box at the bottom of most items (see Figure 20.4) is actually the Links collection. Click the Contacts button to display your default Contacts folder in a dialog box (Figure 20.5), where you can select one or more contacts related to the item. You can also navigate to other contacts folders to pick a contact to link to. Outlook 2002

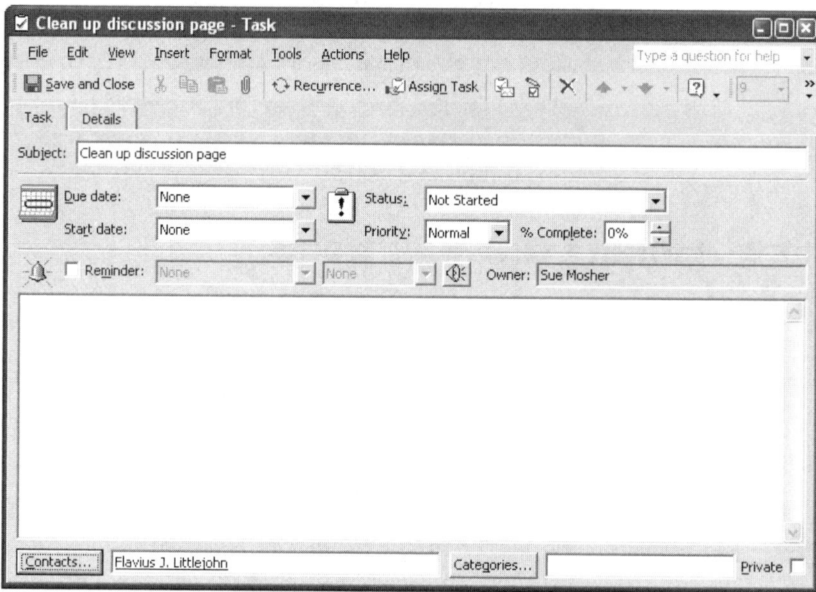


**Figure 20.4** *Choose one or more contacts to link to the current item.*

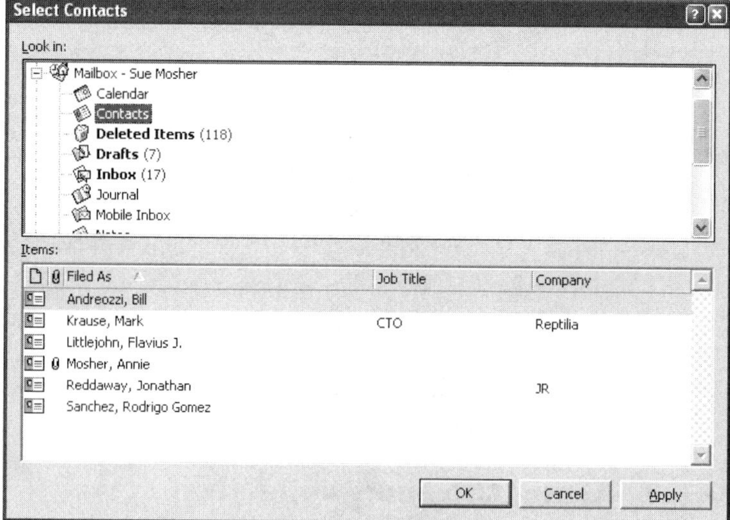


**Figure 20.5** *Users can link to any contact item in any contacts folder.*

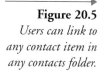

limits the number of linked contacts to less than 30 for performance reasons; Outlook 2000 does not have such a limit.

---

**Note:** Clicking the Contacts button always displays the user's default Contacts folder. Outlook provides no way to display a different folder programmatically. It's up to the user to navigate to some other contacts folder.

---

On a message, the Contacts button and box don't appear on the main page. You'll find them on the Message Options dialog box that appears when you click a new message's `Options` button or the View, Options command in a message you receive.

Another way to establish a link is to type a name into the box next to the Contacts button. If the name appears in your default Contacts folder (or in any contacts folder you've included in the Outlook Address Book), Outlook resolves it to the actual contact when you save the item or press Ctrl+K or Alt+K, just as it resolves a name in a message's To box. However, Outlook does not check the Exchange Global Address List and, in fact, you cannot link to a GAL entry, only to entries in Contacts folders.

If a name is underlined in the Contacts box, the user can double-click it to open the related contact. (Names that are not underlined do not have matching contact entries.) As a programmer, you can gain access to the contact item that a link points to. The `Links` collection provides standard `Add`, `Item`, and `Remove` methods. An individual `Link` object has an `Item` property that returns the actual `ContactItem` object that the `Link` points to, making it easy to retrieve information about linked contacts.

---

**Note:** When programming the `Links.Add` method on a newly created Outlook item, you will need to save the item first.

---

One limitation of the `Links` collection is that the links are broken if the user exports the data, then imports on another machine. Even if a contact name is underlined, double-clicking it will not pop up the related contact. You can, however, use the `ReconnectLinks` subroutine in Listing 20.2 to try to reconnect links to Contact items in the user's default Contacts folder. You can put this code in any VBA module.

**Listing 20.2** *Restoring Connections Using the Links Collection*

```
Sub ReconnectLinks()
    Dim objApp As Outlook.Application
    Dim objNS As Outlook.NameSpace
    Dim objFolder As Outlook.MAPIFolder
    Dim colItems As Outlook.Items
    Dim objItem As Object
    Dim colLinks As Outlook.Links
    Dim objLink As Outlook.Link
    Dim colContacts As Outlook.Items
    Dim objContact As Outlook.ContactItem
    Dim strFind As String
    Dim intCount As Integer
    Dim I As Integer
    Set objApp = CreateObject("Outlook.Application")
    Set objNS = objApp.GetNamespace("MAPI")
    Set objFolder = objNS.PickFolder
    If TypeName(objFolder) <> "Nothing" Then
        Set colContacts = _
          objNS.GetDefaultFolder(olFolderContacts).Items
        Set colItems = objFolder.Items
        For Each objItem In colItems
            Set colLinks = objItem.Links
            intCount = colLinks.Count
            If intCount > 0 Then
                For I = intCount To 1 Step -1
                    Set objLink = colLinks.item(I)
                    On Error Resume Next
                    If objLink.item Is Nothing Then
                        strFind = "[FullName] = _
                          " & Quote(objLink.Name)
                        Set objContact = colContacts.Find(strFind)
                        If Not objContact Is Nothing Then
                            colLinks.Remove I
                            colLinks.Add objContact
                        End If
                    End If
                Next
                If Not objItem.Saved Then
                   objItem.Save
                End If
            End If
        Next
    End If
    Set colContacts = Nothing
    Set objContact = Nothing
    Set objLink = Nothing
    Set colLinks = Nothing
    Set objItem = Nothing
    Set colItems = Nothing
    Set objFolder = Nothing
```

**Listing 20.2** *Restoring Connections Using the Links Collection (continued)*

```
    Set objNS = Nothing
    Set objApp = Nothing
End Sub

Private Function Quote(varInput)
    Quote = Chr(34) & varInput & Chr(34)
End Function
```

**Note:** The problem of losing links is not limited to users with only Personal Folders .pst files. It can also affect Exchange Server users because a common technique for moving a mailbox from one Exchange 5.5 site or container to another is to export the mailbox to a .pst file, then import it into the new mailbox. This loses `Links` connections, as well as custom forms and views that the user may have created.

After the user selects a folder, the procedure checks the `Links` collection on each item in the folder. If any `Link.Item` returns `Nothing` instead of a valid `ContactItem`, the routine tries to locate a matching contact. The `Link.Name` property of an item with a matching contact always displays that contact's `FullName` property. Therefore, the subroutine uses the `Find` method on the Contacts folder's `Items` collection with a search string that incorporates the `FullName` property. If it finds a matching contact, it removes the defective link and adds a new link to that contact.

**CAUTION:** Outlook has a known memory-leak problem when processing large `Items` collections in a `For Each ... Next` loop. If you have folders with thousands of items that need to be relinked, you might want to move a few hundred items at a time into a temporary folder, run `ReconnectLinks`, then move the items back into their original folder. Increasing your Windows page file size might also help you avoid the memory leak.

Another useful application of the `Links` collection occurs when you create a new task to call someone. You can include code in the item's `Write` event handler to look up the contact's phone number and append it to the `Subject` property of the task, or you could get the same functionality by monitoring the user's Tasks folder for new items. Compare the VBA version in Listing 20.3 with the form VBScript version in Listing 20.4. The VBA code is designed to run in the `ThisOutlookSession` module.

**Listing 20.3** *Adding a Phone Number to a Task (VBA)*

```
Private WithEvents m_colTasks As Outlook.Items

Private Sub Application_Startup()
    Dim objNS As Outlook.NameSpace
    Set objNS = Application.GetNamespace("MAPI")
    Set m_colTasks = _
      objNS.GetDefaultFolder(olFolderTasks).Items
    Set objNS = Nothing
End Sub

Private Sub m_colTasks_ItemAdd(ByVal Item As Object)
    Call AddPhone(Item)
End Sub

Sub AddPhone(Item As Outlook.TaskItem)
    Dim objContact As Outlook.ContactItem
    Dim strPhone As String
    If UCase(Left(Item.Subject, 4)) = "CALL" Then
        If Item.Links.Count = 1 Then
            Set objContact = Item.Links(1).Item
            If Not objContact Is Nothing Then
                strPhone = _
                  objContact.BusinessTelephoneNumber
                If strPhone <> "" Then
                    Item.Subject = Item.Subject & " (" & _
                                   strPhone & ")"
                    Item.Save
                End If
            End If
        End If
    End If
    Set objContact = Nothing
End Sub
```

The `AddPhone` procedure looks for the first `Link` object, gets any related contact, and looks up the contact's business phone number. Notice that the VBA and VBScript versions of the `AddPhone` subroutine are identical except for the variable declarations. This is a good example of how modular code can be reused.

### 20.3.3 Linking with a unique identifier

The `Links` collection is limited in that the `Link.Item` can point only to a `ContactItem`. If you need a more flexible linking structure, one approach is to use a unique identifier that allows you to identify positively the exact item being linked to. We'll look at several candidates for such identifiers, beginning with the `EntryID` property.

**Listing 20.4** *Adding a phone number to a task (VBScript)*

```
Function Item_Write()
    Call AddPhone()
End Sub

Sub AddPhone()
    Dim objContact
    Dim strPhone
    If UCase(Left(Item.Subject, 4)) = "CALL" Then
        If Item.Links.Count = 1 Then
            Set objContact = Item.Links(1).Item
            If Not objContact Is Nothing Then
                strPhone = _
                  objContact.BusinessTelephoneNumber
                If strPhone <> "" Then
                    Item.Subject = Item.Subject & " (" & _
                                   strPhone & ")"
                   Item.Save
                End If
            End If
        End If
    End If
    Set objContact = Nothing
End Sub
```

`EntryID` is a unique string that Outlook assigns to each saved item. (An item has a blank `EntryID` until it has been saved.) The advantage of using `EntryID` is that you can quickly retrieve any item using the `Namespace.GetItemFromID` method if you know its `EntryID` and `StoreID`. The chief disadvantage of `EntryID` is that it changes if the user moves the item to a different folder.

Another method of creating a unique identifier is to use the `Session.CreateConversationIndex` method from CDO. Outlook automatically creates unique conversation indexes to identify conversation threads, but CDO provides a method to create a conversation index programmatically. You can use an index string, such as that returned by the `NewConversationIndex()` function in Listing 20.5, for any situation that requires a unique identifier. (You can adapt this procedure to VBA by adding data types to the function and variable declarations.)

One problem with both the `EntryID` and conversation index approaches is that these IDs are designed only for machine-readable applications and are quite long—as many as 140 characters—making them unsuitable for any application, such as a purchase order, in which you might want to show the ID to the user. In Chapter 23, "Exchange Server, Databases, and XML Web Services," you'll see a technique for getting a

**Listing 20.5** *Obtaining a Unique Conversation Index*

```
Function NewConversationIndex()
    Dim objSession
    Dim strCIndex
    Set objSession = CreateObject("MAPI.Session")
    objSession.Logon "", "", False, False
    NewConversationIndex = _
      objSession.CreateConversationIndex
    objSession.Logoff
    Set objSession = Nothing
End Function
```

sequential number from a Microsoft Access database. But if you don't need a sequential number, just a human-readable number, you can use the code in Listing 20.6. The `DateID()` function builds an ID from the current date and time by mapping the month, the hour, and the last two digits of the year to alphabetic characters, leaving the day, minute, and second as numeric.

For example, running the `DateID()` function on May 27, 2003, at 4:14:52 P.M. will return the string `E27C-Q1452`. Running it again about five minutes later will return the string `E27B-Q1952`.

The `DateID()` function will not reliably generate a guaranteed unique ID if used in a high-volume situation, but it's quite suitable for an Outlook form for which the user creates a new item every few minutes, not several items every second. If you want to use it in a multiuser environment, get

**Listing 20.6** *Building an ID from the Current Date/Time*

```
Function DateID()
    DateID = Chr(64 + Month(Now)) & _
                AddLeadingZeroUnderTen(Day(Now)) & _
                Chr(64 + Right(Year(Now), 2)) & _
                "-" & Chr(65 + Hour(Now)) & _
                AddLeadingZeroUnderTen(Minute(Now)) & _
                AddLeadingZeroUnderTen(Second(Now))
End Function

Function AddLeadingZeroUnderTen(strNum)
    If CInt(strNum) < 10 Then
        strNum = "0" & strNum
    End If
    AddLeadingZeroUnderTen = strNum
End Function
```

the user name with the `WSHUserName()` function from Listing 10.10 or, in an Exchange environment, the `GetMailboxUserName()` function from Listing 12.8. Append the user's initials or a few characters from the user name to the string returned by `DateID`.

Once you decide what kind of ID to use, you will need to store it in both items being linked. The `BillingInformation` and `Mileage` fields are available on all Outlook items and can be used for this purpose. You could also create a custom property to hold the ID.

To retrieve a linked item, use the `Items.Find` method, as shown in Listing 20.2, to search the target folder for a matching item.

### 20.3.4 Copying items to a public folder

Outlook does not contain a built-in method to copy items automatically to an Exchange Server public folder, making it difficult to maintain any kind of consolidated view of appointments, tasks, contacts, or journal activity records. One possible solution is to replace the default form for a particular type of item—for example, the Journal form—with a form that makes a copy of each item in a public folder and updates that copy as needed. In Chapter 24, "Deploying Forms and Applications," you will see how to make such a form substitution using a registry entry. Here we'll just consider the code for the form.

To make a self-copying Journal form, create a folder to hold Journal items in the Public Folders hierarchy. For the sake of this example, we'll assume that you have a Company Journal folder at the top of the All Public Folders hierarchy. If you place the folder somewhere else, adjust the path in the code in Listing 20.7. In that Company Journal folder, create a new text property named `Creator`.

Create a new item in the Company Journal folder, and choose Tools, Forms, Design This Form to switch it into design mode. Switch to the (P.2) page. From the Field Chooser, under the User-defined Fields in Folder list, drag the `Creator` property to that page. Choose Form, Rename Page to rename that page to Details or some other appropriate name.

Add the code in Listing 20.7 to the form, along with the VBScript version of the `GetFolder()` function from Listing 18.6. Publish the form to your Personal Forms library or, to make it available companywide, to the Organizational Forms library.

**Listing 20.7** *Automatically Updating a Copy in a Public Folder*

```
Dim m_objCopyFolder
Const olDiscard = 1
Const olFolderInbox = 6

Function Item_Open()
    If Item.Mileage <> "IsCopy" Then
        Call SetCopyFolder
    End If
End Function

Function Item_Write()
    If Item.Size = 0 Then
        If Item.Mileage <> "IsCopy" Then
            Call CopyMe
        End If
    Else
        If Item.Mileage <> "IsCopy" Then
            Call FindAndKillCopy
            Call CopyMe
        End If
    End If
End Function

Function Item_Close()
    Set m_objCopyFolder = Nothing
End Function

Sub SetCopyFolder()
    Dim strFolder
    strFolder = "Public Folders\All Public Folders\Company Journal"
    Set m_objCopyFolder = GetFolder(strFolder)
End Sub

Sub CopyMe()
    Dim objCopy
    Dim objMoved
    Dim strUser
    On Error Resume Next
    If Not m_objCopyFolder Is Nothing Then
        Set objCopy = Item.Copy
        strUser = GetMailboxUserName()
        objCopy.Mileage = "IsCopy"
        objCopy.UserProperties("Creator") = strUser
        Set objMoved = objCopy.Move(m_objCopyFolder)
        Item.BillingInformation = objMoved.EntryID
        objCopy.Close olDiscard
    End If
    Set objCopy = Nothing
    Set objMoved = Nothing
End Sub
```

**Listing 20.7** *Automatically Updating a Copy in a Public Folder (continued)*

```
Sub FindAndKillCopy()
    Dim objNS
    Dim strStoreID
    Dim strEntryID
    Dim objCopy
    Set objNS = Application.GetNamespace("MAPI")
    strStoreID = m_objCopyFolder.StoreID
    strEntryID = Item.BillingInformation
    Set objCopy = objNS.GetItemFromID(strEntryID, strStoreID)
    If Not objCopy Is Nothing Then
        objCopy.Delete
    End If
    Set objNS = Nothing
    Set objCopy = Nothing
End Sub

Function GetMailboxUserName()
    Dim objNS
    Dim objInbox
    Dim strName
    Dim intPos
    Set objNS = Application.GetNamespace("MAPI")
    Set objInbox = objNS.GetDefaultFolder(olFolderInbox)
    strName = objInbox.Parent.Name
    intPos = InStr(1, strName, "Mailbox - ", vbTextCompare)
    If intPos > 0 Then
        GetMailboxUserName = Right(strName, intPos + 9)
    End If
    Set objInbox = Nothing
    Set objNS = Nothing
End Function
```

**Tip:** Did you notice that Listing 20.6 includes a VBScript version of the `GetMailboxUserName()` function from Listing 12.8 to get the name of the Exchange mailbox user?

When the user saves the Journal item for the first time, the `CopyMe` subroutine creates a copy in the target folder established in the `SetCopyFolder` procedure, stamps the copy with the creator's name, and adds the `EntryID` of the copy to the original's built-in `BillingInformation` property.

Upon subsequent updates to the original item, the code uses the `Namespace.GetItemFromID` method to try to locate the copy in the Public Folders store and, if it finds the copy, deletes it, then creates a new copy in the target folder. This brute-force approach is easier to implement than code that tracks which properties have changed and updates only those properties on the copy. In fact, you can use the code in Listing 20.6 for contacts, tasks, or appointments, not just Journal items.

In this case, the `EntryID` is a good linking solution because we are only interested in items in one particular public folder. If the item is moved to some other folder, we don't expect Outlook to be able to find it and update it.

---

**Tip:** Note that this is not true synchronization because changes in the Public Folder item are not propagated back to the mailbox of the user who created the item. You may want to set the permission level for the default user on the folder to nonediting author, so that users can delete their items, but cannot update them in the public folder. All updates, therefore, will propagate from the journal in the user's mailbox items to the public folder.

---

The form code uses the same technique found in Listing 18.13 to mark the copy in order to prevent an endless loop of copies from being created.

---

**Note:** Another approach to the same issue would be to use code in the `ThisOutlookSession` module to monitor the user's Journal folder for new and updated items. The form solution, however, requires only that the user be using the custom form, which can be published to the Organizational Forms library. It does not require any code to be installed locally.

---

## 20.4 Working with custom actions

Custom actions are a unique Outlook technique for creating a new item from an existing item with the option to include data from the original item. Voting buttons are one application of custom actions. Custom actions can also be used to run code that doesn't directly involve creating a new item.

### 20.4.1 A vacation approval form

Let's start with a simple example that builds on the idea of voting buttons. Everyone likes to take vacations, right? However, unless you're the boss, someone must approve your time off. You will create a simple Message form with Approve and Disapprove buttons that a supervisor can use to act on a vacation request. Follow these steps to customize a Message form in design mode:

1. Set the `Subject` text box to read-only, and on the (All Fields) page, enter `Vacation request` as the text for the Subject field.
2. Select the large message body text box at the bottom of the form and drag the top of it down to make some room above the body of the message.
3. In the Field Chooser, create two new fields, `VacationStart` and `VacationEnd`, both as date/time fields. Drag them to the blank space above the message body to create two text boxes. Give these the names `txtVacationStart` and `txtVacationEnd`. Edit their labels so that the form looks like Figure 20.6. On the Value tab of each text box's Properties dialog, change the Format option so that it shows only the day of the week and the date, not a time element.
4. Select the `txtVacationStart` and `txtVacationEnd` text boxes and their labels, and copy them to the Clipboard.
5. Click Edit Read Page to switch to the read layout. Adjust the height of the large-message text box as you did in step 2.
6. Paste the copied text boxes and labels from step 4 into the blank area.

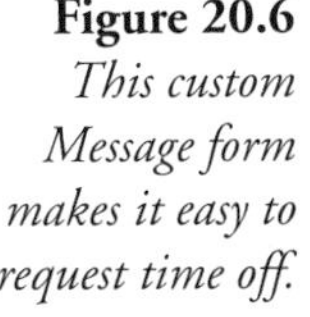

**Figure 20.6** *This custom Message form makes it easy to request time off.*

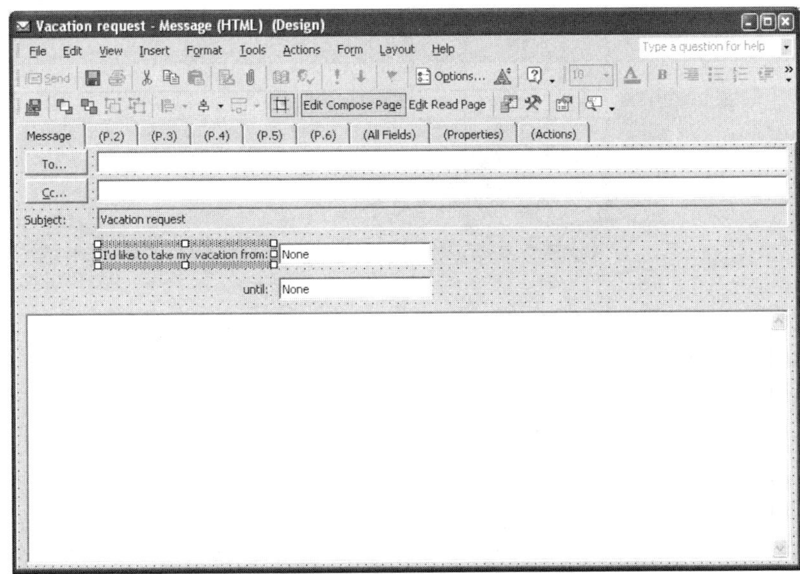

7. Set the `txtVacationStart` and `txtVacationEnd` text boxes on the read layout to be read-only.

---

**Tip:** Did you notice that we're using a Message form, not an Appointment form? This is a good example of how you can put Outlook forms to unexpected uses, based on the different features that each supports. You will see another example of this at the end of the chapter, where we use a custom Post form to generate HTML and plain-text messages.

---

Now, you will make the custom actions that allow the supervisor to respond. The quickest method is to click Options and then type "Approve; Disapprove" in the Use Voting Buttons box. Switch to the (Actions) page of the form to see that two actions, Approve and Disapprove, were automatically added (see Figure 20.7). Select Approve, and then click Properties to see the details for the Approve action (see Figure 20.8).

---

**Note:** The Use Voting Buttons box is not available if you use Outlook 2000 in IMO mode. However, you can still create voting buttons, using the (Actions) page of the form and setting the Address Form Like option to Response, as described in the next section. You can also use the `CreateVoteMessage` procedure found in Listing 10.3.

---

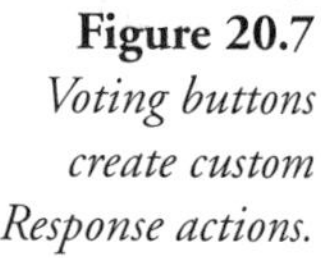

**Figure 20.7**
*Voting buttons create custom Response actions.*

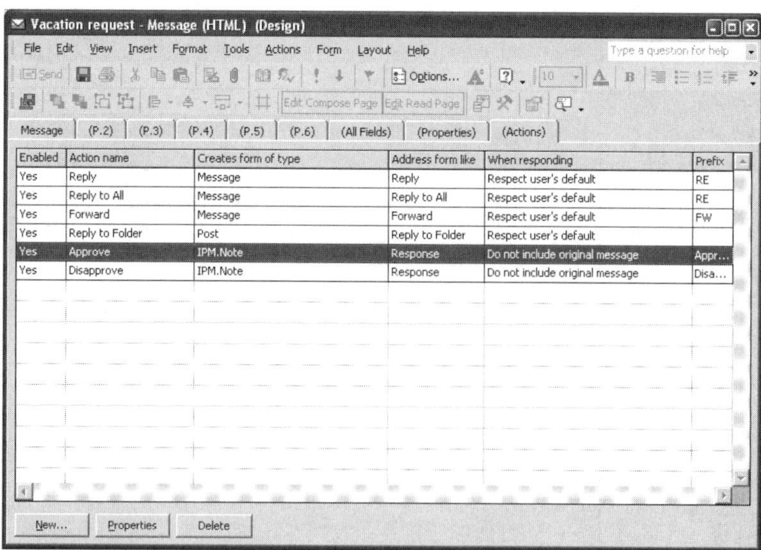


| Enabled | Action name | Creates form of type | Address form like | When responding | Prefix |
|---|---|---|---|---|---|
| Yes | Reply | Message | Reply | Respect user's default | RE |
| Yes | Reply to All | Message | Reply to All | Respect user's default | RE |
| Yes | Forward | Message | Forward | Respect user's default | FW |
| Yes | Reply to Folder | Post | Reply to Folder | Respect user's default | |
| Yes | Approve | IPM.Note | Response | Do not include original message | Appr... |
| Yes | Disapprove | IPM.Note | Response | Do not include original message | Disa... |

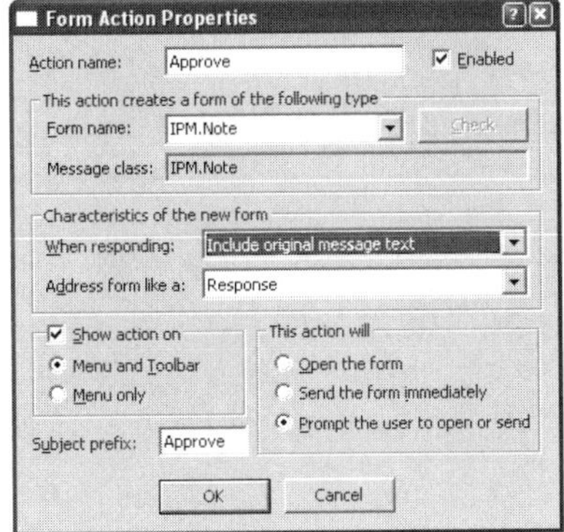

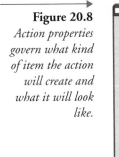

**Figure 20.8** *Action properties govern what kind of item the action will create and what it will look like.*

Next, select each action, then click Properties to make one change so that the supervisor's action will look more like a normal reply; under When Responding, select Include Original Message Text.

Run the form to test it, sending a vacation request to yourself if you don't have a friendly boss to test it with. The recipient should see a message, such as that shown in Figure 20.9, with voting buttons. If you click Approve and choose Edit the Response Before Sending, you will see a standard Message form (see Figure 20.10) with these characteristics:

- "Approve" is the prefix for the Subject field.
- The original sender's text appears in the body of the message.

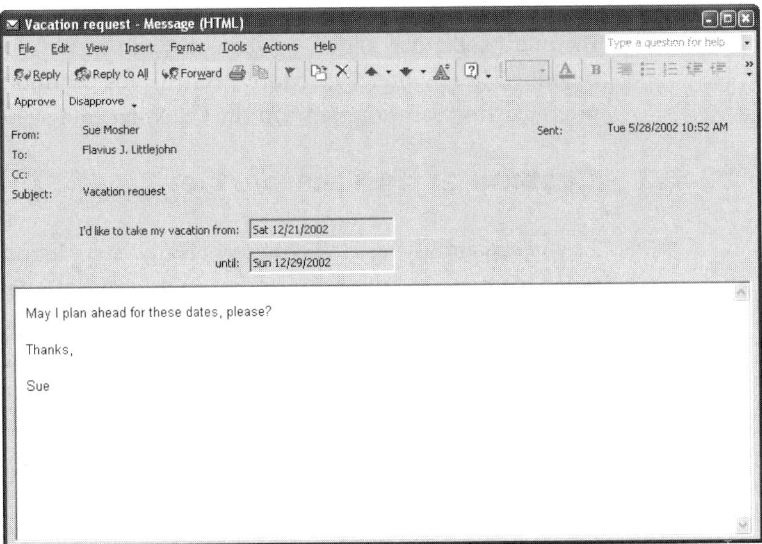


**Figure 20.9** *Click Approve or Disapprove to respond to the vacation request.*

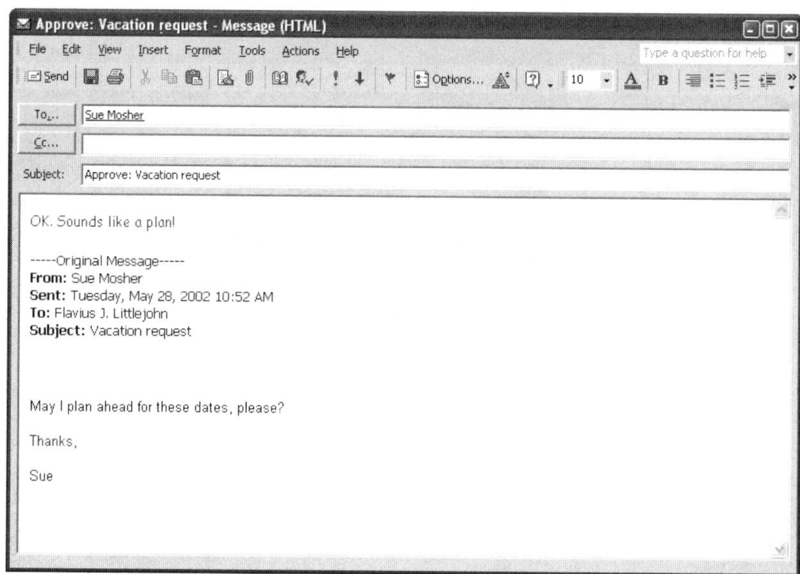


**Figure 20.10** *Clicking one of the custom action buttons produces a new item, using the form specified on the Form Action Properties dialog.*

---

**Note:** Users will see custom action buttons only on sent or saved items. You won't see them while you're composing a new item.

---

You've now built a useful custom action message! After looking at custom action properties, you will enhance the Approve custom action so that it sends back not just a message but also an appointment ready to save to the user's Calendar folder. You can also add the OVC to a custom page, as described in Chapter 19, "More Controls for Outlook Forms," to show the user's existing vacation items in the Calendar folder.

## 20.4.2 Custom action properties

As you saw in Listing 10.3, you can create a new action for an Outlook item object named `objItem` by inserting an appropriate statement, such as:

```
Set objAction = objItem.Actions.Add
```

and then setting the properties of the `objAction` object. Table 20.2 relates the properties of an `Action` object to the settings in the Form Action Properties dialog box (refer to Figure 20.8), showing the corresponding Outlook constants, where appropriate.

**Table 20.2** *Outlook Form Action Properties*

| Form Action Property Settings | Object Property | Possible Values | Outlook Constant (Value) |
|---|---|---|---|
| Address Form Like | `CopyLike` | Reply | `olReply` (0) |
| | | Reply to All | `olReplyAll` (1) |
| | | Forward | `olForward` (2) |
| | | Reply to Folder | `olReplyFolder` (3) |
| | | Response | `olRespond` (4) |
| Enabled | `Enabled` | `True` or `False` | |
| Message Class | `MessageClass` | (Any published form) | |
| Action Name | `Name` | (Any name) | |
| Subject Prefix | `Prefix` | (Any prefix) | |
| When Responding | `ReplyStyle` | Do Not Include Original Message Text | `olOmitOriginalText` (0) |
| | | Attach Original Message | `olEmbedOriginalItem` (1) |
| | | Include Original Message Text | `olIncludeOriginalText` (2) |
| | | Include and Indent Original Message Text | `olIndentOriginalText` (3) |
| | | Prefix Each Line of the Original Message | `olReplyTickOriginalText` (1000) |
| | | Attach Link to Original Message | `olLinkOriginalItem` (4) |
| | | Respect User's Default | `olUserPreference` (5) |
| This Action Will | `ResponseStyle` | Open the Form | `olOpen` (0) |
| | | Send the Form Immediately | olSend (1) |
| | | Prompt the User To Open or Send | `olPrompt` (2) |
| Show Action on | `ShowOn` | Don't Show | (0) |
| | | Menu and Toolbar | `olMenu` (1) |
| | | Menu Only | `olMenuAndToolbar` (2) |

**Table 20.3** *Address Form Usage*

| If You Want to . . . | Address Form Like . . . |
|---|---|
| Send a reply to the sender of the original item | Reply |
| Send a reply to the sender of the original item and any Cc recipients | Reply to All |
| Copy data from fields on one Post form to fields of the same name on a different Post form | Reply to Folder (destination form must be published in the same folder) |
| Copy data from fields on one Task, Contact, or Appointment form to another form of the same type | Forward |
| Have responses tracked on the Tracking tab of the original message in the sender's Sent Items folder | Response |

One of the key functions of a custom action is to create a new item. Custom actions also have a special feature that can copy property values from the original item to the new item. The `CopyLike` property (labeled on the (Actions) tab as Address Form Like) governs how properties are copied from the original item to the new item that the custom action creates. Table 20.3 offers suggestions on when to use which option.

### 20.4.3 Adding code to custom actions

So far, you've been working only with the settings available on the (Actions) page. You can do quite a lot with just those, without writing any code. For example, using the Reply to Folder option, you can create a Post form that inherits data from another Post form. This is very useful in folders for public discussions or for managing complex information, such as help-desk requests.

To enhance custom actions with code, you can use the `CustomAction` event in VBScript code on an Outlook form. The two arguments for the `Item_CustomAction` function are as follows:

`Action` The custom action executed by the user

`NewItem` The new Outlook item that the custom action creates

Use the `Name` property of the action in a `Select Case` block to specify different code for each action. In the case of the Vacation Request form, the code would fit into a structure such as this:

```
Function Item_CustomAction(ByVal Action, ByVal NewItem)
    Select Case Action.Name
        Case "Approve"
```

```
                approval code goes here
            Case "Disapprove"
                disapproval code goes here
            Case Else
                'do nothing
        End Select
    End Function
```

The `NewItem` argument gives you a way of working with the new item that the action creates so you can change its data. You can also prevent the item from being created at all by setting the `Item.CustomAction()` function to `False`. This example sets the `Importance` property to High on the new item created by the `Approve` action, but aborts the creation of a new item for the `Disapprove` action.

```
Function Item_CustomAction(ByVal Action, ByVal NewItem)
   Const olImportanceHigh = 2
   Select Case Action.Name
        Case "Approve"
            NewItem.Importance = olImportanceHigh
        Case "Disapprove"
            Item_CustomAction = False
        End Select
End Function
```

You can now do something very practical with the Vacation Request form—have it automatically create an appointment item and send it back with the approval. All the user has to do is drag the attached appointment to the Calendar folder.

**Note:** If the person approving the vacation had write access to the Calendar folder of the user who sent the request, you could also take a different approach and have the custom action place the appointment item directly in the user's Calendar folder.

First, on the (Actions) page of the form, change the When Responding property of the `Approve` action to Do Not Include Original Message. Then, add the code for the Approve action as shown in Listing 20.8.

Listing 20.8 doesn't affect the operation of the Disapprove action. It enhances just the Approve action by creating a new appointment from the data in the request message and attaching that appointment to the approval message. Because the saved appointment is no longer needed, after it has been attached, the code deletes it from the approver's mailbox. (You'll see another possible role for the created appointment shortly.)

**Listing 20.8** *Enhance a Custom Action with Code*

```
Const olOutOfOffice     = 3
Const olAppointmentItem = 1
Const olByValue         = 1

Function Item_CustomAction(ByVal Action, ByVal NewItem)
    Dim dteStart
    Dim dteEnd
    Dim objAppt
    Dim objAttachment
    Select Case Action.Name
        Case "Approve"
            dteStart = _
              Item.UserProperties.Find("VacationStart")
            dteEnd = _
              Item.UserProperties.Find("VacationEnd")
            Set objAppt = _
              Application.CreateItem(olAppointmentItem)
            With objAppt
                .Start = dteStart
                .End = dteEnd
                .ReminderSet = False
                .Subject = "Vacation"
                .AllDayEvent = True
                .BusyStatus = olOutOfOffice
            End With
            objAppt.Save
            Set objAttachment = NewItem.Attachments.Add( _
                                  objAppt, olByValue, , _
                                  "Your Vacation")
            NewItem.Body = "Your vacation has been " & _
                           "approved. Drag the attached" & _
                           " Appointment to your " & _
                           "Calendar to save it." & _
                           vbCrLf & vbCrLf
            objAppt.Delete
        Case Else
            'do nothing special for other actions
    End Select
    Set objAppt = Nothing
    Set objAttachment = Nothing
End Function
```

Figure 20.11 illustrates the message the user receives after the supervisor clicks the Approve button on a vacation request.

Because you chose Response under Address This Form Like, the user can also look at the original item in the Sent Items folder and, on the Tracking tab, see the date that the request was approved.

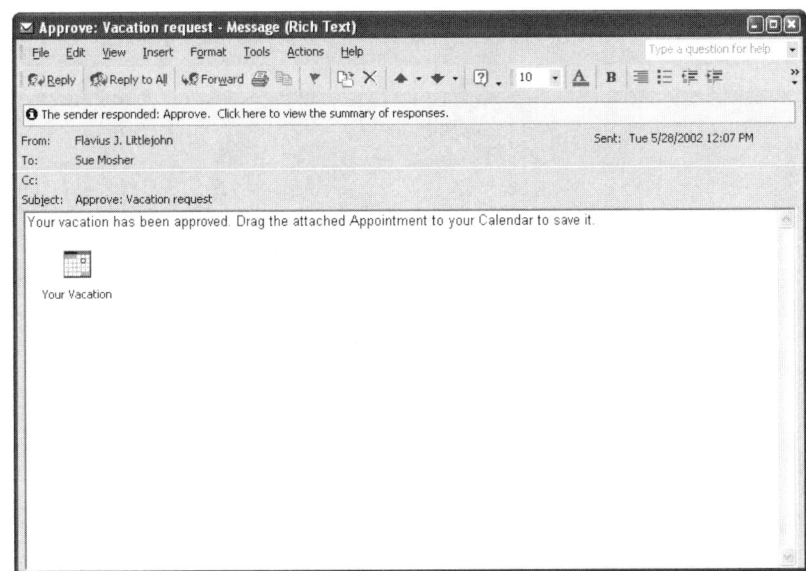


**Figure 20.11** *The user receives not just an approval but also an Appointment item all ready for the Calendar folder.*

We can make two more modifications to the Vacation Request form to incorporate the OVC discussed in Chapter 19. Also, instead of deleting the vacation appointment from the approver's mailbox, we can move that appointment to a public calendar folder, so that users can have a consolidated view of all vacations.

First, rename the (P.2) page as Vacations and add an OVC, as described in Chapter 19. Then, place the code in Listing 20.9 in the Vacation Request form to supplement the code in Listing 20.8. Also add the `GetFolder()` function from Listing 18.6, the `GetFolderPath()` function from Listing 19.4, and the `GetCalFolderPath()` function from Listing 19.5.

Also, replace the `objAppt.Delete` statement in the `Item_CustomAction()` procedure in Listing 20.8 with this code snippet, which copies the appointment to the public folder:

```
objAppt.Subject = Item.SenderName & " - Vacation"
Set objVacFolder = GetFolder(m_strVacFolder)
If Not objVacFolder Is Nothing Then
    objAppt.Move objVacFolder
Else
    objAppt.Delete
End If
```

Note that the `Item.SenderName` expression will trigger an Outlook security prompt, as discussed in Chapter 13, "Understanding Outlook

**Listing 20.9** *Adding Further Enhancements to the Vacation Request Form*

```
Const olFolderCalendar = 9

Function Item_Open()
    Dim objPage
    Dim ViewCtl1
    Set objPage = _
      Item.GetInspector.ModifiedFormPages("Vacations")
    Set ViewCtl1 = objPage.Controls("ViewCtl1")

    With ViewCtl1
        .Folder = GetCalFolderPath()
        .View = "Events"
        .Restriction = "[Subject] = ""Vacation"""
    End With
    Set objPage = Nothing
    Set ViewCtl1 = Nothing
End Function
```

Security." Since the vacation approvals are likely to be performed by a small number of managers, this will probably not be too intrusive. If it is, you could consider modifying the code to get the sender information using Redemption objects.

### 20.4.4 Replacing command buttons with custom actions

When a manager gets a message created with the Vacation Request form, he or she will see voting buttons in the open message and, in Outlook 2002, in the preview pane. What you might find surprising is that the `Approve` and Disapprove actions will also appear on the right-click menu for the message in the manager's Inbox. Also, did you notice that this very functional Vacation Request form has no custom pages (except for the Vacations page to show the OVC) and no command button controls? The custom actions provide functionality without requiring you to develop a separate custom page.

Say that you have a subroutine you want to run. Your first thought is probably to create a command button on a custom page. But if you're working with a Task or Appointment form, whose first page cannot be customized, how does the user know that the custom page contains the button to run your procedure? Chances are, the user might never discover it, just because it's on a separate page.

Custom actions can help alleviate that problem. If you don't need a custom page for some other reason or if, in the case of a Message, Contact, or

**Listing 20.10** *Adding a Forward as vCalendar Command to the Context Menu with a Custom Action*

```
Function Item_CustomAction(ByVal Action, ByVal NewItem)
    Select Case Action.Name
        Case "Forward as vCalendar"
            Item_CustomAction = False
            Set objForward = Item.ForwardAsVCal
            objForward.Display
    End Select
End Function
```

Post form, you don't want to clutter the main page, consider a custom action instead of a command button on a customized page.

For example, the Actions menu in the Calendar folder provides a Forward as iCalendar command, but the right-click menu for an individual appointment has only the regular Forward command. By creating a new Forward as vCalendar action on the (Actions) page on an Appointment form and adding the code in Listing 20.10, any appointments created with the custom form will gain a Forward as vCalendar command on the right-click menu.

---

**Note:** The vCalendar and iCalendar formats are Internet standards for exchanging appointment information; vCal is older than iCal. The `Appointment.ForwardAsVCal` method sends a vCal item, rather than an iCal file, for maximum compatibility with other programs.

---

## 20.5 Using forms over the Internet

Although Microsoft designed the custom forms features in Outlook for use in an Exchange environment, you can exchange voting button messages and custom forms (messages, meeting requests, task requests) via the Internet. Both users must have Outlook, and both must have published the form to their Personal Forms library using the same form name.

When you create a message from a custom form and then send it via the Internet, Outlook constructs a complex Internet message that includes a text/plain message part that any e-mail program can use. It also contains an attachment named Winmail.dat that includes enough information about the form—including the `MessageClass` property—that Outlook recipients can open the item using their locally published copy of the form. If the original message is in HTML format, the message will also contain a text/

html part with HTML content that any HTML-capable mail program can read.

---

**Note:** In Outlook 2000 and 2002, changing the mail format setting for an individual contact or recipient to plain text only has no effect on whether the Winmail.dat attachment is included when you originate a message with a custom form.

---

Normally, this mechanism works fine. If users open the message with a non-Outlook program, the worst that happens is that they see an annoying Winmail.dat attachment that contains no useful information. The non-Outlook recipient can still read the body of the message in plain text or HTML.

However, a major problem occurs if you use a custom form to create a message that contains attachments. Outlook also encodes the attachments in the Winmail.dat file, making them inaccessible to any recipient who is not running Outlook. Therefore, you should avoid using a custom form to send attachments unless you are 100 percent certain that the recipient will open the message with Outlook.

Because of the Winmail.dat and attachment issues, you may prefer to use a custom Outlook form as a data-entry tool, providing text boxes and other controls for the user to enter information, but generating a separate plain text or HTML message using the normal Outlook message form. This message can arrange the data in a tidy format that echoes the data-entry screen. The remaining sections in this chapter explore two such solutions, one for HTML messages and another, exclusive to Outlook 2002, for plain-text messages.

### 20.5.1 Sending a structured HTML message

In both Outlook 2000 and Outlook 2002, you can easily create an HTML-format message in code by setting the `HTMLBody` property to a string of fully tagged HTML text. Setting the `HTMLBody` property forces the format to HTML.

Our example is the Equipment Repair Request form shown in Figure 20.12. The Post button at the left of the toolbar is your clue that this is not a Message form, even though it looks like one. It is actually a custom Post form.

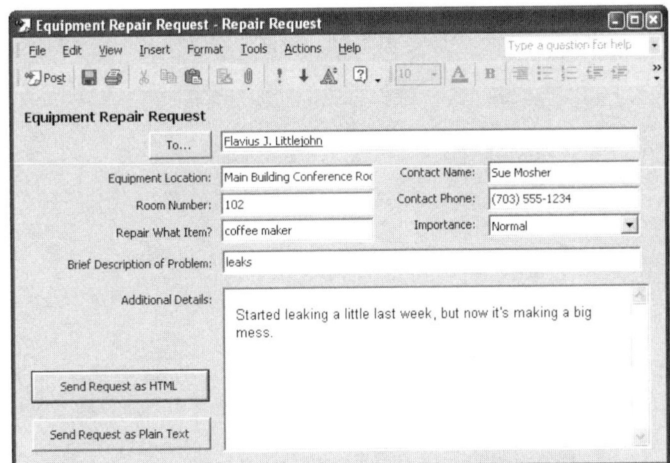

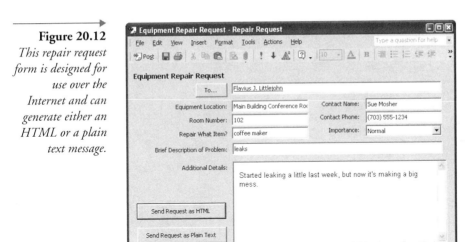

**Figure 20.12** *This repair request form is designed for use over the Internet and can generate either an HTML or a plain text message.*

Post forms are normally used for creating items in folders. However, this application uses a Post form rather than a Message form because of an Outlook quirk: on custom message forms, Outlook disregards the Creates Form of Type setting on the (Actions) tab for the Forward action. When you forward a custom form, Outlook always creates a new instance of the same custom form. On a custom Post form, however, Outlook will respect the Creates Form of Type setting and use a normal Message form (the default for the Forward action).

A Post form normally has no recipients. The To button and box were dragged to the form from the All Mail Fields list in the Field Chooser. The Importance field was also dragged from the Field Chooser, and the large text box for Additional Details is the usual message box that you find on any Outlook item. The form contains the code shown in Listing 20.11. All other text boxes are bound to appropriately named Outlook fields, whose names you see in Listing 20.11. On the (Actions) page of the form, we changed the properties for the Forward action so that When Responding is Do Not Include Original Message and Subject Prefix is blank.

The `Item_Close` and `Item_Write` event handlers prevent the user from saving the Post item, which is intended only for data entry, not for actual storage; they also encourage the user to use one of the two command buttons to send the item. When the user clicks the Send Request as HTML button, the `cmdSendHTML_Click` procedure runs, building an HTML table row by row from the custom properties, and then adding any text that the user has typed in the large-message text box (the `Body` property). The code

**Listing 20.11** *Sending an HTML-Format Message Based on Data Entered in a Post Form*

```
Dim m_blnUserSent
Const olDiscard = 1

Function Item_Write()
    MsgBox "Please click one of the Send buttons when " & _
         "you complete your request."
    Item_Write = False
End Function

Function Item_Close()
    Dim intRes
    Dim strMsg
    If Not m_blnUserSent Then
        strMsg = "You have not yet sent this request. " & _
                 "Do you really want to discard it?"
        intRes = MsgBox(strMsg, vbYesNo + vbQuestion, _
                 "Abandon Repair Request")
        If intRes = vbNo Then
            Item_Close = False
        Else
            Item.Close olDiscard
        End If
    End If
End Function

Sub cmdSendHTML_Click()
    Dim strHTML
    Dim strDetails
    Dim objForward
    strDetails = Item.Body
    strHTML = "<table>" & AddRow("Repair Item") & _
              AddRow("Description") & _
              AddRow("Equipment Location") & _
              AddRow("Room Number") & _
              AddRow("Contact Name") & _
              AddRow("Contact Phone") & _
              "</table>"
    If strDetails <> "" Then
        strHTML = strHTML & "<p>" & strDetails & "</p>"
    End If
    Set objForward = Item.Forward
    objForward.HTMLBody = strHTML
    Err.Clear
    objForward.Send
    If Err = 0 Then
        m_blnUserSent = True
        MsgBox "Request has been sent.", , "Repair Request"
    Else
        MsgBox "Request not sent. Error occurred.", , _
             "Repair Request"
    End If
    Set objForward = Nothing
End Sub
```

**Listing 20.11** *Sending an HTML-Format Message Based on Data Entered in a Post Form (continued)*

```
Function AddRow(strProp)
    Dim objProp
    Dim strRow
    On Error Resume Next
    Set objProp = Nothing
    Set objProp = Item.UserProperties(strProp)
    strRow = "<tr><td><strong>" & strProp & ": " & _
             "</strong></td><td>"
    If Not objProp Is Nothing Then
        strRow = strRow & objProp.Value
    Else
        strRow = strRow & "Property not available"
    End If
    AddRow = strRow & "</td></tr>"
    Set objProp = Nothing
End Function
```

forwards the post, then sets the `HTMLBody` of the forwarding message to the HTML text, and sends the message (shown in Figure 20.13). Note that the `objForward.Send` statement will trigger a security prompt.

If you're well versed in HTML coding, you could easily enhance the table by adding `<font>` and other formatting tags to the strings built by the `AddRow()` function.

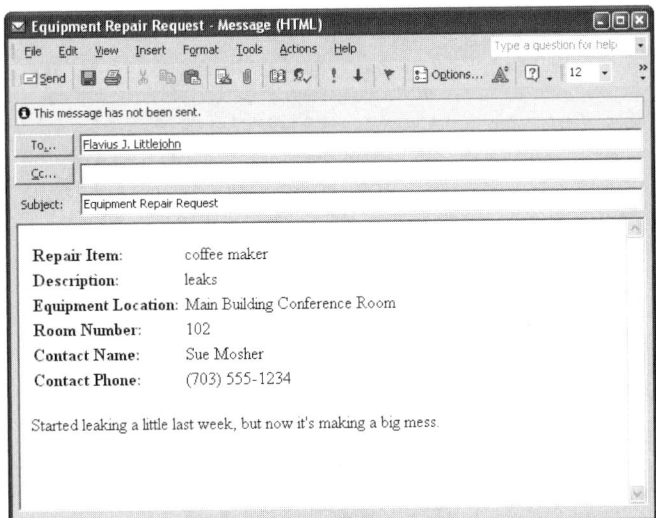


**Figure 20.13** *Compare this outgoing HTML message with the original post in Figure 20.12 and the plain-text version in Figure 20.14.*

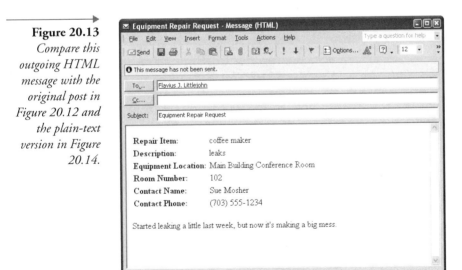

## 20.5.2 Sending a structured plain-text message (Outlook 2002)

Given the widespread use of HTML-format messages to transmit viruses, many users prefer to receive plain-text messages. In fact, starting with Service Pack 1, Outlook 2002 allows users to add a registry entry to force all incoming messages to be viewed as plain text. Any HTML formatting is lost, and the conversion from HTML to plain text is not always pretty. You might, therefore, want to originate the message as plain text. This is difficult to do in Outlook 2000 without using CDO and triggering Address Book security prompts, but Outlook 2002 makes it relatively easy by introducing a new `PostItem` and `MailItem` property, `BodyFormat`, that allows you to force an item to use a specific format.

Listing 20.12 completes the code for the form shown in Figure 20.12 by adding the event handler for the Send Request as Plain Text command but-

**Listing 20.12** *Sending a Plain-Text-Format Message Based on Data Entered in a Post Form*

```
Sub cmdSendPlain_Click()
    Dim strDetails
    Dim strBody
    Dim objForward
    On Error Resume Next
    strDetails = Item.Body
    Item.BodyFormat = 1
    strBody = AddLine("Repair Item") & _
              AddLine("Description") & _
              AddLine("Equipment Location") & _
              AddLine("Room Number") & _
              AddLine("Contact Name") & _
              AddLine("Contact Phone")
    If strDetails <> "" Then
        strBody = strBody & vbCrLf & strDetails
    End If
    Set objForward = Item.Forward
    objForward.Body = strBody
    Err.Clear
    objForward.Send
    If Err = 0 Then
        m_blnUserSent = True
        MsgBox "Request has been sent.", ,"Repair Request"
    Else
        MsgBox "Request not sent. Error occurred.", , _
          "Repair Request"
    End If
    Set objForward = Nothing
End Sub
```

**Listing 20.12** *Sending a Plain-Text-Format Message Based on Data Entered in a Post Form (continued)*

```
Function AddLine(strProp)
    Dim objProp
    Dim strLine
    On Error Resume Next
    Set objProp = Nothing
    Set objProp = Item.UserProperties(strProp)
    strLine = strProp & ": "
    If Not objProp Is Nothing Then
        strLine = strLine & objProp.Value
    Else
        strLine = strLine & "Property not available"
    End If
    AddLine = strLine & vbCrLf
End Function
```

ton. Notice how similar it is structurally to the event handler in Listing 20.11 that sends the HTML version. Also, instead of an `AddRow()` function to build each row in the HTML table, there is an `AddLine()` function to build each line of the plain text message.

Figure 20.14 shows the resulting plain-text message. The key to creating the plain-text message is the `Item.BodyFormat = 1` statement, which sets the format of the Post item to plain text. Outlook always uses the format of the original item to set the format of a forward or reply, so we need to change the format of the original Post item before creating the forwarded message.

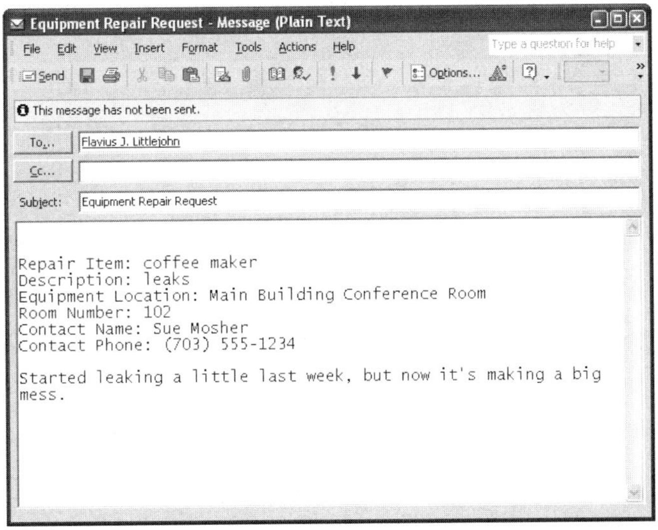

**Figure 20.14** *Compare this outgoing plain-text message with the original post in Figure 20.12 and the HTML version in Figure 20.13.*

## 20.6 Summary

This chapter has wrapped up Part IV, "Outlook Form Design," with information on both basic and advanced techniques. Practical applications have included a vacation request form, a form that automatically keeps an updated copy of itself in a public folder, and a Post form to collect data and send it as a structured HTML or plain text message. You now know how to hide and show form pages and how to avoid problems related to Outlook's forms architecture. You can link Outlook items in several different ways and understand that custom actions are a unique Outlook programming tool to help you generate new items that inherit properties. Custom actions also allow you to add toolbar buttons that run code in your forms without the need for command buttons on a custom page. Finally, you have seen several ways to make Outlook forms work over the Internet. Even if you work in an organization that uses Exchange as its mail/collaboration server, you may want to use these techniques to communicate with external clients and suppliers.

After working so intensely with custom forms, you are probably wondering how you can make existing items use a custom form or how you can use a custom form as your default for messages or other items. Chapter 24, "Deploying Forms and Applications," covers these issues.

In the following chapter, Chapter 21, "Menus, Toolbars, and the Outlook Bar," you will learn many useful techniques for working with Outlook menus and toolbars and the Outlook Bar on the left side of the main Outlook window, including how to run any menu command programmatically.

# *Finishing Touches*

# 21

# *Menus, Toolbars, and the Outlook Bar*

With this chapter, we begin a new section on some of the finishing touches that go beyond simple VBA macros and Outlook forms. You will explore some of the key elements of Outlook's user interface—the menus and toolbars and the optional Outlook Bar that displays shortcuts to folders and files.

Highlights of this chapter include discussions of the following:

- Why menus and toolbars are actually the same thing
- How to make sure that Outlook 2002 is sending messages with the correct account
- How to add a new custom toolbar through code and populate it with controls
- What code can run any menu or toolbar command programmatically
- How to change the toolbars displayed when a user switches folders
- How to write code to add and remove groups and shortcuts on the Outlook Bar

## 21.1 Programming Outlook menus and toolbars

Menus and toolbars are actually both examples of `CommandBar` objects. The `Explorer` and `Inspector` objects include child `CommandBars` collections consisting of all the menus and toolbars. Each `CommandBar` in the collection contains a `CommandBarControls` collection holding buttons, combo boxes, and submenus.

**Tip:** If you use the Object Browser to locate information on the `CommandBar` object, don't look in the Outlook library. The `CommandBar` object is common to all Office programs, so you will find it in the Office library. Where Outlook differs from the other Office programs is that for those programs, the `CommandBars` collection is a member of the `Application` object, not the `Explorer` and `Inspector` objects.

To see what `CommandBars` objects are intrinsic to the currently open Outlook window, run the VBA code in Listing 21.1 and then look in the Immediate window in VBA for a list of menus and toolbars.

**Listing 21.1** *Generate a List of All Menus and Toolbars for the Current Window*

```
Sub EnumCommandBars()
    Dim objApp As Outlook.Application
    Dim colCB As Office.CommandBars
    Dim objCB As Office.CommandBar
    Dim objControl As Office.CommandBarControl
    Dim strWindow As String
    On Error Resume Next
    Set objApp = CreateObject("Outlook.Application")
    strWindow = TypeName(objApp.ActiveWindow)
    Select Case strWindow
        Case "Explorer"
            Set colCB = objApp.ActiveExplorer.CommandBars
        Case "Inspector"
            Set colCB = objApp.ActiveInspector.CommandBars
        Case Else
            GoTo Exit_EnumCommandBars
    End Select
    Debug.Print strWindow & " Command Bars"
    Debug.Print
    For Each objCB In colCB
        Debug.Print "CommandBar: " & objCB.Name
        For Each objControl In objCB.Controls
            Debug.Print vbTab & objControl.Caption, _
                        objControl.ID
        Next
        Debug.Print
    Next

Exit_EnumCommandBars:
    Set objApp = Nothing
    Set colCB = Nothing
    Set objCB = Nothing
    Set objControl = Nothing
End Sub
```

The Immediate window will list toolbars and menus that are currently visible, as well as those that are not currently activated. `Visible` is one of the key `CommandBar` properties listed in Table 21.1. (Constants that apply to `CommandBar` objects in other Office programs, but not in Outlook, are omitted.) Note that you'll get a different list of toolbars and menus depending on whether you're looking at a folder, a contact, a message, or some other type of Outlook item.

---

**Note:** Outlook does not support direct programming of the right-click context menu. The only way to add to the right-click menu is to create a custom action on a custom form, as described in Chapter 20, "Common Outlook Form and Item Techniques."

---

To work with a specific `CommandBar` object menu or toolbar, use its name or index number to retrieve it from the `CommandBars` collection as you would with any other collection. The code in Listing 21.2, for example, toggles the `Visible` property of the Standard toolbar on the currently open item `Application.ActiveInspector` object.

**Table 21.1** *Key CommandBar Properties Supported in Outlook*

| Property | Description |
|---|---|
| `BuiltIn` | `True` if the `CommandBar` is a built-in menu or toolbar (read-only) |
| `Controls` | Returns a `CommandBarControls` object that represents all the controls on the toolbar or menu |
| `Enabled` | `True` if the `CommandBar` is enabled |
| `Left` | The distance in pixels from the left edge of the window to the left edge of the `CommandBar` |
| `Name` | The display name |
| `NameLocal` | The display name in the current language version of Outlook |
| `Parent` | The parent object of the `CommandBar` |
| `Position` | The screen location, using one of these `MsoBarPosition` constants:<br>`msoBarLeft` (0)<br>`msoBarTop` (1)<br>`msoBarRight` (2)<br>`msoBarBottom` (3)<br>`msoBarFloating` (4)<br>`msoBarMenuBar` (6) |

**Table 21.1** *Key CommandBar Properties Supported in Outlook (continued)*

| Property | Description |
|---|---|
| Protection | Whether the toolbar or menu is protected from customization, using one of these MsoBarProtection constants:<br>msoBarNoProtection (0)<br>msoBarNoCustomize (1)<br>msoBarNoResize (2)<br>msoBarNoMove (4)<br>msoBarNoChangeVisible (8)<br>msoBarNoChangeDock (16)<br>msoBarNoVerticalDock (32)<br>msoBarNoHorizontalDock (64) |
| Top | The distance in pixels from the top of the screen or, for docked menus or toolbars, from the top of the docking area to the top of the CommandBar |
| Type | The type of toolbar or menu, using one of these MsoBarType constants:<br>msoBarTypeNormal (0)<br>msoBarTypeMenuBar (1)<br>msoBarTypePopup (2) |
| Visible | True if the toolbar or menu is visible; the Enabled property must be True before Visible can be set to True. |
| Width | The width in pixels |

**Listing 21.2** *Show and Hide the Standard Toolbar*

```
Sub ToggleInspectorStandard()
    Dim objApp As Outlook.Application
    Dim objInspector As Outlook.Inspector
    Dim colCB As Office.CommandBars
    On Error Resume Next
    Set objApp = CreateObject("Outlook.Application")
    Set objInspector = objApp.ActiveInspector
    If Not objInspector Is Nothing Then
        Set colCB = objInspector.CommandBars
        colCB.Item("Standard").Visible = _
          Not colCB.Item("Standard").Visible
    End If
    Set objApp = Nothing
    Set objInspector = Nothing
    Set colCB = Nothing
End Sub
```

### 21.1.1 Floating the Response toolbar

You might have noticed in Chapter 20, "Common Outlook Form and Item Techniques," that the Approve and Disapprove buttons on the Vacation Request form did not stand out from the other toolbars. Voting buttons and other buttons related to custom actions you create on the (Actions) tab

**Listing 21.3** *Float the Response Toolbar for Voting Buttons out of the Menu Docking Area*

```
Dim m_objCB
Dim m_intLeft
Dim m_intTop
Const msoBarTop = 1
Const msoBarFloating = 4

Function Item_Open()
    Call FloatResponseBar()
End Function

Function Item_Close()
    Call ReturnResponseBar()
End Function

Sub FloatResponseBar()
    Dim objInsp
    On Error Resume Next
    Set objInsp = Item.GetInspector
    Set m_objCB = objInsp.CommandBars("Response")
    If Not m_objCB Is Nothing Then
        If m_objCB.Visible Then
            With m_objCB
                m_intLeft = .Left
                m_intTop = .Top
                .Position = msoBarFloating
                .Left = objInsp.Left + 50
                .Top = objInsp.Top + 50
            End With
        End If
    End If
    Set objInsp = Nothing
End Sub

Sub ReturnResponseBar()
    With m_objCB
        .Position = msoBarTop
        .Left = m_intLeft
        .Top = m_intTop
    End With
   Set m_objCB = Nothing
End Sub
```

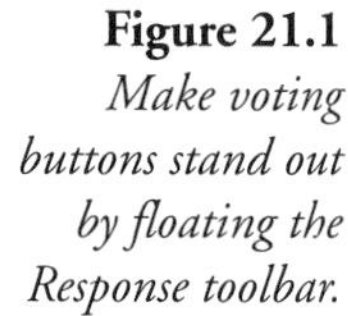

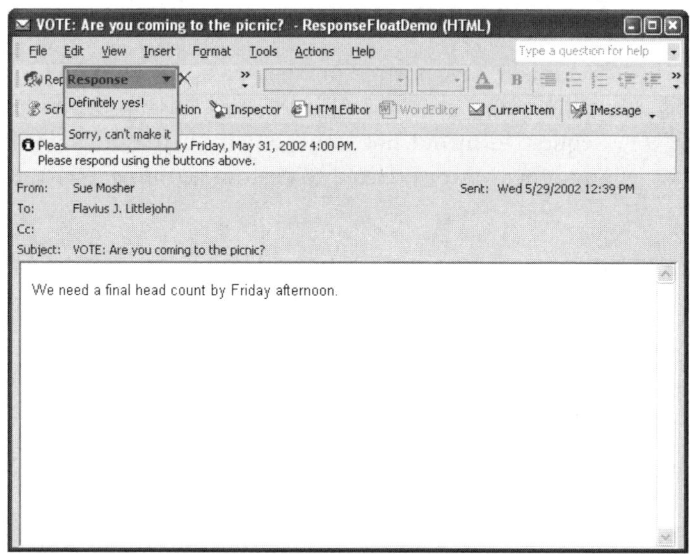


**Figure 21.1** *Make voting buttons stand out by floating the Response toolbar.*

of a custom form appear on a special built-in toolbar named Response. To make it hard for users to miss the Response toolbar, you can add the VBScript code in Listing 21.3 to your form.

The `FloatResponseBar` subroutine moves the Response toolbar out of the docking area so that it floats over the message text, as shown in Figure 21.1, while the `ReturnResponseBar` procedure restores the Response toolbar to its original position when the user closes the item.

### 21.1.2 Working with submenus

To access submenus, you work with the `CommandBarControls` collection. Each submenu on a menu `CommandBar` consists of a `CommandBarPopup` object, which in turn contains its own `CommandBarControls` collection of menu commands.

The `CommandBarControls` collection of a menu or toolbar can contain objects of four types:

| | |
|---|---|
| `CommandBarButton` | A toolbar button or menu command |
| `CommandBarComboBox` | A toolbar or menu combo box |
| `CommandBarPopup` | A submenu |
| `CommandBarControl` | Built-in controls that don't fit one of the other three types of Command Bar control objects |

The commands on a menu are normally implemented as CommandBar-Button objects for individual commands and CommandBarPopup objects for submenus. Each CommandBarPopup object has a child CommandBar object with the same properties listed in Table 21.1 and its own Controls collection. This may seem confusing because the CommandBarPopup object itself has a Controls collection. Just keep in mind that the CommandBar-Popup.Controls collection is the same as the CommandBarPopup.Com-mandBar.Controls collection.

Just as you were able earlier to list all CommandBar objects in Listing 21.1, you can also list menus, their submenus, and all the individual commands. The code in Listing 21.4 builds an Outlook message that includes all menus, submenus, toolbars, and commands for the current folder or item window.

The EnumPopupMenu() function is called any time the EnumAllCom-mands subroutine encounters a CommandBarPopup control (CommandBar-Control.Type = msoControlPopup) and returns a list of all the submenu commands. Notice that the strCmds list of controls includes the Name of any menu or submenu, the Caption for individual commands, and the ID

**Listing 21.4** *Build a List of All Command Bars and Commands*

```
Sub EnumAllCommands()
    Dim objApp As Outlook.Application
    Dim colCB As Office.CommandBars
    Dim objCB As Office.CommandBar
    Dim objControl As Office.CommandBarControl
    Dim objMail As Outlook.MailItem
    Dim strWindow As String
    Dim strCmds As String
    On Error Resume Next
    Set objApp = CreateObject("Outlook.Application")
    strWindow = TypeName(objApp.ActiveWindow)
    Select Case strWindow
        Case "Explorer"
            Set colCB = objApp.ActiveExplorer.CommandBars
        Case "Inspector"
            Set colCB = objApp.ActiveInspector.CommandBars
        Case Else
            GoTo Exit_EnumAllCommands
    End Select
    strCmds = strWindow & " Command Bars" & vbCrLf & vbCrLf
    For Each objCB In colCB
        If objCB.Type = msoBarTypeMenuBar Then
            strCmds = strCmds & "Menu Bar: "
        Else
            strCmds = strCmds & "Command Bar: "
        End If
```

**Listing 21.4** *Build a List of All Command Bars and Commands (continued)*

```
            strCmds = strCmds & Quote(objCB.Name) & vbCrLf
            For Each objControl In objCB.Controls
                strCmds = strCmds & vbTab & objControl.Caption & _
                          vbTab & objControl.ID & vbCrLf
                If objControl.Type = msoControlPopup Then
                    strCmds = strCmds & EnumPopupMenu(objControl)
                End If
            Next
            strCmds = strCmds & vbCrLf
        Next
        Set objMail = objApp.CreateItem(olMailItem)
        With objMail
            .Subject = "Command Bar List"
            .Body = strCmds
            .Display
        End With

Exit_EnumAllCommands:
        Set objApp = Nothing
        Set colCB = Nothing
        Set objCB = Nothing
        Set objControl = Nothing
        Set objMail = Nothing
End Sub

Function EnumPopupMenu(objCtrl As Office.CommandBarControl)
        Dim objCB As Office.CommandBar
        Dim objCBCtrl As Office.CommandBarControl
        Dim strCmds As String
        Set objCB = objCtrl.CommandBar
        strCmds = strCmds & String(10, "=") & _
                  "Begin " & Chr(34) & objCB.Name & _
                  Chr(34) & " menu" & _
                  String(10, "=") & vbCrLf
        For Each objCBCtrl In objCB.Controls
            strCmds = strCmds & vbTab & objCBCtrl.Caption & _
                      vbTab & objCBCtrl.ID & vbCrLf
            If objCBCtrl.Type = msoControlPopup Then
                strCmds = strCmds & EnumPopupMenu(objCBCtrl)
            End If
        Next
        strCmds = strCmds & String(10, "=") & _
                  "End " & Chr(34) & objCB.Name & _
                  Chr(34) & " menu" & _
                  String(10, "=") & vbCrLf
        EnumPopupMenu = strCmds
        Set objCBCtrl = Nothing
        Set objCB = Nothing
End Function
```

for each menu or command. You will see how to use the `ID` property to access an individual control in Section 21.1.3.

---

**Note:** The Actions menu is context sensitive. You will get a different list of commands in each different type of folder or item.

---

### 21.1.3 Accessing menu and toolbar controls

The `CommandBar.Controls` collection supports the standard `Item` method. You can use the value of the `Caption` property of the control. For example, this code fragment sets `objControl` to the Reply button on the Standard toolbar:

```
Set objApp = CreateObject("Outlook.Application")
Set objExplorer = objApp.ActiveExplorer
Set objCB = objExplorer.CommandBars.Item("Standard")
Set objControl = objCB.Controls("Reply")
```

But what if the user has renamed a toolbar button or menu command? If the user renames the Reply command with a new `Caption` of `Send Reply`, the `Set objControl` statement above fails.

An alternative method, one that's also language independent, is to use the `ID` property. The `EnumMenus` subroutine in the previous section created a message that lists the `ID` property for all built-in menu commands.

If you know the `ID`, you can use the `FindControl` method on the `CommandBar` object to return the corresponding control. For example, in Chapter 20, the Equipment Repair Request form displays a Post button, but the form is not actually used to save items, only to send messages with the custom command buttons on the form. Therefore, you might want to disable the Post and Save commands.

---

**Tip:** The `EnumAllCommands` subroutine in Listing 21.4 creates an Outlook message you can save to store a list of commands with their `ID` properties for different Explorer and Inspector windows. You will see that some numbers are repeated—for example, 1 (used on toolbars added by other applications), 761 and 32768 (typically used for lists of items, such as views, toolbars, or dial-up locations), and 190 (used by controls that run VBA macros). Because of the repeated numbers, you cannot use the `ID` to access these controls and should use the `Item` method instead.

---

By running the `EnumAllCommands` subroutine in Listing 21.4, you can discover that the `ID` for the Post button on the File menu is 2988, the `ID` for the Post button on the Standard toolbar is 2575, and the `ID` for Save on both menu and toolbar is 3. If you include the `Item_Open` code in Listing 21.5 in a Post form, both the Post and Save commands will still be visible, but will be disabled. (Note that the code contains examples of both the `Item` and `FindControl` methods.)

When you change the menu or toolbars on an `Inspector` object, those changes persist for new items that you open. Therefore, the `Item_Close` procedure in Listing 21.5 makes the Post and Save commands available again.

In VBA, you can use a slightly different syntax for `FindControl`, using a named argument:

```
Set objCBB = colCB.FindControl(ID:=2575)
```

**Listing 21.5** *Disable Toolbar and Menu Commands That You Don't Want Form Users To Click*

```
Function Item_Open()
   Dim objInsp
   Dim colCB
   Dim objCBB
   Set objInsp = Item.GetInspector
   Set colCB = objInsp.CommandBars
   Set objCBB = colCB.Item("Menu Bar"). _
                Controls.Item("&File").Controls.Item("&Save")
   If not objCBB Is Nothing Then
       objCBB.Enabled = False
   End If
   Set objCBB = Nothing
   Set objCBB = colCB.FindControl(, 3)
   If not objCBB Is Nothing Then
       objCBB.Enabled = False
   End If
   Set objCBB = Nothing
   Set objCBB = colCB.FindControl(, 2988)
   If not objCBB Is Nothing Then
       objCBB.Enabled = False
   End If
   Set objCBB = colCB.FindControl(, 2575)
   If not objCBB Is Nothing Then
       objCBB.Enabled = False
   End If
   Set objCBB = Nothing
   Set colCB = Nothing
   Set objInsp = Nothing
End Function
```

**Listing 21.5** *Disable Toolbar and Menu Commands That You Don't Want Form Users To Click (continued)*

```
Function Item_Close()
   Dim objInsp
   Dim colCB
   Dim objCBB
   Set objInsp = Item.GetInspector
   Set colCB = objInsp.CommandBars
   Set objCBB = colCB.Item("Menu Bar"). _
                Controls.Item("&File").Controls.Item("&Save")
   If not objCBB Is Nothing Then
       objCBB.Enabled = True
   End If
   Set objCBB = Nothing
   Set objCBB = colCB.FindControl(, 3)
   If not objCBB Is Nothing Then
       objCBB.Enabled = True
   End If
   Set objCBB = Nothing
   Set objCBB = colCB.FindControl(, 2988)
   If not objCBB Is Nothing Then
       objCBB.Enabled = True
   End If
   Set objCBB = Nothing
   Set objCBB = colCB.FindControl(, 2575)
   If not objCBB Is Nothing Then
       objCBB.Enabled = True
   End If
   Set objCBB = Nothing
   Set colCB = Nothing
   Set objInsp = Nothing
End Function
```

**Tip:** Network administrators can use system policies to disable a menu or toolbar command permanently using the same `ID` property values that we're using in this chapter's code.

**CAUTION:** Disabling a menu or toolbar control may not be as effective as you might think. In the case of the Equipment Repair Request form, for example, even though the code in Listing 21.5 disables the Post and Save buttons, users can still press Ctrl+S to save an item.

Not only can you disable specific commands, you can also execute virtually any toolbar or menu command programmatically by using the `Com-`

**Listing 21.6** *Execute the Select All Command to Count the Items in a View*

```
Function CountInView() As Long
    Dim objApp As Outlook.Application
    Dim objExpl As Outlook.Explorer
    Dim colCB As Office.CommandBars
    Dim objCBB As Office.CommandBarButton
    On Error Resume Next
    Set objApp = CreateObject("Outlook.Application")
    Set objExpl = objApp.ActiveExplorer
    Set colCB = objExpl.CommandBars
    Set objCBB = colCB.FindControl(ID:=756)
    If Not objCBB Is Nothing Then
        objCBB.Execute
        CountInView = objExpl.Selection.Count
    End If
    Set objCBB = Nothing
    Set colCB = Nothing
    Set objExpl = Nothing
    Set objApp = Nothing
End Function
```

`mandButtonControl.Execute` method. For example, the `CountInView()` function in Listing 21.6 provides a way to obtain the number of items visible to the user in the current view, even if a filter is in place on the view. It runs the Select All command on the Edit menu, and then returns the value of `Application.ActiveExplorer.Selection.Count`.

The next few sections provide more common examples of when executing a menu or toolbar command can add useful functionality to Outlook forms and VBA projects.

**Listing 21.7** *Launch the Insert File Dialog with VBScript Code*

```
Sub ShowAttachmentDialog()
    Dim objInsp
    Dim colCB
    Dim objCBB
    On Error Resume Next
    Set objInsp = Item.GetInspector
    Set colCB = objInsp.CommandBars
    Set objCBB = colCB.FindControl(, 1079)
    If Not objCBB Is Nothing Then
        objCBB.Execute
    End If
    Set objCBB = Nothing
    Set colCB = Nothing
    Set objInsp = Nothing
End Sub
```

### 21.1.4 Displaying the Insert File dialog

On a custom form, you may want to be able to pop up the Insert File dialog either when the user clicks a command button or when the user tries to save the item without a required attachment. The `ShowAttachmentDialog` subroutine is written in VBScript for use on an Outlook form (see Listing 21.7).

### 21.1.5 Automatically showing the Find pane on contacts folders

Both Outlook 2000 and 2002 include a Find command for searching the currently displayed folder. Since searching the contacts folders is a common task for many users, Listing 21.8 provides code for the `ThisOutlookSession` VBA module to automatically display the Find controls whenever the user switches to a folder that contains contacts. To initialize the event handlers, you will need to either restart Outlook or run the `Application_Startup` procedure.

**Listing 21.8** *Automatically Show the Find Controls for the Contacts Folders*

```
Option Explicit
Dim WithEvents objExpl As Outlook.Explorer

Private Sub Application_Startup()
    Set objExpl = Application.ActiveExplorer
End Sub

Private Sub objExpl_FolderSwitch()
    Dim objFolder As Outlook.MAPIFolder
    Dim colCB As Office.CommandBars
    Dim objCBB As Office.CommandBarButton
    Set objFolder = objExpl.CurrentFolder
    If objFolder.DefaultItemType = olContactItem Then
        Set colCB = Application.ActiveExplorer.CommandBars
        Set objCBB = colCB.FindControl(ID:=5592)
        If Not objCBB Is Nothing Then
            If objCBB.State = msoButtonUp Then
                objCBB.Execute
            End If
        End If
    End If
    Set objCBB = Nothing
    Set colCB = Nothing
    Set objFolder = Nothing
End Sub
```

Notice that objCBB is declared not as the generic Office.CommandBar-Control, but specifically as an Office.CommandBarButton object because we know that the Find command on the Tools menu and the Standard toolbar functions as a toggle. For toggle buttons, the CommandBarButton.State property indicates whether the feature is currently active or not. This makes it possible for the FolderSwitch event handler to use the expression objCBB.State = msoButtonUp to determine whether the Find feature is currently turned off and, if it's off, to enable it.

### 21.1.6 Folder-specific toolbars

One simple, practical application of the CommandBars object is to display a particular custom toolbar when the user switches to a certain folder. For example, perhaps you have a Help Desk folder containing custom items. If you initialize an objExpl object variable to fire events (see Listing 21.8), you can use this code snippet to display a corresponding Help Desk custom toolbar that you've already created:

```
Private Sub objExpl_FolderSwitch()
    If objExpl.CurrentFolder.Name = "Help Desk" Then
        objExpl.CommandBars("Help Desk").Visible = True
    End If
End Sub
```

**Tip:** You don't have to create a custom toolbar in code. Just choose View, Toolbars, Customize, and click the New button on the Toolbars tab. You will have to close the VBA window first, though.

### 21.1.7 Sending with a particular account (Outlook 2002)

Strange as it may seem, the Outlook object model contains no method for sending mail with a certain e-mail account. In fact, Outlook 2000 in Corporate/Workgroup mode does not even have a command in the user interface for specifying the account.

Both Outlook 2000 in IMO mode and Outlook 2002 do allow you to specify the sending account when you send a message, but with slightly different techniques. In Outlook 2000 IMO, the user selects the account and sends, all with one command. Outlook 2002 separates the account selection and send commands. This separation means we can check the sending account on the outgoing message and change it if desired.

---

**Note:** Even if the user is viewing multiple Exchange mailboxes, only one Exchange account is available for sending. To change the mailbox that the message appears to be coming from, you can set the `MailItem.SendOnBehalfOf` name property. Whether the recipient sees the mailbox as the From address or a Sent on Behalf of address depends on whether the sender has SendAs or SendOnBehalfOf permission on that mailbox.

---

For example, a user receiving mail from multiple POP or IMAP accounts might want to use only one account for sending all messages. Listing 21.9 provides code for the `ThisOutlookSession` VBA module to check the sending account and prompt the user if it's not the preferred account set in the `strPrefAccount =` statement.

**Listing 21.9** *Check the Sending Account and Give the User the Opportunity To Change It*

```
Private Sub Application_ItemSend(ByVal Item As Object, _
                                  Cancel As Boolean)
    Dim objInsp As Outlook.Inspector
    Dim colCB As Office.CommandBars
    Dim objCBAccounts As Office.CommandBarPopup
    Dim objCBB As Office.CommandBarButton
    Dim strPrefAccount As String
    Dim strMsg As String
    Dim intRes As Integer
    Dim blnAccountFound As Boolean
    ' *** USER OPTION ***
    strPrefAccount = "EMO"
    Set objInsp = Item.GetInspector
    Set colCB = objInsp.CommandBars
    Set objCBAccounts = colCB.FindControl(ID:=31224)
    Set objCBB = objCBAccounts.Controls.Item(1)
    If Not objCBB Is Nothing Then
        If objCBB.Caption <> strPrefAccount Then
            strMsg = "This message will be sent with " & _
                     "the " & Quote(objCBB.Caption) & _
                     " account. " & vbCrLf & vbCrLf & _
                     "Would you rather use your " & _
                     "preferred account (" & _
                     strPrefAccount & ")?"
            intRes = MsgBox(strMsg, _
              vbYesNoCancel + vbDefaultButton1 + _
              vbQuestion, _
              "Send with Preferred Account?")
```

**Listing 21.9** *Check the Sending Account and Give the User the Opportunity To Change It (continued)*

```
            If intRes = vbYes Then
                Set objCBB = Nothing
                blnAccountFound = False
                For Each objCBB In objCBAccounts.Controls
                    If InStr(1, objCBB.Caption, _
                             strPrefAccount, _
                             vbTextCompare) > 0 Then
                        blnAccountFound = True
                        Err.Clear
                        objCBB.Execute
                        Exit For
                    End If
                Next
                If blnAccountFound = False Or _
                   Err.Number <> 0 Then
                   Cancel = True
                End If
            ElseIf intRes = vbCancel Then
                Cancel = True
            End If
        End If
    End If
    Set objCBB = Nothing
    Set objCBAccounts = Nothing
    Set colCB = Nothing
    Set objInsp = Nothing
End Sub
```

Before sending a message, change the statement that sets the value for the `strPrefAccount` variable so that it uses your own preferred account. To check the names of the available accounts, create a new mail message, then click the Accounts button.

**Tip:** If you don't need to change the sending account, just the address that replies will be sent to, you can add a `Recipient` to the `MailItem.ReplyRecipients` collection with the standard `Add` method for a `Recipients` collection.

The key to the technique given in Listing 21.9 is that the first account listed in the Accounts submenu—the one with `Index = 1`—is the account that Outlook will use to send the message unless the user intervenes. Therefore, we can check the `Caption` property of the corresponding `CommandBarButton` against the value set for `strPrefAccount`. This is not the kind of information that you'll find in the documentation on the Outlook object model. It takes a sharp eye for patterns and much testing to discover such behaviors.

### 21.1.8 Adding a new toolbar and controls

You can create a new toolbar in code and populate it with controls for both built-in functions and VBA macros.

Because `CommandBars` is a collection, as with other collections, you use the `Add` method to create a new toolbar. The `Add` method takes the optional arguments listed in Table 21.2. Listing 21.10 creates a new floating toolbar named Sample for the current Explorer window.

---

**Note:** You won't see `msoBarMenuBar` as an option for the `Position` property in Table 21.2. Instead, to replace the built-in menu with one of your own, set the `MenuBar` property of your custom `CommandBar` to `True` and set the `Position` to `msoBarTop`. Only one `CommandBar` object at a time can have `MenuBar` set to `True`.

---

---

**Note:** Outlook does not prevent you from creating multiple toolbars with the same name.

---

**Table 21.2** *Arguments for Adding a CommandBar*

| Argument | Description |
|---|---|
| `Name` | The display name for the command bar; if omitted, Outlook uses a default name such as Custom 1 |
| `Position` | The position or type of command bar, using one of these constants:<br>`msoBarLeft` (0)<br>`msoBarTop` (1)<br>`msoBarRight` (2)<br>`msoBarBottom` (3)<br>`msoBarFloating` (4) |
| `MenuBar` | If `True`, replaces the current menu bar with the new command bar (default = `False`) |
| `Temporary` | If `True`, the `CommandBar` will be removed when Outlook closes (default = `False`) |

**Listing 21.10** *Create a New Sample Toolbar*

```
Function CreateSampleToolbar() as Office.CommandBar
    Dim objApp As Outlook.Application
    Dim colCB As Office.CommandBars
    Dim objCB As Office.CommandBar
    Set objApp = CreateObject("Outlook.Application")
    Set colCB = objApp.ActiveExplorer.CommandBars
    Set objCB = colCB.Add("Sample", msoBarFloating)
    objCB.Visible = True
    Set CreateSampleToolbar = objCB
    Set objCB = Nothing
    Set colCB = Nothing
    Set objApp = Nothing
End Function
```

**Tip:** You can add, modify, or delete a custom toolbar manually. Choose View, Customize, Toolbars, and then switch to the Toolbars tab of the Customize dialog.

After you create a toolbar, you will want to add controls to it. To add a button that duplicates one of the built-in toolbar buttons, you need to know the `ID`, a property of `CommandBarControl` objects. Use the `EnumAllCommands` procedure given in Listing 21.4 to learn what commands are available in a particular Explorer or Inspector window and what the `ID` is for the command you want to use. For example, we already know from using it in Listing 21.8 that the `ID` for the Find command in an Explorer window is 5592. Table 21.3 lists additional arguments, all optional, for adding controls.

**Note:** Controls you create with the `Type` property equal to `msoControlEdit` (2), `msoControlDropdown` (3), and `msoControlComboBox` (4) are all `CommandBarComboBox` control objects. Use the `Text` property of a `CommandBarComboBox` control, as shown in the example in the next section, to retrieve either text typed by the user or a selection from a list.

This code snippet initializes a `colCBControls` object representing the `Controls` collection of a `CommandBar` object (`objCB`) and then adds a button for the built-in Find command:

```
Set colCBControls = objCB.Controls
Set objControl = colCBControls.Add(msoControlButton, 5592)
```

**Table 21.3** *Arguments for Adding CommandBar Controls*

| Argument | Description |
|---|---|
| `Type` | The type of control, using one of these constants:<br>`msoControlButton` (1)<br>`msoControlEdit` (2)<br>`msoControlDropdown` (3)<br>`msoControlComboBox` (4)<br>`msoControlPopup` (10) |
| `ID` | The integer specifying a built-in control |
| `Parameter` | The argument used by Outlook to run built-in controls or by a custom control to store information for the control's VBA procedure |
| `Before` | The number indicating the position of the control on the command bar; if omitted, the control is added at the end |
| `Temporary` | If `True`, the control is temporary and will be deleted when Outlook closes (Default = `False`) |

When you add a custom control to run VBA code, you not only need to use the `Add` method to create the control on the `CommandBar`, but you also must specify what the control should do and how the control should look. Table 21.4 shows the key `CommandBarButton` properties you should consider setting. You can also use these properties to alter the appearance of controls for built-in commands.

**Table 21.4** *Key CommandBarButton Properties*

| Property | Description |
|---|---|
| `Caption` | The text shown on the control |
| `FaceID` | The ID number for the picture shown on a control. You can use the `CopyFace` and `PasteFace` methods to copy and paste the face from one control to another (In Outlook 2002, you can set the picture directly with `Picture` and `Mask`.) |
| `HyperlinkType` | Determines whether the control runs a URL; can be one of these constants:<br>`msoCommandBarButtonHyperlinkNone` (0)<br>`msoCommandBarButtonHyperlinkOpen` (1)<br>`msoCommandBarButtonHyperlinkInsertPicture` (2) |
| `Mask` | Object that represents an image that determines what portions of a toolbar button are transparent (Outlook 2002 only) |
| `OnAction` | The name of the VBA macro to run when the control is clicked or its value is changed |

**Table 21.4** *Key CommandBarButton Properties (continued)*

| Property | Description |
|---|---|
| `Parameter` | Stores information for the control's VBA procedure |
| `Picture` | Object representing the image displayed on a toolbar button (Outlook 2002) |
| `Style` | For a `CommandBarButton` object, sets whether the button is displayed with a caption, an icon, or both; can be any of the following constants:<br>`msoButtonAutomatic` (0)<br>`msoButtonIcon` (1)<br>`msoButtonCaption` (2)<br>`msoButtonIconAndCaption` (3)<br>`msoButtonIconAndCaptionBelow` (11)<br>`msoButtonIconAndWrapCaption` (7)<br>`msoButtonIconAndWrapCaptionBelow` (15)<br>`msoButtonWrapCaption` (14)<br>For a `CommandBarComboBox` object, sets the appearance of the combo box; can be either of these constants:<br>`msoComboNormal` (0)<br>`msoComboLabel` (1) |
| `TooltipText` | The text displayed when the user pauses the mouse over the control; uses the `Caption` value by default |

As you saw earlier in the discussion of submenus, a `CommandBarPopup` object also has child `CommandBar` and `Controls` objects that you use to build the menu for the `CommandBarPopup` object.

## 21.1.9 A toolbar control to launch any message form

The VBA procedure listed in the `OnAction` property must be a subroutine with no arguments. However, the subroutine itself can use the properties of the control to obtain information for use in the procedure.

The `AddFormLaunchCombo` subroutine in Listing 21.11 calls the `CreateSampleToolbar()` function in Listing 21.10, if necessary; adds a `CommandBarComboBox` control; and populates it with a list of favorite published IPM.Note (i.e., Message) forms by using the `AddItem` method, just as you would with a Combo Box control on a form. The `OnAction` property of the control is set to the `RunForm` subroutine, which also appears in Listing 21.11. When the user selects a form from the Run Form control, the `RunForm` subroutine checks the `Text` property of that control and uses that information to create a new item using that form and display the item.

**Listing 21.11** *Add a List of Favorite Forms to a Toolbar*

```
Sub AddFormLaunchCombo()
    Dim objApp As Outlook.Application
    Dim colBars As Office.CommandBars
    Dim objCB As Office.CommandBar
    Dim objCBControls As Office.CommandBarControls
    Dim objControl As Office.CommandBarControl
    On Error Resume Next
    Set objApp = CreateObject("Outlook.Application")
    Set colBars = objApp.ActiveExplorer.CommandBars
    Set objCB = colBars("Sample")
    If objCB Is Nothing Then
        Set objCB = CreateSampleToolbar()
    End If
    Set objCBControls = objCB.Controls
    Set objControl = objCBControls.Add(msoControlComboBox)
    With objControl
        .AddItem "IPM.Note.Info"
        .AddItem "IPM.Note.Notice"
        .AddItem "IPM.Note.Report"
        .OnAction = "RunForm"
        .Style = msoComboLabel
        .Caption = "Run Form"
    End With
    Set objApp = Nothing
    Set colBars = Nothing
    Set objCB = Nothing
    Set objCBControls = Nothing
    Set objControl = Nothing
End Sub

Sub RunForm()
    Dim objApp As Outlook.Application
    Dim objNS As Outlook.NameSpace
    Dim objFolder As Outlook.MAPIFolder
    Dim objItems As Outlook.Items
    Dim objItem As Outlook.MailItem
    Dim objCB As Office.CommandBar
    Dim objCBControl As Office.CommandBarComboBox
    Dim strMessageClass As String
    Set objApp = CreateObject("Outlook.Application")
    Set objNS = objApp.GetNamespace("MAPI")
    Set objCB = objApp.ActiveExplorer.CommandBars("Sample")
    Set objCBControl = objCB.Controls("Run Form")
    strMessageClass = objCBControl.Text
    If Left(strMessageClass, 8) = "IPM.Note" Then
        Set objFolder = objNS.GetDefaultFolder(olFolderDrafts)
        Set objItems = objFolder.Items
        Set objItem = objItems.Add(strMessageClass)
        objItem.Display
    Else
        MsgBox "Not a valid message form", , "Run Form"
```

**Listing 21.11** *Add a List of Favorite Forms to a Toolbar (continued)*

```
    End If
    Set objApp = Nothing
    Set objNS = Nothing
    Set objFolder = Nothing
    Set objItems = Nothing
    Set objCB = Nothing
    Set objCBControl = Nothing
    Set objItem = Nothing
End Sub
```

In addition to the `Text` property, you can also use the `Parameter` or `Tag` property of the control to store information in a new menu command or toolbar option so that a procedure can use it.

## 21.2 Programming the Outlook Bar

The Outlook Bar is the collection of shortcuts optionally displayed on the left side of Explorer windows. The Outlook Bar can hold shortcuts not just to Outlook and system folders, but also to individual files, including program executables, and to Web pages.

You can add and remove both Outlook Bar groups and individual items. You can also program event handlers to react to switching between groups and adding and removing shortcuts and groups.

The Outlook Bar is an object in the `Panes` collection of an `Explorer` object. The Outlook Bar `Pane` object includes a `Contents` child object, which contains the `Groups` collection of Outlook Bar groups. The code in Listing 21.12 displays a message box with the number of groups in the Outlook Bar.

**Listing 21.12** *Count the Number of Outlook Bar Groups*

```
Sub CountOBGroups()
    Dim objApp As Outlook.Application
    Dim objOB As Outlook.OutlookBarPane
    Set objApp = CreateObject("Outlook.Application")
    Set objOB = objApp.ActiveExplorer.Panes.Item("OutlookBar")
    MsgBox "My Outlook Bar contains " & _
           objOB.Contents.Groups.Count & " groups."
    Set objApp = Nothing
    Set objOB = Nothing
End Sub
```

Each `OutlookBarGroup` object contains a child `Shortcuts` collection. Each `OutlookBarShortcut` object in this collection includes `Name` and `Target` properties. The `Target` is set when the shortcut is created and cannot be changed later.

### 21.2.1 Adding groups and shortcuts

To add a new Outlook Bar group, use the `Add` method and provide a name for the group. The code in Listing 21.13 adds a Favorites group.

---

**Note:** Even though Outlook has a `Panes` collection, it will not have more than one item in it—the `Pane` named `OutlookBar`—because the Outlook Bar is currently the only supported `Pane`.

---

The `Add` method also supports an optional *`index`* argument within the Outlook Bar. For example, `objOBGroups.Add("Favorites", 1)` adds the Favorites group as the first group in the Outlook Bar.

The syntax for adding a shortcut to an Outlook Bar group's `Shortcuts` collection is

```
Shortcuts.Add(target, name, index)
```

The target can be either a `MAPIFolder` object or a string representing a system file, a system folder path, or a URL. This code fragment adds a

**Listing 21.13** *Add a Favorites Group to the Outlook Bar*

```
Sub AddFavoritesGroup()
    Dim objApp As Outlook.Application
    Dim objOB As Outlook.OutlookBarPane
    Dim objOBGroups As Outlook.OutlookBarGroups
    Dim objNewOBGroup As Outlook.OutlookBarGroup
    Set objApp = CreateObject("Outlook.Application")
    Set objOB = objApp.ActiveExplorer.Panes.Item("OutlookBar")
    Set objOBGroups = objOB.Contents.Groups
    Set objNewOBGroup = objOBGroups.Add("Favorites", 1)
    Set objApp = Nothing
    Set objOB = Nothing
    Set objOBGroups = Nothing
    Set objNewOBGroup = Nothing
End Sub
```

shortcut to a discussion list for Outlook developers to the bottom of the Favorites group you just created:

```
Set colOBShortcuts = _
  objOB.Contents.Groups("Favorites").Shortcuts
Set objOBShortcut = colOBShortcuts.Add( _
  "http://groups.yahoo.com/group/outlook-dev/messages", _
  "Outlook Developers list")
```

The position *index* within the group is optional. Because the preceding code omitted it, the Outlook Developers shortcut would be added to the bottom of the group.

Outlook 2002 adds one new feature to the Outlook Bar—the ability to set the icon for any shortcut to an .ico file; for example

```
objOBShortcut.SetIcon _
  "C:\Program Files\Microsoft Office\" & _
  "Office10\forms\1033\OOFL.ICO"
```

Many programs besides Microsoft Office install .ico files on your system, which you can use for Outlook Bar shortcut icons.

### 21.2.2 Removing groups and shortcuts

To remove a group or shortcut, use the `Remove` method on a `Shortcuts` or `Groups` collection. You must know the specific *index* number of the shortcut or group you want to remove. The procedure in the next section includes an example. The individual `OutlookBarShortcut` or `OutlookBarGroup` objects do not support the `Delete` method.

### 21.2.3 Maintaining a Favorites group

In Outlook 2000, the Advanced toolbar includes a Previous Folder button that keeps a history of most recently accessed Outlook folders. However, Outlook 2002's Back and Forward buttons in the Advanced toolbar and in the folder bar above the item list do not provide a dropdown list of the history of folders you have accessed. You can create your own list of recently accessed folders with the Favorites group created on the Outlook Bar earlier in the chapter. The code in Listing 21.14 provides a good review of using collection techniques to examine, add, and remove items. The `objExpl_FolderSwitch` subroutine is, of course, an event handler for the `Explorer.FolderSwitch` event, which needs to be initialized, as shown in Listing 21.8. The event handler calls the `AddFolderToFavorites` procedure, passing the current folder as an argument.

**Listing 21.14** *Build a Group of Recently Accessed Folders*

```
Private Sub objExpl_FolderSwitch()
    Call AddFolderToFavorites(objExpl.CurrentFolder)
End Sub

Sub AddFolderToFavorites(objFolder As Outlook.MAPIFolder)
    Dim objApp As Outlook.Application
    Dim objOB As Outlook.OutlookBarPane
    Dim colOBShortcuts  As Outlook.OutlookBarShortcuts
    Dim objOBShortcut As Outlook.OutlookBarShortcut
    Dim intMaxShortcuts As Integer
    Dim I As Integer
    ' *** USER OPTION ***
    intMaxShortcuts = 10
    Set objApp = CreateObject("Outlook.Application")
    Set objOB = objApp.ActiveExplorer.Panes.Item("OutlookBar")
    Set colOBShortcuts = _
      objOB.Contents.Groups("Favorites").Shortcuts
    For I = 1 To colOBShortcuts.Count
        Set objOBShortcut = colOBShortcuts.Item(I)
        If objOBShortcut.Target = objFolder Then
            colOBShortcuts.Remove I
            Exit For
        End If
    Next
    If colOBShortcuts.Count = intMaxShortcuts Then
        colOBShortcuts.Remove intMaxShortcuts
    End If
    Set objOBShortcut = colOBShortcuts.Add( _
                          objFolder, objFolder.Name, 1)
    Set objApp = Nothing
    Set objOB = Nothing
    Set colOBShortcuts = Nothing
    Set objOBShortcut = Nothing
End Sub
```

Here are a few notes on the `AddFolderToFavorites` procedure:

- The `intMaxShortcuts` variable represents the maximum number of shortcuts that you want to keep in the Favorites group. If you right-click the Outlook Bar and choose Small Icons from the pop-up menu, you can see more shortcuts at one time.
- If the target folder already has a shortcut in the group, the original shortcut is removed, and a new shortcut to the folder is added at the top of the group by setting the *`index`* argument of the `Add` method to `1`.
- If the target folder does not already have a shortcut in the group, the oldest shortcut is removed, if necessary, to make room for the new shortcut.

**Table 21.5** *Outlook Bar Events*

| Object | Event | Occurs |
|---|---|---|
| `OutlookBarPane` | `BeforeGroupSwitch` | Immediately before a different Outlook Bar group is opened; can be canceled |
| | `BeforeNavigate` | Before a different folder is displayed as a result of clicking on an Outlook Bar shortcut; can be canceled |
| `OutlookBarGroups` | `BeforeGroupAdd` | Before a new group is added; can be canceled |
| | `BeforeGroupRemove` | Before a group is removed; can be canceled |
| | `GroupAdd` | After a new group has been added |
| `OutlookBarShortcuts` | `BeforeShortcutAdd` | Before a shortcut is added; can be canceled |
| | `BeforeShortcutRemove` | Before a shortcut is removed; can be canceled |
| | `ShortcutAdd` | After a new shortcut has been added |

The result is a Favorites group that constantly updates itself as you navigate from folder to folder. The topmost shortcut in the group always prints to the most recently viewed folder.

### 21.2.4 Outlook Bar events

The objects associated with the Outlook Bar support a variety of useful events for which you can write event handlers. Table 21.5 lists the available events for each object.

## 21.3 Summary

Custom toolbars, menu bars, and Outlook Bar groups and shortcuts make it easy for users to run the VBA subroutines for your Outlook applications and navigate to their favorite Outlook folders. You can also set toolbar buttons or Outlook Bar shortcuts to jump to specific Web pages or even run other programs. Finally, you can tie toolbars, menus, and the Outlook Bar to other Outlook events, displaying only those commands that the user is likely to need in your application.

You have seen many practical applications of toolbar and menu techniques—displaying the Insert File dialog from a form, automatically showing the Find pane in contacts folders, confirming that Outlook 2002 is sending with the correct account, and launching forms from a toolbar button. Even so, we have only scratched the surface of the `CommandBars` object. In Appendix A, you will find additional resources on this topic.

In Chapter 22, you will learn how to produce neatly printed reports from Outlook data, both data in folder views and individual items.

# 22

# *Designing Outlook Reports*

If any single area of Outlook falls short, it's printing and reporting. Outlook's built-in capabilities for regurgitating its data as printed reports and files in other formats are very limited. For example, when you use Outlook's File, Import and Export command, you cannot export user-defined fields. Items that use custom Outlook forms are not exported at all! Furthermore, there is no method for printing a custom form in a format that resembles the on-screen form. An individual form always prints in Outlook's memo style, which produces a simple list of fields.

Because of these major limitations, being able to extract Outlook data into some other format—either a file or a printed report—is an essential skill for Outlook programmers. This chapter discusses how you can export and print from Outlook without programming, using techniques such as Outlook views. You will also see how to push Outlook data into Excel or Word. These reporting techniques can be adapted not just for printed output, but also to produce files of exported data.

Highlights of this chapter include discussions of the following:

- Why folder views are the key to simple tabular reports
- How to use a Word mail merge to build a contact report
- How to build tabular reports with Excel
- How to duplicate the look of an Outlook form with a Word template
- How to print invoices and other reports that combine data from two different folders

Note that the Word mail merge method and all the methods in this chapter that involve programming code are subject to the Outlook address book security prompts.

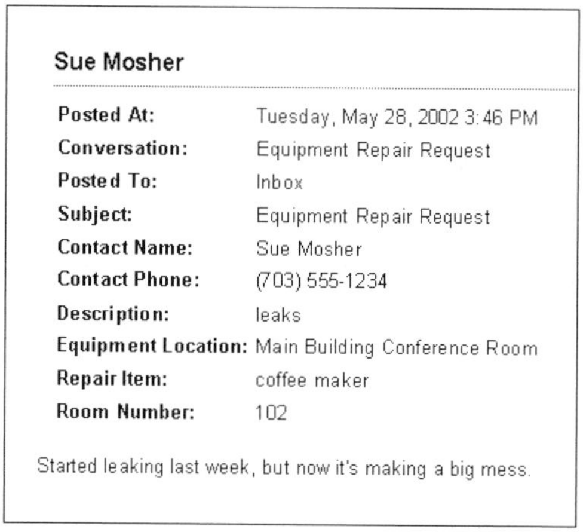

**Figure 22.1** *Printouts of custom Outlook forms look nothing like the form (compare with Figure 20.12).*

**Sue Mosher**

| | |
|---|---|
| **Posted At:** | Tuesday, May 28, 2002 3:46 PM |
| **Conversation:** | Equipment Repair Request |
| **Posted To:** | Inbox |
| **Subject:** | Equipment Repair Request |
| **Contact Name:** | Sue Mosher |
| **Contact Phone:** | (703) 555-1234 |
| **Description:** | leaks |
| **Equipment Location:** | Main Building Conference Room |
| **Repair Item:** | coffee maker |
| **Room Number:** | 102 |

Started leaking last week, but now it's making a big mess.

# 22.1 Built-in report techniques

Users can print individual items or lists from Outlook folders by using the File, Print command. For an individual item, Outlook first prints the built-in fields in a preset order, then prints any custom fields in alphabetical order, and finally prints the contents of the `Body` property. The user cannot change the order of the fields. For example, Figure 22.1 shows the printout that you'd get from the Equipment Repair Request form shown in Figure 20.8.

Printing from a folder view can be a good way to generate a report on multiple items because the user gets pretty much what is displayed on the screen. You have other built-in reporting options, both programmatic and those involving no code at all, if you have Microsoft Word and Excel. The final built-in method that we'll look at involves creating an HTML mail message or post.

## 22.1.1 Printing from customized folder views

Why are folder views important to Outlook reporting? Because almost anything you can show in a view can be printed out. Table views (such as the default view of your Inbox folder) are particularly useful for quick tabular reports on all kinds of Outlook data, including custom properties. Other types of views include timeline (which cannot be printed), card, icon, and day/week/month.

---

**Note:** Can Outlook views be created or modified programmatically? Yes, but only in Outlook 2002, which provides a `View` object with an `XML` property that contains most (but not all) of the view settings. Programming `View.XML`, however, is outside the scope of this book.

---

To create a new view from scratch, choose View, Current View, Define Views. In the Define Views dialog box, click the New button. It is often easier to make a copy of an existing table view and then modify it to suit your needs.

Table 22.1 lists many different ways to customize a view. These techniques can also be accessed by choosing View, Current View, Customize Current View and using the buttons on the View Summary dialog box, shown in Figure 22.2.

**Table 22.1** *View Customization Techniques*

| To Make This Change . . . | Do This . . . |
|---|---|
| Add columns showing other fields | Right-click on any column heading in the view, choose Field Chooser, and then drag fields from the Field Chooser to the view |
| Remove a field | Drag the column heading for the field out of the view |
| Display fields in a different order | Drag a column heading to a new position |
| Change the width of a column | Drag the right border of a column heading to the left to make it narrower or to the right to make it wider |
| Adjust the width of a column to the best fit for the data | Double-click on the right border of the column heading |
| Organize related items by values in a particular field | Right-click the field's column heading, and then choose Group by This Field |
| Sort by particular field(s) | Click the column heading for the field you want to sort by; to sort by up to three additional fields, hold down the Ctrl key as you click the column heading |
| Show only items that meet particular criteria | Choose View, Current View, Customize Current View; click Filter, and set criteria in the Filter dialog box |
| Display data that meets particular criteria in a different font | Choose View, Current View, Customize Current View, and click Automatic Formatting |

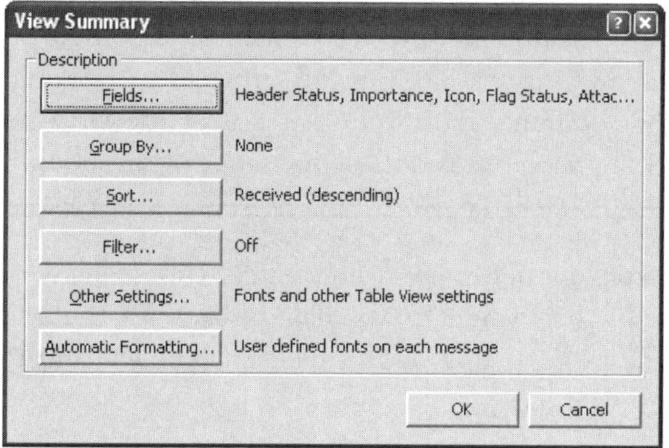


**Figure 22.2** *Modify a view with any of these commands.*

---

**Note:** The Group By feature in Outlook groups related items, such as those with the same category, in a table view and displays the number of items in each group. However, it cannot perform any subtotals or other calculations. If you need subtotals, a good strategy is to use the Excel method in the next section, then add formulas to do the calculations.

---

If a column in a table view is too narrow to show the full data in the field, the print output will also be truncated. To adjust columns accurately

Other Settings
Column headings
Font... 8 pt. Tahoma
Automatic column sizing
OK
Cancel
Rows
Font... 8 pt. Tahoma
Allow in-cell editing
Show "new item" row
AutoPreview
Font... 8 pt. Tahoma
Preview all items
Preview unread items
No AutoPreview
Grid lines
Grid line style: No grid lines
Preview:
Grid line color:
Shade group headings
Preview Pane
Show Preview Pane
Hide header information

**Figure 22.3** *The choices in the Other Settings dialog box depend on the type of view you're modifying.*

so that they print at the width you want, you may need to turn off automatic column sizing by following these steps:

1. Right-click on a column heading, and then choose Customize Current View.
2. In the View Summary dialog box (see Figure 22.2), click Other Settings.
3. On the Other Settings dialog box (see Figure 22.3), clear the box for Automatic Column Sizing, and then click OK twice to return to the view.

Printing from an Outlook view is definitely a what-you-see-is-what-you-get operation. Be sure to use the File, Print Preview command to check whether all your columns fit on the page before you print, especially if you turn off automatic column sizing. To change the margins, choose File, Page Setup, Table Style, and then switch to the Paper tab.

### 22.1.2 Copying data to Excel

One benefit of table views is that you can copy their data to Microsoft Excel with just a few keystrokes and then use Excel for additional formatting or data manipulation. Even custom properties can be exported in this fashion. Follow these steps in any Outlook table view:

1. Add and remove fields from a table view until it shows only the fields you want to copy. (You don't need to worry about column width.)
2. Choose Edit, Select All, then Edit, Copy.
3. Switch to a blank Excel worksheet, and then choose Edit, Paste.

Once you have the data in Excel, you can use Excel's formatting, formula, pivot table, and other features to get a good-looking printout with the summary and analysis that you need. For example, you might want to analyze the messages from an Exchange public discussion folder to find out how many messages are being posted by each person every month.

### 22.1.3 Performing a Word mail merge

Outlook 2000 and 2002 allow you to start a merge to Word directly from any Outlook contacts folder. With that approach, you can even include cus-

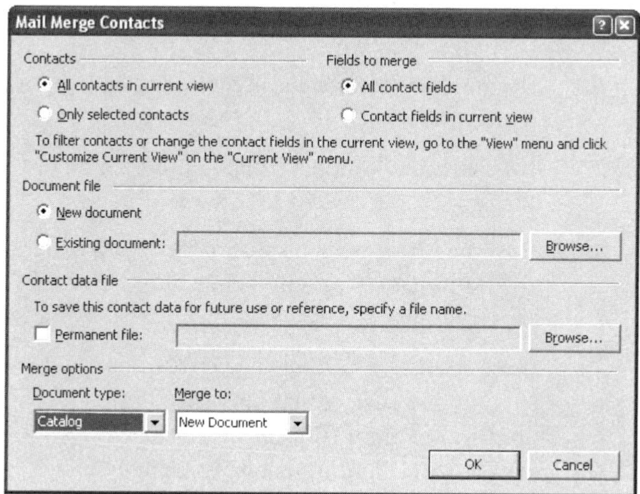


**Figure 22.4** *Perform a mail merge to Microsoft Word from any Outlook contacts folder.*

tom fields in the merge document. Start in the Outlook contacts folder that contains the data you want to print and follow these steps:

1. Select one or more names in the folder.
2. Choose Tools, Mail Merge.
3. Make your choices on the Mail Merge Contacts dialog box (Figure 22.4), then click OK.
4. After Word displays the merge document, add merge fields, other text, and formatting as needed. Save the merge document if you think you might use it again.
5. Click the Merge button in Word.

In Step 3, if you want to build a list or table of items, select Catalog under Document Type. If you want to see custom fields in the Word merge field list, make sure you choose All Contact Fields under Fields To Merge. Any custom fields must be defined in the User-Defined Fields in Folder list in the Field Chooser.

---

**Note:** If you include any e-mail address fields in the merge document, Outlook will display the Address Book–access security prompt.

---

### 22.1.4 Building an HTML message or post

In Chapter 20, "Common Outlook Form and Item Techniques," you learned how to create an HTML message that displays the fields from a custom Outlook form in a tabular format. You can use this same technique to print an item. Taking again the Equipment Repair Request form from Chapter 20 as an example, add a command button named cmdPrint and the code in Listing 22.1.

The `cmdPrint_Click` procedure calls the `AddRow()` function from Listing 20.10. Also compare the `cmdPrint_Click` procedure with the `cmdSendHTML_Click` procedure from Listing 20.10; the main difference is the use of the `PrintOut` method to print an item rather than send it:

```
objPost.PrintOut
```

This method is well suited to forms with a tabular format. You can make the printout as plain or fancy as your HTML coding skills allow.

**Listing 22.1** *Create a Post Item To Print an Item from a Custom Form*

```
Sub cmdPrint_Click()
    Const olPostItem = 6
    Dim objPost
    Dim strHTML
    Dim strDetails
    Set objPost = Application.CreateItem(olPostItem)
    objPost.Subject = Item.Subject
    strDetails = Item.Body
    strHTML = "<table>" & AddRow("Repair Item") & _
              AddRow("Description") & _
              AddRow("Equipment Location") & _
              AddRow("Room Number") & _
              AddRow("Contact Name") & _
              AddRow("Contact Phone") & _
              "<tr><td><strong>Date: </strong>" & _
              "</td><td>" & Now & "</tr></table>"
    If strDetails <> "" Then
        strHTML = strHTML & "<p>" & strDetails & "</p>"
    End If
    objPost.HTMLBody = strHTML
    objPost.PrintOut
    Set objPost = nothing
End Sub
```

---

**Tip:** Any printing that you do from code will use the default printer set for your computer. If you want Outlook to use a different printer, exit Outlook, change the printer in Control Panel, Printers, and then restart Outlook.

---

One advantage of using this print technique is that it's an all-Outlook method self-contained in the original form. The key disadvantage is that you can't get rid of the normal header that Outlook puts on a post printout to show the current user name and Conversation, Posted To, and Subject fields.

## 22.2 Sending output to Microsoft Excel

For reports that require more formatting than Outlook views can provide or in which you want to perform complex data manipulation, Microsoft Excel is a good tool. The row and column layout of an Excel worksheet is very similar to a table view in Outlook and is easy to handle in code.

The feature that makes it possible for you to write code in Outlook to produce reports in Excel is called Office *automation*. You can start an instance of any other Microsoft Office program (or use an existing copy if it's already running), create a new document, and add data to it using the other program's object model.

First, you have to learn the basics of opening a worksheet in Excel and adding data to it. Then, you will look at a specific example, in which you extract the names and addresses from an Outlook distribution list.

### 22.2.1 Understanding Excel report basics

To work with Excel objects in VBA, choose Tools, References, and then check the box for Microsoft Excel 10.0 Object Library. (If you have an earlier version of Excel, check the box for its library.) Put the code in Listing 22.2 in a new VBA module to start a copy of Excel and open a new, blank workbook.

The `GetExcelWS()` function not only returns an `Excel.Worksheet` object that we can work with, but also sets the module-level variable `m_blnWeOpenedExcel` to `True` or `False` depending on whether Excel was already open. The `Set objExcel = GetObject(, "Excel.Application")` statement checks whether Excel is already running. If Excel is not

**Listing 22.2** *Set a Variable To Track the Status of Excel at the Same Time As You Create a Worksheet*

```
Private m_blnWeOpenedExcel As Boolean

Function GetExcelWS() As Excel.Worksheet
    Dim objExcel As Excel.Application
    Dim objWB As Excel.Workbook
    Dim objWS As Excel.Worksheet
    On Error Resume Next
    m_blnWeOpenedExcel = False
    Set objExcel = GetObject(, "Excel.Application")
    If objExcel Is Nothing Then
        Set objExcel = CreateObject("Excel.Application")
        m_blnWeOpenedExcel = True
    End If
    Set objWB = objExcel.Workbooks.Add
    Set GetExcelWS = objWB.Worksheets(1)
    Set objExcel = Nothing
    Set objWB = Nothing
End Function

Sub RestoreExcel()
    Dim objExcel As Excel.Application
    On Error Resume Next
    Set objExcel = GetObject(, "Excel.Application")
    If m_blnWeOpenedExcel Then
        objExcel.Quit
    Else
        objExcel.Visible = True
    End If
    Set objExcel = Nothing
End Sub
```

running, you can create a new instance of Excel with the `Set objExcel = CreateObject("Excel.Application")` statement.

The `RestoreExcel` subroutine uses the value of `m_blnWeOpenedExcel` to put Excel back in its original state after your code runs. A standard framework for populating and displaying or printing an Excel worksheet, therefore, looks like this:

```
Sub GenericExcelReport()
    Dim objWS as Excel.Worksheet
    Set objWS = GetExcelWS()
    If Not objWS Is Nothing Then
        fill the worksheet with data
        objWS.Application.Visible = True
        objWS.Activate
        objWS.Printout
```

```
            objWS.Parent.Close SaveChanges:=False
            Call RestoreExcel
        End If
        Set objWS = Nothing
    End Sub
```

If you want to print the worksheet without showing it to the user, omit the `Application.Visible` and `Activate` statements. If you want to display the worksheet but not print it, omit the `Printout`, `Close`, and `Call RestoreExcel` statements. (There is no need to restore Excel to its former state if you're displaying a worksheet because you will want to leave Excel open.)

The next step is to put data into the worksheet. Within a worksheet, use the `Cells` object to specify a particular cell and put data into it. The `Cells` object takes row and column numbers as parameters using the syntax `Cells(`*`row, col`*`)`. This code fragment puts the text `"My First Excel Report"` into cell A1 (or row 1, column 1) and the text `"End of Report"` into cell E4 (or row 4, column 5) of an `objWS` worksheet object:

```
objWS.Cells(1, 1) = "My First Excel Report"
objWS.Cells(4, 5) = "End of Report"
```

---

**Tip:** Unlike Outlook, Excel includes a macro recorder that turns your keystrokes into VBA code. Choose Tools, Macro, Record New Macro to start the macro recorder. Perform various operations in Excel and click the recorder's Stop button when you finish. Choose Tools, Macros; select your recorded macro; and then click Edit to open the macro in VBA. You can copy code from Excel's VBA window into your Outlook project, editing it as necessary to change the variable names. This can be a useful technique for discovering formatting properties and other methods without reading up on the Excel object model.

---

Another useful Excel object is the `Range` object, which can cover an area that includes more than one cell, even nonadjacent areas. For simple rectangular ranges, you can use the `Cells` object to define a `Range` by its upper-left and lower-right corners. The `MyFirstExcelReport` procedure in Listing 22.3 adds the text from the code snippet above, then gives it bold formatting and displays it to the user. It uses the `GetExcelWS()` function from Listing 22.2.

Use the Object Browser to find out more about Excel objects, properties, and methods.

**Listing 22.3** *Use a Module-Level Worksheet Object Variable for Excel Reports*

```
Sub MyFirstExcelReport()
    Dim objWS as Excel.Worksheet
    Dim objRange As Excel.Range
    Set objWS = GetExcelWS()
    If Not objWS Is Nothing Then
        objWS.Cells(1, 1) = "My First Excel Report"
        objWS.Cells(4, 5) = "End of Report"
        Set objRange = objWS.Range _
          (objWS.Cells(1, 1), objWS.Cells(4, 5))
        objRange.Font.Bold = True
        objWS.Application.Visible = True
        objWS.Activate
    End If
    Set objRange = Nothing
    Set objWS = Nothing
End Sub
```

### 22.2.2 Building a distribution list report

For a practical example of Excel as a report tool, consider the `DistListItem` object in Outlook—a personal distribution list contained in a contacts folder. It holds a list of addresses that can either point to entries in your address books or serve as one-time addresses. The example in Listing 22.4 is designed to run from a toolbar button on an `Inspector` window and work with the currently displayed item (`ActiveInspector.CurrentItem`). It retrieves each member of the distribution list and puts its display name, e-mail address, and address type (such as SMTP for Internet mail) into an Excel worksheet.

Here are a few notes on the code:

- The `DLToExcel` procedure uses the `GetExcelWS()` function from Listing 22.2.
- The syntax for getting Outlook object properties should be familiar, such as `objDL.Subject` for the name of the distribution list.
- The `intStartRow` variable sets the starting location for the list of members (i.e., the first row where data will appear).
- The loop that gets each distribution list member (`objDL.GetMember(I)`) and copies data from three fields to cells in three columns will trigger the Outlook Address Book security prompt because `GetMember()` returns an Outlook `Recipient` object. The `AddressEntry`

**Listing 22.4** *Extract the Members of a Distribution List*

```
Sub DLToExcel()
    Dim objWS as Excel.Worksheet
    Dim objApp As Outlook.Application
    Dim objDL As Object
    Dim objRecip As Outlook.Recipient
    Dim objAddrEntry As Outlook.AddressEntry
    Dim objRange As Excel.Range
    Dim I As Integer
    Dim intRow As Integer
    Dim intStartRow As Integer
    Dim intCol As Integer
    On Error Resume Next
    Set objApp = CreateObject("Outlook.Application")
    Set objDL = objApp.ActiveInspector.CurrentItem
    If objDL Is Nothing Then
        GoTo Exit_DLToExcel
    ElseIf objDL.Class <> olDistributionList Then
        MsgBox _
          "The current item is not a distribution list."
        GoTo Exit_DLToExcel
    End If
    Set objWS = GetExcelWS()
    objWS.Cells(1, 1) = objDL.Subject
    intStartRow = 3
    intRow = intStartRow
    For I = 1 To objDL.MemberCount
        Set objAddrEntry = objDL.GetMember(I).AddressEntry
        With objAddrEntry
            objWS.Cells(intRow, 1) = .Name
            objWS.Cells(intRow, 2) = .Address
            objWS.Cells(intRow, 3) = .Type
        End With
        intRow = intRow + 1
    Next
    intRow = intRow - 1
    Set objRange = m_objWS.Range _
      (objWS.Cells(3, 1), objWS.Cells(intRow, 3))
    For I = 1 To 3
        objRange.Columns(I).EntireColumn.AutoFit
    Next
    objWS.Names.Add _
        Name:=Replace(objDL.Subject, " ", ""), _
        RefersTo:="=" & "" & objWS.Name & _
        "!" & objRange.Address & ""
    objWS.Application.Visible = True
    objWS.Activate
```

**Listing 22.4** *Extract the Members of a Distribution List (continued)*

```
Exit_DLToExcel:
    Set objApp = Nothing
    Set objDL = Nothing
    Set objRecip = Nothing
    Set objAddrEntry = Nothing
    Set objWS = Nothing
    Set objRange = Nothing
End Sub
```

object will also trigger security prompts, so when the prompt appears, you should authorize access for several minutes.

- The `Autofit` method is used to adjust the width of each column in the `Range` object defined for the member list to make sure that the user can see the complete name and address.
- The procedure also assigns a name to `objRange`. Named ranges are an important Excel feature that make it easy to use a particular set of cells for mail merge, import into Outlook, and other functions.

The `For ... Next` block is the heart of the `DLToExcel` subroutine. You can use this type of block to put any kind of Outlook data into Excel cells. For example, if you want to copy data from all items in an Outlook `MAPIFolder` object named `objFolder`, you would set the value for the starting row and use a `For Each ... Next` loop to pick up properties from all items in the folder:

```
intRow = 1
For Each objItem in objFolder.Items
    objWS.Cells(intRow, 1) = objItem.property1
    objWS.Cells(intRow, 2) = objItem.property2
    more code to set property values
    objWS.Cells(intRow, n) = _
      objItem.UserProperties("propertyn")
    intRow = intRow + 1
Next
```

The last line in the `For Each ... Next` loop increments `intRow` so that data input for the next item takes place on a blank new row. After the loop finishes with the last item, the worksheet will contain a block of `intRow` – 1 rows and *n* columns, containing data from *n* fields in `intRow` – 1 items from the folder.

**Tip:** You can make Excel or Word print to a specific printer by changing the value of the `Application.ActivePrinter` property to the name of the printer you want to use, something you can't do with Outlook.

Notice that you can extract data from custom Outlook fields, using the expression `objItem.UserDefinedFields.Find(`*`property`*`)` instead of `objItem.property`. This is a valuable way to export information from custom fields for use in Excel or in another program that can read either Excel data files or delimited files (one of the Save As file formats available in Excel).

### 22.2.3 Formatting Outlook data for Excel

Because Outlook and Excel display data in different ways, you way need some small helper functions to make Outlook data look good in Excel. The functions in this section will help you format date/time, Boolean, and text fields properly.

**Listing 22.5** *Convert "None" Date Values to Null*

```
Function DateToExcel(PropVal)
    If IsDate(PropVal) And _
      PropVal = #1/1/4501# Then
        DateToExcel = Null
    Else
        DateToExcel = PropVal
    End If
End Function
```

**Listing 22.6** *Convert True and False Values to Strings*

```
Function YesNoToExcel(PropVal)
    Select Case PropVal
        Case True
            YesNoToExcel = "Yes"
        Case False
            YesNoToExcel = "No"
        Case Else
            YesNoToExcel = PropVal
    End Select
End Function
```

**Listing 22.7** *Clean Up Text to Fit into Excel Cells*

```
Function TextToExcel(PropVal)
    If VarType(PropVal) = vbString Then
        PropVal = Replace(PropVal, vbCr, " ")
        PropVal = Replace(PropVal, vbTab, "    "
        PropVal = Left(PropVal, 32767)
    Else
        TextToExcel = PropVal
    End If
End Function
```

---

**Note:** The functions in this section do not use data types for the arguments and function declarations for two reasons. First, leaving the typing out makes them suitable for use with VBScript behind Outlook forms. Second, all the functions are designed so that you can pass through data of any type. If the data does not need to be changed to work well in a worksheet, the function returns the data unchanged.

---

Use the `DateToExcel()` function in Listing 22.5 to handle the `#1/1/4501#` date that Outlook displays as "None" when the user has not selected a date.

Use the `YesNoToExcel()` function in Listing 22.6 to convert data in yes/no properties to the strings `"Yes"` and `"No"`. Otherwise, Excel will use the values `-1` and `0`.

Use the `TextToExcel()` function in Listing 22.7 to remove carriage returns and tabs from text and truncate the string to the maximum number of characters an Excel cell can hold. (Excel displays many control characters with an ugly little rectangle.)

## 22.3 Sending output to Microsoft Word

Microsoft Word is an even more flexible reporting tool than Excel. Not only can it handle data in rows and columns like Excel, but it can also reproduce the look of a custom Outlook form, complete with checkboxes. Word reports are also ideal for combining information from different types of Outlook items. For example, you might need an invoice that totals the time you spent working on a particular contact's projects.

### 22.3.1 Understanding Word report basics

The basics of building reports with Word are very similar to the Excel techniques discussed earlier in the chapter. For VBA code, you must first use Tools, References to add a reference to the Microsoft Word 10.0 Library (or an earlier version, depending on what is installed on your system.)

Compare the basic `GetWordDoc()` and `RestoreWord` procedures in Listing 22.8 with the corresponding Excel procedures in Listing 22.2.

**Listing 22.8** *Set Variables to Track the Status of Word at the Same Time As You Create a Document*

```
Private m_blnWeOpenedWord As Boolean
Private m_blnWordPrintBackground As Boolean

Function GetWordDoc(Optional strTemplatePath As String) _
  As Word.Document
    Dim objWord As Word.Application
    On Error Resume Next
    m_blnWeOpenedWord = False
    Set objWord = GetObject(, "Word.Application")
    If objWord Is Nothing Then
        Set objWord = CreateObject("Word.Application")
        m_blnWeOpenedWord = True
    End If
    m_blnWordPrintBackground = _
      objWord.Options.PrintBackground
    If strTemplatePath = "" Then
        strTemplatePath = "Normal.dot"
    End If
    Set GetWordDoc = objWord.Documents.Add(strTemplatePath)
    On Error GoTo 0
    Set objWord = Nothing
End Function

Sub RestoreWord()
    Dim objWord As Word.Application
    On Error Resume Next
    Set objWord = GetObject(, "Word.Application")
    objWord.Options.PrintBackground = _
      m_blnWordPrintBackground
    If m_blnWeOpenedWord Then
        objWord.Quit
    Else
        objWord.Visible = True
    End If
    Set objWord = Nothing
End Sub
```

One difference is the addition of another module-level variable, `m_blnWordPrintBackground`, to store the user's normal setting for background printing, so we can restore it later. (You will usually want to print Outlook reports via Word in the background.) The other change is the addition of an optional argument to create a Word document using a specific template. As you will see, this is the key to making Word printouts that duplicate the look of Outlook form pages.

---

**Tip:** In Word, you can change the default location for templates by choosing Tools, Options, switching to the File Locations tab, and modifying the User Templates location. You can also set a Workgroup Templates location.

---

A Word template can contain boilerplate text, plus bookmarks and fields that you can use to place Outlook data in the text. You can create a template from a new or existing Word document by choosing File, Save As and changing the Save As Type to Document Template.

A standard framework for populating and displaying or printing a Word document looks like this:

```
Sub GenericWordReport()
    Set objDoc = GetWordDoc()
    If Not objDoc Is Nothing Then
        fill the document with data
        objDoc.Application.Visible = True
        objDoc.Activate
        objDoc.Application.Options.PrintBackground = True
        objDoc.Printout
        objDoc.Close SaveChanges:=wdDoNotSaveChanges
        Call RestoreWord
    End If
    Set objDoc = Nothing
End Sub
```

If you want to print the document without showing it to the user, omit the `Application.Visible` and `Activate` statements. If you want to display the document but not print it, omit the `PrintBackground`, `Printout`, `Close`, and `Call RestoreWord` statements. (There is no need to restore Word to its former state if you're displaying a document, because you will leave Word open.)

**Listing 22.9** *Create a Simple Word Document with VBA*

```
Sub MyFirstWordReport()
    Set objDoc = GetWordDoc()
    If Not objDoc Is Nothing Then
        objDoc.Content.InsertAfter _
          "This is the first paragraph. " & _
          vbCrLf & "This is the second paragraph."
        objDoc.Application.Visible = True
        objDoc.Activate
    End If
    Set objDoc = Nothing
End Sub
```

**Note:** As with Excel, you can use the macro recorder to investigate Word's methods and properties, then adapt at least some of the resulting VBA code to your Outlook projects. Many Word macros use the `Selection` object, which represents the currently selected text in a document. However, you will gain flexibility if you use the `Range` object instead. The sample code in this chapter uses `Range`, not `Selection`.

Word provides many different ways to insert text into a document. One that you will see several times in this chapter is the `Range.InsertAfter` method, which adds text after a given area of the document. You can now create your first Word document with VBA. Compare Listing 22.9 with the Excel version given in Listing 22.3.

The `Content` property of a Word document is a `Range` object that represents the entire content of the document. Use the Object Browser to find out more about Word objects, properties, and methods.

## 22.3.2 Duplicating a custom form

As you can imagine, it would be tedious to write code to insert text into a Word document, add data from an Outlook field, then add more text, and then another field, and so on. In addition, it would be very difficult to revise such a report if you wanted to change a few words of text.

A better technique is to lay out the report as a Word document with Word fields acting as placeholders for the Outlook data. The code you write only has to place the data into the fields. It does not need to perform any layout chores; you take care of those simply by editing the Word template as you would a document. As an added benefit, this approach makes it easy to divide up the work. For example, a user who is going to use the printouts could design the template while you write the code.

In this example, we will build a Word template to print out the Equipment Repair Request form shown in Figure 20.12. (You already saw earlier in this chapter how this form looks when printed with the built-in Print command and how to use custom VBScript code to build and print an HTML post.) The template should contain a text box or check box form field for each Outlook property that you plan to print with the exception of properties that may exceed 255 characters. For these, create only a bookmark where you want the text to be inserted. After building the template, we'll add VBScript that you can run from inside the form to invoke the template, fill its fields, then print it.

In a nutshell, here are the steps involved of creating a Word template that can be used to print the data from the Equipment Repair Request form:

1. In Word, press Ctrl+N to create a new document.
2. At the top of the document, type and format the title as you want it to appear on the printout.
3. Choose Table, Insert Table to add a table with columns to match the number of apparent columns in the form's layout. The Equipment Repair Request form, for example, has labels and data controls arranged roughly in four columns, so you should use a four-column table in the Word template. (You will add enough rows for all the fields.)
4. Turn off the borders for the Word table: Choose Table, Select, Table. Next, choose Format, Borders and Shading, and under Setting, choose None, and then click OK.
5. Choose View, Toolbars, Forms to display the Forms toolbar (Figure 22.5).
6. Duplicate the layout of the Outlook form by typing text into a table cell for each label and adding a form field to a table cell for each data field. Use the Text Form Field and Check Box Form Field buttons on the Forms toolbar. Insert a bookmark using the Insert, Bookmark command to position the body of the request.
7. Set the properties for each form field, as described below.

8. Choose File, Save As and change the Save As Type to Document Template. Click the Save button to save the template to the default Word template location on your computer.

To add the form fields described in steps 5 and 6, use the buttons on the Forms toolbar. Click the Check Box Form Field button to duplicate both option buttons and check boxes from the Outlook form. Use the Text Form Field button to duplicate text boxes, combo boxes, and list boxes. Figure 22.5 shows the template with all fields added, plus some formatting for the text.

After the fields and text are in place, you need to set properties for each field. Right-click each shaded field, and then choose Properties to display the options for the selected field. Figure 22.6 shows the Options dialog box for the High check box shown in Figure 22.5.

Under Bookmark, set the name that you want to use for this field in your code. Use a name that's as close as you can make it to the Outlook field name, given that Word bookmarks cannot use spaces or punctuation.

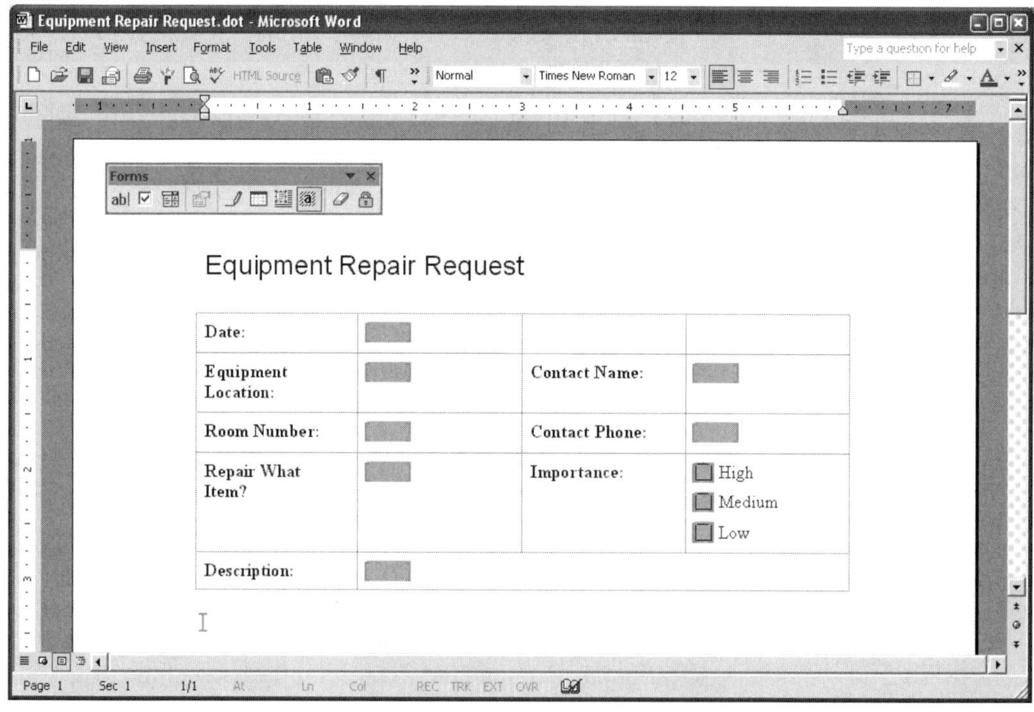


**Figure 22.5** *Use the Forms toolbar in Word to insert form fields that your code can fill with Outlook data.*

Check Box Form Field Options
Check box size
Auto
Exactly:
10 pt
Default value
Not checked
Checked
Run macro on
Entry:
Exit:
Field settings
Bookmark:
High
Check box enabled
Calculate on exit
Add Help Text...
OK
Cancel

**Figure 22.6** *Set a bookmark and other options for each field in the template.*

If you plan to allow users to view the form before printing, you may want to clear the Check Box Enabled option to prevent users from accidentally changing the value of a check box field. For text box fields, the equivalent option is Fill-in Enabled, as shown in Figure 22.7.

Here are a few more tips for working with form fields and templates:

- Before starting your template, compile a list of all Outlook fields that you want to include. Right-click each data control on the source Outlook form and choose Properties to check the field name on the Value tab.
- Use only the Text Form Field and Check Box Form Field buttons on the Forms toolbar to insert fields. Since users won't be filling out this form in Word, you don't need to use the Drop-Down Form Field button at all. Consider using a group of check boxes for fields where

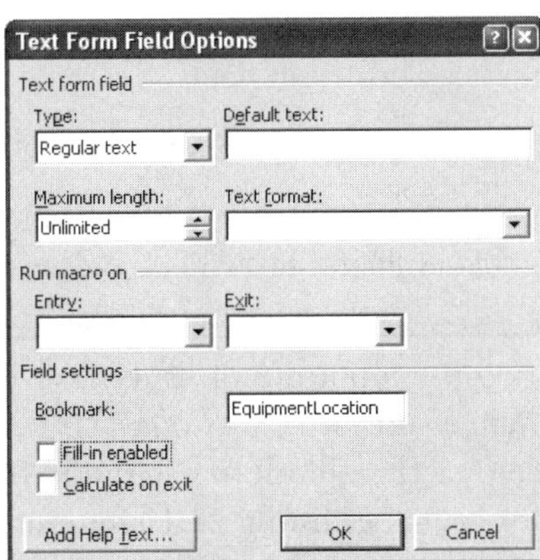


**Figure 22.7** *Set Regular Text as the Type for data that your code will copy from Outlook to text form fields.*

users choose from a built-in Outlook property with a limited number of choices, such as Importance.

- Choose Regular Text as the format for all text fields that you plan to fill with Outlook data. If special formatting is needed, do it in your Outlook code, not in the field properties.
- Don't use a form field in Word to represent the large message box on an Outlook form. Form fields don't handle multiple paragraphs very well; they show boxes where you would expect to have carriage returns and line feeds. Instead, insert a bookmark by itself, without a form field.
- Figure 22.5 shows an I-beam below the table to mark the location of the bookmark for the Details field. To see bookmark locations, choose Tools, Options, View and check the Bookmarks box.
- You really don't have to use form fields at all. Instead, you could use bookmarks without the form fields to set the location for any of your Outlook data fields to be inserted. The advantages of form fields are that the field placeholders are easier to see and format and they include checkboxes.

Next, you need to write the code to print the Equipment Repair Request form from a command button named `cmdPrint` on the form. There are three basic syntaxes for inserting the data into Word—one for check box form fields, one for text box form fields where the data does not exceed 255 characters, and one for text properties that have more than 255 characters or are likely to contain carriage returns and linefeeds. For check box and text box form fields, you work with the document's `FormFields` collection. For bookmarks set for long text properties, you work with the `Bookmarks` collection.

Use this syntax for check box form fields:

```
objDoc.FormFields(CheckBoxFieldName).CheckBox.Value = expr
```

where *`CheckBoxFieldName`* is the bookmark you assigned to the field and *`expr`* is an expression that evaluates to `True` or `False`.

---

**Tip:** For Outlook form option buttons or list boxes with a limited number of choices, you may want to use an `If ... ElseIf ... End If` block or a `Select Case ... End Select` block to determine which check box field value needs to be set to `True`. See listing 22.10 for examples.

---

Use one of these syntaxes for text box form fields:

```
objDoc.FormFields(TextBoxFieldName1).Result = _
  Item.UserProperties(PropertyName)
objDoc.FormFields(TextBoxFieldName2).Result = _
  Item.Property
```

where *TextBoxFieldName#* is the bookmark assigned to the field, *PropertyName* is the name of a custom Outlook item property, and *Property* is the name of a built-in Outlook property.

For long text properties (such as the `Body` property), use a bookmark by itself to mark the location in the document and this syntax to insert text:

```
objDoc.Bookmarks(BookmarkName).Range.InsertAfter _
  Item.Body
```

The complete VBScript code for printing the Equipment Repair Request form is given in Listing 22.10. The first procedure, `cmdPrint_Click`, is the event handler for a `cmdPrint` button that you'd need to add to the form. It starts Word, launches a new document based on the Equipment Repair Request.dot template, and then calls the `FillFields` procedure to push the Outlook data into the document's fields and bookmark. If you want users to review the document before printing, replace the `objDoc.PrintOut` and `objDoc.Close` statements with an `objDoc.Activate` statement.

Listing 22.10 includes VBScript versions of the `GetWordDoc()` function and the `RestoreWord` subroutine. A sample of the printout is shown in Figure 22.8. Notice that it uses different fonts, but that there is no code in Listing 22.10 to perform any font formatting. All the formatting is in the template, which means if you want to change the look of the printout, all you have to do is change the template. The Outlook form code remains the same. Including the printing code in an Outlook form and marrying it to a Word template is a good, flexible solution for creating good-looking printouts.

### 22.3.3 Building reports from related items

To complete your Outlook report skills, you need to be able to combine related Outlook items from two different folders. The example in this section is an invoice listing the hours spent working for a particular contact, as recorded in the Journal folder. This application uses the `Links` collection that you learned about in Chapter 20, "Common Outlook Form and Item Techniques," and introduces techniques for working with Word tables.

**Listing 22.10** *Use a Word Template to Print from a Custom Outlook Form*

```
Dim m_blnWeOpenedWord
Dim m_blnWordPrintBackground
Const wdDoNotSaveChanges = 0
Const olDiscard = 1
Const olImportanceHigh = 2
Const olImportanceNormal = 1
Const olImportanceLow = 0

Sub cmdPrint_Click()
    Dim objDoc
    Set objDoc = GetWordDoc("Equipment Repair Request.dot")
    Call FillFields(objDoc)
    objDoc.Application.Options.PrintBackground = True
    objDoc.PrintOut
    objDoc.Close wdDoNotSaveChanges
    Call RestoreWord
    Set objDoc = Nothing
End Sub

Sub FillFields(objDoc)
    Dim colFields
    Set colFields = objDoc.FormFields
    colFields("RequestDate").Result = Item.LastModificationTime
    colFields("EquipmentLocation").Result = _
      Item.UserProperties("Equipment Location")
    colFields("RoomNumber").Result = _
      Item.UserProperties("Room Number")
    colFields("RepairItem").Result = _
      Item.UserProperties("Repair Item")
    colFields("ContactName").Result = _
      Item.UserProperties("Contact Name")
    colFields("ContactPhone").Result = _
      Item.UserProperties("Contact Phone")
    colFields("Description").Result = _
     Item.UserProperties("Description")
    Select Case Item.Importance
        Case olImportanceHigh
            colFields("High").CheckBox.Value = True
        Case olImportanceNormal
            colFields("High").CheckBox.Value = True
        Case olImportanceLow
            colFields("Low").CheckBox.Value = True
    End Select
    objDoc.Bookmarks("Details").Range.InsertAfter Item.Body
    Set colFields = Nothing
End Sub

Function GetWordDoc(strTemplatePath)
    Dim objWord
    On Error Resume Next
    m_blnWeOpenedWord = False
```

**Listing 22.10** *Use a Word Template to Print from a Custom Outlook Form (continued)*

```
    Set objWord = GetObject(, "Word.Application")
    If objWord Is Nothing Then
        Set objWord = CreateObject("Word.Application")
        m_blnWeOpenedWord = True
    End If
    m_blnWordPrintBackground = _
      objWord.Options.PrintBackground
    If strTemplatePath = "" Then
        strTemplatePath = "Normal.dot"
    End If
    Set GetWordDoc = objWord.Documents.Add(strTemplatePath)
    Set objWord = Nothing
End Function

Sub RestoreWord()
    Dim objWord
    On Error Resume Next
    Set objWord = GetObject(, "Word.Application")
    objWord.Options.PrintBackground = _
      m_blnWordPrintBackground
    If m_blnWeOpenedWord Then
        objWord.Quit
    Else
        objWord.Visible = True
    End If
    Set objWord = Nothing
End Sub
```

**Figure 22.8** *This Word printout duplicates the layout of the form in Figure 20.12. Compare with Figure 22.1.*

Equipment Repair Request

| | | | |
|---|---|---|---|
| **Date:** | 1/1/4501 | | |
| **Equipment Location:** | Main Building Conference Room | **Contact Name:** | Sue Mosher |
| **Room Number:** | 102 | **Contact Phone:** | (703) 555-1234 |
| **Repair What Item?** | coffee maker | **Importance:** | ☒ High<br>☐ Medium<br>☐ Low |
| **Description:** | leaks | | |

Started leaking last week, but now it's making a big mess.

You'll see how to insert data into Word table rows and columns and add a new row to a Word table.

As with the example in the previous section, this solution has two parts—a Word template and Outlook code, in this case VBA code to work with the currently selected contact. No custom form is involved.

Create a template as described in the previous section to provide form fields to match the contact properties that you want to include in the report. We've also added a form field named `InvoiceNum` to hold the invoice number. Next, insert a table—four columns, two rows—below the contact information. This table will hold the data from the Journal folder. You can add column headings to it, but don't insert any form fields. The completed template should look like Figure 22.9. After you create the template, save it as Invoice.dot.

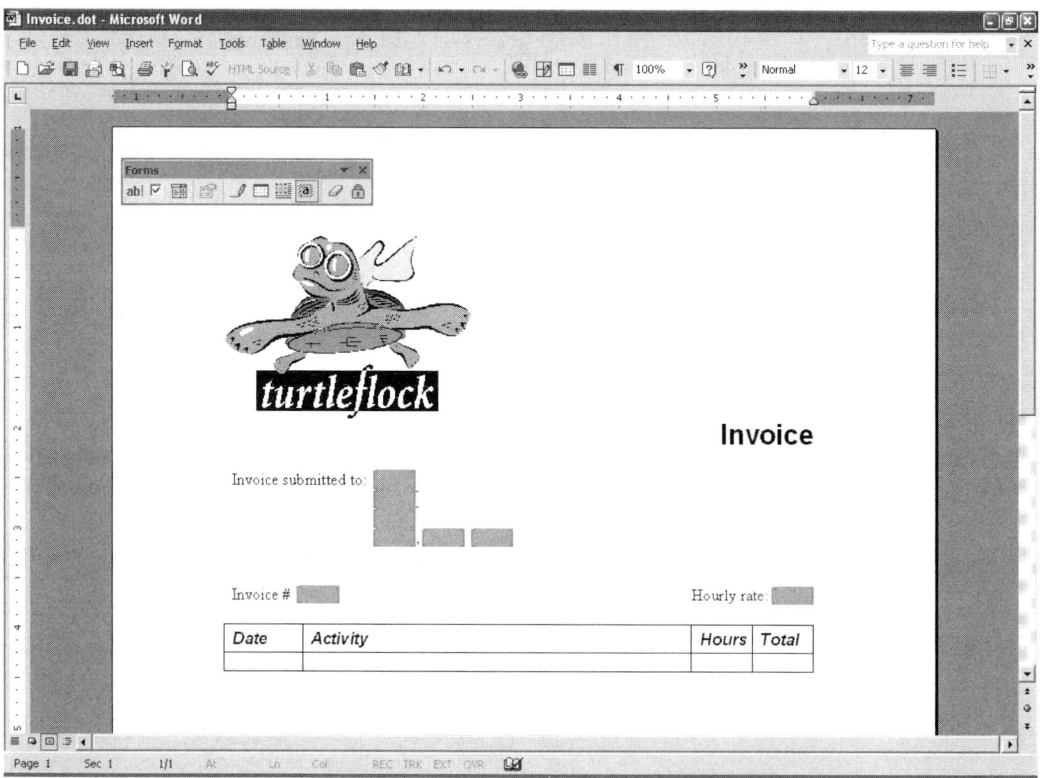


**Figure 22.9** *The basics of an invoice template include form fields and a table, but you can also add other text, formatting, and even a logo.*

The syntax for working with tables in Word is not that different from working with cells in Excel. Use this syntax to assign an object variable to the journal detail table, the only table in the template:

```
Set objTable = objDoc.Tables(1)
```

To add a new row to the table, use this syntax:

```
objTable.Rows.Add
```

Finally, the syntax to fill a cell with data uses the `Cell` object and its *`row`* and *`col`* arguments:

```
objTable.Cell(row, col).Range.InsertAfter data
```

The data should be a string. Do any necessary formatting in your Outlook code.

---

**Note:** Note that you refer to a single cell in a Word table as `Table.Cell(`*`row, col`*`)`, while in Excel, you refer to a single cell as `Range.Cells(`*`row, col`*`)`.

---

Listing 22.11 contains the entire code for the invoice application. You may want to put all the code for the invoice application in a separate Outlook VBA module to make it easier to manage. It makes a few assumptions:

- The hourly billing rate for the contact item is stored in the `BillingInformation` property, and the template includes a matching form field.
- The Journal folder contains only those items that have not yet been invoiced.
- Several procedures are available either as private procedures in the same module or as public procedures in other Outlook VBA modules—`GetCurrentItem()` from Listing 18.7 and `GetWordDoc()` and `RestoreWord` from Listing 22.8, and `DateID()` from Listing 20.5.

Which procedure actually runs the invoice application? It's the `PrintInvoice` subroutine—the only procedure not declared `Private`. The `PrintInvoice` subroutine calls five other routines in turn:

1. `GetWordDoc()` to create a new Word document using the Invoice.dot template and assign it to the `m_objDoc` module-level variable

2. `GetCurrentItem()` from Listing 18.7 to get the currently selected or open contact and assign it to the `m_objItem` module-level variable
3. `DateID()` from Listing 20.5 to generate a unique invoice number based on the date and time
4. `FillContactFields` to fill in the Word form fields in the template with corresponding data from the selected contact, using the techniques described in the previous section
5. `FillTable` to loop through the Journal folder, check each item using the `HasLinkToContact()` function, post entries linked to the contact to the Word table, calculate the charge for each entry, and keep a running total of the charges to post in the last row of the table

**Listing 22.11** *Collate Data from Two Folders into One Word Document*

```
Private m_objDoc As Word.Document
Private m_objItem As Object

Sub PrintInvoice()
    On Error Resume Next
    Set m_objItem = GetCurrentItem()
    If m_objItem.Class = olContact Then
        Set m_objDoc = GetWordDoc("Invoice.dot")
        m_objDoc.FormFields("InvoiceNum").Result = DateID()
        Call FillContactFields
        Call FillTable
        m_objDoc.Application.Options.PrintBackground = True
        m_objDoc.PrintOut
        m_objDoc.Close SaveChanges:=wdDoNotSaveChanges
        Call RestoreWord
    Else
        MsgBox "Please select or open a contact."
    End If
    Set m_objItem = Nothing
    Set m_objDoc = Nothing
End Sub

Private Sub FillContactFields()
    With m_objDoc
        .FormFields("Name").Result = m_objItem.FullName
        .FormFields("Company").Result = _
          m_objItem.CompanyName
        .FormFields("Street").Result = _
          m_objItem.BusinessAddressStreet
        .FormFields("City").Result = _
          m_objItem.BusinessAddressCity
```

**Listing 22.11** *Collate Data from Two Folders into One Word Document (continued)*

```
            .FormFields("State").Result = _
              m_objItem.BusinessAddressState
            .FormFields("Zip").Result = _
              m_objItem.BusinessAddressPostalCode
            .FormFields("Rate").Result = _
              Format(m_objItem.BillingInformation, "Currency")
    End With
End Sub

Private Sub FillTable()
    Dim objApp As Outlook.Application
    Dim objNS As Outlook.NameSpace
    Dim objJournal As Outlook.MAPIFolder
    Dim colJournalItems As Outlook.Items
    Dim objItem As Outlook.JournalItem
    Dim objTable As Word.Table
    Dim curHourly As Currency
    Dim curItem As Currency
    Dim curTotal As Currency
    Dim intRow As Integer
    Dim strContactName As String
    On Error Resume Next
    Set objApp = CreateObject("Outlook.Application")
    Set objNS = objApp.GetNamespace("MAPI")
    Set objJournal = _
      objNS.GetDefaultFolder(olFolderJournal)
    Set colJournalItems = objJournal.Items
    colJournalItems.Sort "[Start]"
    Set objTable = m_objDoc.Tables(1)
    curHourly = CCur(m_objItem.BillingInformation)
    intRow = 2
    strContactName = LinkName(m_objItem)
    For Each objItem In colJournalItems
        If HasLinkToContact(objItem, strContactName) Then
            If intRow > 2 Then
                objTable.Rows.Add
            End If
            objTable.Cell(intRow, 1).Range.InsertAfter _
              FormatDateTime(objItem.Start, vbShortDate)
            objTable.Cell(intRow, 2).Range.InsertAfter _
              objItem.Type & " - " & objItem.Subject
            objTable.Cell(intRow, 3).Range.InsertAfter _
              Format(objItem.Duration / 60, "Standard")
            curItem = objItem.Duration / 60 * curHourly
            objTable.Cell(intRow, 4).Range.InsertAfter _
              Format(curItem, "Currency"
            curTotal = curTotal + curItem
            intRow = intRow + 1
        End If
```

**Listing 22.11** *Collate Data from Two Folders into One Word Document (continued)*

```
    Next
    objTable.Rows.Add
    objTable.Rows.Add
    objTable.Cell(intRow + 1, 3).Range.InsertAfter "TOTAL"
    objTable.Cell(intRow = 1, 4).Range.InsertAfter _
      Format(curTotal, "Currency")
    Set objApp = Nothing
    Set objNS = Nothing
    Set objJournal = Nothing
    Set colJournalItems = Nothing
    Set objItem = Nothing
    Set objTable = Nothing
End Sub

Private Function LinkName(objContact As ContactItem) _
  As String
    If objContact.FullName <> vbNullString Then
        LinkName = objContact.FullName
    Else
        LinkName = objContact.FileAs
    End If
End Function

Private Function HasLinkToContact(objItem As Object, _
  strName As String) As Boolean
    Dim objLinks As Outlook.Links
    Dim objLink As Outlook.Link
    Set objLinks = objItem.Links
    For Each objLink In objLinks
        If objLink.Name = strName Then
            HasLinkToContact = True
            GoTo Exit_HasLinkToContact
        End If
    Next

Exit_HasLinkToContact:
        Set objLink = Nothing
        Set objLinks = Nothing
End Function
```

In Outlook 2000, you need to use a routine such as `HasLinkToContact()` to determine whether a particular journal item has a link to the current contact because the journal items contain no field you can use with a `Find` or `Restrict` to locate linked items. In the next section, however, you will see how to use the `Search` object in Outlook 2002 to locate all items linked to the current contact.

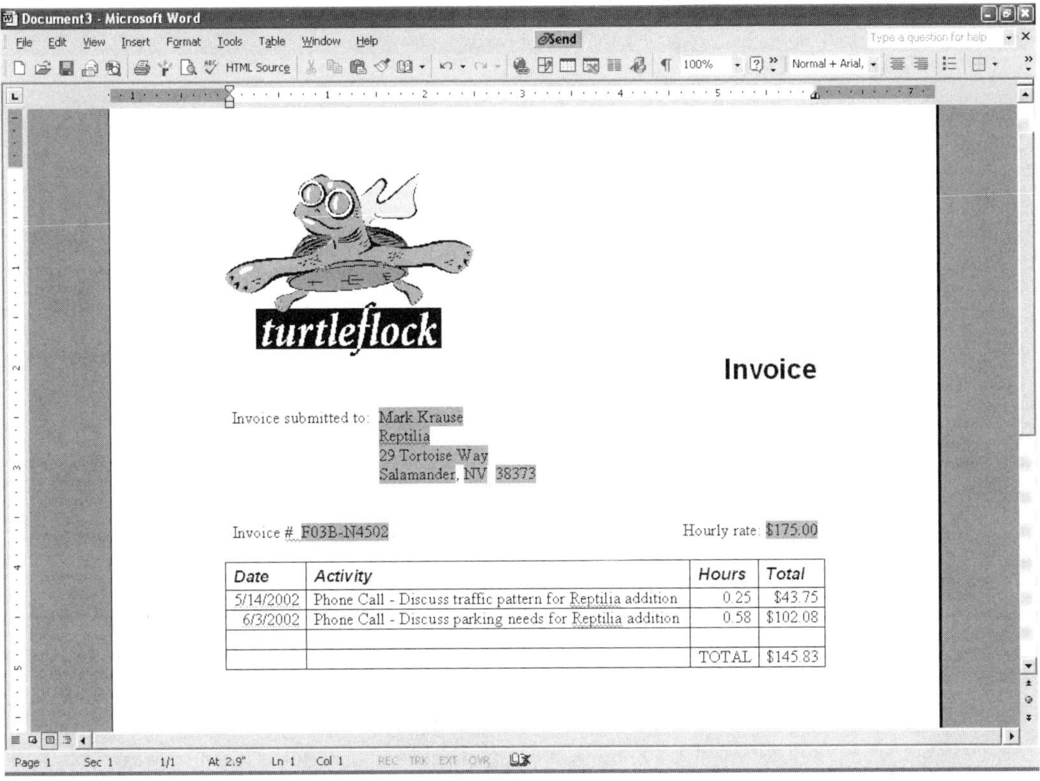

turtleflock

**Invoice**

Invoice submitted to: Mark Krause
Reptilia
29 Tortoise Way
Salamander, NV 38373

Invoice # F03B-N4502

Hourly rate: $175.00

| Date | Activity | Hours | Total |
|---|---|---|---|
| 5/14/2002 | Phone Call - Discuss traffic pattern for Reptilia addition | 0.25 | $43.75 |
| 6/3/2002 | Phone Call - Discuss parking needs for Reptilia addition | 0.58 | $102.08 |
| | | | |
| | | TOTAL | $145.83 |

**Figure 22.10** *This invoice demonstrates how well Word works as a reporting tool to combine items from different folders.*

Figure 22.10 shows the finished product: an invoice produced entirely from Outlook items, but laid out with a Word template.

### 22.3.4 Using Search to report on related items (Outlook 2002)

Checking every item in the Journal folder—as shown in the `For Each ... Next` loop in the `FillTable()` subroutine in the previous section—could be a lengthy process. Outlook 2002's `Search` object, discussed in Chapter 14, "Working with Items and Recipients," can improve the invoice application in two ways. Not only can it search specifically for the linked items in the Journal folder, but it can also search multiple folders, as long as they are in the same Personal Folders file or the user's default Exchange mailbox.

In order to program a search, place this code in the ThisOutlookSession module:

```
Private Sub Application_AdvancedSearchComplete _
  (ByVal SearchObject As Search)
    If SearchObject.Tag = "Links" Then
        g_strSearchStatus = "complete"
    End If
End Sub

Private Sub Application_AdvancedSearchStopped _
  (ByVal SearchObject As Search)
    If SearchObject.Tag = "Links" Then
        g_strSearchStatus = "stopped"
    End If
End Sub
```

Next, place the code in Listing 22.12 in the same module as the PrintInvoice procedure. Edit the PrintInvoice procedure to replace the Call FillTable statement with Call FillTableFromSearch.

---

**Note:** You can use either http://schemas.microsoft.com/mapi/id/{00062008-0000-0000-C000-000000000046}/853a101f or http://schemas.microsoft.com/mapi/id/{00062008-0000-0000-C000-000000000046}/8586001f as the DASL schema property to search for items linked to the current contact. These DASL schema names correspond to the fields that appear in the Field Chooser as Contact and Contacts respectively. The JournalItem and TaskItem objects have a related property called ContactNames that is not available for the AppointmentItem object. The beauty of using the DASL schema property is that it works with all three types of items.

---

Here are a few notes on the code in Listing 22.12:

- GetLinkedItems() is the procedure that actually launches the search. Remember that the Search object produces an asynchronous search. The DoEvents loop waits for one of the events in the ThisOutlookSession module to change the value of g_strSearchStatus.
- We needed to use a Select Case block to handle the three different types of items—appointments, journal entries, and tasks—because the Outlook model exposes different properties for each one.
- In the invoice application in the previous section, we could use the Items.Sort method to sort the items in the Journal folder by the

**Listing 22.12** *Use Outlook 2002's Search Object To Search Multiple Folders for Linked Items*

```
Public g_strSearchStatus as String

Private Sub FillTableFromSearch()
    Dim colResults As Outlook.Results
    Dim objTable As Word.Table
    Dim objItem As Object
    Dim curHourly As Currency
    Dim curItem As Currency
    Dim curTotal As Currency
    Dim intRow As Integer
    Dim intDuration As Integer
    Dim strContactName As String
    On Error Resume Next
    curHourly = CCur(m_objItem.BillingInformation)
    intRow = 2
    strContactName = LinkName(m_objItem)
    Set colResults = GetLinkedItems(strContactName)
    If colResults.Count = 0 Then
        MsgBox "No linked items found"
        GoTo Exit_FillTableFromSearch
    End If
    Set objTable = m_objDoc.Tables(1)
    For Each objItem In colResults
        If intRow > 2 Then
            objTable.Rows.Add
        End If
        Select Case objItem.Class
            Case olAppointment
                objTable.Cell(intRow, 1).Range.InsertAfter _
                  FormatDateTime(objItem.Start, vbShortDate)
                objTable.Cell(intRow, 2).Range.InsertAfter _
                  "Meeting - " & objItem.Subject
                intDuration = objItem.Duration
            Case olJournal
                objTable.Cell(intRow, 1).Range.InsertAfter _
                  FormatDateTime(objItem.Start, vbShortDate)
                objTable.Cell(intRow, 2).Range.InsertAfter _
                  objItem.Type & " - " & objItem.Subject
                intDuration = objItem.Duration
            Case olTask
                objTable.Cell(intRow, 1).Range.InsertAfter _
                  FormatDateTime(objItem.DateCompleted, _
                               vbShortDate)
                objTable.Cell(intRow, 2).Range.InsertAfter _
                  objItem.Subject
                intDuration = objItem.ActualWork
        End Select
        objTable.Cell(intRow, 3).Range.InsertAfter _
          Format(intDuration / 60, "Standard")
```

**Listing 22.12** *Use Outlook 2002's Search Object To Search Multiple Folders for Linked Items (continued)*

```
            curItem = intDuration / 60 * curHourly
            objTable.Cell(intRow, 4).Range.InsertAfter _
              Format(curItem, "Currency")
            curTotal = curTotal + curItem
            intRow = intRow + 1
        Next
        objTable.Sort ExcludeHeader:=True, _
                      SortFieldType:=wdSortFieldDate
        objTable.Rows.Add
        objTable.Rows.Add
        objTable.Cell(intRow + 1, 3).Range.InsertAfter "TOTAL"
        objTable.Cell(intRow = 1, 4).Range.InsertAfter _
          Format(curTotal, "Currency")

Exit_FillTableFromSearch:
    Set colResults = Nothing
    Set objItem = Nothing
    Set objTable = Nothing
End Sub

Function GetLinkedItems(strContactName) As Outlook.Results
    Dim objApp As Outlook.Application
    Dim objSearch As Outlook.Search
    Dim strFilter As String
    Dim strScope As String
    Dim lngCount As Long
    Set objApp = CreateObject("Outlook.Application")
    strFilter = _
        Quote("http://schemas.microsoft.com/mapi/id/" & _
              "{00062008-0000-0000-C000-000000000046}/" & _
              "853a101f") & " = " & SQLQuote(strContactName)
    strScope = "'Calendar', 'Tasks', 'Journal'"
    g_strSearchStatus = ""
    Set objSearch = objApp.AdvancedSearch(strScope, _
                    strFilter, , "Links")
    Do While g_strSearchStatus = ""
        DoEvents
    Loop
    If g_strSearchStatus = "complete" Then
        Set GetLinkedItems = objSearch.Results
    Else
        Set GetLinkedItems = Nothing
    End If
    Set objApp = Nothing
    Set objSearch = Nothing
End Function

Function SQLQuote(MyText) As String
    SQLQuote = Chr(39) & MyText & Chr(39)
End Function
```

`Start` date. You cannot sort a `Results` collection because it contains different types of items. Therefore, the code sorts the Word table on the Date column using the `Table.Sort` method.

- `SQLQuote()` is another handy little helper function. It surrounds text with single quotation marks.

## 22.4 Summary

Making data available through reports is an important programming technique because not everyone who needs to see your data will have Outlook. Printing from Outlook views, exporting to files that can be read by other programs, and using code to send data to Excel are all methods that have a place in your reporting repertoire. Microsoft Word is also an excellent reporting tool, particularly if you need to print from a custom form or combine information from two types of folders. The `Search` object in Outlook 2002 is a powerful new addition that can gather information from several folders.

In Chapter 23, "Exchange Server, Databases, and XML Web Services," we will look at some of the basic issues related to Microsoft Exchange public folders and various ways to connect to databases and XML Web services.

# 23

# *Exchange Server, Databases, and XML Web Services*

Beyond the Outlook screen on your desktop is a wider world of information—some of it stored within your organization and, increasingly, some of it is available through distributed databases and services on the Internet. This chapter will help you make those connections with other information sources, whether they exist as Exchange server public folders, databases, or XML Web services.

Highlights of this chapter include discussions of the following:

- How to use a custom Outlook form to announce a new public folder
- What features a folder home page can add to a public folder
- How to connect to Microsoft Access and SQL Server databases
- Which one line of code can fill a combo box with the contents of a database table
- How to get a unique sequential number from a database
- What new toolkit from Microsoft turns Outlook 2002 into a consumer of XML Web services
- How to use XML Web services to get the local time for a contact, validate a Zip code, and send a fax

## 23.1 Managing Exchange public folders

Outlook works great in a small workgroup with a POP3 or IMAP4 mail server. As you saw in Chapter 20, "Common Outlook Form and Item Techniques," it is even possible to exchange items created with custom forms via Internet mail. However, to get the full benefit of all the collaboration features in Outlook, you need Microsoft Exchange as your mail and collaboration server. Exchange Server supports shared folders with custom forms and views, as well as other programming features beyond the scope of this book, such as server-based event-driven code, workflow, and browser access to data.

One of Exchange Server's key application-building components is the public folder. Public folders can hold any type of Outlook item and can be replicated between Exchange servers in different cities, offering truly global access to your applications. Before adding any public folders, check with the Exchange administrator to find out where in the All Public Folders hierarchy you have permission to create new folders.

### 23.1.1 Setting folder properties

After creating a folder by using the File, New, Folder command, you may want to bring up its Properties dialog to set permissions and other properties. Right-click the folder in Outlook and then choose Properties to display the dialog box shown in Figure 23.1.

On the General tab, you can rename the folder, provide an optional description, and check the folder size. The most important setting on the General tab is the selection under When Posting to This Folder, Use. This sets the default form for the folder—the form displayed when the user presses Ctrl+N, chooses Actions, New, or clicks the New button. In most cases, you can use any published form as the folder default, as long as it

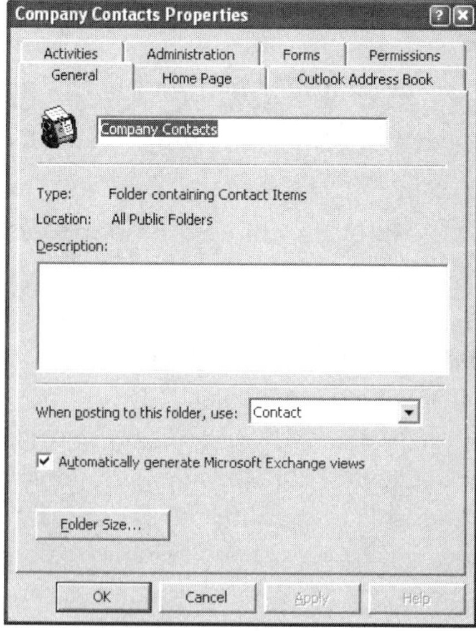


**Figure 23.1** *The Activities and Outlook Address Book tabs appear only on Contacts folders.*

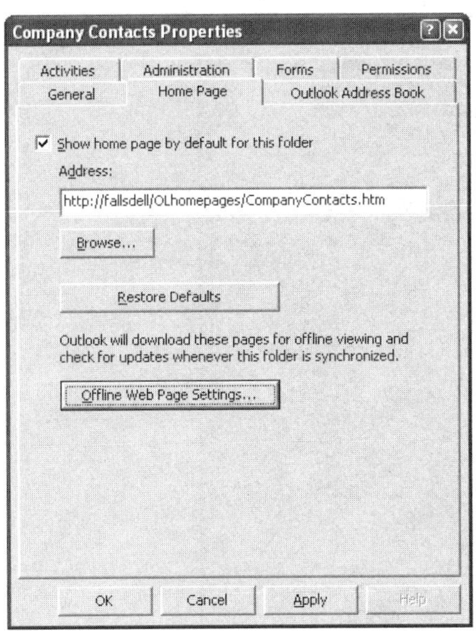


**Figure 23.2** *You can provide a Web page that goes with a folder.*

matches the type of item you designated for the folder when you created the folder. In other words, you can't use a modified Task form as the default for a folder created to hold Appointment items. The other exception is that you can never make a Message form the default for a folder because messages are designed for sending, not posting in folders.

On the second tab, Home Page, shown in Figure 23.2, you can associate a Web page with the folder and show it when the user switches to the folder. You can use any Web page as the folder home page, but Microsoft's intention for this feature is to have more pages like the Outlook Today page, which summarizes information in your own mailbox. Such pages use the OVC, which you already saw in Chapter 19, "More Controls for Outlook Forms." Later in this chapter, you'll see how it fits into a folder home page.

On the Administration tab (see Figure 23.3), set the initial view on the folder, the behavior of items dragged to the folder, and the current access state of the folder. It's common to make the folder available only to owners until you finish modifying and testing its properties. We'll return to the subject of views later in the chapter.

Also on the Administration tab are the Folder Assistant and Moderated Folder buttons, which allow you to add some simple automation to a folder without writing any programming code.

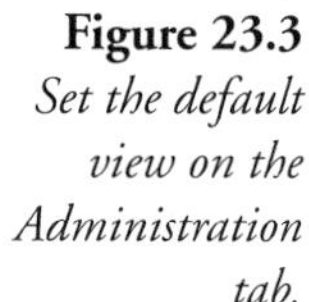

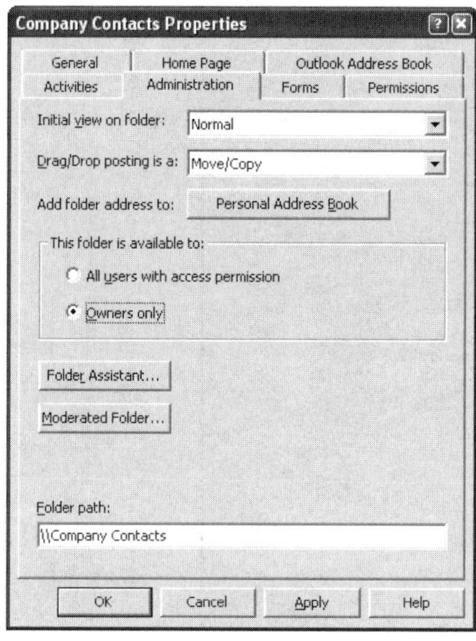


**Figure 23.3** *Set the default view on the Administration tab.*

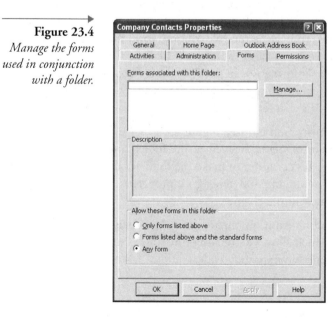

The fourth tab, Forms (see Figure 23.4), helps you manage forms that have been published to the folder's forms library. Use of the Forms Manager is covered in Chapter 24, "Deploying Forms and Applications."

On the Permissions tab (see Figure 23.5), you set permissions for everyone you want to have access to the folder. Click the Add button to add

**Figure 23.4** *Manage the forms used in conjunction with a folder.*

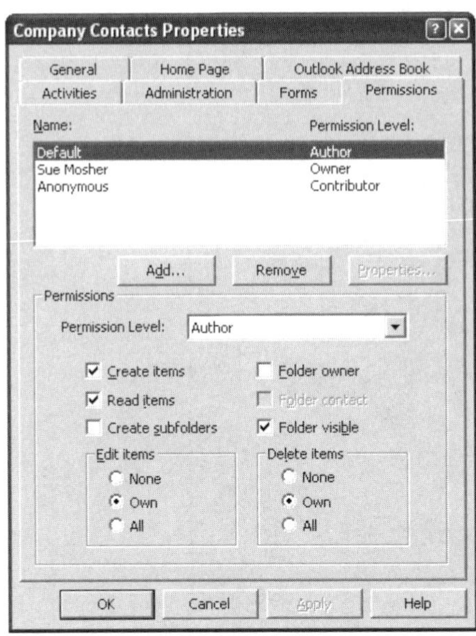


**Figure 23.5**
*Set permissions for a public folder.*

either individual Exchange users or an Exchange security group (Exchange 2000) or distribution list (Exchange 5.5). Then, choose a role from the Roles list, or select from among the individual check boxes and option buttons at the bottom of the Permissions section. Click Apply to set the per-

**Figure 23.6**
*Create activity groups to search for items related to a particular contact.*

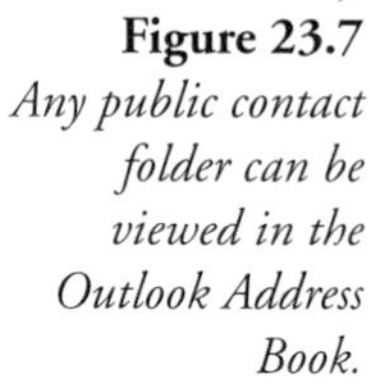

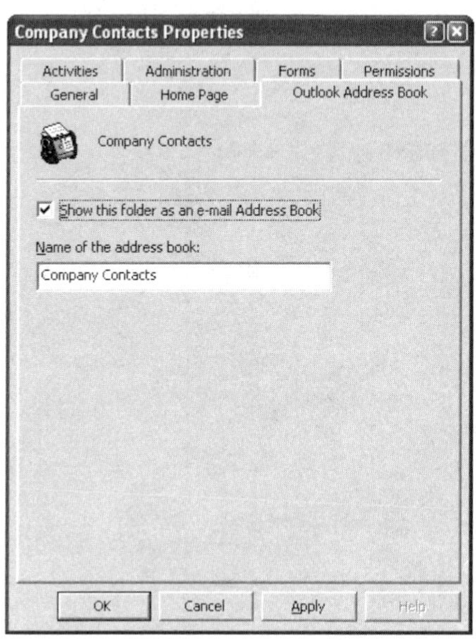


**Figure 23.7** *Any public contact folder can be viewed in the Outlook Address Book.*

missions for each user, group, or list, and then click OK to close the Properties dialog box.

Contacts folders have two additional tabs on the Properties dialog: Activities and Outlook Address Book. You learned in Chapter 20, "Common Outlook Form and Item Techniques," that the Activities tab governs what appears on the Activities page of contact items stored in the folder. However, unlike the Contacts folder in your mailbox, a public folder normally does not have any built-in activity groups (see Figure 23.6). In fact, the idea of activity "groups" is misleading in a public folder context because you can include only one public folder in any "group" as Exchange does not allow searching across subfolders.

The Outlook Address Book tab (Figure 23.7) does not have any settings useful for a folder administrator. These controls affect the display of a public contacts folder in the Outlook Address Book and are specific to each user, not controlled centrally.

Later in this chapter, you will see a custom form for Outlook 2002 that announces a new folder and offers recipients a custom button to add a public contacts folder to the Outlook Address Book.

### 23.1.2 Copying folder design

Setting all those properties probably seems like a lot of trouble. You can copy all or selected settings from one folder to another by following the following steps:

1. Switch to the target folder, the one that you want to copy the settings *to*.
2. Choose File, Folder, Copy Folder Design.
3. In the Copy Design From dialog box (see Figure 23.8), choose the source folder, the one you want to copy the settings *from*.
4. Check the boxes for the design elements you want to copy, and then click OK.

The tricky part about copying a folder design is remembering to start in the target folder and then select the source of the design from the Copy Design From dialog box. Remember that form names should be unique within an organization. You should not have the same name published to two different folders under the same name; if you do, republish the form in one folder using a different name.

Also, copying the folder design does not copy any custom property definitions in the folder. You will have to add those manually or using the code method described in Chapter 24, "Deploying Forms and Applications."

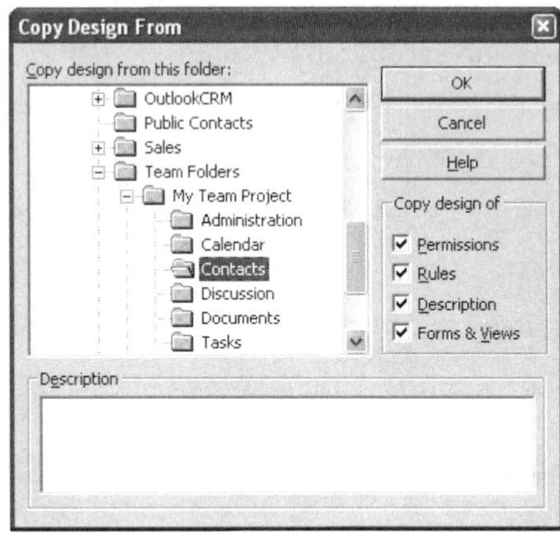


**Figure 23.8** *Copy one or more design elements from an existing folder into a different folder.*

### 23.1.3 Handling folder permissions

Once you move outside the folders in your own Exchange mailbox or in Personal Folders .pst files, keep in mind as you write code that you probably will not have access to every Exchange public folder that you encounter. You should consider these possibilities:

- A particular folder may not be visible to you.
- The folder may be visible in the hierarchy, but the current user may not have permission to view its contents.
- The folder along with its contents may be visible, but the user may not have permission to modify, create, or delete items in the folder.
- If the folder is not visible, any code that walks the folder tree (such as the `GetFolder()` function in Listing 12.7) simply will not find the folder.

### 23.1.4 Managing folder views

We discussed folder views in Chapter 22, "Designing Outlook Reports," but the focus there was on the effect that views have on printed reports. Outlook uses the same views, of course, for displaying data. If you want to restrict the views available on a public folder to only those that you design for the folder, follow these steps:

1. Right-click the folder, and choose Properties.
2. On the Administration tab of the Properties dialog, set the Initial View on Folder to a custom view that you have created.
3. Click OK to close the properties dialog.
4. Choose View, Current View, Define Views.
5. On the Define Views dialog box, check the box for Only Show Views Created for This Folder.
6. Click Close to return to the Outlook folder.

### 23.1.5 New Outlook 2002 folder properties and methods

Outlook 2002 includes several new properties and methods that can help with folder management. These are described in Table 23.1 and discussed earlier in Chapter 12.

**Table 23.1** *New MAPIFolder Properties for Outlook 2002*

| Property | Type | Description |
|---|---|---|
| `AddressBookName` | String | Sets the display name for a contacts folder when it is included in the Outlook Address Book |
| `CustomViewsOnly` | Boolean | Determines whether the folder uses only custom views created for that folder |
| `FolderPath` | String | Read-only path to the folder; can be used to set the `Folder` property of the OVC |
| `InAppFolderSyncObject` | Boolean | Places the folder in the Application Folders send/receive group |
| `ShowAsOutlookAB` | Boolean | Determines whether a contacts folder is included in the Outlook Address Book |
| `Views` | Collection | Collection of customizable `View` objects representing the saved views for the folder |
| **Method** | **Description** | |
| `AddToFavorites` | Adds the folder to the user's Internet Explorer Favorites list so the folder can be opened from the Favorites menu either in Outlook or in Internet Explorer | |
| `AddToPFFavorites` | Adds the folder to the user's Public Folder\Favorites folder so it can be synchronized and used offline | |

Unlike all the other folder properties we've discussed so far, the two settings related to the Outlook Address Book are specific for each user. Therefore, if you want all users to access a particular folder through the Outlook Address Book, you might create a form that notifies the user that the folder is available and provides a button to make it easy for the user to add it to the Outlook Address Book with a specific display name.

Figure 23.9 shows a Message form that makes use of some of the properties in Table 23.1 to provide a very functional announcement of a new folder. It includes a clickable link to display the new folder. For contact folders, it also provides a button to add the folder to the Outlook Address Book using the display name shown on the form. The code for this form is shown in Listing 23.1; it uses the `GetFolder()` function from Listing 18.6.

When an administrator or other user clicks the Select Folder button and chooses a folder, the `cmdSelectFolder_Click` procedure updates the subject and body of the message; saves the folder path in the `BillingInformation` property; and, for contact folders, puts the folder name in the `Mileage` property. When a user receives the message, that user can change

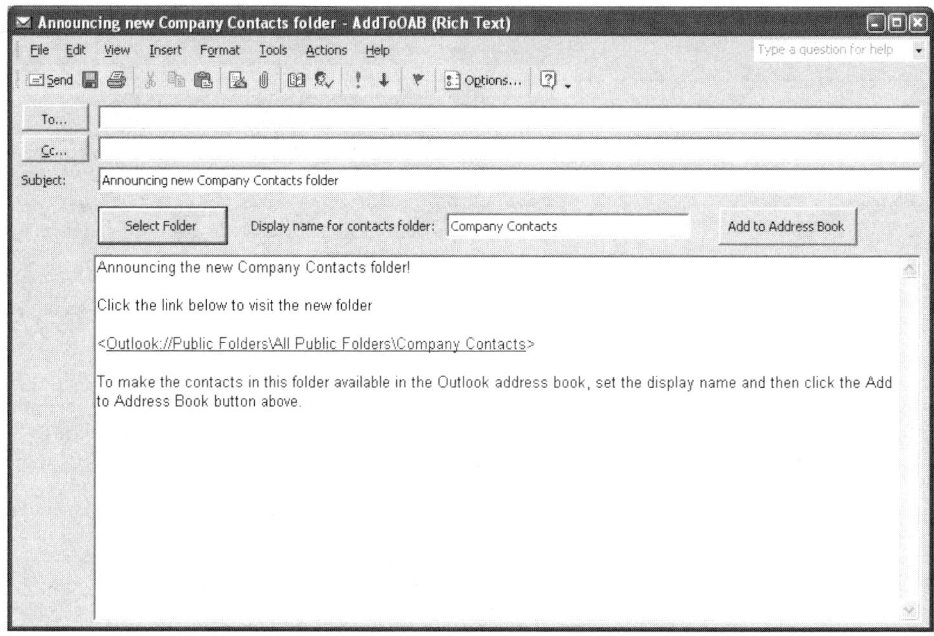


**Figure 23.9** *Use an Outlook 2002 custom form to announce a new public contacts folder.*

the display name as desired and then click the Add To Address Book button to run the code in the `cmdAddToOAB_Click` procedure.

### 23.1.6 Folder home pages

A folder home page is a Web page associated with a folder in Outlook through the setting on the Home Page tab of the folder's Properties dialog, which sets the `MAPIFolder.WebViewURL` property. The Outlook Today page that appears when you open the root of the default information store is a good example (even though it runs from a resource .dll file, not from a separate .htm file). Folder home pages can improve the usability of public folders with enhancements such as the following:

- An explanation of the purpose of the folder and whom to contact if you have any questions
- Hyperlinks, buttons, and other controls that make key functionality more obvious to the user
- Programmable filters to show the data in different ways

**Listing 23.1** *Announce New Folders with an Outlook 2002 Custom Form*

```
Option Explicit
Const olContactItem = 2
Const olFormatRichText = 3
Function Item_Open()
   Item.BodyFormat = olFormatRichText
   If Item.Sent = True Then
       If Item.Mileage = "" Then
           Call DisableOABButton
      End If
   End If
End Function

Sub cmdSelectFolder_Click()
    Dim objNS
    Dim objFolder
    Dim strMsg
    Set objNS = Application.GetNamespace("MAPI")
    Set objFolder = objNS.PickFolder
    If Not objFolder Is Nothing Then
        Item.Subject = "Announcing new " & _
          objFolder.Name & " folder"
        Item.BillingInformation = Mid(objFolder.FolderPath, 3)
        strMsg = "Announcing the new " & _
          objFolder.Name & " folder!" & vbCrLf & vbCrLf & _
          "Click the link below to visit the new " & _
          "folder" & vbCrLf & vbCrLf & "<Outlook://" & _
          Item.BillingInformation & ">" & vbCrLf & vbCrLf
        If objFolder.DefaultItemType = olContactItem Then
            Item.Mileage = objFolder.Name
            strMsg = strMsg & "To make the contacts " & _
              "in this folder available in the " & _
              "Outlook address book, set the display " & _
              "name and then click the " & _
              "Add to Address Book button above."
        Else
          Call DisableOABButton
        End If
        Item.Body = strMsg
    End If
    Set objFolder = Nothing
    Set objNS = Nothing
End Sub

Sub cmdAddToOAB_Click()
    Dim objFolder
    Set objFolder = GetFolder(Item.BillingInformation)
    objFolder.ShowAsOutlookAB = True
    objFolder.AddressBookName = Item.Mileage
    Set objFolder = Nothing
End Sub
```

**Listing 23.1** *Announce New Folders with an Outlook 2002 Custom Form (continued)*

```
Sub DisableOABButton()
    Dim objPage, cmdAddToOAB
    Dim txtContactDisplay, lblContactDisplay
    Set objPage = _
      Item.GetInspector.ModifiedFormPages("Message")
    Set cmdAddToOAB = objPage.Controls("cmdAddToOAB")
    Set txtContactDisplay = _
      objPage.Controls("txtContactDisplay")
    Set lblContactDisplay = _
      objPage.Controls("lblContactDisplay")
    cmdAddToOAB.Visible = False
    txtContactDisplay.Visible = False
    lblContactDisplay.Visible = False
    Set objPage = Nothing
    Set cmdAddToOAB = Nothing
    Set txtContactDisplay = Nothing
    Set lblContactDisplay = Nothing
End Sub
```

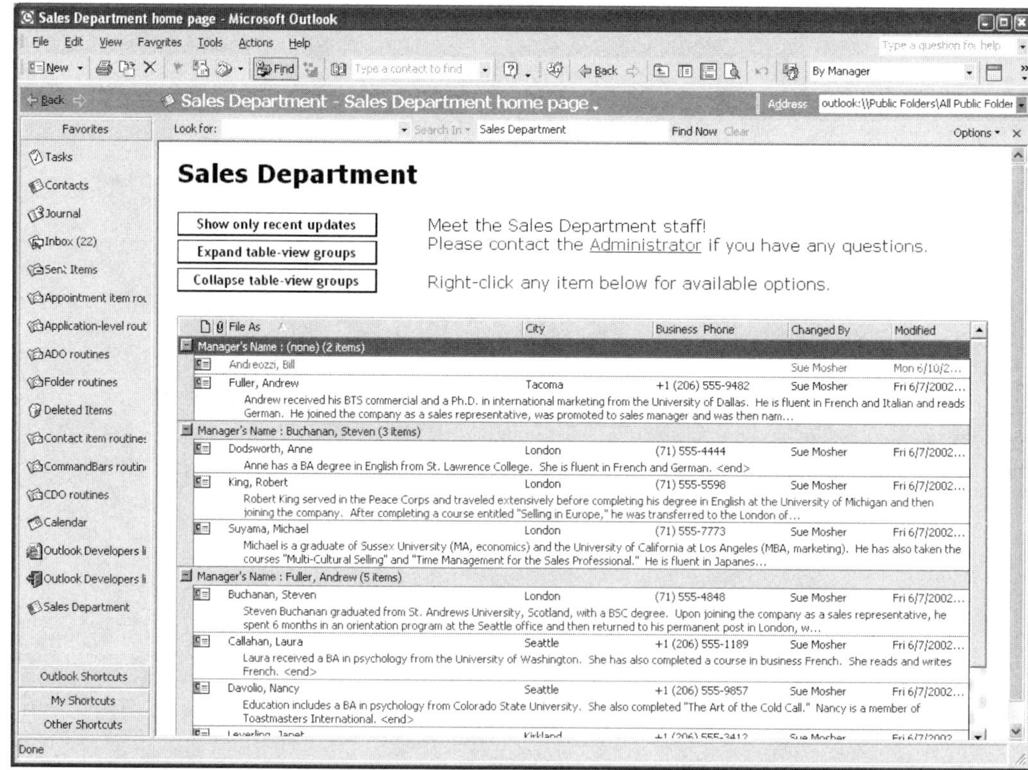


**Figure 23.10** *Use a folder home page to explain a folder and highlight key functionality.*

A key element of virtually any folder home page is the OVC, which you first saw in Chapter 19, "More Controls for Outlook Forms," in the context of an Outlook form. Figure 23.10 shows an example of the OVC placed in the home page for a public Sales Department folder.

---

**Note:** Folder home pages work only in Outlook. If you access the Web page from a browser, you will get different and usually disappointing results. If you want to make a customized page for a public folder available to Web browsers, you should explore the features of Outlook Web Access, which comes with Exchange Server.

---

---

**CAUTION:** If you have Outlook configured to start up in a folder other than Outlook Today, do not set that folder to show a folder home page. If you do, Outlook may hang on startup.

---

You can create a folder home page in any HTML editor, though it's easiest if you have a tool (e.g., Visual Interdev) that provides the same kind of programming aids as the VBA environment. The complete code for the folder home page appears in Listing 23.2. The page consists of the OVC, some explanatory text, and three *hotspots* (text with specific HTML coding) that simulate buttons that the user can click, plus supporting functions and subroutines.

Here are a few notes on the code:

- The title in the `<title>` tag will appear next to the name of the folder when you view the folder in Outlook.
- Inline styles for normal paragraphs, the heading at the top of the page, the hotspot buttons, and the warning text that appears if the user views the page in a browser give the page a consistent look.
- The `codebase` attribute for `ViewCtl1`, the instance of the OVC in this home page, tells Outlook 2000 computers where to find the OVC download on Microsoft's Web site if the latest version is not installed. You could also download the outlctlx.cab file and store it somewhere on your intranet, changing the `codebase` attribute to match.
- Since a folder home page is designed to work only in Outlook, the script is written all in VBScript. You can apply many of the programming skills you've learned working with VBScript in Outlook forms.

**Listing 23.2** *Code for the Folder Home Page in Figure 23.10*

```
<HTML><HEAD>
<TITLE>Sales Department home page</TITLE>
<style type=text/css>
p            { font: 12pt Verdana }
h1           { font: 18pt Verdana ;
                 font-weight: bold }
.button      { text-align: center;
               font: 10pt Trebuchet MS;
               font-weight: bold;
               border-left: solid 1px;
               border-right: solid 2px;
               border-top: solid 1px;
               border-bottom: solid 2px;
               padding-left: 9px; padding-right: 9px;
               padding-top: 1px; padding-bottom: 1px;
               margin-top:4px; margin-bottom:4px }
 .warning    { font: 10pt Verdana ;
                 color: #FF0000; font-weight: bold}
</style>
</HEAD>
<BODY LEFTMARGIN="20">
<h1>Sales Department</h1>
<table border="0" cellpadding="0" cellspacing="0"
        style="border-collapse: collapse" bordercolor="#111111"
        width="100%" id="AutoNumber1">
<tr>
<td width="200">
     <p class="button" id="showme"
          onmouseover="ButtonIn('blue')"
          onmouseout="ButtonOut('black')">
          Show only recent updates</p>
     <p class="button" id="expandall"
          onmouseover="ButtonIn('blue')"
          onmouseout="ButtonOut('black')">
          Expand table-view groups</p>
     <p class="button" id="collapseall"
          onmouseover="ButtonIn('blue')"
          onmouseout="ButtonOut('black')">
          Collapse table-view groups</p>
</td>
<td width="50"> </td>
<td>
<div id="divMain">
<p>Meet the Sales Department staff!<br>
Please contact the
<a href="mailto:administrator@outlookforms.com?subject=
Sales Department page question">
Administrator</a> if you have any questions.</p>
</div>
<div id="divFHP">
<p>Right-click any item below for available options.</p>
```

**Listing 23.2** *Code for the Folder Home Page in Figure 23.10 (continued)*

```
</div>
</td></tr></table>
<p>
<object classid="clsid:0006F063-0000-0000-C000-000000000046"
id="ViewCtl1"
codebase=http://activex.microsoft.com/activex/controls/
office/outlctlx.cab#ver=9,0,0,3203
width="100%" height="410">
<param name="Folder"
      value="\\Personal Folders\Sales Department">
<param name="DeferUpdate" value="0">
</object>
</p>
</body>
<script language=vbscript>
<!--
Dim g_objOL, g_blnIsFHP

Sub window_onload
     g_blnIsFHP = IsFHP()
     If Not g_blnIsFHP Then
          divFHP.innerHTML = "<p class='warning'>" & _
            "Because this page is operating in " & _
            "a browser, some functionality may be " & _
            "disabled. For best results, use Outlook to " & _
            "navigate to the Sales Department folder.</p>"
          Call ButtonDisable(showme)
          Call ButtonDisable(expandall)
          Call ButtonDisable(collapseall)
     End If
End Sub

Function IsFHP()
    On Error Resume Next
    Set g_objOL = ViewCtl1.OutlookApplication
    IF Err Then
          IsFHP = False

    ElseIf Not g_objOL is Nothing then
         IsFHP = True
     Else
         IsFHP = False
     End if
End Function

Function ButtonIn(NewColor)
     If g_blnIsFHP Then
          window.event.srcElement.style.cursor = "hand"
          window.event.srcElement.style.color = NewColor
          window.event.srcElement.style.bordercolor = "brown"
```

**Listing 23.2** *Code for the Folder Home Page in Figure 23.10 (continued)*

```
     Else
          window.event.srcElement.style.cursor = "default"
     End If
End Function

Function ButtonOut(NewColor)
     If g_blnIsFHP Then
          window.event.srcElement.style.cursor = "auto"
          window.event.srcElement.style.color = NewColor
          window.event.srcElement.style.bordercolor = "black"
     End If
End Function

Sub ButtonDisable(ButtonName)
    ButtonName.style.color = "#808080"
    ButtonName.title = _
      "This feature is not available in a browser"
End Sub

Sub showme_onclick
    Dim strDate
    If g_blnIsFHP Then
          If showme.innerText = "Show all contacts" Then
               ViewCtl1.Restriction = ""
               showme.innerText = "Show only recent updates"
               showme.title = "Click to see all contacts"
          Else
               strDate = FormatDateTime(Date - 7, vbLongDate)
               ViewCtl1.Restriction = "[Modified] > '" & _
                 strDate & "'"
               showme.innerText = "Show all contacts"
               showme.title = "Click to see contacts " & _
                 "updated in the last 7 days"
          End If
     End If
End Sub

Sub collapseall_onclick
    If g_blnIsFHP Then
          ViewCtl1.CollapseAllGroups
     End If
End Sub

Sub expandall_onclick
     If g_blnIsFHP Then
          ViewCtl1.ExpandAllGroups
     End If
End Sub
-->
</script>
</html>
```

- The `IsFHP()` function tests whether the page is running as an Outlook folder home page and, if it is not, changes the page to advise the user that functionality may not be available. The `IsFHP()` function also sets a global `Outlook.Application` object. The code in Listing 23.2 does not use this object, but your folder home page code might.
- The `ButtonIn()` and `ButtonOut()` functions run when the user passes the mouse over one of the hotspot buttons, triggering the `onmouseover` and `onmouseout` events. The functions toggle the mouse cursor and the color on the hotspot.
- The Show Only Recent Updates hotspot is a toggle. Its `onclick` event handler uses the `Restriction` property of the view control to change the filter and also changes the displayed text (`innertext` attribute) and the screen tip (`title` attribute).

---

**Note:** `Restriction` is supported only in table and card views. It works much like `Restrict`, but can be unpredictable. For example, the code in Listing 23.2 sets `Restriction` using the `Modified` field. `Modified` is the name that the Field Chooser shows for this property, but its true name in the object model is `LastModificationTime`. If the object model property name doesn't work in a `Restriction` statement, try the field name from the Field Chooser instead.

---

- The `onclick` event handlers for the buttons for collapsing and expanding groups in a table view uses two OVC methods that duplicate commands on Outlook menus.

Though the OVC supports a `<param name="View">` element, you should use it only if you are 100 percent certain that the page will never be viewed from a browser. If you set the `View` parameter, users viewing the page with a browser will always see their own Inbox folder, not the folder you specify with the `<param name="Folder">` parameter. Setting the `ViewCtl1.View` property programmatically will result in a permission error for security reasons if the page is running in a browser. The best practice, therefore, is to make sure that the default view for the folder is set to the view you want users to see when they load the page.

This simple example could be enhanced further in many ways. You could, for example, add a button to initiate a send/receive session with this statement:

```
ViewCtl1.SendReceive
```

You also could include lists of available views and forms, show another folder in a second view control, or add other ActiveX controls to display data from databases. At the high end, the folder home page can evolve into an intranet portal or *digital dashboard* that combines personal data from your own Outlook folders with key corporate information.

## 23.2 Working with databases

Some Outlook applications connect to external databases. The database usage can be as simple as loading choices into a list box or combo box or as complex as synchronizing changes made in Outlook with records kept in a database (which generally requires field-by-field comparisons between the Outlook items and the database records). In this section, we'll look at some basics of making database connections and using database information for some simple, but common, tasks on Outlook forms.

Incorporating database links into your Outlook forms and VBA projects is largely a matter of writing code with ActiveX Data Objects (ADO), an interface that can connect to many different types of databases. To use ADO in an Outlook VBA project, use Tools, References to add a reference to the Microsoft ActiveX Data Objects library. Once you add the reference, the Object Browser will show ADODB in the libraries list.

---

**Note:** The versions of ADO available will depend on your version of Outlook and other software installed on your system. If you are writing code for yourself alone, use the highest version. If you plan to share VBA code with other people, use the highest version that's common to all prospective users.

---

Using ADO is a big topic that deserves a book in itself. In the sections that follow, you'll get the basics of connecting to databases and you'll apply those techniques to some common Outlook tasks—populating a combo box and getting a sequential number as a unique identifier for an Outlook item.

The examples use a sample database for Microsoft Access, the Northwind Traders database, which you can install as part of Microsoft Office setup.

### 23.2.1 Connecting to a database

The basic technique for pulling data with ADO is to connect to a database, open a recordset, and retrieve data in one or more records. Of the different ways to connect to a database, we'll look at two—using a DSN (data source name) and using a connection string.

To create a DSN that points to a database, follow these steps:

1. Run the Data Sources (ODBC) applet from Control Panel. In Windows 2000 and Windows XP, you'll find it under Administrative Tools.
2. On the User DSN tab, click Add, and select the Microsoft Access Driver.
3. On the ODBC Microsoft Access Setup dialog, give the DSN a Name and optional Description.
4. Click Select and browse to the location of the Northwind Traders database on your machine. For Office XP, this will usually be C:\Program Files\Microsoft Office\Office10\Samples\Northwind.mdb.
5. After you select the database, click OK to save the DSN.

---

**Tip:** On the File DSN tab, you can create a DSN that can be shared with other users.

---

The code to connect to a database using ADO and a DSN named Northwind is very simple:

```
Set objADOConn = CreateObject("ADODB.Connection")
objADOConn.Open "DSN=Northwind"
```

Often, you will want to connect to a database located on your network, and then share the code with other people. A DSN-less connection string is useful in that situation. This code snippet builds a connection string to the Northwind.mdb database located on a network share and then opens the database:

```
strConn = "Provider=Microsoft.Jet.OLEDB.4.0;" & _
          "Data Source=\\myServer\myShare\northwind.mdb;" & _
          "Uid=admin;" & _
          "Pwd=;"
objADOConn.Open strConn
```

The `Uid` and `Pwd` parameters are for the user ID and password for the database, if any. A user named "admin" and a blank password are the defaults.

**Listing 23.3** *Connect to an Access Database*

```
Function OpenAccessDB(strDBPath As String, _
  Optional UID = "admin", _
  Optional PWD = "") As ADODB.Connection
    Dim objADOConn As ADODB.Connection
    Dim strConn As String
    On Error Resume Next
    strConn = "Provider=Microsoft.Jet.OLEDB.4.0; " & _
              "Data Source=" & strDBPath & "; " & _
              "User ID=" & UID & "; " & _
              "Password=" & PWD & "; "
    Set objADOConn = CreateObject("ADODB.Connection")
    objADOConn.Open strConn
    If (Err = 0) And (objADOConn.State = adStateOpen) Then
        Set OpenAccessDB = objADOConn
    Else
        Set OpenAccessDB = Nothing
    End If
    Set objADOConn = Nothing
End Function
```

To make it easier to work with Access databases, Listing 23.3 is an `OpenAccessDB()` function that requires only the path to the .mdb file as an argument, although you can also specify optional user ID and password information.

You can use this function to return an ADO `Connection` object that has already been opened and is ready to retrieve recordsets:

```
Set objMyConn = _
  OpenAccessDB("\\myServer\myShare\northwind.mdb")
```

Another type of database that you may see often is Microsoft SQL Server. The `OpenSQLServerDB()` function in Listing 23.4 works much the same as `OpenAccessDB()` except that you need more information to open a SQL Server database. The user ID and password are not optional arguments in this routine, and you must specify both the server where the database is located and the name of the database.

The `Network Library=dbmssocn;` portion of the connection string ensures that the connection is made via TCP/IP instead of Named Pipes, which is the default. Here's an example of how to use the `OpenSQLServerDB()` function:

```
Set objMyConn = _
  OpenSQLServerDB("myServer", "myDatabase", _
                  "My Name", "myPassword")
```

**Listing 23.4** *Connect to a SQL Server Database*

```
Function OpenSQLServerDB(strServer As String, _
  strDBName As String, UID As String, PWD As String) _
  As ADODB.Connection
    Dim objADOConn As ADODB.Connection
    Dim strConn As String
    On Error Resume Next
    strConn = "Provider=SQLOLEDB;" & _
              "Data Source=" & strServer & "; " & _
              "Initial Catalog=" & strDBName & "; " & _
              "User ID=" & UID & "; " & _
              "Password=" & PWD & "; " & _
              "Network Library=dbmssocn;"
    Set objADOConn = CreateObject("ADODB.Connection")
    objADOConn.Open strConn
    If (Err = 0) And (objADOConn.State = adStateOpen) Then
        Set OpenSQLServerDB = objADOConn
    Else
        Set OpenSQLServerDB = Nothing
    End If
    Set objADOConn = Nothing
End Function
```

After you finish working with a database, close any open connections:

```
If objMyConn.State = adStateOpen Then
    objMyConn.Close
End If
```

You can access many other kinds of databases with ADO. Information on different connection strings is readily available on the Internet.

## 23.2.2 Working with database records

The next step, after connecting with a database, is to access a specific recordset. A *recordset* is a collection of database records. It can be a full table from a database or a filtered set of records with only some of the fields from the original table. Some recordsets join data from two or more tables.

To obtain a recordset, create an ADO `Recordset` object and an appropriate Structured Query Language (SQL) statement. Then use the `Open` method on an existing ADO `Connection` object. This code snippet opens the Employees table from the Northwind Traders database using a `Connection` object named `adoNW`.

```
Set rstEmployees = CreateObject("ADODB.Recordset")
strSQL = "SELECT Employees.* " & _
         "FROM Employees;"
```

```
rstEmployees.Open strSQL, adoNW
If rstEmployees.State = adStateOpen Then
    your code for working with rstEmployees
End If
```

The last lines make sure the recordset is actually open before you start using it.

---

**Tip:** This book doesn't have room to cover SQL syntax, but the basics are not hard to learn. Try creating a query in Microsoft Access using the Query Wizard and then using View, SQL View to see the SQL statement for the query. You might also find it useful, especially when you're just beginning to work with ADO and SQL, to add a `Debug.Print strSQL` statement in VBA or a `MsgBox strSQL` statement in Outlook form code after each block of statements in which you build a SQL string. That will let you check the SQL statement's syntax before you use it to get a recordset.

---

Once you have a `Recordset` object, you can use a `Do` loop to work with each record in turn. The record properties are in the `Fields` collection. This code snippet copies the first name and last name of each Northwind employee to the Immediate window:

```
With rstEmployees
    .MoveFirst
    If (.State = adStateOpen) And (Not(.EOF)) Then
        Do Until .EOF
            strName = .Fields("FirstName") & " " _
                      & .Fields("LastName")
            Debug.Print strName
           .MoveNext
        Loop
    End If
End With
```

`EOF` is a property that indicates whether you have reached the end of the recordset. The `MoveFirst` and `MoveNext` methods move through the records in sequence.

If you try this code, you'll see that the names don't print out in alphabetical order. One of the great things about SQL is that you can include things like sorting in the SQL statement. You can also concatenate fields and limit the data returned to just a few fields, improving performance. Listing 23.5 shows a more complicated example that sorts the data and builds the full name from the `FirstName` and `LastName` fields as part of the query.

**Listing 23.5** *Build a Sorted Query with SQL*

```
Sub ListNWEmployeesSort()
    Dim adoNW As ADODB.Connection
    Dim rstEmployees As ADODB.Recordset
    Dim strNW As String
    Dim strSQL As String
    ' ### USER OPTION ###
    ' path to Northwind
    strNW = \\HBWIN2\Office Samples\Northwind.mdb
    Set adoNW = OpenAccessDB(strNW)
    Set rstEmployees = CreateObject("ADODB.Recordset")
    strSQL = "SELECT [FirstName] & " & Quote(" ") & _
             " & [LastName] AS FullName " & _
             "from Employees " & _
             "ORDER BY Employees.LastName;"
    Debug.Print strSQL
    rstEmployees.Open strSQL, adoNW, _
      adOpenForwardOnly, adLockReadOnly
    With rstEmployees
        .MoveFirst
        If (.State = adStateOpen) And (Not(.EOF)) Then
            Do Until .EOF
                Debug.Print .Fields("FullName")
                .MoveNext
            Loop
        End If
    End With
    rstEmployees.Close
    adoNW.Close
    Set adoNW = Nothing
    Set rstEmployees = Nothing
End Sub
```

The first `Debug.Print` statement shows that `strSQL` has this value:

```
SELECT [FirstName] & " " & [LastName] AS FullName from
Employees ORDER BY Employees.LastName;
```

The second `Debug.Print` statement gets the data from the `FullName` field assigned in the SQL statement as the concatenation `[FirstName] & " " & [LastName]`.

The `adOpenForwardOnly` and `adLockReadOnly` parameters in the `rstEmployees.Open` statement are options to improve performance by specifying that the code will move only sequentially through the recordset, not forward and back and that we're opening the recordset for read-only access.

As with a `Connection` object, you should always close a `Recordset` object when you have finished using it:

```
rstEmployees.Close
```

With that basic background in opening databases and looping through recordsets, we can now take up some examples that you can apply to Outlook programming projects.

### 23.2.3 Populating combo boxes

One very common database application is to populate combo boxes on Outlook forms. In this example, we'll build a combo box using the `Categories` table in the Northwind database. Code behind the form will take the user's choice from the Categories combo box and use that to populate a second combo box with products from that category, so that the user can select a favorite product for a contact.

The first step, before you do any coding, is to look at the structure of the two database tables we'll be using—Categories and Products—and determine what fields we need. If you look at the Northwind `Products` table in design view, you'll see that the `ProductName` is a text field, but `CategoryID`—the field that provides a link to the Categories table—is a number, not the name of the category. This means that the Categories combo box on our form will need to contain both the number and the name for each category.

The customized page for this example, shown in Figure 23.11, shows the two combo boxes—along with appropriate label controls. The `cboProduct` control is bound to a user-defined property, `Product`. The `cboCategory` control is unbound. We don't need to store the product category in the item because we are using it only to filter the Products combo box. These advanced property settings turn the `cboCategory` control into a multicolumn combo box with the first column hidden:

```
BoundColumn     1
ColumnCount     2
ColumnWidths    0 pt;130 pt
```

The code for the form is in Listing 23.6. Both combo boxes are filled from the database when the form opens. Then, when the user selects a category, the `cboCategory_Click` event handler passes the `CategoryID` (from the first hidden and bound column in the `cboCategory` control) to the

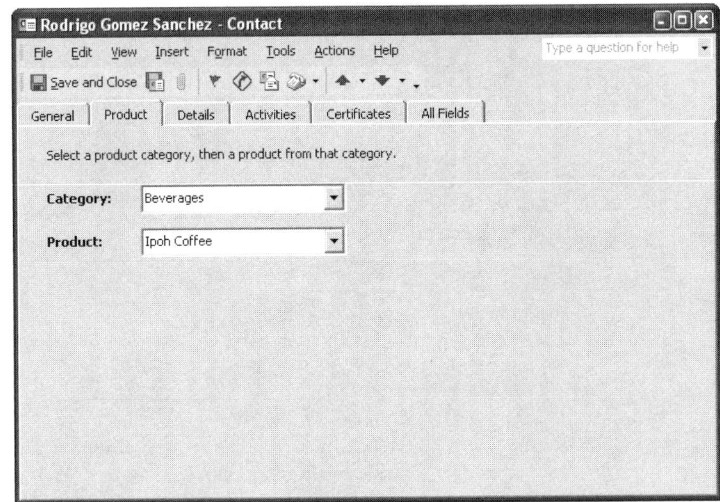


**Figure 23.11** *Fill combo boxes using ADO to connect to a database.*

`FilterProductList` procedure, which updates the values for the Product combo box.

---

**Tip:** Listing 23.6 includes a VBScript version of the `OpenAccessDB()` function from Listing 23.3.

---

The syntax for opening a database and recordsets should seem quite familiar now. The main difference between the `FillProductList` and `FilterProductList` routines is this `WHERE` clause in the SQL statement:

```
"WHERE [CategoryID] =" & CatID & " "
```

to filter by the `CategoryID` field.

For both combo boxes, we use the `Recordset.GetRows` method to return a two-dimensional array of values from the recordset. The first dimension is the number of rows, while the second dimension is the number of columns. This makes it possible to set the `Column` property of the combo box directly to the array from the recordset, as in the following statement:

```
cboCategory.Column = rstCats.GetRows
```

That's right! Once you have a recordset that contains only the rows and columns that you want to use in the combo box, it takes just one line of code to fill the control.

**Listing 23.6** *Populate Combo Boxes from ADO Recordsets*

```
Option Explicit
Dim m_adoNW
Dim cboProduct
Dim cboCategory
Const adOpenForwardOnly = 0
Const adLockReadOnly = 1
Const adStateOpen = 1

Function Item_Open()
    Dim strNW
    Dim objPage
    On Error Resume Next
    ' ### USER OPTION ###
    ' path to Northwind
    strNW = "\\GXWIN2K2\Office Samples\Northwind.mdb"
    Set m_adoNW = OpenAccessDB(strNW, "admin", "")
    If Not m_adoNW.State Is Nothing Then
        Set objPage = _
          Item.GetInspector.ModifiedFormPages("Product")
        Set cboProduct = objPage.Controls("cboProduct")
        Set cboCategory = objPage.Controls("cboCategory")
        Call FillCategoryList
        Call FillProductList()
    End If
End Function

Function Item_Close()
    On Error Resume Next
    If m_adoNW.State = adStateOpen Then
        m_adoNW.Close
    End If
    Set m_adoNW = Nothing
    Set cboCategory = Nothing
    Set cboProduct = Nothing
End Function

Sub cboCategory_Click()
   Call FilterProductList(cboCategory.Value)
End Sub

Sub FillCategoryList()
    Dim rstCats
    Dim strSQL
    On Error Resume Next
    Set rstCats = CreateObject("ADODB.Recordset")
    strSQL = "SELECT [CategoryID], [CategoryName] " & _
             "from Categories " & _
             "ORDER BY [CategoryName];"
    rstCats.Open strSQL, m_adoNW, _
                 adOpenForwardOnly, adLockReadOnly
```

**Listing 23.6** *Populate Combo Boxes from ADO Recordsets (continued)*

```
    If rstCats.State = adStateOpen Then
        cboCategory.Column = rstCats.GetRows
        rstCats.Close
    End If
    Set rstCats = Nothing
End Sub

Sub FillProductList()
    Dim rstProds
    Dim strSQL
    On Error Resume Next
    Set rstProds = CreateObject("ADODB.Recordset")
    strSQL = "SELECT [ProductName] " & _
             "from Products " & _
             "ORDER BY [ProductName];"
    rstProds.Open strSQL, m_adoNW, _
                adOpenForwardOnly, adLockReadOnly
    If rstProds.State = adStateOpen Then
        cboProduct.Column = rstProds.GetRows
        rstProds.Close
    End If
    Set rstProds = Nothing
End Sub

Sub FilterProductList(CatID)
    Dim rstProds
    Dim strSQL
    On Error Resume Next
    If CatID <> "" Then
        Set rstProds = CreateObject("ADODB.Recordset")
        strSQL = "SELECT [ProductName] " & _
                 "from Products " & _
                 "WHERE [CategoryID] =" & CatID & " " & _
                 "ORDER BY [ProductName];"
        rstProds.Open strSQL, m_adoNW, _
                    adOpenForwardOnly, adLockReadOnly
        If rstProds.State = adStateOpen Then
            cboProduct.Column = rstProds.GetRows
            rstProds.Close
        End If
    End If
    Set rstProds = Nothing
End Sub

Function OpenAccessDB(strDBPath, UID, PWD)
    Dim objADOConn
    Dim strConn
    On Error Resume Next
```

**Listing 23.6** *Populate Combo Boxes from ADO Recordsets (continued)*

```
        strConn = "Provider=Microsoft.Jet.OLEDB.4.0; " & _
              "Data Source=" & strDBPath & "; " & _
              "User ID=" & UID & "; " & _
              "Password=" & PWD & "; "
    Set objADOConn = CreateObject("ADODB.Connection")
    objADOConn.Open strConn
    If (Err = 0) And And (objADOConn.State = adStateOpen) Then
        Set OpenAccessDB = objADOConn
    Else
        Set OpenAccessDB = Nothing
    End If
    Set objADOConn = Nothing
End Function
```

There's one more thing to notice about the code in Listing 23.6: Because we know that we'll be using the database more than once—each time one of the combo boxes is filled—the `m_adoNW` variable for the database is declared at the module level and instantiated in the `Item_Open` event handler. That makes it available to all the other procedures in the form's script, without the need to make the database connection again.

### 23.2.4 Getting a sequential number

Now that you've seen a VBScript database example, let's do one with VBA. In this case, you'll need to create an Access database with a single table named Counter. The table has one field—`ID`—with the data type set to AutoNumber. We can use the `GetNewNumber()` function in Listing 23.7 to query this database and table every time we need a sequential number for a purchase order. You will need to adjust the value of the `strPath` variable to point to the Counter.mdb database on your system.

**Tip:** The normal starting number for an AutoNumber field is 1. However, Access Help has a topic entitled "Change the starting value of an AutoNumber field" that explains how to set the starting number for an AutoNumber field by using an append query. Access will then increment the number by 1 each time you add a new record with the `GetNewNumber()` function.

Adding a new record with the `AddNew` method increments the `ID` field. The code finishes up by deleting the newly created record since it is no longer needed.

**Listing 23.7** *Use an Access AutoNumber Field to Generate Sequential Numbers*

```
Function GetNewNumber()
    Dim adoConn As ADODB.Connection
    Dim rstCounter As ADODB.Recordset
    Dim strPath As String
    Dim strSQL As String
    Dim strName As String
    ' ### USER OPTION ###
    ' path to counter database
    strPath = "C:\Ch23\Counter.mdb"
    Set adoConn = OpenAccessDB(strPath)
    strSQL = "SELECT [ID] FROM Counter;"
    Set rstCounter = CreateObject("ADODB.Recordset")
    rstCounter.Open strSQL, adoConn, _
                    adOpenDynamic, adLockOptimistic
    rstCounter.AddNew
    rstCounter.Update
    GetNewNumber = rstCounter.Fields("ID")
    rstCounter.Delete
    rstCounter.Close
    adoConn.Close
    Set adoConn = Nothing
    Set rstCounter = Nothing
End Function
```

Using this function is easy. For example, maybe you want to assign an account number to new client contacts. You could use the `CreateNewClientContact` procedure in Listing 23.8, for example, to create a new contact, put a unique number in the `Account` property, add Client as a category, and then display the new item.

**Listing 23.8** *Add an Account Number to a New Contact*

```
Sub CreateNewClientContact()
    Dim objApp As Outlook.Application
    Dim objContact As Outlook.ContactItem
    Set objApp = CreateObject("Outlook.Application")
    Set objContact = objApp.CreateItem(olContactItem)
    With objContact
        .Account = GetNewNumber()
        .Categories = "Client"
        .Display
    End With
    Set objApp = Nothing
    Set objContact = Nothing
End Sub
```

Once you have a unique number in the `Account` property for this contact, you can use that number to mark other items related to this contact, using the linking ideas discussed in Chapter 20, "Common Outlook Form and Item Techniques."

---

**Tip:** By default, Access opens databases so they can be shared by other users. You could conceivably have several tables in one database, each table generating a different series of unique numbers.

---

## 23.3 Using XML Web services (Outlook 2002)

XML Web services are a relatively new collaboration mechanism that allows you to exchange information with other applications across the Internet. Many XML Web services provide lookup functions that can be useful to Outlook (e.g., validating a Zip code based on an address). Some, such as the fax transmission service you'll see later in this chapter, may also process information you submit and send it on to another application.

Different types of client applications can connect to XML Web services, not just Outlook or even just Microsoft programs. What's exciting about these services is that they make it possible to connect to remote databases with a minimum amount of code on the client. In most of the examples you'll see in this chapter, just two lines of code do all the work.

---

**Note:** XML stands for Extensible Markup Language and looks superficially like HTML coding in that it contains tags enclosed in angle brackets like <this>. However, where HTML is primarily concerned with formatting, XML concentrates on structure. It provides an organized way to describe fairly complex structures, using a plain-text syntax that can be easily transmitted over the Internet.

---

To make XML Web services incredibly easy to program in Office XP, Microsoft provides an Office XP Web Services Toolkit that you can download (see Appendix A—there is no comparable version of the toolkit for Office 2000). The toolkit has two key features. First, a search tool helps you locate XML Web Services on the Internet. Then, after you locate a service that you want to incorporate into your VBA project, the toolkit creates a proxy class module for all the methods and properties of the service. This means that your VBA code can treat the service just like another object; you won't need to worry about most of the details of how XML Web services actually work.

In many cases, to use the Web service in your VBA project, you need to write just two lines of code! One creates a new instance of the class that the Web services Toolkit builds, while the other provides an input to the service and accepts the service's output. In essence, you can use such Web services just as you use built-in functions and those functions you write yourself. The difference is that these Web service "functions" exist on the Internet.

---

**CAUTION:** The word "Web" in "XML Web services" should be a tip-off that the techniques in this section will work only when you are connected to the Internet. Some also require that you register and pay for the service. The services used for the demos were all publicly available, free services at the time this chapter was written. However, it is possible that the owner of a Web service may discontinue it at some future date.

---

Users running Outlook 2002 on Windows XP should be able to import and use your VBA code for XML Web services with no additional components required. Users with earlier versions of Windows will need to install either the Office XP Web Services Toolkit or the SOAP Toolkit 3.0 Redistributable Files, which are available on Microsoft's Web site.

### 23.3.1 Searching for XML Web services

To use the search tool, in the VBA environment choose Tools, Web Services References. In the Web Services References dialog, click the More button to display the entire search details. By default, the dialog searches at http://uddi.microsoft.com/inquire, but you can substitute another site that supports the Universal Description, Discovery, and Integration (UDDI) registry. Enter keywords and/or a business name, and then click Search.

If you don't get any matching results, you can also retrieve a list from any site that publishes a directory of services. One site with a registry of many XML Web services is http://www.xmethods.net. As you can see in Figure 23.12, the URL to access their list of XML Web services is http://www.xmethods.net/default.disco.

Retrieving the list of available services may take quite a few minutes. If you already know what service you want to use, you can skip the search step and connect directly to the URL for the service's Web Services description

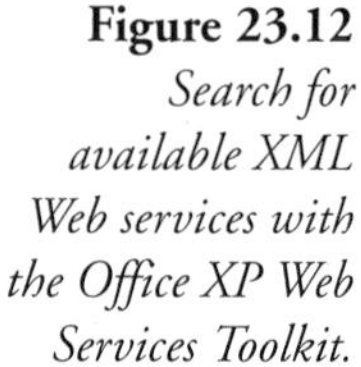

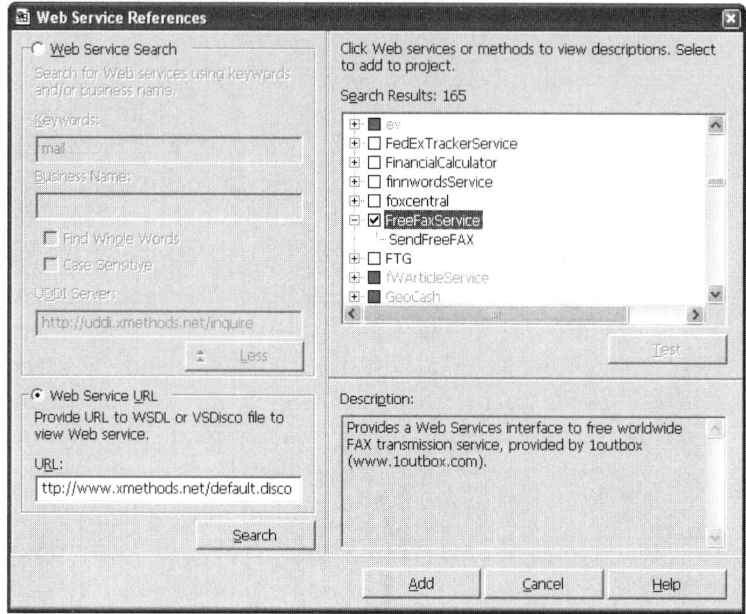


**Figure 23.12** *Search for available XML Web services with the Office XP Web Services Toolkit.*

language (WSDL) file, which contains all the information that VBA needs to use the service.

After you retrieve the list of XML Web services, select a service and click Add to have the Toolkit create a new class module in VBA to proxy the service's methods. The remaining sections in this chapter look at several examples of XML Web services that you can use with Outlook and show how to provide inputs to and read outputs from the services.

### 23.3.2 Checking the local time by Zip code

It's time to call the client, but you're geographically challenged and aren't really sure what time zone the client is in. The LocalTimeByZipCode service provides a lookup to give you the local time for any U.S. Zip code. To create the `clsws_LocalTime` class shown in Listing 23.9, point the Web Services References tool to the service's page at http://www.alethea.net/webservices/LocalTime.asmx?WSDL, click Search, and then click Add.

As you probably noticed, `wsm_LocalTimeByZipCode()` is the only public procedure in Listing 23.9. To connect to the LocalTimeByZipCode service and retrieve the time, your code simply instantiates a class instance and passes the Zip code to that function:

```
Dim TimeService As New clsws_LocalTime
strTime = TimeService.wsm_LocalTimeByZipCode(strZip)
```

**Note:** The class modules created by the Web Services References tool for the other Web services samples in this chapter are very similar to Listing 23.9 and, therefore, won't be shown.

**Listing 23.9** *Use the Office XP Web Services Toolkit To Build a Class Module for Each XML Web Service*

```
Private sc_LocalTime As SoapClient
Private Const c_WSDL_URL As String = _
  "http://www.alethea.net/webservices/LocalTime.asmx?WSDL"

Private Sub Class_Initialize()
    Set sc_LocalTime = New SoapClient
    sc_LocalTime.mssoapinit c_WSDL_URL
End Sub

Private Sub Class_Terminate()
    On Error GoTo Class_TerminateTrap
    Set sc_LocalTime = Nothing
    Exit Sub

Class_TerminateTrap:
    LocalTimeErrorHandler "Class_terminate"
End Sub

Private Sub LocalTimeErrorHandler(str_Function As String)
    ' SOAP Error
    If sc_LocalTime.faultcode <> "" Then
        Err.Raise vbObjectError, str_Function, _
                  sc_LocalTime.faultstring
    ' Non SOAP Error
    Else
        Err.Raise Err.Number, str_Function, Err.Description
    End If
End Sub

Public Function wsm_LocalTimeByZipCode _
  (ByVal str_ZipCode As String) As String
    On Error GoTo wsm_LocalTimeByZipCodeTrap
    wsm_LocalTimeByZipCode = _
      sc_LocalTime.LocalTimeByZipCode(str_ZipCode)
    Exit Function

wsm_LocalTimeByZipCodeTrap:
    LocalTimeErrorHandler "wsm_LocalTimeByZipCode"
End Function
```

**Listing 23.10** *Get the Current Time for Any U.S. Zip Code*

```
Sub WhatTimeIsIt()
    Dim TimeService As New clsws_LocalTime
    Dim objItem As Object
    Dim strZip As String
    Dim strTime As String
    Dim strMsg As String
    Set objItem = GetCurrentItem()
    If objItem.Class = olContact Then
        strZip = Left(objItem.MailingAddressPostalCode, 5)
        If Len(strZip) = 5 And IsNumeric(strZip) Then
            strTime = _
              TimeService.wsm_LocalTimeByZipCode(strZip)
            strMsg = "The current time in zip code " & _
                     strZip & " is:" & vbCrLf & vbCrLf & _
                     vbTab & strTime
            MsgBox strMsg, , "What Time Is It?"
        End If
    End If
    Set objItem = Nothing
    Set TimeService = Nothing
End Sub
```

Listing 23.10 shows how that could work in the context of Outlook, by using the Zip code from the current contact. It uses the `GetCurrentItem()` function from Listing 18.7.

You can run the `WhatTimeIsIt` macro any time you're connected to the Internet, looking at an Outlook contact with a U.S. address, and need to know what time it is at that location.

### 23.3.3 Understanding SOAP

The first line in Listing 23.9 offers a clue as to what's happening behind the scenes:

```
Private sc_LocalTime As SoapClient
```

SOAP is the acronym for Simple Object Access Protocol. SOAP is a technique for exchanging information designed for Internet use by any kind of client that can make a Web connection via HTTP (as your browser does) and package data into a stream of XML text.

When you ran the installation for the Office XP Web Services Toolkit, the setup program also installed the Microsoft SOAP Type Library if it was not already present on your system, and set a reference to that library in VBA. `SoapClient` is one of the objects in that library.

This line in the class module declarations sets a constant to the location on the Web for the WSDL data that defines the LocalTimeByZipCode service:

```
Private Const c_WSDL_URL As String = _
"http://www.alethea.net/webservices/LocalTime.asmx?WSDL"
```

When you create a new instance of the class, the following line in the `Class_Initialize()` procedure initializes the `SoapClient` object and connects it via the Internet to the Web service's WSDL definition:

```
sc_LocalTime.mssoapinit c_WSDL_URL
```

Once that happens, SOAP handles all the details of formatting an XML stream to send to the Web service. All your code has to do is pass in a string and get a string back from the `wsm_LocalTimeByZipCode` function.

### 23.3.4 Validating Zip codes

The LocalTimeByZipCode service example used a contact's Zip code to look up the time, but a more common task is looking up the Zip code for an address or validating that an address has the correct Zip code. EraServer.NET offers a ZipCodeResolver service for personal, noncommercial use. The first step is to point the Web Services References tool to http://webservices.eraserver.net/zipcoderesolver/zipcoderesolver.asmx?WSDL in order to add a new `clsws_ZipCodeResolver` Class module for the service, as described in the previous example.

The `GetFullZip()` function in Listing 23.11 takes the street address, city, and state as arguments and returns a full ZIP+4 zip code.

A practical use for this function might be to validate silently and, if necessary, update Zip codes whenever a user creates or modifies an item in the Contacts folder. To accomplish that, declare an `Items` object `WithEvents` in the `ThisOutlookSession` module, instantiate it when Outlook starts, and provide event handlers for the `Items.ItemAdd` and `Items.ItemChange` event handlers. Listing 23.12 shows the necessary event handlers.

**Listing 23.11** *Add the ZIP+4 Code to Any U.S. Address*

```
Function GetFullZip(strStreet As String, _
  strCity As String, strState As String) As String
    Dim ZipResolver As New clsws_ZipCodeResolver
    GetFullZip = ZipResolver.wsm_FullZipCode _
                 ("0", strStreet, strCity, strState)
End Function
```

**Listing 23.12** *Set Up Event Handlers To Watch for New and Modified Contacts*

```
Dim WithEvents colContacts As Outlook.Items

Private Sub Application_Startup()
    Dim objNS As Outlook.NameSpace
    Set objNS = Application.GetNamespace("MAPI")
    Set colContacts = _
      objNS.GetDefaultFolder(olFolderContacts).Items
    Set objNS = Nothing
End Sub

Private Sub colContacts_ItemAdd(ByVal Item As Object)
    If Item.Class = olContact Then
        Call UpdateZips(Item)
    End If
End Sub

Private Sub colContacts_ItemChange(ByVal Item As Object)
    If Item.Class = olContact Then
        Call UpdateZips(Item)
    End If
End Sub
```

Both the `ItemAdd` and `ItemChange` event handlers call the `UpdateZips` procedure in Listing 23.13. It uses the `GetFullZip()` function from Listing 23.11 to resolve the Zip code from the contact's address properties and update the contact properties as needed.

The `UpdateZips` subroutine saves the contact only if the Zip codes needed to be updated.

### 23.3.5 Sending a fax from an Outlook form

Our final example uses the FreeFAX fax transmission service from http://www.OneOutBox.com. This free service is supported by volunteers who provide outbound fax transmissions in different geographic areas, including most of North America and many other countries. (They often add advertisements to the cover sheet.) As in the previous examples, the first step is to point the Web Services References tool to the WSDL file for the service at http://www.OneOutBox.com/wsdl/FreeFaxService.wsdl and generate the `clsws_FreeFaxService` class module.

The parameters required to send a fax are shown in Table 23.2, with descriptions taken from the WSDL document that defines the service. (Because a WSDL file is simply an XML document, you can open it right in Internet Explorer 5.0 or later.)

**Listing 23.13** *Check the Zip Codes on Any Contact*

```
Sub UpdateZips(objContact As Outlook.ContactItem)
    Dim strStreet As String
    Dim strCity As String
    Dim strState As String
    Dim strZip As String
    With objContact
        If .BusinessAddressStreet <> "" Then
            strStreet = .BusinessAddressStreet
            If .BusinessAddressCity <> "" Then
                strCity = .BusinessAddressCity
                If .BusinessAddressState <> "" Then
                    strState = .BusinessAddressState
                    strZip = GetFullZip(strStreet, _
                      strCity, strState)
                    If strZip <> .BusinessAddressPostalCode Then
                        .BusinessAddressPostalCode = strZip
                    End If
                End If
            End If
        End If
        If .HomeAddressStreet <> "" Then
            strStreet = .HomeAddressStreet
            If .HomeAddressCity <> "" Then
                strCity = .HomeAddressCity
                If .HomeAddressState <> "" Then
                    strState = .HomeAddressState
                    strZip = GetFullZip(strStreet, _
                      strCity, strState)
                    If strZip <> .HomeAddressPostalCode Then
                        .HomeAddressstalCode = strZip
                    End If
                End If
            End If
        End If
        If .OtherAddressStreet <> "" Then
            strStreet = .OtherAddressStreet
            If .OtherAddressCity <> "" Then
                strCity = .OtherAddressCity
                If .OtherAddressState <> "" Then
                    strState = .OtherAddressState
                    strZip = GetFullZip(strStreet, _
                      strCity, strState)
                    If strZip <> .OtherAddressPostalCode Then
                        .OtherAddressstalCode = strZip
                    End If
                End If
            End If
        End If
    End With
    If Not objContact.Saved Then
        objContact.Save
    End If
End Sub
```

**Table 23.2** *Input Parameters for the FreeFAX Service*

| Parameter | Description |
|---|---|
| `Sender` | Your e-mail address so that delivery notices can be forwarded to your attention |
| `ToNum` | The international dialing code of the recipient fax machine, including country and area codes (e.g., in the USA, dial 17035551212); nonnumerics within the string are ignored |
| `Name` | Delivery information at the destination, such as name and mailstop; may include spaces (or _) and `RETURN` (or /) |
| `Text` | The contents of the fax to be delivered; will be formatted roughly 80 characters wide on the page; no limit |

The `SendFreeFaxToContact` subroutine in Listing 23.14 provides a place for you to set a `strMyAddress` variable to your own return address so that you can be notified when the fax has been delivered.

Even though all the code for working with XML Web services in the previous sections is in VBA, you may be able to connect to the services from an Outlook form. Microsoft has a documented but unsupported method that calls functions and subroutines in the `ThisOutlookSession` module. You can invoke such procedures with the syntax `Application.procedure`.

**CAUTION:** Even though this technique of calling a procedure in the `ThisOutlookSession` module seems to work in both Outlook 2000 and 2002, it is unsupported, which means there's no guarantee it will work in the next version of Outlook or even that it will work all the time in current versions.

To make the `SendFreeFaxToContact` available from a form, place it in the `ThisOutlookSession` module, not in a normal code module, and declare it as a `Public` subroutine. You will also need to remove the data typing for the arguments because Outlook form code has only variant type variables. It should look like this:

```
Public Sub SendFreeFaxToContact(objContact, strText)
```

The form shown in Figure 23.13 is an example of how you might construct a form for sending faxes with this service. Based on a Post form, it has three components—the Contacts field and button dragged from the Field Chooser, the usual message control, and a Send Fax button. The `Item_Open`

**Listing 23.14** *Use an XML Web Service To Send a Contact a Fax*

```
Sub SendFreeFaxToContact _
  (objContact As Outlook.ContactItem, strText As String)
    Dim FreeFax As New clsws_FreeFaxService
    Dim strMyAddress As String
    Dim strFaxNum As String
    ' ### USER OPTION ###
    strMyAddress = "nobody@slipstick.com"
    strFaxNum = objContact.BusinessFaxNumber
    If strFaxNum <> "" Then
        FreeFax.wsm_SendFreeFAX strMyAddress, strFaxNum, _
          objContact.FullName, strText
        MsgBox "Your fax was sent to " & strFaxNum, , _
               "Send Free Fax"
    End If
    Set FreeFax = Nothing
End Sub
```

procedure in Listing 23.15 sets the format to plain text, because the FreeFax service sends only text. When the user clicks the Send Fax button, the `cmdSendFax_Click` procedure runs, calling the `SendFreeFaxToContact` subroutine in the `ThisOutlookSession` module for each linked contact that has data in the `BusinessFaxNumber` property.

A few minutes after you send the fax, the FreeFax service should send a message back to the notification address you provided to let you know whether the transmission was successful.

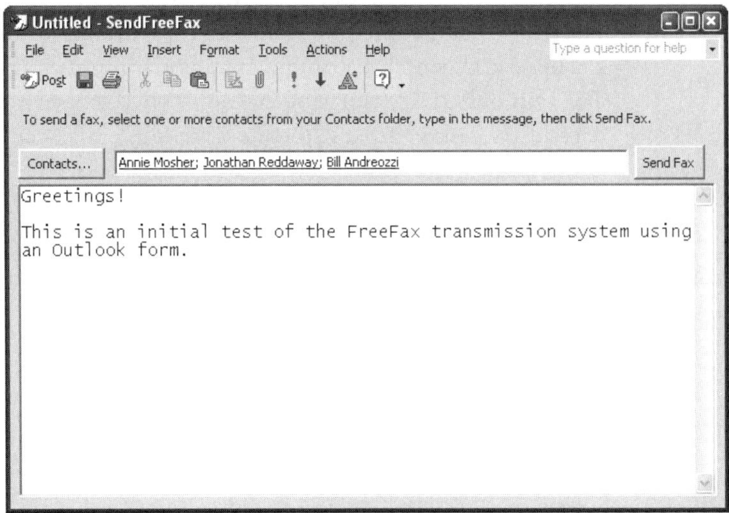


**Figure 23.13** *Even an Outlook form can make use of XML Web Services.*

**Listing 23.15** *Call a Procedure from the ThisOutlookSession Module*

```
Function Item_Open()
    Const olFormatPlain = 1
    Item.BodyFormat = olFormatPlain
End Function

Sub cmdSendFax_Click()
    Dim objLink
    Dim objContact
    On Error Resume Next
    For Each objLink In Item.Links
        Set objContact = objLink.Item
        If objContact.BusinessFaxNumber <> "" Then
            Application.SendFreeFaxToContact _
              objContact, Item.Body
        End If
    Next
    Set objLink = Nothing
    Set objContact = Nothing
End Sub
```

## 23.4 Summary

Connections to Exchange, databases, and XML Web services can transform Outlook from a customizable personal productivity tool into a platform for collaboration both within your organization and with other entities. In this chapter, you have learned how to set up public folders on Exchange and give them a more friendly face with a folder home page. You can now populate list box and combo box controls on Outlook forms with records from a database and generate a unique, sequential number any time you need one. For Outlook 2002, you've seen how XML Web services that perform such services as looking up a Zip code or sending a fax can be incorporated into Outlook projects with as few as two lines of code.

The final chapter considers the issues you are likely to encounter when you decide to share your Outlook applications with other users.

# 24

# *Deploying Forms and Applications*

By now, you should have quite a few Outlook forms and VBA code modules that you're eager to share with other people in your organization. In this chapter, you learn how to make them available to your colleagues.

Highlights of this chapter include discussions of the following:

- How to publish an Outlook form programmatically
- How to convert existing data to a custom form
- What code to use to import to a custom form
- How to use the Forms Manager to move and delete forms
- How to recover the password from a custom form
- How to share an Outlook VBA application with other users
- What tools you need for creating Outlook applications as Component Object Model (COM) add-ins

## 24.1 Deploying forms

You have already digested many techniques for deploying forms. In Chapter 15, "Outlook's Six Basic Forms," you saw how to publish a form to a forms library or save it as an Outlook template .oft file. In Chapter 23, "Exchange Server, Databases, and XML Web Services," you learned how to set the default form for a folder—a particularly useful technique in Exchange Server public folders.

You'll need to use code (or a utility) to handle these other key form deployment tasks:

- Converting existing items to a custom form
- Replacing a default form

- Importing data to a custom form

We'll also cover another crucial issue when using forms in Outlook folders—ensuring that the fields in the forms and the items created in the forms are defined in the folder and vice versa.

### 24.1.1 Distributing forms to remote users

You have probably already realized that one way to distribute a form to remote users is to save it as an .oft template file and e-mail it to the users, along with instructions on how to publish it to the Personal Forms library.

---

**Note:** In a Microsoft Exchange Server environment, the synchronization process ensures that remote users have the latest version of forms stored in folders set for offline use. However, there is no offline copy of the complete Organizational Forms library. Offline users will have only the forms from that library that were used in messages they received. They will also have any forms published to public folders that were synchronized. In addition, you may want to provide a mechanism to distribute other forms—such as the monthly report for a traveling sales representative—to those off-site users.

---

An alternative is to skip the instructions and provide a script that will open the form and install it. Each Outlook item includes a `FormDescription` object that defines the properties of the form. Once you retrieve this object from the item, you can set its `Name` property and then publish the form with the `PublishForm` method to the user's Personal Forms Library or any other forms library.

You can use the code in Listing 24.1 to create a script that users can run to install forms. Create a new text file with Notepad, add the code, and save it as Install.vbs. (You could also use a script editor, if you prefer.) Zip the Install.vbs files along with any forms template .oft files into a single .zip file using a utility such as WinZip. After the users extract the files to a folder, they can run the Install.vbs file to publish all .oft files in that folder to their Personal Forms libraries.

---

**Note:** If the user has a version of Outlook that predates the Outlook E-mail Security Update and the form has code, the user will see an Enable/Disable Macros prompt. However, the user's response to this prompt does not matter. The form will be published regardless.

---

**Listing 24.1** *Install Forms with a Script*

```
Option Explicit

Dim objOL, objExpl, objFormItem, objFormDesc, objFile
Dim strScriptName, strScriptPath, strForms, strFormName
Dim intLoc
Dim colFiles
Dim fso
Const olPersonalRegistry = 2
On Error Resume Next
Set objOL = CreateObject("Outlook.Application")
If Not objOL Is Nothing Then
    strScriptName = WScript.ScriptFullName
    intLoc = InStrRev(strScriptName, "\")
    strScriptPath = Left(strScriptName, intLoc)
    Set fso = CreateObject("Scripting.FileSystemObject")
    Set colFiles = fso.GetFolder(strScriptPath).files
    For Each objFile In colFiles
        strFormName = objFile.Name
        If LCase(Right(strFormName, 4)) = ".oft" Then
            Set objFormItem = _
              objOL.CreateItemFromTemplate(objFile.Path)
            If Err.Number = 0 Then
                Set objFormDesc = objFormItem.FormDescription
                intLoc = InStrRev(strFormName, ".oft")
                objFormDesc.Name = _
                  Left(strFormName, intLoc - 1)
                objFormDesc.PublishForm olPersonalRegistry
                strForms = strForms & vbTab & _
                           strFormName & vbCrLf
            Else
                MsgBox Err.Number & " - " & Err.Description
           End If
        End If
    Next
    If strForms <> "" Then
        strForms = "The following forms were published to " & _
               "your Personal Forms library: " & _
               vbCrLf & vbCrLf & strForms & vbCrLf & _
               "You can launch any of these forms " & _
               "by clicking New | Choose Form and " & _
               "switching to the Personal Forms library."
    Else
        strForms = "Errors occurred during attempted publication."
    End If
    MsgBox strForms, , "Published Outlook Forms"
End If
Set objFormDesc = Nothing
Set objFormItem = Nothing
Set objOL = Nothing
Set objFile = Nothing
Set colFiles = Nothing
Set fso = Nothing
```

The `Name` property is used to set the `MessageClass` property of the form when it is published. You can also have a separate `DisplayName`, which the user sees in the Choose Form dialog box. If you don't set a value for `DisplayName`, Outlook will use the value from the `Name` property.

Don't forget that to exchange information with someone via the Internet using custom Outlook forms, both sender and recipient need to have the form published under the same name.

### 24.1.2 Matching form and folder fields

Outlook is sometimes referred to as a *semistructured* database. This means that while there is a default data structure for items stored in a particular folder, any individual item may contain a custom property that is not defined as part of the folder or on any other items in that folder. In that case, you cannot use the `Find` or `Restrict` method to search for items that have a particular value for that property. You also will not see the item-only custom fields on the list of user-defined fields available for use in folder views.

Conversely, an individual item created with a custom form may be missing a custom property defined in the folder. For example, consider a tasks folder with a custom `ProjectStatus` field added to the folder. A table view can show that property, and with in-cell editing turned on, users can set the value for individual items by typing the value into the view. However, if an item is using a custom form that doesn't include the `ProjectStatus` property, setting a value for that property will one-off the item, with the negative consequences described in Chapter 20, "Common Outlook Form and Item Techniques."

The ideal situation, therefore, is a three-way match between custom properties in the folder, in any custom form used to create items in the folder, and in the items themselves. The biggest challenge is achieving that congruence when you decide to use an existing form in a different folder. For example, if you make a form available to someone else, either by publishing it in the Organizational Forms library or using the method in the previous section, the other user probably will not have the required fields in his or her folders. The same is true if you decide to use a form in a newly created folder.

Unfortunately, Outlook provides no straightforward way to copy a set of custom properties from one folder to another: Publishing a custom form to a folder's forms library does not propagate custom properties to the folder, nor does the File, Folder, Copy Folder Design command that can copy forms, views, permissions, and other folder-design features.

---

**Note:** As you learned in Chapter 17, "Extending Form Design with Fields and Controls," when you create a new custom property for a form, it is also defined in the parent folder of the item. This may be either the default folder for that type of item or the folder where the form was published, depending on exactly how you launched the form that you're designing.

---

Three methods are available to deploy custom property definitions to a new folder:

- Copy an entire folder
- Create new fields manually using the Field Chooser
- Create new fields programmatically

If you already have a folder that contains not just the form you want to use, but also the custom properties, views, and other folder design elements, you can copy that folder elsewhere in the hierarchy to create a new folder with exactly the same characteristics. This is a very good method to use when one department in an organization wants to start using a folder-based application developed for a different department.

Creating new fields using the Field Chooser can be tedious, but it is the only method available for formula and combination fields.

For other types of fields, you can use the code in Listing 24.2 to create a field in the target folder to match each custom property in a custom form. Before running it, open an existing or new item using your custom form. The `MakeUserPropsInFolder` procedure will prompt you to select the target folder.

Here's how it works: The code creates a normal item in the target folder (a `PostItem` if the folder is for mail and post items), then loops through the custom form item's `UserProperties` collection of custom properties. For each custom property, it creates a matching property in the folder item's `UserProperties` collection, which in turn automatically creates a property definition in the folder. After the loop is completed, the folder item is deleted. Some error tracking is included, because the `UserProperties` collection can behave oddly, appearing to contain what are in fact built-in properties.

**Listing 24.2** *Create Folder Fields Programmatically To Match Form Fields*

```
Sub MakeUserPropsInFolder()
    Dim objApp As Outlook.Application
    Dim objNS As Outlook.NameSpace
    Dim objInsp As Outlook.Inspector
    Dim objFolder As Outlook.MAPIFolder
    Dim objItem As Object
    Dim objProp As Outlook.UserProperty
    Dim objDummy As Object
    On Error Resume Next
    Set objApp = CreateObject("Outlook.Application")
    Set objNS = objApp.GetNamespace("MAPI")
    Set objFolder = objNS.PickFolder
    If Not objFolder Is Nothing Then
        Set objInsp = Application.ActiveInspector
        If Not objInsp Is Nothing Then
            Set objItem = objInsp.CurrentItem
            If objFolder.DefaultItemType = olMailItem Then
                Set objDummy = _
                  objFolder.Items.Add("IPM.Post")
            Else
                Set objDummy = objFolder.Items.Add
            End If
            objDummy.Save
            Debug.Print "Folder: " & objDummy.Parent.Name
            For Each objProp In objItem.UserProperties
                If objProp.Type <> olCombination And _
                   objProp.Type <> olFormula And _
                   objProp.Type <> olOutlookInternal Then
                    Debug.Print vbTab & objProp.Name
                    objDummy.UserProperties.Add _
                      objProp.Name, objProp.Type, True
                    If Err Then
                        Debug.Print vbTab & "  Error: " & _
                          Err & " - " & Err.Description
                        Err.Clear
                    End If
                End If
            Next
        End If
    End If
    objDummy.Delete
    Set objDummy = Nothing
    Set objItem = Nothing
    Set objProp = Nothing
    Set objFolder = Nothing
    Set objInsp = Nothing
    Set objNS = Nothing
    Set objApp = Nothing
End Sub
```

### 24.1.3 Converting existing items to a new form

Many times, you'll want to make existing items use a newly published custom form. For example, you may have a Contacts folder with hundreds of items that you want to display in a new, customized Contact form. Converting data from one form to another is a matter of changing the `MessageClass` property of the individual items. You can run the VBA macro in Listing 24.3 to update items in a folder to use a custom form instead of one of Outlook's default forms. The user selects the folder from the Select Folder dialog and supplies the name of the custom form via an input box.

---

**Note:** Don't forget that CDO is an optional Outlook component, but one that I recommend all Outlook developers install. The code in Listing 24.3 will produce errors if CDO is not installed.

---

Because Outlook suffers from memory leaks when processing large numbers of items, Listing 24.3 uses CDO for the actual looping through the items in the folder. The `DoCDOLogon` and `DoCDOLogoff` procedures from Chapter 10 are available to handle a `g_CDOSession` variable so that we can use CDO's `Folder` and `Message` objects.

---

**Note:** The `DefaultMessageClass` property of the folder does not indicate whether a custom form is the default form for that folder. It always returns the name of one of the built-in classes. This means that you can use it to test whether a given form is appropriate for the folder. However, you cannot use it to discover the class of the default form for the folder.

---

The foregoing code does some checking to make sure that a folder has been selected, and then uses a CDO `MessageFilter` object to filter out any items that are not using the default Outlook form. You may want your routine to do additional validation—perhaps to change only items that are already using a particular custom form, rather than changing only items that are using the default form.

The syntax for `MessageFilter` is quite different from that for Outlook's `Find` and `Restrict` methods. To use `MessageFilter`, you set the value for either a built-in property, such as `Type` (which is the same as `MessageClass` on an Outlook item), or add to the `MessageFilter.Fields` collection, setting the desired value for the new field.

**Listing 24.3** *Apply a New Form to Existing Items*

```
Public g_CDOSession as MAPI.Session

Sub UpdateMessageClass()
    Dim objApp As Outlook.Application
    Dim objNS As Outlook.NameSpace
    Dim objFolder As Outlook.MAPIFolder
    Dim objCDOFolder As MAPI.Folder
    Dim colCDOMessages As MAPI.Messages
    Dim objCDOMessage As MAPI.Message
    Dim objFilter As MAPI.MessageFilter
    Dim strClass As String
    Dim strFolderClass As String
    Dim strMsg As String
    Dim strTitle As String
    Set objApp = CreateObject("Outlook.Application")
    Set objNS = objApp.GetNamespace("MAPI")
    Set objFolder = objNS.PickFolder
    If Not objFolder Is Nothing Then
        strMsg = "Change all items in folder to what class?"
        strTitle = "UpdateMessageClass"
        strClass = InputBox(strMsg, strTitle)
        strFolderClass = objFolder.DefaultMessageClass
        If InStr(1, strClass, strFolderClass, _
                 vbTextCompare) Then
            Call DoCDOLogon
            Set objCDOFolder = _
              g_CDOSession.GetFolder(objFolder.EntryID, _
                                    objFolder.StoreID)
            Set colCDOMessages = objCDOFolder.Messages
            Set objFilter = colCDOMessages.Filter
            objFilter.Type = strFolderClass
            For Each objCDOMessage In colCDOMessages
                objCDOMessage.Type = strClass
                objCDOMessage.Update
            Next
            Call DoCDOLogoff
            strMsg = "Updated items in " & objFolder.Name & " Folder"
            MsgBox strMsg, , strTitle
        Else
            strMsg = "The class you specified is not " & _
                     "the normal type for this folder. " & _
                     "No items will be updated."
            MsgBox strMsg, , strTitle
        End If
    End If
    Set objFilter = Nothing
    Set objFolder = Nothing
    Set objCDOFolder = Nothing
    Set objCDOMessage = Nothing
    Set colCDOMessages = Nothing
    Set objNS = Nothing
    Set objApp = Nothing
End Sub
```

### 24.1.4 Replacing a default form

Even though you cannot edit the default Outlook forms, in Outlook 2000 and 2002, you can replace any of the default forms with a custom form to add functionality that the standard form does not include. For example, you might want to use a Message form that includes additional custom reply actions.

Microsoft provides a Forms Administrator tool (see Appendix A) to make the necessary Windows registry change for Outlook 2000. (As with all work in the registry, be sure to make a backup first.) If you run the tool with Outlook 2002, it puts the registry change in the wrong key. However, you can export a .reg file from the Forms Administrator and adapt it to work for Outlook 2002 simply by changing the key from HKCU\Software\Microsoft\Office\9.0\Outlook\Custom Forms to HKCU\Software\Microsoft\Office\10.0\Outlook\Custom Forms. Once you make that change, run the .reg file to import the entry into the registry.

---

**CAUTION:** Replacing any default form is not a trivial matter. You must take care to ensure that your replacement form includes all the functionality of the default form in addition to any special operations you have designed into the custom form. Also make sure that you enter the correct form name. The Forms Administrator tool does not check to make sure that the form name you enter is a valid, published form of the correct type.

---

The registry entries have two separate effects on new and existing items. Existing items will open in the form whose message class you specified in the tool, but the `MessageClass` property on the items will remain that of the default form. However, for new items, the `MessageClass` will be that of the custom form that was substituted. If you later remove the substitution registry entry, the `MessageClass` does not change. Therefore, if you want the items to revert to the built-in default form, you will need to change the `MessageClass` on the items using code similar to that in Listing 24.3.

Alternatively, you can use code in the custom form to reset the `MessageClass` on new items to the default form. For example, this code ensures that contacts will always be associated with the IPM.Contact form, even if they're created with a substitute custom Contact form:

```
Function Item_Write()
    Item.MessageClass = "IPM.Contact"
End Function
```

After you add the substitution information to the registry, Outlook will use the substitute form instead of the original form whenever you open an item of this type.

To remove a substitution, you can either run the tool again or just delete the registry entry in the Outlook\Custom Forms key.

### 24.1.5 Importing to a custom form

As you learned in Chapter 22, "Designing Outlook Reports," Outlook does not allow you to export directly to custom forms or custom fields using its File, Import and Export command. The same limitations apply to importing data. You must write custom code to copy the data field by field.

---

**Note:** It is also not possible to program Outlook's built-in Import and Export feature to automate importing or exporting even when custom fields or forms are not involved.

---

The exact code, of course, will depend on the source file. You must use the right syntax for any particular source to get the source records and fields. If the data is in a delimited file, a document that can be opened in a Microsoft Office program, or a database you can access with ADO, you can use VBA to write the code that follows this basic sequence:

1. Open the source file or database.
2. Create a new Outlook item using the custom form.
3. Get the first record from the source file or database.
4. Get the first field from the source.
5. Copy the data from the first source field to the corresponding field in the Outlook item.
6. Repeat steps 4 and 5 for all the fields you need to import.
7. Save the Outlook item.
8. Repeat steps 1 to 7 until you run out of source data.

For example, in Chapter 22, "Designing Outlook Reports," you learned how to use the Excel `Worksheet.Cells` object to put data into a particular cell. You can also reverse the process and create new Outlook items by reading the data from each row of cells to create a new contact. The `ExcelDL-`

ToContacts subroutine in Listing 24.4 uses a worksheet created with the DLToExcel procedure in Listing 22.4.

**Listing 24.4** *Create New Contacts from Data in an Excel Worksheet*

```
Dim m_blnWeOpenedExcel as Boolean

Sub ExcelDLToContacts()
    Dim objExcel As Excel.Application
    Dim objWB As Excel.Workbook
    Dim objWS As Excel.Worksheet
    Dim objRange As Excel.Range
    Dim objApp As Outlook.Application
    Dim objContact As Outlook.ContactItem
    Dim intRowCount As Integer
    Dim I As Integer
    On Error Resume Next
    m_blnWeOpenedExcel = False
    Set objExcel = GetObject(, "Excel.Application")
    If objExcel Is Nothing Then
        Set objExcel = CreateObject("Excel.Application")
        m_blnWeOpenedExcel = True
    End If
    On Error GoTo 0
    Set objWB = objExcel.Workbooks.Add("C:\ExcelDL.xls")
    Set objWS = objWB.Worksheets(1)
    Set objRange = objWS.Range("test")
    intRowCount = objRange.Rows.Count
    If intRowCount > 0 Then
        Set objApp = CreateObject("Outlook.Application")
        For I = 1 To intRowCount
            Set objContact = _
              objApp.CreateItem(olContactItem)
            With objContact
                .FullName = objRange.Cells(I, 1)
                .Email1AddressType = objRange.Cells(I, 3)
                .Email1Address = objRange.Cells(I, 2)
                .Save
            End With
        Next
    End If
    objWB.Close False
    Call RestoreExcel
    Set objExcel = Nothing
    Set objWB = Nothing
    Set objWS = Nothing
    Set objRange = Nothing
    Set objApp = Nothing
    Set objContact = Nothing
End Sub
```

As you can see, to write import code you need to know quite a bit about the source data. In this example, you need to know:

- The location of the source data file
- The named range that contains the data to be imported
- What data is present in each column of the range and which Outlook property it matches

Writing import routines is hard work, especially if you have dozens of fields to copy. Be sure to test carefully.

### 24.1.6 Importing from a comma-delimited file to a custom form

Many programs can export to comma-delimited files. In a comma-delimited file, each line is a record. The fields in the record are separated by commas. Since this is such a common format, it's useful to know how to open a comma-delimited file and read its data. In Chapter 10, you learned how to use the `FileSystemObject` from the Scripting Runtime to write Outlook data to a file. Now, let's reverse the process and read the data in a comma-delimited file back into Outlook items. Don't forget that you need a reference to the Microsoft Scripting Runtime in your VBA project.

To create a simple example, open Notepad, and type in these three lines:

John Doe, Lake Cleanup

Alice Channing, Air Quality

Marsha Kuong, Water Quality

Save the file as Project.csv. This gives us a comma-delimited file of people and the projects they're working on that we can import.

---

**Tip:** One way to create a comma-delimited file of exported Outlook data—including custom properties—is to push data from Outlook into Excel using the techniques discussed in Chapter 22, "Designing Outlook Reports," and then save the file as a comma-delimited file rather than as an Excel worksheet. Another method would be to use the `FileSystemObject` techniques from Chapter 10, "Working with the Object Models," to create a new text file directly.

---

The default Contact form doesn't have a `Project` field, does it? Create a custom form with a `Project` field: Open the default Contact form in design mode, create a new text field named `Project`, and drag the `Project` field to the P.2 page. Publish the form to your Personal Forms library or Contacts folder with the message class IPM.Contact.Project.

Now, you're ready to see the code to import the data in the Project.csv file to new items created with the IPM.Contact.Project form. The `ImportProjectCSVToOutlook` subroutine in Listing 24.5 does the following:

- Prompts the user for a file name and then opens that file
- Converts each line from the file into an array of fields
- Creates a new custom Outlook item using the IPM.Contact.Project form
- Copies the data from the array into the corresponding Outlook properties
- Saves the Outlook item
- Repeats the above process until it runs out of data

The `AtEndOfStream` property provides a convenient way to determine when the code has processed all the data in the file, while the `ReadLine` method allows the code to process one line (i.e., one record) at a time. You could adapt this code to process any number of fields, but as with the Excel example in the previous section, you need to know in advance which field in each comma-delimited record matches which Outlook property.

## 24.2 Managing forms

You already know how to publish custom forms to the different forms libraries. For moving and deleting forms, Outlook provides a Forms Manager feature. One task that the Forms Manager cannot handle is recovering the password from a custom form. Because the password is exposed as a property, it's easy to write VBA code for that chore.

### 24.2.1 Using the Forms Manager

To move published forms between locations and remove forms that you no longer need, use the Forms Manager. This tool is not available if you have Outlook 2000 in IMO mode.

**Listing 24.5** *Import Data from a Comma-Delimited File to a Custom Form*

```
Sub ImportProjectCSVToOutlook()
    Dim objApp As Outlook.Application
    Dim objNS As Outlook.NameSpace
    Dim objContacts As Outlook.MAPIFolder
    Dim objContact As Outlook.ContactItem
    Dim fso As Scripting.FileSystemObject
    Dim objStream As Scripting.TextStream
    Dim strFileName As String
    Dim strLine As String
    Dim arr() As String
    strFileName = _
      InputBox("File to import:", "Import to Outlook")
    If strFileName <> "" Then
        Set fso = _
          CreateObject("Scripting.FileSystemObject")
        If fso.FileExists(strFileName) Then
            Set objStream = _
              fso.OpenTextFile(strFileName, ForReading)
            Set objApp = _
              CreateObject("Outlook.Application")
            Set objNS = objApp.GetNamespace("MAPI")
            Set objContacts = _
              objNS.GetDefaultFolder(olFolderContacts)
            Do Until objStream.AtEndOfStream
                strLine = objStream.ReadLine
                arr = Split(strLine, ",")
                Set objContact = objContacts.Items.Add _
                                 ("IPM.Contact.Project")
                With objContact
                     .FullName = arr(0)
                     .UserProperties("Project") = arr(1)
                     .Save
                End With
            Loop
            objStream.Close
        End If
    End If
    Set objNS = Nothing
    Set objContacts = Nothing
    Set objContact = Nothing
    Set objApp = Nothing
    Set objStream = Nothing
    Set fso = Nothing
End Sub
```

To start the Forms Manager, choose Tools, Options from Outlook's main menu, and then switch to the Other tab. Click Advanced Options, then Custom Forms, then Manage Forms. You can also open the Forms Manager by right-clicking the name of an Outlook folder, choosing Properties, switching to the Forms tab, and then clicking Manage.

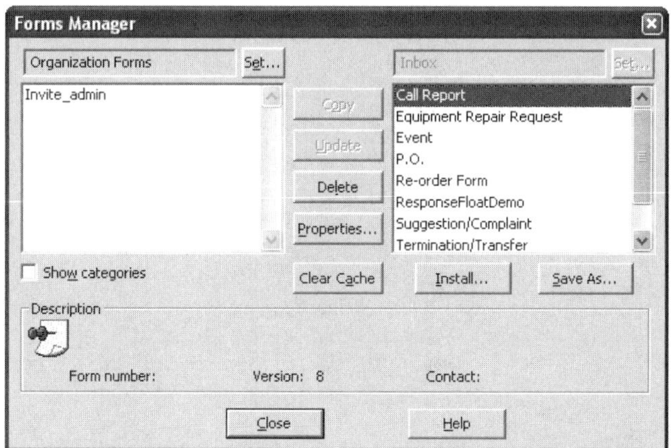


**Figure 24.1** *The Forms Manager, Outlook's tool for maintaining forms, appears only in Outlook 2002 and in Outlook 2000 in Corporate or Workgroup mode.*

In the Forms Manager dialog box (see Figure 24.1), use the Set buttons to select a folder or library. You can then use the Copy, Update, and Delete buttons to manage forms, or the Properties button to find out more about a form.

---

**Note:** The Save As button on the Forms Manager allows you to save a form as an .fdm file. The Install button imports an .fdm file into a forms library. However, since the Forms Manager is so difficult to reach through the Outlook user interface, this method of installing forms is less convenient than the others discussed in this chapter.

---

For example, if you have successfully tested a form in your Personal Forms library, you might want to copy it to the Organizational Forms library and then delete it from your Personal Forms library. Remember that you must have appropriate permissions from the Exchange Administrator to put a form in the Organizational Forms library and must be a folder owner to add to a folder forms library.

### 24.2.2 Recovering a form's password

Someone creates a custom form, password-protects it to safeguard the code, then leaves the company without providing the password. Is the form now blocked from further modifications? Fortunately, getting the password for an Outlook form is simple; the `FormDescription` object, which contains key information about the form, includes a `Password` property. The VBA code in Listing 24.6 pops up the value of the `Password` property in a

**Listing 24.6** *Recover the Password from a Custom Form*

```
Sub GetFormPassword()
    Dim objApp As Outlook.Application
    Dim objInsp As Outlook.Inspector
    Dim objFD As Outlook.FormDescription
    Dim strMsg As String
    Set objApp = CreateObject("Outlook.Application")
    Set objInsp = objApp.ActiveInspector
    If Not objInsp Is Nothing Then
        Set objFD = objInsp.CurrentItem.FormDescription
        If objFD.Password <> "" Then
            strMsg = "The password for this form is:" & _
                     vbCrLf & vbCrLf & objFD.Password
        Else
            strMsg = "This form has no password."
        End If
        MsgBox prompt:=strMsg, Title:="Get Form Password"
    End If
    Set objFD = Nothing
    Set objInsp = Nothing
    Set objApp = Nothing
End Sub
```

message box. Before running it, open an item that uses the custom form. You can either open an existing item or use the File, New, Choose Form command to create a new item using the custom form.

After you retrieve the password with this macro, you may want to open the form in design mode—entering the password in the prompt that appears—and remove the password protection completely. On the (Properties) page, clear the Protect Form Design box to remove the password protection. You can also set a new password with the Set Password button.

## 24.3 Distributing VBA applications

So far in this chapter on deployment, the focus has been on Outlook forms. What about your VBA applications? Can they be distributed as easily?

No, it is not as easy simple to distribute Outlook VBA applications as it is with Office programs, such as Word and Excel, where you can embed VBA inside documents (more on that shortly). These are the methods available to you:

- Import and export
- Automate Outlook from another program
- Write a COM add-in

COM add-ins are the recommended method for distributing Outlook VBA applications on any significant scale, but they require techniques beyond the scope of this book. I have included a few notes on COM add-ins later in this chapter, and you'll find other useful references in Appendix A. If you need to share your code with just a few other people, try one of the other methods.

**CAUTION:** I do not recommend that you try to replace another user's entire VBAProject.OTM file with a copy of your own VBA project file. Doing so would wipe out any VBA code that the other user had already written. Import and export provides a better method of swapping code modules.

### 24.3.1 Importing and exporting VBA modules

It's simple, but it works. VBA includes both Export File and Import File commands on its File menu. With these, you can export from VBA, then give the exported file to someone else to import. The exported files use these file extensions:

Modules, .bas files

Forms, .frm files

Class modules (including `ThisOutlookSession`), .cls files

One catch with importing files is that you will get an error if the imported file duplicates any form name or public procedure name in the currently open project. Also, you cannot import directly into your `ThisOutlookSession` module. You would need to import the saved class module and then copy and paste the imported module's procedures into the existing `ThisOutlookSession` module.

### 24.3.2 Automating Outlook from another Office application

Remember how in Chapter 22, "Designing Outlook Reports," you used automation code in Outlook to create printed output in Excel and Word. You can also reverse the process and put code to automate Outlook into macros attached to a Word and Excel document or template. Then, distribute that file to other users. Both Word and Excel documents include events that fire when a document opens, so it's easy to have a document display a

VBA form or run code. You can also add a command button to an Excel worksheet or a double-clickable field to a Word document to run a macro on demand.

Take the `ImportProjectCSVToOutlook` procedure from the previous section as an example. Here are the steps to follow to make it run from a Word document:

1. In Outlook VBA, place the `ImportProjectCSVToOutlook` procedure in a separate module.
2. Choose File, Export File to save the module as ImportProjectCSV.bas.
3. Open a new document in Word, and press Alt+F11 to switch to Word's VBA environment. You should be in a project named Project (Document1). (The document number may be different if you have more than one unsaved document open in Word.)
4. Choose Tools, References to set a reference to the Microsoft Outlook 9.0 (or 10.) Object library.
5. Choose File, Import File to import the ImportCSV.bas file into the Project (Document1) project. (You could also copy the code directly from the Outlook VBA window to the Word VBA environment without going through the export and import steps.)

That's all there is to it! Switch back to the Word document, and press Alt+F8 to bring up the Macros dialog box. You should see `ImportProjectCSVToOutlook` as an available macro. Try running the macro to make sure it works.

---

**Tip:** One of the benefits of using a Word document to distribute VBA code to perform Outlook tasks is that you can include an explanation of the application in the same document.

---

If you want to have the macro run when the user opens the Word document, switch back to the Word VBA window. Look in the Project Explorer under Project(Document1) and then under Microsoft Word Objects for ThisDocument. Double-click ThisDocument to display the code module for the document itself. From the dropdown list at the top left of the module window, select Document. From the list at the top right, select Open. This places a shell for the `Document_Open` procedure in the document. Add one line of code to the procedure to call `ImportCSVToOutlook`. The finished procedure should look like this:

```
Private Sub Document_Open()
    Call ImportCSVToOutlook
End Sub
```

Now, close and save the Word document, perhaps naming it ImportCSVToOutlook.doc. When you open it, if the Word macro security setting permits, the `ImportCSVToOutlook` procedure should run, just as it did when you ran it from Outlook's VBA window.

If you prefer to have the user read some instructions and then double-click a Word field to run the procedure, follow these steps:

1. In the VBA project for the Word document to which you added the Outlook code, remove the `Document_Open` subroutine that calls `ImportCSVToOutlook`.
2. Switch from VBA back to the document itself, and type in whatever explanatory text you'd like the user to read.
3. Choose Insert, Field to display the Field dialog box.
4. From the Field Names list on the right side of the Field dialog box, choose Macro Button.
5. In the box where you see MACROBUTTON, type a space, then the name of the macro (`ImportProjectCSVToOutlook`), then another space, then To Import, Double-Click Here.
6. Click OK to save the MACROBUTTON field.

You should now see the text "To Import, Double-Click Here" in the document; you can test it by double-clicking it. You may want to use shading, highlighting, or a border to set it off from the rest of the text. To run the code, the user just double-clicks on the field.

### 24.3.3 Creating COM add-ins

COM add-ins are separately compiled Dynamic Link Library (.dll) files that hook into Outlook or other Office programs. Typically, a COM add-in project includes a combination of Class modules, modules, and forms. It may have its own entries in the Windows registry to track user preferences. In other words, COM add-ins are complex.

You can create and compile COM add-ins either with Visual Basic or with Office XP Developer, the programmer's edition of Office. Office XP Developer edition includes an add-ins template that makes the process a little easier, and you'll find other resources in Appendix A.

An Outlook COM add-in typically loads when Outlook starts and either responds to specific Outlook events or provides toolbar buttons to invoke the new functionality included in the add-in. To enable and disable COM add-ins already installed on your system, choose Tools, Options, switch to the Other tab, click Advanced Options, and then click COM Add-ins.

## 24.4 Summary

Whether you want to concentrate on Outlook forms or build programs in VBA or do a bit of both, your job as a programmer is not finished until you make those applications available to the people who need to use them. Publishing to the forms libraries is the primary way to deploy Outlook forms, while COM add-ins are the way to go if you are distributing high-end applications written in VBA. For the small tasks that you run as macros from toolbar buttons, export and import may be good enough.

I hope this book has given you a solid introduction to Outlook programming. I encourage you to explore the additional resources listed in Appendix A to see other techniques and discover source code that you can incorporate into your own projects.

# Resources for Outlook Programming

All the source code for the VBA code listings and Outlook forms discussed in this book are available on the Internet at http://www.outlookcode.com. You can also go there to comment on the book and get a list of errors in the text.

A book of this size could never cover everything you might want to know about Microsoft Outlook programming. Fortunately, there are other books, many resources available on the Internet, and excellent discussion forums where you can encounter other Outlook programmers, both casual and professional. This appendix highlights general resources and specific topics that deserve more coverage than this book could accommodate.

## A.1 Books on Outlook programming

Randy Byrne, *Building Applications with Microsoft Outlook Version 2002* (Microsoft Press, 2001, ISBN 0-7356-1273-0).

This book takes you from using the Outlook building blocks that you've encountered in this book to building enterprise-level applications of many kinds. It includes information on building COM add-ins and digital dashboards, working with Exchange Server and SharePoint Portal Server, trusting COM add-ins under the Outlook E-mail Security Update, and using controls such as the PivotTable List. Sample applications cover contact management and shared activities.

Raffaele Piemonte and Scott Jamison, *Developing Applications Using Outlook 2000, CDO, Exchange, and Visual Basic* (Addison-Wesley, 2001, ISBN 0-2016-1575-4).

This book is valuable if you are programming for older Outlook clients, because of its comparative tables of properties and methods available in Outlook 97, 98, and 2000.

Dwayne Gifford, *Outlook 2000 VBA Programmer's Reference* (Wrox, 1999, ISBN 1-8610-0253-X)

This is a desk reference on the Outlook 2000 object model.

Additional Outlook and Exchange developer books are listed at http://www.slipstick.com/dev/books.htm.

## A.2 Web resources for Outlook programming

I have posted dozens of articles and additional Outlook programming samples on my Slipstick Systems Outlook & Exchange Solutions Center Web site at http://www.slipstick.com/dev/.

The Microsoft Developers Network maintains a support area for Outlook and other Microsoft Office applications at http://msdn.microsoft.com/office with articles and sample applications. Microsoft publishes information about known Outlook programming bugs, patches, and additional how-to sample code in the Microsoft Knowledgebase at http://support.microsoft.com/search/. You will find the VBScript language reference at http://msdn.microsoft.com/library/en-us/script56/html/vbscripttoc.asp.

Perhaps the key sample for exploring VBA (and even more, Visual Basic) programming with Outlook is the Items Command Bar application from http://www.microeye.com/resources/itemsCB.htm. This sample illustrates the following key concepts, among others:

- Overall framework for building a COM add-in for Outlook
- A "wrapper" class module for handling `Explorer` events from all open folder windows, not just the ActiveExplorer window
- Best practices for working with toolbars and custom toolbar buttons

## A.3 Outlook programming discussion groups

The free Outlook-dev discussion list has more than 1200 Outlook developers as members and provides both e-mail and Web interfaces. Information on joining the list is available at its Web site at http://groups.yahoo.com/group/outlook-dev/.

Microsoft provides several public Outlook programming newsgroups available via NNTP or Web interface, chief among which are

- microsoft.public.outlook.program_addins
- microsoft.public.outlook.program_forms
- microsoft.public.outlook.program_vba

If your local NNTP server does not carry these, you can also access them via the Web at http://communities.microsoft.com or http://groups.google.com. Google provides several years of newsgroup archives.

## A.4 Outlook programming tools

In addition to the forms design and VBA tools built into Outlook and the Redemption library discussed in Chapter 13, "Understanding Outlook Security," I recommend that you obtain at least one tool for digging deep into Outlook's data structure. The tool provided by Microsoft, Mdbvu32.exe, is available on the Exchange Server CD but has a difficult interface and little documentation. A third-party tool, Outlook Spy, available from http://www.dimastr.com, allows you to drill down into Outlook object properties. not just with Outlook but also with CDO and Extended MAPI, and to write short test scripts. It also makes it easy to look up `CommandButton.ID` property values and monitor events.

Office XP Developer is an expanded version of the Office XP suite that includes many developer tools, including a code librarian, a COM add-in designer, and a code commenter and error handler that work with VBA.

## A.5 Specific Outlook programming issues

This section highlights resources for specific Outlook programming topics mentioned in this book.

### A.5.1 A.5.1 Outlook object model

Micro Eye provides diagrams of the Outlook 2000 and 2000 object models, suitable for printing in color, at http://microeye.com/resources/ObjectModel.htm and http://microeye.com/resources/ObjectModel2002.htm. The Outlook forms Help topic "Outlook Fields and Equivalent Properties" provides a mapping of field names visible in the user interface with the actual property names.

### A.5.2 Collaboration Data Objects

You can get the Help file for CDO, Cdo.hlp, from the Exchange Server CD or from the CDOLive Web site (http://www.cdolive.com/start.htm), which provides independent support for CDO developers. An online version is available at the Microsoft Developers Network Web site at

http://msdn.microsoft.com/library/en-us/cdo/html/_olemsg_overview_of_cdo.asp

The article at http://www.cdolive.com/cdo10.htm on "Property Tags and Types" is particularly valuable for learning about how CDO fields map to Outlook properties.

### A.5.3 FileSystemObject

References and sample code for scripting with the `FileSystemObject` are available at

http://msdn.microsoft.com/library/en-us/script56/html/jsfsotutor.asp.

### A.5.4 Explorer and Inspector events

The Items Command Bar application from http://www.microeye.com/resources/itemsCB.htm demonstrates a "wrapper" class module that handles Explorer events from all open folder windows, not just the ActiveExplorer window. This technique can also be applied, to some extent, to Inspector windows, but it has serious limitations because of the way Outlook handles some new messages.

### A.5.5 Outlook security

The following Web pages provide additional information and tools for dealing with the Outlook E-mail Security Update:

- Slipstick Systems information on the Outlook E-mail Security Update can be found at http://www.slipstick.com/outlook/esecup.htm.
- The Outlook Security Features Administrative Package for Outlook 98 and 2000 is available at http://www.microsoft.com/office/ork/2000/appndx/toolbox.htm#secupd.

- The Outlook Security Features Administrative Package for Outlook 2002 is available at http://www.microsoft.com/office/ork/xp/appndx/appa11.htm.
- Outlook Redemption can be found at http://www.dimastr.com/redemption/.

### A.5.6 DASL

DASL is the acronym for DAV Searching and Locating; DAV itself is an acronym for Distributed Authoring and Versioning. This syntax is used to construct searches with the Outlook 2002 Search object. Exchange 2000 uses it extensively, as does SharePoint Portal Server. A good place to start learning about the DASL search syntax is with the SharePoint documentation at

http://msdn.microsoft.com/library/en-us/spssdk/html/_overview_of_the_select_statement.asp

A set of lists that map Outlook display field names to DASL properties can be downloaded from http://www.slipstick.com/files/schema.zip.

### A.5.7 vCard, vCal, and iCal

Information on these Internet standards for exchanging contact and calendar data among different clients is available from the Internet Mail Consortium at http://www.imc.org/pdi/.

### A.5.8 Outlook View Control

The Outlook View Control (OVC) for Outlook 2000 can be downloaded from http://office.microsoft.com/downloads/2000/outlctlx.aspx.

The version of the OVC that ships with Outlook 2002 has a security problem. To obtain a safe version, visit the Microsoft Office Download Center at http://office.microsoft.com/Downloads/default.aspx, and download and install the latest update for Outlook 2002. Any update from August 16, 2001, or later will have the more secure OVC.

The Microsoft Knowledgebase provides additional information on the OVC for Outlook 2000 (http://support.microsoft.com/support/kb/articles/Q281/6/18.asp) and 2002 (http://support.microsoft.com/support/kb/articles/q291/4/07.asp).

### A.5.9 One-off forms

The CDOLive code sample at http://www.cdolive.net/samples/?item=CleanUpOneOff shows how to clean up the MAPI properties that cause an item to exhibit one-off symptoms.

The Microsoft Knowledgebase (the URL is given in Section A.2) has many articles on the different properties and methods that can cause one-off forms.

### A.5.10 CommandBars

The Items Command Bar application from http://www.microeye.com/resources/itemsCB.htm shows how to build a custom toolbar, add items to launch forms, and ensure that the toolbar doesn't duplicate itself when the user opens more folders.

### A.5.11 Digital dashboards

Digital dashboards are Web portals, often built for company intranets, that combine different types of personal and organizational information, using the Outlook View Control to display a user's own data. A good resource for getting started with digital dashboards is http://www.digidashlive.com.

### A.5.12 XML Web services

You can download the Microsoft Office XP Web Services Toolkit from http://msdn.microsoft.com/msdn-files/027/001/827/Search.asp. Follow the Documentation link from that page for addition information, including sample code.

If you want other people to use your XML Web services VBA modules, they will need to install either the Office XP Web Services Toolkit or the SOAP 3.0 Toolkit Redistributable Files, which you can obtain from http://www.microsoft.com/downloads/release.asp?ReleaseID=41252.

### A.5.13 Deploying Forms

You can download the FormsAdmin.exe tool for replacing a default form with a custom form from http://www.microsoft.com/office/ork/2000/Appndx/toolbox.htm#outladm.

### A.5.14 COM add-ins

The Items Command Bar application from http://www.microeye.com/resources/itemsCB.htm shows how to build a COM add-in that properly shuts itself down when Outlook closes and uses. For other samples and references, see http://www.slipstick.com/dev/comaddins.htm and the books listed above.

# B

# *Files Blocked by Outlook Security*

Table B.1 lists the file types that Outlook 2002, Outlook 2000 with Office Service Pack 2, and Outlook 2000 with the Outlook E-mail Security Update consider dangerous and, therefore, block from access both in the user interface and in code solutions using the Outlook object model and the CDO object model.

This list was complete at the time of publication, but Microsoft may add or subtract from it in future versions.

For more on Outlook security features, see Chapter 13, "Understanding Outlook Security."

**Table B.1** *Attachments Blocked by the Security Update*

| File Extension | File Type |
|---|---|
| `.ade` | Microsoft Access project extension |
| `.adp` | Microsoft Access project |
| `.asx` | Windows Media Audio or Video shortcut (blocked only in Outlook 2002 builds earlier than 10.0.3005) |
| `.bas` | Visual Basic class module |
| `.bat` | Batch file |
| `.chm` | Compiled HTML Help file |
| `.cmd` | Windows NT command script |
| `.com` | MS-DOS program |
| `.cpl` | Control panel extension |
| `.crt` | Security certificate |

**Table B.1** *Attachments Blocked by the Security Update (continued)*

| File Extension | File Type |
|---|---|
| `.exe` | Program |
| `.hlp` | Help file |
| `.hta` | HTML program |
| `.inf` | Setup information |
| `.ins` | Internet naming service |
| `.isp` | Internet communication settings |
| `.js` | JScript script file |
| `.jse` | Jscript encoded script file |
| `.lnk` | Shortcut |
| `.mda` | Microsoft Access add-in program (blocked only in Outlook 2002) |
| `.mdb` | Microsoft Access program |
| `.mdt` | Microsoft Access workgroup information (blocked only in Outlook 2002 SP-1 and later) |
| `.mdw` | Microsoft Access workgroup information (blocked only in Outlook 2002 SP-1 and later) |
| `.mde` | Microsoft Access MDE database |
| `.mdz` | Microsoft Access wizard program |
| `.msc` | Microsoft common console document |
| `.msi` | Windows Installer package |
| `.msp` | Windows Installer patch |
| `.mst` | Visual Test source files |
| `.ops` | Office XP settings (blocked only in Outlook 2002 SP-1 and later) |
| `.pcd` | Photo CD image |
| `.pif` | Shortcut to MS-DOS program |
| `.prf` | Microsoft Outlook profile settings (blocked only in Outlook 2002) |
| `.reg` | Registration entries |
| `.scf` | Windows Explorer command (blocked only in Outlook 2002) |
| `.scr` | Screen saver |

**Table B.1** *Attachments Blocked by the Security Update (continued)*

| File Extension | File Type |
|---|---|
| `.sct` | Windows script component |
| `.shb` | Shell scrap object |
| `.shs` | Shell scrap object |
| `.url` | Internet shortcut |
| `.vb` | VBScript file |
| `.vbe` | VBScript encoded script file |
| `.vbs` | Visual Basic script file |
| `.wsc` | Windows script component |
| `.wsf` | Windows script file |
| `.wsh` | Windows Script host settings file |

C

# *Key Procedures You Can Reuse*

The functions and subroutines in Table C.1 are those you are most likely to want to use as building blocks in your own Outlook forms and VBA modules.

**Table C.1** *Building-Block Procedures*

| Name | Listing Number | Description |
|---|---|---|
| `AddFormLaunchCombo` | 21.11 | Add a list of favorite forms to a toolbar |
| `AddPhone` | 20.3 | Update a `TaskItem` with a phone number from a linked contact |
| `AddPST` | 12.1 | Opens a Personal Folders file |
| `ComplexProcedure` | 10.8 | Boilerplate framework for adding a log file to a complex procedure |
| `ConfigurePublicContacts` | 12.10 | Configures a public Contacts folder for offline and address book use (Outlook 2002) |
| `CopyAttachments` | 10.9 | Copies attachments from one Outlook item to another |
| `CountInView()` | 21.6 | Returns the number of items displayed in the current folder view |
| `CreateFollowUpTask` | 6.2 | Creates a `TaskItem` based on information in the currently open `AppointmentItem` |
| `CreateSenderContactRed` | 14.15 | Adds a contact with a mail message sender's information using the Redemption library to avoid security prompts |
| `CreateVoteMessage` | 10.3 | Creates a voting button message after prompting the user for the buttons' text |
| `DateID()` | 20.6 | Builds an ID from the current date |

**Table C.1** *Building-Block Procedures (continued)*

| Name | Listing Number | Description |
|---|---|---|
| `GetLinkedItems()` | 22.12 | Returns a `Results` collection of all items in the Calendar, Tasks, and Journal folders related to a particular contact (Outlook 2002) |
| `DeleteAttachments` | 7.3 | Deletes all attachments in any Outlook item |
| `DeleteAttachmentsCh09` | 9.1 | Is an enhanced version of `DeleteAttachments` with greater user interaction |
| `DoCDOLogon, DoCDOLogoff` | 10.4 | Initializes and ends a CDO session |
| `EnumAllCommands` | 21.4 | Builds a list of all command bars and commands |
| `EnumCommandBars` | 21.1 | Generates a list of all menus and toolbars for the current window |
| `EnumStoresCDO` | 12.2 | Displays a message box listing all information stores available to Outlook with information on the type of store |
| `GetCDOItemFromOL()` | 10.5 | Returns the CDO Message object corresponding to a given Outlook item |
| `GetCurrentItem()` | 18.7 | Returns the currently selected or open Outlook item |
| `GetFolder()` | 12.7 | Returns a `MAPIFolder` object from a folder path string (VBA version) |
| `GetFolder()` | 18.6 | Returns a `MAPIFolder` object from a folder path string (VBScript version) |
| `GetFolderPath()` | 19.4 | Returns a string path for any `MAPIFolder` object |
| `GetFormPassword()` | 24.6 | Returns the password for a custom form |
| `GetFromAddressCDO()` | 13.5 | Returns the sender's e-mail address using CDO |
| `GetFromAddressR()` | 13.6 | Returns the sender's e-mail address, avoiding security prompts by using the Redemption library |
| `GetFullZip()` | 23.11 | Returns the ZIP+4 code to any U.S. address using an XML Web service (Outlook 2002) |
| `GetMailboxUserName()` | 12.8 | Returns the user's Exchange mailbox name without triggering Outlook security prompts (VBA version) |
| `GetMailboxUserName()` | 20.6 | Returns the user's Exchange mailbox name without triggering Outlook security prompts (VBAScript version) |
| `GetNewNumber()` | 23.7 | Returns a sequential number from an Access database Auto-Number field |

**Table C.1** *Building-Block Procedures (continued)*

| Name | Listing Number | Description |
|---|---|---|
| `GetOLItemFromCDO` | 10.6 | Returns the Outlook item corresponding to a given CDO Message object |
| `GetOneName()` | 14.11 | Returns one name that the user selects from the address book, avoiding security prompts by using the Redemption library |
| `GetOtherUserCalendar()` | 12.6 | Opens another Exchange user's Calendar folder |
| `HasAppFolders()` | 12.9 | Returns `True` or `False` depending on the availability of the Application Folders send/receive group (Outlook 2002) |
| `HasRequiredCategory()` | 18.14 | Returns `True` or `False` depending on whether the Categories property includes at least one category from a prescribed list |
| `IsInDefaultStore()` | 12.4 | Returns `True` or `False` depending on whether an object is in the default information store |
| `IsOLSecure()` | 13.1 | Returns `True` or `False` depending on whether the version of Outlook includes the E-mail Security Update (VBA version) |
| `IsOLSecure()` | 13.2 | Returns `True` or `False` depending on whether the version of Outlook includes the E-mail Security Update (VBScript version) |
| `MakeUserPropsInFolder` | 24.2 | Updates a folder to add custom properties from the currently displayed custom form |
| `MsgToContactRedemption` | 13.4 | Sends a message to the currently selected contact, avoiding security prompts by using the Redemption library |
| `NewConversationIndex()` | 20.5 | Returns a unique string for use when you need a unique identifier |
| `NextBusinessDay2()` | 14.4 | Returns the date *x* business days from a given day, taking into account weekends and items in the Calendar folder marked as holidays and vacations |
| `OpenAccessDB()` | 23.3 | Returns an `ADO.Connection` object by opening an Access database (VBA) |
| `OpenAccessDB()` | 23.6 | Returns an `ADO.Connection` object by opening an Access database (VBAScript) |
| `OpenSQLServerDB()` | 23.4 | Returns an `ADO.Connection` object by opening a SQL Server database |
| `Quote` | 12.6 | Returns any input as a string surrounded by double quotation marks |

**Table C.1** *Building-Block Procedures (continued)*

| Name | Listing Number | Description |
|---|---|---|
| `ReconnectLinks` | 20.2 | Reconnects items in a folder chosen by the user to the linked contacts in the Contacts folder |
| `RemoveUserProps` | 10.2 | Removes all custom properties from the currently displayed item |
| `ReplaceCat` | 6.3 | Replaces one category with another for all items in the current folder |
| `ResolveAndSendViaRed()` | 14.14 | Returns `True` or `False` depending on whether all addresses in a message could be resolved; if `True`, sends the item, avoiding security prompts by using the Redemption library |
| `SelectionFramework` | 14.3 | Boilerplate for processing selected items in a folder |
| `ShowAttachmentDialog` | 21.7 | Launches the Insert File dialog |
| `ShowsComposeLayout()` | 18.5 | Returns `True` or `False` depending on whether a custom form is displaying the compose layout rather than the read layout |
| `SQLQuote` | 22.12 | Returns any input as a string surrounded by single quotation marks |
| `StampDate` | 14.7 | Stamps the date and current user's name on an Outlook item |
| `UpdateMessageClass` | 24.3 | Changes the `MessageClass` property for all items in a chosen folder |
| `WSHListSep()` | 10.11 | Returns the user's list separator for use in handling Categories and other built-in keywords fields where the user's language settings are not known (VBA version) |
| `WSHListSep()` | 18.14 | Returns the user's list separator for use in handling Categories and other built-in keywords fields where the user's language settings are not known (VBScript version) |
| `WSHTimeZoneOffset()` | 10.12 | Returns the number in minutes that the user's time zone differs from Greenwich Mean Time |
| `WSHUserName()` | 10.10 | Returns the user's Windows logon name using Windows Script Host to avoid Outlook security prompts |
| `YearsSinceDate()` | 6.1 | Returns the number of years between two dates |

# Index